The Renaissance of Islam

(Translated From the German of Adam Mez)

By

Salahuddin Khuda Bakhsh

and

D.S. Margoliouth

KITAB BHAVAN
New Delhi-110002

KITAB BHAVAN
Publishers, Exporters & Importers
1784, Kalan Mahal, Darya Ganj
New Delhi - 110 002 [India]

Phones : *3274686, 3263383*
Telex : *31-63106 ALI IN*
Fax : *91-11-3263383*

ISBN 81-7151-124-4

First Edition 1937
2nd Reprint 1979
3rd Improved Edition with
New Typesetting 1995

Fonts : Garamond Light–11 Pt.

Published by:
Nusrat Ali Nasri for Kitab Bhavan
1784, Kalan Mahal, Darya Ganj
New Delhi - 110 002 [India]

Printed in India at:
Seema Offset Printers
Choori Walan,
Delhi - 110 002 [India]

Contents

Foreword

My brother, Salahuddin, began his last work on Islamic Studies—a translation of Professor A. MEZ'S "DIE RENAISSANCE DES ISLAMS" from German into English on the 16th of July, 1927. He completed twenty-three and a half out of the twenty-nine chapters by July, 1931, when unfortunately he was taken ill and died on the 9th of August, 1931.

The translation of the last five and a half chapters, which was left unfinished, was very kindly done by Dr. Margoliouth, (p. 570) Professor of Arabic in the University of Oxford, who had taught my brother Arabic when the latter was a student at Oxford in the late nineties. The first seventeen chapters of the book as well as chapters 23 to 29 were published in the magazine "Islamic Culture" at Hyderabad between the years 1928 and 1933.

After my retirement from the Indian Police Service in August, 1934, I went to England. There my sister-in-law, Mrs. Evelyn Khuda Bakhsh, told me that she had carefully preserved the unpublished translations of the Renaissance of Islam by her husband, and that she desired to have the entire work published in the form of a book. I suggested to her that she should write to Mr. Marmaduke Pickthall, the Editor of "Islamic Culture", and ask him if he would publish the book, as most of the translated chapters had already appeared in his magazine. This my sister-in-law did, and she received a reply from Mr. Pickthall to the effect that he could not undertake the publication but would have no objection to her getting the translations printed in the form of a book anywhere in England or in India. We then decided to try and have the book published here, and as I was returning to India I brought the manuscripts back with me.

It was beyond my means to defray the entire cost of the publication of the book, so I approached my friend, Mr Syed Abdul Aziz, Barrister-at-Law, the then Hon'ble Minister of Education to the Government of Bihar, and he very kindly sanctioned a substantial grant of money to enable me to accomplish my purpose. But for the generous aid given by the Government of Bihar this book would have remained unpublished, and perhaps lost to the world for ever.

Shahabuddin Khuda Bakhsh

Patna,

June 1937.

Introductory Note

The author of the work which is here given an English dress, Adam Mez (born 1869, died 1917) well known to Arabic Scholars by his edition of the curious book *Abul Kasim ein Bagdader Sittenbild* (Heidelberg, 1902) left the German original of his *Renaissance des Islams* at his death in typescript, practically complete, yet not quite ready for the press.

The task of preparing it for the printer was undertaken by Dr. Reckendorf, whose Preface, dated June 1922, contains no memoir of the author, and little more about the work itself than that it was meant to portray the momentous changes in Mahomedan civilization which took place in the fourth century of Islam (tenth century A.D.) with reference to their origin on the one hand and their incidental continuance on the other; further that the author was dissatisfied with the title, but could think of nothing more appropriate.

It is indeed clear that the word *Renaissance* has associations which do not quite correspond with the theme described. Applied to Christian Europe it means restoration of something that had been lost; the recovery of of classical (i.e. Greek) art, literature and Science, which during the Dark and the earlier middle ages had been neglected.

The institutions which form the subject of Mez's researches were not so much recovered as introduced; and though South Arabian archaeology has revealed the existence of a wonderful civilization in that part of the peninsula, this was rarely, if ever, the source of the innovations in the Islamic Empire.

Whether the title chosen be felicitous or not, this work is a notable monument of its author's learning, which was both wide and deep. It reveals exhaustive study of Arabic literature, both printed and manuscript, with a mass of illustration from works in other languages, both European and Oriental. Access to the source of the statements in the text is facilitated by constant reference in the margin.

Something of the sort had been previously achieved by A. von Kremer in his *culturgeschichte des Orients unter den Chalifen* (*Vienna*, 1875-7), since whose time the sources of information have been enormously increased. Fresh materials are indeed still rapidly accumulating; but Mez's work is a masterly compendium of all bearing upon its subject that had been ascertained up to its time.

The Translator, Mr. Salahuddin Khuda Bakhsh, who had studied at the University of Oxford, in his busy life as barrister and Professor at the University of Calcutta, found time to produce numerous original works connected with Islam and its history, and to give English dress to important German treatises dealing with these subjects, enriching them with his own observations: thus von Kremer's brochure *culturgeschichtliche Streifzuge* in the second edition of the translation is swollen into two stout volumes (*Islamic civilization*, Calcutta 1929, 1930). Since his Oxford days he had maintained regular correspondence with the present writer, and when he undertook to translate the *Renaissance* for the Hyderabad magazine Islamic Culture asked me to peruse and make observations on the typescript before sending it to press, which I was very willing to do. The last batch of typescript was returned to me by post, marked "Addressee Dead", a great shock and grief to me, thus learning that I had lost a valued friend of long standing, while the world had lost a man peculiarly well qualified to interpret East to West and West to East, owing to the variety of his attainments and the width of his sympathies. How wide they were was apparent to anyone who visited his overflowing library, bequeathed, I understand, to that which bears the name of his family at Bankipore (Patna).

His translation of this work having stopped at Section 24, at his widow's request I translated the four remaining sections. It was gratifying to learn that the whole was to be collected from the parts of Islamic Culture and published in book form. A Spanish translation by Salvador Vila was issued in 1936 among the *Publicaciones de las Escuelas de Estudios Arabes de Madrid y Granada*.

Oxford, D.S. Margoliouth

July 1937.

THE RENAISSANCE OF ISLAM[1]

I. THE EMPIRE

In the 4/10 century[2] the Empire again sank back to its pre-Arab condition. Individual States, with natural as opposed to artificial boundaries, were formed, as has always been the case except for short intervals in the history of the East. In the year 324/935 the disintegration was complete. The small States were but fragments of one and the same Empire and the historian thus makes the inventory of the liquidation : West Iran is Buwayyid, Mesopotamia Hamadanid, Egypt and Syria render homage to the Ikhshidids, Africa to the Fatimids, Spain to the Omayyads, Transoxiana and Khorasan to the Samanids, South Arabia and Bahrain to the Karmathians and Jurjan to the Dailamites, Basra and Wasit to the Barids; while naught but Baghdad and a portion of Babylonia owned the Caliph's actual sway[3].

Already in the year 324 Masudi likens the situation to the Diodochi States that grew out of the Empire of Alexander the Great (Masudi, I, 306; II, 73 et sqq). And yet the fiction of the supremacy of the Caliph at Baghdad is in no way dissipated or impaired. Masudi himself speaks of the Empire of the 'Commander of the Faithful' as extending from Farghana and the Eastern frontier of Khorasan to Tangier in the west, 3,700 parasangs; from the Caucasus to Jedda, 600 parasangs[4].

---

(1) Mez, *Die Renaissance Des Islams*. Heidelberg, 1922.

(2) The first is the Muslim and the second the corresponding Christian era.

(3) Misk, V, 554 ; Ibn al-Jauzi 58a ; Ibn al-Athir, VIII, 241 *Kitab-al-Uyun*, Berlin, IV, 153 b ; Abulfeda under A.H. 223.

(4) Masudi, IV, 38, according to Fizari.

The local rulers (*Ashab-al-Atraf or Muluk-al-Tawaif*) acknowledge the suzerainty of the Caliph, and in the first instance cause prayer to be offered for him in the mosque, and purchase their titles from him, and send annual presents to him. Thus, when the Buwayyid, Adad-ud-Dowlah, conquers Kirman in 358/968, he obtains the Charter of Confirmation from the Caliph[1]. Like an Emperor of the Holy Roman Empire, with but small power over the German nation, the Caliph, though recognized as titular head, possessed dignity without substantial authority. But the idea of the Caliphate was once so overwhelmingly sublime that even the Spanish Omayyads would not assume the title of 'Commander of the Faithful,' but were content with the appellation 'Caliphs' Sons,' (Banu-l-Khulafa). The Fatimides caused the first breach. They aspired to be not merely temporal sovereigns but genuine successors of the Prophet. Thus, after the conquest of Kairowan in 297/909 they assumed the title of Caliph[2]. Since then the practice of calling oneself 'Commander of the Faithful' has spread. In the year 342/953 even the 'petty Sunnite ruler of Sigilmash, south of Atlas, takes on the once awe-inspiring title of 'Commander of the Faithful[3].' When Abd-al-Rahman heard in Spain that the Fatimids were calling themselves 'Commanders of the Faithful'; he too in the year 350/961, adopted that title[4]. This prevented emancipated Islam from effecting any association with definite political boundaries. The fatherland of the Muslim thus extended further and further, and the idea of a Muslim Empire, unknown to Masudi, emerged into light. While, in the case of Islam, this meant an extension of territories; in the case of the Holy Roman Empire of German nationality the lapse of centuries produced the very opposite results, namely, its shrinkage into a smaller and smaller compass.

---

(1) Misk, VI, 323.

(2) *Kitab-al-Uyun*, IV, 69a Berlin.

(3) Bekri, 151, Ed. Slane.

(4) Abulfeda, under A. H. 350 ; Maqqari, 1,212.

For Mukaddasi, the Muslim Empire extends from the extreme east at Kashghar to remote Sus on the Atlantic, and requires ten months to traverse[1]. According to Ibn Haukal it is bounded on the East by Inida and the Persian Gulf; on the West by peoples of the Sudan who dwell on the shores of the Atlantic; on the North by the countries of the Romans, the Armenians, the Alans, the Arrans, the Khazars, the Russians, the Bulgarians, the Slavs, the Turks, the Chinese; on the South by the Persian Sea[2]. Within these borders the Muslim travelled under the shadow of his faith, and, wheresoever he went, found the very same God, the very same prayer, and the very same laws and customs. There was, so to speak, a practical code of citizenship of this Muslim Empire, for the faithful in all these countries was sure of his personal freedom, and could on no account be made a slave[3].

Nasir-i-Khusru, in the 5/11th century, travels dauntlessly through all these countries. It was not unlike what happened in Germany in the 18th century.

The Fatimid Caliph, however, stands in strong opposition to his rival, the Abbasid Caliph. Outside Africa, Yaman and Syria pray for him. 'In every valley he has his agents[4]. The following little story shows what they thought he could do. Sultan Adad-ud-Dowlah had a silver lion affixed to the stern of his gondola in Baghdad. This was stolen. In vain was the earth turned upside down in search for it. People conjectured that the Fatimids had sent some one to commit the theft[5]. In the year 401 a Beduin chief, Shaikh of Agel, who held Anbar and Kufa, went the length

(1) p. 64.
(2) 10 f.
(3) Only some sectarian eccentrics like the Karmathians taught different views.
(4) Fihrist, 189.
(5) Ibn Al-Jauzi, fol. 118 a.

of causing, under the very nose of the Abbasids, prayers to be offered for the Egyptian Caliph, Al-Hakim, until he was brought to his senses by the Buwayyid Baha-ud-Dawlah[1]. It was some comfort to the Caliph at Baghdad that the newly-risen star, Sultan Mahmud of Ghazni, always showed great respect, annouced his victories; detailed his troubles to him. When in the year 403/1012 the Fatimid Al-Hakim wrote a letter to get him over to his side, Mahmud sent the letter to the Abbasid Caliph after tearing it and spitting on it[2]. Over Mekka and Medina sharpest was the friction in the holy territory; for their possession was of much greater importance then than before. There was no occasion before to discuss the insignia of the true Caliph, but now, in view of the disputes regarding the position of the Caliph, the theory was put forward that the true Caliph was the one who held the holy territory[3]. This theory constituted the basis of the calim of the Ottoman Caliphs to the Caliphate. The *Tertii Gaudentes* in these disputes for the possession of the holy towns were the Alids, of whom the Hasanids had always been wealthy and influential round about Medina. Without any opposition from the other two powerful claimants—the Caliphs of Baghdad and Egypt—the Medinite Alids conquered Mekka about the middle of the 4/10th century. But the thing to note is that, at the end of the century, the holy territory wears the same aspect as it does today[4] : Mekka, instead of Medina, becomes the centre of political gravity, and the Sharifs become the custodians of the Holy Towns[5].

Geographically at this time the Empire of Islam has once more become purely Oriental. After Charlemagne the Mediterranean had become a Saracenic sea. At the beginning of the 4/10th century the Abbasids successfully maintained

(1) Ibn al-Athir, IX, 157 ; Ibn Taghribardi, 107.
(2) Ibn Taghribardi, 114.
(3) Masudi, 1, 362.
(4) Very great changes have taken place since the days of Mez Tr.
(5) Snouck-Hurgronje, *Mekkah*, 1, 59.

their western frontier against the attacks of the Byzantines. From the pulpits of the capital, victories were exultantly announced. In the year 293/904 Muslim pirates captured Thessalonica, second town of the Byzantine Empire, "a great town guarded with walls, outposts, turrets," and took 22,000 inhabitants as slaves[1].

But in 314/924, with the occupation of Malatias[2], began the forward march of Greece. In 331/941, after a serious discussion, and upon the advice of the aged Wazir Ali Ibn Isa, the portrait of Christ, preserved in Edessa, was made over to the Christians by way of ransom for Muslim war-prisoners. With great *eclat* it was brought to Hagia Sophia[3]. Masudi mourns over the weakness of Islam in his days. He laments the victories of the Romans over the faithful; the desolation of the roads used by pilgrims; the cessation of the holy war. Victorious has Islam been hitherto, says he, but now is its stately column broken, its foundation overthrown. "Such is the case in 332/942 in the Caliphate of Muttaqi, the Commander of the Faithful. May God improve our condition[4]!"

In this century the Byzantine Empire had the good fortune of having at its head three extraordinarily able generals, following one another in succession : Nicephorus Phokas, John Zimiskes and Basil Bulgaroktonas[5]. The last, by far the ablest of the three, ruled for 55 years. In 350/961 Nicephorus conquered Crete, the chief centre of Muslim pirates, after an eight months' siege. Five years later fell Cyprus, and with it passed away the unquestioned supremacy of Islam in the Mediterranean. In 351/962

(1) Joannes Cameniata, one of the prisoners, *Corpus Script. Historiae Byzant.* Bonn, 491, 589.

(2) Misk, V, 249.

(3) Yahya ibn Sa'id, 98.

(4) Masudi, II 43 et sqq.

(5) Finlay, *History of Greece*, Vol. II. pp. 323 et sqq. Tr.

Nicephorus marched into Aleppo. Mopsuesta surrendered in 354/965 and finally Tarsus, the strongest bulwark of Islam, after the inhabitants had been reduced to live upon dead bodies for food[1]. In 357/968 Nicephorus conquered Hamah, Emesa and Laodicea. In the winter following fell the apparently invincible Antioch[2]. When in the year 362/972 Mesopotamia was fearfully devastated, and even Nisibin was plundered, the people rose at Baghdad with the rage of despair and the Mesopotamian and Syrian fugitives stopped religious services, broke up pulpits, and attacked the Caliph's residence at such close quarters that they could be shot at from the windows of the palace[3]. In the year 363/974 Baalbec and Beyrut were captured. From Beyrut the miracle-working status of Christ was taken by the Conqueror and placed in one of the palaces of Constantinople. Damascus escaped on payment of an annual war tax of 6,000 dinars[4].

In the south, however, the Muslims maintained the Nubian frontier of the quondam *Imperium Romanum*. In the year 332/943 Masudi writing from Egypt says : the Nubians pay to the Empire up to to-day a tribute which they call baqt (pactum). It is made over to the representative of the Egyptian governor in Assuan[5]. In the year 344/955 the Nubians even lost their frontier town Ibrim (Primis)[6]. In the extreme south-west Andagust, the great commercial emporium of the Western Sahara, already becomes a Muslim town, and constitutes the most advanced post towards Central Africa[7].

(1) Yahya ibn Sa'id, 123 ; Misk, VI, 254, 272.

(2) Yahya, 131 ; Michael Syrus, 551.

(3) Yahya, 140 ; Ibn al-Jauzi, 104 c; Ibn al-Athir, VIII, 455 ; Abul Mahasin, II, 436.

(4) Yahya, 145. cf. Jean Ebersolt, *Le grand palais de Constantinople.* Paris, 1910. p. 22.

(5) Masudi. III. 39.

(6) Yahya, 114 ; Maqrizi, *Khitat*, 1, 198.

(7) According to Mahallabi, writing in the 70th year of the 4/10th

The retreat in the West corresponds to a steady advance in the East. In the year 313/925 Baluchistan, hitherto heathen, was conquered[1]. In the year 349/960 the inmates of 20,000 Turkish tents accept Islam[2]. And while at the end of the 3/9th century the last town of the Empire, so far as the Turks were concerned, was Asfigab; the admission of Bogra Khans into the circle of Muslim princes pushed the frontier on to the basis of Tarin[3].

For Mukaddasi the empire of Islam extends right up to Kashghar[4], and in the year 397/1006 Khotan is Muslim. At this very time Mahmud of Ghazni sets out on his conquering expenditions and subdues large tracts in India for Islam. "The token of alliance with Indian Kings was the cutting off of a finger." Mahmud had a collection of many such fingers[5].

Whether the dissolution of the Abbasid Caliphate into fragments means a downward course to us, who merely judge by quantity and the so-called unity, is beside the question here. World-empires depend for their existence either upon a gifted ruler or upon a brutal caste—in either case they are unnatural.

---

century, even in Rankan, on the river Niger, the King and the majority of the people are said to be Muslims (Yaqut. IV, 329). But In Bekri and Ibn Sa'id (who comes later) they are called heathens.

(1) Misk, V. 249.

(2) Misk. VI, 240 ; *Kit-al-Uyun*, IV, fol 67a.

(3) Yaqubi, BG VII, 295. By a later Persian writer the town is identified as Sairam, 17 Km. east of Kunkent. This agress with the position assigned to it by Ibn Khuradadbih. This identification is accepted by Levih (Archaeological Journey to Turkistan, p. 35) and by Grenard (JA 1900, t, 15, p. 27.). But this is improbable as Sam'ani who knew Central Aisa very well speaks of Asfigab as a large town (in Abulfeda, Geogr. ed. Reinaud, p. 494). Yaqut (1,250) expressly reports that in 616/1219. Asfigab was destroyed by the Mogols but Chauchung in Nov. 1221 visits the town of Sailan, (Bretschneider, Mediaeval Researches, 1, 74).

(4) p. 64.

(5) Jauzi, fol. 18b.

The Egypt of Ikhshidids, the Kafurs and the Fatimids does not convey a bad impression; even the Samanids in the East receive a good testimony[1]. But bad times had come over Baghdad.

For the first time in 315/927 the town fell into the hands of ruffians who became more and more audacious with the progressive weakness of the Government[2]. The very worst times were those which intervened between the death of Bagkams and the entry of the Buwayyids, 329-334 (940-945 A.D.).

Like a presage of the fall of the Caliphate, the great dome of the palace of Mansur came crashing down in a tremendous storm in the year 329/940—the dome which constituted the crown and glory of Baghdad[3].

In the year 331/942 Ibn Hamdi, chief of a robber band, plundered the town under the protection of Ibn Shirzad who, as Secretary to the Turkish Commander-in-Chief, stood at the head of the Government. From his and his companions' share of the booty Ibn Hamdi had to make a monthly payment of 15,000 dinars to Ibn Shirzad for which he received regular receipts and statements of account.

Thus the citizens kept guard with signal trumpets and could no longer sleep in peace[4]. Houses in the town were deserted and their owners actually paid money to people to live therein and keep them in repair. Many baths and mosques were shut up[5]. To these was added the eternal strife between Sunnah and Shiah, accompanied by constant incendiarism. The large conflagration of 362/972 reduced 300 shops and 33 mosques to ashes and destroyed 17,000

(1) Ibn Haukal, 341 et sqq.
(2) Ibn al-Athir, VIII, 125.
(3) Jauzi, fol. 67a; *Kit-al-Uyun*, IV, 190a.
(4) *Kit-al-Uyun*, IV, 205b.
(5) Jauzi, 72a.

lives. It is said to have been caused by the government itself to end the town fights. Thus began the migration to the eastern side of the town which even to-day is by far the more populous[1]. In the following year Ibn Shirzad succeeded the Commander-in-Chief on his death. He imposed such heavy taxes that many merchants left the town. The insecurity became so appalling that robbers broke into the house of a Qadhi who, in climbing the roof, to effect his escape, fell down and was killed[2].

In Mukaddasi's time Baghdad had vacant spaces and sparse population which dwindled day by day. I fear, says he, that it will become like Samarra[3].

That part of the town which formerly, at noon, was the centre of a lively concourse of traders and customers; namely, the corner where the cobblers, and cotton traders' streets met, was in 393/1000 the playground of sparrows and pigeons[4]. Larger and more populous than Baghdad was then the capital of Egypt. It has remained since the greatest town of Islam.

---

(1) Yahya 141 ; Ibn al-Athir, VIII, 462.

(2) *Kit-al-Uyun*, IV, 229?.

(3) Mukaddasi, (Eng. tr. by Azoo) p. 120. Tr.

(4) Wuz. 116. Le. Strange, *Baghdad*, p. 77. Tr.

II. THE CALIPHS

When, in the year 295/907, a vacancy of the throne was imminent the Wazir one day rode home from the palace, accompanied, as usual, by one of the four chief ministers. He discussed with him the question of succession to the Caliphate. Personally he declared for the son of the Caliph Al-Mutazz but the other—the later Wazir Ibn Al-Furat—dissuaded him from his choice, arguing that one should not choose as Caliph him who knows the house of one, the land of another, and the garden of the third, who is affable and courteous to people, who knows life and has grown wise by experiece. He suggested the young prince Al-Muqtadir. The Wazir realized the position and Al-Muqtadir was duly raised to the throne[1]—a boy of thirteen whose sole joy consisted in obtaining holidays from school[2].

By reason of minority his election was, infact, illegal, and an honest Qadhi actually lost his life for concientious scruples to do homage to him on that ground[3]. But the mandarins had miscalculated. The boy's mother—a Greek slave—ruled firmly with her party; appointed and dismissed; and prevented plunder of the State treasury. Her strength of character is revealed by the way in which she guided the studies of her grandsons. While the later Caliph Al-Radhi sat reading his books, there came the eunuchs[4] of his grandmother with a white piece of cloth. They wrapped the books therein and left the prince angrily behind. After

(1) *Kitab-al-Uyun*, IV, 58 (b).
(2) Wuz. 116.
(3) *Arib*, 28.
(4) See the interesting note of Burton on eunuchs. *Arabian Nights*, Vol. I., 70 *Supplemental Nights*. Tr.

two hours they brought back the books in precisely the same condition in which they had taken them. Thereupon the prince said to them : "Tell him who enjoined you to do what you have done that these are purely learned and useful books on theology, jurisprudence, peotry, philology, history, and are not what you read, stories of the Sea, the history of Sindbad and the fable of the Cat and the Mouse." Suli, the prince's friend, who related this story, fearing lest they should report who was with him and the consequences of such a report, went up to the eunuchs and begged them not to convey the prince's message. They rejoined : We have not understood the learned message, how are we to repeat it[1] ? Deposed by rebels twice for a couple of days or so, Muqtadir sat for twenty-five years on the throne, but always under the shadow of his mother. Compelled by his retinue, but contrary to her and his own wishes, once and only once did he undertake a campaign. He fell in battle. His head was cut off; his dress, even the mantle of the Prophet, was torn off; and a soldier, out of sheer campassion, covered his bare body with a heap of grass. Of stout build, rather undersized, of pale complexion, he had small eyes with large pupils, a handsome face and a fine reddish beard[2]. Everything that is reported of him points to a sweetness and gentleness of disposition. When the Wazir reported to him that a monthly grant of 300 dinars was made for musk in his food and yet the Caliph took no biscuits or at least but a few, he laughed and forbade retrenchment, on the ground that people perhaps needed money for other necessary expenses[3].

But he was fond of wine[4].

His half-brother al-Qadir was chosen because, unlike

---

(1) Al-Suli, *Auraq*, Paris, 4836, p. 9.7*.

(2) Masudi, *Tanbih*, 377 ; Misk, V, 379. Arib 1,76; *Kit al-Uyun*, IV, 129a.

(3) Wuz. 352.

(4) Dhahabi, *Tarikh al-Islam*. Amedroz, *Kit. al-Wuzara*, p. 11.

him, he was not a minor, nor had he a mother to take him under her wing[1]. He, also, was stoutly built and was of reddish complexion. He had large eyes, a thick beard and was slow of speech[2]. When the insurrection of 317/929, which had set him up as Counter-Caliph, was quelled, he crying *Nafsi, Nafsi, Allah, Allah,* begged his brother for his life[3]. But he himself is said to have been a hard drinker, a miser, a hypocrite and prompt at shedding blood[4]. He managed to rid himself of the Commander-in-Chief, Muins, and succeeded in effecting considerable retrenchments[5]. But, as he would not voluntarily abdicate, he was blinded, and was, indeed, the first of the Caliphs and Princes of Islam to endure that fate[6]. This practice was learnt from the Byzantines. After this incident he lived for seventeen long years in the home where he had resided as a Prince. He is said to have become so poor that he could not afford anything but a cotton coat and a wooden sandal (qabqab khashab[7]). Walking in his simple garb and with his face covered, he was yet, once, recognized as a former Caliph by a Hashimite who presented him with a thousand dirhams and accompanied him home[8].

His nephew Al-Radhi (322-29/933-940) was only 25 when proclaimed Caliph. He was thin, short of stature, and brown in complexion. He had a sharp chin and a snub nose[9]. He understood and loved peotry and song, and has left behind a collection of his own poems. He was a collector of crystal ware, and spent more on it than on anything else[10].

(1) *Arib*, 181.
(2) Masudi, *Tanbih*, 388 : *Kit.al-Uyun* IV, 141b.
(3) *Kit.al-Uyun*, IV, 123 b.
(4) Masudi, *Tanbih*, 388 ; Misk, V, 424 ; Arib 185.
(5) Misk, IV, 419. Masudi, *Tanbih*, 388.
(6) Ibn al-Athir. VIII, 333.
(7) *Kit.al-Uyun*, IV, 120a.
(8) Masudi *Tanbih*. 388 ; *Kit.al-Uyun*, 183b.
(9) Al-Suli, *Auraq*, 27.
(10) Al-Suli, *Auraq*, 27.

Besides, he had a passion for pulling down old and erecting new buildings in their places. Specially fond was he of laying out gardens[1]. He was very generous by nature, but his limited means prevented free scope to his generosity. His people once found him sitting on a coil of rope, watching building operations. He invited them to take their seats on other coils by his side : This done, he ordered each coil to be weighed and its weight paid to the occupant in gold and silver pieces[2].

A learned man raved before him of a beautiful girl he had seen with a slave-dealer. On return home he found the girl waiting there for him. The Caliph, had purchased her for him[3]. Only one fault did his friends find with him; he gave himself up to too much pleasure and, contrary to the advice of his physician, overfed himself[4]. He died at the age of 32, after having made all necessary preparations for the washing of his dead body. He ordered the coffin to be prepared and even chose his shroud. He put them in a box with the inscription : Preparations for the other world[5].

His reign, however, did not quite pass off unstained by blood. Cunningly he lured Ibn Maqlah, the former Wazir, into a trap ; had a number of his relatives arrested and killed; of course, only such as had aspired to the throne after him or had caused homage to be done already[6].

In his twenty-sixth year his half-brother Al-Muṭtaqi ascended the throne. He, too, was of stout build, of fair complexion, with round blue eyes, with meeting eye-

---

(1) Ibn al-Jauzi, fol. 54a.
(2) Ibn al-Jauzi fol. 54a.
(3) Ibn al-Jauzi, fol. 54a, according to Al-Suli.
(4) He suffered from stomach troubles.
(5) *Kitab-al-Uyun*, IV, 182a.
(6) *Kitab-al-Uyun*, IV, 220a.

brows, short nose and reddish hair[1]. He did not indulge in wine. He zealously fasted and gave no entertainments. His only companion was the Qur'an none else would he have besides it[2]. But ill-luck never forsook him. On the night before his circumcision a bath collapsed, killing the slave-girls who were preparing themselves for the festivity. All his chamberlains suddenly died, with the result that no one cared to accept service under him. When at a celebration on the Tigris he drove through the town and crowd cheered him, a scaffolding gave way, and later a number of courtiers, women and children were drowned by the river suddenly overflowing its banks[3]. Even when on the throne this ill-luck persistently doggeg his footsteps. He was the first Caliph who, seeking for help, left the *Town of Peace*[4] and roamed about with the defeated Hamadanids in Mesopotamia. He refused the protection of the Egyptian Ikhshidids. The Turkish general, whom he trusted, betrayed him for 600,000 dirhams which a pretender to the throne had offered him, and had him blinded by an Indian slave[5]. He lived for 24 years after this tragedy and died in his own house[6]. His successor Al-Mustakfi, who waded to the throne in shame and infamy, was the son of a Greek slave-girl[7]. He had a fair complexion, long nose, big eyes, small mouth, a full beard. He was corpulent and rather tall. He had a strong liking for negro women[8]. Situated as he was between a grasping wife, whose intrigues had raised him to the throne, and the Turks actually ruling the town, he could

---

(1) Masudi, *Tanbih*, 397, *Kit.al-Uyun* IV, 220a.

(2) Ibn al-Jauzi, 66b.

(3) *Kitab-al-Uyun*, IV, 221b.

(4) Ibn al-Athir, VIII, 304.

(5) *Kitab-al-Uyun*, 219a.

(6) Yahya ibn Sa'id, 101.

(7) Masudi, *Tanbih*, 398; *Kitab-al-Uyun*, IV, 22a, merely mentions her as a slave.

(8) *Kitab-al-Uyun*, IV, 239a.

hardly be happy. Finally came the Buwayyids, who, at the very first conference, forced upon him a Wazir whom he had sworn never to appoint. The Chamberlain Duka thus relates: I was present on this occasion. Resisting, the Caliph yielded. But I saw his eyes full of tears at the strangeness of the demand[1]. When on the point of being deposed, he voluntarily abdicated on condition that none of his limbs was maimed or mangled[2]. But his successor, brother of his predecessor, in revenge for what had been done to his brother, had him blinded. No one was prepared to excute this punishment. A slave, however, whom he had once caused to be whipped when Caliph, undertook the task[3]. The later Caliphs reconciled themselves to a position of inactivity, and thus managed nominally to rule for long years. After a stroke of apoplexy Al-Muti' resigned in favour of his son—Al-Ta'i—who was deposed in the eighteenth year of his rule. For twelve years he lived after his deposition in honourable captivity under his successor. Very little is known of these later Caliphs. Al-Muti's mother, a slave of Slavonic nationality, was more famous than her son. She was a whistler. With a petal in her mouth she warbled wondrous notes with remarkable skill. She could imitate all singing birds[4].

Al-Ta'i was strong and handsome and of fair complexion. He held at bay a powerful stag, which knocked every one down and which no one dared to touch, until the carpenter removed his horns[5].

Al-Qadir was pious and kind; two-thirds of his meals he distributed to different mosques[6]. He used to dye his

---

(1) *Kit.al-Uyun*, IV, 232a.
(2) Ibid, IV, 238a.
(3) Ibid, IV, 238b.
(4) Kit. al-Uyun, IV, 240.
(5) Ibn al-Jauzi, fol. 106a.
(6) Ibn al-Jauzi, 132b.

long beard; put on ordinary dress; visit with the people the sanctuaries of the saints at Baghdad, such as those of Ma'ruf and Ibn Bessar, and indulge in all kinds of adventures. He even wrote a theological work, in the orthodox Sunni strain, which was read out every Friday in the circle of theologians in the mosque of Mahdi[1].

Against these fleeting shadows the splendid succession of the African Caliphs stands out in striking contrast. From the very begining among them, the Caliphate passed from sire to son. This practice was their salvation; for it spared them blood-stained disputes regarding the succession. To this was added a statesmanlike attitude in their dealings. When the Governor of Syria wrote direct to Al-Muizz (341-365/952-975), ignoring the legitimate channels, the Caliph took him to task and returned the letter with unbroken seals. The most brilliant of these Caliphs was Al-Aziz (365-386/975-996). Stalwart, of tawny complexion, with reddish hair and large blue eyes, a dauntless hunter, a connoisseur of horses and precious stones, he is the first example of that large-hearted Saracenic chivalry which made so deep and lasting an impression upon the West. The Caliph beat and captured the Turkish leader who had conquered Ascalon and had caused the Egyptian army to pass under a bare sword, but he took no revenge upon him. In fact, he made over his own tent to him ; supplied him with horses; met all his needs; returned his signet to him and allowed him the company of his friends among the prisoners of war. At the first interview he caused a cup a syrup to be handed over to him and when the Turk hesitated, thinking that it might perchance contain poison, the Caliph drank first[2].

And, finally, there looms on the horizon the extraordinary figure of Hakim! Sometimes he sat by day with

---

(1) Ibn al-Jauzi, 132a ; Al-Subki III, 2.

(2) Yahya ibn Sa'id, 155.

candle light; sometimes he spent the night in darkness[1]. As he loved, with a few companions, to roam about the streets of Old Cairo at night, the merchants kept their shops open and well-lighted. And thus the Bazars were as lively at night as they were during the day[2]. Except those that were used for hunting, he ordered all dogs to be destroyed, as their barking disturbed him in his nightly adventures[3]. When a disease unfitted him to ride, he had himself carried by four men in a litter—restless, ill at ease by day and by night. On these occasions he received prayers and petitions in which only one line on a page was permitted to be written. The petitioners were only allowed to approach him on his right side. He ordered them to present themselves at a certain place on the following day. He kept his orders and gifts in his sleeve and personally distributed them among the petitioners[4]. He never put a curb on expenses. He was lavish and kind to his people. Law and justice reigned triumphant under him. And yet no great man was quite sure of his life, for he pounced upon his best friends with a morbid suddenness. Much as he liked the black eunuch Ain, he yet had his right hand cut off. But this did not prevent the bestowal of favours upon him. He, indeed, conferred the most honourable titles upon him and installed him in most responsible offices. Suddenly, one day, he cut out his tongue, only to reward him afterwards yet more lavishly[5]. Of his whimsical treatment of Christians and Jews hereafter.

Towards the end he roamed about in the desert; allowed his hair to grow until it reached his shoulders; never trimmed his nails; never changed his black woollen mantle and blue head cloth reeking with dust and perspiration.

---

(1) Ibn Tagharibardi, 63.
(2) Yahya Ibn Sa'id, 185.
(3) Yahya, 188.
(4) Yahya, 217.
(5) Yahya, 218.

The learned Christian Yayha compared him to Nebuchadnezzar who, after the manner of the beasts of the field, lived with nails like the claws of eagles and hair like a lion's mane because he had destroyed the Lord's Temple. Yahya was considerate enough, however, in describing the Caliph's disease as melancholia, and said that they should have put him into a bath of violet oil to impregnate his withered brain with sweet scented moisture.

III. THE PRINCES OF THE EMPIRE

Their title is Amir. Even the royal princes were so called—only the eunuch Kafur in Egypt felt quite content with the appellation of 'Ustad[1]'. The Amir-al-Omara, at the court of the Caliph, originally had no connection with this title. He was the Commander-in-Chief. This title was also borne by the Field-Marshal Munis, who never considered himself of the rank of a prince. For the princes of the Empire there was no official mark of distinction. Prayer was offered for them in the mosque, as to the governor, after prayer for the Caliph. Only in Babylonia, where the Commander of the Faithful himself resided and personally carried on the administration, was it deemed derogatory to his dignity to mention the name of any other along with his at the service in the mosque. In the year 323/934 the Chief Chamberlain, Mohammed ibn Yaqut, had already arrogated all powers to himself, and compelled the ministers to report everything to him and to do nothing except over his signature. The result was that the Wazir was reduced to a shadow, without work or authority[2]. When the preachers of Baghdad prayed for him the Caliph dismissed them all[3]. In the following year, however, the Caliph had to yield, and the name of Ibn Raiq was openly mentioned in the prayers at the mosques. This meant the acknowledgment of a prince under him in Babylonia[4].

(1) Yahya, 124. In the East 'Ustad' was the title of Wazirs. Ibn al-Amir is so called [Misk, vi, 220]; another, Ibn Taghribardi 34. Today the coachman is called 'Ustad' in Cairo. In India the word 'Ustad' is used for a teacher—teachers of all kinds. Tr.

(2) Misk. V, 474.

(3) Al-Suli, *Auraq*, 83.

(4) 'Sultan', at this time, is only used of the Caliph and *Dar-us-Sultan* is

Among these princes the Hamadanids strike us as representatives of the worst class of Beduins (Lane-Poole, *Mohammadan Dynasties* pp. 111-13 A.H. (317-394/929-1003). On the occasion of the conference at Mosul, the Caliph Radhi took up his residence in a house and so did his Commander-in-Chief Ibn Raiq; whilst the Hamadanid pitched his tent by the cloister. You are mere Beduins, said Ibn Raiq, contemptuously to the Hamadanid (*Kit. al-Uyun* IV, 182 *b*). Of their bad government, their plundering propensities, their oppression of the peasantry, their destruction of trees, their constant violations of engagements and promises, we shall speak elsewhere. The founder of the dynasty treacherously murdered the Wazir who had accompanied him on a pleasure-ride (*Kit. al-Uyun*, IV, 60-a) and Nasir-ad-Dawlah, in a cowardly fashion, killed Ibn Raiq in his own Hamadanid tent[1]. In their own house strife and insubordination were rife. Not merely flagrantly so in the Mesopotamian branch, but elsewere as well— as shown by the murder of Abu Firas by his nephew, the son of Saif-ad-Dawlah[2]. Among them it was only Saif-ad-Dawlah who was distinguished by brilliant achievements and a certain degree of chivalry. The Greek authors note that he often fell into tactical errors because he was too conceited and never asked any one for advice lest it might be said that he conquered through others (Abulfeda, *Annales*, under

the palace of the Caliph at Baghdad. The statement of Ibn Khaldun [III, 420] that Muizz-ud-Dawlah adopted the title of 'Sultan' is incorrect. According to the later Egyptian writer Abul Mahasin [II, 252] the special title of the rulers of Egypt was at first Pharaoh and later 'Sultan.' Even al-Zuhri [9/15th century] thinks that the only rulers legitimately entitled to that title are those of Egypt. This fits in with the word 'Soldan,' current in mediaeval Europe, to signify the ruler of Egypt. The later Amirs of Baghdad do not seem to have been mentioned in prayers until Adad-ud-Dawlah in 368/979 received this honour which no king had had before or after. Misk, VI, 499.

(1) Misk, 60 ; VI, *Kit.al-Uyun*, IV, 182b.

(2) Ibn al-Athir, VIII, 334; Ibn Khall. according to Thabit ibn Sinan, See Dvorak, Abu Firas, 114 sqq.

349). But despite his brilliant achievements he was always defeated by the Turkish Cheifs Tuzun and Begkem.

Out of the old Empire the Baridis, likewise, carved their fortune[1].

(1) "Al-Baridi. This *nisba* was borne by three borthers, Abu 'Abd Allah Ahmad, Abu Yusuf Ya'kub and Abu'l-Husain, who played an important part in the period of the decline of the Abbasid Caliphate under al-Muktadir and his successors. The head of this family was the first mentioned Abu'Abd Allah, who, not content with the unimportant offices which the Caliph's vizier 'Ali b. 'Isa had given him and his brothers, obtained from his successor Ibn Mukla (*q.v.*) the government of the province of al-Ahwaz and other important offices for his brothers in return for a present of 20,000 dirhams (316/928). They managed to make such good use of their opportunities that when they were involved in the fall of the vizier scarcely two years later the ransom of 400,000 dinars demanded for their freedom by Muktadir was paid without difficulty. After the assassination of al-Muktadir in 320 (932), Abu 'Abd Allah was able to do as he pleased and by unheard of extortion and deeds of violence to enrich himself, while his brothers were restored to their offices and did likewise. This continued in the reign of the Caliph al-Radhi (322-329=934-940) because their old friend, the Vizier Ibn Mukla, had again gained power in this period. Instead of giving the revenues of the provinces governed by them to the Caliph's treasury, they kept them to themselves by false statements and bribery. This state of affairs could not go on for ever and when Ibn Raik (*q.v.*) under the title of Amir al-Umara had gained control of the Caliphate (324=936), the Caliph advanced witn an army against Abu 'Abd Allah, after all the subterfuges contrived by that cunning man to gain the favour of Ibn Raik had failed. But Abu 'Abd Allah knew what course to take ; he escaped to the Buwayyid 'Imad al-Dawla in Fars and persuaded him without much trouble to conquer al-Ahwaz and al-Irak. When an opponent to Ibn Raik arose in the Turk Bedikem (*q.v.*) Abu 'Abd Allah took the side first of one then of the other according to circumstances, and after Bedikem's victory in 326 (938) he was appointed by him Vizier of the Caliph. He was deposed soon afterwards, however, but as Bedikem had perished early in the reign of al-Muttaki (329=941), he seized Baghdad for a brief period but after a few weeks was forced by the mutinous troops to return to Wasit. In the following year 330 (932) he sent his brother Abu'l-Husain with troops against Baghdad so that the Caliph and Ibn Raik had to seek refuge with the Hamdanids of Mosul. Abu'l

For long they were the actual rulers of Babylon. More like secretaries than soldiers (Misk, VI, 154), they yet boldly fought many a time. In greed and short-shightedness they did not yield to the Hamadanids. The first really disastrous time for Baghdad was the year 330/941 when a Baridi conquered Baghdad and the Caliph fled to Mosul. Already in March he raised the land-tax, oppressed the landlords, imposed heavy capitation taxes on Christians and Jews, levied an enormous additional tax on wheat, took away a portion of their wares from the merchants, and exacted compulsory loans from the populace[1]. Before Muizz-ad-Dawlah, the last Baridi fled to the Karmatheans in South Arabia. But he was subsequently reconciled to the new order of things, returned to Baghdad, and was even included

Husain made himself so detested by his oppressions there that the Hamdanids had no difficulty in driving him from Baghdad and even from Wasit. The brothers were able to assert themselves in Basra although they had to wage a costly war with the lord of 'Oman, who had come against Basra with a fleet and had already taken Obolla 331 (942). Fortunately for them the fleet was set on fire and the enmy was forced to retire to 'Oman. There and other wars consumed Abu 'Abd Allah's wealth and although he did not hesitate to have his brother 'Abu Yusuf murdered to gain his accumulated treasures, they availed him little, for he himself died the same year 322 (944). The third brother Abu'l-Husain soon came into conflict with his own followers who recognised Abu'l-Kasim, the son of Abu 'Abd Allah as their master, and escaped with great difficulty to the Karatian prince of al-Bahrain. With the latter's help he laid siege to his nephew in Basra, till he came to terms with him. Soon afterwards he again began intriguing and went to Baghdad to try to obtain the governorship of Basra and so, far from being successful, he was executed there in 333 (945) after a trial. His nephew Abu'l-Kasim in the following year made peace with the Buyid Muizz al-Dawla, though only for a brief period, for in 335 the latter sent troops against him and in 336 (947) advanced in person against Basra and forced him to flee to the Karmatians of al-Bahrain. He then ceased to play any active part in politics though he was ultimately pardoned by Muizz al-Dawla and did not die till 349 (960)." *Ency. of Islam.*

(1) Misk, VI, 158 ; *Kit.al-Uyun* 192a.

among the table companions (Nudama) of Muizz-ad-Dawlah[1].

Compared to these robber princes, the soldiers hailing from northern countries who established their throne within the confines of the Empire were veriable fathers to the people. The Samanids pretended to be Persians and traced their descent from the Sassanids. At the end of the 3rd/9th century they reached their highest splendour : Transoxiana, Media, and the whole of Iran up to Kirman were under their rule. But within their own kingdom there flourished almost independent States ; for instance, Sigistan (Afghanistan) still belonging to the Saffarids, prayed, true enough, for the ruler of Bukhara, but merely paid him a tribute. The vastness of their Empire necessitated the establishment of a kind of vice-royalty. They themselves resided in Bukhara, but their Commander-in-Chief (*Sahib-al-Jaish*) had his seat at Nishapur, which under the Tahirids had become the capital of Khorasan[2]. Mukaddasi—possibly for personal reasons—cannot sufficiently extol their mode of life, their attitude towards learning and learned men. They excused them from kissing the ground before them. Even if a tree was to rise against them, says Mukaddasi, it would instantly wither away[3]. Even when the powerful Adad-ud-Dawlah, who conquered everybody else, marched against the Samanids, God destroyed his army and made over his State to his enemies[4]. The Dailamites, to be sure, did take the whole of Iran from the Samanids but after a hard fight. Almost every

---

(1) *Kit. al-Uyun*, IV, 247. On the word 'Nudama,' see Burton, *Arabian Nights*, Vol. I.. p. 46. "Nadim" denotes one who was intimate with the Caliph, a very high honour and a dangerous one. The last who sat with 'Nudma' was Al-Radhi bi'llah A.H. 329/940. See Suyuti, *History of the Caliphs*, Eng. tr. Tr.

(2) Vambery, *Bokhara*, Chapters IV and V. Tr.

(3) For Mukaddasi, see Khuda Bukhsh, *Studies : Indian and Islamic*, 159-162.

(4) Misk, VI, 377.

year Subuktagin, the general of Muizz-ud-Dawlah in Baghdad, had to hasten to Rai with help to the brother of his master conducting operations against the Samanids there.

Twenty years after Mukaddasi had lavished his praises, the kingdom of the Samanids was crushed between the Turks of the North and the South and the last of the House was killed in flight. To the Caliphs of Baghdad the Samanids always remained unswervingly loyal and never failed to send in presents. In the year 301/913 Ahmed Ibn Ismail even applied to the Caliph for the post of *Sahib-al-Shurtah* (Prefect of Police) which had fallen vacant by the death of the last of the Tahirids. Like a Governor to his Sovereign the Samanid Nasr sent the head of a slain rebel to the Caliph.[1]

The future, indeed, belonged to the people of the mountain ranges of Northern Persia—hitherto in the background. Of all their generals who ruled West Iran, after the death of Yusuf ibn Abissagh the Dailamite Merdawigh is the most attractive personality to the chroniclers. Islam sat lightly upon him. Like an unbeliever, he took the sons and daughters of the empire into slavery—50,000 to 100,000 women and children. Like unbelivers the inhabitants of Hamadan were put to the sword[2], and so the Iranians in the year 320/932 created a scene before the Caliph's palace in Baghdad. They questioned the authority of the Government to tax when it was not in a position to stand by the faithful with help and protection. A band of pious men met one of Merdawigh's generals before Dinawar. Their leader carried an open Qur'an in his hand and implored them to fear God and to spare the faithful who had committed no crime. But he is reported to have struck him in the face with the Holy Book and then run his sword through him[3].

(1) *Kit.al-Uyun*, IV, 190b.

(2) Masudi, IV, 23 et sqq.

(3) Masudi, IX, 24.

Merdawigh was an optimist with large schemes. He aspired to restore the Persian Empire and to destroy that of the Arabs[1]. He wore a diadem set with precious stones, according to the old Persian style, sat on a golden dais, in the midst of which stood the throne. In front was a silver dais covered with carpets and in front of that again were placed gilded chairs for the magnates of the realm. He meditated the conquest of Baghdad; he thought of rebuilding the palace of Chosroe at Ctesiphon and of ruling the world therefrom[2]. His soldiers feared his pride. He found the magnificently planned winter celebration in Ispahan mean and paltry, because to the eye, (intent upon the wide, wide world), everything appeared small and insignificant. With difficulty the Wazir succeeded in inducing him to show himself to the people. On this day of festivity all saw discontent legibly inscribed on his face. In his mantle he wrapped himself and lay down in the tent with his back against the entrance without uttering a word[3]. Along with 50,000 Dailamites he had 4,000 Turkish slaves[4] whom he unwisely preferred to his own people who, for that reason, hated him with intense hatred[5]. Despite his preference for the Turkish guards, one day he forced them, when they had awakened him from his sleep by the noise in saddling their horses, to lead their horses by the rein and carry the saddles and trappings on their backs. By way of revenge for this sort of treatment they surprised him in his bath and killed him[6]. His brother Wasmigir and his nephew Kawus, however, managed to retain a small principality high up in the north of Iran. His heritage devolved upon the leaders of the mercenaries from the Persian mountains—the Buwayyids.

(1) Al-Suli, *Auraq* (Paris) 81.
(2) Masudi, IX, 27 ; Misk, V, 489.
(3) Misk, V, 480.
(4) Masudi, IX, 26.
(5) Al-Suli, *Auraq, 81.*
(6) Misk, V, 482.

The Buwayyids were so strange to Arab culture that Muizz-ud-Dawlah, as the ruler of Baghdad, needed an interpreter for an Arab audience[1]. By cunning and soldierly qualities they rose. Without compunction they passed from one commander to another who paid them better. When Makan was beaten they begged for leave and said : they did not wish to lay upon him the heavy burden of their salaries and upkeep. If things went better, they would return[2].

One of their great qualities was to know how to make, and always to have, a reserve of money. Tradition tells us that to the founder of the dynasty, in a moment of great need, a serpent showed a hole in which a treasure lay buried[3]. By bribing the Wazir of Merdawigh they were able to plunder the rich sectarians (Khurramites) residing in their castles on the highlands of Kerag. With this money they tempted and won over a large number of their own countrymen serving in other armies. Thus to conquer the Caliph's troops and to occupy Southern Iran was an easy matter to them. Moreover they treated the prisoners with kindness and clemency and straightway took them into their service[4]. Rukn-ud-Dawlah, the ruler of Rai, for fear that he might have to spend a single dirham from his treasury, neglected the administration of the country and was prefectly content with the revenues he received—whatever they were[5]. Adad-ud-Dawlah acquired an immense fortune. Even in later times, which were by no means very prosperous, Fakhr-ud-Dawlah (d. 387/997), according to the testimony of his contemporary Ibn al-Sabi, left behind 2,875,284 dinars, 100,860,790 dirhams and treasures of all kinds which were carefully noted down. He was a miser.

(1) Misk, V, 435.

(2) Misk, V, 435.

(3) Misk, V, 464.

(4) Misk, V, 444.

(5) Misk, VI, 357.

The keys of his store-rooms were kept in an iron purse, from which he never parted[1]. Even Baha-ud-Dawlah (d. 403/ 1012) was niggardly with every dirham and gathered together treasures such as none of his House had done before[2].

Another feature of this family was its strong solidarity and strict discipline, at all events in the first generation. This must be credited to the personality of Ali, who later received the title of Imad-ud-Dawlah. To him, indeed, this House owes its splendour. When the third brother, Muizz-ud-Dawlah, already the ruler of Babylon, paid his official call on him, he kissed the ground before him, and remained standing, though bidden to sit down[3]. After the death of the eldest the supreme authority devolved upon the second brother Rukn-ud-Dawlah in Rai, to whom Muizz-ud-Dawlah rendered unhesitating obedience[4].

Muizz-ud-Dawlah, on his death-bed, commanded his son to obey Rukn-ud-Dawlah and to consult him in all important matters and also to show respect to his cousin Adad-ud-Dawlah, older in years than him[5]. But when Adad-ud-Dawlah wanted to wrench Babylon away from his unworthy cousin, Rukn-ud-Dawlah, father of Adad-ud-Dawlah, rose from his seat, rolled on the ground, foamed at the mouth, and for days neither ate nor drank. He said : I saw my brother Muizz stand before me, biting his finger for my sake, saying : O brother, you had assured me of the safety of my wife and children.

At the order of the indignant father, Adad-ud-Dawlah marched out of Baghdad where he had built a palace for

(1) Ibn Taghribardi, 821.
(2) Ibn al-Jauzi, fol. 159b.
(3) Ibn al-Athir, VIII, 353.
(4) Ibn al-Athir, VIII, 336
(5) Misk, VI, 298.

himself[1].

Imad-ud-Dawlah's was not a royal figure. He was rather a good businessman, endowed with the shrewdness of a peasant. He had arranged with the Caliph for the grant of Persia in fief as against the payment of a million dirhams. The Wazir had expressly warned his ambassador not to part with the banners and robes of honour—the insignia of investiture—without payment. But Imad-ud-Dawlah forcibly took these away and, of course, paid nothing[2].

Rukn-ud-Dawlah's fidelity, clemency and justice are praised[3]. To the Marzuban who fled to him with 'his horse and his whip' he made many beautiful presents—the like of which Miskawaihi had never seen. The historian was then the librarian of the Wazir in Rai and hastened with many others to the palace to see the procession with the presents[4].

Rukn-ud-Dawlah's Wazir suggested to his master to take over the country of the fugitive as he was not strong enough to administer it effectively. But Rukn-ud-Dawlah peremptorily rejected this proposal as unworthy of him. Miskawaihi, who must have known him well through his master, calls him a 'high-minded man[5]' but complains that he made the life of his Wazir, Ibn al-Amid, a burden unto him. Although behaving better than other Dailamites—Miskawaihi says—he acted like soldiers after victory. He took what he could and never thought of the morrow. He showed great weakness in dealing with his soldiery, who worried the people so much that some rode away to the desert to confer as to how they should satisfy them.

Moreover, he thought that his rule must stand or fall

(1) Misk, VI, 444.

(2) *Kit.al-Uyun*, IV 146a.

(3) Ibn al-Athir, VIII, 493.

(4) Amedroz, *Islam* III, 335 ; Misk, VI, 280 ff. [Eng. tr. vol V, 232].

(5) Amedroz, *Islam* III, 336 ; Misk, VI, 293.

with the Kurds and, acting on that belief, he never interfered with these robbers. When it was reported to him that a caravan had been looted and the cattle driven away, he merely rejoined : People must live[1].

Muizz-ud-Dawlah, Prince of Babylon, was curt in his behaviour and was readily moved to anger. He insulted his Wazirs and court officials[2]. He even buffeted his Wazir, al-Muhallabi. But in his illness he softened[3]. At every attack—he suffered from stone in the bladder—when he felt that he was dying, he had the lamentation for the dead done for himself in conformity with the custom of the Dailamite mountaineers. He was always ready to shed tears. Weeping, he begged his Turks, in a battle which was already almost lost, to make one whole-hearted, desperate effort under his leadership[4].

He treated the Caliph, who was in his power, with soldierly arrogance. He confiscated the property of his Wazir, al-Muhallabi, after his death, although he had served him for thirteen long years; and extorted money from his servants even down to his boatmen. His behaviour disgusted all, without exception[5]. On his new palace in the north of Baghdad, he spent 13 million dirhams which he mercilessly extorted from his supporters[6].

He never bestowed a thought on the rights of the people. He placed his army in civic quarters at Baghdad, a heavy burden to the citizens. He gave cultivable lands in fief to his soldiers. Under him the inspecting officers lost all influence; public works were no longer undertaken; the

(1) Misk, VI, 354 et sqq.
(2) Misk, VI, 194.
(3) Misk, V, 210.
(4) Misk, VI, 217.
(5) Ibn al-Athir, VIII, 405.
(6) Misk, VI, 293. Ibn al-Athir, VIII, 398. According to Ibn al-Jauzai, 1,000 million dinars.

soldiers took up lands on trial, sucked them dry, and then exchanged them for fresh ones. But he encouraged the mending of dams and personally carried soil for the purpose. The entire army followed his example. Thus he made the districts of Nahrwan and Badaraya once more fertile, and the people of Baghdad loved him for that[1]. His son Bakhtyar was endowed with immense physical strength. He once held a powerful ox by the horns so that it could not move[2]. In all other respects he was a thorough failure. He niether kept his promise nor his threats; talked but did nothing[3]. He spent his time in hunting, eating, drinking, music, joking, cock-fights, and with dogs and loose women. When he had no money to go on with he deposed the Wazir, took away his money, and appointed another in his place[4]. According to a more lenient view, he was interested in valuable books; in slave-girls, traind in various arts ; and in fine Arab horses which he loved to exercise in the desert[5]. When his Turkish boy favourite was taken prisoner he neither ate nor drank, he sighed and fretted ; and whenever the Wazir or a general came to him with important affairs he never ceased to ventilate his grief, with the result that he suffered in dignity and public esteem[6].

Adad-ud-Dawlah was the only real royal personality of this House. His rule, in the end, extended from the Caspian Sea to Kirman and Oman. Not in vain did he again, for the first time in Islam, bear the old title of *Shahan-Shah*, reckneod before as blasphemous[7]. The title continued in his House, as the revival of an old Oriental practice. He

(1) Misk, VI, 219. See Guy Le Strange, *Lands of Eastern Caliphate*, p. 80 Tr.
(2) Ibn Taghribardi, 19.
(3) Misk, VI, 386.
(4) Misk, VI, 389.
(5) Misk, V, 419.
(6) Misk, VI, 469.
(7) Wuz, 388 ; Yaq. *Irshad*, II, 120.

carried the stamp of his northern lineage. He had blue eyes, reddish hair[1]. The Wazir called him Ibn Abu Bakr, the manure dealer, becuae he resembled a man of that name who sold manure to the gardeners of Baghdad[2]. He was cruel in his dealings. He caused the Wazir Ibn Baqiyyah who had worked against him and who had been delivered to him, already blinded, to be trampled to death by elephants—the first instance of this punishment in Islamic history[3]. Another Wazir, who felt himself unable to carry out an order given to him, committed suicide for fear of his displeasure[4]. But he was equally severe upon himself. When once a girl so thoroughly captured his heart that she took him away from his work, he had her instantly removed (Ibn al-Jauzi, fol. 120 a).

Like everyone anxious effectively to govern an extensive Empire he provided for quick news-service. The courier who came late was punished. Thus he arranged to get the post from Shiraz to Baghdad in seven days ; that is a daily ride of more than 150 kilometres. He also developed and improved the espionage system. 'Every word that fell in Egypt came to his ears, and the people were on their guard even before their wives and slaves." He swept the streets of Baghdad clear of thieves. An instance is mentioned by Ibn al-Jauzi (*Kit. al-Adkiya*, p. 38, according to the *Tarikh* of Hamadani)

(1) Yaq. *Irshad*, V. 349.

(2) Ibn Khall. Nr. 709 from the *Uyun-al-Seyar* of Hamadani.

(3) Misk, VI, 481. [Eng. tr. Vol. V p. 304].

(4) Misk, VI, 514. But much has been unjustly imputed to him. Thus Ibn Taghribardi relates (pp. 159 et sqq) that he sued for the hand of the Hamadanid princess, Jamilah, but was refused. This angered and enraged him. He took everything away from her and reduced her to absolute poverty. According to another legend he compelled her to live in the prostitutes' quarter and on that account she drowned herself in the Tigris. As a matter of fact the girl, true to her brother, a mortal enemy of Adad-ud-Dawlah, fled with him. After his death she was delivered to Adad-ud-Dawlah who put her, along with her slavegirls and women companions, into his harem : Misk, VI, 507.

where he poisoned them like rats. He restored order in the Arabian and even in the more notorious Kirmanian desert, with the result that pilgrims had no more exactions to submit to or inconveniences to put up with. On the pilgrim-routes he dug wells and constructed cisterns and protected Medina by a wall. He renovated the half-ruined capital, Baghdad; built mosques and laid out bazars; repaired the bridges over the great canals, which had become so damaged that women, children and animals fell into the water while using them ; made the bridge on the Tigris, which could only be used with risk to life, broad, spacious and safe, protected it with railings, appointed guards and supervisors; restored the famous garden which had become the 'haunt of dogs and depository of corpses'. He made the wealthy classes repair the dilapidated weirs. He redug the canals which had become choked with mud, and built mills on their banks: he patched up the holes in the dams and planted a colony from Fars and Kirman on the waste lands[1]. But, all this notwithstanding—Babylonia was merely an appendage. The centre of his rule was always Persia. There the chief Qadhi resided. At Baghdad he only had four deputies to represent him[2]. Indeed Adad-ud-Dawlah is said to have whole-heartedly despised Baghdad. He is reported to have said: In this town only two, worthy of being called men, I found; but when I closely examined them I discovered that they were Kufans and not Baghdadis at all[3]. He established a richly endowed bazar for seed-sellers and made arrangements for the cultivation of foreign fruits. Thus he introuduced indigo plantation in Kirman[4]. At Shiraz he built a magnificent palace with 360 rooms[5]. At Baghdad he enlarged the immense palace of the late Field-Marshal

(1) Misk, VI, 509 ff. On the Province of Fars, see Guy Le Strange, *Lands of the Eastern Caliphate*, p. 248.

(2) Misk, VI 502.

(3) Supplement to Kindi, (Ed. Guest) p. 574.

(4) Misk, VI, 509; Ibn al-Jauzi, 119b.

(5) Muq 449.

Subuktagin by purchasing the hosues round about, and built a high masonry aqueduct to conduct, through desert and suburbs, water to his park. He used elephants for pulling down houses and consolidating the soil. He was the first to use elephants in the Muslim army[1]. Death prevented the execution of his further and yet more extensive building schemes[2]. He was up before dawn, had a warm bath, said his morning prayer, and this done, he conversed with his intimate friends. Then he transacted the business of the day and breakfasted—his physician being always present. After breakfast he slept till midday. The afteroon he dedicated to his friends, to recreation and to music[3]. He had very able teachers[4]. He loved learning ; gave stipends to theologians, jurists, philologists, physicians, mathematicians, and mechanics[5] ! Of his library we shall speak later. As a rule he studied a great deal and used to say : When I have mastered Euclid I shall give 20,000 dirhams in charity ; when we have done with the book of the grammarian Abu Ali I shall give 50,000 dirhams in charity. He loved poetry, paid the poets, and preferred the company of the literati to that of his generals[6]. He was well-versed in lyrical poetry[7]. Tha'labi even cites Arabic verses which are said to be his, but they are nothing more than mere empty rhymes. Notwithstanding all this, his treatment of Sabi was ungracious—Sabi was then master of Arabic prose. To the philosophers he assigned a large room in his palace, next to his own suite, where they could discuss matters undisturbed. Even to the preachers and to the *muezzins* (those that call to prayers) he assigned salaries. He made provision for the poor and the foreigners who lived in mosques, and established an immense hospital

(1) Misk, VI, 464.
(2) Al-Khatib al-Baghdadi, *Tarikh Baghdad*,, Ed. Salmon, p. 56 et. sqq.
(3) Ibn al-Jauzi, fol. 120.
(4) Kifte, 226.
(5) Ibn al-Jauzi, fol. 120a ; Ibn al-Athir, VIII, 518.
(6) *Yatimah* II, 2 ; Ibn al-Jauzi, fol. 120a.
(7) *Irshad*, V, 286 Ibn al-Jauzi, *Kit.al-Adkiya*, 38.

at Baghdad. On the birth of every son he gave away 10,000 dirhams as alms and, when by a favourite wife, 50,000 ; for every daughter 5,000 dirhams. Even of the welfare of his non-Muslim subjects he was not oblivious. He allowed his Wazir, Nasr ibn Harun, a Christian, to build anew a church and cloisters which had been destroyed, and to give money to needy and indigent Christians[1].

A father to his people, however, he never was. He remained a foreign despot, who knew how to feed his flock to shear it all the more effectively. He increased old burdens, created fresh ones, and extorted money in all manners and shapes[2]. He had, in the end, an annual revenue of 320 million dirhams. He wished to make it 360 million—a million a day. "He hoarded dinars and did not despise a single dirham[3]."

The final verdict of Miskawaihi, who had personally served him, runs thus : If Adad-ud-Dawlah had not had some slight-faults, which one does not care to mention when enumerating his numerous good qualities, he would have attained the pinnacle of earthly achievements and I should have hoped eternal bliss for him in the world to come[4].

His talent for rule shows itself in the selection of his subordinates. Over Media he appointed the Kurd, Bedr ibn Hasanawaihi (d. 405/1014). Brave and just, he gave to the poor and widows 1,000 dirhams in alms every Friday. To the cobblers between Hamadan and Baghdad he made an annual payment of 3,000 dinars, to provide needy pilgrims with foot-wear. For shrouds he assigned a monthly gift of 20,000 dirhams. Moreover, he built bridges and three thousand new mosques and inns. Never, indeed, did he

(1) Misk, VI, 511; Ibn al-Athir, VIII, 518.
(2) Ibn al-Athir, IX, 16.
(3) Ibn-al-Jauzi, fol. 120b.
(4) Misk, VI, 511.

pass by a spring without founding a village there. For the holy town and the protection of pilgrim-roads, he paid 10,000 dinars every year. He provided for the construction of reservoirs and cisterns and for the storage of provisions at the stations on the roads leading to the holy towns. He gave money to the Alids at Kufa and Baghdad, to the Qur'an readers, and to the indigent nobility[1]. The Amir-al-Juyush (d. 401/1010), too, came from the school of Adad-ud-Dawlah. In the year 392/1002 he was sent to Baghdad to restore order there. He made the town, a prey hitherto to the robbers, so safe and secure that a slave could be sent out at night carrying a silver salver with gold pieces without any one interfering with him[2].

After Adad-ud-Dalwah the Buwayyids produced nobody of any usefulness or importance. Finally, the last sources of revenue gave way, and Jalal-ud-Dawlah[3] had even to sell his store of cloth in the bazar. He had no chamberlains, no servants, no porters. Not even had he any one to announce the hours of prayers[4].

Bejkem and Ikhshid[5] represented the Turks in the circle of Muslim princes. Both were capable soldiers and efficient rulers. But they made no outward display. The first was a veritable condottiers. From Makan he went over to Merdawigh, and after the latter's death—he is said to have had a hand in his murder—with a few hundred Turks and Persians he joined Ibn Raiq in Babylonia. The former soldiers of Merdawigh continued under his command[6]. It was not a large body of men, 300 in all. At Ibn Raiq's behest he wrote to his former comrades in Iran and many

(1) Ibn al-Jahiz, fol. 161b.
(2) Ibn al-Jauzi, fol. 156b.
(3) See Lane Poole's *Moh. Dynasties*, pp. 139 et sqq.
(4) Ibn al-Jauzi, fol. 182, 184b.
(5) On the Ikhshidids, See Lane Poole, *Moh. Dynasties, p. 69*.
(6) *Kit. al-Uyun,* IV, 147 a.b.

responded, and joined him[1]. Then he meddled in politics, removed the name of Ibn Raiq from his banners and shields, drove him out of Baghdad, and became himself the Amir of Babylonia. He had then 700 Turks and 500 Persians under his command[2]. The Caliph, who preferred him to his predecessor[3], conferred upon him the honourable title of Nadim (Table-companion[4]). But this Turkish[5] soldier had no use for the literary friends of the Caliph. The only one whom he took to was the famous physician Sinan ibn Tahbit[6]. He begged him to cure him of the tendency to sudden outbursts of anger and to point his faults out to him.

Bejkem was wonderfully courageous. With 290 Turks he put 10,000 men of the Baridi to flight (*Kit. al-Uyun*, IV, 154 b). Within sight of the enemy he swam with his Turks across the Dajla and attacked the enemy who had reckoned upon perfect safety there. His Persians came after him in boats[7]. When he was with the Caliph in Samarra and there heard that Ibn Raiq was proceeding from Baghdad to Syria he expressed a desire to go to Hit acorss the desert to seize him. But the Caliph would not permit this, because Ibn Raiq had been assured an undistrubed passage.

To Baghdad he brought many an uncouth practice of his earlier military life. When he tried to extort money from people by placing pans full of glowing charcoal on their bodeis, it was pointed out to him that the practice of Merdawigh should not be introduced at the residence of the Caliph.

(1) Misk, V, 508.
(2) *Kit.al-Uyun*, IV, 163b.
(3) Al-Suli, *Auraq*, 55.
(4) *Kit. al-Uyun*, IV, 166b.
(5) On Bedjkem, see the *Ency, of Islam* ; see also Weil, *Cesch, d. Chalifen*, Vol. II. pp. 664 et. sqq. Tr.
(6) Misk, VI, 26 et sqq.
(7) *Kit. al-Uyun*, IV, 164.

The Baghdadis disliked him for his objectionable ways and rejoiced when Ibn Raiq suddenly attacked Baghdad in his absence[1]. The mob and the street boys jeered at him, calling after him "half of Bejkem's moustache has been shaved off." When they saw a Turk in a high cap they cried out : Fly away, our Amir is not Bejkem[2]. He held, however, the status of a prince in consequence of his having founded a colony in Madain.

The grandfather of Mohamed ibn Tughj came from Turkistan under the Caliph Mutasim who, for the first time, enlisted Turkish soldiers in large numbers. His father rose to be governor of Damascus, but was disgraced and died in prison. His son enjoyed the 'sweet and bitter of life'. Ibn Tughj, every now and then, took military service under some general or other, and at one time even served as falconer to a nobleman. In the service of the governor of Egypt he distinguished himself by courage and heroism. This served as a stepping-stone to a governorship and eventually to the independent rule of Egypt[3]. He ruled as many countries as the most powerful Pharaoh : Egypt, Syria, Yaman, Mekka, Medina[4]. No wonder then, that he should refuse the

(1) *Kitab al-Uyun*, 179a.

(2) Bejkem was appointed Amir-al-Umara in 326/Sept. 938 in place of Ibn Raiq. He first directed his attention to the Hamadanids who would not pay tribute. He proceeded to Mosul against the Hamadanid Hasan. While he was away Ibn Raiq suddenly appeared in Baghdad. Bejkem had to make peace with Hasan in 327/938 and to return to the capital. A peace settlement was soon reached with Ibn Raiq, by the terms of which the latter received the governorship of Harran, Edessa, Kinnesrin with the district on the upper Euphrates and the frontier fortresses. In 329/941, Bejkem was surprised and slain in an expedition by some Kurds. See *Ency. of Islam*. Sub. Bejkem. Tr.

(3) In 318 he became governor of Damascus and in 321 Governor of Egypt. He did not take over the office, however, till 935 (323 A.H.), in 938 (327) he assumed the title of Ikhshid, and in 941 (330 A.H.) Syria was added to his dominions, and Mekka and Medina in the following year. The Ikhshidids ruled from 935-961. Tr.

(4) *Kit. al-Maghrib*, 20.

invitation of the Caliph Mustakfi to accept the insecure principality of Baghdad after the death of Ibn Tuzum[1].

Ikhshid was corpulent and had blue eyes. He was so strong that none could stretch his bow. He suffered from attacks which could not be precisely diagnosed[2]. Egypt fared well under him. He maintained order and issued a full-valued dinar[3]. His army was the most impressive army of his age. When in the year 333/944 he came to the Euphrates the inhabitants of Raqqah and Rafiqah were amazed at the number, orderliness, and equipment of his army. They had never seen the like of it[4]. In him credulity and greed formed a useful alliance. In cold blood he proceeded to extort money from all rich officials—friends or foe. Most of them deserved their fate.

Fond of ambergris, he received it as a present from all quarters and, of these presents, from time to time, he held an auction sale[5]. Stories are told of him how he did not shrink from making even small profits. And yet he never took to rack or torture, and spared women from extortions[6]. He venerated holy men (Salihun) and used to ride to them to invoke their blessings. "Muslim ibn Ubaidullah Al-Husain tells me: I described to Ikhshid a holy man in el-Qarafah, called Ibn al-Musayyab and lo! he rode with me to him, begged him for his blessings, rode on and said to me : Come, now I shall show you another holy man. I went with him to Abu Sulaiman Ibn Yunus and there I saw a fine old man sitting on a padded mat. He rose to meet Ikhshid and asked him to sit on the mat. Thereupon Ikhshid said to him : O Abu Sahl, utter some words of the Qur'an upon me, for the

(1) *Kit. al-Uyun*, 227b.
(2) *Kit. al-Maghrib*, 39.
(3) *Kit. al-Uyun*, IV, 208b.
(4) Ibid, IV, 212.
(5) *Kit. al-Mughrib*, 35.
(6) *Kit. al-Maghrib*, 15, 37.

wind of the desert has hurt me. Then the Holy man stretched his hand under the mat ; brought out a piece of clean, folded cloth ; put it over his head and uttered words of the Qur'an on him[1]."

Ikhshid loved to hear the Qur'an read out to him and, on such occasions, wept[2].

Once he had a wonderful experience. A man from Babylonia stood on the well of Zemzem in Mekka and called out : O ye people ; I am a foreigner ; yesterday I saw the Prophet of God who thus spoke unto me : Go to Egypt, present yourself before Mohamed ibn Tughj and tell him from me that he is to set Mohamed ibn al-Maderai free (the great Persian financier). The caravan proceeded to Egypt and the foreigner with it. They came to Fustat, Ikhshid heard of the matter, sent for him and questioned him : What have you seen? He related the story. How much have you spent over your journey to Egypt? 100 dinars was the reply. Thereupon Ikhshid rejoined : Here are 100 dinars from me. Return to Mekka and sleep at the very same spot again and tell the Prophet that you conveyed his message to Mohamed ibn Tughj, but he replied : I have such and such an amount to get from him—he named a heavy amount—and if he pays it back to me I shall forthwith set him free. The man answered : I shall not make jokes with the Prophet. With my own money I shall return to Medina and go to the Prophet of God, and appear before him, awake and not in sleep, and shall tell him : O Prophet of God ! I have conveyed your message to Mohamed ibn Tughj and this is his reply. After saying this the man got up, but Ikhshid held him back and said : The matter has now taken a serious turn. We only intended to test you. You shall not leave before I have set him free[3].

(1) *Kitab al-Maghrib*, p. 34.
(2) Ibid, p. 37.
(3) *Kitab-al-Maghrib*, p. 35.

He sent a messenger to him and set him free. In the year 331/942, a report came from Damietta that a robber whose hand had been cut off as punishment and who had done penance and had lived as a servant of God in a mosque, had got back his hand. Ikhshid sent for the man to Old Cairo and bade him relate his story. I saw in dream, he said, the roof of the mosque opon and three men descend—Mohamed, Gabriel, and Ali. I begged the Prophet to restore my hand to me. He did so, and I awoke with my hand restored. From Damietta a letter came stating that many trustworthy people testified to having seen him once with his hand cut off. Ikhshid gave presents to the man of miracle and was amazed at the power of God. Later it was discovered that all this was pure imposture and the excitement caused by the story gradually died out.

IV. CHRISTIANS AND JEWS

What distinguished the Muslim Empire from Christian mediaeval Europe is the fact that within the borders of the former, unlike the latter, lived a large number of people of other faiths than Islam. These were the professors of 'protected religions' who, from the outset, hindered and thwarted the political unity of the Islamic Empire. Relying upon agreements and rights resulting therefrom, churches and synagogues always remained as something foreign to the State and never could form part of it. The Jews and Christians took good care to see that the 'House of Islam' continued in an unfinished state. The result was that the faithful always felt themselves as conquerors and not as citizens. The feudal idea never, indeed, perished—in fact it set up principles surprisingly modern. The necessity, however, to live side by side created an atmosphere of toleration, absolutely unknown to Mediaeval Europe. This toleration found expression in Islam in the creation of the science of Comparative Religion and its enthusiastic cultivation. Apart from conversions to Islam these different groups subsisted, sharply divided one from another. As in the Byzantine Empire punishment for conversion to Islam was death, so also in the Empire of the Caliph conversion of a Muslim to Christianity meant capital punishment for him[*][1].

(*) *Kit. al-Uyun, fol.* 209a.

(1) Attempts at reconversion must, of course, precede this punishment. From early Fatimide times the following is reported : It was reported to the Qadhi that an eighty year old Christian had accepted Islam, but was reconverted to his faith. He was asked to return to the faith of Islam, but he declined to do so. The Qadhi brought the matter to the notice of the Caliph, who made over the man to the Chief of the

Mixed marriages were out of the question ; for a Christian woman, according to her laws, could not marry a non-Christian and a Christian man, according to the law of the Church, could only marry a non-Christian woman if she and her children became Christians. In the case of a Muslim woman this was an absolute impossibility. The laws of the Empire further guaranteed that protected religions did not in any way collide with each other—no Jew could become a Christian and *vice versa*. Only conversion to Islam was

police. This officer sent the man to the Qadhi, with instruction to summon four assessors to reconvert him. If he repented—so ran the order—he was to get 100 dinars but if he persisted in his refusal he was to be killed. He was duly asked to accept Islam but he refused and was, accordingly, killed and his body was thrown into the Nitle (Supplement to Kindi, Ed. Guest, p. 593). In Seruj (Mesopotamia) in the 3/9th century an all-too zealous Muslim, who wanted to reconvert the apostates who had gone back to the fold of the Church, by all kinds of ill-treatment, was beaten and imprisoned under orders of the Qadhi (Mich. Syrun, p. 535). Says Abul 'Ala (8449/1057. *Luzumiyyat*. Bombay Ed. 250) : "The Christian accepts'Islam not out of conviction but from greed. He seeks power or fears the judge or else wishes to marry". Even high ecclesiastics accept Islam. Upon them the angry Church Chroniclers cast terrible aspersions. About the end of the 2/8th century the Nestorian Metropolitan of Merv, who was publicly convicted of pederasty, accepted Islam and traduced the Christians at Court (Barhebreus. *Chron. Eccles.* III., 171 et sqq).

About 360/970 the Bishop of Azerbaijan accepted Islam after being caught in the very act of fornication with a Muslim woman (Ibid, 247). In the year 407–1016 a metropolitan of Tikrit, who was threatened by his deacons with removal from office for fornication, accepted Islam and adopted the name of Abu Muslim, and took many wives. The Christian chroniclers report with satisfaction that, at the court of the Caliph, he was no longer respected as before when he was the representative of his congregation. In the end he became beggar (Elias Nisibenus, 226 ; Barhebr. *Chron. Eccles.* III., 287 et sqq.) Even in Spain, in the 3/9th century, a high church authority—Bishop Samuel of Elvira, who was deposed for evil living– became a Muslim (Graf Baudissin *Euloguis und Alvar*, 1872, p. 162). In the 3/9th century Abul 'Aina, expressed himself in a humorous way when he was made to wait in the ante-chamber of the Wazir, a convert to Islam, because he was at prayer : *'every thing new has its speical charm.'*

allowed (Sachau, *Syrische Rechtsbucher*, 11,75,170). No Christian could inherit from a Jew and *vice versa*. No Christian or Jew could inherit from a Muslim, and no Muslim from a Christian or a Jew either[1].

In the year 311/923 the Caliph issued an edict to the effect that goods of an heirless protected-subject should devolve upon the members of his community ; while those of a Muslim should go to the treasury[2].

In the second half of the fourth century an edict, in favour of the Sabians, emphasizes that Muslim authorities should not interfere with the laws of inheritance of the Sabians, remembering the words of the Prophet : 'One does not inherit between different religions[3].'

Along with the Jews and Christians the Zarathustrians too were recognised in the 4/10th century as protected subjects[4]. Like the former they too had a chief who represented them at court and with the Government.

And yet there was a difference between the three.

Through all the dangers and difficulties, attendant upon the growth of the loose confederation that arose out of the Empire, the Jews had managed to maintain their political status unimpaired. The Zarathustrians were but a remnant of a people, never fully conquered in their inaccessible homes. The condition of the Christians, living in the once Sassanid Empire, where they had already acquired the status

---

(*) Any attempt by a Muslim forcibly or by unfair pressure to convert a Christian subject who paid the tribute was also punishable with death. The law existed in the Turkish Empire in our day. 'Ed. I.C.'

(1) In the Letters patent to a Qadhi this point is specially emphasised. Paris. Arab MSS. 5907 fol. 126.

(2) Wuz. 248.

(3) *Rasa'il* of Sabi, Leyden, fol. 211a.

(4) See the note at the end of this Chapter.

of protected subjects, was less favourable than either that of the Jews[1] or even of the Christians who had been inhabitants of the provinces forming part of the quondam Byzantine Empire. "Thus the chiefs of the Zarathustrians and Jews enjoyed hereditary dignity and were called kings. They paid their taxes to their respective chiefs. Such never was the case with the Christians[2]." The chiefs of the Magians and Jews are temporal sovereigns, says the Jacobite patriarch at an audience with the Caliph, but he, on the contrary, is a spiritual chief and can only inflict ecclesiastical punishments, such as removal of bishops and priests from their ranks and excommunication of laymen from the Church[3]. By the transfer of the centre of government to the East the Nestorian catholics, chief of the Eastern Christians, became the head of the Christians in the Muslim Empire. He was chosen by his Church, but his appointment was confirmed by the Caliph and, like other high officials, he received his letter of appointment from him. One such letter, dated 533/1139 runs thus "A lawful assembly of the Christians has selected you to shepherd their affairs ; to administer their trust properties ; to adjust differences between the strong and the weak among them. According to an old, well-established practice they have submitted their nomination and, as Imam, I give permission to you to act as the Catholicos of the Nestorians in the 'Town of Peace' and in the rest of the Muslim countries, and also to be an 'authority' over the Greeks and the Jacobites and the Melkites throughout the Empire, with full power to wear the robe of the Catholicos in your divine service and in other religious gatherings. I further direct that no metropolitan, bishop or deacon is to share with you the honour of wearing

---

(1) Noldeke, Tabari *Ubersetzung*, 68, note.

(2) Michael Syrus, 519. "At Moeul the people pay a gold piece annually. Of the amount realised from the Jews half went to their chief and half to the government" (R. Petachja, 275).

(3) Dinoys of Tellmachre, 148. Barhebreaus, 1372.

robes or carrying the insignia of office[1]. Should any one act contrary to your decision he will be forthwith punished. The Caliph commands that you should be treated as your predecessors have been treated in the past. He further commands that you and your community be protected in life and property ; that everything is to be kept in good condition and that your burial ceremony is to continue as before. The capitation-tax is to be levied only once a year, and then only upon those of sound mind and sufficient means, and women and children are to be excluded from the operation of this rule. Finally, the existing laws are in no way to be tampered or interfered with. You shall mediate between the Christian sects in their disputes and help the weak in his rights against the strong."

The patriarch of the Jacobites also had to get a letter of appointment from the reigning Caliph and, on that account, had to go to Court on the occasion of every fresh accession[2]. But about 302/912 he was forbidden by the Caliph to take up his residence at Baghdad[3].

Christians who were Nubian subjects had a privileged position in the Empire. They paid taxes to their own king, who kept special tax-collectors in Muslim territory. When one of them became a Muslim, the son of the Nubian king, who happened to be at Baghdad on a visit, had him forthwith put in chains[4].

Of the head of the Jewish community the Muslims have very little to say. According to Jewish report he passed through hard times in the 4/10th century[5]. In the sixth

(1) The insignia of the Catholicos were a crozier and a hgih cap burtullah, Jahiz, Bayn, II 76; Baihaqi, ed. Schwally, 566.

(2) Michael Syrus 519.

(3) Barhebraeus, 1,275, Observation I.

(4) Mich. Syrus, 532 ; Barheb. I. 384.

(5) H. Graetz, *Gesch. der Juden* v, pp. 27 6 et. sqq. As to the Muslim account, Goldziher *Rev. Ẹtud. Juives* viii, 121 ff. According to the

century Benjamin of Tudela and Petachja of Regensburg speak of the head of the Jewish community. The division of Islam into the Caliphate of Baghdad and that of Cairo had apparently also affected the organization of Jewish community. Thus we hear of the *Roshgalutha* at Baghdad, (to whom the title of *Sayyadana* (our Lord) was given by the Muslims, whose commands were obeyed only East of the Euphrates[1] and of the *Sar hassarim* (Prince of Princes) in Cairo who appointed rabbis in Syria and Egypt—the dominion of the Fatimides[2].

This isolated position of the Cairene *Nagids* was artificially created by the Fatimide opposition to all things Baghdadian. We have a letter of an Egyptian head of the community (dating from the XIIth century, directly after the fall of the Fatimides) to whom an objectionable leader of prayer had been given from Baghdad[3]. The number of Jews in the Muslim Empire (excluding the West is stated by Benjamin (who travelled in A.D. 1165) to be somewhere near 300,000. Twenty years later Rabbi Petachja assesses their number in Babylon alone at 600,000[4]. To the Syria of the 4/10th century these figures are not applicable, for the political measures of the Crusaders had practically destroyed the Jewish community within their jurisdiction[5]. Benjamin fixes the inhabitants of the Ghetto of Jerusalem at four[6]. Petaachja did not find even one. According to the report of Bailo Morsillius Georgius, dated October 1243, there were

---

popular belief the Jewish chief is to have such long arms that he may touch the knee with his finger tips. *Mafatih al-Ulum*, ed. Van Vloten, p. 35.

(1) Benjamin, 61, according to P. also at Damascus and Acco.

(2) Benjamin, 98.

(3) *Mitteil Samml. Erzh.* Rainer V. 130.

(4) p. 289.

(5) On the Jews in the Middle Ages, See Depping, *Die juden im Mittelalter*. Stuttgart, 1834 Tr.

(6) Only one MS. has the figure 200.

only nine adult Jews in that third of Tyre which belonged to the Venetians[1].

According to Benjamin, on the other hand, there were 3,000 Jews under Muslim rule in Damascus—according to Petachja 10,000 and 5,000 in Aleppo. But they were very plentiful on the Euphrates and the Tigris, just as they were very plentiful at that time on the Rhine and Mosel. On the Tigris they were particularly so. From Nineveh down the Tigris there were Jewish communities in all the towns and villages[2]: in Jazirat ibn Omar 4,000 ; Mosul 7,000 (according to P. 6,000) ; in Harbah, the most Northern town of Babylonia, 15,000 ; in Ukbara and Wasit, 10,000 each town. But it is somewhat surprising that at Baghdad itself there were only 1,000 Jews[3]. The Jewish towns on the Euphrates were Hillah with 10,000 ; Kufa with 7,000 ; Basra with 2,000 Jews. In the beginning of the 4/10th century Sura and Nahr Malik were almost entirely Jewish[4]. Towards the East the Jewish community were more and more numerous : Hamadan 30,000 ; Ispahan 15,000 ; Shiraz 10,000 ; Ghazni 80,000 ; Samarqand 30,000[5]. Makaddasi confirms these figures of the 4/10th century. In Khorasan, he says, there are many Jews and few Christians[6] ; in Media more Jews than Christians[7]. There were, however, only two towns of the Empire in the East which were called 'Yahudiyyah,' towns of the Jews ; one was situated near Ispahan and the

---

(1) Tafel and Thomas, *Urkunden zur alteren Handels und Staatsqeschichte der Republik Venediq*, Vienna, 1856. II, 359.

(2) Petachja, 279.

(3) p. 19 ; Pet, 280. Today there are over 40,000 Jews there with 21 synagogues. Obermeyer, *Modernes Judentum*, p. 23. Vienna 1907. The latest edition of B reads 40,000. This neither agrees with P nor fits in with the amount of the capitation-tax.

(4) Ibn al-Kifti, 194.

(5) The numbers are merely conjectural as P did not visit the East. One little Arab town of Khaibar is said to have counted 50,000 Jews.

(6) P. 323.

(7) P. 394.

other east of Merv. In Khuzistan Muqaddasi found few Christians, and not many more Jews or Zarathustrians[1]. In Fars the Magians were more numerous than the Jews ; the Christians even fewer than the Jews[2] .

In Arabia itself there were more Jews than Christians. In Qurh–the second great town of Hijaz—the majority of the population was Jewish[3]. For Egypt Benjamin's figures are much lower[4] ; Cairo 7,000 ; Alexandria 3,000 ; the Deltaic towns about 3,000 and 600 in all in the commercial centres of Upper Egypt.

The numerical strength of the Christians can be only very imperfectly fixed. The assessment of taxes in Babylonia under Omar I shows some 500,000 souls, liable to capitation-tax. This suggests about a million and a half of protected subjects inclusive of Jews[5]. According to the Egyptian census of the 2/8th century there were five million Copts paying capitation-tax. This indicates the existence of some 15 million Coptic Christians[6]. At the beginning of the 3rd/9th century Baghdad yielded 130,000 dirhams and at the beginning of the 4/10th century 16,000 dinars in capitation-tax[7]. Both figures show some 15,000 non-Muslim subjects liable to taxation. Of these 1,000 must have been Jews. We

(1) P. 414

(2) P. 439. A writer of the XIVth century tells us that little Persian towns of Abarquh was noted for the fact that there the Jews were not allowed to stay more than forty days. After that period if they continued to live there they forfeited their life. Hamadallah Mustawfi. G. Le Strange, 1903, P. 65.

(3) Maq. P. 184.

(4) This agrees with Maq (P. 202) "few Jews." In antiquity they are said to have constituted more than an eighth of the population. (Caro, *Wirtschaftsgeschichte*, 1, 27.)

(5) Ibn Khurd. p. 14.

(6) Accordig to the census of 1907 Egypt shows only twelve million inhabitants.

(7) Ibn Khurd.p. 125 ; according to Qod (p. 251) the capitation-tax for the year 204/819 was 200,000 dirhams.

can thus, with tolerable certainty assume, the Christian population to have been somewhere between 40 to 50,000 at Baghdad. The only two towns, between the Euphrates and the Tigirs, where Ibn Haukal finds a preponderance of the Christian population, are Edessa and Tekrit, the head-quarters of the Jaqcobites, and the seat of their patriarch. Some of its old chruches and cloisters go back, says Ibn Haukal, to the times of Jesus and the apostles[1]. In Babylonia, chiefly in Southern Persia, there was a considerable population of the Zarathustrians[2]. A riot is reported between them and the Muslims in 369/979 in Shiraz. Their houses were plundered and Adad-ad-Dawlah punished every one concerned in it[3]. But as a rule Shiraz was very peaceful. Makkadasi is surprised that the Zarathustrians there bear no distinguishing marks and that the whole town is bedecked on the occasions of the feasts of the infidel. When in the year 371/981 the chief of the Sufis died, Muslims, Jews, and Christians formed the funeral *cortege*. In the Eastern Persian desert only al-Qarinain was inhabited by the Zarathustrians, who mostly lived by letting out donkeys on hire and roamed about in all directions[4].

About the end of the 2/8th century under the Caliph Amin, the Sabian community flourished for the last time. "Then paganism once again attained its splendour in Harran. Attired in costly clothes, decked with myrtles and roses, with little bells attached to their horns, oxen were led, through the streets, followed by flute-players[5]." In the twentieth year of the fourth century (*i.e.* tenth century A.D.) the Caliph sent for the opinion of the Inspector of Industries at Baghdad regarding them. The opinion was as follows : "They should be killed, for they are neither Christians nor

(1) P. 156.
(2) Muq. p. 126.
(3) Ibn al-Athir, VIII, 522.
(4) Qod, 209.
(5) Mich, Syrus, 497.

Jews, but are worshippers of stars." It cost the Sabians a great deal to pacify the Caliph[1]. An edict, issued about the middle of the century, reaffirmed the protection promised to them and they were permitted to live in Harran, Raqqah and the Osrhcene[2]. But about 400/1009 they had almost disappeared. Ibn Hazm fixes their number approximately at forty[3]. Legally no calling or profession was closed to the protected subjects. In those lucrative occupations, such as banking, large commercial ventures, linen trade, land-ownership, medical profession, the Christians and Jews were thickly represented and firmly established[4].

They so arranged among themselves that in Syria, for instance, most of the financiers were Jews and most of the physicians and 'scribes' Christians[5]. Even at Baghdad the head of the Christian community was the Court physician, and the Court banker the head of the Jewish community[6].

In the lowest class of tax-payers were the Jewish money-changers, tanners, shoe-makers, and particularly dyers[7]. At

---

(1) Subki, II, 193.
(2) *Rasa'il* of Sabi. Leydon, fol. 211a.
(3) *Kit.al-Fisal*, II, 115.
(4) Abu Yusuf, *Kit. al-Khiraj*, 69.
(5) Maq. 183.
(6) The physician Gabriel and his colleague Michael chose, for instance, the Nestorian Catholicos in the year 210/825 (Barheb. *Chron. eccles*, III, 187). In a poem of Abu Nawas (d. circa 195/810) there occurs : "I questioned my friend, Abu Isa and the wise Gabriel and said : Wine is gratifying unto me. To this he rejoined : Too much of it kills; but four doses, for each element, are permissible.'

And in far off Nisabur sings a poet : 'When I found my body full of ailments and pain in my joints, I sent or a *Shaikh* of the capitation-tax payers whose father's brother was a Patriarch and whose mother's brother a Catholicos' (Yathimah, IV, 306).
(7) *Kit. al-Khiraj*, 69 ; Maq. 183. 'Like a sandal from the shop of the Jew Ibn Esrah' says Abulqasim (ed. Mex. 42). The Jews of Ispahan specially carried on humble trades, such as those of cupping, tanning, fulling and, worked as butchers, Abu Nuaim, Leyden MS. fol. 11a.

Jerusalem Benjamin of Tudela (12th century) found the Jews in complete monopoly of the dyers' trade[1]. Even the twelve Jews that lived at Bethlehem were all dyers[2]. Wherever, indeed, there lived even a single Jew in a locality he was certain to be a dyer[3].

In the Hanafite and Hanbalite laws the life of a protected-subject was placed on precisely the same footing as that of a Muslim—a most important principle indeed. The very same blood money was payable in either case. According to Malik, however, the murder of a Christian or of a Jew could be atoned for on payment of half the amount required in the case of a Muslim; according to Shafa'i by a third and in the case of a Parsi by a fifteenth part only[4].

It was regarded as an offence to say to a Muslim : You Jew, you Christian[5].

The Government never interfered with the worship of the tolerated-subjects ; in fact, it looked with favour upon the frequently noisy celebration of Christian feasts[6].

In the case of failure of rain the Government actually ordered processions of Christians with their Bishop at the head, and of Jews with trumpeters[7].

Monasticism continued in peaceful prosperity[8]. For

(1) p. 35.
(2) p. 40.
(3) pp. 32, 43, 44, 49.
(4) Yahya ibn Adam, 55 ; Sachau, *Muh. Recht*, 787. In Gaul, for instance, the *Wehrgeld* for a free Frank was twice as much as for a Roman citizen.
(5) Qodamah, Paris, Arab. 5907.
(6) In theory, they were not allowed to carry banners, crucifixes, torches, (*Kit. al-Khiraj*) but this prohibition was never actually enforced.
(7) Diony. V. Telmachre, 176. See Guy Le Stange, *Baghdad during the Abbasid Caliphate*, p. 212 et. Sqq. Tr.
(8) Guy Le Strange, *Baghdad under the Caliphate*, p. 207 et sqq. [Tr].

instance, it is reported of Dair Qura, about 100 kilometres South of Baghdad, a mile east of the Tigris : "a fine, charming, thriving cloister, containing 100 small cottages for the monks—each with one occupant. A monk was allowed to sell his cottage to another—the price varying from 50 to 1,000 dinars[1]. Every one of these little cottages stood in the midst of a fruit garden, where all kinds of fruits, date-palms, and olive-trees grew, yielding an income between 50 and 200 dinars. Right through the grounds of the monastery, which were enclosed by a high wall, there flowed a canal. On these grounds the festival of the Cross was celebrated and the people flocked to it[2]."

The largest monastery of Egypt was that of St. Anthony, south of Cairo, in the desert, three days' journey from the Nile, high up on a hill. It owned rich estates and possessed property in the town. Within the walls of this monastery, besides a large vine-yard, vegetable gardens, three springs and various fruit trees, there were as many as 3,000 date-palms[3].

In the Byzantine Empire the State-Church proceeded far more drastically against fellow-Christians of differing sects that did Islam against her protected-subjects. When in the 4/10th century the Emperor Nicephorus reconquered the Syrian territory he specially assured the inhabitants that he would protect them from the harassing interferences of the State-Church. This promise notwithstanding, he insulted the Jacobites as much as he could ; for instance, compelled them to leave Antioch. The Jacobite chronicler calls the Imperial

(1) It is reported that about the year 300/912 parents used to purchase a cell for a son joining the monastery. Yaqut, *Irshad,* II, 24.

(2) Schabusti' *Book of the Cloister*, fol, 115b, also Streck, 284. On the Mesopotamian monk life up to the 3/9th century, See Budge, *Book of Governors*, CXLCII ff.

(3) Abu Salih, ed. Evetts, fol. 54*b*. As poverty was insisted upon by the monastic rules of Egypt, the Egyptian monasteries were built on quite a different plan from those of Syria.

patriarch more perverse than the Pharaoh and more sacrilegious than Nebuchadnezzar. From the reconquered Melitene the Jacobite Patriarch, along with seven theologians, was taken and imprisoned at Constantinople and the great Church there was made over to the Orthodox community[1]. The Patriarch died in exile at the Bulgarian frontier ; one of his companions perished in prison ; another was stoned in front of the gate of the Imperial Palace. Three abjured their faith and were rebaptised but found no peace after, becoming the butt of ridicule. The leaders of the Syrian church found it impossible to continue their residence at the seat of the 'Orthodox' patriarch and had, accordingly, to remove to Amida, the more tolerant country of the infidels[2].

The State-church forbade the use of bells to the Armenian Christians[3].

Often enough the Muslim police had to interfere when the different Christian parties fought each other. Thus in the 3/9th century the Governor of Antioch appointed an officer to whom the Christian community paid 30 dinars per month, who was posted near the alter and whose duty it was to see that members of contending parties did not murder each other[4].

In the Christian community at Tinnis (Egypt) great trouble arose in the 20th year of the 4/10th century over the election of a bishop. "Father did not speak to his son nor wife to her husband." In the end they had to invoke the aid of the Government which put a seal on the door of the main church[5].

---

(1) Michael Syrus, 556 ff.

(2) Barheb. 1,432 ff.

(3) Schlumberger, *Epopee Byzantine*, 68. Just as the English Church acted towards the Catholics right up to the 19th century, and the Spanish and Chilian churches even later towards the Protestants.

(4) Mich, Syrus, 517.

(5) Yahya ibn Sai'd, Paris, 83b.

About the year 200/815 the Caliph Mamun wanted to give to the protected subjects[1] complete freedom regarding their faith and the management of their ecclesiastical affairs. Every community of whatever persuastion—even if it consisted of only ten souls—was to be permitted to choose its own spiritual chief and such an one was to receive the Caliph's recognition. But in consequence of the agitation of the various Church dignitaries the C aliph stayed his hand.

As regards the construction of churches the Sassanids showed greater toleration than did the later Roman Law which forbade the erection of new synagogues to the Jews and only permitted the repair of those in ruins. In Islam, the Persian and the Roman, the milder and the harsher views, were indiscriminately applied. At times new churches were allowed to be built ; at others old churches in ruins were not permitted to be repaired. The pious Governor of Egypt, between 169 to 171/785-787, destroyed all the newly-built churches there although he was offered 50,000 dinars as bribe. This fact the chronicler states with admiration. His successor, however, permitted the re-construction of those Churches and the theologians decreed that construction of churches was part of the economic system of the country and argued that such was the correct view from the fact that all existing churches in old Cairo were built under the Islàmic sway[2]. When about the year 300/912 in Tinnis (Egypt) a church was destroyed, the Government helped the Christians in rebuilding it[3]. In the year 326/938 the Christians gave money to the Egyptian Amir to induce him to sanction the repair of a church in ruins. He replied : First bring legal opinion on the subject. Ibn al-Haddad decided that permission should be refused and so did the Malekites, but Mohamed ibn Ali held, on the other hand, that it was

(1) Sachau, on the legal position of the Christians in the Sassanid Empire. *Metteil. des Sam. fur Orientalische Sprachen* X, 2.

(2) Kindi, Ed. Guest, 131.

(3) Yahya ibn Sa'id, Paris, fol. 81 a.

permissible to make improvements and to rebuild churches in ruins. On this decision being made public, the people set fire to his house and called upon him to forthwith repent and recant. The populace raved, barricaded the streets, and surrounded the church. The soldiers were called in to restore order, but stones were thrown at them and the ruler recalled them. Then he summoned the Mufti Abu Bakr ibn al-Ḥaddad who had decided against the Christians and spoke to him thus : "Go to the church. If it is not entirely in ruins, let it stand or else pull it down. May God curse them!" He took an architect with him who with candle in hand examined the church and reported : It can still continue for 15 years, then a part of it will collapse. The remainder will, however, continue for another forty years, and then, if the building is unattended to, the entire structure will fall down. Upon this report the Amir forbade repairs. In 366/976 it was, however, repaired ; this was just before the completion of forty years and the church was saved[1].

In the hospitals of the Capital, protected-subjects were treated in precisely the same way as Muslims. Only in the year of the plague at the beginning of the 4/10th century, the wazir directed the Caliph's physician, in charge of medical aid and medicines, outside the capital, to attend to Muslims first[2]. The dead were, of course, buried separately. It is, however, stated that in the year 319/931, on the occasion of the floods in Tekrit, a Babylonian town, the dead, both Muslims and Christians, were buried together with the result that it was impossible to distinguish the grave of one from that of the other[3]. There were no ghettoes for Christians and Jews, although people of the same faith lived close to each other. In Baghdad, for instance, Christian cloisters were to be found in all parts of the town.

(1) Tallquist, 321, f. Supplement to Kindi, p. 554.
(2) Ibn al-Kifti, Ed. Lippert, 194.
(3) Ibn al-Athir, VIII, 174.

As the Muslim Law was only meant for Muslims, people of other faiths were left to seek remedy in their own Courts. These courts, so far as we are aware, were exclusively ecclesiastical. The heads of the churches acted as Judges and, in fact, published several law books. Their jurisdiction extended not merely to marriage and inheritance but also to most of the disputes occurring among Christians. With these disputes the State did not concern itself. But the protected-subject was not debarred from seeking relief in a Muslim court. This, however, was regarded with displeasure by the Church. The catholicos Timotheus (cir, 200/800) published rules, intended for removal of all excuses to Christians for seeking relief in Islamic courts, on the ground of want of legal assistance in their own system[1]. And SS 12 and 13 of this Book of Rules imposes upon every one, seeking relief from Islamic courts, punishment such as penance, alms, sack cloth and ashes[2]. His successor even decreed excommunication for it. In the year 120/738 the Qadhi of old Cairo first sat in the mosque to deal with cases of the faithful, and then on the steps, to deal with those of the Christians[3]. Later the Qadhi there set apart a day in the week at his residence to hear cases of Christians. The Qadhi who acted in 177/793 actually took the Christians inside the mosque. In any case the Islamic State did not compel any protected-subject to submit to the jurisdiction of the Qadhi if he was not so inclined[4]. But once he submitted to his jurisdiction the trial proceeded according to Muslim Law and he had to abide by it[5].

In the laws issued by the patriarchs which have come down to us, only ecclesiastical punishments are mentioned:

(1) Sachau *Syrische Rechtbucher*, II, 57.
(2) Ibid, 67, p. 169.
(3) Kindi, Ed. Guest, 351.
(4) Maverdi, Ed. Enger p. 109.
(5) Thus in the draft of a Qadhi's patent in Qodamah [written shortly after 316/928] Pairs, Arab. 5907.

for instance, reprimand before the assembled community ; standing in sackcloth and ashes before the church ; payment of atonement-money to the church ; exclusion from the church, the sacrament and Christian burial[1]. For instance the punishment for one who assaults another Christian is prohibition from attending church or receiving sacrament for two months. Every Sunday he is to stand in sackcloth and ashes and give alms to the poor according to his means[2]. We also learn from a reliable Spanish source that there too the Christians settled their disputes among themselves and that only in cases of capital sentence had the Qadhi to be consulted. They placed the condemned criminal before the Qadhi, submitted proofs, and if he said '*bene est*' the offender was put to death[3].

According to R. Petachja the chiefs of the Jewish community in Mosul were permitted to punish their own people even in cases where a Muslim was concerned. There was there a Jewish prison where the offenders were incarcerated[4].

The disability which the non-Muslims felt most keenly was one which they shared with slaves ; namely their incompetence to depose in a law court. According to certain jurists they could not depose even against one of their own people. Others, however, made some exceptions[5].

(1) Sachu, *Syr Recht.* II p. VI.

(2) Ibid, p. 681.

(3) Graf Baudissin, *Eulogius und Alvar*, p. 13.

(4) P. 275.

(5) Sachau, *Muh. Recht.* 739 ; Kindi, 351. According to the patent in Qodamah (Paris Arabe 5907, for. 12*b*) the Qadhi was to allow Christians and Jews as witnesses against one another. On the other hand Christian courts, in Muslim countries, had to accept, though not willingly, the testimony of a Muslim against a Christian. Only they insisted that the witness was God-fearing and unobjectionable—qualities equally required by the Qadhi in the witnesses before him. *Syr. Rechtbucher*, II, 107.

As a return for the protection accorded to them by Government the tolerated subjects paid capitation-tax each according to his means : 12, 24, 48 dirhams, and in countries of gold currency, 1,2,3 dinars, per head per annum. It was a tax in commutation of military service ; only adults capable of bearing arms paid it.

Cripples and monks, if they were not self-supporting, were exempted[1].

Even in the Byzantine Empire every non-Christian Jew and Magian, had to pay one dinar annually per head[2] and, in the conquered countries, the Christians imposed capitation-tax upon all Muslims[3]. Naturally the major portion of the tolerated-subjects paid the lowest amount. Thus Benjamin of Tudela reports that the Jews pay one gold piece per head in all Muslim countries[4]. Likewise Petachja : The Jews of Babylon pay no tribute to the Caliph—only a gold piece annually to Resgalutha[5]. In October 1243 the Venetian Bailo Marsilius Georgius reports from Tyre : Every male Jew, as soon as he reaches his fifteenth year, pays to our officer one *Bisantius*, on the feast of All-Saints[6].

Notwithstanding different currencies, the amount actually paid by each individual was practically the same, any variation being due to fluctuations in the exchange.

At the beginning of the 3/9th century the Egyptian

(1) According to B. of T. (p. 77) and Marsilius, 15 was the lowest age for the payment of capitation-tax. In the Persian Empire it was 20 (Noldeke, Tr. of Tabari 247).

(2) Ibn Khurd, p. III.

(3) Ibn Haukal, 127. In the year 358/969 when Basilios capture Aleppo, along with other taxes every adult had to pay one dinar per head. Ibn Sa'id, fol. 98b.

(4) p. 77. Compare the Chinese traveller on the Persian capitation-tax. Noldeke. Traus. of Tahari, 246. Anm. 2.

(5) pp. 275, 228.

(6) Taiel und Thomas, II, 359.

government was satisfied with the payment of half-a-dinar. But in 300/1,000 the Egyptian patriarch Georgius imposed upon each adult-male member of his flock 1½ dinars instead of half-a-dinar as before[1].

When on a visit to Egypt about the year 200/815, the patriarch Dionysius thus reports of the famous linen-weaving town of Tinnis : Although Tinnis has a considerable population and numerous churches we have never witnessed greater distress than that of its inhabitants. When we enquired into the cause of it they thus replied : Our town is encompassed by water. We can neither look forward to a harvest nor can we maintain a flock. Our drinking-water comes from afar and costs us 4 dirhams a pitcher. Our trade is exclusively that of linen which our women spin and we weave. We get from the dealers half-a-dirham per day. Although our earning is not sufficient to feed our dogs we yet have to pay 5 dinars a head in taxes. They beat us, imprison us and compel us to give our sons and daughters as securities. For every dinar they have to work for two years as slaves. Should a girl or a woman get a child while with them, they make us swear that we would not claim them. It is not uncommon to exact a fresh tribute before such a woman is set at liberty. The patriarch replied : According to the Law of Mesopotamia they were to pay the capitation-tax in this order : rich 48, middle class 24, poor 12 dirhams per year[2]. The taxes were collected in instalments of six, five, four, three, two dirhams[3].

In the beginning this tax was collected from the

(1) *Mitteil, aus den Samlungen* Rainer II/III, 176 ff.

(2) Mich. Syrus, p. 516. In Syria the pig was an object of special taxation. Bailo of Tyre reports that up to his time every Christian who killed or sold a pig had to pay four dinars to the king. The Venetians abolished this tax. Tafel and Thomas, *Urkunden zur alteren Handels und Staatsgesch. der Republik Venedig,* Vienna 1856. II, 350.

(3) As in the Persian Empire, Tabari (Noldeke's trans.) p. 242 ; Dionysius, 61, Yahya ibn Adam, p. 56.

Babylonians every month, apparently because the Muslims received out of it their pension month by month. Such also was the case in Spain[1] in the 3/9th century. But later in the year 366/976 it was ordered to be collected in the first month of the year. Women, minors, old men, people out of work, indigent and unmarried monks, were exempt from payment[2]. On payment a paper receipt was usually given. In harsher times they tied the quittacne-receipt round the neck and put a stamp on the hand of the protected-subject[3]. This was an old Babylonian custom. The slave there carried a small cone of burnt clay bearing his and his master's name (*Mashriq*, V, 651). The Talmudic Jews marked their slaves by a seal either on his neck or on his coat (Krauss, *Talmudische Archaeologie*, II, 89).

In the year 500 A.D. the Governor of Edessa fastened a leaden seal round the neck of those poor of the town who received a ration of a pound of bread per day[4].

The old jurists Abu Yusuf and Yahya ibn Adam do not say a word about this practice. Apparently it was but rarely enforced. At all events Dionysius of Tellamachre (d. 845 A.D.) mentions it as an exceptional procedure to send a tax-collector, accompanied by a stamper, who was to stamp the name of the town or of the village on the right hand

---

(1) Leovigildus, *Dehabitu Clericorum* (Esp. Sagr, XI) : *Vectigal quod Omni lunari Mense pro Christi nomine solvere cogimur.* Eulogious Memoriale, 1,247 : *quod Lunariter solvimus cum gravi mocrore tributum*, according to Graf Baudissin, *Eulogius und Alvar*, p. 10.

(2) *Rasail* of Sabi p. 112, ed Ba'abda, 1898.

(3) In Egypt under the last Omayyads every monk had to wear an iron ring round his wrist and every Christian a signet of the shape of a lion on his hand. Maqrizi, *Khitat, I.* 492.

(4) Joshua Stylites, ed. Wright, 42. Even in Strassburg of the XIVth century the poor of the town had to carry a public badge [Brucker, *Strasburger Zunft-und Polizeiverordnungeu*, p. 61]. In China of the 9th century the enrolled prostitutes carried a copper label of the Emperor round their necks. [Renaud, *Relation des voyages*, 69].

and on the left the word "Mesopotamia' and to tie two discs round the neck, one bearing the name of the town and the other the name of the district. For every three men they exacted a stamp-fee of three dirhams. Dionysius further states that they also noted in their register the name, the personal description, and the native-place of the tax-payer. This caused great excitement, for it led to the detection of many strangers against whose name fictitious residence, as stated by them, were recorded. If this method had been pursued to its legitimate conclusion, it would have caused greater mischief than ever. When the stamper saw that he had not enough work on hand he proceeded into the surrounding country and seized everyone he met. More than twenty times he visited the whole of the neighbourhood and was not satisfied until he had brought all the inhabitants to book, not one escaping him. Thus happened what the prophet Daniel and the Apostle James had said : All men received the stamp of this animal on their hands, on their breasts, on their backs[1].

It is apparent that the patriarch does not mention the discs and the stamps as something of common occurence.

A Basran poet of the first period of the Abbasids, however, sings :

"Love for her is stamped on my neck,
"It is stamped where the seal is
impressed on the protected subjects[2]."

According to a writer quoted by Jahiz (d. 255/869) it is the sign of an inn-keeper to put a seal on the neck of a protected-subject[3]." One such disc, found in the neighbourhood of Hamadan, dates from the first year of

(1) Dionys. of T. ed. Chabot, 148.
(2) Aghani, III, 26.
(3) Bayan, I, 41.

the 4/10th century. We have, indeed, direct proof that in the first quarter of the same century a sealed quittance-receipt was given on payment of this tax[1].

The ordinary clergy were not exempt from the capitation-tax; but monks, living on charity, like other beggars, were[2]. In Egypt, for the first time in 312/924, capitation-tax was imposed on monks and bishops and on all monasteries in Upper and Lower Egypt and of the Sinai Peninsula. A number of monks thereupon travelled to Baghdad and complained to the Caliph Muqtadir. He forthwith directed that as in the earlier times, nothing was to be taken from monks and bishops[3].

Even in 1664 A.D. all Europeans, all unmarried members of the Coptic church, the Patriarch, and all Turks, *i.e.* Muslims, were free from capitation-tax in Egypt[4].

The collection of the capitation-tax was just as harsh and severe as was that of other taxes, though, according to law, all severity was banned. The canonical law forbade these old, tried methods, such as assault, torture, exposure in the sun, pouring of burning oil on the head. According to it, the defaulting tax-payer was only to be kept in custody until he paid up his dues[5].

Regarding the regulation as to dress, Harun al-Rashid, in the year 191/807[6], ordered the protected subjects to use cord instead of belts, stitched caps, and to refrain from using foot-wear of the same kind as that of the Muslims. Instead of a tassel they were to have a wooden knob on their saddle.

---

(1) Masudi, IX, 15.
(2) Abu Yusuf, p. 70.
(3) Yahaya ibn Sa'id, 83.
(4) M. Wanslebs, *Beschreibung von Aegypten*, p. 57.
(5) *Kit. al-Khiraj*, p. 69.
(6) Tabari, III, 713.

Instead of the horse-saddle their women were only permitted the use of the donkey-saddle[1].

In the 2/8th century the Jews wore a tall hat which has been likened by certain writers to a mile-stone or to a pitcher[2]. The Christians in those days used a burnoose, but when the tall-hat (qalansuah) went out of fashion among Muslims it became the distinguishing token of a Christian[3].

In the old regulations no special colour is mentioned. The use of a special colour evidently was a purely local custom[4]. Jahiz (d. 255/869) describes the Babylonian custom: the proper wine-dealer must be a protected-subject bearing the name of Adin, Mazbar, Azdankad, Misa or Sluma and wearing a black and white spotted dress and having a seal on his neck.

At the time of Harun al-Rashid, the faithful of Misr abused, in the mosque, a Qadhi whom they hated, but the Qadhi stood at the door of the mosque and called out : *Where are the fellows in honey-coloured mantles ?* Where are the sons of whores ? Why doesn't one of them say what he wants to enable me to see and hear him[5].

By an edict of the Caliph in 325/849 honey-coloured head-gear and girdles were, for the first time, prescribed for non-Muslims. He who used a Qalansuah (a pointed cap) like that of a Muslim, has to fasten two buttons of a colour different from that used on Muslim caps. The slaves of Christians and Jews were to have a honey-coloured patch four fingers in diameter on their chest and on their back. Also they were forbidden to use a small soldier's belt. They

---

(1) *Kit. al-Khiraj, 75.*

(2) Kindi, ed. Guest, p. 424. In Egypt it was called 'burtullah.' In the East it formed part of the dress of the Catholicos.

(3) *Mustatraf* II, 222 a, R; *Mufid al-Ulum*, 200 a; R.

(4) Jahiz, Bayan I, 14 I

(5) Kindi, p. 390.

were, however, permitted a broad band round their waist. On their housedoors a wooden figure of the devil was to be nailed[1]. According to an ordinance of the year 239/853 they were not to ride on horses but only on mules and donkeys[2]. All these measures, however, were of no avail. The protected subjects simply disregarded them. Already in the year 227/885 the people of Baghdad rose against the Christians who, in defiance of the regulation, rode on horses[3]. And about the 90th year of this very century Ibn al-Mutazz once again complains that Christians give themselves airs, riding on mules and using horse-saddles (Ibn al-Mutazz, *Diwan*, II, 9 ; Abul Mahasin, II, 181). Four year before the beginning of the 4/10th century all these measures were revived and re-inforced. And yet through the whole of this century (*i.e.* the 4th/10th century) we hear nothing of these rules. In any case they lay dormant. With the ascendancy of orthodoxy in the 5/11th century they were once again taken more seriously.

In 423/1031 the Catholicos of the Christians and the Ras-al-Ghalut of the Jews pledged themselves in a solemn assembly on behalf of their brethern-in-faith, who wanted to place themselves on an equal footing with Muslims, that they would once again carry their distinguishing marks. At this time, as never before, the rule came into force that protected subjects were not to build their houses higher than those of the faithful. So far as I am aware Mawardi is the first to mention this fact[4]. The idea soon makes its way

(1) Tabari III, 1389 et sqq ; Maqrizi, *Khitat*, II, 494. The Sabians also had to wear a special coloured dress. Yatimah, II, 45. In the West, for the first time in 1215 A.D. the Lateran Council demanded a distinguishing sign for the Jews. Probably this was due to the knowledge of such practices in the East.

(2) Tabari, III, 1419. Even in the Constantinople of the XIIth century no Jew was to ride a horse. Benjamin of Tudela, p. 24.

(3) On this occasion the cloister of 'Khalil Yasu' was demolished. Elias Nisibenus, 188. According to Tabari this happened in the year 272.

(4) Enger's edition, p. 428.

into the West, where in 1205 Pope Innocent III complains that the Jews at Sens have built a synagogue which overtops a neighbouring church[1].

There was as much jeering and ill-will between religions as between the races. They spoke of the stench of the Jews[2]. The Christians were dubbed wine-bibbers (especially on Easter day[3]). Their nuns and choir boys were slandered as corrupt and of easy virtue.. The Sabians were taunted for their hard-heartedness towards each other[4].

It was, indeed, known to cultured Muslims that Christianity, more than any other religion, preached love and meekness and, knowing this, they noticed how little its professors lived up to its teachings. Jahiz (d. 255/869) states that all sharp practices come from the Greeks, notwithstanding compassion being the key-note of their religion[5]. Al-Beruni declared it a noble philosophy which gives the shirt to him who takes away the coat ; which offers, when struck on one, the other cheek ; which blesses an enemy and prays for all. But men are not philosophers and since the conversion of the Emperor Constantine, adds the author, the sword and the lash have been the instruments of the Christian government[6].

The most amazing feature of the Islamic Government is the number of non-Muslim officers in State service. In his own Empire the Muslim was ruled by Christians[7]. Old is the complaint that the decision over the life and property of Muslims lay in the hand of protected subjects[8]. To Omar I is

---

(1) Caro, I, 296.
(2) Ibn Kuťaiba, *Adab al-Katib*, p. 26.
(3) Yatimah, III, 97.
(4) Ibn al-Kifti, 398.
(5) *Kit. al-Haywan*, 1, 55.
(6) *India*, Translation II, 161.-
(7) For Syria, Muq. 183 : for Egypt *Yahya* ibn Sa'id, Paris fol. 122a.
(8) Ibn Kutaiba, *Uyun of al-Akhbar*, 99.

ascribed a warning against making Christians and Jews State officers[1].

Twice in the 3/9th century even the War Ministers were non-Muslims with the result that the 'defenders of the faith' had to kiss their hands and obey their commands[2]. Like Muslims, Christian and Jewish officers were sworn in. The Diwan al-Insha[3], composed about 840/1436, mentions the Jewish 'formula of oath' and states that it was drafted by Fazl ibn al-Rabi, Chancellor of Harun, and has served since then as a model for later times.

Against the domination of protected subjects, so galling to true Muslims, were the anti-Christian movements directed[4]. In 235/849 the Caliph decreed that none but a Muslim was to hold a public office and, in consequence thereof, even the office of the recorder of the level of the water of the Nile was taken away from Christian overseers. But ten years later this very Caliph placed the constructions of his palace in charge of a high Christian officer[5] and by 296/909 the Christian 'State-Officers' had become so powerful that the Caliph Muqtadir had to resuscitate the ordinances against them[6]. Christians and Jews were to hold no other appointments except those of physicians and tax-collectors[7]. But Muqtadir's order was so ridiculously unworkable that his own Wazir had four Christians among

(1) Ibn Kutaiba, Ibid, p. 62.

(2) Wuz, 95.

(3) Paris, MS. 4439.

(4) Kindi, 203.

(5) Tabari, III. 1438.

(6) *Arib*, 30,

(7) Abulinahasin, II, 171. The papyruses show that in Egypt there was a large number of Christian tax collectors. One of them in the year 349/960, actually had the cross impressed upon his seal. Karabacek, *Mitteilungen* II/III, p. 168.

It was Omar II, Omar ibn Abdul Aziz, the Umayyad–Ed. "I.C'.

the nine privy Councillors, who were daily guests at his table[1]. Christian officers were found everywhere. Such already was the case among the Tahirids[2] in the 3/9th century. And, in the year 319/931, one who sought the Wizarat, had to ingratiate himself into the favours of Ibrahim, the Christian secretary of the Amir, and Stephan, secretary of the Field-Munis[3].

To get on in the world one had to call attention to his Christian connection. "My family is connected with yours, says an applicant for a post under the government. My forefathers held important offices in the Byzantine Empire. In the days of Mutadid a crucifix fell from the hand of my grandfather, Ubaidullah ibn Sulaiman, and, when the people saw it, he said : it was an amulet of our women-folk, who conceal it in our dress without our knowledge[4]." He had calculated correctly. Under the very same Muqtadir who wanted to remove Christians from public offices, this flatterer of the Christians became his Wazir. At the head of the intriguers against the all-powerful Munis stood the eunuch Muflih. His Christian secretary, also a eunuch, then wielded the greatest influence[5]. In the year 324/935 died Stephan, the Christian superintendent of the Caliph's private chest[6]. The first Buwayyad also employed a Christian secretary[7] ; when the Wazir of Adad-ad-Dawlah proceeded to Basra he left behind a Christian as his representative at the capital[8]. The Caliph al-Tai (363-381/993-991) had a Christian secretary[9], and in the second-half of the same

(1) Wuz, 204.
(2) Schabusti, Berlin, fol. 51a.
(3) Misk V, 352.
(4) Arib, 164.
(5) Ibid, 112.
(6) Al-Suli, *Auraq*. Paris ; 96.
(7) Misk, V. 465.
(8) Misk VI, 310.
(9) Ibn al-Hajjaj, *Diwan x*, p. 18.

century both Adad-ad-Dawlah (d. 372/982) at Baghdad and the Fatimid Caliph al-Aziz at Cairo had Christians for their Wazirs. The former sought and obtained permission of his master to rebuild churches and cloisters and to help his needy brethren with money[1].

Later the Muslim jurists laid down that a Christian or a Jew could hold the post of a Wazir (Wizarat al-taufid), provided he was not vested with absolute powers[2]. At the Egyptian Burah at the beginning of the 3/9th century, sat a Christian district magistrate who every Friday donned the black Abbasid official dress, girded the sword round his waist and rode to the mosque, accompanied by his guardsmen. There he halted. His representative, a Muslim, went into the mosques, prayed and preached and then ruturned to his chief outside[3]. Under the orders of the Amir a Muslim saint, who is said to have bidden the Christian secretary of the Viceroy to dismount, was thrown to the lions[4].

In the year 389/999 the Christian Secretary of State of Egypt, Fahd, was ordered to prosecute all who after the death of the Qadhi was accused of embezzling funds belonging to orphans, depositories, etc. He sold the property left by the Qadhi and dismissed all who had held responsible offices under him, including some most influential Muslim clerics[5].

Despite these unnatural conditions even Christian chroniclers report but few disturbances in the 4/10th century between Muslims and non-Muslims. In the year 312/924 the people in Damascus plundered a great church and took

(1) Misk VI 511 ; Ibn al-Athir, VIII, 518.
(2) *Iqd al-Farid* of Abu Salim (d. 652) p. 147.
(3) Eutychius *Corpus Script. Christ, Orient*, p. 58.
(4) Abulmahasin ; II, 233.
(5) Supplement to Kindi, Ed. Guest, p. 595. 597.

away 200,000 dinars' worth of property in crucifixes, cups, dishes, incense-burners, cushions.

They also plundered a number of monasteries. About the same time at Ramla three churches were destroyed but, by the order of the Caliph, were rebuilt[1]. On the other hand the bishop could get nothing when he came to Baghdad to complain about the church of St. Mary at Ascalon which was burnt down by Muslims. It was said to have been done with the help of the Jews who had collected wood and set fire to it and had gone on the roof with red-hot rollers to melt the leaden sheet which covered the roof. The result was that the lead melted away and the pillars collapsed[2].

In the year 329/937 some churches in Jerusalem were plundered by Muslims[3]. In the year 381/991 two Muslims abused a Christian astronomer who did not wear his distinguishing badge. He complained to his chief who put the two offenders into custody. Thereupon two churches were plundered and the Catholicos ended the unhappy affair by rich presents[4]. There was also excitement over a report that a pig had been found in a mosque. It was said to have been thrown in by Christians. In the year 392/1002 the people of Baghdad were roused to anger by the report of the murder of a Muslim. They set fire to a church which in collapsing caused the death of quite a number of people[5].

In the year 403/1012 the funeral of the daughter of a Christian physician, married to a high Christian officer, took place during the day with the accompaniment of candles, drums, litanies, monks, and women hired to weep. A Hashimid found all this objectionable. He stoned the coffin.

(1) Yahya, fol, 81a.
(2) Yahya, f. 84b.
(3) Yahya, f. 82b.
(4) Barhebraeus, *Chron. Eccl.* III, 259.
(5) Wuz, 443 ; Ibn al-Jauzi, fol. 147 b ; Barhebraeus, *Chron, eccles.*, III, 262 et sqq.

Thereupon a clerk of the Christian officer cut his head open with his club. The Christians then fled with the cropse into the church in the Greek quarter. The people were inflamed; copies of the Qur'an were displayed in the bazars ; the doors of the great Mosque were closed and a procession appeared before the Caliph's palace. The Caliph ordered the officer to surrender the offending clerk, but he refused. This was followed by a fight in front of his house.

An Alid was reported to have been killed. This news enraged the populace still more. Prayers were suspended and some Christians killed. After long negotiations the clerk was surrendered to the Caliph, but after some time was again released[1]. At Baghdad these were mere isolated occurrences. The relations were strained them in Egypt only. There a united church and a non-Arab people stood in opposition to the Arabs. Not until the end of the century did the Christians of Egypt begin to forget their Coptic language[2]. In the first two centuries one Coptic rebellion followed another. In 216/831 the last of them was put down. And yet the entire middle class of Egypt was Christian. The Arabs understood the Copts as little as once the Greeks understood the Egyptians, despite the fact that Copts managed to introduce into the traditions of the Prophet sayings favourable to themselves. On of these spurious traditions thus lays down the role of the Coptic clerks in the State : "The Copts will help the faithful to the path of piety by removing worldly cares from them[3]."

(1) Ibn al-Jauzi, Berlin, fol. 159 a.

(2) This is best explained by what Maq., who was there in the third quarter of the 4/10th century, reports : The Christians speak Coptic [p, 203] ; while the Bishop of Ashmunian [Egypt] writing about 400/1010, reports that he had translated the Coptic and Greek documents into Arabic as most of the people do not understand those languages sufficiently well. *Historia Patriarcharum Alexandrinorum*, ed, Seybold, Beirut, 1904., p. 6. The Coptic popular poetry of the 10th century A.D., known to us, is purely ecclesiastical.

(3) Abu Salih, ed, Evetts, fol. 286. from the *Fadail Misr* of Kindi, Maqrizi, *Khitat*, I,24 et sqq.

As States-Officers these Copts did their work so effectively that most of the Christian disturbances of Egypt might be put down to their credit.

About the middle of the 4/10th century a successful military operation of the Byzantines found its echo in Egypt. When in the year 389/960 Syria was devastated by the Byzantines, a disturbance which broke out in the old mosque of Cairo after the Friday prayer culminated in the destruction of two churches[1]. And when, in the following year, the Emperor Nicephorus won back Crete for the Christians, the so-called Imperial church of St. Michael at Cairo was plundered. It remained closed for a long time, the doors having been blocked with earth[2].

The first Fatimids showed to the protected subjects a toleration amazing in sectarian chiefs such as they were. They had Jewish physicians who were not required to accept Islam[3]. At the court of Muizz nothing could be done without the help of some Jew or other. The cunning renegade Ibn Killis knew this and thus largely depended for support on his former brethren in faith[4]. The rationalistic tendency of the Ismailites made public disputations between Muslims and Christians possible for the first time in Islam[5]. Under Aziz the friendly attitude of the court towards Christians grew. He had, indeed, relations among the Christian clergy; of these Aristes became the Archbishop of Misr. The Caliph, indeed, had great regard for the Christians in general.

No idle song did the poet sing when he sang : "Become

(1) Yahya ibn Sa'id, fol, 92 a.
(2) Yahya, fol. 92b. Graetz.
(3) *Gesch der Juden*, V. 4th Ed. p. 266.
(4) de Goeje, Z.D.M.G. 52, 77. According to Ibn al-Jauzi [Bodl, Uri 670 year 380] [See Lane-Poole's Egypt. Tr.]
(5) Guyard, *Grand Maitre des Assassins*, p. 14. [Long before the Ismailites public disputations were held between Christians and Muslims, See Khuda Bukhsh, *Studies : Indian and Islamic*, p. 58 Tr.].

Christian, for Christianity is the true religion ! Our time proves it so. Worry not about anything else : Yaqub, the Wazir, is the Father ; Aziz, the Son, and Fadl, the Holy-Ghost." When the people asked for the punishment of the poet, the Caliph begged Ya'qub and Fadl to forgive the author[1]. Later this very Caliph made the Christian Isa, son of Nestorius, his Wazir and appointed Manassah, the Jew, his representative in Syria. This was too much. The people clamoured for the removal of them both and the Caliph acquiesced in their demand[2]. Under this Christian Wazir there was an attack upon the Christians.

Disquietened by the conquests of the Emperor Basil in Syria, the Egyptian Caliph fitted out a fleet in the year 386/996 which was burnt down in the dock-yard. The people suspected the Greek merchants and killed 160 of them. From the Greeks the attack passed on to the native Christians. Churches were plundered and the Nestorian bishop fatally wounded. The Wazir, however, restored order. Sixty-three offenders were seized. Every one of these had to draw a lot from under a piece of cloth. On one was written "Thou wilt be killed' ; on another 'Thou wilt be whipped' ; and on the third 'Thou wilt be set free.' And thus everyone was dealt with according to the lot he drew[3].

In the year 393/1003 the fanaticism of al-Hakim began to burst into flame[4]. Noticing the Caliph's attitude, the people

(1) Ibn al-Athir IX, 82.

(2) Ibid, IX, 81.

(3) Yahya, fol, 113a. : Maqrizi, *Khitat*, 1,195., The judgment really was not meant to be carried out, for the author adds that the condemned one was taken through the town with the head of a murdered man tied round his neck. No other instance of this kind is reported from the 4/10th century.

(4) The history of al-Hakim is most exhaustively told by de Sacy in his *Expose de la religion des Druzes* p. CCLXXVIII et. sqq. Only, de Sacy has not used the continuation of Eutychius by Yahya ibn Sa'id, a contemporary of al-Hakim and a sober and trustworthy reporter.

took to destroying churches and the Caliph to replacing them by mosques. Among such mosques was the famous al-Azhar. But this was not all. The old regulation regarding 'dress' was now renewed and reinforced. The Christians, moreover, had to carry heavy wooden crosses round their necks ; public festivals and ringing of bells were proscribed; the crosses outside the churches were broken down and their traces effaced. Famous churches such as the Church of the Holy Sepulchre at Jerusalem and the great cloister of al-Qosair, on the Moqatta mountain chains, were destroyed. Even the graves in the great cemetery were violated. This Hakim never intended or wished to be done and he stopped it as soon as he heard of it. Despite all this, the Caliph appointed the Christian Mansur ibn Sadun his Wazir that very year and throughout this period employed Christian physicians. A list of capable Muslims eligible for the post of clerks was ordered to be made with a view to appointing them instead of Christians ; for hitherto all clerks, officers, physicians of his empire, without exception, were Christians. On Thursday, the 12th of Rabi II of 403/1012, clerks, tax-gatherers, physicians with the bishops and priests met together and walked weeping, bare-headed and bare-footed, to the Palace and, on reaching it, kissed the ground before it. Al-Hakim sent an officer to receive the petition and gave a gracious answer. On the Sunday following, the 15th of Rabi II, there came forth an order that the cross round the necks of Christians should be much heavier, its arms were to be two feet long and a finger's breadth its thickness. The Jews too were ordered to wear balls, five pounds in weight, round their necks in commemoration of the calf's head which they were supposed to have worshipped.

Many distinguished Christian officers accepted Islam.

It is only from his work that the chronological sequence of events can be accurately fixed for the first time. The account of the other contemporary, Bishop Severus, is more a pious legend.

Others followed suit with the result that for many a day together no Christian was seen in the streets. Many, indeed, only pretended to be Muslims, such as Muhass ibn Badus who was killed in 415/1024 when Finance Minister. They found his corpse uncircumcised although he had sent for the man to perform the operation[1].

On the contrary, in the Provinces most of the Christians and Jews retained their respective religion. Many thousands of churches and cloisters were destroyed and the Christians had actually to pay for their destruction. Of the cloisters in Egypt only two were spared, at Alexandria. The Sinai cloister surrendered all its treasures, and apart from heavy payments, owed its salvation to the impossibility of destroying its massive masonry walls[2].

Later, when the incense of the newly preached religion of the Druses reached the Caliph's nostrils, and he strove to set it in competition with the old Islam, the religions of the protected subjects ceased to provoke his anger. When in the year 419/1019 it was reported that the Christians had assembled in their houses to celebrate the Lord's Supper and even those of them that had accepted Islam had taken part in it he did not worry about it. The very same year he restored the endowments to the Sinai cloister and rebuilt the cloister of al-Qosair[3].

Under his successors things, went back to earlier practice. Christians were again allowed to conduct public processions. The only thing that reminded the people of the mad Caliph was the black turban and the black girdle which most of the Copts have ever since worn.

---

(1) Al-Muhasibi [d. 420/1029] apud Becker, *Beitrage zur Geschichte Aegyptens*, 1,61.

(2) Yahya, fol. 122.

(3) Yahya, fol. 131a.

Already in the year 415/1024 the Coptic Feast of the Epiphany was celebrated with the old splendour and under the patronage of the Caliph himself. From 436-439/1044-1047 a converted Jew was the Wazir in Cairo, and under him the Persian Jews Abu Sa'd and at-Tustari administered the State[1].

Thus did a poet sing :

"Today the Jews have reached the summit of their hopes and have become aristocrats.

"Power and riches have they and from among them are Councillors and princes chosen.

"Egyptians, I advise you, become Jews, for the very sky has become Jewish[2] !"

---

(1) Yahya, fol. 133*b*. The regulation regarding dress must have been renewed from time to time. Thus under the Qalaunid al-Nasir in 8/14th century the Christians were directed to wear blue, the Jews yellow, and the Samaritans red head-bands. The Samaritans, even to this day, in Palestine, wear a red hat-band.

(2) Suyuti, *Husnul- Muhadharah*. II, 129.

V. SHI'AH

In the 4th/10th Century the oldest counterpart of the official Caliphate, Kharijism, bad lost its importance[1]. As small theological Separatists, Kharijis were found scattered over the centre of the Empire. At the beginning of the century they caused in Eastern Mesopotamia a few disturbances.[2] Only on the frontiers they still maintained their strength,—right back in Afghanistan[3], and in the West where the Berbers on either side of the Straits of Gibraltar cast in their lot with them[4].

The Mahdite Shi'ahs, the Karmathians and the Fatimids, however, continued the Kharijite struggle against the Caliphate, an indication that the old Islamic regime was at an end. The revival of the essentially old oriental ideas in Shia'ism at the expense of Islam constitutes the distinguishing feature of the spiritual movements of the 4th/10th century. Wellhausen's researches have shown that Shia'ism was not, as it was formerly believed to be, a reaction of the Iranian spirit against Islam[5]. Of this view the geographical expansion of the sect in the 4th century affords

---

(1) For Kharijism, See Brunnow's Monograph translated by Khuda Bukhsh under the title of *Kharijites Under The First Omayyads*, Muslim Review, 1927. Tr.

(2) Masudi, V, 320.

(3) Muq., 323.

(4) Gold-ziher. They were Ibadites, specially Makkarites, Z. D. M. G. 41, 31 Sqq. The Eastern section adhered to the stricter Sufrite views. About 400/1,000 all other parties of the Kharijites had died out. To-day the Arabs of Oman and the countries in East Africa, under their sphere of influence, are the only important remnants of the Kharijites.

(5) *Oppositionsparteien*, 91.

strong confirmation. Already at the end of this century Khawarizimi called Babylonia the classic soil of Shia'ism[1] and Kufa, with the grave of 'Ali, its head-quarters.

"He who craves the martyr's crown need only go to the *Dar-al-bittish* at Kufa and say : May God have Mercy on 'Othman Ibn 'Affan.[2]"

In the course of the 4th/10th century the new teaching laid its hold upon Kufa's old rival city, the city of Basra. It was said of the latter in the 3rd/9th Century : "Basra is for Otham ; Kufa for Ali"[3], where Suli (d. 330/942) took shelter when persecuted for a declaration in fovour of Ali[4]. Already in the 5th/12th century Basra had no less[5] than thirteen places of worship dedicated to the memory of 'Ali. There, even in the great mosque, a relic of 'Ali was exhibited : a piece of wood 60 feet in length, 5 spans in breadth and four inches thick which he is said to have brought from India[6].

From the earliest times Syria, indeed, had been an unfavourable soil for the Alid propaganda. Even at the beginning of the 4th/10th century Nasa'i was trampled to death in the mosque at Damascus for not citing any tradition of the Prophet in praise of Muawiya and for giving 'Ali precedence over him[7]. I do no know how, but only in Tiberias Shi'ahs were found ; half of Nablus and Kades as also the major portion of Transjordania were Shi'ite[8]. Despite the Fatimid rule this sect made no appreciable advance. That

(1) *Rasa'il*, ed. Constant., 49.
(2) *Tarikh Baghdad*, Paris, fol. 14b. Only the suburb of Kunash was Sunnite.
(3) Jahiz, *opuscula*, 9.
(4) Muq., 126.
(5) Nasir-i-Khusru 87.
(6) Nasir-i-Khusru.
(7) Muq., 179.
(8) Ibn Khall., Wustenfeld 1,37, Subki, *Tabaqat* II, 84.

Nasir-i Khusru found Tripoli in the year 428/1037 Shi'ite[1] is explained by the fact that the *Banu Ammar* there, one of the many small frontier dynasties, were Shi'ites and, apparently, put into practice the barbarous principle *Cujus regio, ejus religio* ; a principle which never found favour in Islam, much less legal acceptance. With the exception of the towns, Arabia was positively Shi'ite, and even among the towns Oman, Hajar, and Sa'dah were predominently Shi'ite[2]. In the Province of Khuzistan, lying next to Babylonia, Ahwaz, the capital, at least was half Shi'ite, and in Persia, it was only near the coast-tracts, lying close to Babylonia and in intimate touch with Shi'ite Arabia, that Shia'ism found its adherents[3].

In the entire East, however, the Sunnah absolutely reigned supreme ; only the inhabitants of Qumm were extreme Shi'ites who had separated from the Community[4], and avoided the mosque until Rukn-ud-Dawlah compelled them to attend service there. The fact that Qumm was once occupied by the partisans of the rebel Ibn Al-Ash'ath accounts for this curious position of affairs there. In Kufa Ibn Al-Ash'ath's son was brought up. The Sunnites made fun of the fanaticism of the Qummites. Once a zealous Sunnite was appointed Governor over them. He heard that by reason of their hatred to the Companions of the Prophet no one named Abu Bakr or Omar could be found there. Lo! he summoned the people one day and thus spoke to their chief : 'I swear by the Mighty God that unless you produce before me a man among you named Abu Bakr or Omar I

---

(1) p. 42.
(2) Muq., 96.
(3) Muq., 415.
(4) Muq., 395. A Shi'ite woman, from Qumm represents Shia'ism in a poem in *Yatimah*, IV, 135. The Shi'ites also, dominated in the small Quhastanian town of Raqqah (Muq., 323). Already in the 3rd century the Qummites paid 30,000 dirhams for a linen sleeve of an Alid's coat.

will deal severely with you. They asked for three days' time. They zealously ransacked the town and spared themselves no pains. At last they found one bearing the name of Abu Bakr, a poor wretch, barefooted, naked, squint-eyed, the most hideous of God's creatures. His father was a foreigner who had settled down at Qumm, and hence the name. When they appeared before the Governor with him, he reprimanded them. You bring the most hideous God's creatues, said he, to me and thus trifle with me. And forthwith he ordered them to be beaten. Thereupon a wit among them thus addressed the Governor : "Do what you please, Amir, but the air of Qumm will not produce an Abu Bakr of more comely appearance than the one before you." The Governor laughed and pardoned them[1].

At Qumm the fanatical party of the Ghurabiyyah[2] were powerful. In honour of Fatima, daughters inherited, to the exclusion of sons, among them[3]. In the year 201/816 another Fatima, daughter of the eighth Imam, al-Ridha, was buried there. Thus Qumm, next to Mashed, is the most coveted burial place of the Persians, Isfahan[4] on the contrary, was still, when Muqaddasi passed through it, so fanatically prepossessed in favour of Muawiya that he almost came to grief there. It was the very reverse of Qumm. In the year 345/956 there was a great uproar at Isfahan because a member of the garrison, a Qummite, had insulted a name held sacred by the Sunnites. People attacked each other and fell, and shops of the Qummite merchants settled there were looted[5]. Towards the end of the century Hamadani ascribes the decay of Nisabur and the misfortune of the Province of Quhistan to the diffusion of the Shi'ite doctrines

(1) Yaqut, IV, 176.
(2) On Ghurabiyyah, see Friedlander, *On the Heterodoxies of the Shi'ites* ; pp. 56 Sqq. Tr.
(3) Subki, *Tabaqat*, II, 194.
(4) Muq., p. 399.
(5) Ibn al-Athir, VIII, 388.

there. At Herat one already heard a boy say at the market-place that Mohamed and 'Ali cursed the Taim, to whom Abu Bakr, and the Adi, to whom 'Omar' belonged[1].

So far indeed Shia'ism had not conquered the lands which it owns to-day, but it was well on the way towards that consummation. Even persecution helped its cause forward. Theologically the Shia's are the heirs of the Mut'azilahs whose lack of tradition-mindedness was particularly helpful to them. In the 4th/10th century there was actually no real system of Shi'ite theology. The Shi'ite Amir 'Adad-ud-Dawlah merely adapted himself to the views of the Mut'azalites. Only the Fatimids had a regular Shi'ite system which, as Muqaddasi expressly points out, agreed in many points with the Mut'azalites[2]. Except on the question of Imamat, on all fundamental doctrines the Zaidites are in perfect agreement with the Mut'azalites[3]. Moreover, an edict of the Caliph, dated 408/1017, assumes close connection between the Shi'ites and the Mut'azalites. Among other things it forbids the Shi'ite doctrine of *Rifd* to the Mut'azalites[4].

The method of Ibn Babuyah al-Qummi, chief exponent of the Shi'ite learning in the 4th/10th century, in his *Kitab-al-ilal*, recalls to our mind that of the Mut'azalites, who claimed absolute omniscience for themsevles. Like Mut'azalism, Shai'ism possessed ample scope for all manner of heresies. Already the Shi'ite leader Ibn Muawiya (2nd/8th century) gathered round him heretics of all shades of opinion. One of these was later executed for denying the resurrection and maintaining that human beings were not unlike vegetables[5]. In the year 341/952 Muizz-ad-Daulah

(1) *Rasa'il*, 424 *sqq* Ibn Haukal, 268.
(2) Ahmed ibn Yahaya, ed. Arnold, p. 5.
(3) Maqrizi, *Khitat*, II. 352.
(4) Ibn al Jauzi, 166b.
(5) Wellhausen, *Oppositionsparteien*, 99.

set at liberty some preachers of the doctrine of the transmigration of the soul. Of these one asserted that he harboured the spirit of 'Ali ; another the spirit of Fatima and the third the spirit of the angel Gabriel[1]. These doctirnes, notably those of rebirth and the transmigration of souls, are found alike in Shia'ism, Mut'azalism and Sufiism. There common source is the Christian Gnosis[2]. In Babylonia, about 300/900, we encounter the view that 'Ali was a second Christ. In 420/1029 the Shi'ite preacher at Baghdad prayed first for the Prophet, and then for 'Ali who had 'conversed with a skull ;' a story based upon the legend of Christ having brought the dead back to life. In Islam for long continued the idea that Christ was at once human and divine[3]. Many of the pathetic incidents of Passion Friday are introduced into the 'Ashura feast. Qummi (d. 355/966) states : Every time a man sees the heaven red like fresh blood or the sun on the wall like a red mantle he is to recal the death of Husain. Fatima, upon the same analogy became the 'Blessed Virgin,' (*Batul*)[4]. And finally these were Shi'ites who taught that Husain was not really killed but, like Jesus, appeared so to men[5]. Possibly even the dress of the Shi'ahs has some connection with the white vesture of the Gnostic sect. Originally the Shi'ahs too wore a white dress. 'White dress and black heart,' tauntingly exclaims Ibn Sakkarah. One of their cranks wore a black dress, saying that the heart only need be white[6]. The Karmathians had white banners. The Fatimid Caliphs and preachers wore white dresses[7]. The

(1) Abul Mahsain, II, 338.

(2) It is not necessary to ascribe the specific idea of the Messiah to the South Arabian Jews who are set down as the authors of this doctrine. Friedlander Z.A. 23 24.

(3) Ibn al-Jauzi, fol. 178 a.

(4) Qummi, Berlin, *Kit. al-Ilal*, fol. 77b. Fatima is called so because she never had her period.

(5) Al-Qummi, *Kit. al-Ilal*, Berlin, fol. 135a.

(6) Yat., II, 206.

(7) Al-Qummi, *Kit.al-Ilal*, Berlin, fol. 131a. Ali Dede (*Kit al-Awail Wal*

green colour, the distinguishing token of the Alids to-day, was decreed by the Egyptian Sultan Shaban ibn Husain (d. 778/1376)[1].

The only new feature of the Shi'ite theology of that time was the attempt to shape traditions to suit 'Ali and his house[2]. This naturally provoked the hearty contempt of the Sunnite savants. Someone, about the year 300/912, cited a tradition of the Prophet upon the authority of 'Ali and his family. What kind of a chain of tradition is that ? contemptuously questioned Ibn Rahawaihi. Both parties freely invented traditions and such, indeed, had been conspicuously the case since the earliest times. Already Ibn Ishaq, the biographer of the Prophet, is said to have interspersed his book with Shi'ite poems. On the other hand Urwanah (d. 147/764) forged stories favourable to Muawiya which have found a place in the historical work of Madaini[3]. And if a poet[4] about the year 300/900 ascribes the learned fables of the Shi'ahs to their lack of traditions, Muqaddasi, at the chief mosque at Wasit, hears a saying of the Prophet set in proper theological form : God on the Day of Resurrection will seat Muawiya by his side, perfume him with His own hand and then present the creation as a bride to him. I asked why, says Muqaddisi. The lecturer replied : Because he fought 'Ali. I called out : You have lied, you false believer. Whereupon said the lecturer : Seize this Shi'ah ! The people rushed upon me but an officer, recognising me, drove them

---

Awakhir) cites poetical quotations in proof of this fact. In 204 from Khorasan Mamun entered Baghdad wearing green dress and carrying green banners [Ibn Tafur, ed. Keller, fol. 2a.] Green banners floated on the occasion of the *Naubahar* at Balkh [Mas. IV, 43]. Perhaps this way the distinctive colour of Khorasan.

(1) Ibn al-Jauzi, Berlin, fol, 35a.

(2) E. g. Nasir-i-Khusru, p. 48 ; Abul Mahasin, II, 408.

(3) Goldziher in *Kultur der Gegenwart* ; Wuz., 170 ; *Irshad*, VI, 400, 94.

(4) Mas'udi, VIII, 374.

away[1]. At Isfahan the same traveller had to combat the statement of a spiritual chief that Muawiya was a Prophet and, in doing so, once more ran into danger[2]. But in truth 'Ali was no more the apple of discord at the time of Muqaddasi. Long past were the days when an Abbasid Caliph, like al-Mutawakkil, associated only with those that hated 'Ali. Of these one used to insert a cushion inside his dress, uncover his bald head, dance and sing : Here comes the bald, big bellied Caliph, *i.e.*, 'Ali[3]. On the whole the Sunnites treated 'Ali with great courtesy and consideration[4]. They were anything but hostile to him. Hamadani (d. 398/1008), who has some very harsh things to say against the Shi'ites and who defends 'Omar against the vituperations of the Khawarizimi[5], has himself composed a sort of elegy on 'Ali and Husain[6].

The wild cursing of the first three Caliphs such as was indulged in by the Shi'ites, was most abhorrent to the Sunnites. In 402/1011 there died at Baghdad a Sunnite savant who had heard at Karkh, the Shi'ite quarter of the town, the Companions of the Prophet reviled and abused. He vowed that never would he set his foot there again, and never indeed did he go beyond the Qantarah al-Serat[7]. When a Shi'ite was punished as such, the judgment never referred to 'Ali, the reason stated always being : He has slandered Abu Bakr and 'Omar[8].

---

(1) p. 126. Through a spirit of sheer opposition Muawiya was made into a saint ; "Even today [in the year 332] M's. grave, at the small gate at Damascus, is an object of Pilgrimage. A house is built upon it and every Monday and Thursday it is decorated" [Mas., V. 14].
(2) p.399 Ibn al-Jauzi, Berlin, fol. 60b ; Abulfeda *Annales* , year 236.
(3) Sarasin, *Das Bild 'Alies bei dem Historikern der Sunnah.*
(4) *Rasa'il* 424 ff.
(5) *Diwan*, Paris, pp. 90 ff.
(6) *Rasa'il*, 58.
(7) Ibn-al-Jauzi fol. 29b
(8) Abulfeda, year 351.

When in 351/962 Muizz-ad-Daulah adorned the mosques of Baghdad with the usual Shi'ite inscriptions of curses and imprecations and when these were blotted out over night, his clever Wazir el-Muhallabi counselled him to let Muawiya's name alone remain in the new inscriptions, omitting those of the others[1]. Many Alids had made their way to Egypt which was but rarely connected by a firm bond with the throne of Baghdad. In 236/850 the Caliph al-Mutawakkil, who had interned the Arab Alids at Samarra, caused the Egyptian branch of the family to be collected and sent to Iraq, each male obtaining 30 dinars and each female 15 dinars from the Governor. Thence they were banished to Medina[2]. Many Alids managed, however, to evade this measure and soon after rebelled, with the result that the successor of Mutawakkil was constrained to write to Egypt that no Alid was to have any land in fief or to be permitted to use a horse or to leave the capital or to own more than one slave. In case of a law suit, it was further ordained, he was disqualified as a witness[3]. No wonder then that, in the fifties, Egypt witnessed one Alid insurrection after another. In the 4th/10th century the Shi'ite unrest manifests itself in Egypt and the cause of the Alid nobles becomes the cause of the Shi'ites. On the Ashura Day of the year 350/961 feelings became so strained that an actual fight took place between the Shi'ahs and the Sunnite military, consisting mostly of Sudanese and Turks. Of every one the soldiers enquired : Who is thy uncle ? and attacked every one who did not answer : "Muawiya"[4]. One of the excited Sudanese roamed about the streets shouting : 'Muawiya is the uncle of 'Ali'—a saying which became the anti-Shi'ite war-cry of the

(1) Aghani, XIX, 141.
(2) Kindi, 198.
(3) Kindi, 204.
(4) This seems to have been a common Sunnite confession of faith. Nafta waihi [d. 323] relates a witticism:— They said to a Shiah: Thy mother's brother [khal] is Muawiya ! Upon which he rejoined : That I do not know. My mother is a Christian and that is her business. [Yaqut, *Irshad* 1, 313]

Egyptians. The Government maintained order as best it could. In the year 353/964, however, a well-known Shi'ah was scourged and detained in custody, where he died.

Over his grave a fight took place between the troops and his supporters. But when with Gawher[1] power passed to the Shi'ites, upon the slightest provocation the people raised the anti-Shi'ite cry : 'Muawiya is the uncle of 'Ali ! For instance when in 361/972 a blind woman, who used to go about reciting in the streets, was imprisoned, a crowd forthwith began invoking the names of the Companions of the Prophet odious to the Shi'ahs and calling out : 'Muawiya is the uncle of the faithful and of 'Ali.' The Governor gave in, announced in the mosque that the woman was arrested only for her own safety and instantly released her[2]. Even an insurrection of the Sunni money-changers, the most docile of political elements, is reported[3].

On the whole the Fatimid Government acted with wisdom and moderation. The only thing it did was to give all good appointments of judges and jurists to the Shi'ahs. They even allowed the public celebration of the anit-Shi'ite festival, started by the Sunnites in 362/973 in commemoration of the day when the Prophet and Abu Bakr, taking shelter in the cave, evaded and escaped the enemy. Canopies were put up on the streets and bonfires lighted.

Here too Hakim constitutes an exception. In the year 393/1002 his Governor at Damascus had a Maghrabite taken round the town on a donkey to the place of execution with a crier proclaiming in front of him : This is the reward of him who loves Abu Bakr and 'Omar. In the year 395/1005 Hamki's reforming rage reached its height. Along with other things he enjoined curses on Abu Bakr, 'Othman, Mauwiya,

(1) Lane-Poole, *Egypt*, 99. et. 599 Tr.
(2) Maqrizi, *Ittiaz*, 87.
(3) Maqrizi, *Khitat*, 339 Sqq.

etc., even upon the Abbasids, to be inscribed outside the mosques, walls of houses and archways. This was most offensive to his Sunnite subjects[1]. In 396/1005 he interdicted lamentation and recitation in streets on the Ashura day on the pretence that peple stood before shops and exacted money. He permitted lamentations, however, in the desert[2]. In 399/1099 came the usual reaction and Hakim forbade imprecations of those old, honoured men of Islam[3]. The Shi'ahs could not, however, make much headway in conversion. Muqaddasi found Shi'ahs in the city only, and at one spot in the Delta[4]. In the West the town of Naftah on the Algerian-Tunis frontier acquired the reputation of being the stronghold of Shia'ism and was accordingly named the smaller Kufa[5]. The political decline of the Fatimids caused an ebb in the tide of Shia'ism.

In all intellectual movements Baghdad signalized itself as the real capital of the Islamic world, for here all sects and doctrinal opinions found a shelter and a home[6]. But in the 4th/10th century the two chief camps there were those of the Hanbalities and the Shi'ites[7]. The Shi'ites specially had their supporters in the bazar quarters of Karkh. Not until the end of the 4th/10th century did they extend beyond the great Bridge and occupy the quarter round the Bab-al-Taq[8]. Towards the Western side of the town for long they

(1) Ibn Tagribardi, 91; Ibn al-Athir, IX, 126. According to the former he was executed ; according to the latter only banished from the town.

(2) Yahya ibn Sa'id, fol. 116a. In the same year the pilgrim-caravan is said to have been called upon to revile the first three Caliphs. This of course was not done, but it caused a great scandal. Maqrizi, *Khitat*, 1, 342.

(3) Maqrizi, *Khitat*, 431 ; Kindi, supplement, 600.

(4) Ibn Sa'id, fol. 199a.

(5) p. 202.

(6) Bakri, 75.

(7) Muq., 126. According to Muq., the chief fault of the Hanbalites was the hatred of the Alids.

(8) Wuz, 37.

could not spread. There the Hashimids[1], notably in the quarters near the Basra Gate, formed a close community. They were zealous opponents of the Shi'ahs. Even Yaqut found the Sunnites there and the Shi'ites in Karkh[2]. Despite the energetic persecutions of Mutawakkil, so powerful were the Shi'ites in Babylon, about the end of the 3rd/9th century, that the Wazir[3] in 284/897 advised the Caliph, who wanted the Omayyads publicly reviled from the pulpits—the edict has come down to us—that such a measure would merely benefit the Alids, who were scattered all over the country and found much favour with the people[4]. In 313/925 the Baratha Mosque is for the first time mentioned as the meeting-place of the Baghdad Shi'ites[5]. The Caliph ordered their removal, only 30 persons were found at prayer who were compelled to hand over seals of white clay which were surreptitiously distributed by Faitmid emissaries to people with Shi'ite leanings[6]. The mosque was eventually levelled to the ground, and, to leave no trace behind, the land on which it stood was annexed to the adjacent grave-yard[7]. The year 321/923 witnessed a significant event. The North-Persian courtier Yalbaq desired the renewal of the imprecations on Muawiya from the pulpits, but the Hanbalites incited the people against it with the result that there was unrest and excitement[8]. In 323/935 it was

(1) Ibn al-Athir, IV, 146.
(2) Under Karkh, Baghdad ; Guy Le Strange, *Baghdad*, 95, Tr.
(3) Wuz, 483.
(4) Tabari, III, 2164 Sqq.
(5) Guy Le Strange, *Baghdad*, pp. 95, 154 Tr.
(6) Ibn al-Jauzi, fol. 29b. There were sharpers at Baghdad who lived by selling rosaries and clay-plates to the Shi'ahs which they passed off as coming from the grave of Husain (yat. III). The clay plates are even sold today (called *Tabaq*, vulgarly *Taboq*). The Shi'ahs put these in front of them when at prayer, so that their brows may touch them each time they prostrate themselves.
(7) Ibn al-Jauzi, fol. 67a.
(8) Misk. gives it in details, V. 413 ; Ibn al-Athir mentions it briefly, VIII, 204 ; Abul Mahasin II, 259.

promulgated that no two Hanbalites should meet in the streets as they always stirred up strife. The Caliph issued an edict against these unruly subjects and the edict has come down to us. He reproaches them for regarding the Shi'ahs as 'unfaithful' : for attacking them in streets and elsewhere, forbidding them to make pilgrimage to the graves of the Imams ; and for reviling the pilgrims as heretics, while they themselves make pilgrimage to the grave of one who was of the people without a noble lineage or connection with the Prophet, prostrate themselves before his monument and pray at his grave. Unless they desist from their wicked ways he will proceed against them with fire and sword[1]. In 328/ 940, at the instance of the Amir Begkem, the Baratha Mosque was rebuilt for the Sunnites, bearing on the porch the name of the Caliph Al-Radhi. His successor Al-Muttaqi had the pulpit of the Mansurah Mosque (which had hitherto been preserved in the treasury which bore the name of Harun-al-Rashid) brought to the new mosque, which was consecrated in 329/941[2].

The Hamadanids were the first Shi'ite dynasty to meddle in the affairs of Baghdad. At first this interference was of a kind to draw upon them the scron of all the world. The Shi'ite Hamadanid helped Prince Ibn al-Mutt'azz, well-known for his pronounced anti-Shi'ite tendencies, to the throne[3]. Things however, changed when, after a short time, the Dailamites, who had been converted to Islam by an Alid, became rulers of Baghdad. Shortly after his arrival Mu'izz-ad-Daulah ignominiously deposed the Caliph, assigning this, among other reasons, that the Caliph had imprisoned the chief of the Shi'ites. In 349/960 the Shi'ites were able to

(1) Later some theological colouring was given to this edict. Abulfeda, *Annales* year 323.

(2) Ibn al-Jauzi, fol. 67a ; Ibn al-Athir, IX, 278 ; Misk., VI, 37 only reports the completion of the mosque without an details.

(3) Ibn al-Athir, VIII, 13.

close their mosques against the Sunnites with the result that the latter had no other place of worship left to them except the Baratha Mosque[1]. In 351 Mu'izz-ud-Daulah caused the Shi'ites inscriptions to be put upon the walls of the mosques, but they were removed by the people at night. In the following year he introduced solemn wailings and lamentations for Husain on the 10th of Moharram, Ashura Day, the chief festival of the Shi'ahs. The bazars were closed; the butchers suspended their business ; the cooks ceased cooking ; the cisterns were emptied of their contents ; pitchers were placed with felt coverings on the streets ; women walked about with fallen tresses, blackened faces, torn dresses, striking their faces and wailing for Husain. Also pilgrimages were made to Karbala[2]. On this day, says Biruni, common people have an aversion to renewing the vessels and utensils of the household[3]. In the same year, on the 18th of Dhulhijjah, the celebration of the day of the 'Pond of Khumm' (the day on which the Prophet is said to have nominated 'Ali as his successor) was officially introduced at Baghdad[4]. On this day, on the other hand, Mu'izz-ud-Daulah ordered the usual accompaniments of a festive celebration. Tents were pitched ; carpets were laid down ; valuable things were exhibited ; with blowing of trumpets and beating of drums a huge bonfire was lighted in front of the office of the Chief of Police. On the following morning camels were slaughtered and pilgrimages were made to the grave of the Quraishites. The Sunnites returned the compliment by celebrating the day of the death of Husain as a day of rejoicing. They dressed themselves up on this day in new garments with various kinds of ornaments, and

(1) Ibn al-Athir, VIII, 397.

(2) Wuz., 483 ; Ibn al-Jauzi, fol. 93b ; Ibn al-Athir VIII, 403, 407 ; Abul Mahasin, II, 364. The usual Passion play of modern times is nowhere mentioned. *Rasa'il*, Constant., *p. 37*.

(3) Al-Beruni, [Sachau's tr., p. 326 tr.]

(4) Ibn al-Jauzi, fol. 95b ; Ibn al-Athir, VIII, 407 ; according to Abul Mahasin [II, 427] erroneously in the year 360.

painted their eyes with stibium ; they celebrated a feast and gave banquets and parties, eating sweetmeats and sprinkling scent on each other. Even traditions were made to dwell upon the felicitous character of this day. They believed that one who painted antimony round his or her eyes on this day would be spared running eyes throughout the year[1].

Thus does Qummi (d. 355/966) frequently urge : He who mourns on the 'Ashura Day will be happy on the Day of Resurrection. He who calls it a day of blessing (yaum barakah) and gathers anything into his house that day will derive no good from it. Such an one will rise on the Day of Resurrection with Yazid and find his way to the lowest depths of Hell[2]. After the fall of the Fatimids the Sunnite Ayyubids converted according to the Syrian custom the 'Ashura Day, hitherto regarded as an official day of mourning, into one of rejoicing and festivity[3]. The Sunnites even invented a direct counter celebration. Eight days after the Shi'ite mourning for Husain they mourned, on their part, for Mus'ab ibn Zubair and visited his grave at Maskin on the Dujail, just as the Shi'ites visited the Kerbala. And, indeed, eight days after the 'Feast of the Pond' the Sunnites set up a counter-feast, the celebration of the day on which the Prophet and Abu Bakr concealed themselves in a cave. They celebrated this feast in precisely the same way as did the Shi'ites their "Feast of the Pond". On Friday the 25th Dhul Hijjah, 389/999 this celebration took place for the first

---

(1) Qazwini, Cosmogr. I, 68. Biruni further adds : Such was the custom in the nation during the rule of the Benu Umayya, and so it has remained also after the downfall of this dynasty (Chronology of Ancient Nations, p. 326). On the Ashura day Biruni [p. 327] says : Some people say that Ashura is an Arabicised Hebrew word, *viz.*, Ashur, *i.e.*, the 10th of the Jewish Month Tishri, in which falls the fasting Kippur ; that the date of this fasting was compared with the months of the Arabs, and that it was fixed on the 10th of their *first* month, as it, with the Jews, falls on the 10th of their *first* month.

(2) *Kit. al-Ilal*, fol, 99b.

(3) Maqrizi, *Khitat*, 1, 490.

time[1]. During these celebrations there was the usual friction between the two parties, and some strong rulers therefore prohibited both these celebrations[2]. On one such celebration, even at the residence of the Caliph, the cry was heard: 'Hakim ya Mansur', referring to the hereditary enemy at Cairo. This was a trifle too much for the Caliph. He sent his palace-guards to the help of the Sunnites and the Alids came thereupon begging for pardon for the insult so offered to him. In 420/1029 the Shi'ite preacher of the Baratha Mosque was arrested for heretical teachings. In his place a Sunnite was sent, who ascended the pulpit with a sword in conformity with the Sunnite and not the Shi'ite practice. The people greeted him with a shower of bricks. His shoulder and nose were fractured and his face was covered with blood. This angered the Caliph and he wrote an indignant letter. In the end the chief of the Shi'ahş apologised and appointed another in his place with necessary instructions[3].

It is significant of the sudden and rapid rise of the Shi'ahs in the 4/10th century that then, for the first time, their two great sanctuaries were definitely located in Babylonia. Hitherto there was an uncertainty about the grave of 'Ali. Even in 332/994 Mas'udi thus writes: "Some look for the grave of 'Ali in the mosque at Kufa[4], others in the citadel there, and yet others by the side of Fatima's grave at Medina". According to others the camel which carried the coffin went astray and 'Ali found his final resting-place somewhere in the territory of the tribe of Tai[5]. The Shi'ite Hamadanid Abul Haija (d. 317/929) adorned the place at

(1) Wuz., 371 Ibn al-Jauzi, Berlin, fol. 143.

(2) Thus by Maullim in 382 [Ibn al-Jauzi, fol. 134a] and by Amid al-Juyush in 392 and 406 [Wuz., 482 f; Ibn al-Jauzi, 147b ; Ibn al Athir, IX, 184].

(3) Ibn al-Jauzi, fol. 178a.

(4) So also Ibn Haukal 163.

(5) Masudi, IV, 289, VI, 68.

Meshed 'Ali—which today passes for the grave of 'Ali, with a huge domed mausoleum resting on a number of quadrangular cloumns, with doors on each side. The Wazir ibn Sahlan vowed, during an illness, that should he recover he would encircle the mausoleum with a wall, and this vow he fulfilled in the year 401/1041. The first great man, to my knowledge, buried there at his request, was a high officer from Basra who died in 342/953[1]. Of the rulers, 'Adad-ud-Daulah was the first to be buried by the side of Ali's grave, he having been interred at first at the Dar-ul-mulk at Baghdad[2]. This very 'Adad-ad-Dawlah[3] had the grave of Husain at Karbala, which had been destroyed, ploughed over and sown at the instance of the Caliph Mutawakkil, adorned with a monument[3]. In the 4th/10th century a monastery near Merv[5] boasted of being the proud possessor of the head of the Prince of Martyrs ; this head was said to have been taken in 548/1153 from Ascalon to Cairo[6]. Ibn Taimiyya (d. 728/1328) declares it to be a fiction of fools[7]. Already in 399/1009 a Wazir at Rai had given directions for his dead body to be taken to Karbala for burial. His son enquired of the Alids whether he could puchase land for 500 dinars by the side of Husain's grave for his father's burial. The Alid replied that he would accept no money from those who take shelter in the neighbourhood of his ancestor. Thus the son secured a place without payment[8]. The interior of the sanctuary at Karbala has been for the first time described by Ibn Batuta in the 8/14th century. Of the old times we only hear that the sarcophagus was covered with a piece of

(1) Ibn al-Athir, VIII, 380.

(2) Ibn al-Athir, IX, 13.

(3) Tabari, III, 1407. Satires regarding this by Ibn Bessan have come down to us. Ibn Bessan died 302 A.H.

(4) He also renovated the grave of Fatima al-Qummi. Hamadani *Rasa'il*, 435.

(5) Muq., 46, 333.

(6) Maqrizi, *Khitat*, 427.

(7) Schreiner, Z.D.M.G., Vol, 53, p. 81.

(8) Yaqut, *Irshad*, 1. 68.

cloth and that candles were kept burning around it[1]. The piety of another Buwayyid Prince built a mosque over the grave of Rida at Tus, the most beautiful in Khorasan[2].

---

(1) Ibn al-Athir, IX, 203. Ibn Taghribardi, p. 123.
(2) Muq., 333.

NOTES

(1) For a brief account of Shiahism, See Johannes Hauri's *Islam* (pp 89 et. Sqq.)

(2) For more detailed information, see Goldziher's *Mohammed and Islam*.

On p. 222 Goldziher says : It is an elementary fact that Islam appears in two forms ; Sunnite and Shi'ite. This division, as we have already seen, arose through the question of succession. The party, which even during the first three caliphates secretly recognized the rights of the Prophet's family, without, however, entering upon an open conflict, protested, after the fall of their pretenders, against the usurpers of the later non-Allite dynasties. Their opposition was first directed against the Omayyads, later, however, against all succeeding dynasties who did not tally with their legitimistic ideas. To all their disqualifications they oppose the divine right of the descendants of the Prophet through the children of Ali and Fatima. Thus, as they condemn the three caliphs who preceded Ali as impious usurpers and oppressors, they also oppose secretly, or, if the opportunity for strife offers, openly the actual formation of the Moslem State in all times to come.

The very nature of this protest easily led to a form in which religious factors were predominant. In place of a caliph raised to the supreme rule by human device, they recognized the Imam as the only justifiable worldly and spiritual leader of Islam, divinely called and appointed to this office. They give the preference to the designation Imam as more in accord with the religious dignity of the chief recognized as such by virtue of his direct descent from the prophet.

On p. 230, he discusses the inherent difference between theocratic rule of the caliph in Sunnism and of the legitimate Imam in Shiahism.

For Sunnite Islam the caliph exists in order to insure the carrying out of the tasks of Islam, in order to demonstrate and concentrate in his person the duties of the Moslem community. "At the head of the Moslems"—I quote the words of a Moslem theologian— "there must stand a man who sees that its laws are carried out, that its boundaries are kept, and defended, that its armies are equipped, that its obligatory taxes are raised, that the violent thieves and street robbers are suppressed, that assemblies for worship are instituted, that the booties of war are justly divided, and other such legal necessities, which an individual in the community cannot attend to." In a word, he is the representative of the judicial, administrative and military power of the State. As ruler, he is none other than the successor of his predecessor, chosen by human act (choice or nomination by his predecessor), not through special qualities of his person. The caliph of the Sunnites is in no sense an authority in doctrine.

"The Imam of the Shi'ites on the contrary is the leader and teacher of Islam by right of personal qualities given to him by God, he is the Heir of the Prophet's Ministry. He rules and teaches in the name of God's Just as Moses could hear the call from the burning bush: "I am Allah, the Lord of the worlds" (Sura 28, V. 30) , so it is the direct message of God which is given to the Imam of each age. The Imam possesses not only the character of a representative of a rule sanctioned by God, but also supernatural qualities, raising him above ordinary men and this in consequence of a dignity not 'accorded to him, but by virtue of his birth and rather a consequence of his substance.

"Ever since the creation of Adam a divine substance of light has passed from one chosen successor of Adam to the next, until it reached the loins of the grandfather of Mohammed and 'Ali. Here this divine light divided itself, and passed in part to 'Abdallah, the father of the prophet, and in part to his brother Abu Talib , the father of 'Ali. From the latter this divine light has passed from generation to generation, to the present Imam. The presence of the pre-existent divine light in the substance of his soul makes him the Imam of his age and gives him extraordinary spiritual powers far surpassing human abilities. His soul substance is purer than that of ordinary mortals, "free from evil impulses, and adorned with sacred forms". This is more or less the idea which moderate Shi'ism has of the character of its Imam. In its extreme form (as we shall see). 'Ali and the Imam are raised into the vicinity of the divine sphere, aye into its very midst. Although this transcendental theory is not clothed in definite, uniform, dogmatic terms it may be regarded as the generally recognised Shi'ite view of the character of the Imams".

On p. 254 et sqq he calls attention to some erroneous views about Shiahism still widely prevalent.

(a) The mistaken view that the main difference between Sunni and Shi'ite Islam lies in the fact that the former recognizes, in addition to the Koran, the Sunna of the Prophet as a source of religious belief and life, whereas the Shi'ites limit themselves to the Koran and reject the Sunna.

This is a fundamental error involving a complete misunderstanding of Shi'ism, and has arisen largely from the antithesis in the nomenclature between Sunna and Shia. No Shi'ite would allow himself to be regarded as an opponent of the prinçiple of the Sunna. Rather is he the representative of the true Sunna, of the sacred tradition handed down by the members of the prophet's family, while the opponents base their Sunna on the authority of usurping "Companions" whose reliability the Shi'ites reject.

It very frequently happens that a great number of traditions are common to both groups ; differing only in the authorities for their authenticity. In cases where the Hadiths of the Sunnites favour the tendencies of the Shi'ites, or at least are not opposed to them, Shi'ite theologians do not hesitate to refer to the canonical collection of their opponents. As an example we may instance the circumstance that the collections of Bukhari and of Muslim, as well as of other collectors of Hadiths were used at the court of fanatical Shi'ite vizier (Tala' ibn Ruzzik) as subjects for pious reading at the sacred Friday gatherings.

Tradition is therefore an integral source of religious life among the Shi'ites. How vital a role it plays in Shi'ite teachings may be inferred from the circumstance that 'Ali's teaching about the Koran and Sunna, as above set forth (page 43), is taken from a collection of solemn speeches and sayings of 'Ali, handed down by the Shi'ites. Reverence for the Sunna is therefore as much of a requirement for the Shi'ites as for the Sunnites. This is illustrated also in the abundant Sunnite literature of the Shi'ites, and the discussions attached thereto, as well as in the great zeal with which the Shi'ite scholars fabricated Hadiths, or propagated earlier fabrications which were to serve the interests of Shi'ism. We must therefore reject the supposition that the Shi'ites in principle are opposed to Sunna. It is not as rejecters of the Sunna that they oppose its adherents, but rather as those faithful to the family of the Prophet and its followers—that is the meaning of the word Shi'ite—or as the elite (al-khassa) as opposed to the common people (al-amma) sunk in error and blindness.

(b) It is also an erroneous view which traces the origin and development of Shi'ism to the modification of the ideas in Islam, brought about by the conquest of and spread among Iranic nations.

This widespread views is based on an historical misunderstanding, which Wellhausen has overthrown conclusively in his essay on the *"Religios-politischen Oppositions-Parteien im alten Islam"*. The Alite movement started on genuine Arabian soil. It was not till the uprising of al-Mukhtar that it spread among the non Semitic element of Islam. The origins of the Imam theory, involving the theocratic opposition against the wordly conception of the State; the doctrine of the Messiah into which the Imam theory merges and the belief in the parousia in which it finds an expression, as we have seen, can be traced back to Jewish-Christian influences. Even the exaggerated deification of 'Ali was first proclaimed by 'Abdullah ibn Saba, before there could possibly have been a question of the influence of such ideas from Aryan circles, and Arabs joined the movement in great numbers. Even the most marked consequences of the anthropomorphic doctrine of incarnation (see above page 233) owe their origin in part to those who are of indisputable Arabian descent.

Shi'ism as a sectarian doctrine was seized upon as eagerly by orthodox and theocratically minded Arabs as by Iranians. To be sure, the Shi'ite form of opposition was decidedly welcome to the latter, and they readily identified themselves with this form of Moslem thought, on whose further development their old inherited ideas of a divine kingship exercised a direct influence. But the primary origins of these ideas within Islam do not depend on such influence; Shi'ism is, in its roots, as genuinely Arabic as Islam itself.

(c) It is likewise a mistaken view that Shi'ism represents the reaction of independent thought against Sunnitic incrustation.

Quite recently Carra de Vaux has advocated the view that the opposition of Shi'ism against Sunnitic Islam is to be regarded as "the reaction of free and liberal thought against narrow and unbending orthodoxy."

This view cannot be accepted as correct by any student of Shi'itic doctrines. To be sure, it might be urged that the cult of 'Ali forms to such an extent the centre of religious life among the Shi'ites as to remove all other elements into the background. (See above page 231). This feature cannot, however, be regarded as characteristic of the principles underlying Shi'itic doctrines, which in no respect are less strict than those of the Sunnites. Nor should we be led astray in the historical appreciation of the principle of Shi'ism by an increasing lack of regard among the Shi'ite Mohammedans of Persia for certain restrictions demanded by the ritual. "In giving the preference to infallible personal authority as against the force of general public sentiment, the Shi'ites set aside those potential elements of liberal thought, which mainfest themselves in the Sunnitic form of Islam". It is the spirit of absolutisms rather which permeates the Shi'itic conception of religion.

On the Shiahs and the Mutazalites. Goldziher (pp. 249-250) says:—

The connection between the prevailing dogmatism of the Shi'ites and the doctrines of the Mutazilites seems to be maintained as a definite fact and finds an unmistakable expression in the declaration of the Shi'ites authority, that the doctrine of the hidden Imam is a part of the teaching of those who accept the *adl* and *tauhid* which represent the Mutazilite teachings. It is in particular a branch of the Shi'ites known as the Zeiditic which is even more closely and more consistently to the Mutazilite doctrines than is the Imamitic.

The Mutazilite influence has maintained its hold on the Shi'itic literature up to present time. It is a serious error to declare that after the decisive victory of the Ash'arite theology the Mutazilite doctrine ceased to play any active part in the religion or the literature. The rich dogmatic literature of the Shi'ites extending into our own days refutes such an assertion. The dogmatic works of the Shi'ites reveal themselves as Mutazilite expositions by their division into two parts, one embracing the chapters on "the unity of God" and the other the chapter on "justice" (above, page 110). Naturally the presentation of the Imam doctrines, of the infallibility of the Imam are also included. But even in regard to this latter point it is not without significance that one of the most radical of the Mutazilites, al Nazam agrees with the Shi'ites. And it is especially characteristic of the Shi'itic theology that their proofs for the theory of the Imamate are based entirely on Mutazilite foundations. The absolute necessity of the presence of an Imam in every age and the infallible character of his person are brought into connection with the doctrine, peculiar to the Mutazilites, of an absolutely necessary guidance through divine wisdom and justice (page 111). God must grant to each age a leader not exposed to error. In this way Shi'itic theology fortifies its fundamental point of view with the theories of Mutazilite doctrine.

I will conclude this note with the words with which Goldziher closes the chapter on Asceticism and Sufiism (p. 197):

"Ghazali's writings are constantly belittling all dogmatic formulas and heir-splittings which set up the claim of having the only means of salvation. His dry, academic speech rise to the heights of eloquent pathos when he takes the field against such claims. He has championed the cause of tolerance in a special work entitled "Criterion of the Differences between Islam and Heresy". In it he declares to the Moslem world : that harmony in the fundamentals of religion should be the basis of recognition as a believer, and that the deviation in dogmatic and ritualistic peculiarities, even if it extends to the rejection of the Caliphate recognized by Sunni Islam, which would therefore include the Shi'ite schism—should offer no ground for heresy. "Check your tongue in regard to people who turn to the Kiblah".

Words which inspired the Islamic word with large liberalism in the past and which will assuredly uplift it in the future !

VI. THE ADMINISTRATION

Within the Caliphate the Provinces formed more or less a loose confederation. The central authority dealt with them not through departmental ministries, but every Province had its own Board (Diwan) at Baghdad which managed its own affairs. And every such Board consisted of two sections : the general (Asl) which concerned itself with the assessment and collection of taxes[1] and with the problem of husbanding and augmenting the taxable resources of the people, *i.e.*, the administration; and secondly the purely financial section (Zimam)[2]. The Caliph Mutadid (279-289/892-902), the ablest ruler of the 3rd/9th century[3], incorporated the Provincial Boards into one Central Board (Diwan-ad-Dar)[4], with three branches : the Eastern Board (Diwan al-Mashriq); the Western Board (Diwan al-Maghrib) ; and the Board for Babylon (Diwan al-Sawad). And the Caliph, at the same time, placed the finance Boards of the three branches under one chief[5] ; with the result that the new century witnessed the division of the administration into two departmental

(1) Qodamah (d. 337/948), Paris, *Arabe* 5907, fol. 10. "Asl" has this very sense in the document in Wuz., 11.

(2) On this see Amedroz, J.R.A.S., 1913, ff. See also Misk., VI, 338. At the head of this Board a financier was generally placed. Even small Boards such as the Board for the administration of the property of a Caliph's wife, had these two sections, with a Superintendent at the head of each. Misk., V. 390.

(3) Never did the highest offices of the Empire—those of the Caliph, the Wazir, the Minister (Sahib Diwn) and the Commander-in-Chief—work so harmoniously together as they did under this Caliph, Wuz., 189.

(4) The great Court-Diwan was also called Diwan ad-Dar al-Kabir, Wuz., 262.

(5) Wuz.; 77.

ministries : the Ministry of the Interior (Usul) and the Ministry of Finances (Azimmah). A number of offices (also called Diwan) were placed under these great ministries, for every Province had its own office. But as the Chancellor of the Empire (Wazir), President of the Central Board, personally administered the Province of Babylon, some of the Babylonian provincial offices were treated as Imperial offices. No sharp line of division between the Central and Provincial offices was ever drawn.

The different Boards may thus be summarised :—

1. The War Office (Diwan al-Jaish). It consisted of two branches : the department of pay (Majlis al-Taqrir) and the recruiting department (Majlis al-Muqabalah). Individual corps, such as Life-guards and various provincial levies, were specially dealt with[1].

2. The Board of Expenditure (Diwan an-Nafaqat) at Baghdad, chiefly busied itself with the requirements of the Court. As the largest part of Babylonia was leased out, the tax-farmers had to meet the necessary expenses. This board consisted of :—

(a) The office dealing with pay and salary (Majlis al-Ghori), chiefly the salaries of Court-Officials (Hasham);

(b) The office dealing with provisions (Majlis al-Anzal). It settled accounts with suppliers of bread, flesh, animals for purposes of food, sweets, eggs, fruit, fuel, etc.

(c) Office of Camp-followers. It dealt with fodder for horses, wild animals maintained at State expense, with the *personnel* of the stable and other attendants. Finally it dealt with building accounts, surveyors, architects ; with dealers of gypsum, bricks, lime and clay, with teak-wood

(1) Qodamah, Pairs, fol. 2b.

sellers and teak-wood cutters, carpenters, painters and gilders.

(d) Office for contingencies (Majlis al-Hawadith)

(e) The Drafting office.

(f) The Copying-department[1].

3. The office of the State-treasury (Diwan Bait al-Mal). At Baghdad it was the controlling authority between the Board of Expenditure and the Ministry of the Interior. The statement of revenues came in here before it went to the Ministry. All orders of the Board of Expenditure had to be countersigned by the head of the State-treasury[2]. In 314/926 it was ordered that the daily account (Ruz-nameghat) of the Baghdad treasury should be submitted to the Wazir week by week. Hitherto the practice had been to submit monthly accounts in the middle of the following month[3].

4. The Comparing Board (Diwan al-Musadarin)[4] : orders for payments were drawn up here in duplicate—one remained in this office, and the other was forwarded to the Wazir.

5. The Despatch Board was called Diwan er-Rasa'il in the East and Diwan el-Insha in Fatimid Egypt[5]. At the beginning of the Vth century the head of this Board at Baghdad drew an annual salary of 3000 dinars (about 30,000 marks), besides fees which came to him from the numerous documents and letters of appointment which were drawn up here along with the correspondence of the Prince, which

---

(1) *Ibid*, fol, 8a-9b.
(2) Qodamah, fol. 8.
(3) Misk., 5,257.
(4) Wuz., 303, 306.
(5) 'Insha' is used in the East for the drafting office. *Mafatih el-ulum*, ed. Van Vloten, 78 ; Wuz., 151, 216.

was the main business of the Board[1].

6. The General Post Office (Diwan al-Barid)[2]. Its chief supervised the officers of the post-roads and was in charge of their salaries. He had to have intimate knowledge of the roads, for he had to advise the Caliph regarding his tours and the despatch of his troops. Above everything he must needs enjoy the confidence of the Caliph, for reports from all quarters came to him and it was his duty to send them on to their proper destination and to see that reports of post-masters and other reports were laid before the Caliph[3].

Highly developed was the news service of the Empire. The ruler at Baghdad once sent a shoe to Ibn Tulun in Egypt which came from the house of his mistress, the very existence of whom none but intimate friends knew. With such a system no life was quite safe[4]. The Post-master was chiefly the official reporter (Sahib al-Khabar) ; his spies ('ain) supplied him with information. This system is a Byzantine legacy. Already under the Emperor Constantine the Great, his colleagues, who bore the very same name of *Veredarii*, acted as informers[5]. And just as reporters today, the literati then took to reporting as a means of livelihood[6]. In the appointment-letter of a postmaster, dated 315 A.H., one of

(1) Yaqut, *Irshad*, 1, 242.

(2) Qodamah (writes about 315-927) VI' 184 (de Goeje's ed).

(3) Maqrizi, *Khitat*, II., 180.

(4) Maqrzi, *Khitat*, 180.

(5) J. Burckhardt, *Die Zeit Constants des grossen*. 3rd, p. 70. In the first century of the Muslim rule an Egyptian Post-master acts as an official reporter of the acts of the Prefect. ZA, XX, 196.

(6) In the 3rd/9th century the evil tongue of the poet Ibn Bassam was silenced by making him a post-master (Masudi, VII, 271) ; Yaqut, *Irshad*, V. 322 ff. As a reward they allowed another poet to choose a post-mastership among the post-masterships of Khorasan (*Yatimah*, IV, 62). The post-master of Nisabur possessed the largest number of books even in that learned town (Ibn Haukal, 320). The Maghribi Ibn Khaldun, on the other hand, regards the post-mastership as part of the military system (*Muqaddamah*, I. 195).

the duties assigned to him was to report in detail on tax-collectors, the cultivation of land, the position of the subjects, the way in which judicial officers lived, the working of the mint and the office dealing with Government pensioners. He was further to keep an account of the couriers within his jurisdiction, their number, their names, their salaries and also of the roads, the mileages and the stations thereon, and to see that the postal bags were speedily despatched. The reports of each individual department, such as the judiciary, police, taxation, were to be kept separate[1]. Not only was it his duty to report matters of political importance but also matters of interest. In 300/912 the Post-master of Dinawar reported, on the information of a confidant in another town, that the mule of such and such a person had given birth to a young one which was a wonder to all[2] the world. "I sent for the mule and the young one, and found the mule of light brown colour and the young one well-developed with perfect limbs and a hanging tail."

7. The Caliph's Cabinet (Diwan at-Tauqi)[3]. To it came the petitions directed to the ruler after they had been enquired into at the office of the Royal Household (D. ad-Dar). After disposal they were returned to the Diwan ad-Dar, which referred them to their respective departments[4]. The order was written on the petition itself and was a triumph of concentrated brevity on the part of the ruler or of his secretary. The marginal notes of the Barmecide Ja'far, who administered this cabinet for the Caliph Harun, are said to have been collected by collectors who paid a dinar apiece for them[5].

---

(1) Qodamah, Paris fol. 15. ff.
(2) *Arib.* 39.
(3) Khuda Bukhsh, *Orient under the Caliphs,* 236 Tr.
(4) Qodamah, Paris, fol. 20a.
(5) Ibn Khaldun, *Kit. al-Ibar*, 1, 206.

8. The Diwan al-Khatam (The Board of Signet)[1] where the orders of the Caliph were sealed after they had been compared in different Boards and offices[2].

9. The Diwan al-Fadd (The Board for breaking the seals). Here the official correspondence of the Caliph was opened. Formerly all correspondence went straight to the Caliph, but later it came to the Wazir who passed it on to the respective ministries. Thus the Diwan al-Fadd became the Wazir's Board, with a Secretary as the chief of the office. In the ministry for Babylonia this office apparently retained its earlier name : Majlis al-Askudar[3]. These two offices were placed under a single chief, who drew a monthly salary of 401 dinars (about 400 marks)[4].

10. The Imperial Bank (Diwan al-Gabedah)*. Into this Imperial Bank flowed the commission for changing smaller into bigger coins, the exchange commission, the interest on advances, fines for non-payment in due time and other items. Private persons paid in large sums for managing provincial banks which they exploited and robbed[5].

---

(1) *Orient under the Caliphs*, p. 237.

(2) Qodamah, fol. 20b.

(3) Qodamah, fol. 21b.

(4) Wuz., 178. This passage is somewhat obscure. It appears to me that formerly all correspondence addressed to the Caliph went straight to the palace and was opened there. Later this system was done away with and the practice came into vogue for the Wazir to deal with all correspondence and distribute it to the respective ministries. While the former arrangement lasted, an official in the palace presumably opened the correspondence and placed it before the Caliph. This official, who was directly responsible to the Caliph, must have had his bureau (Diwan al-Fadd) at the Palace. Later when the Wazir took charge of correspondence, the Diwan al-Fadd became the Wazir's Cabinet, with his Secretary in charge thereof. This apparently was Additional work imposed upon the Secretary. Being thus added to the office of the Secretary to Diwan al-Fadd formed part of the general Secretariat under the charge of the Secretary. No other explanation suggests itself to me. Tr.

(*) *Ghibtah*—Ed. "Islamic Culture."

(5) Qodamah, fol. 20b.

11. The Board of Charity (Diwan al-Birr was-Sadaqah)[1]. At the beginning of the 4th/10th century the ministers (Sahib diwan) were of three different grades[2]. The minister for Babylon drew the largest salary, 500 dinars (circa 500 marks) per month[3] ; others drew a third of his salary. Under the Caliph al-Mutadid (279-289/892-902), 4,700 dinars a month (circa 50,000 marks) were allotted in the budget for all the various employees of the ministers, from the heads of departments down to door-keepers and gatherers of rags and waste-paper. To this amount was to be added the pay of the Wazirs, the clerks of the pay-offices, and the treasury-staff. These salaries were met from fines and retrenchments, and therefore the amount of their salaries depended upon their care and vigilance in the dicharge of their duties[4]. The salaries were paid in the first week of the month[5]. At the beginning of the 4th/10th century the practice,—later very much in favour--was introduced of paying less than the whole of the twelve months' salary. In 314/926 most of the officers received only ten months' pay and, as generally happens, officers on the lowest rung of the ladder suffered the most. Post-masters and pay-officers received only eight months' pay[6]. On the other hand, by multiplication of offices in the same hand an attempt was made to compensate for the loss. About the year 300/912 one and the same officer held the Ministry of the Interior, the Presidentship of the Diwan at-Tauqi and of the Bait-al-Mal[7].

At the head of the Provinces the Amir (Commander of the army), and the 'Aamil (chief of the civil administration) stood side by side. The 'Aamil really was the tax-gatherer,

(1) Misk., V. 257.
(2) Wuz., 156.
(3) Wuz., 314.
(4) Wuz., 20.
(5) Wuz., 81.
(6) Wuz., 314 ; Misk., V. 257.
(7) Wuz., 77.

for it was his main duty to remit the contribution of the province to the State-Treasury. He also had to defray the necessary expenses of administration. The central treasury merely concerned itself with the Court, the Ministers, and matters connected with Baghdad[1]. The two heads of the Province shared the same ceremonial privileges[2] at court functions, and the general orders of the Wazir came simultaneously to both[3]. In rank, however, the Commander was higher, in the sense that to him fell the privilege of leading the people at prayer—a privilege which always marked him out as the foremost Muslim in his own jurisdiction[4]. If the two got on well together, they could do anything they pleased,—as did for instance the Amir and Aamil of Faris and Kirman in 319/931. They remitted for a considerable length of time no revenues to Baghdad[5]. But where these posts were held by one man he was as good as an independent ruler of the province. For this very reason the high-spirited Turkish general Begkem would not proceed to Khuzistan in 325/937 unless they put him in charge at once of the 'army and taxes'[6]. Officially the position of Ahmed ibn Tulun and of Ikhshid was that of the Amir, but in reality they were independent rulers of Egypt.

At the end of his chronicle Dionysius V Tellmachre (d. 229/834) complains of the crowd of officers who in every way devour the bread of the poor[7]. For instance, in the small town of Raqqah on the Euphrates, there were *(a)* a qadhi, *(b)* a taxing-officer, *(c)* a commander of the garrison, *(d)* a post-master to report the affairs of the town *(e)* an administrator of the Crown-lands (Sawafi), *(f)* a Police-

(1) Wuz., 11 ff.
(2) Wuz., 156.
(3) Wuz., 50.
(4) E.g. Tallquist, 15.
(5) Ibn al-Athir, VIII, 165.
(6) Ibn al-Athir, VIII, 252.
(7) Michael Syrus, 538.

officer[1]. This full complement of local function—aries was found in every one of the 36 districts of the Samanid government[2]. The greater portion of this all too numerous staff was done away with when the Wazir, who appointed them, vacated office. Unemployed, they then roamed about the streets of the capital and intrigued until their party was once again in power, exactly as is the case in Spain today, and was some time ago in the United States. Or else they made the province unsafe. Once when a former official came with a letter of recommendation from Baghdad to a Governor of Isfahan he impatiently called out : You are a pest to the country, you unemployed fellows ! Every day one of you appears before me, praying for alms or a post. Even if I had all the wealth of the world it would not suffice for you all[3].

The shrewd 'Adad-ud-Daulah made advances to these unemployed during their period of unemployment, and on their appointment he realised the money advanced to them[4].

In Egypt the Ikhshid was the first to give fixed salaries to officers[5]. The Fatimids adopted his system almost in its entirety. They evidently intended to partition the State among their supporters. Gawhar retained all the officers in their posts, but he associated a Maghribi with each of them[6]. But when the Maghribis proved themselves to be a greater

(1) According to Michael Syrus [p. 541]—his account is somewhat obscure-the post of the Chief of the police was incorporated in that of the military commander. And yet the Caliph issued a separate patent for the Cheif of the Police (Sahib Ma'anah), Qodamah, Paris, fol. 145.

(2) Ibn Haukal, 307. Like Khorasan, Babylonia also was divided according to the duo-decimal system into 24 circles with 12 districts each. Wuz., 258.

(3) *Kit. al-Faragh*, II, 10.

(4) Ibn al-Athir, IX, 16.

(5) Tallquist, 39 ; Maqrizi, *Khitat*, I, 99.

(6) Maqrizi, *Ittiaz*, 78.

source of trouble, the attempt to replace the older, the entirely Christian officialdom was abandoned. According to the account of the Fatimid administration that has come down to us, the Wazir, like his Baghdad colleague, drew a monthly salary of 5,000 dinars. The salaries of the ministers at Cairo were, indeed, much smaller. The chief of the Correspondence Board (Diwan al-Insha) drew 120 ; the head of the Treasury (Bait al-Mal) 100 ; the other departmental heads 70 to 30 dinars per month. On 40 dinars (about 400 marks) the chief of a Board in Egypt appointed an officer who carried on correspondence on his own responsibility[1].

As opposed to the army, where we meet almost exclusively with names of slaves, the Civil Service shows nothing but names of freemen in its cadre[2]. The Persians especially took to the civil service. In the earlier days to them belonged the Barmacides, in the later the Maderaites and the Firajabites[3]. A great deal of the work of the official was akin to that of a merchant, and the Persian was to be sure the cleverest merchant of the realm. Even to-day the Austrian official who organized the Persian postal-service reports : Every Persian feels himself capable of doing anything that may be entrusted to him. He will not hesitate to assume and discharge the duties of a high civil office to-day and an equally high military office to-morrow[4]. This is an old Persian trait. The Persian Secretary of the Baghdadi Sultan Bakhtiyar felt such confidence in himself that he

(1) Yaqut. *Irshad* 238.

(2) 'Such names as Yaqut, Gawhar, Yalbaq imply that their owners were originally slaves. By *freie* and *unfreie* Mez means names of 'freedom and names of slaves.' For this note I am indebted to Prof. Margoliouth. Tr.

(3) Istakhri, 146. These civil servants were of five kinds : (*1*) clerks in the Despatch Office ; (*2*) clerks in the Tax Office ; (*3*) clerks in the War Office ; (*4*) clerks attached to courts ; (*5*) clerks in the Police Office ; Baihaqi, ed. Schwally, 448 ; more exhaustively in the *Jamharah* of Saizari, Leiden, fol. 99a ff.

(4) *Aus Persian,* Wine 1882, 184.

sought the appointment of a Marshal (isfahsalar) and had, on that account, to flee in 358/969 from Baghdad[1]. And yet the training of an official was quite different from that of a jurist or of a savant. His was a temporal education (Adab) with a mere working knowledge of theology. And this difference reflected itself even externally. The official never used the *Tailasan*[2] of the savant but the *Durra'ah* (a garment with an opening or slit in the front. It was always of wool without any lining).

When the Wazir al-'Utbi pressed the learned Ibn Dha (d. 378/988) to accept the presidentship of the 'Diwan er-Rasa'il' he made it clear to him that acceptance of the office would not mean his exclusion from the guild of savants, for that office in Khorasan was a juristic office[3]. On the other hand the Caliph refused to appoint a learned man as his Wazir, on the ground that it would be said everywhere that he had no *Katib* in his dominions available for such a post[4].

(1) Misk., VI. 326 ff.

(2) *Tailasan* is a 'scarf' or 'hood' (academic) which lies on the shoulder. It appears from Arab authors that the *Tailasan* was also sometimes worn round the turban. See Lane *S.V.* Browne, *Lit. Hist. of Persia,* 1.335 ; Dozy, *Noms de Vetements chez les arabes,* 278 sqq ; *Burhan-i-Qati.* S.V.). The *Tailasan* was also worn by Judges. "Sometimes I have spoken," says Muqaddasi in his *Ahsan ut-Taqsim* (p. 7), "in a terse way implying rather than expressing details. Thus, for instance, my words regarding Ahwaz : "There is no sanctity in its mosque." I mean thereby that it is full of swindlers, low and ignorant people who arrange to meet there. Thus the mosque in never free from people who sit there while others are engaged in prayer. It is the gathering-place of importunate beggars and a home of sinners. And such is also my remarks about Shiraz. I say "there are a large numbers of people there with Tailasans," By this I mean that the Tailasan is alike the dress of the gentlemen, the learned and the ignorant. How often have I not seen drunken people turning their Tailasans upside down and trailing them behind themselves ! When I sought admission at the Wazir's wearing a Tailasan I was refused admission; it would, perhaps have been otherwise had I been recognized, but I was always asked in when I went wearing a *Durr'ah.*" I am indebted to Dr. Siddiqi of Dacca of this note. Tr. See Yaqut *Irshad* 1234 : Muq. 440.

(3) es-Subki, II. 166.

(4) Wuz., 322.

This pure body of secular officers constitutes a striking contrast between the Muslim Empire and the Europe of the Early Middle Ages where the clerks consisted of none but classical scholars. This indeed was not to the best advantage of Islam, for the official world, absorbed in its work and content with its small intellectual inheritance, rarely took part in the higher intellectual activities of the day. The official world was a safe refuge to the laity from the storm and stress of intellectual and spiritual strife. Even to-day the self-complacent effendi is a great hindrance to progress,—as great, perhaps, as the narrow-minded theologian. Pious legend traces the fundamental rules relating to officers and judges to Omar I. He is said to have imposed four obligations on his officers : *(a)* never to ride a horse ; *(b)* never to use fine linen ; *(c)* never to eat dainty dishes ; *(d)* never to close the door[1] against the indigent, and never to keep a hajib[2].

And in the 3rd/9th century money played an ugly role in the official circles. Everything was to be paid for[3], even the very office itself, and money had to be found in all possible ways. The head of the office made money by drawing salaries of employees who were either not required or were not employed at all. Moreover he falsely showed on the list various employees as jurists and clerks, and debited to the treasury larger sums than were actually spent on the purchase of paper (for use in his department)[4]. The civil head ('Aamil) of Egypt drew a splendid salary of 3,000 dinars (about 30,000 marks) a month. Of course out of this amount he had to defray the expenses of his office, besides the presents to the military chief, the Court and the Wazir. Even the favourite wife of a Caliph complained that she

(1) *Kit. al-Khiraji;* Wuz., 66

(2) 'Hajib' literally means 'one who does not let people in or one who prevents people's access to the door.

(3) Wuz., 263.

(4) Misk., V., 344.

was badly served by the officials, and the Caliph thereupon advised her to make presents to them to put them in better humour[1]. The poet Ibn el-Mut'azz (d. 296/908) calls the officers "Choleric Nabateans", with full bellies ; while he describes the people as thin and lean[2]. And the pious people of those times grouped officers and sinners together, not unlike the "publicans and sinners" of the New Testament. A pious engraver refused to engrave a precious stone of an officer for 100 dinars, whereas he did the same thing for a merchant for 10 dirhams. Another pious man refused 500 dinars which a merchant offered as a gift to him. His friends, however, talked him over by arguing that one might refuse to have anything to do with government moneys, for such moneys were always under the shadow of suspicion, but no such suspicion rested on the self-acquired money of a merchant[3]. And yet another was taunted for sitting at dinner with an officer. He apologised by urging that the food-stuff was lawfully pruchased[4]. One day when Ahmed ibn Harb was sitting with the Chiefs and distinguished men of Nisabur who had called on him, his son came into the room drunk, playing a guitar and singing. He passed impudently through the room without greeting them. When Ahmad observed their astonishment, he asked : What is it ? They rejoined : We are ashamed to see this lad pass thee by in such a condition. Thereupon Ahmad replied : He is to be forgiven. One night my wife and I partook of food sent to us by a

(1) Wuz., 184 ff. "Mutadid made a grant of an estate to a favourite, but the head of the Diwan delayed giving effect to it, and on her complaining to the Caliph, he told her that the proper way for her, as for others, was to approach the official with the customary presents. On her doing this the grant was passed and the official boasted thereafter of having taken a present by the Caliph's order." Amedroz., J.R.A.S., 1908., PP. 431-2 Tr.

(2) *Diwan* , II, 14. It is true that he had unhappy experiences at Court. For thirty years he wrote in prose and verse to officials without getting anything. (Wuz., 115).

(3) Ahmad ibn Yahya, ed. Arnold, p. 44.

(4) Ibid., 61 ; 56.

neighbour. That very night this boy was conceived. We went to sleep without saying our prayer. Next morning we enquired of our neighbour where the food came from which he had sent us and we were informed that it came from a government-servant at whose house there was a wedding-feast[1]. In saying goodbye to an officer some said seriously, some in joke : Do penance for thy appointment. When an emeritus, attracted by a fat pay, accepted an office, he was called 'apostate'[2]. General opinion indeed hardly regarded the charge of corrupt administration of an office as slanderous.The chroniclers are amazed to find high officers honest. Thus it is expressly reported of the deceased head of the public treasury in 314/926 that he left no money behind[3]. It frequently happened that officials, suspected and even convicted of malpractices, were left in their posts or were reinstated after they had paid up their fines. But such was not always the case. We are told on good authority that Ikhshid, otherwise a sound financier, was the author of this system[4]. When anything untoward happened to an official his more successful colleagues opened a subscription-list to lighten the burden of his punishement[5]. It needed the eccentric Hakim cut off in 494/1013, for embezzlement, the hands of a ministerial chief like those of an ordinary criminal. But this very Caliph placed him again in 409/1018 at the head of the pay-office. In 418/1027 he made him his Wazir[6].

The unnatural condition of the civil service under the Caliphate brought its own Nemesis, namely, the craving for titles and the use of involved phraseology in official

(1) *Kashf el-mahjub*, 366.
(2) Misk., V., 244.
(3) *Arib*, 128.
(4) Tallquist, 39.
(5) Wuz., 306, 308.
(6) *Becker, Beitrage Zur Gesch. Agyptens*, 1, 34 ; according to el-Musabbihi (420).

documents, which began in the 4th/10th century and has continued to this day. They assigned great importance to inflated court style in speech and address, but notable it is that the subscription— in contrast to the European practice—was marked with brevity. Hitherto the mode of address had simply been : To the father of N. from the father of N. Al-Fadl b. Sahl introduced about 200/815 the form "To N.N. May God preserve him. From N.N."[1]. Thenceforward the development became very rapid. We have list of the different grades of addresses which the Wazir used in the beginning of the IVth century. The commanding officer in Syria was to be addressed : "May God strengthen thee, preserve thy life, make his goodness perfect in thee and bestow His favours on thee". The engineer was to be addressed : "May God protect and forgive thee." The lowest grade of officers, such as country post-masters and government bankers, were to be only addressed with "May God preserve thee[2]". At the beginning of the century, the magnates and Wazirs were addressed as "our master" (Sayyadana) or our patron (Maulana), and in the second person 'thou'. In 374/984 two Wazirs were already given the title of "the exalted Sahib," and were addressed as "the master, my patron, my leader" in the 3rd person[3].

What matters to me, sings Khawarizmi (d. 383/993), if the Abbasids have thrown open the gates of honour and surnames. They have conferred titles on a man whom their ancestors would not have made the doorkeeper of their lavatory. Though plentiful the titles, few are the dirhams in the hands of these our Caliphs[4].

---

(1) Eutychius (d. 318/930) p. 54 ; according to a very good authority.

(2) Wuz., 153 ff.

(3) Taghribardi, 34. Even the Christian Wazir Isa ibn Nestorius was spoken of as 'our sublime master" (Sayyadana el-ajall). Yahya ibn Sa'id, fol. 112a. Wuz., 153 ff.

(4) Yatimah, VI, 145.

In 429/1037 the Chief Qadhi Mawardi received the title of Aqda'l-Qudat, Highest Judge. Certain theologians took exception to it. On their part, however, they declared it legal to call the Amir Jalal-ad-Daulah 'Great King of Kings,' a title which Mawardi regarded as the usurpation of God's title. Later all judges were called Aqda'l-Qudat[1].

In this respect too the Caliph Hakim tried to go back upon existing conditions. After freely distributing at first all kinds of titles, in 408/1017 he repealed all save the seven highest. But soon the old practice was re-introduced[2]. The Secretary of the Caliph al-Qadir (381-422/991-1031) is said to have introduced as the ordinary mode of court-address Al-Hadhrah. Even in this small matter the practice of the 4th/10th century obtains in the Orient to-day. He is said to have addressed the Wazir, for the first time, as 'thy exalted wazirite presence' (al-hadhrat al-aliyat al-waziriyyah). This very man is said to have introduced for the first time the expression "the most sacred, prophetic presence," in addressing the Caliph instead of the older, simpler term "Caliph,," and this innovation soon became the general practice. The strangest term, the appellation of the Caliph as "service" goes back to him. Thus I read a passage in the handwriting of the Qadhi ibn Abi'l-Sawarib : "The servant of the most sublime 'service' such and such[3]." The Caliph al-Qaim conferred upon his Wazir (killed in 450/1058) three titles:—Rais al-Ru'asa, (Chief of·Chiefs), Sharf al-Wuzara (honour of the Wazirs), Jamal-al-Wara (Beauty of Creation[4].

On the other hand, in the judicial department, the original mode of address continued ; in his letters the Chief Judge always addressed judges by their names[5].

---

(1) Yaqut, *Irshad*, V, 407.

(2) Yahya ibn Sai'id 222.

(3) Wuz., 148 ff.

(4) *Tarikh Baghdad*, J. R. A. S. (1912) 67.

(5) Wuz., 148 ff.

On Fridays and Tuesdays all offices were closed. Thus the Caliph al-Mutadid (279-289/892-902) is said to have ordained the holiday on Friday because it was a day of prayer and also because his teacher had always given him a holiday on that day, and on Tuesday because in the middle of the week people needed a day for rest and a day to themselves for the management of their own private affairs[1].

(1) Wuz., 22.

VII. THE WAZIR

With the end of the feudal state and the rise of bureaucracy the Wazir steps into light under the first Abbasid. The Omayyads knew of no such official[1]. In the beginning of the 4th/10th century the chancellor was further defeudalized, the caliph taking away from him the administration of the Abbasid family estates, which yielded his predecessors an annual income of 170,000 dinars ; a fixed salary at first of 5,000 and later of 7,000 dinars was assigned to him[2]. But as compared with the other officials he held a position of exceptional importance. He received stipends for his sons, 500 dinars a month for each, indeed a minister's salary[3].

The most noticeable change was that in the empire originally founded on a military basis, the Wazir, the chief clerk, stood higher in rank than all the generals. The mighty official hierarchies of the earlier Orient were once more revived. When in the year 312/924 the all-powerful marshal Munis returned to Baghdad, the Wazir proceeded on his barge to him—"a thing which no Wazir had ever done before"—to congratulate him on his safe arrival. On his departure the Marshal kissed his hand[4].

Like the other officials at the beginning of the 4th/10th

---

(1) Al Fakhri, ed Ahlwardt, 180. (For the earlier history of the Wazir, see my *Contributions to the History of Islamic Civilization*, pp. 242 et sqq. Tr).

(2) Wuz. 280, 350, Misk, v, 268.

(3) Wuz., 23. In the Fatimid Empire even all his brothers received 2-300 Dinars a month, Maq. 1,401.

(4) Wuz, 50 sqq. ; Misk v. 214.

century the Abbasid Wazir generally used the Darra'ah (mantle), Qamis (coat), Mubattanah (shirt), and the Khuff (shoes)[1]. The official colour was black[2].

At Court festivities the Wazir wore the Court-dress (Thiyab al-Mauhib), Qaba (Gown), and the sword, suspended from his girdle (Mintaqah) ; the only piece of civil dress on him then was the black Imamah (turban)[3]. This costume was solemnly bestowed upon him by the Caliph on his appointment of office. In a procession of courtiers, generals, officers, he was fetched from and escorted back home, and the historian takes pains to state that a wazir once, on such a festive occasion, wanting to pass water, alighted at the house of an officer, whose salary he increased for this accommodation[4]. On his return home the wazir received the congratulations of the people in the

---

(1) Wuz, 325.

(2) In the poem of Isfahani apud Al Fakhri, ed. Ahlwardt. 334.

(3) Sabusti, *Kit. ad-diwanat.* fol. 66 a; Misk, VI, 45, 46 ; Yaqut *Irshad,* V. 356. In 319/931 the people were surprised to see the Wazir on a festive occasion in a soldier's cap (Shashiya) and with a sword suspended from his shoulder-belt (Arib, 165). We know of the daily routine of a Wazir about 275/888. He rose towards the end of the night and prayed till sunrise. Then he received people who had come to pay respects to him. This done, he rode to the Caliph's palace where he discussed matters with him for full four hours. Then on return home he dealt with the affairs of those present and absent until midday. He then took his meal and rested. Late in the afternoon he occupied himself with State finances. An abstract of all income and expenditure was laid before him. This done, he looked into his own affairs and matters concerning his own servants. He then conversed and took rest (Sabusti, Berlin, fol. 118 b.). About the middle of the 4th/10th century the Buwayyid Wazir at Rai used to go to office before sunrise with candles and beacon-grates [Yaqut, *Irshad,* V, 358]. Also at the end of the 5th/11th century the Wazir went early in the morning [after sunrise] to the office, came home at 10 o'clock, remained undisturbed till midday and after that did what he pleased. [es-Subki, III, 141].

(4) *Arib,* 164.

order of their rank. The Caliph sent him money, robes of honour, incense, food and drink, and ice[1].

Even the routine of the Wazir's work about 300/913 has come down to us, with a note that he kept up his earlier habits as the head of a department. His counsellors saw him early in the morning. To each he then assigned the papers connected with his department with necessary directions. In the evening they brought the papers back for inspection and remained on till night. When the work was over and papers connected with expenses, orders, accounts had been laid before him and dealt with, the Wazir adjourned the meeting by rising from his seat[2]. At these meetings each officer, with his inkstand in front of him, occupied a fixed seat facing the wazir, the chief secretary sitting straight in front of him.[3]

Of important documents the wazir kept a copy in his archives which, as a rule, after his fall, made their way to the house of his successor[4]. When in 304/916 Ibn al-Furat succeeded 'Ali ibn 'Isa these papers filled up a whole house to the ceiling. We also read of a bamboo chest in which private papers were kept, and on the lid of which the wazir had made a list of its contents[5].

Up to 320/932 the former palace of Sulaiman ibn Wahb, with a circumference of 200,000 yards, on the Eastern Bank of the Tigris (called also Dar-al-Mukharrim), had been the official residence of the wazir. Later they realized a fabulous sum of money by the sale of this extensive plot of land in one of the most expensive quarters of the town. They

---

(1) Wuz., 31.
(2) Wuz., 235.
(3) Yaqut, *Irshad*, 1, 342.
(4) Wuz., 208.
(5) Wuz., 59 ; Misk. V. 253.

parcelled it out into numerous plots and sold them to various people, using the sale-proceeds as the donative of the Caliph Qahir to his troops[1]. The palace of one of the Caliph's sons was then assigned to the wazir[2]. In front of the Wazir's office so many foot-soldiers were quartered as guards that thirty men could be sent out at a time for special purposes[3]. At the great audience of the wazir armed guards stood in readiness in the hall to escort persons specially honoured, and always the wazir, from the hall. They marched in front with drawn swords. The guard is said to have consisted of as many as 200 soldiers[4].

The wazir generally went to Court only on the days of audience, which at the beginning of the century were Mondays and Thursdays[5]. On these occasions one of the four Secretariat chiefs used to ride to the palace with him[6]. There he had a special house set apart for him, where the courtiers paid their official call on him until he was summoned to the Caliph. From 312/924, however, the wazir waited at the house of the Court-Marshal, an indication of his waning power[7]. At the meeting he sat opposite to the Caliph. On these occasions in his left hand he held a beautiful inkstand which was suspended from a chain. The demands of yet more exacting ceremonials of later times (about 300/913) required a Chamberlain to stand by the wazir holding his inkstand[8]. On days other than the audience-days the wazir had a representative at Court[9], but the courtiers kept him informed of all that happened at the

(1) Misk, V, 410 ; Wuz. (pp. 23) mentions 173, 346 ells as its measurement.
(2) Misk. V, 391.
(3) Wuz., 121.
(4) Wuz., 112.
(5) Wuz., 241 ; 352.
(6) Ibn al-Athir, VIII, 7 ; *Kit. al-Uyun*, IV, Berlin, fol. 586.
(7) Wuz., 368.
(8) Wuz., 342.
(9) Al-Fakhri, 392 ; Maqrizi, Khitat, II 156.

Palace[1]. In 300/913, when the Caliph wanted to appoint a Wazir, he drew up a long list of candidates and sent it to his confident who, by reason of old age, was constrained to give up his appointment as Wazir. He made his note against each name. But when this very retiring wazir suggested the appointment of a Qadhi as his successor the Caliph resented the suggestion. He would be laughed at, said he, by the Princes of Islam and peoples of other faith were he to do such a thing ; for they would then assuredly say that either there is no competent official (Katib) for such an appointment in his dominion, or that he has gone astray in his decision[2]. But about this very time the Qadhi Al-Merwazi of Bokhara (d. 334/946) became the wazir of the Samanid Prince of Khorasan[3].

The tendency of the times was to create a caste out of every high official position. Like the clan of the Qadhis, there grew up the clan of the wazir. The wazir's sons formed a special caste, the highest in the official circle[4]. Even the post became hereditary. In his eighteenth year the son of the wazir Ibn Muqlah succeeded his father[5] ; in his twenty-fourth the son of Amid[6]. The family of Khaqan furnished four wazirs in seventy years, and in fifty years that of Banu-l-Furat a similar number. Amid was the Wazir of Mu'izz-ud-Dawlah, founder of the Buwayyid dynasty. His son and grandson became wazir of Rukn-ud-Dawlah in Iran. Ten members of the Banu Wahib, originally Babylonian Christians, held the highest officers in succession. Of these four actually were wazirs[7]. The wazir nominated in 310/931, and belonging to this family, was a spendthrift in his

(1) Wuz., 267 ; For Cairo, Ibn al-Athir, IX, 82.
(2) Wuz. 322.
(3) Flugel, *Die Klassen der hanafitischen Rechtsgelehrten*, 296.
(4) Ibn al-Jauzi, Berlin, fol. 66 a.
(5) Syuti *Husn al-Muhadhara II, 127.*
(6) Yaqut Irshad, V. 356.
(7) Amedroz, JRAS, 1908 p., 418 ; *Yatimah*, III 359.

youth, who had run into debts. He was so hard pressed by his creditors that the Qadhi had to put him under the Court of Wards. The efficient Marshal Munis accordingly apprehended that he would mismanage as wazir the State-finances just as he had mismanaged his own[1]. The matter appeared all the more serious as the Wazir essentially was Finance Minister. He had to prepare the budget ; impose or annul[2] taxes ; realize revenue from the provinces[3]. In 303/915 the troops, clamouring for more pay, had already burnt his cattle and killed his horses in the stables[4]. In the 4th/10th century the barques of the wazir were invariably wrecked on the financial rock. When in 334/946 the wazir heard that the troops were blaming him for delay in the payment of their salary he sheared his head, washed himself with hot water, wrapped himself up in his shroud and prayed all night. The soldiers eventually killed him. He was a theologian. He fasted every Monday and Thursday and always prayed to God to let him die in power[5].

The most critical year in the history of the Wazirs is the year 334/946. With the entry of the Buwayyids into Baghdad the Chancellor of the Amir (Chief administrator) also received the title of Wazir ; whereas the Chancellor of the Caliph ceased to be addressed as such[6]. Strictly speaking there was now no Wazir any longer. Hilal as-Sabi, in his "History of the Wazirs" mentions the most prominent Chancellors of the 4th/10th century and divides them into (a) Wazirs of the Abbasid dynasty and the *Kuttab* (clerks) of the Dailamite period[7]. Thus even Gauhar, at the conquest of Egypt, refused in the beginning the title of Wazir to Ja'far

(1) Amedroz, 1908, 431.
(2) Ibn al-Athir VIII, 51.
(3) Wuz., 239 Ibn al-Athir, VIII, 713.
(4) *Arib*, 58.
(5) Ibn al-Jauzi, fol. 75.
(6) Misk, VI, 125 ; Mas'udi, *Tanbih*, 39.
(7) Wuz., 3.

ibn al-Fadl since he was not the Wazir of the Caliph[1]. To the Fatimids, at first, the name itself was apparently to profane ; their highest official was the Qadhi. The second Egyptian Caliph, Al-'Aziz was the first to appoint a Wazir, the Jewish convert Ibn Killis (d. 380/990) ; and even at a later period, in the presence of the Wazir, the chief Qadhi could not be addressed as Chief Qadhi for the simple reason that that was regarded as a fitting title only of the Wazir[2]. Maqrizi expressly states that after the death of Ibn Killis 'Aziz appointed no other Wazir. Nor did Hakim either. Only in the 5th/11th century under Zahir was this office resuscitated under the name of Wisatah (a channel of communication)[3], but the people did not make any refined or subtle distinction. The Christian Yahya ibn Sa'id living about the year 400/1010, always speaks of Wazirs.

Under the princes of the Empire the office of the Wazir undergoes a change. Of the old Wazirs of the Empire, Al-Fadl ibn Sahl (Wazir of the Caliph Mamun) had borne the title of *Durri Asataini* (master of two dominions), apparently because he could wield both the pen and the sword[4], but the military aspect was not emphasised or brought into prominence. A clever general, Al-Hasan ibn Makhlad, was, for the first time appointed Wazir or the Caliph al-Mu'tamid, but he was deposed in 272/885[5]. On the other hand we find the Wazirs of the Samanids and the Buwayyids active alike as the head of the army and as the chief of the

(1) Maqrizi, *Ittiaz*, 70.

(2) *Qalqashandi*, 9 tr. by Wustenfeld (A. C. G. W. 1879), 185.

(3) Khitat, 1. 439.

(4) *Arib*, 165.

(5) Al-Fakhri altogether omits Ibn Makhlad who held office between Sulaiman ibn Wahb and Ibn Bulbul-i-Masudi, VIII, 39 ; Tabari, III, Index.) The statement that Ibn Bulbul united 'the pen and the sword' is to be put down to this omission of Ibn Bulbul's predecessor. Moreover we do not hear of any military activities of Ibn Bulbul; on the contrary Tabari III, 2110) expressly states that he was only employed in the chancery.

Chancery[1]. Even so distinguished a man of letters as Sahib had to lead an expedition when Wazir[2].

The decline in the dignity of the Wazir, like the decline in morals, is amply evidenced by the fact that the irritable Buwayyid Mu'izz-ud-Dawlah in 341/952 condemned at Baghdad his Wazir Al-Muhallabi, a member of the Omayyad aristocracy, to 150 stripes and imprisonment[3]. But this indignity notwithstanding, he took him back as Wazir. But before doing so he first enquired whether it was possible for him to do so after the treatment he had meted out to him and, to his entire satisfaction, he found a precedent in the conduct of the condottiere Merdawaigh, who had his Wazir once so severely beaten that he could neither walk nor sit and yet he placed him in charge of the office again. In 362/973 Mu'izz-ud-Dawlah's unworthy son appointed a Court Chief his Wazir[4]. His cousin the Sultan Adad-ud-Dawlah, had his Wazir, Abu'l Fath Ibn al-Amid arrested, blinded and his nose cut off[5]. Adad-ud-Dawlah compelled his cousin to have his Wazir, the former chief, blinded and sent to him for conspiring against him. When sent, Adad-ud-Dawlah had him taken round the camp and then trampled to death by an elephant. Under orders his dead body was impaled on Tigris Bridge[6]. A beautiful elegy was penned by a poet over this unfortunate man, who to be sure had many a cruel act to his credit:—

(1) For the Samanids, for instance, Mirkhond, Hist. of the Sam. Ed. Wilkin, 72, 84. for the Wazirs of Muizz-ud-Dawlah, Saimari and Muhallabi, Misk, VI, 211, 434 ff ; for Adad-ud-Dawlah, Misk, VI, 451, 482 ; for the Wazir of Baha-ud-Dawlah, Ibn al-Athir, IX, 138.

(2) Ibn al-Athir, IX, 39.

(3) Misk, VI, 190 ff ; Ibn al-Athir, VIII, 375.

(4) His duty had been to carry food on his shoulder, covered with a towel, and to taste it before serving it. Misk VI, 362 ; 396 ; Ibn al-Athir, VIII, 462. People made fun of him saying 'from plate to the Wizarat'. Ibn al-Jauzi, fol. 104 a.

(5) Ibn al-Athir, VIII, 497.

(6) Misk VI, 481 ; Yahya ibn Sa'id, Paris, fol. 105 a ; Ibn al-Athir VIII, 507.

As the Earth was but too narrow to gather in
thy virtues
They made air thy grave and wind thy
shroud[1].

Adad-ud-Dawlah introduced two innovations into the office of the Wazir : first, he appointed two Wazirs simultaneously ; and secondly, of the two one, Ibn Mansur Nasr ibn Harun, was a Christian. Nasr remained as Governor of his tribal homeland, Faris ; but the other al-Mutahhar ibn Abdallah accompanied him to Baghdad. Al-Mutahhar was a proud man and when he failed to sweep the Babylonian swamps clear of the robbers who infested them, he opened up the arteries in his two arms with his knife, for he preferred to die rather than to appear before his master with his work undone[2].

His successor merely became the *locum tenens* of the Wazir, who resided in Shiraz. But this experiment was unsuccessful as the two constantly collided with each other[3]. Following his father's example, in the year 382/992, Baha-ud-Dawlah, residing in Shiraz, appointed two Wazirs, one of these being his Governor in Babylon[4]. After the death of Sahib (d. 384/994) who, for a long time, held the wizarat with distinction, a disgraceful bargaining for this post began in Iran. A successor was chosen, but as another high officer offered eight million dirhams for it, whereas the one already chosen had offered only six for his retention in office, the prince graciously excused two millions to each of the rival candidates and appointed them both, with the result that ten million dirhams made their way into the prince's pocket.

(1) Ibn al-Athir. Thus also writes Nadim al-Arib of Ahmed Sa'id el-Baghdadi, 143 ; Ibn Taghribardi, 20.
(2) Misk VI, 513 f; Yahya ibn Sa'id, Paris, fol. 107 a; Ibn al-Athir, VIII, 514.
(3) Misk. VI. 515 ; Ibn al-Athir, IX, 66.
(4) Ibn al-Athir, IX, 66.

They jointly issued and signed orders ; they mutually helped each other in sucking the country and, in the event of a war, they cast lots as to who should lead the army. But this position of affairs was not of long duration ; it ended by one getting the other assassinated[1]. And, finally, the Christian Wazir of the East found a counterpart in Egypt. In 380/990 the Fatimid Caliph Al-'Aziz appointed the Christian 'Isa, son of Nestorious, his Wazir[2].

To the passion for titles, evidencing itself about 400-1010, even the Wazirs fell victims,—-a clear proof of the degeneration of the society of that time. In 411/1020 the Amir of Baghdad conferred upon his Wazir the princely prerogative of having the drum beaten, before prayer time, in front of his house. He also designated him 'the great Wazir' (Wazir-al-Wuzara)[3].

At Cairo the Caliph al-Hakim soon followed the example of conferring the fateful title of Wazir-al-Wuzara. The historian Hilal as-Sabi (d. 447/1055) mournfully refers to it as one of the pomposities of the times[4].

In 416/1025 the Wazir at Baghdad simultaneously received a number of titles : Alam-ud-Din (Insignia of Religion); Sa'd-ud-Dawlah (good fortune of the dynasty) : Amin-al Mulk (Trusted one of the Empire); Sharaf-al-Mulk (glory of the Empire)[5]. This was a prelude to the conditions now obtaining in the Orient. As against his titleless predecessors, the title bedecked Wazir was a shadowy, powerless phantom.

---

(1) Yaqut, *Irshad*, 1, 71 ff.
(2) Yahya ibn Sa'id, fol. 112 f. He indeed, did not officially hear the title of Wazir.
(3) Ibn al-Jauzi, 168 ab.
(4) Hakim died 411-1020. Yahya ibn Sa'id, fol. 128 a.
(5) Wuz., 201.

WAZIRS IN THE 4TH/10TH CENTURY

Outstanding is the figure of 'Ali Ibn al-Furat, who in 296/909, in his fiftieth year, succeeded his brother al-Abbas as Wazir. He was immensely rich. His contemporary, the Historian As-Suli[1], thus speaks of him: Never have we heard of a Wazir other than Ibn al-Furat who, while in office, possessed in silver and gold, in movable and immovable property, ten million dinars (about 100 million marks)[2]. He held court in grand style. He paid five thousand monthly pensions, varying from a hundred dinars to five dirhams[3]. He regularly gave away twenty thousand dirhams every year in stipends to poets ; not counting occasional rewards and gifts for panegyrics[4]. Of those who constantly sat at his table nine have been mentioned as his privy councillors. Of these four were Christians. For two long hours fresh dishes were served[5]. For his underlings he kept a kitchen large enough to serve a whole regiment of troops : 90 sheep, 30 goats, 200 fowls, 200 partridges, 200 pigeons were daily consumed. Five bakers baked wheaten-bread day and night ; sweets were always in preparation. In the house there was a large drinking-hall where stood a capacious cistern of cold water. All who needed found drink there : infantry, cavalry, police, clerks. To officers, courtiers, civil servants, the cup-bearers, clothed in the finest embroidered Egyptian linen, with towels over their shoulders, offered *sherbat*[6]. His palace was a town in itself ; seven of his tailors had their quarters there. On the walls lay hanging rolls of papyrus for the use of applicants and complainants, who thus spared the trouble of buying them[7]. On the day of his investiture wax and

(1) Ibn al-Jauzi, fol. 173 a.
(2) *Arib*, 37.
(3) Wuz., 142.
(4) Wuz., 201.
(5) Wuz., 240.
(6) Wuz., 195.
(7) Wuz., 176.

papyrus rose in price as, to everyone who came to congratulate him, he gave a mansurain paper roll and a candle ten pounds in weight. The cup-bearer on that day used 40,000 pounds of ice[1]. Throughout his Wizarat he kept up the practice of presenting a candle to all who left his palace after dusk. In 311/923 he established a hospital at Baghdad and sanctioned for its maintenance 200 dinars from his private purse[2].

An aristocrat born and bred, on assuming charge of his office, with his own hands, he burnt without reading a list of his enemies drawn up by some one for him[3]. After his deposition he would rather die than ransom himself with the money of his supporters[4]. When the director of taxes sent on an order of his which looked like a forgery, and intimated to him that he had detained the bearer in custody, Ibn al-Furat wrote back (knowing that it was forged) that it was genuine for, said he 'one who even in Egypt expected something good by the use of his name and authority was not to be put to shame[5]. 'And when the fallen Wazir 'Ail ibn 'Isa bowed as low as he could before him, kissed his hand, and rose even in the presence of his young ten-year-old son, Ibn al-Furat declared that in misfortune his lever (meaning his cheerful disposition) increased like that of a camel[6]. By long service he had become thoroughly familiar with all the pranks and tricks of the official life. In a masterly fashion he unravelled the tangled financial skein of the Empire, and in more ways than one justified his successor's glowing tribute on his death : "Today has financial skill

(1) Wuz., 63.
(2) Ibn al-Jauzi, Berlin, fol. 23. (See Custom *Intro. to the History of Medicine,* pp. 208-10 Tr.
(3) Wuz., 119. This is also related of the Caliph Mamun. Tabari, III. 1075.
(4) Wuz., 98.
(5) Wuz., 113 ; Ibn al-Jauzi, *Muntazam,* fol. 28.
(6) Wuz., 307.

passed away[1]." In politics, cool and calculated was the old Wazir's judgment : "At bottom to rule is naught but a game of chance, a piece of jugglery. When one does that well, it is called 'Politics'." Another maxim of his was : "In matters of government, progress, even if not always in the right direction, is preferable to standing-still." And yet another : "If you can fix up a matter with the librarian or the Secretary, do so, without bringing it up before the Wazir"[2].

And yet cold-bloodedly he plundered the treasury. Already in conspiracy with his brother he largely swindled the State[3].

His critics recalled the fact that, when his property was confiscated, money-bags were found bearing the seals of the master of the privy-purse of the Caliph[4]. One of his officers tells us that in a few minutes he made away with 70,000 dinars. "After the insurrection of Ibn-al-Mut'azz, I along with Ibn al-Furat fixed the main items regarding the largesses that were to be paid to the troops and made arrangements for payment thereof. When Ibn al-Furat had finished with this business he got into his 'Flyer' and proceeded to the Mu'alli river. There he called a halt. The crew took the boat to the bank and he thus spoke to me : Order the treasurer Abu Khorasan to bring another 70,000 dinars to me and debit it to the account of the largesses." Thereupon said I to myself : "Have we not already settled all the items ? What is this additional amount for ?" but indited what he directed. Then he signed, handed it over to a servant and said : "Leave not the treasury until thou bringest the money to my house." He, then, proceeded on. The money was duly brought and made over to his Treasurer[5].

(1) Wuz., 283.
(2) Wuz., 119.
(3) Wuz.,134.
(4) Wuz., 139
(5) Wuz., 134.

His former companion and later rival, 'Ali ibn'Isa, also of an old official stock, was the very reverse of him[1]. Pious, he fasted by day and devoted half of his income to pious uses[2]. In contrast to Ibn al-Furat, even towards the Caliph he never adopted a fixed rule of behaviour[3]. To the philologoist al-Akhfash at a full audience he gave such a rough and rude reply that the 'world became black before him and he died of grief[4]. 'Ali ibn 'Isa was never slovenly in dress. He took his shoes off only in the *Harem* or when he went to sleep[5]. He worked day and night[6] and, when exhausted, he retired to a recess near the door, which was screened off by a curtain and where cushions were placed to enable him to rest before resuming work[7]. That he lost his sense of dignity in misfortune we have already seen. From sheer piety he proceeded against Christian officials[8], and from pure scruples he would not let his sons take up any appointment during his term of office[9]. He sought to obviate deficit in the budget by effecting economy ; by lowering the salaries of guards and officers ; by stopping, among other things, the usual distribution at Court or to officials of flesh on the Baqr-id Day. He strove to prevent embezzlement of public funds. But Ibn al-Furat taunted him by saying that he concerned himself with the morals of the people and was anxious whether the geese of the Baghdad ponds were not cheated out of their food, forgetting the most important thing of all—the abuse of public revenues[11]. Another officer reckoned that the Wazir, in one hour, got

(2) Ibn al-Jauzi, Berlin, fol. 76b.

(3) His contemporary as-Suli in Suyuti's *Husnul-Muhadhera*, II, 126.

(4) Wuz., 312.

(5) Yaqut, *Irshad*, V, 225.

(6) Wuz., 325.

(7) *Arib*, 130.

(8) Wuz., 325.

(9) Wuz., 95. According to Bar Hebraeus he had even Christian advisers in the Ministry.

(10) Wuz., 266.

(11) Wuz., 260.

twenty dinars but he occupied himself with trifles which were not worth the money he received in pay[1]. Notwithstanding this pious frame of mind, he lied after his fall to the Caliph in stating that he merely possessed 3,000 dinars. It was immediately shown that he had a deposit of 17,000 elsewhere and, within a short time, he actually promised to pay in to the State 300,000 dinars : ¼ within thirty days and the balance later[2].

Later he was reproached for having sworn that his landed property was only worth 20,000 dinar, whereas it was actually worth 50,000 and this discovery to 'Ali "was not unlike giving him a stone to swallow"[3]. Never were his hands clean, and his extreme mildness to the two financiers, who then sucked Syria and Egypt dry, could never be defended or justified[4].

Between these two Wazirs Mohamed b. Khaqan acted for two long years[5]. He belonged to the circle of high court nobility ; in fact, was the son of a Wazir. The verdict on him, not unlike the verdict on many a democratic leader, was : Careless and affable, yet mean and cunning. When asked for a favour he would beat his breast and say: Yes, with great pleasure ! This habit won for him the name of the 'breast-beater.' He was a greater favourite of the people than of the nobility[6]. His portrait is adorned, now with harmless, comical, now with poisonous anecdotes, originally related of others. His practice was to appoint, then immediately to depose, and then again to reinstate officers and this not because of the absence of a sense of responsibility on his part, but rather on account of a craving

(1) Wuz., 351.
(2) Wuz., 288.
(3) Misk, V, 19.
(4) Wuz., 280.
(5) *Kit. al-Wuzara*, Ed. Amedroz.
(6) Wuz., 276. p. 39 Tr.

to secure the customary fee for appointments[1].

At an inn at Hulwan seven officers are reported to have met who were appointed to one and the same office within twenty days ; at Mosul five[2]. In eleven months he is said to have appointed eleven prefects for the important district of Baduraya, of which a great part of Baghdad formed part.

Thus, at the beginning of the century, three Wazirs stand out in bold relief, each wholly different from the other, the common feature between them being their rapacity in robbing the State-treasury.

Because he did not belong to the official circle, Hamid ibn-al-'Abbas, who became Wazir in 306/918, constitutes a great exception to the general rule[3]. He began life as a revenue-farmer and rose steadily to fame and fortune. He was more than eighty when he assumed the office of Wazir but, despite his elevation, he retained his farming lease. As he was quite ignorant of Secretariat work he merely bore the name and wore the uniform of the Wazir. 'Ali ibn 'Isa, the former Wazir, really did the work. Not without reason then did a poet satirize him by saying : We have a Wazir with his nurse[4]. And the people called one, the Wazir without the official robe, and the other, the official robe without a Wazir inside it. When the Caliph felt a misgiving that 'Ali ibn 'Isa might not care to act as a subordinate, after having been the chief, the former revenue-farmer rejoined: The clerk is not unlike a tailor who now makes a coat for 10, and now for 1,000 dirhams. The clerical staff retaliated with contempt. And when he addressed his fallen predecessor in coarse language the latter scornfully replied: "I

---

(1) Contemporary stories about him. Al-Fakhri Ed. Ahlwardt 314.

(2) Wuz., 263 ; Fakhri, 313. Kufa grew out of the Persian district of Mah el-Kufa.

(3) Amedroz *Intro. to Wuz, a biographical sketch*, p. 18.

(4) *Kit. al-'Uyun*, IV, 95 a.

am not to be treated like a farmer at the weighment of his corn." He displayed a luxury characteristic of an upstart. He kept 1,700 chamberlains (Hajib) and 400 armed mamluks. The crew of his barge consisted of white eunuchs, the most expensive to employ.

On a quarrel with the black court-eunuch, Muflih, he threatened him by saying that he had a good mind to purchase 100 black eunuches, call them Muflih and make a present of them to his slaves[1]. He was, indeed, generous. When a courtier complained to him that he had come to the end of his stock of barley he handed over an order for the supply of 100 kurr of barley to him (a kurr was about 3,600 pounds). For his kitchen he paid 200 dinars (about 2,000 marks) a day. No one left his house at a meal-time without food ; even the vistors' servants were provided with a meal. And thus many a time 40 tables were laid. He made a gift of a house to the Caliph which cost him 100,000 dinars[2]. While on a drive he once saw the burnt-down house of a poor man. He forthwith ordered that unless it was rebuilt by the evening he would be most unhappy and it was, accordingly, done at great cost[3].

And yet he shamelessly speculate in corn, stored it away in his barns at Babylon, Khuzistan and Isfahan and thereby caused a serious riot.

Another Ibn Muqlah (born at Baghdad 272/835 came from humble conditions of life[4] : in his sixteenth year he took service and through Ibn al-Furat rose into eminence[5].

---

(1) Ibn al-Athir, VIII, 102.

(2) Ibn al-Jauzi, fol. 19 a.

(3) Ibn Jauzi, 26. ab

(4) When he had become Wazir, a friend of his earlier days, the poet Jahiz, reminded him of times when "bread was still coarse and there was no horse at the door or a barge on the bank." Ibn al-Jauzi, fol. 64b.

(5) *Kit. al-Uyun* VI, fol. 77a.

In the school of the latter he learnt the art of amassing wealth within a few years. Under the first three Caliphs of the century he acted as Wazir three times, and, when Wazir, built a magnificent palace on the most valueable land in the capital. A great believer in astrology, he gathered astrologers round him and, upon their advice, laid the foundations of the palace after sunset. The most notable part of the palace was the fine, laticed garden where only palms were conspicuous by their absence. There birds of all kinds were collected together, nor were gazelles, wild cows, wild donkeys, ostriches and camels absent. He made all kinds of breeding experiments. When it was reported to him that a water-bird had mated with a land-bird and had laid eggs he gave 100 dinars to the informant[1]. A daring intriguer was he, and to his intrigues is ascribed the deposition of the Caliph al-Qahir (322/934).[2] He incited the Caliph and the general Bejkem, against the then real ruler of Baghdad, Ibn Raiq, who had confiscated his property[3]. But the Caliph played him false in spite of the fact that he had fixed the interview in consultation with the astrologers[4], and as punishment his right hand was cut off[5]. This was all the more cruel as Ibn-Muqlah was one of the most renowned calligrapers of all times, and the chief founder of the new Arabic script which for centuries continued in use[6]. But he, instead of using the left hand, tied a reed-pen to his right arm, and thus wrote on[7]. But the punishment had no deterrent effect upon him. He went his way inciting and reviling as before. Three years later his tongue was cut out.

(1) Ibn al-Jauzi fol. 64 ab.
(2) Misk. V, 447.
(3) *Kit. al-Uyun*, IV, 157 a.
(4) Ibid, b.
(5) Ibid 160 b. 161 b. The physician Thabit describes how he found the arm after it had cut off. Misk, V, 581.
(6) The library of Adad-ud-Dawlah at Shiraz possessed a Quarn in 30 vols. copied by him, Yaqut, *Irshad*, V, 446.
(7) *Kit. al-Uyun* IV, 162 a.

He died in custody and the chroniclers describes how he, who once was a powerful man, fond of show and splendour, held the string at the well with his mouth while he emptied the bucket[1].

Another Wazir drank at night and had the usual next morning headache. Even the opening of the correspondence he made over to different officers, and committed the charge of most important affairs to Abu Faragh Isra'il, a Christian. Everything that he did was with a view to extort money (Misk., V, 247).

About the middle of the century Abu Muhammad al-Hasan al-Muhallabi acted with great success as Wazir in Babylonia. He was descended from an old Islamic noble line, the family of Muhallab ibn Abi Sufra[2]. His ancestral-home was Basra, where in the 3rd/9th century they still owned magnificent houses[3]. To the later Wazir things were very hard at beginning. At one time he had not even enough money to purchase meat for his journey. A friend advanced him the money and later received 750 dirhams from him[4]. As Wazir he held possession of Baghdad (in the fateful year (334/946), until Mu'izz-ud-Dawlah's entry there[5]. In 326/938 we find him first as deputy (wali) to the finance minister, Abu Zakariyya as-Susi[6] ; then as deputy to the Wazir, from whose jealousy he had much to suffer later on[7]. After the death of the wazir in 339/950 Mu'izz-ud-Dawlah made him his 'secretary' : six years later he received the title of Wazir[8]. His friend al-Isfahani, author of the great "Book of

(1) Ibid, fol. 162 a.
(2) Yat. II, 8.
(3) Thalibi, *Kit. al-Mirwah*, 129 b.
(4) al-Hamawi, *Tamarat al-auraq*, I,82.
(5) Misk V, 121.
(6) Misk, V, 575.
(7) Yaqut, *Irshad*, III, 180.
(8) Misk, VI, 214.

Songs," applauds only his virtues as 'secretary[1]' but he was also an efficient general, as for instance, with great courage he repelled the attack of the Yamanite Arabs against Basra[2]. He died on a campaign undertaken for the conquest of Oman in 352/963, after holding for 13 years the highest official position in the State. He genuinely cared for order ; he restored the older and the juster system of taxation ; he caused the *hajib* of the chief Qadhi to be almost whipped to death for molesting women who came to the Judge for justice[3]. But the low cunning with which he traced the property of deceased officers excites our disgust, though such conduct was not deemed derogatory even to the dignity of Caliphs and Amirs, and Miskawaihi refer to it with admiration[4]. On the other hand people were shocked at Mu'izz-ud-Dawlah for confiscating Muhallabi's entire property immediately after his death and extorting money from all connected with him, down to his boatmen. In Mu'izz-ud-Dawlah, Muhallabi had a hard task-master[5]. On one occasion, under his orders, 150 stripes were administered to him. Nor did Mu'izz-ud-Dawlah treat his Turkish marshal Subuktagin any better, though he enjoyed his complete confidence[6]. But, all this notwithstanding, Muhallabi, in matters of importance, did exercise great influence. He prevailed upon Mu'izz-ud-Dawlah to retain Baghdad as his residence add even to build his famous palace there[7]. The members of his round table were the most renowned scholars and authors of the day[8]. At these gatherings wine and plea-

(1) Yat, II, 278.
(2) Misk, VI, 190. [Vol, IV, 393 ; Vol. V. 304, 330 Eng. Tr.]
(3) Misk, VI, 168 ff. [Eng. tr. Vol. V, pp. 199-200 ; See also pp. 128 et. Sqq. specially pp. 130-138 ; Character of Muhallabi, pp. 153 et Sqq. Tr.].
(4) Misk, V. 244.
(5) Misk, VI, 248.
(6) Misk, VI, 258.
(7) Misk, VI, 241.
(8) Misk, VI, 242.

sure recklessly rioted. Even Miskawaihi, in his cold and brief portraiture of the Wazir, speaks of his generosity[1]. Once Muhallabi was presented with a beautiful inkstand set with precious stones. Officers talked in whispers about it. One thought he could make very good use of it by selling it and living on the proceeds of its sale, while Muhallabi might go to the devil. Hearing of this, Muhallabi presented the inkstand to him[2]. The Qadhi At Tanukhi thankfully relates how he graciously sent for him, the young son of an old companion, and provided him with a judicial sinecure, and showed his esteem for him in the presence of the chief Qadhi, an old enemy of his father, by talking seemighly seriously in a low voice to him, on a solemn occasion, as if he was discussing some State secret. "The next morning the chief Qadhi almost carried him on his head[3]."

The most famous Wazir, at the end of the century, was Ibn Abbad, in Rai, surnamed the 'Sahib'[4]. Chancellor of the Iranian Buwayyids (d. 326/928, d. 835/995). From a schoolmaster he rose to a royal position. The young prince, for whom he secured the empire, yielded to him in everything and honoured him in every conceivable manner[5]. On his death he was mourned like a prince[6]. He was fired with great literary ambition. His panegyrists compared him to Harun al-Rashid. Like him, he gathered the best intellects round him. With masters of Baghdadian and Syrian literature such as ar-Radhi, as-Sabi, Ibn al-Hajjaj, Ibn Sukkera, Ibn Nubata he corresponded[7]. Of theological works alone he

(1) Misk, VI, 166.

(2) Ibn al-Jauzi fol. 91 b.

(3) Yaqut, *Irshad*, VI, 253 ff.

(4) He was the first to bear the title of 'Sahib' [Taghribardi, 56]. About 400/1010 the 'Amid el-Juyush' is so called. (*Diwan or-Radhi*, I, 231). Later every Wazir and, in our time dregs of society, such as publications and butcher's boys are so called. Taghribardi, 56.

(5) Yaqut, *Irshad*, II, 273.

(6) Taghribardi, 57.

(7) Yaqut, III, 32.

possessed 400 camel-loads and yet he was reproached for knowing nothing of theology[1]. True he devoted himself more to such studies as Logic, Mathematics, Music, Astronomy, Medicine ; he even wrote a medical treatise[2]. He could not afford to be as generous towards men of letters as is related of the earlier patrons of poets. He generally gave 100 to 500 dirhams and a dress, and only rarely 1,000 dirhams[3]. He particularly liked, and made gifts of light silk[4]. His staff, accordingly, dressed mostly in multi-coloured silk. The poet az-Zafrani once asked Sahib for a floral silk-dress such as he had seen his staff use. The Wazir replied : "I have heard of Ma'n ibn Zaida that a man said to him : Give me an animal to ride, O Prince ! He is reported, thereupon, to have given him a camel, a horse, a mule, a donkey and a slave-girl, saying : "If I but knew another animal for riding purposes in God's creation I would assuredly have given even that to you." And so we now present unto thee *Jubba*, shirt and coat, trousers, turban, handkerchief, a wrapper, a mantle and socks of floral silk. Had we but known of another wearing apparel which could be made of floral silk we would have presented that also unto you[5].

It was Sahib's misfortune to have incurred the displeasure of the sharpest tongue of his time. We have the laudatory letter which Abu Hayyan al-Tauhidi addressed to him at the beginning of their correspondence ; a correspondence which ended with vituperative effusions. Vivid, striking, it is a perfect model of the masterly Arabic diction of the century.

---

(1) Yaqut, *Irshad*, II, 274. 315.

(2) Yaqut, III, 42 ff.

(3) Yaqut, *Irshad*, II, 304 ; Yaqut, *Irshad*, VI, 276. The poet al-Maghrabi begs 500 dinars of him but Ibn Abbad tells him : be merciful and make it 500 dirhams.

(4) Yat. III, 33 ; Yaqut, *Irshad*, II, 320, III, 34.

(5) Yaqut.

The portrait of the Wazir Ibn al-Amid (d. 369/971), painted by Miskawaihi, who for many years was his librarian, leaves a powerful impression behind. Tauhidi ridicules the historian by saying that his misfortune was that he constantly uses expressions such as "Muhallabi has said," "Ibn al-Amid has said," and so on until the reader wearies of them. To begin with Miskawaihi applauds his memory[1] : "Several times he told me that in his young days he used to bet his comrades and the scholars with whom he associated that he would commit to memory a thousand lines in one day ; and he was far too earnest and dignified a man to exaggerate. In addition he was sole master of the secrets of certain obscure sciences which no one professes, such as mechanics, requiring the most abstruse knowledge of geometry, and physics, the science of abnormal motions, the dragging of heavy weights, and of centres of gravity, including the execution of many operations which the ancients found impossible, the fabrication of wonderful engines for the storming of fortresses, stratagems against strongholds and stratagems in campaigns, the adoption of wonderful weapons, such as arrows which could permeate a vast space, and produce remarkable effects, mirrors which burned a very long way off. He could, for his amusement, scratch the form of a face on an apple in an hour—a face so fine that another could not do it with all the appropriate instruments in a number of days. His letter to Ibn Hamdan has been preserved. It speaks of the decay and the building-up of the Province of Fars[2] and is one from which it is possible to learn the whole duty of a Wazir. He was the preceptor of Adad-ud-Dawlah, the most efficient ruler of that century and Adad-ud-Dawlah never referred to him as his master[1]. Ibn Amid even headed the army in the field but on account of gout he had to be carried in a litter. He

(1) Miskawaihi (Eng. tr. by Prof. Margoliouth, Vol. V., 295 Tr.)
(2) Ibid, p. 298. Here Miskawaihi speaks of Ibn Amid's difficulty in establishing a reign of justice.

modestly listened to those who expounded a subject and not perhaps till months or even years after would he show himself at a discussion a thorough master of it. Exceedingly difficult was his position between a prince who, though ruling his soldiery by lavish liberality, had nothing to give for useful administrative purposes and the Dailamite tribesmen intent on exploiting the subjects. But despite difficulties the Wazir restored order and Miskawaihi reports that he even put the leaders of the army in such fear that they trembled when they saw him in a reproaching mood. 'This I have often seen' says the historian. But he was aware of the envious temper of the Dailamites and he knew that they could only be ruled by simple and unostentatious methods. But when his son began to spend money freely and enter into rivalry with the Dailamite magnates, inviting them to games, to hunting expeditions, to dinners and drinks, the father foresaw the shipwreck of his house and died of suppressed grief.

(1) Ibid, p. 302.

VIII. FINANCES

Although the Muslim legislation on the subject of taxation seems clear and simple enough in the works of theorists from Abu Yusuf to Mawardi and in the collection of Traditions, it was in reality complicated, diverse, and difficult. The contrast between the systems of finance in the provinces which were formerly Byzantine and Persian respectively is not done away with ; further in pre-Arab times there was a difference between the systems of taxation current in Syria, Egypt and North Africa just as there was between the Babylonian, Khorasanian and South Persian systems.

Only those taxes which were purely Islamic were consistently maintained in the whole Empire : the poll-tax paid by Christians and Jews and the alms paid by Believers. These were calculated by the month, as was also the case with the rents on hereditary tenements, on mills and city sites, etc., etc., and the monthly payments in all these cases followed the lunar year. Actually, the lunar Calendar was only followed in their exaction in those great cities which were less dependent on the harvest. Taxes in the country had to be arranged to suit the needs of the cultivator, and his sowing and harvest, which involved the solar year[1]. This solar year was the Coptic and Syrian in the portion of the empire which had formerly been Greek, the Persian in the East. In the latter the collection of taxes started with the new year[2]. This was natural in the earliest period, when the

(1) Maqrizi, *Khitat*, 1,273, who here draws upon a special work, *the history of al-Mut'adid* by 'Abdullah ibn Ahmad ibn Abi Tahir.

(2) In the further East, Afghanistan and Transoxians, the land-tax was levied in two annual instalments. Ibn Hakal, 1, 308, 341.

new year began with the summer solstice which was harvest-time[1]. At our period it started at the commencement of spring, before harvest, hence the Caliphs in the 3rd/9th century at times endeavoured to institute at different fiscal New Year. Mutawakkil fixed it for June 17th in 243/857, but died before making his innovation effective. It is asserted that the Caliph al-Mut'adid noticed when hunting that the corn was still quite green, while the officials were already trying to collect the taxes. Consequently in 281/894 he enacted that the fiscal year should commence on July 11th, and at the same time had the different calendars of the fiscal bureaux harmonized. The East had to adapt itself to the West. Whereas the Persian calendar intercalated a month after every 120 years the Caliph enacted that a day should be intercalated after every four years according to the Greek and Syrian systems[2]. Since, however, on religious grounds the lunar year could not be abolished ; there were now two concurrent years of different lengths, which occasioned serious confusion ; for instance, the lunar year (*as-sanatu'l hillaliyah*) 300 was distinguished from the fiscal year (*assanatu'l Kharajiyah*) 300, and since the two years ultimately synchronised so little "that the fiscal year called 300 came after a lunar year which had already passed, and as it was improper to attach a thirteenth month to a lunar year, since then the sacred months would be displaced, and as the taxes of a whole year would have been lost" it was decided in the year 350/961 to drop a fiscal year once in 32 years, and so harmonize to a certain extent between the two methods of calculation. The fiscal year 350 was immediately renamed 351. The enactment worked out by Sabi is preserved[3].

---

(1) Al-Biruni *chron.* p. 216.

(2) Maqrizi, 275 ; al-Biruni, Chron. 32 ff : Tabari, III, 2143 ; *Rasa'il es-Sabi*, 213.

(3) *Rasa'il es-Sabi*, 209 ff : Maqrizi, 1, 277 Prof. Margoliouth writes to me : The words "die *monatsjahressteuern zu kurz gekommen waren*" [in Mez] are far from clear. Suppose lunar year 300 to end when

Another peculiarity of the Muslim financial system was that the Provincial tax-offices served as State-treasuries. Out of the revenues the ordinary expenses were defrayed and soldiers paid, the balance only being remitted to the central treasury[1]. Thus the money remitted to the central treasury was only meant for the court, the garrison of the capital, the ministries, and the East of Baghdad, belonging, according to Law, to Court. The western portion, that is to say the real town itself, formed part of the district of Baduriya[2].

The Khawarazmi introduces us to the system of book-keeping obtaining in a Khorasanian Customs-office in the 4th/10th century[3]. We find there:—

> The amount of assessed taxes (Qanun)[4], the amount paid by each tax-payer on account of the tax assessed, the journal containing daily income and expenditure, the amounts totalled up at the end of every month. The yearly account : this was a register in which

---

fiscal year 300 begins. If we make them synchronize by adding a month to lunar year 300, so that they coincide for one month, the dues for that one month will be liable to be paid for the whole year 300. It does not seem to me that the expedient resorted to avoided that difficulty. Tr.

(1) Misk, V, 193 : Al-Faragh 1, 51 : Ibn Hakal, 128 : *Mafatihu ulum*, 54. Even in the provinces of the Byzantine Empire the prefect defrayed, directed out of the revenue, the expenses of the province. The practice, among the Ommayyads, is said to have been for the carrier of taxes to be accompanied by ten men from the particular province who swore before the Caliph that nothing but what was permissible had been taken and the soldiers and all, entitled to be paid, have been paid. *Ajbar Makhmua*, 22 ff : Abulfoyyad, according to Simonet *Hist. de los Mozarbes*, 158. In all statements in the budget and rent-rolls the actual amont must be understood.

(2) Wuz., 11 ff. [Guy Le Strange, *Baghdad*, 1 p. 51, 315.—Tr.]

(3) *Mafatihu'l 'Ulum*, 54.

(4) In the post-Diocletain period *Qanun* is the common term for regular taxes. Wilken, *Griech, Ostraka*, 378.

> amounts paid in were systematically entered for easy reference. The statements were shown in three columns : first, the amount taxed : second, the amount actually collected; and third the difference between the two. In most cases the amount paid in was less than the amount assessed. The quittance receipt for the tax. Final settlement. Release.

We possess the Imperial Budget of the year 306/918. It is based upon the statement of accounts of the year 303. Similar to what we find in the books of individual tax-officers, here, too, revenues are set against expenses ; and expenses, exactly as with us, are divided into ordinary and extraordinary expenses. And, as is frequently the case with us, it closes with a deficit. Therein the taxes of Babylonia, Khuzistan, Faris, and Iran are shown only in current coin ; whereas, even up to 269/873, payment of taxes is shown both in coin and in kind. This indicates a distinct progress in the financial administration of the Eastern part of the Empire. In the Syrian and Mesopotamian provinces, on the other hand, taxes were yet assessed both in kind and current coin[1]. The steady growth of the practice of noting down taxes in current coin only and the consequent disappearance of the earlier picturesque customs made the accounts simple and uniform and, at the same time, strikingly different from the diversified tax-list of the western countries during the Middle Ages.

Only of the town of Asbigah in Turkistan, on the extreme frontier of the empire, it is reported that it sent in an annual Khiraj (land-tax) of four copper coins and a broom[2]. About

(1) Kremer, *Einnahmebudget der Abbasiden,* 309, 323 ; Qodamah, 239: Wuz, 189.

(2) Muq, 340. This statement is confirmed by Yaqut,(*Geography* 1,249), according to which Asbigah is the only town in Khorasan and Transoxiana which paid no khiraj, for as the greatest frontier town it needed its revenue for military purposes.

the year 300/912 it became customary to send in with the tribute and the taxes some curios to the Court. In 299/911 with the Egyptian revenue, came a he-goat with milking udder[1] ; in 301/913 from 'Oman a white parrot and a black gazelle[2] ; and in 305/917 again from 'Oman black antelopes and a black bird which spoke Persian and Indian languages better than any parrot[3].

An important form of landed property throughout the Empire was the fief (Iqta)[4]. Both in the East and the West it was of ancient origin. Abu Yusuf[5], writing expressly about the East, says : the hereditary lease (the fief) is a Persian institution. In the West it is a Roman institution. In this way here, as in the East, the crown-lands and *agri deserti* passed from the government to the private individual[6]. The tax, payable by the tenant, was determined by the individual contract but, according to the theorists, tenants only paid a tenth of the proceeds[7]. They, indeed, were not better off than the ordinary landholders. In a work of the 4th/10th century an anecdote is related which runs thus. Hurun al-Rashid expressed a wish to invest his physician with a fief but the latter begged for money instead to by land, urging

(1) Ibn al-Jauzi, Berlin fol. 6a.

(2) Ibn al-Jauzi, fol. 9a.

(3) Ibn al-Jauzi, fol. 15 b.

(4) Aghnides *Intro. to Moh. Law* (Columbia University, 1916) pp. 484 sqq. Tr.

(5) *Kit. al-Khiraj*, 32. Along with this there was the lease for life but of this there is very little talk (*Mafatihu'l-'Ulum*, 460).

(6) Becker, *Z A* 1905, 301 ff.

(7) Qodamah, Paris, fol. 90a : Tenth-land is of six kinds : (a) Lands, whose owners have become Muslims and who are still in possession thereof. Such as is the case in Yaman Medinah and Taif. (b) Wasteland cultivated by the faithful, (c) Fiefs. (d) The quondam enemy land distributed by the Caliph among the faithful. (e) The quondam Persian crownlands. (f) Lands, (as is the case in military frontiers) abandoned by the enemy and occupied by the faithful. Along with the *Diwan el-Khiraj* there was a special Tax-office for manorial estates (Diwan addiya). Khuda Bukhsh, *orinet under the Caliphs*, p. 235 et sqq.

that he had no fief in his landed possessions.[1] There was, indeed, a large number of cases where it was argued whether the land in dispute was a fief or an ordianry taxable landed property ; the landholders maintaining the former, the tax-officers urging the latter[2]. By confiscation or abandonment— the latter was oftener the case on account of heavy taxation— fiefs constantly escheated to Government. Thus, under the Safarids, in the 3rd/9th century so many land-owners, liable to taxes, emigrated from Fars that the then Government felt itself constrained to realize the entire amount of the taxes from those who had remained behind. This cumulation of taxes weighed heavily upon the country. When the province reverted to the Empire, a Persian deputation went to the Caliph at Baghdad (303/915) praying for the discontinuance of the practice of exacting cumulated taxes (takmilah) : in other words the practice of making up the deficit of taxes from those that still retained lands[3]. In the East this practice appears to have been somewhat exceptional. In Egypt, on the other hand, the liability of the community to pay the taxes due from those that had left was the rule. In Mesopotamia this rule applied only to the capitation-tax. In France the responsibility of the community for taxes was only done away with shortly before the Revolution ; in Russia not until 1906.

The Government, indeed, retained other lands in its direct possession as crown lands (*Diya Sultaniyyah*). In prosperous times crown lands were always augmented by purchase of other lands[4] but in times of stress the very opposite was the case. In 323/935 the government had to sell some crown lands to pay back a loan[5]. When the Government was weak, these crown lands were always in

(1) *Kit. al-faragh*, II. 103.
(2) Wuz. 220.
(3) Wuz, 340 ff : *Kit. al-'Uyun*, fol. 81 a.
(4) Qodamah, 241.
(5) Misk, V, 505.

danger of being absorbed by neighbouring landed proprietors[1].

To escape the burden of taxation smaller landlords were wont to hold lands in the names of the more powerful ones. The result was that these lands appeared in the names of the latter and, instead of the land-tax, paid only the tenth due from fiefs[2]. The possession, indeed, remained with the actual owners who were at liberty to sell or to deal with them as they pleased. This was an old device. Through large landed-possessions this practice came into vogue in Byzantine Egypt. The existence of such a practice is even reported during the Omayyad times[3] but in the 4th/10th century we find a special book in the tax offices of Khorasan dealing with such cases[4]. About 300/912 strikingly common was this practice in tax-ridden Fars[5]. In the East these small landlords never lost their proprietory right as they did in Egypt, where, in 415 A.D., their position as clients was secured and ratified by law[6].

Moreover, to the treasury came in a fifth of the treasure-trove ; a fifth of the things raised from the mines or found in the sea ; the sale proceeds of slaves of untraceable owners; stolen properties recovered from robbers and, finally, the treasury was the ultimate heir when no legal heir was forthcoming[7]. The rule, regarding the ultimate succession of the treasury in case of an heirless decease, applied only to the case of an heirless Muslim. Thus the property of Khatib al-Baghdadi (200 dinars) passed, after

(1) Wuz, 131 : *Kit.al-Faragh*, 1, 50.
(2) See the note at the end of this chapter Tr.
(3) Qodamah, 241.
(4) Khwarezmi, *Mafatih al-Ulum*, 62.
(5) Istakhri, 158.
(6) Matthias Gelzer : *Studien zur Byzantinischen Verwaltung Agyptens* 72 ff.
(7) Qadamah, Paris 1907, fol. 91a : Schmidt, *Die occupatio im Islamischen Recht*, Islam, 1,300 ff.

his death, to the State[1]. According to a saying of the Prophet : "A Muslim cannot inherit from an unbeliever and *vice-versa*" ; the Caliph in 311/923 rules that the property of heirless Christians and Jews should pass on to their respective communities and not to the state[2].

Among the jurists many principles, surprisingly modern were fought out, such as the principle that property should go to the state in preference to distant kindred. And this was all the more significant as, according to many jurists, even some near relations could *only* inherit such shares as were definitely fixed by the Qur'an, with the result that the treasury often became their co-heir[3]. In the 3rd/9th century under the Caliph al-Mut'amid (256-279/869-892) a special department dealing with Inheritances (*Diwan al-Mawarith*) was established . a splendid pound for greedy officials to fish in[4].

---

(1) Yaqui, *Irshad*1,252.

(2) Wuz, 248.

(3) (There are three classes of heirs in the Hanafi Law : (1) Sharers, (2) Residuaries, and (3) Distant kindred. 'Sharers' are those who are entitled to a prescribed share of the inheritance. 'Residuaries' are those who take no prescribed share but succeed to the 'residue' after the claims of the sharers are satisfied. 'Distant kindred' are all those relations by blood who are neither 'sharers' nor 'Residuaries.' The question as to which of the relations belonging to the class of 'sharers' or 'Residuaries,' or 'distant kindred' are entitled to succeed to the inheritance depends on the circumstances of each case. Tr.) In the absence of 'sharers' the Shaf'ite assign to the State the surplus left after distribution among the Residuaries (Sacha, *Muh, Recht,* 211 and 247). In 283/896, the Caliph al-Mut'adid decreed that distant kindred should be taken into consideration. (Tabari, III 2151) ; Abulfeda, *'Annales*, year 283, according to the *Tarikh* of Qadhi Shahabu'ddin (d. 642/1244) Muqtafi followed al-Mut'adid and in 300/912 renewed that law. In 311/923 this very Caliph annulled his law and ordained that, in case of failure of 'near relations', the surplus was to be divided among the 'Residuaries, with the result that the state and the 'distant kindred' got nothing. In 355/966 the Amir Mui'zz-ud-Dawlah enforced the older practice (Ibn al-Jauzi, fol. 98b: 100a).

(4) According to the edict of the year 311, *Arib*, 118.

"Woe to him whose father dies rich ! Long does he remain incarcerated in misfortune's home, the unrighteous officer saying unto him : How do I know that you are the rich man's son ? And when he rejoins : "My neighbours and many others know me," they pluck his moustache one by one, assault him, knock him about, until strength ebbs away from him and he faints. And in the dungeon he languishes until he flings his purse to them[1]."

Thus complains Ibn al-Mut'azz at the end of the 3rd/9th century.

The Caliph al-Radhi, did indeed, control the princely greed for capturing inheritances ; for when the Sultan of Babylon confiscated a large inheritance he compelled him to restore the spoil to the rightful claimant[2].

Saif-ud-Dawlah, however, officially confiscated inheritances. In 333/944 he appointed Abu Husain Qadhi of Aleppo. When confiscating the properties of the dead, Abu Husain was wont to say : "The inheritance is Saif-ud-Dawlah's, mine the commission only[3].

Great was the temptation to treat the property of deceased strangers as heirless and, as such, to confiscate it. Some such practice was, indeed, legalized in England in the 13th Century but in Islam it was never applied to the property of deceased Muslims.[4]

In 401/1010 a considerable sum of money was brought to the Buwayyid Governor at Baghdad, which had been left by a deceased Egyptain merchant, with the information that he was heirless. The Governor, however, ruled that nothing which was unlawful should find a place in the

(1) *Diwan*, 1, 131.
(2) Al-Sufi, *Auraq* Paris 4836; 147.
(3) Wustenfeld, *Die Statthalter von Agypten*, IV. 35.
(4) Caro, *Soziale und Wirtshaftsgehschichte der Judcn* 1.317.

treasury and that the money should not be touched until further enquiry. Some time after a brother of the deceased came from Egypt with a document empowering him to receive the heritage and he duly obtained delivery thereof. The report spread and throughout Egypt resounded the fame of the Governor who heard it with pleasure and satisfaction[1].

Different, however, was the case with people of other faiths. In the XIIth Century the Rabbi Petachja fell ill at Mosul and his case was declared hopeless by the physicians. "There, according to law, the Government takes half of the property of every Jew that dies : and as the Rabbi was well-dressed they said : he must be rich, for the government officials have already come to take his property *as though he was dying.*" A portion of the property of the rich, in many instances, was taken away in their life-time. The practice, indeed, grew up of exacting a part of the ill-gotten gains of officials; not unlike Napoleon I, who extorted for the State large sums from his enormously wealthy marshals. Even the merchants, whom they fleeced, probably had made good business out of their dealings with the State.

Thus, in describing the oppressive rule of Mut'amid, Ibn al-Mut'azz says:—

"And to many a prosperous merchant possessed of gold and precious stones it was said : with you the Government has large deposits. And he rejoined : no, by God I have neither little nor much. I have only made money in trade and never have I cheated.

But they fumigated him with smoke from burning-straw and singed him with heated bricks until life became a burden to him, and, dispirited, said he, would that all this money were in hell ! He gave them what they wanted and then was he sent away, stiff and weary and sad[2].

(1) Ibn al-Athir, IX, 158.

(2) *Diwan*, 1, 131.

In Hilal (Wuz, 224 ff) the list of such instances only shows cases of officials and bankers who dealt with the government. In the literature of romance not a single case appears of Government confiscating private property in this unjust fashion. Ibn Muqlah, the Wazir, hated Abu'l-Khattab but he could not find any administrative reason (Ta'riq Diwani) to extort money out of him[1] for he had left Government service twenty years before and was living peacefully in retirement at home. Let us trace the growth of this practice. At the beginning of the 4th/10th century it was regarded in the light of punishment but later, on any pretence it was resorted to against all who had dealings with the government and were suspected of foul play. The Ikshid viceroy of Egypt, who outdid all other princes in extortion between 300/912 and 350/960, vigorously pursued this policy of confiscation. "He took from every one what he could ; especially, armed slaves of distinguished men with their weapons, horses, liveries and incorporated them in his body-guard[2]." And he who escaped this fate while living was sure to lose his property after death. This became a settled practice with the Ikhshid. When an officer, a stranger, or a rich merchant died he prevented the heirs from taking possession of the property until they had paid him a certain amount of money[3]. Thus in the year 323/934 he took 100,000 dinars from the heritage of the cotton merchant Sulaiman, the richest merchant of the country[4].

At the death of Muhallabi, (d.352/963) who had served for 13 long years, Mu'izz-d-Dawlah confiscated his entire property and extorted money from all his servants, "not even the muleteers and boatmen or even those who had served him for a single day excepted[5]." This provoked general

(1) Misk. V, 398.
(2) Tallquist, p. 16/17.
(3) Tallquist, 36.
(4) Tallquist, 17.
(5) Misk. (Eng. tr.), Vol. V, p. 213, "With his death," says Misk, "the

horror and aroused universal resentment among the people. And when Sahib, who had ruled North Persia as the all-powerful Wazir for many years, died, his house was forthwith put under guard and the Prince personally conducted a search and found a purse with receipts for 150,000 dinars deposited elsewhere. He at once had the deposits collected and all that was found in his house and treasury taken away to the palace[1].

In these circumstances every artifice that could be employed was employed to thwart the treasury in its designs upon the inheritances. They deposited their properties with different persons[2] and showed them in their books under false names[3]. When the Wazir Ibn al-Amid, put to death in 366/976, saw that there was no longer any hope for him, he flung the inventory of his property—money and goods—into the oven, saying to his judges : 'Of my hidden property not a single dirham shall go to your master'. Even torture failed to secure a clue from him[4]. After Bejkem's death (326/941) the Caliph al-Muttaqi, a very pious ruler, went forthwith to his house, dug everywhere, and got two millions in gold and silver[5]. He even had the soil washed and thereby recovered another sum of 36,000 Dirhams[6]. But Bejkem had buried some of his treasury in the desert. He is said to have killed those who helped him in burying the treasures but Thabit ibn Sinan declares this to be a piece of falsehood. Bejkem himself has described the process to Thabit as follows : "I thought about the treasure which I have buried in my palace and it occurred to me that some accident might prevent my having access to my palace, in which case I

---

generosity and nobility of the clerical profession came to an end."

(1) Yaqut, *Irshad*, 170.

(2) Wuz, 74.

(3) Ibn la-Jauzi, 193 b.

(4) Yaqut, *Irshad*, V. 350.

(5) Ibn al-Jauzi, Berlin, fol. 68a.

(6) Misk VI, 39.

should lose not only my property but my life, since one in my position cannot live without wealth. So I buried some in the country, knowing that I could not fail to have access to the country. I have been informed that people defame me with a story that I murder my companions on these occasions. I assure you that I have never killed any one in that way. I will tell you what I used to do. When I wished to make an expedition for the purpose of burying treasure, I used to have mules laden with empty chests brought to my palace. In some of the chests I would place the treasure after which I would lock them. Into the rest I would introduce the men who were to accompany me while they were on the mules' back ; I would then cover the chests, lock them and lead the mules, taking the rope which led the train and sending away the attendants of the mules, which I would myself lead to the place which I wanted. When I was by myself in the middle of the country, I would let the men out of the chests, they having no idea where they were ; I would then have the treasure taken out and buried in my presence, while I made some private marks. After this I would make the men get back into their chests, which I would then cover and lock. I would then lead the mules to such place as I chose, and there let the men out. They neither knew where they had gone nor by what way they had returned and no murder was necessary[1]."

To seize the property left by the treasurer (d. 350/961), whom Mu'izz-ad-Dawlah always regarded as poor, the Wazir resorted to the arts of a detective. By those methods he eventually succeeded in tracing the treasure to the room of his Nubian barber and in discovering the actual amount and the exact spot. These were inscribed in secret letters on the back of a scale-pan of a weighing machine.

The death of a well-to-do man was a veritable catastrophe

(4) Misk (Eng. tr.), Vol. V. pp. 11-12 Tr.

to his family and friends. His bankers prevented inspection of his will by officials in order that they might not know how and where his property was deposited. But all this notwithstanding, the family, in the end, had to buy itself off by payment of large sums ; in some cases amounting to as much as 50,000 dinars[1]. According to the strict law of Islam customs duty is forbidden and yet everywhere customs—offices were found[2]. The Jurists solved the difficulty by bringing customs-duty under the heading of Poor-tax (zakat)—at all events, so far as the Muslims we concerned. Hence the fiction that a merchant could have free passage across the frontier for a year, should he pay the customs-duty once during that year. But he had also to pay 10 per cent on all cash that he took along with him. In reality the tariff varied very much. At Jeddah, the port of Mekka, they levied half a dinar on every camel-load of wheat;

(1) Misk, VI, 248.

(2) Qalqashandi, Wustenfeld, 162. According to theory, the non-Muslim merchant has to pay on the frontiers the very same customs-duty as Muslims ; generally 10 per cent on his wares. On payment he receives a pass, available for a year which releases him from any further obligation to pay custome-duty during that period (Sarakhshi d. 495/1102) in his commentary on Shaibani. *MS. Ledien* in de Goeje: *Internationale Handelsverkeer in de Middleeuwen, Verslagen en Me'dedeelingen der K. Akad. V. Wetenschapen, 1909, 265*). But on this point there is no consensus of opinion among the learned. Some fix the customs duty on foreign merchants at 5 per cent ; only on imported wine 10 per cent had to be paid [Yahya b. Adam, 51]—others fix the customs-duty at 10 per cent all round [*Kit al-Khiraj*, 78]. According to Shafai this 10 per cent, customs-duty may be increased or decreased by half as the exigencies of the State may require. In any case this was a purely personal tax and, when the same merchant happened to come again within the year with goods, he had nothing to pay except according to mutual agreement [Qalqashandi, 164]. In the 5/11th century the Greek, the Spanish and the Maghribian ships had to pay the tenth to the Sultan at Tripoli [Nasir Khusru]. The word tenth,' in the end assumed merely the meaning of 'customs-duty.' The commercial treaties of 1154 and 1173 A.D. with the Pisans fix customs at 10 per cent. [Sehaube, *Handelsgeschichte der rom. Volker*, 149.] [See the note at the end of this chapter, Tr.]

on every bale of Egyptian linen 2 or 3 dinars according to quality ; on a camel-load of wool 2 dinars. At Qulzum (Suez) they levied on every camel-load 1 dirham. Even at other Arabian ports customs-duty was levied, but the rate was generally lower. The ships, coming from the West to Egypt, paid customs-duty at Alexandria ; those from Syria at Farama[1]. The different Arab potentates had their own custom-houses with different tariffs[2]. One of these levied half dinar on every load, most of the others only charged one dirham.

Babylonia was richly blessed with sea, river and street tolls. On occount of its exacting searches and harassing interferences Basra bore a bad reputation. There in Muqaddasi's time lay the frontier between the territory of the Caliph and that of the Karmathians and, at the gate of the town, were located face to face custom-houses of the two powers ; so that on a single sheep as much as four dirhams (double its worth) was levied. The gate, indeed, opened for only an hour a day (Muq. Eng. tr. p. 217). At Yahudhiya, the merchant quarter of Isfahan, 30 dirhams were imposed as *octroi* for every camel-load (Muq. 400). In one of the provinces of Sind the customs-duty was differentiated according as the merchandise came from other

(1) Muq. 104.

(2) "The provinces of this country" says Muqaddasi, "are under separate governments. Al-Hijjaz has ever belonged to the sovereigns of Egypt. Al-Yaman belongs to the Al-Ziyad dynasty whose origin is of Hamadan. Ibn Tarf has Athar and over San'a an independent governor rules, who is, however, subsidized by Ibn Ziyad in order to read the Khutbah in his name. Sometimes 'Aden would be wrested from their hands [on the break-up of the Ziyadite kingdom Aden passed into the hands of the Banu Man who had held a semi-independent rule over it since the days of Al-Mamun]. The family of Qahtan are in the mountains. They are the oldest dynasty in Al-Yaman. The Alawiyah of Sadah read the Khutbah in the name of the Al-Ziyad dynasty. 'Uman belongs to Ad-Dailam. [It came under the power of the Dailamites in A.H. 355. See Ibn al-Athir, VIII, 419] and Hajar to the Qaramitah. Al-Ahqaz is ruled by a native chieftain" Azuh's.tr. pp. 158-59. Tr.

parts of Sind[1].

As was the practice everywhere in ancient times here too export duties were charged. According to jurists the frontier garrisons are to search the travellers, to take away arms and slaves from them, to inspect their papers to see if they contain any information relating to the faithful[2]. In Transoxiana they charged for a passage across the Oxus for every male slave 70 to 100 dirhams ; for every Turkish slave girl 20 to 30 dirhams and for a camel 2 dirhams. For the luggage of the passenger a charge of 1 dirham was imposed[3]. In the small South Arabian town of Athar only export duty was levied[4]. Kirman, amazingly rich in dates, only perhaps paid the export prize. There the drivers of caravans exporting 1,00,000 camel-loads of dates to Khorasan, received a reward of one dinar per head from the government[5].

The custom's searches in 'Oman were particularly said to be objectionable[6]. In the 6th/12th century the Spanish Ibn Jubair complains of the conduct of the custom officers at Alexandria : "Scarcely had we arrived when the Government officials boarded the boat to take charge of everything that was there. Every Muslim was produced one after another : his name, his personal description, the place he came from—all was noted down. Everyone was questioned as to the goods and the cash that he had with him. On all he had to pay *zakat* (poor tax) without any enquiry whether he had paid it already or not for the year. As most of the travellers were on pilgrimage by sea they had nothing with them except provisions for the journey[7].

(1) Muq. 485.
(2) *Kit al-Kiraj*, 117.
(3) Muq, 340.
(4) Muq, 485.
(5) Muq. 124.
(6) Muq, 105
(7) Provisions for the journey, according to the jurists, were exempt from duty. Qalqashandi. Wustenfeld, 162.

For these they had now to pay the poor-tax without being asked whether a year had or had not elapsed since the last payment. Ahmad ibn Hasan was brought ashore for information regarding the Maghrib and the goods on the boat. He was taken to the authorities, then to the Qadhi, then to the custom officers, then to a band of the Sultans's servants, and was interrogated about everything. They commanded the faithful to unpack their luggage, their provisions. Guards were quartered on the bank to see that everything was actually brought into the customs office. They then questioned the passengers one after another. Everyone's luggage was brought in until the customs office became choked full. This was followed by searches of things—big and small—and everything was thrown pell-mell. They felt the pockets of travellers to see if there was any thing there. When this was done they made them swear if they had anything else besides. In this process and owing to a pressing crowd, many things were lost. After a degrading and humiliating scene the travellers were sent away. We prayed to God for a liberal reward for all our troubles.[1]"

The assumption, made in all seriousness from the very beginning of Islam, that the Empire was the empire of the faithful, led to the separation of the State-treasury (Bait al-mal) from the privy-purse of the sovereign (Bait mal al-khassah). But as one and the same person could draw from both without accounting to any one, it was but a matter of his own conscience how far he would keep the two separate[2]. In later centuries touching stories were invented regarding the care and attention which Abu Bakr and 'Omar bestowed on the moneys of the faithful. And yet an understanding did exist that in the event of the exhaustion

(1) Ibn Jubair, 351.

(2) A certain check lay in this, that the Wazir [the Finace Minister] was at the same time the chief of the privy-purse and as such had to countersign the orders of the Steward of the Royal Household. Wuz. 140.

of the treasury the privy-purse could be drawn upon to meet the situation[1]. We know from a letter of the Wazir Ibn 'Isa that the Caliph Al-Mu'tadid (279-289/892-901) and even the parsimonious Muqtafi (289-295/901-7) placed the privy-purse at the disposal of the State[2]. Under al-Mutadid, however, it was still something uncommon. When in the absence of the Wazir, his son, who was representing him, borrowed money of the Caliph for purposes of State, the father wrote to him saying that he had committed an offence against them both. He should have raised the money from the merchants and paid interest to them out of his and his father's money. Under Al-Muqtadir (295-320/907-932) the privy-purse was, indeed, very largely drawn upon ; always, to be sure, on the understanding that the moneys, so drawn would be repaid. In 319/931 the Wazir laid before the Caliph a deficit of 700,000 dinars (7 million marks) on account of urgent State expenditure, and saw no other way out of the difficulty than payment by the Head of the State. But to the Caliph this suggestion seemed monstrous and he very gladly accepted the offer of an aspirant to office who undertook to pay the entire sum, and a million dirhams, over and above that amount, to the privy-purse of the Caliph. This benefactor was installed as Wazir but, in the following year, he was deposed as they discovered that he manipulated accounts to his own advantage[3]. In 329/940 the Wazir asked for and obtained 500,000 dinars from the Caliphs' privy-purse for the pay of the troops.

As the spiritual head, the Caliph had to meet out of his own purse the expenses of the pilgrimage and the annual campaigns against the unbelievers. He had also to pay for the ransom of prisoners and the entertainment of foreign

---

(1) Thus, in our own days, the Sultan 'Abdul Hamid supplied money to the State-Treasury from his own immense fortune.

(2) Wuz, 284.

(3) Misk, V, 351 : Ibn al-Athir, VIII, 176.

ambassadors[1]. On the other hand the entire appanage and the court were maintained at the State cost[2].

We possess a statement of the sources of income to the privy-purse dating from the 4th/10th century[3] :—

1. Ancestral Property. Among the Abbasids Harun al-Rashid is said to have left the largest amount in cash : 48 Million dinars, *i.e.*, about 480 million makrs. But the Caliph al-Mutadid (279-289/892-901), by economy and good management, increased his cash to over 9 million dinars. This immense sum was considered so extra-ordinary that people ascribed to him all manner of schemes which he had in view as soon as the savings amounted to 10 million dinars. He wanted, it is reported, to reduce the land-tax to a third. He wanted, so it is also said, to melt down the gold pieces into one single block to be placed before the gate of his palace that the princes might know that he had at his command 10 million dinars and that he did not need their help. But he died before he actually got together 10 million dinars[4]. His successor Al-Muqtafi (289-295/901-907) raised the privy-purse to 14 million dinars[5].

2. Land-tax and tax paid for lands held in fiefs in Persia and Kirman, *i.e.*, the net income (after deduction of

---

(1) Wuz, 22. It was, therefore, not very unnatural for the Wazir to ask the Caliph al-Muqtadir for the cost of the Baqra'id feast but the Caliph resented the demand. Wuz. 28.

(2) Wuz, 10 ff.

(3) Musk, V, 381 ff.

(4) Wuz, 189. For his private treasure he built a house the joints of which were filled with lead. The money was kept in purses bearing the stamp of the treasure responsible for them. [Wuz 139]. Other princes of the 4th/10th century kept their money in chests. Only the far sighted Ikhshid, Princes of Egypt kept his money in the armoury in sacks made of net-work of steel-wire, where no one suspected it to be. Tallquist, 43.

(5) Besides Misk, see Wuz, 290 [p. 139 other figures are mentioned]; Elias Nisibenus, [b. 364/974] p. 200. According to Muh, ibn Yayha.

expenses). From 299/911 to 320/932 the annual amount that came in was 23 million dirhams of which 4 millions were credited to the treasury and the rest (19 millions) to the privy-purse. True, the Caliph had to meet extra-ordinary expenses of these Provinces ; *e.g.*, in 303/915 he had to pay 7 million dinars for their reconquest[1].

3. Moneys from Syria and Egypt. In theory the Capitation-tax levied upon the Jews and Christians should come to the private treasury of the Caliph as the representative of the faithful and not to the State-treasury[2].

4. Moneys that came in by way of 'compensation' confiscation, and inheritance[3].

5. Moneys from the land-estates and land-tax in general from Babylonia and Khuzistan.

6. Savings : The last two Caliphs of the 3rd/9th century used to lay by every year 1 million dinars. By such econmy, after a reign of 25 years, al-Muqtadir is said to have saved over 700 million marks ; that is to say, double the amount of Harun al-Rashid. But after the Karmathian trouble of the year 315/927 there was only half a million dinars (5 million marks) left in the privy-purse[4].

---

(1) This amount is arrived at by a comparison of the statements : the campaign and the donative cost 10 millions (Misk.), of which, according to Wuz. (p. 290), the donative cost 3 millions.

(2) Ibn al-Jauzi, 196b.

(3) The Caliph inherited the property of the eunuchs and childless freedmen of the family. And as these were high-salaried officer, wealth flowed into the Caliph's treasury. Thus in 311/923 died the old general and armed slave Yanis al-Muwaffaqi whose house was guarded by 1,000 picked soldiers and who, from his landed estates only, drew an income of 30,000 dinars (Arib, 115). In 302/914 died Bidah, "the most trained, the most beautiful, the most talented, and the most coquettish of Ma'mun's slave-girls leaving behind a considerable sum of money, jewellery, landed-estates and country houses. The Caliph confiscated them all," *Arib, 54.*

(4) Misk, Eng. Tr. pp. 203-204, Vol. IV. Tr.

Fars always was the most difficult province to govern and because of its complicated system of taxation it served as a rare training ground for administrators[1]. Says Muqaddasi: "Ask not about the multiplicity and oppressiveness of its taxes." He appears to have read in a book in the library of 'Adad-ud-Dawlah that the Persians of Fars were so drilled into obedience that they became the most patient of men under injustice[2]. They were weighed down under most oppressive of taxes and knew not what justice was[3]. In 303/915 Fars was by far the most heavily-taxed of all the provinces[4]. Not for nothing does Balkhi devote to Fars the longest of his political excursus[5]. Already under the Sassanids diversified may have been the constitution of this mountainous country ; un-approachable rocky castles, forests and a landed aristocracy constituted a perfect feudal frame-work. Most of the lands there were held in fiefs[6] and yet the financial system was so minutely worked out that even the ordinary labourers on the crown-lands had to pay their taxes in dirhams[7].

The taxes were assessed on the basis whether the land could be irrigated and, if irrigated, could be irrigated by or without machinery. In cases where the irrigation was not by means of machinery they paid a certain sum which was made the standard of assessment. Two thirds of this amount was raised on lands irrigated by machinery, and only one half on lands which could not be irrigated at all[8].

Fruit culture (the vine was included in it in Islam) was

---

(1) Istakhri, 146.
(2) Muq, 451.
(3) Muq, 448.
(4) Von Kremer, *Einnahmebudget,* 308.
(5) Istakhri, 156 ff : Ibn Haukal, 216.
(6) Muq, 421.
(7) Istakhri, 158.
(8) Istakhri, 157.

freed from taxation by the Caliph Mahdi but at the instance of the corn-dealers in 303/915 this privilege was withdrawn and heavy taxes were imposed. The vine-planters, henceforth, paid for every 150 A.R. of irrigable vine 1425 dirhams as tax[1]. For every palm-tree a quarter of a dirham was charged[2]. Mills and rose-factories belonged to the Caliph[3]. In the towns of Fars the Bazar-ground belonged to the government who realized rent—the houses, of course, belonged to the owners.

All taxes, beyond the recognized canonical taxes (such as land tax, poor-tax, capitation-tax on Christians and Jews) were regarded as illegal by Muslim jurists. And thus the pious Wazir 'Ali ibn 'Isa removed indirect taxes (Maks) in Mekka and the wine-tax in Mesopotamia[4]. And for this very reason precisely, the Egyptain Caliph Al-Hakim, when he wanted to be pious, removed all taxes and tolls beyond those sanctioned by Law. His successor, however, soon restored them[5]. Just as Fars was famous for land-tax[6], so was Egypt famous for indirect imposts. The lists of the Fatamid times show everything as taxable—scarcely was the air immune from taxation[7]. Over and above the authorized legal amount—one twelfth of the net sum was charged as 'discount' ; one tenth as 'exchange' and one per cent as stamp duty[8]. The Arab historians, assuming that the administration was conducted on the basis of the canonical Law, call. Ibn Mudabbir, the director of the Finances in Egypt in 247/861, "Satan's clerk " who introduced these illegal

---

(1) Wuz, 340 : Istakhri, 157.
(2) Muq, 452.
(3) Istakhri, 158.
(4) *Kit. al-'Uyun*, IV. fol 81. These are the *Dara'ib al-khamar in* Ibn Haukal, 142.
(5) Yahya ibn Sa'id, Pairs, fol. 123a, 133b.
(6) See Balkhi's *Province of Fars* (tr. by G. Le Strange) pp. 83-85 Tr.
(7) Maqrizi, 1, 103.
(8) Ḥafmeier, *Islam*, IV, 100 ff.

exactions[1]. But, as a matter of fact, these were not innovations, they were already in existence under the Ptolemies the Romans and the Byzantines. "People involuntarily asked if there was anything in Egypt which was not taxed" (Wilcken, *Grieschische Ostraka*, 410) ; and, evidently the old Islamic time did not lay a restraining hand upon fiscal exploitations. (Taxes on shops were for the first time revived both at Baghdad (Yaqubi, II, 481) and in Egypt (Kindi, ed. Guest, 125) under the Caliph al-Mahdi, 158-169 (775-786).

Muqaddisi (p. 213) reports that in Tinnis, a Peninsula known for its weaving trade, taxes were so oppressive that the people, about the year 200/815, complained to the Patriarch who happened to be passing through the town that they were compelled to pay five dinars a year, an amount which was difficult for them to find and that no quarter was given or mercy shown in realizing it.

The old practices continued, down to the minutest detail. The singular position which Alexandria once held as a separate district for purposes of taxation, she continues to hold at the beginning of the 4th/10th century of the Muslim era. In the budget it is stated : " Egypt and Alexandria[2]." Even later Qalqashandi mentions that Alexandria pays taxes direct to the privy-purse of the Sultan[3].

Even the Pharaonic theory of the State-ownership of the land, inherited by the Ptolemies the Romans, and the Byzantines, plays an important role in the Arab theories of

(1) Maqrizi, *Khitat*, 1, 103. He declared that when he administered Babylonia—West and East—he finished his work by the evening, but in Egypt business kept him occupied many a night through. (Ibn Haukal, 88). Also the Christian Wazir 'Isa ibn Nestorious is mentioned by his contemporary and fellow-Christian Ibn Sa'id as one who imposed many new taxes (p.180).

(2) Von Kremar, *Einnahme-budget*, 309.

(3) Tr. by Wustenfeld, 158.

taxation. Nor is the old Ptolemaic principle of monopoly lost sight of. Speaking of the first Fatimid times Muqaddisi says : The taxes are very heavy in Egypt, especially in Tinnis, Demietta and on the banks of the Nile. The Copts of Shata are only allowed to use materials stamped by the Government and effect sales through Government brokers. And whatever was sold was entered in book kept by a government official. Not until the entry, indeed, was the stuff allowed to be rolled, tied with bast, packed into cases. All, who had anything to do with any of these processes, had to be paid a fee. Something more was exacted at the gate of the harbour and before the boat sailed she was thoroughly searched. On Every bag of oil one dinar was levied at Tinnis and heavy were the imposts at Fostat, on the Nile. I was told that at Tinnis the daily customs duty was to the exent of 1,000 dinars and there were quite a number of such places on the banks of the Nile, in Upper Egypt, and on the coast near Alexandria[1]. In the second half of the 4th/10th century it became a general practice in the East to levy duties on sales of goods. Towards the end of his reign 'Adab-ud-Dawlah (d. 372/982) introduced a tax on the sale of horses and household utensils and established a monopoly in ice and flowered silk. Hence the angry verses: "A toll lies on all the markets of Babylon and a tax of a dirham on things sold therein[2]". When in 375/985 'Adad-ud-Dawlah's son sought to levy a tenth of the price on sale of genuine silk and woollen stuff, the town rebelled and compelled the withdrawal of the measure[3]. In 389/998 this measure was again re-introduced and as before, it led to an open rebellion. The people prevented the Friday service in the old town and set fire to a house where tax-rolls were kept. The rioters were punished, but only the tax on genuine

(1) Muq, 213.
(2) Jauhari, Dict. S. Mks.
(3) Ibn al-Jauzi, Berlin, fol. 123b : Ibn al-Athir, IX, 16-23 according to the *Taghi* of the contemporary Sabi.

silk was retained. Thus every piece, as it came out of the loom, was stamped. But taxes did not stop with articles of luxury. In 425/1033 the saintly Dinawari[1] impressed upon the prince the mischief which the imposition of the salt-tax caused to the people. It was accordingly repealed and the announcement was made in the sermon at the mosque. At the door of the mosque curses were inscribed on him who would impose the salt-tax again. The salt-tax, then, brought in an annual revenue of 2,000 dinars[2].

The Egyptians, indeed, never protested or rose against these taxes.

In Syria the taxes on merchandise were light and continued to be so even under the Egyptian Caliphs[3]. Only there existed, particularly in Jerusalem, the rule that goods could not be sold save in authorized market-places, which had to pay heavy sums to government[4]. The peculiar feature of this province was the 'Himayah', the licence tax, as for instance 'license' for keeping a carriage. These 'licenses' yielded quite as much as the high land-tax in force[5]. The taxes and imposts varied according to the ruler. Since 330/941, says Ibn Haukal, the taxes depended upon people who tried to swindle each other and people whose one aim was to make hay while the sun shone. No one thought of or cared for the country[6]. This very traveller saw the Syrian

(1) Wuz, 368.
(2) Ibn al-Jauzi, fol. 188a.
(3) Muq. says: Taxes are not heavy in Syria with the exception of those levied on the Caravansaraies (Fanduk) : here, however, the duties are oppressive. The property-tax, called Himayah, also is heavy. 'Himayah' literally signifies 'Protection.' It was an uncanonical tax levied on goods and premises, and of the nature of a ('license') granting the protection of the State to the occupier and possessor. Description of Syria by Muqaddasi (circa 985 A.D.) Trans. by Guy Le Strange, pp. 91, 92. Tr.
(4) Muq, 167.
(5) Muq, 189.
(6) p. 128.

budget for the year 296/908, which showed 39 million dirhams after the deduction of official salaries[1].

In these two countries—Egypt and Syria—the State-chest were in the form of dome-shaped structures standing on high columns within the chief mosque. At Fostat the State-chest stood in front of the pulpit. It had an iron-door with a lock. Access to the door could only be had by means of wooden steps. On account of the State-chest the mosque was cleared and closed at night[2]. Was this an old Egypto-Syrian practice ? In ancient times, was the Church-chest similarly kept ? Was the church in Byzantine times at once the Temple and the State-treasury ?[3]

Down to late in the 4th/10th century leases of royal domains were renewed every four years in the chief mosque[4]—also an old Egyptian practice.

Through the greater half of the century (up to 370/980) Mesopotamia stood under the almost independent Hamadanids. These Bediun princes, of whom only Saif-ud-Dawlah, in Aleppo, showed any splendour or possessed any chivalry, oppressed their subjects with the supine indifference of nomads. They were by far the worst rulers of the century. Compared with them, the Turkish and Persian rulers were angels of benignity. Characteristic of their nomad upbringing was their aversion from trees. When Alepoo, in 333/944, held out against the troops of 'Adad-ud-Dawlah, they cut down all the beautiful trees in the neighbourhood which, according to the contemporary poet Sanaubari

(1) *Mafatih al-Ulum*, 54.

(2) Ibn Rosteh, 116 : Muq, 182. It is mentioned that at Barda, at the foot of the Caucasus, the treasury, according to the Syrian practice, stood on nine columns in the mosque. It had a leaden roof and iron doors. Istakhri, 184.

(3) cf. Wilcken, *Clriech, Ostraka*, 149.

(4) Maqrizi, *Khitat* 1, 82.

constituted its most striking charm[1]. They forcibly pruchased the greatest portion of the lands in Mesopotamia for a tenth of their actual value. In his long life, Nasir-ud-Dawlah is said to have converted the entire distirct of Mosul into his private property[2]. He had fruit trees cut down. He replaced them by crops such as cotton, rice and others. Many emigrated. The entire tribe of the Banu Habib, cousins of the Hamadanids, went over with 12,000 (one MS. has 5,000) horse men to the Greeks, where they found a friendly welcome and whence they vigorously plundered their quondam, unfortunate home. The property of the unhappy emigrants was naturally confiscated by the Princes. "Many, however, preferred to remain in Muslim countries out of love for their home where they had spent their youth. But they had to make over half of the entire harvest and the Prince assessed and fixed their share of taxes, as he pleased, in gold and silver."

In 358/968 the district of Nisbis alone yielded five million dirhams a part form the capitation-tax, which brought in 5,000 dinars ; wine-tax which brought in 5,000 dinars ; taxes on domestic animals and vegetables which brought in 5,000 dinars and the taxes from mills, baths, shops and crown-lands which brought in 10,000 in dinars. After the expulsion of the Hamadanid trees were replanted and vineyards restored[3].

It is not surprising, then, that about 370/980 Ibn Haukal declares the Hamadanids and the Spanish (Caliph Abdal-Rahman III to be the richest prices of the time[4]. In 368/978 'Adad-ud-Dawlah stored away in his strongest castle treasures worth about 20 million dirhams[5]. And yet there

(1) Wustenfeld, die *Stathalter ven Agypten*, IV, 36.
(2) Misk, VI, 485.
(3) Ibn Haukal, 140 sqq.
(4) Dozy, II, 57.
(5) Misk, VI, 496. Misk was entrusted with the counting of the booty.

was constant quarrel for tribute both with Baghdad and Byzantium[1].

In the East which, in the course of the century paid homage to different princes, specially to the Samanids and the Buwayyids, taxation in the 4th/10th and 3rd/9th centuries was fairly uniform. Ibn Haukal states this to be the case even with Afghanistan. He gives the best certificate to the Samanids for having devised a sound and uniform system of financial adminstration for the whole of the extreme north and the east of the Empire. Says Ibn Haukal : "The taxes are lower and yet the salaries of officers higher than anywhere else. The taxes are collected twice a year and yield 40 million dirhams per annum. The salaries are paid every quarter and amount to 5 millions a quarter—half of the revenue. The State-officers, such as the Qadhis, tax-collectors, civil servants, heads of the Police and post-masters of a particular district receive the self-same pay which is fixed according to the taxable resources of the district. The great difference between the income and the expenditure points to just and mild adminstration of the taxes[2]."

In Fars, in 309/918, under 'Adad-ad-Dawlah, the most outstanding ruler of the century, the revenue rose from 18, 87, 500 to 21,50,000 ; that is to say it increased by one-sixth of the original amount. He could thus afford to spend freely and secure an annual revenue of three and a quarter million dinars, for, as Ibn al-Jauzi[3] says, "he valued the dinar and despised not even the smallest copper coin[4]."

(1) For instance, Elias Nisibenus, p. 215, according to Thabit b. Sinan, Ibn Sa'id, 61ff.

(2) Ibn Haukal, 341.

(3) Ibn Balkhi, *J.R.A.S.*, 1912, p. 889.

(4) Ibn al-Jauzi, Berlin, fol. 120 b. There another authority sets down his revenue at 320 million dirhams ; a further proof that a dinar was only werth 10 dirhams. He wanted to raise his revenue from 320 to 360 millions ; that is to say, a million per day.

On the whole Egypt also maintained an equally high level. In the 3rd/9th century the all too powerful Ibn Tulun managed to extort about 5 million dinars from the country. In the troublous times about the middle of the 4th/10th century it yielded 32,70,000 dinars a year and about the end of the century under the Wazir Ya'qub ibn Killis it rose again to four million dinars[1]. Of a general financial collapse there can be no talk. Everywhere it depended upon the man at the helm of the State. In 355/965 the Wazir represented to the Buwayyid Rukn-ud-Dawlah that the district of Adherbaijan would yield 50 million dirhams if he personally assumed the administration. To a weaker administrator, he pointed out, it cannot yeild more than 2 millions at the outside because of the fiefs of the Dailams and Kurds and the difficulty of forcibly realising taxes from such as were powerful and headless of their obligation and because of waste and want of care.

Only in Babylonia the taxable resources of the country declined and this decline shows itself in the second half of the 3rd/9th century. About 240/850 Ibn Khurdadbih estimates the revenue of Babylon at 78 million dirhams. About 290/893 a large portion of Babylon, about half, is leased out for two and a half million dinars[2]. The Budget of the year 306/918, however, only shows just a little over one and a half milion dinars—less than a third[3]. The revenue, indeed, increases somewhat in the 4th/10th century. In 358/968 Ibn Fadl leased out Babylon for 42 million dirhams[4]. Later 'Adad-ud-Dawlah only offered 30 million dirhams for it[5]. Very violent was the contrast from the early times, for

(1) Abu Salih, ed. Evetts, fol. 23a.

(2) Wuz, 10. The statement (Wuz. 188) that under this very Caliph, al-Mutadid, Babylon yielded the same revenue as it did under 'Omar I, does not fit in with the figures.

(3) Von Kremer, *Einnahmebudget*, 312.

(4) Ibn Haukal, 169/178.

(5) Misk, VI, 440.

then "the land-tax of Babylon constituted the largest sum in the world[1]" but now 'Adad-ud-Dawlah affirmed that he would rather have title from Babylon and revenue from Arragan (the coast land in Fars)[2]. The main reason for the decline was the gradual conversion of the country into a swamp, due to maladministration. The peasants were compelled to emigrate. Most of the people of Mosul, for instance, were Arabs who, in the 4th/10th century, had come to Mesopotamia to cultivate the alluvial lands[3]. Thus Babylonia was unable to contribute anything to the central treasury.

The lopping off the Province of Fars from the Empire by the Saffarids caused the first financial embarrassment to the Baghdad Government. This criais, in the 70th year of the 3rd/9th century suggested, for the first time, the idea of compulsory loans. Al-Muwaffiq proposed to the Wazir "loans from merchants and also an imposition of a sum of money upon them, upon the Wazir (himself), upon the clerks and treasury officials to meet the expenses of the equipment and despatch of an army to Fars." But the Wazir was not very pleased with the proposal[4]. When, about the year 300/912, money from the Province of Ahwaz, which had been farmed out, came in in driblets, the Government at Baghdad made the Jewish Financier Joseph, son of Phinehas, advance money to make up the deficit[5]. In the year 319/931 the Government of Fars and Kirman conspired together to hold back the revenue in the future, with the result that the Wazir was compelled, for the first time, to sell crown-lands of the value of 50,000 dinars[6] and also to

(1) *Aghani*, IV, 79.
(2) Muq, 421.
(3) Ibn Haukal, 143.
(4) Sabusti, *Kit. al-Dhiyarat*, Berlin, fol. 119a.
(5) Wuz, 178.
(6) In such circumstances the neighbouring land-lords combined together and purchased the land for much below the real value ; Ibn Hamdun, *J.R.A.S.*, 1908, 434.

take a loan of half the amount of the taxes realizable in 320/932. Thus for the year 320 very little in the way of taxes was left. Moreover he had to borrow 200,000 dinars (2 million marks) at the rate of 1 per dirham per dinar, that is to say seven per cent per month[1]. In 323/934 the loan could not be repaid. The Wazir was, therefore, compelled to give the creditors in part orders upon the treasury officials of Babylonia and in part to sell domain-lands[2]. In 324/935 the Wazir again borrowed from rich merchants ; and State properties, such as houses near the wall of the old town etc., etc. had to be sold to repay the loan[3].

In the method of collecting taxes the bad pre-Islam practices now recur. The tax-farming in the East began with the Government loan, which was adopted for the first time under the Caliph al-Mut'adid (279-289/892-901)[4]. At that time "the world was deserted and the treasuries empty." It took quite a long time to collect the taxes and yet, in spite of all retrenchments, they required 7,000 dinars per day to meet the necessary expenses. Two shrewd officers induced a capitalist to advance this sum as against the taxes of some of the districts of Babylonia. With this device the Wazir and the Caliph were delighted for it was at once novel and ingenious[5]. With the exception of the manorial estates, the tax roll of 303/915 shows Ahwaz and Wasit as farmed out[6].

---

(1) Misk, V, 342, 345, 364 : Ibn al-Athir, VIII. 165.

(2) Misk, V. 505.

(3). Al-Suli, Auraq, p. 103.

(4) See Von Tischendorf, *Lehnwesen in den Moslim, Staaten*, Leipzig, 1872 Tr.

(5) Wuz, 101 et sqq.

(6) Von Kremer, Fars, was also farmed out but as the leasee neglected to pay, it was taken away from him and brought back under State control (Wuz. 340).

IX. THE COURT

Black and white were the colours of the Caliphs in the 4th/10th century. When in the year 320/932 the Caliph Muqtadir took his last ride[1], fully aware of its serious significance, he dressed himself in the most solemn attrie. He wore a silvery *qafatan* and a black turban, and bore the mantle of the Prophet on his shoulder and carried a staff in his hand[2]. In front of him rode the Crown-prince, like the Caliph, dressed, in Qafatan and white turban. In the 4th/10th century the Abbasid rulers usually wore the high-pointed cap (*Qalansuwah*) and the Persian cloak (*Qaba*)—not unlike those worn by his distinguished subjects—colour raven-black[3].

Black too was the purse in which the Caliph daily put in alms at the morning-prayer[4]. Black likewise was the

(1) (Misk, IV, 265 Tr.)

(2) *Arib*. 177 ; Ibn al-Jauzi, fol. 436. Staff and mantle were the distinguishing tokens of the Caliph ; *Diwan of Rida*, 313. The mantle was believed to be mantle of the Prophet, *Ibid*, p. 543. Ikhshid, the viceroy of Egypt, used a silvery qafatan like that of the Caliph and forbade its use to others (Tallquist, 30).

(3) Mas'udi, VIII, 169, 377. The Mamluk Sultans wanted closely to imitate the dress of the old Caliphs, which was as follows : (1) a black turban, the point of which fell between the shoulders ; (2) a coat, (Jubbah) of black silk with fairly wide-sleeves and without embroidery ; (3) a Beduin sword carried according to Beduin fashion on the felt side and suspended by a belt passing over the right shoulder. This sword is said to have the sword of 'Omar I (Qatremere, *Mameloucs*, I 133).

(4) It was 200 dirhams and was distributed among *the poor* women residing near the Palace (Wuz, 19). Abul Mahasin states that Ibn Tulun spent 1000 dinars daily in alms. Many of these, Tulunide figures are purely imaginary.

banner of the Caliphate (*'alam al-Khilafat*) bearing in white the inscription 'Mohamed is the messenger of God' (*M. rasul allah*)[1].

The Fatimid Caliphs at Cairo adopted the 'Alid colour, which was white. Their banners were white or blood red and a poet likens them to anemones (Abu'l Mahasin, II, 460; Sabusti, the *Book of Cloisters,* Berlin, fol. 128 b.) The coronation of the Caliph took place thus : he attached his banner to a pole and received the signet of office. It was marked by absolute Arab simplicity (Misk, V, 454). But in the case of Amirs the coronation was a real one, according to the old heathen fashion : a diadem, set with precious; sotnes, was put on their head and a neck-chain and two gold arm-buckles also set with precious stones, were put upon their person[2]. In the 3rd/9th century the usual court livery was red. For a special state

---

(1) *Misk*, V, 294. The Abbasid crown-prince, at the end of the 4th/10th century—so also the Amirs of the Empire—carried two banners, one black and another white. Abul Mahasin, II, 34, ; *Arib* 177; Ibn al-Jauzi fol. 43b. 112b.

(2) The (*Taj*) crown was set with precious stones, such as was Saif-ud-Dawlah's (prince of Aleppo) at the reception of the Greek ambassador in 353/964 (Yahya b. Sa'id, fol 84a). The gold neck-chains were even in ancient Egypt a distinguishing token of a warrior (ZDMG, 41, 211). They were conferred as a mark of honour, about 300/912 cn victorious generals (*Arib*, 35). The conqueror of the Karmathians got two gold arm-buckles in addition to the neck-chain (*Arib*, 3). Ikhshid, the ruler of Egypt, seems to be the first prince who, as such, was invested with a neck-chain and two arm buckles. In 324/935 the Caliph sent them through his Wazir. The bazars and the streets of old Cairo were decorated with trappings and curtains and carpets ; the doors of the chief mosque were covered with gold-embroidered brocade. Thus with his insignia rode Ikhshid to prayer, his Wazir by his side. Tallquist, 17 f. His predecessor Khumarwaihi had received only the crown but no chains (Kindi, 240). Neck-chains and arm-buckles continued even under the Fatimids as marks of honour for generals, and this in spite of the canonist of Islam, who severely forbade the use of gold ornaments. (Khuda Bukhsh, politics in Islam, p. 220 and the note. Tr.)

occasion the Caliph directed that every one should be supplied with a new and different coloured dress in addition to the red jacket and the pointed cap[1]. At solemn audiences in the 4th/10th century the attendants stood before the Caliph, attired partly in black and partly in white[2]. Over the Abbasids, as over the Fatimids, hovered the state-umbrella (*Shamshat al-Khalifah* ; in Egypt, *Mizallah*). Of this they saw or heard very little at Baghdad. In 332/943 this state-umbrella was even carried in front of the Amir as a signal mark of honour[3]. In the African Cairo it was reckoned as a symbol of majesty and matched the dress of the Caliph[4]. And, indeed, the highest token of the supremacy of the Caliph of Baghdad was the announcement by drum, timbal and trumpet of the five daily prayers by the guards of his palace. Only at Court-mourning did this announcing-music stop for a few days[5]. Desperately did the Caliph defend this supreme prerogative against the Amirs, but in vain. From 368/976 Adad-ud-Dawlah caused the drum to be beaten at the gate of his residence at three prayer-times ; from 418/1027 Jalal-ud-Dawlah extended it to four prayer-times ; and finally, in the year 396/1014, like the Caliphs, the Amir had the drum beaten at all the five prayer-times. Like his costume, unostentatious was the title of the Caliph : the simple "Prince of the Faithful[6]." But since the second "Abbasid—according to what precedent we know not—the Caliph received a special pious name immediately after the homage was done

(1) Sabusti, Berlin, fol. 68b.

(2) *Kit. al-Uyun*, IV, 236.

(3) *Kit. al-Uyun*, IV, fol. 225b.

(4) Maqrizi *Khitat*, II, 280 according to Musabbihi (d. 420/1029) ; Abul Mahasin 285 ff, Wustenfeld, Qalqashandi, 173. To the Barbarous practices of the Fatimids belongs also the superstitious carrying of the coffin of their ancestors on campaigns (Ibn Taghribardy, 10).

(5) Ibn al-Zauzi, fol. 114 a, 175b, 197 b; Ibn al-Athir, IX, IX, 215.

(6) The adoption of the appellation of Imam-al-Haq by al-Mustakfi, in 334/945 (along with the title of 'Prince of the Faithful.') was but a challenge to the claims of the Shi'ite and the Fatimid Imams, Ibn-al-Jauzi, fol. 73 b; Abul Mahasin, II. 308.

to him[1]. In 322/933 the Caliph asked his friend As-Suli, the savant and famous chess-player, to draw up a list of titles with a view to enabling him to select one out of them. Suli—we have it from him—submitted to the Caliph thirty titles with a recommendation in favour of Al-Murtadha billah (Pleasing unto God'). He was indeed so very sure of the acceptance of his recommendation that he actually composed a long poem with the rhyme 'Murtadha'. But the Caliph rejected the recommendation on the ground that an unfortunate pretender had once borne that title, and he selected the title of 'Al-Radhi for himself. The poem was flung into water but Suli made use of it in his history and thus saved it for posterity. Later he composed a poem with the rhyme Radhi but, unfortunately, it is lost.

The Secretary of the Caliph Qadir (381-422/991-1031) for the first time introduced the circumscription 'His most holy, prophetic presence 'for the Caliph—a circumscription which became the general fashion. Even the extraordinary practice of referring to the ruler as "Service" goes back to this Secretary. Says Hilal : I have seen in the hand-writing of the Qadhi ibn Abi's-sawrib : 'the servant of the high "Service" of such and such[2].

In full strength was the rage for titles among the Amirs, the highest dignitaries, and the official circles. All were distinguished as friends, helpers, supporters of the "dynasty[3]." Al-Biruni (d. 447/1055) says : When the 'Abbasids had decorated their assistants, friends, enemies indiscriminately with vain titles compounded with the word 'Dawlah', their empire perished[4].

(1) The Samanid rulers, while living bore a different name from that which they bore after death, *Muk.* 337.

(2) Hilal (447/1055), 148 ff.

(3) Wali-ud-Dawlah, the oldest of these Dawlah titles, was conferred upon the Wazir Abul Qasim (d. 291/903). Even in Egypt we came across a title in 286/899 (Biruni, 132 ff; Ibn Sa'id fol. 133b.

(4) (Sachau, 129. Eng. tr. Tr.).

In the second half of the 4th/10th century they took to double titles. 'Adad-ud-Dawlah (supporter of the dynasty)[1] was also adorned with the title of 'Taju'l Millah' (Crown of Religion). And finally to three titles. Baha-ud-Dawlah (Beauty of religion) was called, Diya al-Millah' (Light of Religion) and 'Ghyath al-Ummah, (Help of the community). Everywhere these Dawlah-titles flourished : among the Samanids, among the rulers of the North and the East, as also among the Fatimids. In 382/992 the Turkish Bogra Khan assumed the title of Shihab-ud-Dawlah (Flame of the dynasty). Even entirely un-Islamic, nay quite balsphemous, designations, came into fashion. The Buwayyids were the first to confer on their Wazirs titles which really belonged to God : the only one (Auhad) ; the most excellent of the excellent (Kafi'l Kufat) ; the unique among the excellent (Auhad al-Kufat). Other princes called them even 'Prince of the World' (Amir al-'Alam) and 'Lord of the Princes' (Sayyid al-Umara). And it is precisely this which calls for Biruni's censure : May God inflict ignominy on them in this world and show them and to others their weakness[2].

Finally the Caliph Qadir (381-422/991-1030) is said to have conferred on Mahmud of Ghazni, for the first time, the most fateful of all titles—the title of Sultan[3]. But when in 423/1031 the Amir of Baghdad sought the title of 'As-Sultan al-Mu'azzam Malik-al-Umam' (The Powerful ruler, King of the nations), Mawardi, the plenipotentiary of the Caliph, refused it on the ground that the 'Sultan al-Ma'azzam' was none other than the Caliph himself. The socond portion was modified into 'Malik-ud-Dawlah' (King of the Dynasty)[4]. And when, 429/1037, the Buwayyid ruler arrogated to

(1) d. 372/982.
(2) Sachau, 131 Tr.
(3) Ibn al-Athir, IX, 92: **Ali Dede**, fol. 89 a, according to the *Tarikh al-Khulafa* of Suyuti. Titles in the Roman Empire, Gibbon, II, 169, Bury's ed. Tr.)
(4) Ibn al-Jauzi, fol. 184 b.

himself the very ancient heathen title of 'Shahinshah al'Azam, Malik al-muluk' the people rebelled and pelted with stones the preacher who announced it at prayer[1].

Although the court-theologians sought to prove that 'King of the Kings of the Earth' was no divine title, yet the old traditional title of 'Chief Qadhi', 'Judge of Judges' was strongly taken exception to by serious-minded people, and the well-known Mawardi, author and publicist, actually threw up the post of a judge on that account[2]. But this title survives even today. Hilal as-Sabi did not approve even of the title of Al-Ghalib (The Conqueror) which, in 391/1001, the Caliph conferred upon his successor. He supported his objection by a reference to the well-known inscription on Alhambra (There is no conqueror (*Ghalib*) save Allah[3].

The power of conferring titles was the exclusive prerogative of the Caliph. From him alone they derived their validity and for this prerogative he was amply paid. In fact towards the end of the 4th/10th century it constituted his main source of income. After much bargaining the Amir of Baghdad had to pay in 423/1031 for the title of 'Malik-ud-Dawlah' 2000 dinars, 30,000 dirhams, 10 sus of floral silk, 100 pieces of valuable brocade and 100 pieces of ordinary brocade, 200 mann (weight) of aloes, 10 mann of camphor, 1,000 mithqal (weight) of ambar, 100 mithqal of musk and 500 Chinese dishes—besides other gifts to individual courtiers[4].

---

(1) Gibbon, Bury's ed. Vol. II. p. 282 Tr.

(2) Ibn al-Jauzi, 193 a; Subki, II, 305. He belonged to the table-companions of the newly-title Amir. According to this history he kept himself aloof from him. But the prince sent for him and yet his relation with him did not change. His firmness redounded to his credit.

(3) Suli finds fault with this *laqab* (surname) even for the Caliph as it is forbidden by Surah 49, V. II. See Wuz, 420 ; *Auraq* Peris, Arab, 4836, 3.

(4) Ibn al-Jauzi, 184b.

In other directions, too, court etiquette had markedly developed. In fact it assumed the form which it has retained up to the present time. About 200/800 Ma'mum was addressed as 'Thou' like any one else[1]. About 300/900 Muqtadir too was mostly thus addressed,[2] although the practice of referring to the Caliph in the third person, such as 'Prince of the Faithful' etc., had already come into fashion. At the end of the century it was not considered good taste to address an educated man by such a familiar term as 'Thou'. At the beginning of the 4th/10th century a governor is for the first time addressed at the reception of the Caliph by a name (*ism*) which has a somewhat official ring about it, but which to express greater friendliness is changed into his *Kunyah* (father of so an so)[3]. In the 5th/11th century even the Caliph himself is not supposed to address any of his friends in public except by name—the use of *Kunyah* (father of so and so) being reserved for private conversation[4]. Al-Ma'mun shook hands with the patriarch Dionysius as he was wont to do with all whom he wished to honour[5]. When the Field Marshal Munis took leave of the Caliph at the beginning of the 4th/10th century he kissed the Caliph's hand[6]. As a special mark of honour they kissed the feet of those higher in rank ; friends of equal status kised the shoulder[7]. Thus did the servant-girls offer welcome to Telemachos, kissing his shoulder and the crown of his head[8]. On special ceremonial occasions the Amir Bejkem kissed the Caliph Radhi's hand and feet[9].

---

(1) Ibn Taifur. ed. Keller.
(2) For instance, Wuz, 229; *Arib*, 176.
(3) Ibn Said, ed. Tallquist, 40.
(4) Ibn Abi Usaibah. I. 216.
(5) Mich. Syrus.
(6) Hamadani, Paris, fol. 201 a.
(7) Wuz 358.
(8) Odyssey, XXI, 224.
(9) as-Suli, 54, 423, the driver of the swine and cattle-heard does the same to Odysseus XXI, 234.

The old Arab Muslims regarded kissing the ground in front of a man as an invasion of God's privilege. The Byzantine ambassadors standing before the Caliph Muqtadir in 305/917 would not do so, as the Muslims were excused this part of the court etiquette at Byzantium. In a sotry dating from the 4th/10th century a timid clerk is represented as wishing to kiss the ground before the chief of the police, who rebukes him thus : Don't do that. 'Tis a custom aomng tyrants[1].

In the 30th year of the same century the Amir of Egypt threw himself on the ground before the Caliph. When Ikhshid met the Caliph, the former had already dismounted and, like an attendant, had a sword, a belt and a quiver. Several times he kissed the ground, then he stepped forward and kissed the Caliph's hand[2]. Muhammad Khaqan called out to him : Mount the horse, Muhammad ! then, again : Mount the horse, Abu Bakr! He is said to have done this under instructions from the Caliph. But Ikhshid remained standing before the Caliph, leaning on his sword. But when, eventually, being induced to mount his horse he attended on the Caliph with a whip over his shoulder,—a thing he had never done before, Ikhshid boasted of this and the Caliph was delighted. Thereupon the Caliph spoke to Ikhshid : For thirty years I confer the province upon thee and with thee I associate Angur as thy Governor. On this Ikhshid kissed the ground several times, and both on his son's behalf and his own for being addressed by his surname made a similar present to the Caliph as he had made before[3].

On the coronation of the Amir 'Adad-ud-Dawlah in 369/979 the court ceremonial was seen at its best. At the reception hall sat the Caliph armed with the Caliph's sword,

(1) Al-Khatib, *Tarikh Baghdad*, ed. Salon, 56 ; Misk, V, 124 briefly states: 'they kissed the ground'.

(2) Al-Faragh. 1, 54.

(3) Tallquist, 40

before him lay the Qur'an of 'Othman, on his shoulder rested the mantle and in his hand lay the staff of the Prophet. On either side stood the nobility. The Turks and the Dailamites lined up unarmed and then followed their Prince. When it was told to 'Adad-ud-Dawlah that the eye of the Caliph was upon him he kissed the ground. Dismayed at this form of obeisance a General asked him in Persian : O King, Is he God ? 'Adad-ud-Dawlah then stepped forward and twice kissed the ground, and twice did the Caliph invite him to come nearer and yet nearer to him. Then he kissed the feet of the Caliph. The Caliph thereupon laid his hand upon him and thrice told him: Be seated ! —and yet he would not sit. Then said the Caliph : I have sworn that thou shalt sit down. Then he kissed the stool placed to the right of the Caliph and sat down. The Caliph thereupon solemnly made over to him the administration of all his lands. This was followed by his retirement into an adjoining room where he was invested with robes of honour ; the crown was placed on his head and the banner handed over to him. Three days after the Caliph sent him presents, among them a mantle of Egyptian cotton, a gold dish and a crystal flask. The drink in the flask[1] was so stale and scanty that it seemed as if someone had drunk out of it, although it was tied with a silken string. In Fatimid Egypt veneration for the Caliph went still further. When in 366/976 the appointment-letter of the new Qadhi was read out in the mosque of Al-Azhar 'the reader', whenever the name of Mu'izz or any one of his House was mentioned, made a sign to the audience to prostrate themselves on the ground[2]. Likewise on the same occasion in the year 368/1008, the Qadhi kissed the ground each time the name of al-Hakim was mentioned[3]. Indeed the people in the bazar prostrated themselves whenever this

(1) Ibn al-Jauzi, fol. 116a.

(2) Supplement to Kindi, 598.

(3) Prof. Margoliouth wrties to me : The reference given by Mez to Al-Kindi is inaccurate (pp.136 ; 138). His 'der' can only mean the Qadhi.

Caliph's name was mentioned (Ibn al-Jauzi, fol. 150 b.). But when this very Caliph reverted to the old Islamic ideals he forbade kissing of the ground before him, and the use of 'Maulana' (our Lord) in reference to him. But under his successor Zahir the older practices, such as they existed under his forebears, revivied (Yahya ibn Sa'id, fol. 132 b.).

Most of the people prostrated themselves even before Ibn Ammar, the administrator of the empire : the select few however kissed his stirrup, and those that were intimate his hand and knee[1].

About this time a courtier of the ruler of Bukhara is held up as the highest model of court-propriety. While talking to his ruler, a scorpion crept into his shoe and stung him several times but he remained unmoved. Only when he had done with him and was alone, did he pull off his shoe[2]. At the court of Ikhshid an elephant and a giraffe were exhibited. All, slaves, soldiers, servants were taken up with them, but the eyes of Kafur never left those of his master for fear he might require him and find him perchance inattentive[3]. In 332/944 Mas'udi loves to dwell upon such court-etiquette. He speaks with praise of a Hudailite who, in conversation with the Caliph Saffah, did not stir when a storm blew a tile into the middle of the hall[4], and of a courtier of a Persian king who on a ride was so engrossed in listening to the story of the Prince that he and his horse fell into a stream. Ever since that incident, says the historian, he enjoyed the king's fullest confidence[5].

In official correspondence, even among themselves, the

---

(1) Maqrizi, *Khitat* II, 36.

(2) Ibn al-Ahtir, VIII, 196 ; in *Muh. el-Udaba* . (I, 117) this story is related of 'Abdul Malik and Hajjaj.

(3) Tallquist, 47.

(4) *Muh al-Udaba* relates this very story of a Samanid courtier.

(5) Mas'udi, VI, 122ff.

Amirs speak of the Commander of the Faithful in terms of highest respect, referring to him as 'Our Lord' (Maulana). They even speak of themselves as his Freedmen (Maula)[1]. Even in letters to a third person they always begin with the formula : Our lord, the Prince of the Faithful in well,—God be praised or thanked for it[2]. Indeed everything is represented as his command[3]. In the distant Rai, in the vicinity of the modern Tehran, the Wazir presents to his prince on New Year's day a huge gold medal bearing on one side the names of the Caliph, the Prince and the place of coinage, and on the other some verses[4]. In his personal intercourse with the Amirs the Caliph had to experience the effects of his dwindling power. The Turk Bejkem never drank at home without seeing that his cupbearer drank first out of the vessel ; similarly when the Amir dined with Al-Radhi, the Caliph tasted all food and drink before the Amir, and could not be induced to alter this practice even at Bejkem's earnest entreaty[5].

The Caliph's dignity sufferred most under Al-Mustakfi (333/334/944-946), who fell entirely into the clutches of an ambitious Persian woman. She ruled the Court and the staff, and the palace was thrown open to all indiscriminately, even to those personally unknown to the Caliph. The Caliph received them all. For the love of this women he showered upon the Amir Tuzun unheard of honours and prerogatives.

---

(1) They no longer speak of themselves as slaves (Abd), as did Tekin of Egypt even about the year 300/912. (*Uyun al-Hadaiq,* IV Berlin, fol. 125b).

(2) E.G. *Rasa'il* of Sabi, Leiden, fol. 76 b.

(3) Ibid, fol. 124 b; we have put the matter up before the 'Prince of the Faithful' and he has thus issued his orders. etc. Ibid fol. 202 Muiz-ud-Dawla to the Yamanites : the 'Prince of the Faithful,'—may God strengthen him! — signifies his intention to us and urges us on to such and such things.

(4) Ibn al-Athir, IX, 41.

(5) as-Suli, *Auraq*, Paris, 54.

Tuzun was permitted to ride in the palace-grounds where not even a Caliph had ridden before. Even the state-umbrella of the Caliph was borne before him[1].

Unfortunately for the Caliph the Dailamites were Shi'ites and as such had no respect for him. Hitherto the palace revolutionaries had merely deposed and killed Caliphs but now, for the first time, he was subjected to public-indignities. In 334/945 when he sat in Solemn session surrounded by his people according to their respective rank, Mu'izz-ud-Dawlah came up to him, kissed the ground before him and then the hand of the Caliph, lo ! two of his Dailamite soldiers rushed in, loudly uttering something in Persian. The Caliph, presuming that they wished to kiss his hand, stretched it out to them. And instantly they seized him, brought him down to the ground, tied his neck with his truban and dragged him out into the hall. Muizz-ud-Dawlah sprang to his feet. Wild was the confussion and shrill the trumpet-sound[2]. The Caliph was taken to the Sultan's palace and then blinded[3]. But the clever and circumspect. 'Adad-ud-Dawlah showed honour to the Caliph once again a thing which had completely gone out of fashion[4]. And yet even he, when he proceeded to Baghdad in 370/980, desired the Caliph to meet him at the Bridge of An-Nahrawan. "This was the first time that a Caliph went out to meet an Amir[5]."

At the time of Al-Mutadid (279/289/892-901) the court establishment consisted of :—

1. The *Princes of the Caliph's house.*

2. The *Palace-Staff*—About 1000 dinars was the daily expenditure. Of this sum 700 was meant for the whites, to

(1) *Kit. al-Uyun*, iv, 222 ff.
(2) Misk (Eng. tr.) Vol. V., pp. 89—90 Tr.
(3) Yahya ibn Said. fol. 86 b : Misk, V, 124.
(4) Ibn al-Athir, VIII, 339.
(5) Ibn al-Jauzi, 117 a.

whom all the actual porters (*Bawwab*) belonged, and 300 for the blacks, mostly the Caliph's slaves[1]. As the latter received only a small wage they were provided with bread.

3. *Freedmen*—These were mostly the former white slaves of the Caliph's father (*Mamalik*). From among them were recruited 25 chamberlains (*Hujjab*), and their deputies (*Khulafa al-Hujjab*) 500 in number[2]. At the last battle in which al-Muqtadir took part one of these threw himself upon his master to protect him and was killed[3]. In 329/940 the title of chief Hajib (*Hajib al-Hujjab*) was for the first time conferred[4].

4. *The Guards*—In the Baghdad garrison the regiments, under different commanders, consisting partly of their armed slaves, formed definite units,—*e.g.*, the regiment of the Greek Johannes Janis (Janiseyyah), the regiment of the eunuch Muflih (Muflihiyah). The other units consisted mostly of the royal slaves, or were chosen from among the expert horsemen and archers of the royal army (*'Askar al-Khassah*). Out of these a regiment of body-guards, *Mukhtarin* (the selected), was chosen. The body-guard of Khumarwaihi in Egypt was also called "the selected[5]." They did military service at audiences and acted as escorts of the Caliph.

5. The rest of the court-staff were the private secretaries, Qur'an-readers, Muazzins, astronomers, officers-in-charge of clocks, story-tellers, jesters, couriers, standard-bearers, drummers, trumpeters, water-carriers, workmen from goldsmiths to carpenters and saddlers ; the five

(1) According to an authority not always very reliable in its computations these blacks numbered 4.000 strong (*Tarikh Baghdad*, ed. Salmon, 51).

(2) Cf. Misk, V, 541 ; T. *Baghdad*, ed Salmon 49, 51.

(3) Misk, V, 379.

(4) Abu'l-Mahasin, II, 295.

(5) Abu'-Mahasin, II, 65.

marshals under an equerry, the fifth being in charge of camels ; hunters, menagerie-keepers, valets-de-chambre, cook, physicians-in-ordinary, crew of the court-boat, lamp-lighters, etc.

6. *Ladies* : for their daily expenses 100 dinars were assigned[1]. We have no correct information as to their exact number. Khawarezmi asserts that in Mutawakkil's harem there were 12,000 ladies[2], but the much older Mas'udi fixes the number at 4,000, and one MS. reads only 400[3]. About the year 300/912 the *harems* were under the control of two stewardesses, one the Caliph's, the other his mother's. Prisoners of State of high rank were committed to the custody of the former for mild incarceration ; as was the case with the Wazir Ibn al-Furat in the year 300/912[4], and with the Hamadanid Prince and the Wazir 'Ali ibn 'Isa in the year 303/915[5].

The Caliphs' consorts were mostly Greek or Turkish slave-girls ; their origin made no difference ; and this produced kaleidoscopic uncertainty in the offices connected with the court and the higher administrative posts. Every one of these ladies sought to confer as brilliant a distinction as possible on her, relations and kinsmen. Already the father of Rashid had introduced at court his brother-in-law, first a slave and later a freedman ; subsequently he appointed him Governor of Yaman[6]. The maternal uncle of Muqtadir, a Greek, bearing the slave-name *Gharib* (the rare one), exercised great influence at court and was addressed as 'Amir'[7]. The chief court-stewardess of the Caliph's mother,

(1) Wuz, 11 ff.
(2) Khwarezmi, *Raza'il*, 137.
(3) Masudi, VII, 276.
(4) *Arib*, 109, Wuz. 105.
(5) *'Uyun el-Hada'iq*, Berlin, fol. 132a. (See Bowen, *'Ali ibn Isa*, p. 159 Tr.)
(6) Ya'qubi, II, 481.
(7) *Arib*, 49.

a Hashimite, succeeded in securing the position of "Marshal of the nobility (*Naquib*) of the 'Abbasids and the "Alids" for her brother. But then entire nobility opposed this appointment with the result that he had to surrender his office, the most distinguished one at court, in favour of the son of the former incumbent[1]. The experience of the Caliph's mother, as the pivot of court-intrigues and wire-pulling, was so bitter that the choice of the next Caliph was determined by the fact that he had no mother living at the time of his accession[2].

About the year 300/912, 11,000 eunuchs are said to have been at Court[3] : according to another account 7,000 and 700 chamberlains[4]. Whereas an authentic old report fixes at 700 the total number of eunuchs and court attendants[5].

As at the Old Persian court[6] the sovereigns of the late Roman Empire gathered together at meals and at carousing banquets companions whom they called 'Friends of the Caesar[7].' About 200/813 the Caliph Ma'mun, on his return to Baghdad, also had a list prepared of men whom he wished to entertain at his table (*Nudama*)[8]. According to the wish of the Caliph the list included literati, savants, courtiers, military men. From this list of the *Nudama* of the Caliphs Mu'izz-ud-Dawlah only selected the physician Sinan

(1) *Arib*, 47.
(2) *Arib*, 181 ; *Kit. al-Uyun*, IV, 131 b. She had died immediately after the birth of Al-Qadir. *Kit. al-Uyun*, IV, 66 b.
(3) Abu'l-Mahasin, II, 482 ; *Tarikh Baghdad*, 49. According to the Qadhi et-Tanukhi (d. 447/1055).
(4) *Tarikh Baghdad*, 51.
(5) Sabusti, *Book of Coisters*, fol. 68b.
(6) (Says Gibbon (Bury's Ed. Vol. II, p. 283 ; also see note 57 Tr.) : Antonious, a Roman subject of Syria, who had fled from the oppression and was admitted into the council of Sapor, and even to the Royal table, where, accroding to the custom of the Persians, the most important business was frequently discussed. Tr.)
(7) *Fihrist*, 61.
(8) Sabusti. Berlin, fol 21a.

ibn Thabit. The table-talks of the Caliph Mu'tamid (256/279/ 869-892) have been collected and preserved[1]. The Table-Companions drew a salary[2].

As-Suli describes the first gathering of the Table-companions of Ar-Radhi 322/326/933-940). They sat in strict order. To the right sat first the old Prince Ishaq ibn al-Mutamid ; then As-Suli, the savant and chess-player ; then a philologer, private-tutor of a Prince, and Ibn Hamdun, scion of an old court nobility. To the left sat three literary courtiers of the family of Munajjim and two Beridis of high official descent. The proceedings began with the recitation of laudatory poems. This was followed by a complaint from Ar-Radhi regarding the heaviness of the burden his new dignity had imposed upon him in those troubled times. But the complaint was forthwith softened by the comforting assertion that he had not selfishly sought the throne, and the optimistic belief that God would help him in the fulfilment of his duty. This led on to talk about the constant fear he was in of his predecessor. He did not behave, said the Caliph, like an uncle towards his nephew. Suli consoled him by reference to the example of the Prophet, who too had to suffer much at the hands of his uncle, Abu Lahab, regarding whom the Almighty actually revealed a *surah* in the Qur'an. "On that night we sat for three hours drinkind wine. Radhi having given up wine, did not, however, join us[3]." The table-companions sitting on the opening night, to the right and the left, formed two shifts for alternate evenings[4].

---

(1) Masudi, VIII, 102. Ma'mun once enjoyed himself with his companions by suggesting that each should cook a special dish (Sabusti, Berlin, 80 a).

(2) *Fihrist*, 61.

(3) As-Suli, *Auraq*, Paris, 4836, II ff.

(4) Ibid., 143 ff.

Suli particularly praises Ar-Radhi for constantly inviting later several companions at a time to his drinking-parties, whereas the earlier Caliphs had drinks provided only for two at a time, one for himself and one for a companion[1]. Large drinking-bowls full of wine and cups with water were placed before the guests to enable them to take as much as they pleased ; whereas in earlier times cup-bearers handed round the cup. Even Suli tells us of drinking-competitions at which the winner showed his empty bumper to the Caliph. This practice however became in the end too nauseating for him and he likened them to the urine-flasks shown to the physician[2].

Particular rulers are said to have had special signs of their own for indicating the dissolution of these convivial gatherings. Yazdajerd said : "The night is advancing." Shapur: " 'Tis enough, O men." 'Omar : "'Tis time to pray." 'Abdul Malik : "If you please." Rashid : "Subhan Allah." ; and Wathiq passed his hand over his temples[3].

The court-establishment consumed large sums. For the kitchen and bakery 10,000 dinars (100,000 marks) were alloted per month. Merely for musk a monthly sum of 300 dinars was paid into the kitchen though the Caliph did not care much for it in his food, and at the most had but a little in his biscuits[4]. In addition to these sums, the following payments are shown per month : 120 dinars for water-carriers, 200 dinars for candles and oil, 30 dinars for medicine, 3,000 dinars for incense, baths, liveries, arms, saddles and carpets[5].

---

(1) For instance Al-Wathiq (227-233/841-847) had a day in the week for each companion.

(2) As-Suli. *Auraq*, Paris, 4836, 71.

(3) *Muh. al-Udaba*, 1, 121.

(4) Wuz, 351.

(5) Wuz., 16-18.

In the *Harem* of Khumarwaihi food said to be so plentiful that the cooks sold it in the streets. "He who had a guest, went to the gate of the *Harem*, and found expensive food for sale at a small price—food such as could not be found elsewhere[1]."

When the Caliph Qahir wanted seriously to economise he sanctioned only one dinar for fruit for his table,—formerly the amount spent was 30 dinars a day. As for courses at meals they were limited to twelve, and instead of 30 sweet-dishes the Caliph ordered only so much as was enough for him[2]. The evil day had already come. In 325/937 the number of chamberlains was reduced from 500 to 60[3]. In 334/945 Muizz-ud-Dawlah took the control of the finances completely away from the Caliph and only allowed him 2,000 dirhams for his daily expenses[4]; less than half the amount he spent before[5]. Two years later, instead of the pension, he assigned to him lands chiefly at Basrah, which, along with his private means, made up a total of about 200,000 dinars a year. In course of time, however, the Caliph's income dwindled to 50,000, about half a million marks per year[6]. Moreover since 334/945, at the death or deposition of a Caliph, the practice of plundering the palace until nothing was left came into vogue[7]. In 381/991, on the deposition of Tai, the populace for the first time plundered the palace in the fullest sense of the term and took away

---

(1) Maqrizi, *Khitat*, 1,316.

(2) *Arib*, 183.

(3) Misk, V, 541.

(4) Misk, V, 125 ; Ibn al-Jauzi, 78 b.

(5) Both in 280/893 and 330/941 the court-expenses were reckoned at 5,000 dirhams per day.

(6) Ibn al-Jauzi, 78 b.

(7) Yahya 86 a ; Misk V, 124. Already at the death of Radhi the Sultan took away the carpets and untensils that pleased him [Ibn al-Athir, VIII, 176. At the depostion of the Wazirs in 299/911 and 318/930 their houses were plundered. Wuz, 29 ; Ibn al-Jauzi, fol. 40 a].

marble, lead, teak-wood and lattices[1]. On the death of a Pope the Roman people proceeded likewise. We notice at this time, a remarkable similarity between the Pope and the Caliph inasmuch as the Caliph now assumes more and more the role of a Pope,—namely, the premiership of the entire Muslim church. The disappearance of the last traces of the Babylonian Church-state uncommonly fortified his spiritual character.

When in 423/1032 the Sultan with three courtiers rowed in a boat in the garden of the Caliph's palace and amused himself under a tree with music and wine, the Caliph on hearing of it sent two Qadhis and two chamberlains to urge upon him the impropriety of such conduct at that place, whereupon the Sultan apologised[2].

Even in these later times the role of the Caliph is very simple and unecclesiastical as compared with that of the Byzantine Emperor, who is greeted in the circus as a second David, and a second St. Paul, and revered as High Priest, and whose day, as is shown by the Book *De-Ceremoniis,* was spent between churches, altars, and pictures of saints.

(1) Ibn al Jauzi, fol. 130 b; Ibn al-Athir, IX, 56.

(2) Ibn al-Jauzi, fol. 185 a/b. (In this story the Caliph takes upon himself the task of reproving the Sultan for debauchery in the Caliph's garden. This implies that his garden was sacred, and that the Caliph had the right to reprove the Sultan for immorality. Prof. Margoliouth. Tr.).

X. THE NOBILITY

The Arabs said : 'Ashraf un-nasab', *i.e.*, nobility lies in blood. Above everything else the aristocrat should be brave and generous[1]. Too calculating a nature was deemed unaristocratic ; the aristocrat should be prudent, but must feign improvidence[2]. Unlike that of a clerk which is small[3], his head should be big[4]. He should have a thick growth of hair on the forehead, a high nose, a broad-cornered mouth[5]. He should have a broad breast and shoulders, a long forearm and long fingers[6], but not a round face. Unaristocratic was affectation in dress or in gait. They said : A Sayyid may make up his turban as he pleases[7]. Under the 'Abbasids mankind was divided by a courtier into four classes :—

(1) The ruler, whom merit has placed in the foremost rank ;

(2) The Wazir, distinguished by wisdom and discrimination,

(3) The high-placed ones, whom wealth has raised aloft ;

---

(1) In this connection, see Goldziher's *Muruwwa und Din* in his *Muh. Studien,* Tr.

(2) Ibn Qutaiba, *Uyun el-Akhbar*, 271, ed. Brockelmann.

(3) *Ibid.*, 270.

(4) Qalqashandi, Subh-el-Asha, 43.

(5) The latter also is the chief characteristic of a noble horse.

(6) The chief of the Jews was so aristocratic that when he was standing erect, his fingers touched the knee. Those of the Mehdi of the African Senusiyyah even touched the earth in such a posture. (Hartmann, AFR. 1, 266.)

(7) *Kit. anba nugha el-abna* of Zafar al-Makki (565/1170) Ms. Berlin, fol. 16b, f.

(4) The middle class (*ausat*) who were attached to the other three classes by their culture.

The rest of mankind were described as mere scum, a marshy brook and lower animals who knew of nothing save food and sleep[1].

Thus the aristocrat made money and achieved political successes—two very common things then. The disregard of blood, particulary on the mother's side, went so far that all the Caliphs, since the 3rd/9th and 4th/10th centuries, were sons of Turkish or Greek slave-girls ; nay at the beginning of the 3rd/9th century even the son of a black slave-girl nearly succeeded to the Caliphate[2]. And yet Islam established an aristocarcy of blood which survives even today. At the head of this aristocracy stood the kinsmen of the Prophet' or 'Banu Hashim ;' 'members of the House of the Prophet' or 'People of the House.' As kinsmen of the Prophet they drew a salary from the Government, and with their entire suite were exempt from the Poor-tax (Sadaqah)[3]. Nay, they had their own Court[4].The Naqib (Marshal), appointed by the Caliph, was their judge.Not only at Baghdad, but in very large town, such an one was appointed. At Wasit, Kufah, Basrah and Ahwas he was called 'marshal of the 'Alids'[5]. About 351/961 Ibn Tabataba was the marshal of the Egyptian 'Alids[6]. Even under the Fatimids the marshal of the 'Alids was a notable dignitary of the Court[7]. The letter of appointment of the Baghdadian marshal of the Talibids (354/965) has come down to us. It is apparent

(1) Ibn al-Faqih, Bibl. Geog. V, 1,

(2) Ibrahim, son of Al-Mahdi, by a black slave girl, was absolutely black, corpulent and coarse. He, on that account, was called the 'dragon' (*Guruli matali el-budur* 1, 13).

(3) Jahiz, Opus, 7.

(4) Mawardi, ed. Enger, 165.

(5) Ibn al-Jauzi, 115 a.

(6) Ibn Sa'id, ed. Tallquist, 49.

(7) Musabbihi, *apud* Becker, *Beitrage*, 1. 33.

from it that even complaints of ordinary Muslims against a Talibid were heard by this officer[1].

Until the 4th/10th century the two opposing branches of the Prophet's family—the Abbasids who succeeded to power and the Talibids who suffered—were under one and the same Naqib (Marshal)[2]. But at the end of the century each had his own chief, and that indeed because the 'Abbasids had declined, while the other had risen in power and would no longer endure tutelage. The conditions thus called into being were a fore-shadowing of the present state of things.

Both the 'Alids and the 'Abbasids were addressed as Sharif[3]. It appears from *Arib*[4] that the 'Alids had no speical distinguishing signs of their own. The green turban appears as their mark quite late in order of time,—not indeed till the 8th/14th century[5].

To the descendants of the Prophet residing at Baghdad, but nowhere else, one dinar a month was doled out under Mu'tamid (256-279/870-892)[6], but under his successor it was cut down to ¼th of a dinar per month. 4,000 such pensioners are said to have been at Baghdad at that time, and this fits in with the item in the Budget, *viz.*, 1,000 dinars per month under this head[7]. In 209/824 they assert the number of the 'Abbasids to be 33,000[8]. Jahiz writing about the same time, fixes the 'Alid strength at 2,300[9].

(1) *Rasa'il* of Sabi, Ba'abda, 153.
(2) *Arib*, 47.
(3) For the 'Alids, At-Tanukhi ; Al-Faraj, II, 43 ; Yaqut, *Irshad* 1, 256, for the Hashimids.
(4) p. 49.
(5) The green colour as the 'Alid colour was fixed for the first time by the Egyptian Sultan Sha'ban-Ibn Hussain (d. 778/1376).
(6) That is to say about 10 marks.
(7) Wuz, 20.
(8) Tabari, III, 969 ; *Kit. al-'Uyun* 351.
(9) *Fusul*, London, fol. 207a.

The chiefs of the Hashimids (Mashaikh) drew special pay, which is shown in the Budget along with the pay of the preachers at Baghdad : 600 dinars in all[1]. Even the 'Abbasid princes (*Aulad al-Khulafa*) received a special, but not a very handsome, pension. Al-Mu'tadid (279-289/892-902) allowed to the children of his grandfather—princes and princesses—a special increment of 1,000 dinars between them; to his own brothers and sisters 500 dinars a month between them ; whereas to the rest of the relatives only 500 dinars per month between them[2]. Basrah, the only non-Shite court of importance next to Baghdad, was the centre of this discontented band. In the eighties of this century three persons, one of them being a descendant of the Caliph Mahdi, another of Ma'mun and another of Wathiq, found themselves there[3].

The Wathiqi had been a preacher at Nisibis, but being involved in an intrigue, was dismissed from his post. On dismissal he came to Baghdad. Thence he proceeded to Khorasan where he tried in vain for an appointment as post-master or secular judge. Disappointed, he went over to the Turks, gave himself out as the crown-prince of Baghdad, succeeded in bringing about the explusion of the Samanids and the establishment of his own rule at Bukhara. The Caliph in consequence sent a public letter on his account to the north[4]. After the failure of his plan there he secretly resided again at Baghdad, but to escape the designs of the Caliph he once more went over to the Turks. He roamed all over the East and was eventually stranded at the court of Mahmud of Ghazni[5], who incarcerated him in a castle, where he died. The Ma'muni, on the other hand, a poet, wanted to conquer

(1) Wuz, 20.

(2) Wuz, 20.

(3) *Yatimah*, IV, 37, 112.

(4) The public letter, says Prof. Margoliouth, was a refutation of the man's claim, as appears from Hilal, 421. Tr.

(5) Wuz, 421 ff ; *Yatimah*, IV, 112 ff ; Ibn al-Athir, IX, 117 f.

Baghdad with the help of the Samanid troops and set himself up as Caliph. He died soon, however, before he was forty[1]. With the help of the ever-effective belief in the Madhi, a son of al-Mustakfi (deposed 334/945) tried in his fiftieth year to secure the empire for himself. His emissaries preached to those who "supported justice and resisted injustice" to fight the enemies of the Faith and to restore it to its original purity. In those troubulous days they found a large following even in the highest circles of Baghdad. They assured the Sunnites that the expected Madhi was an 'Abbasid, and the Shi'ites that he was an 'Alid. Even the general Sebuktagin went over to his side but when he, a Shi'ite, heard that it was an affair of the 'Abbasids he forsook the cause and suppressed the movement. The matter ended by the Caliph cutting off the nose of the pretender and his brother[2].

Apart from their pension the Hashimids were given posts out of which money was made with an easy conscience. The office of the leader of prayers in towns was mostly held by them[3]. The Imam of the first mosque of Baghdad, who died in 350/961, was a Hashamid, and so also at this time was the Imam of the Amr mosque at old Cairo[4]. And Hashimids also were the two chief judges appointed in 363/974 and 394/1004[5].

At the end of the century an 'Abbasid prince acted as a preacher at Nisibis[6]. The very lucrative position of the leadership of the annual pilgrim-caravan was always held by a Hashimid. For the first time since the rise of Islam a Talibid was given that post of honour in 204/849 and that because Ma'mun wanted to use the Alids against his brother.

(1) *Yatimah*, IV, 94 ; Ibn al-Athir, IX, 71.
(2) Misk, VI, 315 ff.
(3) Ibn al-Jauzi, fol. 90 b.
(4) Supplement to Kinid, ed. Guest, 575.
(5) Ibn al-Jauzi, 105 b, 141 b.
(6) Wuz, 421.

For three years he held that post, when it once more reverted to the Hashimids, who retained it till 336/947[1]. It then passed into the hands of the 'Alids, who appointed 'Alids as their representatives and deputies[2]. In all pious gifts the kinsmen of the Prophet came in first for their share. At the time of Ahmad ibn Tulun, the Egyptian Ibn ad-Dajah gave 2,000 dinars to a Tailbid ; other magnates displayed similar munificence[3]. The Wazir 'Ali Ibn 'Isa, early in the 4th/10th century, made an annual grant of 40,000 dinars for the benefit of the 'Alids, 'Abbasids, descendants of the Ansar and Muhajerun, and the two holy towns[4]. In one single day the mother of the Caliph Al-M'uti gave to the 'Abbasids and the 'Alids over 30,000 dinars[5]. In one of his letter Abu'l A'ala apologises for having sent so little to an 'Alid[6]. Proverbial was the 'Alid who 'takes but does not give[7]."

How small a pittance was the monthly dole of ¼ dinar may be inferred from the fact that both the 'Alids and the 'Abbasids lived in grovelling poverty !

We even come across a Hashimid as a petty spy. In the great famine of 334/945 Hashimids were sentenced to death for eating their children[8]. At the residence of the Wazir As-Sahib in North Persia an 'Alid presented himself as an itinerant story teller[9]. The poet Ibn al-Hajj (d. 391/1001) speaks of an ill-famed Hashimid female singer[10]. While the

(1) Mas'udi, IX, 69.
(2) Ibn al-Jauzi Berlin, fol. 129b ; Ibn al-Athir, IX, 54. The leadership of the Egyptian pilgrimage continued in the hands of the Hashimids. Supplement to Kinid, 475.
(3) Yaqut, *Irshad*, II, 159.
(4) Wuz, 322.
(5) Ibn al-Jauzi, 74 a.
(6) *Rasa'il*, ed. Margoliouth 35.
(7) *Kit. al-faragh*.
(8) Yahya ibn Sa'id, fol. 87 a.
(9) *Muh al-udaba*, II 295.
(10) Tallquist, 48.

Egyptian viceroy Kafur was out riding a member of his staff violently pushed back a beggar-woman. For this the Governor wanted to cut the delinquent's hands off but the woman interceded on his behalf. This kindly office greatly amazed Kafur who asked for her name, taking her to be a woman of noble descent. She professed to be an 'Alid. Kafur was desconcerted and observed : "The Devil maketh us forget these people." After that he sanctioned a great deal of alms for Alid women[1]. The "uncles of the Prophet" belonged to the quarrelsome strata of the metropolitan populace[2].

When in 306/918 there was a delay in the payment of their salary, a Hashimid crowd fell upon the Wazir, while he was coming out of his office, abused him, tore off his cloth and dragged him from his horse. The Caliph ordered some of these offenders to be wihpped, transporting the entire lot in chains to Basrah. There, in that condition, they were led through the town on donkeys. After this was done they were lodged in a house close to the prison. The Governor treated them well, and in secret even gave money to them. Moreover after 10 days arrived the order for their release[3].

With the growing strength of the Shi'ites in Baghdad the Abbasids, specially those residing at Basrah-Gate became more and more restive[4]. The energetic Wazir Al-Muhallabi (*circa* 350/961) was constrained to keep a number of the Abbasid leaders in custody in the small towns of Babylon, whence they were only released after the Wazir's death[5]. To end the eternal dispute between the Shi'ites and

(1) Wuz, 331.

(2) The immediately preceding anecdote deals with a brawl between members of the two Imperial families.

(3) *Arib*, 75.

(4) Ibn al-Athir, IX, 110.

(5) Wuz., 331.

the Sunnites at Baghdad, in which the fiery spirits on either side incited their adherents to take up arms, the general sent there to restore and maintain order had 'Alid and 'Abbasid tied together in pairs and drowned in the Tigris[1].

The time, longlooked for by the 'Alids, had at last come. Everywhere their power waxed, while that of the 'Abbasids waned. In Khorasan for instance Mukaddasi find many rich 'Alids, but not a single resident 'Abbasid there[2]. The 4th/10th century reveals conditions which obtain there today. The House of Muhammad is exclusively represented there by the 'Alids. All promoted and subserved their cause—the Karmathians and the Fatimids. In the Perisan mountains they founded an 'Alid Empire. After the middle of the century they conquered Mekka and, instead of Median, made Mekka the capital of the Holy Lands, and cunnighly managed to turn the fierce rivalry of Baghdad and Cairo to the advantage of the newly-established centre of the Shi'ite power.

Shi'ites were the new rulers in the East and the West, *viz.*, the Hamadanids and the Buwayyids. The increasing veneration of the Prophet even encircled his descendants with heightened splendour. When Kafur once was riding, the whip fell out of his hand ; a Sharif picked it up and handed it over to him. Verily, said Kaful, willingly would I die now ! What other ambition can I have after a son of the Prophet hands my whip to me. Shortly after this incident he died[3]. At the beginning of the 4th/10th century not only in the Shi'ite Tiberias could nothing be done without the help of the 'Alid chief there[4], but even the very impartial Ikhshịd, ruler of Egypt, had constantly about him two of these gentlemen : the Hasanid 'Abdullah b. Tabataba and the Hussainid Al-Hasan ibn Tahir, "who never left his side

(1) Wuz., 464 ; Ibn al-Jauzi, fol. 147.
(2) Muq, 323.
(3) Tallquist, 47.
(4) Snouck Hurgronje, Mekka, 1, 56 sqq.

but who were mutually hostile to each other.[1]" The latter negotiated and effected a peace with Saif-ud-Dawlah for him[2] and in 327/939, by his diplomacy, averted a Babylonian invasion[3]. The same year another 'Alid, by his influence with the Karmathians, secured a free and safe passage for the pilgrims which had been closed for 10 years[4]. In the Shi'ite houses of the Buwayyids and the Hamadanids they were the approved madiators in family disputes. Considering how lucrative this attitude of intermediaries was, it was inconvenient for them when they were ultimately compelled by the Baghdad Government to follow suit[5] as against the Fatimids, and repudiate these as no true Scions of 'Alid stock.

In the year 403/1012 an order of the Baghdadian Amir went forth to the officers which warmly recommended the claims of the 'Alids to them—a thing which had never happened before[6]. But simultaneously with this order the balck-official dress of the 'Abbasids was prescribed for the marshal of their nobility (Naqib), which no 'Alid had worn before. With this measure the earlier, stronger 'Abbasid cousin declared himself defeated[7].

---

(1) Tallquist, 18.

(2) Tallquist, 42.

(3) Tallquist, 25.

(4) Ibn al-Jauzi, fol. 60a.

(5) 'Follow suit' means here taking the definite line which the Government had adopted. Prof. Margoliuth. Tr.

(6) Diwan of Rida, 210. ["This is based on an error. The heading of the poem in the Diwan of Radi (as his name should be spelt) merely states that Radi was made overseer of the Alawids throughout the empire : previously there had been local *Nuqaba* . Moreover it is not true that this was the first occasion on which an 'Alawid wore "the black robe" : according to Radi's Diwan (p. 541) he appeared in such a robe at the Caliph's court in 382. Wearing balck meant acknowledging the Caliph's authority, and in the order of 382 Radi states emphatically that only the 'Abbasids have the right of succession to the Prophet." I am indebted to Prof. Margoliouth for this note. Tr.].

(7) Ibn al-Jauzi, fol. 158b : Ibn al-Athir, IX, 170.

The descendants of the first three Caliphs now play no distinguished part. When a body of Qur'an-readers complained against Al-Omari, the Qadhi of Egypt, to the Caliph Harun, the latter enquired whether there was still a descendant of 'Omar I employed in the *Diwan*. But when they found none, he sent the complainats away[1]. His successor Bakri, appointed by Amin, came so poor to Egypt and had such bad luck with his land that he could not pay the land-tax. The officer who dealt with his case cried out : Is the son of the companion of our Prophet and his successors to be so harassed on this account ? His debt is my debt,—I shall pay it year by year[2]. In modern Egypt, on the other hand, along with the descendants of the Prophet those of Abu Bakr and 'Omar constitute the Muslim airstocracy.

Ever since the beginning of the XIXth century the Bakris or the Siddiqis especially have been in possession of lucrative clerical offices there[3].

An 'Othmani, a descendant of the Caliph 'Othman, went about begging in all the streets of Nisibis about the year 400/1009 to the great discredit of his pious ancestor. Even he, such as he was, was called Sharif[4]. Such is the main outline of the ecclesiastical aristocracy[5] of Islam.

The pre-Islamite nobility had maintained themselves most tenaciously in the stronghold of feudalism, to wit, in the forests, mountains and castles of Fars. There the old

---

(1) Kindi 415. In 388/998 died the savant Al-Khattabi, a descendant of Zaid ibn Al-Khattab brother of 'Omar I (Yaqut, *Irshad,* II, 81).

(2) Kindi, 416.

(3) Hartmann, MSOS, 1909, 81.

(4) *Yatimah*, IV, *293 f.*

(5) To these also belonged the descendants of the first 'Helpers' of the Prophet. They too had a marshal (Naqib) at Baghdad and were provided with gifts from the pious. Ibn al-Jauzi, 112a : *Kit. al-fragh,* II, 2.

families were honoured. There they inherited Government offices from sire to son from the earliest to the present time[1]. Chivalrous conduct was held in high esteem among them. Purity from foul talk, abstinence from intercoure with loose women, striving after the highest attainable elegance at home, in dress, and at table[2] was their dominant note. Of the Omayyad nobility only the Mahalibah, descendants of Muhallab ibn Abi Safra, knew how to maintain their position and prestige. Basrah was their seat where they lived in lordly mansions[3]. In the great slave insurrection of 3rd/9th century one of these played a conspicuous role in the hope that the 'Abbasid rule might end[4] ; another, about the middle of the 4th/10th century, became the Wazir of 'Adad-ud-Dawlah.

Even the Qadhi family of the Banu Abi'l-shawarib pretended to be related to the Omayyads, and therefore to the rulers of Cordova and those of Multan[5].

The free 'Abbasid armed nobility (the *abna-ud-Dawlah*), who had come with the 'Abbasids from Khorasan, were still in power in the 3rd/9th century and were distinguished by their splendid horses and equipment. In the 4th/10th century they were supplanted by slaves, or emancipated knights, by Turks and Persians.

Even the last descendants of the Tahirids—who in the 3rd/9th century ranked next to the reigning dynasty—maintained at the close of the 4th/10th century a miserable existence at the Court of Bokhara.

But they did not lack imagination[6]. In the entire north,

---

(1) Ibn Haukal, 207.

(2) Thalibi, *Kit. al-Mirwah*, 129f.

(3) *Kit. al-Uyun*. IV, 6 b.

(4) Mas'udi, 1. 377.

(5) See the poems on them in *Kit. al-'Uyun*. IV, 70a ; Jahiz. *Opuscula*. 15 See Prof. M, *Arab Historians*, p. 139.

(6) *Yatimah*, IV. 7 ff. 11

right up to the country of the Turks, they were called by the Roman-Byzantine appellation of 'Patricians' (Batariqa)[1].

Of the great families of his time Ibn Rosteh (end of the 3rd/9th century) has some interesting tales to tell. The family of Ibn Ashath is said to have descended from a Persian shoe-maker. They owed their wealth to the childless Jew whom the shoe-maker's aunt had wedded. The Mahallibids sprang from a Persian weaver. The House of Khalid ibn Safwan went back to a peasant woman of Hira, who while pregnant fell into Arab hands. The family of Al-Jahm originated from a run-away slave who falsely claimed Qoraishite nobility, and that of the opulent and princely Abu Dulaf from the Christian bankers of Hira. The Court-marshal Al-Rabi, founder of an influential line of officials, is said to have been a worthless, illegitimate son of an unchaste slave-girl[2].

(1) They are so addressed by a poet of Turkistan, *Yatimah*, IV, 81.
(2) Ibn Rosteh, 207 f.

XI. THE SLAVES

All owned slaves : Muslims, Christians, and Jews. Only the Christian Chruch, now and then, felt conscience stricken and pointed out that "in Christ there is neither slave nor free[1]. It strove, at least, to ban slave-trade among its congregation[2]. It was particularly astonishing to Muslims that slave-girls in Christian and Jewish homes were not sexually at the disposal of their masters[3]. The Law or Oriental Christianity regarded sexual relations of the master with his slave-girls as pure fornication, punishable with excommunication from the church[4]. Where such a thing happened the lady of the house was to remove the delinquent by sale. Were the slave-girl to bear a child to her Christian master, the child was to be brought up as a slave to the entire disgrace of the fornicating parent. The caliph Mansur once sent three beautiful Greek slave-girls and 3,000 gold pieces to the physician Georges. The physician accepted the money, but sent the girls back with a message that "with such I shall not live in the house, for to us, Christians, only one wife is allowed, and I have one in Belafet." For this the Caliph praised and admired him[5].

(1) For instance *Syr, Rechtsb.* 2, 161. The Ethiopian thinker, Zar'a Ya'qub (Circa 1600 A.D.), in his criticism of Islam and Christianity, reproaches the former for destroying the equality and brotherhood of man by sanctioning in slave-trade since all mankind address God as "father" (*Philosophi abessini* ed. Littman, p. 11 of the translation.).

(2) *Syr, Rechtsb*, 2 165. In Islam, too, there is a tradition of the Prophet: 'The worst of humanity is he who sell men.' Al-Qummi, *Kit. al-Ilal* Berlin, fol. 206 (b).

(3) *Le Livre de la creation*, ed, Huart, IV, 38 and 46 of the translation.

(4) Sachau, *Rechtsb*, 2, 161.

(5) Elias Nisibensis (about 400 of the Hegira) in the *Corpus Scriptorum Orientalium Christianorum*, 179.

On the other hand a child, born of a Muslim from his slave-girl, became immediately free[1]. The mother, too, could neither be alienated nor sold and, indeed, after the death of the master, became free. It is curious to note that even several masters could, at one and the same time, possess and co-habit with a slave girl[2].

While in the Byzantine Empire it was forbidden to people of other faiths to hold Christian slaves[3] (even the Christian Church in the Islamic Empire forbade Christians to sell Christian salves to non-Christians on pain of ex-communication[4]) the Muslim Law permitted Christians and Jews to own Muslim slaves[5].

In the 4th/10th century, Egypt, South Arabia, and North Africa, were the chief markets for black slaves. Their Caravans brought gold and slaves from the south. About the middle of the 2nd/8th century 200 dirhams was the average price of a slave[6]. The Abyssinian Kafur, later ruler of Egypt, is said to have been purchased for 18 dinars in 312/924; a very small price considering he was a eunuch[7]. In 'Oman they paid between 250-300 makrs for a good negro slave[8]. About 300/912 a sweetly pretty girl" fetched 150 dinars (1,500 marks)[9]. When the Wazir As-Sahib (Ibn Abbad) purchased a Nubian male slave, for 400 dinars[10], the price

---

(1) At least the first child. On the position of subsequent children the schools differed. The Hanafite view in d'Ohssen, VI, 11-12. The Shafiite view in Sachau, *Muh. Recht*; 174.

(2) al-Kindi, 338.

(3) Cod. Just: C.I. Tit. 9 and 10.

(4) Sachau, *Recktsbucher*, 2, 109, 147.

(5) Sachau, *Muh Recht*, 173.

(6) Aghani, III. 55.

(7) About 180 marks, Wustenfeld *Die Statthalter von Agypten*, IV, 47.

(8) *'Aj'aib el-Hind*, 52. For an ordinary slave in the Byzantine Empire they then paid 240 marks. Vogt, Basile 1,383.

(9) *Guruli Matali elbudur*, 1, 196.

(10) Ibn al-Wardi, 46.

was considered a trifle excessive ; for even pretty dark-coloured Nubian girl, the most highly prized as concubines, could be had for 300 dinars[1].

The relative sterility of the Negro-women in the Northern countries accounts for the Muslim world not being flooded with imported negroes and their bastards[2].

Like the negro-servant today the black house-slave was chiefly employed as door-keeper[3]. In a society which, above everything else, valued good poetry and fine music, artistically talented and trained boys and girls would inevitably be in great demand. A famous musician, at the time of Al-Rashid, had often as many as eighty slave girls in training[4]. And for such girls so trained the price was from 10 to 20,000 marks[5]. Some of the poorer artists gave lessons at the houses of great slave-dealers[6]. Of the professional female singers in the Capital in 306/918 there were very few who were not slaves[7]. As with us, famous singers and female artists had their fancy prices. About 300/912 a female singer was sold in an aristocratic circle for 13,000 dinars (130,000 marks), the broker making 1,000 dinars[8]. In 326/937 Ibn Raiq—ruler of Mesopotamia—paid 1,400 dinars for a female singer, a sum regarded as extravagant by the people[9].

As regards prices, the white slaves—aristocracy of the slaves—stood on quite a different footing. A good-looking,

---

(1) Idrsi, Ed. Dozy, 13.
(2) Jahiz, *Opusc*, 78.
(3) Report of a Chinese in the XIIIth century A.D. in Fr. Hirth : *Die Lander des Islam nach Chinesischen Quellen*, 55.
(4) *Aghani*, V, 6.
(5) Michael Syrrus, ed. Chabot, 514 where Mahdi is confounded with Ibrahim al-Mausili.
(6) *Aghani*, XXII, 43.
(7) Aba'l-Qasim, ed. Mez.
(8) Ibn al-Jauzi, fol. 88a.
(9) Al-Suli, *Auraq*, 142.

but untrained, white slave-girl fetched 1,000 dinars or more[1]. To Khwarezmi, 10,000 dinars were offered for a slave-girl[2]. When in 4th/10th Century, by reason of reverses on the western frontier, the one source of supply—Byzantium and Armenia—was closed, the price of the white slaves went up[3]. For the citizens and the clients of the Empire could not be made slaves accoridng to Law ; particularly not, as in other countries, for commission of crimes. Even Muslim parents could not sell their children ; as the Jewish father might sell his daughters who were under age[4]. Even when in the 3rd/9th century the Egyptian Christians were taken prisoners in an open rebellion and were sold as slaves at Damascus, the procedure was regarded as unlawful and provoked fierce resentment.

On the other hand, for those sects which claimed Islam as their monopoly, other Muslims stood outside the pale of Law. In the century of the Karmathians, this became a matter of great importance, for the theory permitted them to make their captives slaves. And thus many peaceful citizens in Arabia, Syria and Babylon, suddenly found themselves robbed of their freedom. In an attack on the pilgrim-caravan of the year 312/924 about 2,000 men and 500 women were marched off as slaves to the Karmathian capital. Among the victims was the philologer al-Azhari (d. 370/980) who was assigned as booty to certain Beduin adventurers. For two years he roamed about as a slave with them in the desert. This captivity enabled him to gather together rich material for his 'Dictionary'[5].

---

(1) Istakhri, 45.

(2) *Yatimah*, IV, 151.

(3) Muk, 242 [See Roberts, *Social Laws of the Qur'an* pp. 55-56. For fuller notes on the subject see at the end of the Chapter. Tr.]

(4) Krausz, *Talmud, Arch*, II, 84 ; *Le Livre de la creation*, ed. Huart, p. 38 of the translation. The sale of a Muslim Circassian girl is forbidden by the Canon Law to this day.

(5) His own account of the matter. Yaqut, *Irshad*, vi, 299.

In the rest of the empire the supply of white slaves was confined to Turks and members of that inexhaustible race which has given the caste its European name, "the slav(e)s." The latter was rated higher than the former as merchandise. Says Khwarezmi[1] : We take to Turks when no other slaves are available. The chief article of export from Bulgar—capital of the Volga Bulgarians—was slaves who were thence taken to the Oxus[2]. Samarqand was the greatest slave-market noted for the supply of the best white slaves, and depending like Geneva or Lausanne of our time on its educational industry[3]. The second channel of import for slaves of Slavic nationalities lay through Germany to Spain and the Mediterranean harbours of Provence and Italy[4]. The slave-dealers in European were almost all Jews. The slaves came almost exclusively from Eastern Europe as is the case today with the "white slave traffic[5]." With the slave-trade there is clearly connected the settlement of Jews in the East Saxon towns of Magdeburg and Merseburg (Caro, *Wirthschaftageschichte der Juden*, 1,191). In the transport of slaves they were well-fleeced at any rate by the Germans : the Coblenz customs-regulation exacted four dinars for every slave (Caro, 1,192) and the Bishop of Chur levied two dinars per head at the Wallenstadti Customs-House (Schaube, 93).

---

(1) *Yatimah*, IV, 116.

(2) *Muk*, 395.

(3) Ibn Haukal, 368.

(4) The prohibition of the Venetian Doge in 960 to board slaves on a steamer referred only to Christian slaves (Schaube, *Handels-gesch. der rom. Volker*. 23). The treaty of Venice with the Emperor Otto the Great [967 A.D.] forbids only Christians of the royal territory to buy or sell slaves [Ibid 6]. Even much later in Genoa slave-delarers were a striking phenomenon (Ibid, 104).

(5) Bishop Agobard of Lyon [9th century A.D.] mentions in his book *de insolentia Judaeorum* some instances of Jews stealing or even purchasing Frankish Christian children for sale to Spanish Muslims. I have taken this passage from Baudissin's *Euloigus und Alvar* Leipzig, 1872, p. 77.

Finally the third route for the slave-trade likewise led from the western Slave countries, then at war with Germany and consequently productive of human merchandise, to the East over Prague. Poland and Russia—a route followed by Rabbi Petachja in the 6th/12th century. In the 4th/14th century Prague was the starting-point, being a centre of the then slave-trade. Saint Adalbert gave up his bishopric in 989 A.D. because he could not redeem all the Christians whom a Jewish dealer had purchased[1].

In the towns they had a slave-market (*Suq erraqiq*) in charge of a speçial officer. We possess detailed information about a slave-market built at Samarra in the 3rd/9th century. It consisted of a quadrangle intersected with alleys. The houses contained lower and upper rooms and stalls for slaves[2]. It was a degrading punishment for a slave of the better class to be sold in the market instead of at a private house or through a prominent dealer[3]. The reputation enjoyed by slave-dealers was not unlike that of the horse-dealers of today. An Egyptian Governor was denounced from the pulpit as "a mendacious slave-dealer.[4]" "How many brown girls, of impure colouring have been sold as gold blonde ! How many decrepit ones as sound ! How many stodgy ones as slim and slender ! They paint blue eyes black, yellow cheeks red, make emaciated faces chubby, remove the hair from the cheek, make light hair deep black, convert the straight into curly, thin into well-rounded arms, efface small-pox marks, warts, moles and pimples. One should not buy slaves in markets held on festival or similar days. How often then has a boy been mistakenly purchased for a girl ! We have heard a slave-dealer say : "A quarter of a dirham of Henna increases the value of a girl by 100

(1) Caro, 1, 191 ff.
(2) Yaqubi, *Geography*, 259.
(3) Misk, VI, 391.
(4) Kindi, 110.

dirhams." They made the hair appear longer by tying on to the ends similarly coloured hairs. Bad odour from the nose was remedied by scents and teeth were whitened by potash and sugar or charcoal and powdered salt.

The dealers advised the girls to make themselves pleasant to the old and bashful, but to be reserved and distant with the young to inflame their passion and to capture their hearts. They coloured the finger tips of a white-girl red ; of a black one red and yellow-gold ; thus imitating nature which works with flowers through opposites."

These statements come from an Introduction by the well-known Christian physician Ibn Botlan (first half of the 5th/11th century) to the art of making good purchases of slaves. This little book combines with theory a good deal of ancient practical experiences in the traffic of slaves.

"Indian women are meek and mild but they rapidly fade away. They are excellent breeders of children. They have one advantage over other women : It is said : 'On divorce they become virgins again.' The men are good house-managers and experts in fine handicrafts, but they are apt to die from apoplexy at an early age. They are mostly brought from Qandahar. The women of Sind are noted for slim waist and long hair. The Medinite woman combines suavity and grace with coquetry and humour. She is neither jealous nor bad-tempered nor quarrelsome. She makes an excellent songstress. The Mekkan women is delicate, has small ankles and wrists and languishing eyes. The Taifite, gold-brown and slim, is full of fun and levity but is lacking in fecundity and is liable to die at child-birth. On the other hand, the Berber woman is unrivalled for breeding. Pliant to a degree, she accommodates herself to every kind of work."

"According to the broker, Abu 'Othman, the ideal slave is a Berber girl who is exported out of her country at the age of nine, who spends three years at Medinah and three at Mekka and at sixteen comes to Mesopotamia to be trained in elegant accomplishments. And, thus, when sold at twenty-five, she unites, with her fine racial excellences, the coquetry of the Medinite, the delicacy of the Mekkan, and the culture of the Mesopotamian woman.

"At the markets negrosses were much in evidence ; the darker the uglier and the more pointed their teeth. They are not up to much. They are fickle and careless. Dancing and beating time are engrained in their nature. They say : were the negro to fall from heaven to the earth he would beat time in falling[1]. They have the whitest teeth and this because they have much saliva. Unpleasant is the smell emitted from their armpits and coarse is their skin.

"The Abyssinian woman, on the other hand, is weak and flabby and frequently suffers from consumption. She is ill-suited for song and dance and languishes in a foreign country. She is reliable and has a strong character in a feeble body. The women of Bujjah (between Abyssinia and Nubia) have golden complexion, comely countenance, delicate skin, but an unlovely figure. They must be taken out of their country before circumcision, for often it is done so clumsily that the bones become visible. The men are brave but are prone to steal and so, they should not be trusted with money. And for this reason, precisely, they make bad house-managers. Of all the blacks, the Nubian woman is the most adaptable and cheerful. Egypt agrees with her, for as at home she drinks the Nile water there too. Elsewhere she is liable to the diseases of the blood.

"Fair skinned, the Turkish women are full of grace and

(1) The negro must always dance. Like the German when he has shaken off the work-day mood he feels an unconquerable passion to sing. The negro, similarly, on every occasion takes to his *Ngoma* K. Weulie, *Negerleben in Ostafrica*, 84.

animation. Their eyes are small but enticing[1]. They are thick-set and are inclined to be of short stature. There are very few tall women among them. They are prolific in breeding and their offspring are but rarely ugly. They are never bad riders. They are generous ; they are clean in their habits ; they cook well ; but they are unreliable.

"The Greek woman is of red-white complexion, has smooth hair and blue eyes. She is obedient and adaptable, well-meaning, faithful and trustworthy. The man are useful as house-managers, because of their love of order and disinclination to extravagance. Not infrequently they are well-trained in some fine handicraft.

"The Armenian is the worst of the white, as the negro is of the black. They are well-built, but have ugly feet. Chastity is unknown and theft is rampant among them. But they know not avarice. Coarse is their nature and coarse their speech. Let an Armenian slave be an hour without work and he will get into mischief. He only works under the threat of the cane or the stress of fear. When you find him lazy—it is simply because he delights in laziness and not because he does not feel equal to work. You must then take to the cane, chastise him and make him do what you want."

Even in the earlier centuries the practice had grown up of calling male and female slaves not "Slaves" but boys and girls. As always this too was alleged to be a command of the Prophet. Piety, and chivalry, moreover forbade corporal chastisement of slaves. "The worst man is he who takes his meal alone, rides without a saddle-cloth or beats his slaves" is a noble sentiment handed down by Abu'l Laith as-Samarqandi (d. 387/997) as a saying of the Prophet[2]. In the

(1) A poet of the 4th/10th century praises the Mongolian eyes of the Turkish boys in these words "too small for the eye-stick" (Yaqut, V, I 82).

(2) *Bustanal-'arifin* [*Tanbih al-ghafilina*]. Cairo (1304) P. 222.

4th/10th century even the language of the Qur'an "the faithful are brothers" is put forward in condemnation of one who beats his slaves. "Be a friend to thy slave and let a slave be a friend to thee" is put into rhyme[1].

In the description of an ideal Yamanite chief, about 500/ 1,106, it is expressly stated that he never beat a slave[2]. Even under the first Omayyads an Egyptian Qadhi grants freedom to a slave-girl who has been hurt by her mistress. She is made over to a pious family which assumes responsibility for her and her education[3].

The Christian Church of the East threatened with excommunication those who, directly or by refusal to maintain, forced their slave-girls into prostitution[4]. The Muslim brothel was mostly worked with slave-girls, as many stories show. The Law, indeed, ignores it as it professes to give no quarter to prostitution. As against this attitude of the Muslim Law the Chruch has preserved a trace of the spirit of ancient frankness.

The recommendation of Qur'an is to marry orphans, "pious servants and handmaidens[5]." Very beneficent, indeed, was the principle which enabled the slave to buy his freedom and, this particularly so, as both male and female slaves could engage independently in work. Mas'udi tells of a slave who was a tailor that he paid two dirhams daily to his master, keeping the rest of his earnings for himself[6]. Moreover it was regarded as a good and pious deed to grant, by will and testament, freedom to a certain number of one's slaves. Thus in the 3rd/9th century the

---

(1) Abu Hayyan at Tauhidi, *Riṣ. fi's-ṣaddaqa* (Const. 1301) p. 169.
(2) '*Umara al-yamani*, ed. Derenbourg, 9.
(3) Al-Kindi, 317.
(4) Sachau, *Mitteilungen des Orient,* Seminars, X, 2, p. 93.
(5) Qur'an, 24, 32.
(6) Mas'udi, IV, 344.

Caliph al-Mu'tasim directed the emancipation of 8,000 slaves on his death[1]. This same Caliph ordered, at the bloody storming of an Armenian fortress, that the families taken into slavery should not be separated or torn asunder[2].

The favourite salve-girl of a well-to-do merchant could proceed very far : she could show herself surrounded by female attendants fanning her[3].

On the night of the 15th of Ramadhan, the well-known preacher Ibn Samun spoke of sweets. A slave-girl of a rich merchant happened to be among the audience. The next evening a slave brought 500 biscuits to him, each containing a gold-piece. The preacher brought the gold pieces back to the merchant who told him that they had been sent with his consent[4]. Even the male slave could capture the master's heart. Such is the delight which the Oriental takes in one who combines beauty with intelligence. Thus does the poet Sa'id al-Khalidi praise one of his slaves[5] :—

" Not a slave but a son is he with whom God has blessed me,

" On his cheeks are roses, anemones, apples and pomegranates,

" All arranged in rows as in a garden brimming with beatury and bloom.

" Cheery, witty, unique, a fine sparkling gem—above all else,

" The holder and trustee of my purse.

Never do I miss anything

" He spends but, to my extravagance, he objects

(1) Mich. Syrus, 543.

(2) Mich. Syrus, 537.

(3) *Mughrib* of Ibn Sa'id, Tallquist, 15.

(4) Ibn al-Jauzi, Berlin, fol. 142 b.

(5) *Ma'alim et-Talkhis* Berlin, fol. 15 b.

" But, in spending, he never forgets the rule of the golden mean.

" Conversant, like myself, with *ars poetica* — he

" Strives ever and anon to improve himself therein.

" Connoisseur of poetry, he accurately assesses the worth of fine diction.

" He looks after my books, and under his care

" They all keep fine.

" He folds my clothes and keeps them like new.

" Among mankind he is the best of cooks

" When alone with him he lets the wine freely flow

" When I laught, happy he is ; when I rage, he is in fear and trembling.

" In literary circles this excellent slave became a proverb[1]."

The poet Kushagim of Aleppo, (d. 330/941), too, make a touching reference to his slave Bishr[2] : "Who will now, look after my inkpot, my books, and my cups as he did ? Who will fold and glue the paper ? Who, in cooking, will make the lean rich ? Regardless of the opinions of others— he always thought well of me. Loyal he ever remained even when the trusted one failed." Ma'arri does not omit to send his greetings to the slave Muqbil in a letter addressed to his master : "though black of hue, he is more to us than a Wazir whose love and loyalty cannot be relied upon[3]."

Highest was the rank of the armed slave who "bore in his knapsack not only the staff of the marshall" (Munis, Jauhar) but even the sceptre of the Sovereign (Kafur in Egypt, Subuktagin in Afghanistan). Already at the beginning of the 'Abbasid rule a Turkish slave was the governor of

(1) The 'alibi, *'Umad al-Mansub,* Z D M G, VI, 54. We learn there that he was also called Ressas.

(2) Diwan, 181 ff.

(3) *Letters*, ed. Mergoliouth, 41.

Egypt (162-164/779-781) of whom Mansur used to say :

"There is the man who fears me and not God[1]." Of pederasty we need not speak here.

The ideas were precisely the same here as in the Frankish empire where also *freedmen* attained the highest position of honour and, as such, received the homage and obedience of free-men. There, too, quondam slaves were especially generals, governors and royal guardians[2]. But in the East the slave rarely succeeded in permanently getting the better of the freeman as was the case with the European slave ; for the continuance of the institution of slavery stood in the way of the effacement of the distinction between the slave and the freeman[3].

On the whole, opinion was not very favourable to the slave. "When the slave is hungry he sleeps ; when satiated, he fornicates," ran a saying and the poet Mutanabbi sings : "Expect nothing good of a man over whose head the slave-dealer's hand has passed[4].'

And so thought Homer :—

"See, the ruling Zeus robs half of the manhood from him on whom dawns the day of servitude[5]."

But despite all favours of fortune, legal guarantees and the happy position of the modern Oriental domestic slave we must not paint in too roseate a colour the status of the Muslim slave in the Middle Ages.

In the 4th/10th century all the provinces indeed swarmed

---

(1) *Al-Kindi*, 123.
(2) Chr. Meyer, *Kulturgesch, Studien*, 91.
(3) This is not borne out by the facts Tr.
(4) Diwan, 546.
(5) Ody, XVII, 322.

with run-away slaves and the governors were specially advised[1] to arrest them, to put them in custody and, whenever possible, restore them to their owners.

The slave, turned out on the streets, by the Chief of the police (Nazuk), brought tears to his master's and a katib's eye when he begged to go back to him. The latter he made weep the more because of the dinar he had given him[2].

The run-away slaves are likely to have been mostly agricultural slaves. Even the army of the only dangerous slave insurrection of the century (3rd/9th century) consisted of the negroes who cleared out the salt-marshes at Basrah till they came to be productive soils. The salt-hills piled up by the negroes were mountains high. Then thousands of them were employed on the canals of Basrah[3].

(1) *Rasa'il* of Sabi Baabda.
(2) *Kit. al-Faragh*, 1, 54.
(3) *Kit. al-Uyun*, Berlin, IV, fol. 7 a.

NOTE

1. The Acquisition of Slaves

"The greatest of all divisions, that between freeman and slave, appears as soon as the barbaric warrior spares the life of his enemy when he has him down, and brings him home to drudge for hím and till the soil." The two main causes of slavery are want and war, and of these two it may be said that war is the more potent. And so with the Muhammadans, the acquisition of slaves was chiefly connected with warfare. Surah 47 (verse 4 f.) runs thus :—

"When ye encounter the unbelievers, strike off their heads, until ye have made a great slaughter among them ; then bind (the remainder) in fetters. (5) And After this give (the latter) either a free dismissal, or exact a ransom, until the war shall have laid down its arms."

The usual expression for female slaves in the Qur'an as we have already seen is, "that which your right hands possess."

It will be seen that there is nothing in the Qu'ran regarding the purchase of slaves.

According to Muhammadan Law, a slave is (i) a person taken captive in war, or carried off by force from a foreign hostile country, and being at the time of capture an unbeliever. (ii) The child of a female slave whose father is (a) a slave, or (b) is not the owner of the mother of the child, or (c) is the owner of the mother but, who does not acknowledge himself to be the father. (ii) A person acquired by purchase.

War and slavery, as one would expect, are also closely bound together in the Old Testament. In Num. chap. 31, the children of Israel are commanded to wage a war of vengeance against the Midianites. And in verse 7 ff, we read : —

"And they warred against Midian, as the Lord commanded Moses and they slew every male......(9) And the children of Israel took captive the women of Midian and their little ones", etc.

As far as strangers were concerned, the Israelites were allowed to buy, sell, or transfer their male and female slaves. So we read in Lev. 25, 4 ff :—

"And as for thy bondmen, and thy bondmaids, which thou shalt have ; of the nations that are round about you, of them shall ye buy bondmen and bondmaids. (45) Moreover of the children of the strangers that do sojourn among you, of them shall ye buy, and of their families that are with you, which they have begotten in your land ; and, they shall be your possession. (46) And ye shall make them an inheritance for your children after you, to hold for a possession ; of them shall ye take your bondmen for ever."

As among the Muhammadans slave consist partly of children of female slaves, and partly also of those that are acquired, so in the Old Testament we have the two expressions, "he that is born in the house" and "he that is bought with money." This shows us that among the Israelites as among the Muhammadans the number of slaves might be multiplied by birth. This, of course, is true of all peoples who trade in slaves ; since the slaves are the "possession" of their masters, their children also belong to them.

A further agreement between the Muhammadan and Old Testament laws consits in the limitation of slaves to foreigners. In Lev. 25, 39 ff., we read :—

"And if thy brother be waxen poor with thee, and sell himself unto thee ; thou shalt not make him to serve as a bondservant :— [40] as an hired servant, and as a sojourner, he shall be with thee ; he shall serve with thee unto the year of jubilee. [41] then shall he go out from thee, he and his children with him......[42]...... they shall not be sold as a slave is sold."

And so with the Muhammadans, who are strictly forbidden to take believers as slaves. The Muhammadan like the Israelite is to regard his fellow-believer as a brother.

Among the Babylonians, however, it was otherwise. Salves were recruited both from within and without. If a son, whether natural or adopted, sinned against his parents, his father could sell him as a slave. And likewise the husband had the right to dispose of a quarrelsome wife for money. Also the captured enemy naturally took the position of a slave ; especially did the white [light-complexioned] slave from Gutium and Shubarti at that time appear to be much desired.

II. The Treatment of Slaves

We have already seen how the Qur'an insists upon the just and humane treatment of the widow and orphan. And a like treatment is demanded also for slaves ; and that in accordance with the teaching that all men belong to God, [and] are therefore in a certain sense alike. So we read in Surah XVI, 73 :—

"God hath caused some to excel others in wordly possessions; yet those who thus excel do not give of their wealth unto those whom their right hands possess [their slaves], so that both may have an equal share thereof. Do they, therefore, deny the beneficence of God?" Also Sura 4, 40 :—

"Honour God, and associate none with him ; and show kindness unto parents, relations, orphans, the poor, the neighbour who is of kin to you, and he who is not, and to your trusted friend, and the traveller, and to those whom your right hands possess ; for God loveth not the arrogant and the proud."

In the year before his death, the Prophet, during a farewell pilgrimage at Mina, delivered an address to his followers, in which, among several other injunctions, we find the following : —

"And your slaves ! see that ye feed them with such food as ye eat yourselves, and clothe them with the like clothing as ye wear yourselves; and if they commit a fault which ye are inclined not to forgive, sell them ; for they are the servants of the Lord, and are not to be tormented."

If Muhammad could not abolish slavery, he has certainly done what he could to secure for slaves humane treatment. And if present-day Muhammedans disregard his injunctions, it is not fair to hold the Prophet hismelf responsible for it. Also, as already observed, it must not be forgotten that the legislation of the Qur'an was enacted for a seventh-century people. The position and treatment of slaves among the ancients in different lands naturally differed in accordance with the character of the various peoples, as well as the character of the slaves themselves, that is *e.g.*, whether they be foreign or home-born. And there was also a difference of treatment by the same peoples at different times. But if the enactments of the Prophet had only been faithfully observed by his followers, the treatment of slaves in Muhammadan countries would in all cases compare very favourably with what it was among the ancients.

Also the treatment of slaves, as enacted in Muhammadan law, taken all in all, can only be regarded as just. As we have already seen in the case of adultery, female slaves were held to be less guilty than free women, and consequently their punishment was to be less severe. And especially did the Law enact that they should be sufficiently supported, and not made to suffer.

On the other hand, it must be remembered that slaves, like any other property, were transferable. A Muhammadan has the right to sell his concubine, at least as long as he has no child by her. And even if he have a child by her, he can always deny the paternity (although this does not often happen). And in any case, the slave would have to continue to serve him, and be his concubine, that is unless he, when she has borne a son to him, presents her with her freedom by way of compensation.

III The Emancipation of Slaves

The founder of Islam not only insisted upon the humane treatment of slaves, but also that it should be made possible for them to secure their freedom, when they had shown themselves worthy of it by their conduct. Accordingly the emancipation of slaves among the Muhammadans must be regarded as a meritorious act. Surah XXIV, 33 reads :

"And those of your slaves who desire a deed of manumission, write it for them, if ye have a good opinion of them, and give them of the wealth of God, which he has given you."

The manner in which this emancipation is brought about in Muhammadan countries varies. Sometimes complete and immedate emancipation is granted to a slave gratuitously, or for a money compensation to be paid later. This is done by means of a written document, or by a verbal declaration in the presence of two witnesses, or again by the master presenting the slave with the certificate of sale obtained from the former master. Also, in conformity with the Command in Surah XXIV, 33, future emancipation is sometimes agreed upon to be granted on the fulfilment of certain conditions ; or more frequently, on the death of the owner. In the latter case the owner cannot sell the slave with whom the agreement has been made. Also, as the owner cannot alienate by will more than one-third of the whole property that he leaves, the Law ordains that, if the value of the said slave exceed that portion, the slave must obtain, and pay to the owner's heirs the additional sum. We shall see further on that for certain offences, such as manslaughter, etc., the freeing of a captive is reckoned as part-punishment.

It is not impossible that prophet to some extent at any rate, was acquained with the Old Testament enactments concerning the emancipation of slav :s (cf. Deut, 15 12 ; Ex. 21, 5 ff ; Jer. 34, 15, 17 ; Ezek, 46 (17). While, however, the Old Testament deals only with the emancipation of Israelite slaves who had become bondmen through debt Muhammad speaks of the emancipation of all slaves. Roberts, *Social Laws of the Qur'an* pp. 53, 60.

Also Doughty, *Arabia Deserta*, 1, 554 ; Lane *Modern Egyptians*, 168; Snouck Hurgronje, *Mekka* II, 18 ff.

XII. THE SAVANT

The 3rd/9th century developed those who had a knightly and courtly education into litteratures (*adib*) of the debased type of the modern journalists who will speak on every subject. This, naturally, constrained the savants to take to specialization : "He who would be a savant (*'alim*) should cultivate a particular branch of learning (*fann*) but he who would be a litterateur, let him range over the entire domain of learning".[1] A number of profane sciences grew out of the old belles-letters (*adab*). Hitherto only theology and philosophy possessed systematic method and scientific style, but now philosophy and history and even geography adopted their own method and style. No longer content with merely amassing copious and varied material, they become practical, they begin to systematize and they feel a sense of responsibility. How brief, now, become the prefaces to books ! And a striking illustration of this is the preface to the Fihrist composed in 377/987 : "God, help with thy Grace ! The Soul craves for facts and not for theories. And, precisely for this reason, we restrict ourselves to these words since the book itself will show—if God wills—what we have aimed at composing it. We seek God's help and blessings !"

A further change was effected by the separation of Jurisprudence from the Theology with the result that the learned world was rent in twain —the world of jurists and that of savants proper (*'ulama*). The vast mass of students, who worked for a living, attached themselves to jurists ; for only through the jurists, who represented Law and Ritual, was it possible to secure the posts of judges and preachers.

---

(1) Ibn Kutaibah, according to the *Mikhlat* of Amuli, 228.

Says Jahiz in a well-known passage : Our experience is that the study of traditions or the exegesis of the Qur'an up to fifty years will not qualify a man as 'Jurist' or render him eligible for a judicial post. These honours can only be attained by studying the writings of Abu Hanifa and such like and by committing to memory legal formulae for which a year or two are amply sufficient. One who does this is appointed after a short time, judge over a town, nay, over an entire, province.[1]

The advance of theology—rendered possible by jettisoning the juristic ballast—and the spirit of the new age raised the ideal of the savant to a remarkable altitude.

"Learning only unveils herself to him who wholeheartedly gives himself up to her : who approaches her ; with an unclouded mind and clear insight ; who seeks God's help and focusses an undivided attention upon her ; who girds up his robe and who, albeit weary, out of sheer ardour, passes sleepless nights in pursuit of his goal rising, by steady ascent, to its top most height and not to him who seeks learning by aimless flights and thoughtless efforts or who, like a blind camel, gropes about in the dark. He should not yield to bad habits or permit himself to be led astray by vicious tendencies. Nor must he turn his eyes from truth's depth. He should discriminate between the doubtful and certain, between genuine and spurious and should always stand firm by the clear light of reason." Thus wrote Mutahhar in 355/966.[2]

The clerk (*katib*) was the representative of profane learning. He was already severely distinguished from the theologian by his dress who used *Tailasan* and, in the East

(1) Goldziher, *Muh, Studien*, II, 233. The young Ghazzali was very much distressed when a theologian addressed him as 'jurist' Subki, III, 259.

(2) Fd. Huart. 1, 5.

at least, the Chinband[1].

Persia, the worldly province, was the head-quarters of the 'clerk'. In its capital, Shiraz, he was more honoured than the theologian[2]. The East, on the other hand, was the paradise of the savant where the theologian even today enjoys an esteem unrivalled elsewhere in the world[3]. When in the 5th/11th century a great theologian travelled through Perisa, the inhabitants, with their wives and children met him wherever he went, touched his sleeve to invoke his blessings and took the dust off his sandal as if it was medicine. Merchants, artisans flung their wares upon his train : fruits, sweets dresses, furs. Even cobblers were not behindhand. Sufi women threw garlands of roses at him in the hope that he might touch them and they might thence draw magical power[4].

Every mosque of importance is likely to have had a library for, hitherto, it was the practice to bequeath books to them[5]. The Library at Merv is said to have had as nucleus the books brought there by Yazdagerd[6]. The magnates also took a pride in collecting books. At the end of the 4th/10th century every one of the three great rulers of Islam—of Cordova, of Cairo, and of Baghdad—was a lover of books.

---

(1) See Khuda Buksh. *Contributions to the History of Islamic Civilization, vol. II* (Second Edition) : *Educational system of the Muslims* where this word is explained in note.

(2) Muk, 440.

(3) This passage appears confused and is certainly, inaccurate. Tr.

(4) Subki, III, 91.

(5) Margoliouth, Abul Ala's, *Letters*, XVI.

(6) Ibn Taifur, *Kit. Baghdad,* ed. Keller, fol. 62 a. Even at a later time Yaqut praises a library at Merv where he worked for 3 years. In his time there were 12 libraries there : of these one possessed some 12,000 volumes. The administration was very liberal and a savant continually had 200 volumes at a time with him without giving any security. (One dinar being the average value of each book). Yaqut, *Geog Dictionary, vol. IV*, 509.

Al-Hakam of Spain had his agents all over the East to collect first copies of books that were written. The catalogue of his library consisted of 44 Fasculi, each of 20 folios, containing merely the titles of books. At Cairo before the Caliph Abdul Aziz (d. 386/996) mention was made of the *Kit-Al-Ain* of Khalil ibn Ahmad. He sent for it and the librarian immediately brought over 30 MSS, among them, an autograph copy of the author. A dealer offered the Caliph a MS of the *'History of Tabari'* for which he had paid 100 dinars. The Caliph, in his library had more than 20 MSS of this work, including an autograp copy of the author. Of the *Jamharah* of Ibn Duraid he had 100 MSS[1]. Later writers even presume to know the actual number of books there. In the printed edition of Maqrizi the number is estimated at between 160 and 120,000 volumes[2]. Ibn al Tuwair : The library had departments, divided into sections, each section with a door on hinges and with locks. It contained more than 200,000 volumes[3]. Poor is the comparison which the western libraries of this period offer. In the 9th century the Cathedral library of Cosntance possessed 356 volumes, the Benedictbeuren[4] library in 1030 just over 100 volumes and the Cathedral library of Bamberg in 1130 only 96 volumes[5]. Mukaddasi was shown over the library of Adad-ud-Dawlah by the Chief Bed-maker *Rais-al-far-rushin*. The library formed a building by itself. It was in charge of a superintendent (*wakil*) a librarian (*khazin*) and an inspector (*mushrif*). Adad-ud-Dawlah had collected there every book composed up to his time in every branch of learning. The library consisted of a large ante-room and a long arched hall with rooms on all sides. In the walls of the hall and the

(1) Thus reports the generally trustworthy Musabbihi (d. 420/1029), a contemporary (*apud* Maqrizi, *Khitat,* 1,408), we must not forget that the numerals vary in different copyists.

(2) Maqrizi, *Khitat*, 1, 409.

(3) Ibid.

(4) Village in Upper Bavaria.

(5) Th. Gottlieb, *Uebermittelalterliche Bibliotheken*, 22, 23, 37.

rooms he had inserted cupboards of veneered wood two yards long by three broad with doors which were let down from above. The books were all piled upon shelves. Every branch of learning had its own cupboards, and catalogues, in which the names of the books were registered. Only distinguished people were allowed admission into the library[1]. The three passionate lovers of learning of the 3rd/9th century were the oft mentioned Jahiz, Fath ibn Khaqan, a magnate of the Court, and Qadi Ismail ibn Ishaq. Never did a book come to Jahiz's hand but he read it from cover to cover, be it what it might. Finally he hired the shops of the book-dealers to read the books there on loan. A later authority even invents for him a bibliophile's death. He used to heap up books high around him and one day the heap fell upon him and killed him[2].

Whenever he left the Caliph's table for some business or other Ibn Khaqan pulled a book out from his sleeve or his shoe and read it until his return. And this he did even in the privy. "I always found Qadi Ismail ibn Ishaq either reading a book or shifting books[3]," says Ibn Nadim.

Sijistani (d. 275/888) had a wide and a narrow sleeve made : the first was intended for books but the other served no purpose[4].

About the middle of the 3rd/9th Century the courtier Ali ibn Yahya Munajjim established a beautiful library on his estate which he named the 'Treasure-house of Wisdom, (*Khizanat al-hikmah*). From all parts of the world people flocked there and were entertained at the proprietor's cost. There also came with the pilgrim caravan the astronomer

---

(1) Muk, 449. Mez's rendering has been corrected.

(2) Abulfida, *Annales*, year 255.

(3) *Fihrist*, 116; Yaqut; *Irshad*, VI, 57; *Gurar al-fawaid of* Mur-tadha, Tehran, 1272.

(4) Abulmahasin II, 79.

Abu Ma'shar from Khorasan. He visited the library and was so captivated by it that "he forgot both Islam and the pilgrimage[1]."

An Isphanian theologian and landowner (d. 272/885) is said to have spent 300,000 dirhams on books[2]. Even a Court Marshal at Baghdad who died in 312/924 left behind books worth more than 2,000 dinars[3]. In 357/967 among other things, 17,000 bound volumes were confiscated belonging to a rebellious son of the Amir of Baghdad[4]. In 355/965 the house of the Wazir Abul Fadl ibn Amid was so thoroughly plundered by itinerant religious warriors' that nothing was left behind to sit upon or to drink water from. The historian Ibn-Miskawaihi was then his librarian who thus proceeds : The Alid Ibn Hamzah sent carpets and utensils to him, but his heart was troubled about his books, for nothing was dearer to him than books. And he had plenty of them, dealing with all sciences and every branch of philosophy and literature—more than a hundred camels' load. When he saw me, he asked me about them and I informed him that they were as safe as before and that no one had touched them. He was delighted and said : you are a child of fortune. Every thing else can be replaced but these can never be. I noticed how his face lighted up. He added : bring them to me tomorrow at such and such a place. I did as I was told, and of all his possessions they alone were saved.

Sahib ibn Abbad (d. 384/994) refused the invitation of the Samanid Prince to become his Wazir on the ground, among others of the difficulty of removal ; having 400 camel-loads only of theological works. The catalogue of his library filled 10 volumes. Under Sultan Mahmud of Ghazni, who

(1) Yaqut *Irshad*, V 46.
(2) Abu Nu'aim, *Tarikh Ispahan*, Leiden, fol. 51 b.
(3) Suli, contemporary and courtier in *Arib*, 121. Suli himself had a big library. Ibn al-Jauzi, 796.
(4) Misk, VI, 314; Ibn al-Athir, VIII, 431.

proved himself a Maecenas neither to Firdausi nor to Beruni, the books were consigned to the flames[1].

The Qadi Abul Mutrif of Cordova (d. 420/1,011) was a great collector of books. He always had six copyists to work for him. Wherever he heard of a beautiful book he sought to secure it, making extravagant offers for it. He never lent a book, but would willingly get it copied and make a gift of it without hesitation. After his death his books were sold for a whole year in his mosque ; fetching 400,000 dinars for the collection[2]. The Baghdadian savant Al-Baiqani (d. 425/1,033) required 63 baskets and two trunks for the transport of his books on removal[3].

The Manichaeans had already shown delicate taste and fancy in the get-up of their books. In 311/923, at the public gate of the castle at Baghdad, the portrait of Mani, together with 14 sacks of heretical books, was burnt. Gold and silver fell out of them. The supporters of the schismatic Al-Hallaj (executed in 310/921) also imitated the Manichaeans in this respect. Their books were written in gold on Chinese paper, were encased in silk and brocade, and were bound in costly leather[4].

The State-papers of the Byzantine Chancery are always mentioned as works of art. In 326/937 a letter of the Byzantine Emperor came to the Caliph—the Greek text in letters of gold and the Arabic translation in letters of silver[5]. Somewhat later another letter was sent to the Caliph of Cordova in letters of gold on sky-blue leather. It was encased in a cylinder of chased silver with the portrait of the emperor in coloured glass on the cover. That entire work of art was

(1) Yakut, *Irshad*, II, 315.

(2) Ibn Bashkuwal, 1, 304 F.

(3) Wustenfeld, AGGW, 37 Nr 335.

(4) *Arib*, p. 90, according to Misk.

(5) Ibn al-Jauzi, 59 a.

enveloped in brocade[1]. The poems of the Caliph Mutamid were likewise inscribed in letters of gold[2]. The Wazir Ibn Abbad (d. 386/996) personally drafted the letter of appointment of his chief Qadi Abdul Jabbar, and himself copied it in a most extravagant fashion. It consisted of 700 lines, each line on a folio and the entire work fitted into an ivory case, which looked not "unlike a thick column"[3]. In the 5th/11th century this work, along with another bibliographical rarity, was presented to the Wazir Nizam el-Mulk. The latter was a Qur'an, the variants of which were in red, between the lines, the explanation of uncommon expressions in blue, and passages of practical import in gold[4].

The book-lovers' greatest joy consisted in MSS of famous scribes.

But along with libraries another form of literary endowment came into existence. It combined the collection of books with instruction or, at least, with remuneration for work done in the libraries. The poet and savant Ibn Hamdan (d. 323/935)—a distinguished nobleman of Mosul—founded in his native town a 'House of Learning' (*dar-al-'ilm*) with a library possessing books on every branch of learning. It was open to all who wished to make use of it. For the poor paper was provided free. For himself the founder set apart a place where he declaimed his verses or those of others and dictated historical and juristic notes[5]. The Qadi Ibn Hibban (d. 354/965) bequeathed to the town of Nisabur a house with "library and quarters for foreign students and provided stipends for their maintenance." The books were

---

(1) Maqq, ed. Dozy, 1, 257.
(2) Es-Suli, to whom the Caliph el-Muktafi had shown it. Apud Shabushti, 396.
(3) Es-Subki, *Tab*, II, 230.
(4) Es-Subki, II, 230.
(5) *Irshad*, II, 420.

not to be lent out[1]. A courtier of Adud-ud-Dawlah (d. 372/ 982) built at Ram-Hormuz on the Persian Gulf—as at Basrah—a library where those who read or copied received a grant. At Ram-Hormuz a Mutazilite theologian always lectured on Mutazilite principles. In 383 the Buwayyid wazir Sabur ibn Ardashir (d. 415/1,024) founded a 'House of Learning' (*dar-al-ilm*) on the west side of Baghdad[2]. Besides, 10,400 volumes, mostly authors' autographs, and copies belonging to celebrated scholars, it possessed 100 copies, of the Qur'an written by the Banu Muklah[3]. The management was in the hands of two Alids and a Qadi.

Further Ar-Radi, poet and registrar of the Alids, (d. 406/ 1,015) established one such 'House of Learning' for students (*Talabat ul-ilm*); making necessary arrangements for their needs (Diwan, Beyrut I, 3). The name signifies the change. The old institutions, which were libraries, pure and simple, were called the 'Treasure-house of wisdom' *Khizanat al-Hikmah*—the newer ones. 'The House of Learning' (*Dar al-ilm*) in which the library was merely a speical section. Even in Egypt such academies were founded. In 378/988 Aziz purchased a house by the side of Al-Azhar and endowed it for 35 theologians who held their sittings for learned discussions every Friday in the mosque between the midday and the after-midday prayer. Thus, the Islamic academy, which is still the greatest academy in Islam, dates from the

(1) Wustenfeld AGGW, 37.

(2) Muk. 413; Fihrist, 139, (Ibn Khall, 1,250, Prof. Margoliouth says that it was founded in 381, in a part of Baghdad called 'between the two walls' in the quarter of Karkh, *Letters of Abul Ala*, XXIV, Tr.).

(3) Ibn Khall, II, 80; Ibn Jauzi, fol. 135 a. The library was burnt down in 450/1058. Ibn al-Athir, IX 247. Books which earlier were in possession of famous men, are of special importance in theological literature for they furnish in a manner a chain of tradition and a guarantee of accuracy. For this reason the reader carefully noted his name on the cover of the book. In Yaqut's *Irshad* (vi, 359) it is noted how the librarian of this library was shown that the books were being eaten by worms.

4th/10th century. The wazir Ibn Killis established a private academy. He is reported to have spent 1,000, dinars every month for professors, copyists and book-binders[1]. In 935 the Caliph al-Hakim founded a *Dar-al-ilm* at Cairo in which he gathered together books out of the different libraries in the citadel. It was thrown open to all. Besides the lecturers who lectured there—he appointed a librarian and two assistants[2]. Pen, paper and ink were supplied free of cost.

We possess the budget of this institution. Its maintenance cost 257 dinars a year.

Among other items of expenses :—

Paper	....	....	90	Dinars.
Pay of the Librarian	....	....	48	Dinars.
Pay of the Servants	....	....	15	Dinars.
Pay of the Officer in charge of Paper, Ink and Pens of reed	....	....	12	Dinars.
Repairs	....	....	12	Dinars.
Drinking-water	....	....	12	Dinars.
Abbadan mats	....	....	10	Dinars.
Felt-Carpet for winter	....	....	5	Dinars.
Covering for winter	....	....	4	Dinars.
Repair of Door Curtains	....	....	1	Dinar.

Al-Afdal shut up the library, because it became the centre of religious strife and sectarian disputes[3]. Theological and juristic lectures were mostly delivered at the mosques where the audience formed a circle in front of the lecturer who, whenever possible, took his place with his back to a pillar[4].

(1) Yahya ibn Sa'id, his contemporary and countryman, fol. 108 a.

(2) Yahya, fol. 116 a.

(3) Maqrizi, *Khitat* II, 458.

(4) Muk, 205. In 314/926 the Tigris, near Mosul, was frozen with the result that one could actually ride across it. To celebrate the occasion

If any one posted himself near such a circle, people called to him to turn towards the class. At the chief mosque of Cairo Mukaddasi reckoned 120 such circles in the evening[1]. The most famous educational centre of the empire then was the oldest chief mosque of Baghdad—the mosque of Mansur[2]. The Khatib al-Baghdadi is said to have taken, while on a pilgrimage, three draughts from the well of Zemzem, each draught signifying a wish : that he might compose a history of Baghdad, that he might be allowed to dictate traditions at the mosque of Mansur, and that he might be buried near the grave of Bisr el-Hafi. For fiftty years, there sat in this mosque, by one and the same pillar Naftawaihi (d. 323. 935), chief of the Zahirite school of Jurisprudence[3].

Within the theological circle, lectures of the canonists, dealing with professional learning, drew the largest audiences. And yet, compared with the figures to-day, the number is relatively small, whence we can infer that the number of competing teachers was great. Abu Hamid al-Isfaraini, (d. 406/1,015) the most renowned jurist of the century, called the second Shafi'i drew only 3 to 700 disciples at the mosque of Ibn al-Mubarak at Baghdad where he lectured[4].

The most famous lecturer in jurisprudence at Nishapur, the great centre of learning in the East, and an audience of over 500 on Firday the 23rd of Moharrum, 387/997[5] ; a successor of his—the "incomparable" Juwaini (d. 478/1085) had a daily audience of 300[6] ; whereas, to-day, for instance,

Abu Zikrah sat in the middle of the river with a circle of audience around him to whom he dictated notes. Ibn al-Jauzi, fol. 31 a.

(1) Yaqut *Irshad,* 1, 246.

(2) Guy Le Strange, *Baghdad,* p, 33. Tr.

(3) *Irshad* 1, 809.

(4) Wustenfeld, AGGW, 37, Nr. 287; *es-Subki,* III, 25; Ibn al-Athir, IX, 183, mentions 400.

(5) Nawawi, *Tahdhib,* ed Wustenfeld, 307; Subki, II, 170.

(6) Subki, II, 252.

in the God—forsaken Kashghar (East Turkistan) the first professor lectures, sometimes in our days, to an audience of 500[1].

They counted the students from the number of ink-pots which they put before them ; for the ink-pot was the most important part of a students equipment[2].

The enraged audience of the famous Tabari flung ink-pots at him when he said something which they did not approve of[3]. On the death of the lecturer, students smashed the ink-pots and broke their pens of reed and went about the town shrieking and lamenting. At the death of the above-mentioned Juwaini, who also was a famous preacher, his pulpit was thrown down and the entire Nishapur shared the academic grief. "The gates of the town were closed and instead of a head-gear they covered the head with a handkerchief[4]."

People brought their books to college in a receptacle called 'flask', doubtless with academic humour[5].

In earlier times dictation (*imla*) was counted as the highest stage of instruction[6]. In the 3rd/9th century it was largely resorted to by theologians and philologers. The Mutazilite el-Jubbai is said to have dictated 150,000 leaves and yet he was never seen to refer to any book except the calendar of Khwarezmi[7]. Abu Ali al-Qali dictated five volumes[8]. The student made a note on the leaf of his note-

(1) Hartmann, *Chinesisch-Turkestan*, 45.
(2) Nawawi and Subi.
(3) Yaqut, *Irshad*, VI, 436.
(4) Wustenfeld, AGGW, 37 Nr 365; Subki, II, 257.
(5) 'Qarurah'—probably this word was used for a case Cf. Dozy, Yaqut, *Irshad*, II, 10.
(6) Suyuti, *Muzhir*, I, 30; apud Goldziher, S. W. A. 69, 20.
(7) Ahmad Ibn Yahya, ed. Arnold, 47.
(8) Suyuti.

book : "Lecture, dictated by our Shaikh N.N., at such and such a place, on such and such a day[1]."

In the 4th/10th century, however, the philologer gave up the Theologian's method of teaching. Instead of dictating notes he took to explaning and commenting (*Tadris*) upon a work, read out by one of his pupils, "not unlike the method pursued in explaining compendiums" (*Mukhtasarat*). Abul Qasim Ez-Zajjaji (d. 339/950) is said to have been the last to dictate lexicography[2]. As expressly stated by Suyuti, in the sphere of theology, dictation, however, continued to be the approved method. When that vain wazir, Saheb ibn Abbad (d. 385/995) dictated traditions he naturally had a number of sycophants as his audience who took down notes. Each copyist had six others attached to him, each of whom repeated the dictation to the other[3]. But dictation, here, too showed signs of decline and only a few savants preferred it to *Tadris*[4].

The history of the *Kitab al Yaqut* of Mutarriz (d. 345/956) shows how a book grew out of dictation. From the 24th of Moharrum 326/936 he dictated *dic ad diem* this book until completed. To this he added a great number of notes and supplements. Abu Ishaq et-Tabari, then, read the book out before him, the students listening and he making further additions to it. Then from Dhulqada of 329/940 to Rabi II of 331/942 Abul Fath read it out to him when the notes of the best pupils were compared and yet further additions made by the author. Then he added fresh chaplers and supplements which Abu-Mohamad Wahb took down. This done, Abu Ishaq et-Tabari had once more to read the book

(1) Subki III, 259.
(2) Ahmad ibn Yahya,. ed Arnold 47.
(3) Yaqut, *Irshad*, II, 312.
(4) Ahmad ibn Yahya, 63. At the time of Haji Khalifa the traditionists seem to have finally abandoned dictation Marcais, *Le Taqrib de en-Nawawi* JA. 1901, 18 p. 87.

over to him. Then the final shape was given, the author promising to make no further additions[1].

The altered mode of instruction called new educational institutions into being. The predominance of *Tadris* gave birth to the *Madrasahs:* the main reason being that with *Tadris* went hand in hand *Munazarah* (disputation) and the mosque was hardly deemed a fit place for such a method of study and instruction.

In this sphere, too the 4th/10th century moulded the form which exists to this day. Tradition, as a whole, points to Nishapur—then the greatest centre of learning in the East—as the birth-place of the *Madrasah*. The best authority—Al-Hakim, the historian of the Nishapurian Savants, says that the first *Madrasah* was founded there for the benefit of his contemporary Isfaraini (d. 418/1,027)[2]. The *madrasah* of Ibn Furak (d. 406/1,015) can only have been a few years younger[3]. Both Isfraini and Ibn Furak were ardent disciples Al-Ashari and must have preferred dogmatic discussions—even *Tadris*—to simple transmission of traditions[4]. A third Nisapurian (d. 429/1,037) who built a *madrasah* for the savants in front of his house was a chief *mudarris* (lecturer) and a disputant (*munazir*)[5].

In the great colleges the assistant professor sat on a raised seat enjoining silence and repeating the words of the professor for the benefit of those who were at a distance

(1) *Fihrist* 76.

(2) Subki, *Tabaqat*, III, 111, 137. Maqrizi (*Khitat*, II, 363) thinks that the *madrasah* of Baihaqi (d. 454/1,062) was the first and Dhahabi that of Nizam-ul-Mulk. (Subki, III, 137). In Jauhari the word is not found but in Hamadani it occurs, *Ras.* p, 247.

(3) Subki, III, 52.

(4) Ribcra seeks to establish in his interesting essay '*Origen del Colegio Nidami de Baghdad*' [reprinted in his Opuscula] that the madrasah originally was a *Karramite* institution. But there is no proof for this theory.

(5) Subki, III, 33.

from him. At the theological lectures the professor began: Praise be to God and blessings on his Prophet. Then he caused verses of the Qur'an to be recited by one of his pupils with a fine voice. This done, the professor prayed for the town and his pupils. The assistant professor then enjoined silence invoking the name of God and praising the Prophet. Next he addressed the professor saying : May God be gracious to thee, whom wilt thou quote ? And each time the name of prophet or a saint occurred, he pronounced the prescribed Formula.[1]

About 300/912 a teacher began with the Qur'an, and its various readings then passed on to the sayings of the Prophet and, whenever a strange proposition or an uncommon expression occurred, he explained, discussed and questioned his audience as to the sense[2]. Students were allowed at the lecture to get up and question the teacher, as the history of a philologer (d. 415/1,024) shows. First one rose and asked : O Abu Ubaidah ! What is that ? Then a second and a third. Since all three asked silly question, Abu Ubaidah took his sandals, ran into the mosque and called out; How come all the cattle to be herded in my room today[3]!

This pious scruple against transmitting traditions which had previously existed, had not yet quite disappeared[4]. Birqani (d. 425/1,034) tells us that his teacher was always reluctant to teach tradition. His pupils, whenever he spoke

(1) Nawawi, *Taqrib*, JA, 1901, 18 p. 88. That this also obtained in the 4th/10th century is showed by the order of the Khatib "that this formula is to be loudly recited."

(2) Yaqut, *Irshad* VI, 282.

(3) Yaqut, *Irshad*, V, 272.

(4) Goldziher Z. D. M. G. Vol. (1907), p. 861. See also Samarqandi's *Bustan el-arifin* (p. 10) where one says: I have met 120 companions of the Prophet and there was no traditionist among them who did not wish some one other than himself to repeat traditions and no *mufti* among them either who did not prefer some one other than himself to decide.

to any one, were wont to step aside and, without his knowledge, to make notes of traditions which he wove into his conversation[1]. Another actually refused to teach tradition until he was seventy[2]. And yet the transmission of tradition was an act of worship and required a certain amount of purification. "It is desirable that the transmitter of traditions should purify, perfume himself and comb his beard before beginning his lecture. He is to sit upright in a dignified posture. He is to take severely to task any one who interrupts him. But he himself should be polite and courteous to all[3]."

From the 2nd/8th and 3rd/9th centuries we hear of people, who seeking intercession for a sick or needy person, throw a slip of paper before an honoured theologian while sitting with his circle of students around him. The professor picks it up, it utters a prayer and the students confirm it with *Amin*. Then the instruction proceeds. The following story comes from the 4th/10th century.

One day, during his *wizarat*, Saheb ibn Abbad, intending to dictate notes, showed himself, in the fashion of a theologian, in a veil and chinband and said: "You know my zeal for theology"—his statement was confirmed by the audience. He, then, proceeded: "I am always pre-occupied with this subject. Whatever I have spent, in acquiring a knowledge of it, from childhood up to now, has come from my father's and grandfather's purse and yet I have not kept free from lapses. God and you are my witnesses that I do penance to God for any sin committed." He owned a house which he named the 'house of penance.' There he was wont to remian for some weeks (doing penance), taking care that the validity of his penance was testified to by canonists. On completion of the penance he dictated notes. To every

(1) Marcais in the *Taqrib* of Nawawi J. A. 1901. 17 p. 196 note 2.
(2) Subki *Tabaqat* II, 161.
(3) *Taqrib* pp. 18, 85 ff, (J.A. 1901). From Ghazzali Marcais quotes that Sufian Thauri always seated the poor in the very first rank.

copyist some six others attached themselves, of these six every one passed on the dictated matter to others[1]. Darqutni (d. 385/995) silently prayed while the students read aloud before him. He called attention to mistakes by saying: '*Subhan Allah.*' We are also told as an example of his acumen that he corrected mistakes by citations from the Qur'an[2]. A theologian, who died in 406/1,015 began his lectures by recitations from the Qur'an and traditions and, during the whole time, never moved a limb till he was quite exhausted[3]. Bahili always sat at the lecture which he delivered once a week behind a curtain for fear that his pupils might look upon him and the populace with one and the same eye. On account of deep pre-occupation with God he had become frenzied and never knew what length his lecture had reached until remined of it[4]. Theological lecture concluded with a prayer, prefaced by *Qumu*, stand up[5].

Opinion was naturally divided as to the age when study should begin. Some recommended that the study of tradition should not commence until the 30th year; others not until the 20th. In the VIth century Qadi Iyadh of Cordova (d. 544/ 1, 149) states the opinion of experts to be that the study of tradition should not be taken up before the age of 5. In support of this view, even a tradition from Bukhari (*'Ilm*, ch. 18) is cited and Nawawi, who died in 476/1,083, states this to be the general rule in his time. The famous Humaidi is said to have been carried on his father's shoulder for instruction[6]. And, for this reason, indeed, notices of learned men invariably refer to the age when they commenced to attend lectures.

Rare are the instances of boys of six attending lectures.

---

(1) *Irshad*, II, 312. (For his life, see, Ibn Khall, II, 239).
(2) Subki, II, 312. (*ibn Asakir on Dictation*, Ibn Khall, II, 253 Tr.).
(3) Ibn *al-Jauzi*, fol. 163 a.
(4) Subki, *Tabaqat*, II, 257.
(5) Subki, *Tabaqat*, II, 192.
(6) *Taqrib*, J. A. 1901. 17, p. 193.

The famous Qadi Tanukhi (d. 384/994) belongs to this rare group[1]. Abu Nu'aim of Ispahan, the greatest traditionist of the age, began attending lectures at eight[2]. But generally they commenced at 11. At the age of 11 the famous Khatib[3], three of his disciples, and Ibn al-Jauzi's[4] began attending lectures.

There were teachers, indeed, who would not, at their lectures, admit beardless youths for fear of love-intrigues. An ardent, youthful shcolar, had to use, in consequence, a false beard[5].

There was a difference of opinion even as to the age when one should teach theology. Nawawi seems to think that one could do so at any age provided an audience is found. The old teacher should cease to lecture when he feels that through age or blindness he mixes up traditions[6]. As a poor student, Isfaraini, the greatest Shafiite jurist of the 4th/10th century, worked as a porter[7]. Others went through their course of study by sleeping on the *minaret* of the mosque in which they heard lectures.

It is related of the wazir Ibn al-Furat (d. 312/924) that, during his *wazarat*, he allowed 20,00 dirhams as a permanent annual grant to poets, apart from individual donations or gifts for panegyrics. In his last *wizarat* he thought of his

---

(1) Ibn al-Jauzi, fol. 130 b.
(2) Subki III, 8.
(3) *Tarikh Baghdad*, J. R. A. S. 1902, p. 50.
(4) Ibn al-Jauzi, fol. 137 b.
(5) Wustenfeld, *Schafiiten*, AGGW 37, Nr. 88.
(6) *Taqrib*, J A (1901) 18 p 50. The later theorists are very severe upon blind theologians. Some even refuse to regard them as trustworthy traditionists, an indication of the value set upon writing and a corresponding decline in the high esteem in which memory was held in the past. The Khatib rules : We are to look upon a blind theologian or traditionist in the same light as an uneducated person with eyes. Ibid, p. 63.
(7) AGGW, 37 Nr 28.

students and said: Perhaps they can ill-afford to spare a penny or even less to buy ink and paper. It is, then, my duty to help and provide them with these. And he, according by, sanctioned 20,000 dirhams out of his own purse for these[1].

This story suggests that institutions for students were not common then. Moreover, the larger portion of this grant, as is expressly stated, was diverted to other purposes. The poor scholar—when not a jurist or official— earned a living as copyist, as did the Christian Yahya ibn Adi (d. 364/974). One of the outstanding philosophers of the 4th/10th century, who twice transcribed the entire commentary of Tabari on the Qur'an, used to copy as many as 100 leaves in twenty-four hours[2]. Abu Hatim, who for 50 years worked as copyist at Nishapur, thus expresses himself: "Copying is a wretched, accursed business. It secures neither bread to the living nor a shroud to the dead[3]." By copying Daqqaq (d. 489/7,096) maintained mother, wife, and daughter. In course of a year he copied of *Sahih* of Muslim. He once dreamed that on the Day of Judgment he was absolved and " as I was through the gate of Paradise" says he, "I threw myself at full length on my back, put one leg on the other and called out 'ah, now, by God, I am rid of copying[4]'."

The imposture of the copyists was regarded as a misfortune of learning[5]. Extremely conscientious savants copied their libraries out for themselves[6], whenever possible.

Private tuition did not bring in much. A whole band of

(1) Yaqut *Irshad*, 1,255 Wuz. 201 f.
(2) *Fihrist* 264; Kifti, 361.
(3) *Yatimah* III, 319.
(4) Yaqut, *Irshad*, VI, 337.
(5) *Yatimah* , IV, 122,
(6) Often, particularly in the account of the lives of the Malekite jurists, e. g., *Bibl. Arab-hisp.*

savants; *e. g.*, the entire Hanafite school, Ahmad Ibn Hanbal, Sufyan Thauri and other, declare it unlawful for teachers to take money for instruction in Qur'an and tradition[1].

Others considered it lawful but placed the traditionist higher who "only taught for the sake of heavenly reward." Even Nawawi in the 8th/13th century refused to accept the salary, assigned for his post, at Ashrafiyyah.

After an unremunerated lecture of the sort mentioned the pupils said: May God reward thee ! Where upon the teacher replied: May God let it profit ye[2].

In 346/957 there died a famous Khorasanian teacher, who became so hard of hearing, from his thirtieth year, that he could not even hear the braying of a donkey. When he went to the mosque to deliever lectures he invariably found it full of people who carried him on their shoulder to his seat. He would receive no remuneration for his lectures but earned a living as copyist[3]. Jauzaki (d. 388/998) said : "10,00,000 dirhams have I spent on Traditions but not a single dirham have I earned thereby." An Alid, wishing to present 300 dinars to the famous, Khatib al-Baghdadi, who happened to be at the masque of Tyre, placed the sum on his prayer carpet. The Khatib took up the prayer carpet in anger and left the mosque. The Alid had to pick up the gold pieces from the fissures in the mat[4].

To become a school-master, as the later famous Abu Zaid al-Balkhi (d. 322/933) became, meant 'Sour bread and a despised occupation[5]." Jahiz has written a book on school-masters which is full of fun and of anecdotes, descriptive

(1) Muk. *Bustan el-arefin*. Marcais, *Taqrib*, J A (1901) 17 p. 143.
(2) Subki, II, 297.
(3) Ibn al-Jauzi, fol. 87.
(4) Subki, II, 169.
(5) Subki, III, 14.

of their helplessness and folly. "As stupid as a school-master" was a familiar proverb.[1] Greek comedy may be responsible for much of this, for in it the shcool-master is a stock comic figure[2]. But it was averred in all seriousness that the oaths of weavers, sailors, and those who let animals on hire have no validity in law and those of the carriers of loads and school-masters but partial validity[3]. Ibn Habib (d. 245/859) counsels : when you ask one regarding his business and he answers, School-mater ! then give him a cuff[4]. Ibn Haukal reports[5] : "The daily consumption of onions has made the Sicilians weak-minded with the result that they see things otherwise than as they are. As an illustration they regards the school-masters, of whom there are more than 300, as the noblest and the most important members of their community and out of them make confidants and choose assessors in their courts. But we all know how cribbed and confined is the understanding of the school-masters and how light-headed they are ! Through cowardice and fear of fighting they have resorted to their occupation."

The School-master was paid at times in kind. Proverbial is the School-master's kitchen for its heterogeneous content. It was great or small, good or bad according to the purse or the generosity of the pupils' parents. Jahiz said of a school-master.

> Their cakes and bread, that is no good—
> A plague upon such work and food[6].

(1) Yaqut, *Irshad*, 1,141.
(2) Jahiz, *Bayan* 1,100.
(3) Ibn Kutaibah, *Uyun al-Akhbar*, 93.
(4) Yaqut, *Irshad*, VI, 473.
(5) p. 86.
(6) Tha'alabi, Kit. *umad el-mansub* ZDMG, VI. There was no school on Tuesdays and Fridays (Ibn al-Mutazz II, 1 ; Abulqasim, LVII). For later times *Alif Ba* 1,208; *Madkhal*, II, 168. Children wrote with chalk on boards (Muk, 440). Straps were used *for chastisement. Yatimah*, II, 63.

More happily placed were private-tutors (*muaddib*) in rich houses. An ordinary teacher received about 60 dirhams for tuition; exceptionally competent ones not quite a thousand[1]. A private tutor of this sort received 70 dirhams per month at the house of an officer of Abdullah ibn Tahir in the 3rd/9th century but he stood under the supervision of his own teacher who had recommended him and who occasionally examined the boys and had the power of removing him, if necessary[2]. Most fortunate, indeed, were the tutors of princes. Such a position was held by distinguished philologers. Mohamed ibn Abdullah Ibn Tahir, one of the most generous men of his time, allowed to the grammarian Tha'lab, the resident private tutor of his son, a house close by the palace where he and his pupil lived, receiving daily seven rations of black bread, a ration of wheat bread, seven pounds of meat, forage for horses, and a stipend of 1,000 dirhams[3]. In 302/914 the son of the Wazir celebrated at Baghdad the admission of his son to the school-room with an invitation to 300 guests—officers of all rank and status. The private tutor received, 1,000 dinars as present[4]. In the shcool-room of princes a slave of his tutor stood by the side of the little Mamun to take the board from his hand, wipe it and, again, hand it back to him[5]. At court, savants were always welcome and received pension. They were classed under two headings : (1) Jurists (*Fuqaha*) and (2) Theologians (*'Ulema*). The third and the best paid group was that of the *Nudama* (messmates of the sovereign) of the Caliphs. The same individual could draw simultaneously all the three stipends. It, then, made up 300 dinars a month with free quarters[6]. The philologer Ibn

(1) Jahiz, *Bayan*, 1, 151.
(2) Yaqut, *Irshad*, 1 122.
(3) Yaqut, *Ieshad*, II, 144.
(4) *Kit al-uyun Wal-hadaig.*, Berlin, fol. 125 b.
(5) Baihaqi, ed, Schwally, 620.
(6) *Fihrist*, 51.

Duraid (d. 321/933) received from Al-muqtadir 50 dinars per month when he came destitute to Baghdad[1]. Al-Farabi (d. 339/950) received from Saif-ud-Dawlah, the ruler of Aleppo, one dirham per day and was quite satisfied with it[2]. Rarely, indeed, do we read of a sarvant, at this period, concerning himself with any business or craft as a means of livelihood. Sibghi (d. 344/955), however sold dye. In his shop met all the traditionists of the day[3]. He bequeathed this, his house, 'the House of Law' (*Dar as-Sunnah*) to a savant as *Madrasah* and made a suitable endowment for it[4]. Diligh (d. 351/962), who was at once a savant and a successful merchant, died leaving behind 300,000 dinars (3 million marks). He sent his collection of books to a colleague, inserting between every two folios a gold piece. He used to say : 'There is nothing in the world like Baghdad, nothing in Baghdad like the *Qatiah*, nothing in *Qatiah* like the *Derb-Abi Khalif*, nothing in the *Derb-Abi Khalif* like my house[5].

Another who lived in old Cairo had tailoring as his sole means of subsistence. Every week he made a coat (*Qamis*) for a dirham and two danaqs and maintained himself thereby—not accepting even a drink of water from any one[6]. Another Cairene savant (d. 494/1,101) maintained himself by selling robes of state to the aristocracy[7]. But Mutarriz (d. 345/956), the greatest philologer of his age, endured life-long privations; for occupation with learning hindered him from earning a livelihood[8]. And the celebrated philologer Ibn Faris (d. 369/979) speaks of the dirham as the best

(1) Wistenfeld AGGW, 37 Nr 92.
(2) Abulfida, *Annales*, year 339.
(3) Subki, II, 168.
(4) Subki, III, 66.
(5) Subki, II, 222.
(6) Subki, II, 102.
(7) Subki, III, 297.
(8) Abulfida, *Annales*, year 345.

physician for his malady and wishes that he had 1,000 dinars that the blocks heads might serve him[1].

At the end of this period the Muslim savant becomes eligible for privy councillorship. The young Isfaraini (d. 418/ 1,027) was the first of his guild in Nisapur to receive a title—the title of Rukn-ud-din (pillar of religion)[2]. Then also came into view, yet only as a mark of honour, the later important title of the '*Shaikh-ul-Islam*. Both the Asharites and the Persian conservatives conferred that title upon their chief theologian[3].

Nor were comic pictures of the professors wanting. The grammarian Tha'lab and Al-Mubarrad used so to take each other off, that the audience, enthralled and spell-bound hastened from the lecture of one to that of the other[4]. Another once boasted : I have never forgotten anything and continued : Slave, hand me my shoes. Lo ! rejoined the slave: You have them on[5].

The famous philologer Ibn Khaluyah was learned but coarse. Once at a social gathering at the palace of Amir Saif-ud-Dawlah he struck the peot Mutannabbi with his keys in the face and caused him to bleed[6].

And Naftawaihi was as famous for his learning as he was notorious for filth and bad odour.

The strain caused by his work affected the mind of the lexicographer Jauhari (died about 390/1,000). After he had

(1) Yaqut, *Irshad*, II, 9.
(2) AGGW, 37, Nr. 316. Already a savant (d. 356/966), who was held in great esteem at the court of Bokhara, ranked higher than the Wazir and was addressed as the great master (Shaikh Jalil). Subki, II, 86.
(3) Subki, III, 47, 117.
(4) *Irshad*, II, 149.
(5) *Irshad*, VI, 209.
(6) Ibn Khallikan Wustenfeld's ed. I, 65.

dictated his dictionary up to the letter *DAD* he went up to the roof of the old mosque at Nisapur and called out : Ye people ! I have accomplished something this side of the grave such as no man has accomplished before. Now I will achieve something for the other side of the grave such as no man has hitherto achieved. He tied two door-leaves with a piece of string under his arms, mounted to the highest point in the mosque and tried to fly. He fell to the ground and died[1].

(1) Yaqut, *Irshad* II, 269.

XIII. THEOLOGY

In the 4th/10th century Muslim theology passed through its greatest epoch ; namely, its emancipation from jurisprudence whose hand-maid it had hitherto been. Even in the 3rd/9th century all theological works of note bear juristic impress. This change must be set down to the credit of the Mutazilites. Throughout the 3rd/9th century they propounded purely theological questions and, now, they challenged their opponents to reply. They were the first Muslim party which was free from all juristic leanings. And even in the 4th/10th century—of the five greatest groups in which Islam was then divided, namely; Sunnah, Mutazilah, Murjiah, Shiah and Kharijites—they were the only party of pure dogmatism (Kalamiyyah)[1]. They conceded complete liberty with regard to particular rules of law (*Furu'*) and taught that every jurist was free to follow his own lines[2]. Thus there were Mutazilites in every shade of juristic school, even among the Traditionists, (*Ashab el-hadith*) whom people are inclined to regard as born enemies of the Scholastics.

The Sufis again were avowed opponents of all juristic schools (*ilm ed-dunya*). Makki (d. 386/996) applied to it (*ilm ed-dunya*) an alleged saying of Christ : The base savants are not unlike a stone on the mouth of a canal. They would neither themselves drink the water nor would they let it fertilise a field. Such are the wordly-wise savants[3]! They sit upon the road leading to the next world. They neither move

---

(1) Muk, 37.

(2) Muk, 38; Ahmad Ibn Yahya, 63

(3) Muk, 439.

on themselves nor yet do they let the servants of God move on to Him. Or, again, they are not unlike white washed graves, externally well-cared for but within replete with the bones of the dead[1].

And the Sufis won the day. In the following century Ghazzali—the pioneer of the later Muslim orthodoxy—declared jurisprudence to be something *worldly* and *untheological*[2]. In fact we notice among the Sufis a tendency to penalise all sciences. Ibn Khafif (d. 371/981) had to conceal his ink-pot in his breast-pocket and paper in his waist-belt for fear of the brethren[3].

Once again they opposed the Gnosis the inner understanding, to knowledge, the theology. "O, Wonder ! how is he, who knoweth not how the hair of his body grows black or white, to know the creator of things?" Thus Hallaj (d. 302/914) ridicules learning ![4] Elsewhere he tells us : I saw a Sufi bird with two wings. He did not understand my business so long as he flew. And he questioned me about purity (Safa), and I replied : Clip thy wings off by the scissors of self-annihilation, or else thou wilt not be able to follow me. But he rejoined : My wings I need to fly. One day he fell into the sea of understanding and was drowned[5]. On the other hand others, like Junaid (d. 289/901), have expressly placed Theology (*'ilm*) above *Gnosis (Ma'rifah)*[6]. As a matter of fact the list, for instance, of the Shafiite savants exhibits a number of Sufis. The Sufiite Theology is by far the most important and successful as being the movement in the learning of that time which harbours the strongest religious forces. It imported into and impressed upon Islam

(1) Makki, 141.
(2) Goldzihar, *Zahiriten*. 182.
(3) Amedroz. *Notes on Some Sufi Lives*, JRAS, 1912, 554.
(4) *Kit. et-tawasin*, ed Massignon, 73.
(5) *Kit. et-tawasin*, 30.
(6) Ibid, 195.

three special features of its own which, even today, constitute by far the most important and effective features of its religious life. They are: A firm faith in God, the order of Saints, and the Prophet'e cult.

The study of the Qur'an and Tradition, enjoined as a religious duty upon every believing Muslim, male and female[1], increased more and more, but the 4th/10th century inaugrated the modern practice of permitting the transmission of traditions, independently of personal intercourse, even without a special permission from the teacher[2]. The result was that in the place of the old-fashioned travelling, the individual traditionists took to the study of books. Thus Ibn Yunus ed-Sadafi (d. 347/958) could become the head of the traditionists in Egypt without travelling or hearing any one outside Egypt[3].

Yet it was some time before the savant, in search of traditions, was less frequently to be found wandering in the streets or putting up at inns than the merchant or official. In 395/1005 died Ibn Mandah, 'the last of the travellers', that is to say, the most famous of those who travelled about the empire to hear traditions. He collected 1700 traditions and brought home 40 camel loads of books[4]. Abu Hatim of Samarqand heard about a thousand teachers from Tashkend to Alexandria[5]; an Afghan savant heard over 1200[6]. And yet Ghazzali—the most outstanding figure in the theological world—undertook very few journeys for purposes of study.

---

(1) Samarqandi *Bustan al-arifin*, Cairo, (1304.) p. 3.
(2) Goldziher, *Muh. Studien* II, 190 ff. Nawawi mentions some savants who considered written transmission as valid. Even the canonical collections themselves called many instances of this mode of transmission into being. JA (1901) p. 226.
(3) Suyuti, *Husnul Muhthera*, 1, 164.
(4) Zarqani, 1,230; Goldziher, *Muh. Studien*, II, 180.
(5) Subki, *Tabaqat*, II, 14.
(6) Subki, III, 114.

Outside his home, Tus he heard lectures in the North, in Jurjan, and studied later at Nisapur, the great university town of his country. That was all. How conflicting in the 4th/10th century were views regarding the subject of travel is manifest from the *Bustan al-'Arifin* (p. 18 ff) of Samarqandi! And significant, too, is the fact that Naibakhti calls the well-known Abul Faraj al-Isfahani (d. 356/967), author of the *Kitab al-Aghani,* from whom even the renowned Daraqutni heard traditions, 'the greatest liar' because he used to frequent the market of the book-dealers, lively and stocked with books, purchase a heap of manuscripts there, bring them home and make extracts there from[1].

The traditionists, however, were considered the most prominent of learned men and were, in fact, most influential in the empire. Historians faithfully note their deaths and hand down strange stories of their feats of memory. Abdullah Ibn Sulaiman (d. 316/928) went from Baghdad to Sijistan. At Baghdad he was so profoundly esteemed that he lectured at the residence of the wazir 'Ali Ibn Isa and the Government erected a pulpit for him. He did not take with him a single book to Sijistan. From memory he dictated 30,000 traditions. The Baghdadians thought that he was playing the fool with the people and sent a messenger there whom they engaged for six dinars. He took notes, returned home, and it transpired that only six traditions of the lot could be at all taken, exception to and of these six only three were found spurious[2].

Ibn Uqwah (d. 332/943) boasted of carrying 52,000 traditions with their respective authorities in his head[3]. The Qadi of Mosul who dies in 355/966 is said to have known 20,000 traditions by heart[4]. And in 401/1010 died a savant

(1) *Tarikh Baghdad,* ed Krenkow, JRAS, 1912, p. 71.
(2) Ibn al Jauzi, fol. 36 a; Subki, II, 230.
(3) Ibn al-Jauzi, fol. 726.
(4) Goldziher, *Muh. Studien,* II, 200.

in Egypt who possessed a long roll of 87 yards, on both sides of which were written the beginnings of Traditions known to him[1].

Theologians recall with pride a story of the poet Hamadani (d. 398/1007) who fancied himself because he could repeat a hundred verses on hearing them once. He used to speak slightingly of the respect shown by the people to the memorising of traditions. Someone sent him a chapter of tradition and gave him a week's time to commit it to memory. At the end of the week the poet returned the document with the observation : Who can retain this in memory ? Mohamed, son of X and Jafar, son of X, after X and then various names and expressions[2].

With what speed tradition was taught may be inferred from the fact that the Khatib heard the entire *Sahih* of Bukhari in five days and that from a lady[3]. The two greatest traditionists of this century are Abul Hasan 'Ali al-Daraqutni (d. 385/995) and Al-Hakim of Nisapur (d. 405/1014). In the following century their mantle fell upon the Khatib al-Baghdadi (d. 403/1012).

Their work was cut out for them by the collection of traditions which had been finished in the 3rd/9th century with their divisions and contractions. And they fulfilled their task either by fresh collections as did Daraqutni by composing a *Book of Sunnah* and helping the Egyptian Wazir Jafar ibn el-Fadl, who had theological ambitions, to prepare a *Musnad* for a handsome sum[4] : or by composing

(1) *Sukkardan* Margin of *Mikhlat*, 185.

(2) Subki, III, 661.

(3) Yaqut, *Irshad*, 1,247. He heard traditions from the famous Karunah of Merv whom also Ibn Baskuwah (1,133) has mentioned.

(4) Yaqut, *Irshad*, II, 408. The pupils of Muslim have specially composed fresh *Sahihs; e.g.* Abu Hamid (d. 325) and Abu Sa'id (d. 353), Subki, *Tabaqat*, II, 97, f.

Istidrak and *Mustadrak* (supplements) such as those of Daraqutni or of Hakim—both being of opinion that a great deal of good material had escaped the earlier writers[1]. Or yet again by collecting parallel reports, according to other authorities (*Mukhraj* or *Mustakhraj*) as was done by almost every reliable traditionist of the 4th/10th century.

In this century a special literature arose on doubtful readings (*Tashifat*) : both Daraqutni and the Khatib wrote on the subject[2].

From the very beginning criticism of traditions concerned itself with individual authorities (*Marifat-rejal el-hadith*), with the ascertaining of their names and the determination of their position as reliable (*thiqat*) or weak (*du'afa*) traditionists. Nor was the consideration of the qualities required in a perfect traditionist lost sight of. Yahya ibn al-Khattan (d. 198/914) is said to have composed the first book of this kind[3]. After the comparison of classical text they proceeded to scrutinize the authorities therein and wrote books on the traditionists mentioned in the two *Sahihs* The demand for an uninterrupted chain of traditionists[4] led on from the biography and critical estimate of the individual traditionist to a general history of these witnesses. Thus arose the chronicles of the 3rd/9th century, such as those of Bukhari (d. 256/870) ; the great *Tabaqat* of Ibn Sa'd (d. 230/845), arranged according to time and place; and the so-called '*Histories of the Towns*' in the 3rd/9th and the 4th/10th centuries which reached their summit of excellence in the *History of Nisapur* by Al-Hakim (d. 406/1015)—he is said to be more exhaustive in biographical

(1) Goldziher *Muh Studien*, II, 241. Daraqutni's successors are mentioned in Nawawi 1, 17.

(2) Goldziher, II, 241.

(3) Marcais, *Taqrib* of Nawawi, JA, 1900, 16 p. 321.

(4) This question is said to have been first raised by Shafi-i (d. 204). (Ibn Abd el-Barr (d. 463); see Marcais, *Taqrib*, JA 1900, 16, p. 321.

details than even the Khatib—in the Tarikh of *Ispahan* by Abu Nu'aim (d. 430/1039).

The works of the Khatib '*On the cases of fathers who obtained tradition from sons*' and '*The Companions of the Prophet who handed down traditions to the generation following them*', show the subtle critical technic which had then come into being[1]. This biographical knowledge, then, enjoyed the highest esteem. The Qadi Abu Hamid of Marv (d. 362/972)—renowned as a teacher of the great Abu Hayyan at- Tauhidi—considered biographical literature as 'an ocean of decisions and an equipment of Qadis'. He maintained that the acuteness of jurists depended upon the extent of their biographical studies[2].

Most admired in the Khatib was his keenness in detecting genuineness or otherwise of a document by the anachronism of the subcription[3].

In the 4th/10th century Karabizi (d. 378/988) wrote the work on the names and surnames of traditionists which, by common consent, has been set down as the most authoritative for all times[4].

In earlier times historical studies were held in such bad odour among theologians that Ibn Ishaq (d. 151/767) is said to have made fun of a historical student by asking him "who was the actual standard-bearer of Goliath"[5]. But, now, at the beginning of the 4th/10th century Zingi mentions as lectures on 'traditions' only historical subjects such as the *History of the Mubayyidah*, the death of Hajar ibn Adi, the Shiite leader, *the Book of the Battle of Siffin* and *the Book*

---

(1) Yaqut, *Irshad*, 1,248.
(2) Subki, II, 83.
(3) *Irshad*, 1,249.
(4) Marcais *Taqrib* of Nawawi, JA (1901), 18, 135.
(5) Goldziher *Muh. Studien*, II, 207.

of the Battle of the Camel[1]. But later the wind veered once again. Nawawi reproaches Ibn Abd-el-Barr (d. 463/1071) for injuring his book by incorporating historical information therein[2].

The theory of the criticism of tradition also was elaborated in the 4th/10th century. Ibn Abi Hatim al-Razi (d. 327/239) has constructed a whole ladder of epithets for the transmitters : (*Thiqah,* trustworthy ; *Mutqin,* exact; *Thabt,* Solid; *Hujjah,* Authority; *Adl-hafiz,* Good memory ; *Dhabit* Sure ; *Sadiq,* veracious ; *Mahallu-huess-idq,* inclining to veracity ; *La ba's bihi,* harmless)[3].

Khattabi (d. 388/998) is said to have been the first to fix the three main classes of traditions : Perfect (*Sahih*), Good (*Hasan*), and Weak (*Da'if*). Daraqutni (d. 385/995) defined the *'taliq'* and Hakim (d. 405/1015) placed, once and for all, the science of tradition (*Usul el-hadith*) on an independent basis, on such a scale and thoroughness, that it retains its position even today. Here the later centuries did nothing more than add matters of secondary importance.

Even the external form of treatment—that is, the division into a number of *Anwa* (sections)—they accepted and retained as in the days of Al-Hakim[4]. From him too, dates the practice of the scribes to place a dot in the middle of the circle, indicating thereby the termination of a tradition after collation[5]. (This means that the scribes used to indicate the end of a tradition by putting a sign thus : O, After collation the circle was supplied with a point within : O).

---

(1) Wuz, 202.

(2) *Taqrib, JA (1901),* 18 p. 123.

(3) Nawawi, *Taqrib,* JA (1901), 17 p. 146; Goldziher, *Muh. Studien,* II, 142.

(4) Nawawi, JA (1900), 16 p. 330 Sqq. Ibn Hibban (d. 354) had already divided these into *Anwa* p. 487 note (1).

(5) Nawawi, JA (1901), 17, p. 528.

The Qur'an-readers play the second role in the theological world. Mukaddasi never fails to mention the school of reading obtaining in every province, but for the 'readers' themselves he entertains no regard or affection. He notes greed, pederasty, and hypocrisy as their chief *traits*[1]. Even this branch of learning was divided up by Ibn Mujahid about the year 300/912[2].

On or about this time there were fierce disputes on the question of the true text of the Qur'an. Government even took to persecution ; for Ibn Shanabud (d. 328/939) was scourged under orders of the wazir Ibn Muqlah and had to recant six different variants in the reading of the Qur'an in the following manner. "Mohamed ibn Ahmed ibn Ayyub says: I had read texts differing from the text going back to Othman and approved by the companions of the Prophet. I see clearly now that they were wrong. I atone for my mistake and renounce my opinion, for the text of Othman is the right rext which no one should reject or call into question[3]."

And yet he left behind pupils, of whom, one Shanabudi is mentioned as a famous 'reader', who dies as late as 387/997[4]. His variants and those of the others have come down to us. They are perfectly harmless. But here, they took every thing all—too seriously, for the doctrine of the world of God left them no option in the matter. The theologian Al-'Attar (d. 354/965) defended, in an exegetical work, some of the readings differing from the official redaction and stood firmly by the text without vowel-points urging that in

(1) Muk, 41.

(2) Died 334/945. He had a thick beard and a large skull. He read the Qur'an, so the people believed, even in his grave. Jauzi, *Muntazam*, fol. 56 a.

(3) Suli, *Auraq*. Paris, fol. 52; *Fihrist*, 31; *Irshad*, VI, 300 ff; Noldeke, *Gesch. d. Korans*, 274.

(4) Suyuti, *de interpretibus Corani*, 37; Misk, V, 447; Ibn al-Jauzi fol. 54 a.

classical Arabic any punctuation which yeilded a sense was permissible. He was reported to Government and was asked to appear before Jurists and "readers" and make atonement. His recantation was put into writting and was countersigned by all. Despite all this—to the end of his days it is said he clung to his own private reading and passed it on to his pupils[1].

In 398/1008 once again there emerged into light a Qur'an which differed from the official redaction and which was stated to be the copy of the famous dissenter Ibn-Masud. It was burnt by Qadi. About midnight a man appeared and cursed the man who had burned it. He was killed on the sopt[2].

Not unlike the four schools of jurisprudence the seven canonical schools of reading supplanted in the 4th/10th century most of the differing readings[3] ; even the arbitrary selection of eight schools of readings is the work of this century. (Noldeke, *Geschichte des Korans,* 299). An Egyptian theologian who died in 333 A.H. wrote on the differences in the *seven* schools of readings. (Suyuti, *Husnul Muhadhera,* 1,332,234). Another Egyptian who died 401 on the *eight.*

It was not at all a recognized practice in the 4th/10th century to explain the Qur'an. Tabari relates that in old days a pious man, passing by a place where the Qur'an was being explained, called out to the teacher: 'Better would it be for thee to have the tamburin played at thy back than to sit here[4], and, according to Samarqandi, Omar, seeing a Qur'an with a man, where every verse was explained, asked for a

---

(1) Ibn al-Jauzi, fol 98 a; *Irshad,* VI, 499.

(2) Suyuti, *de interpretibus Corani,* 37; Musk, V, 447; Ibn al-Jauzi, fol. 98 a ; *Irshad,* VI, 499.

(3) Ibn al-Jauzi, 152 b, Subki, *Tabaqat,* III, 26.

(4) Noldeke, *Gesch. des Korans.* 278; *Fihrist.* 31; Samarqandi, 73.

pair of scissors and cut it into pieces[1]. Out of pious scruples the philologer Asma'i is said never to have explained anything in the Qur'an or the tradition; not even such words and phrases, analogies and etymologies as were common to them both[2].

Tabari, however, manages to cite instances of the 'Companions of the Prophet'—and preeminently of Ibn Abbas[3]—who busied themselves with the exposition of the Qur'an ; but his '*polemics*' (p. 26 sqq) show that the party which absolutely repudiated it was very strong. At last a saying of the Prophet was cited to effect a compromise : "however interprets the Qur'an according to his own light will go to hell". Every interpretation of the Qur'an had, therefore, to be ultimately traced back to the Prophet— no private judgment being permitted[4]. Only linguistic explanations were allowed (p. 27).

But, in spite of this limitation in the interpretation of the Qur'an much could be dexterously said which really had no place there. Tabari's own commentary, which is praised for its felicitous union of tradition and judgment, shows this[5].

The otherwise extremely liberal Samarqandi has expressed a definite opinion disallowing, though a Hanafite, every scientific explanation. In the interpretation of the Qur'an, according to him, at most it is permissible to employ elucidatory traditions; *i.e.*, to adopt the form in which the Chapter headed "Interpretation of the Qur'an" in Bukhari and Muslim is composed, and which was practised by the second class of exegetes discussed by Suyuti, (*de. inter Korani*, Text p. 2.).

---

(1) Tafsir, 30.
(2) *Bustan al-arifin*, 74 ff.
(3) Suyuti, *Muzhir*, II, 207 ; Goldziher, SWA, vol. 72, p. 630.
(4) *Tafsir* 1, 26.
(5) For instance, vol. I, 58 'on *Predestination*'.

The new element in the interpretation of the Qur'an in this and the preceding century was the very enthusiastic and independent co-operation of the Mutazilites. Of their leader Al-Jubbai, his son-in-law Ashari, at once his pupil and his opponent, complains that not once in his commentary has he referred to an older commentary but has solely relied upon the promptings of his heart and those of his demon[1]. But, again, the orthodox refused to follow the lead of this very Ashari because they persisted in literal interpretation of "doubtful" passages[2]. The Mutazilite philologer Ali Ibn Isa el-Rummani (d. 385/995) wrote a commentary on the Qur'an. Sahib ibn Abbad (d. 385/995) on being questioned, if he, too, had written one, replied: 'Ali ibn Isa had left nothing for him to do'[3].

The Mutazilite Nakkas[4] who died at Baghdad in 351/962 and who 'lied in tradition' composed a commentary of 12,000 leaves. Abu Bakr of Edfu (d. 388/988)[5] wrote one in 120 volumes. In the following century, however, he was outstriped by the Mutazilite Abdus-Salam al-Qazwini (d. 483/1090) who commented upon the Qur'an in 300 volumes of which seven dealt only with the sura *Fateha*[6]. We obtain an idea of the method of this school from the fact that the Mutazilite Ubaidullah al-Azdi (d. 387/997) collected together 120 different views concerning the meaning of 'in the name of God the merciful and compassionate[7] . Hetherto no Muslim sect had disregarded the Qur'an. For all it was the central armoury to draw weapons from for warfare and, thus,

(1) Spitta, *el-Ashari*, 128.

(2) Goldziher, ZDMG, 41, p. 59. According to Ibn Khaldun, *Hist. Berb*, 1,299.

(3) [illegible]mad ibn Yahya, ed. Arnold, 65; Suyuti, *Mufasserin*, 30.

(4) *Fihrist*, 33; Yaqut, VI, 496.

(5) Suyuti *Husnul Muhadherah*, 1,233.

(6) Suyuti, *de interp. Corani*, 19; Subki (*Tabaqat* III, 230) speaks of 700 volumes.

(7) Suyuti, *de interp. Corani*, 22. In Mutazalite exegesis its enemy Ibn Kutaibah can only cavil at trfles. (*Mukhtalif, el-hadith*, 80 ff.).

like all holy books, it had to suffer from a great deal of exegetic subtlety. The Sufis and Shiahs; notorious as *Ahl ta' wilat,* freely used the tried method of allegory.[1] Everywhere the Shiites detected personal allusions : By the "Cow" which God ordered the Jews to sacrifice, Ayesha was meant[2] and the Gods Jibt and Tagut[3] were none else than Muawiya and Amr ibn al-As[4].

The scientifically-trained like Abu Zaid al-Balkhi (d. 322-934), who had studied philosophy, astronomy, medicine, natural sciences under Al-Kindi at Baghdad stood in the opposite camp. In his letters on the *Nazm el-Quran* (composition of the Qur'an) he takes the words in their literal sense[5]. In his enquiry into the allegories he arrived at such negative conclusions that a highly-placed Karmathian withdrew the pension he had hitherto paid him[6].

Even philology, had become so exacting then as to set up a special ecclesiastical vocabulary different from the common usage[7]. And the entire school of the *Zahirities* emphasised the literal interpretation of Law and preeminently of the Qur'an, as their main principle. But for obvious reasons none of them embarked upon commentary of the Qur'an. The literal interpretation of the Qur'an had as little attraction for Muslims then as it has today.

Arab, Jewish and Christian legends of the Qur'an and the tradition were indeed a notable field of fierce controversy[1]. There theology was confronted with miracles— *recognizing only the Pre-Islamic Prophets as real*

---

(1) Goldziher, *Zahiriten*, 132.
(2) Sura, 2,63.
(3) Sura, 4,54.
(4) Ibn Kutaiba, *Mukhtalif el-hadith*, 84.
(5) *Irshad* , 1, 148. The book is not mentioned in the *Fihrist.*
(6) *Fihrist*, 138.
(7) Goldziher, *Zahiriten* 134.

miracle-workers. And so it is that the most conspicuous Qura'nic scholar of his time Ahmad eth-Tha'labi (d. 427/ 1036) composes as his most important work his *'Histories of the Prophets[2]'*.

To some miracles were the most cherished possessions of their faith. They would much rather have the history of the camel that flew than of the camel that walked or much sooner hear of a false vision than of an established fact[3].

Whereas others rejected them *a priori* and yet others transformed them into amazing allegories.

The famous physician Al-Razi about 300/912 wrote on the other hand a book on the "Impostures of Prophets". Mutahhar dose not even once dare to refer to its contents for it corrupts, says he, the heart, weans it from piety and fosters hatred towards the Prophets[4].

The conjunction of the Qur'an and reason yielded precisely the same amusing result as we find in the exegesis of the Protestant Rationalism.

We must, for God's sake, even deny that in the 'Flood' innocent children were drowned. It was suggested that for 15 years before the 'Flood' God had sealed the womb of every woman so that the evil fate might only overtake the guilty. Another looked upon the Ark of Noah merely as a symbol of his religion and the 950 years of life, which the Qur'an credits him with, as the duration of his preaching. Another contended that the wonderful She-Camel which came out of a mountain to the Prophet Saleh was merely a

---

(1) Suyuti, *Mufassarin.*

(2) Already Abu Rajah (d. 335/946) composed a poem of 30,000 verses on the *'History of the world and of the Prophets.'* Abul Mahasin II, 319; Subki II, 108.

(3) Sura, 34, V. 2.

(4) Mutahhar, IV. 113.

symbol of a specially compelling proof. A third shrewdly hinted that the Prophet had concealed the camel in the mountain and simply fetched her out. A fourth made a yet more lively suggestion; namely, that the camel stood for a man and a woman[1]. Other maintained that Abraham who, according to the Qu'ran, remained unscathed in a burning oven, had smeared himself with a fire-proof oil and referred to similar tricks among the Indians[2]. Of the birds Ababil, which drove the advancing Abyssinians back with stones from Mekka—a widespread explanation wás that they perished by reason of the fruit, water and climate of Yaman[3]. The 'spring of melted metal' which God caused to flow for Solomon[4] was explained away as Solomon's mining activity. The famous hoopoe which Solomon missed at the review[5] was put down as the name of a man, the talking ants[6] as timid, the demons as proud, powerful, crafty men who acknowledged his sway.

The only miracles, outside the Qur'an, which systematic theology took notice of, were miracles of the Prophet. Though disowned by the Qur'an—yet the traditions of the 3rd/9th century reckoned some two hundred of them[7]. The rationalists, however, interpreted them in the light of reason. Thus the enemies, surrounding the house of the Prophet, were blinded not in point of fact but by rage and hate and so did not notice his escape. Not yet did the devil himself personally oppose the Prophet in the council house at Mekka but a man with devilish disposition[8].

Even good Muslims, in cultured circles, who professed

(1) Mutahhar, III, 22; IV, 44.
(2) Mutahhar III, 56.
(3) Mutahhar, III, 189.
(4) Sura, 34, V. 2.
(5) Sura, 27, V. 18.
(6) Sura 27, V. 18.
(7) Mutahhar, IV, 112 f.
(8) Mutahhar, IV, 163.

to accept these miracles, did not do so in good faith.

In 355/966 Mutahhar el-Makdisi composed his '*Creation and History*' specially to defend Islam against the all-too-credulous story-tellers and the unbelieving doubters. He is never weary of re-iterating that only the Revelation and trustworthy traditions are binding upon him. Nevertheless we note his joy when he succeeds in justifying a miracle before the Bar of Reason, "mother of all sciences". To those who consider the assumption of Enoch to heaven, related by tradition, impossible he thus replies: there are more wonderful things still, for instance, the cloud sailing in the sky and the Earth, standing firm despite its weight[1].

To those who deny the possibility of Jona's history, namely, of a living person existing in the womb of an animal—he puts forward the case of an embryo, living and breathing in the mother's womb[2].

And again he shows his secret satisfaction in the rationalistic explanation of Prophetic miracles by giving enthusiastic assent to the view that the very same phenomenon may be a miracle at one time and not so at another. He specially refers to the Qur'an as one such instance of relative miracle admitting thereby that, in other time, such a performance may be within human reach and accomplishment. And thus he strays into assertions which Muslims can only regard as the assertions of a crazed heretic[3].

The Prophet is reported to have promised : 'God will, at the beginning of every century, send a man from my house to make their religion clear to them.'

---

(1) Mutahhar, III, 14.
(2) Mutahhar, III, 116.
(3) Mutahhar, IV, 164.

The later savants have drawn up a list of these 'revivalists' (Mujaddidun), of whom each must have been born at the beginning of his century. (The text has 'died' but the meaning is evidently 'born').

About the year 400/1010 the choice lay between three candidates of equal worthlessness. In 300/912 the only one whose claim could be seriously entertained was Ashari (d. 325/937)[1]. This indeed, indicates impoverishment in the domain of official theology; representing the most acute intellects of the day. The Mutazilites, then, raised all kinds of problems. As a sect they were as little opposed to the Sunnis *then* as were the Shiahs. This opposition does not come to light till the 5th/11th century[2]. Not unlike the Sufis, their difference with the majority of the faithful in the 4th/10th century was still a purely theological difference[3]. In religious rites they, for the most part, followed the orthodox school. And yet there were Shiite Mutazilite like the Zaidite and even Alids like Da'i Abu Abdullah—a pupil of Abu Abdullah el-Basri[4]. Other famous Shiite Mutazilites were Rawendi and the philologer Rummani (d. 384/994)[5]. Their masters were almost all Persians who had emigrated to Mesopotamia or had settled down in Isfahan. Jubbai (d. 303/915) has even written a commentary on the Qur'an in Persian. Their central theme was theology in a narrow sense; at its inception, the relation of God to the good and evil in

(1) Goldziher *Zur Charakteristik es-Suyutis*, SWA, Vol. 69, 8 ff. People also held different views on the question whether there should be only one reformer in every century or one in every branch (of learning). Dhahabi held the letter opinion and placed, in the fourth century, Ibn Suraij at the head of Jurisprudence, Ashari at the head of theology, and Nasa'i at the head of tradition. Subki, *Tabaqat*, II, 89.

(2) Ibn Hazm, *Milal*, II, 111.

(3) Mutahhar, 1, 13.

(4) Ahmad Ibn Yahya, *Kit. el-milal*, ed. Arnold, 63.

(5) Suyuti, *Mufassirin*, p. 74.

the world[1]—in other words, the *doctrine of Predestination*, which had an intense fascination for the Zarathustrian cast of mind. The leading Mutazilite chief of the time, Ibn al-Hudail al-Allaff, is said to have celebrated his greatest dialectic triumph actually against the Magians[2]. At the end of the 3rd/9th century Mutazilism produced the most doughty champion of the dualistic view—Ibn al-Rawendi—who most violently opposed his own sect and was ultimately denounced to Government[3].

In the 4th/10th century, at least in Isfahan[4], neither the Mutazilites nor the Sufis could escape the fate of being attached to Ali as their founder[5]. Khawrezmi even expressly states that the Mutazilites (the Sufis also claimed him) were devoted to the Church-father Hasan of Basra with the same love and devotion as the Shiahs were to Ali, the Zaidites to Zaid, and the Imamites to the Mahdi[6]. There were also stray influences of Gnostic speculations such as the theories of the first creation and of the Logos Demiurgos[7].

In the 4th/10th century there were but few who[8]

(1) Spitta, *Ashari*, 87.
(2) Ahmad ibn Yahya, 26 f,
(3) Ahmed ibn Yahya ed. Arnold, 53 f.
(4) Ibid, 61 f.
(5) Arnold 5 f.
(6) Yatimah.II, 120.
(7) Ibn Hazm, *Milal*, IV, 197.
(8) Ibn Hazm, *Milal*, II, 112. Those few who gnawed still at the old bone 'free-will' were called 'Qadarites'. The significance of this word is not easy to explain. For ibn Kutaibah (*Mukhtalif*, p. 98) the Qadarites are the supporters of the doctrine of the free-will who "appropriate all power to themselves"— their opponents being 'Jabariyyah.' But that is *lucus a non lucendo.* In the earlier days, however, the defenders of 'Predestination' were so called (Qadarites) "who place all their sins to the credit of the Almighty." (Ahmad ibn Yahya, ed. Arnold, p. 12). In the 3rd/9th century strictly speaking they taught that God had created good and the devil evil (Ibn Kutaibah, *Tawil Mukhtalif el-hadith,* Cairo, 1326, p. 5; Spitta, *el-Ashari, p. 1:1).* For this dualism people called them, 'the

speculated on sin and predestination ; the outstanding topic then was the unity and attributes of God.

The advancement, in the domain of speculation, must be ascribed to the influence of Greek philosophy which in the 3rd/9th century caused a lively ferment[1]. But it is to be noted that its definite influence mainfests itself only upon the higher stratum of the *Mutakallimun* (theologians), upon such as An-Nazzam and Jahiz ; nor is its influence absent from Christian theology which, throughout this period, busies itself with the purification of the conception of God[2]. In making this very question, namely, the question of the purification of the conception of divinity, the central theme of their discussions the Mutazilites not only made it the main dogma even of modern Muslim theology but gave a peculiar turn to Arab philosophy, which, with its speculations on

---

Zoroastrians of Islam' ; (Ibn Kutaibah, 96) and related of them the old story where a Qadarite recommended Islam to one of other faith. To that recommendation he replied that he would wait until God so wished it. Thereupon the Qadarite rejoined : God wished so long ago but the devil has stood in the way. Thereupon the Jew or the Christian—whoever he was—answered : I remain with the stronger of the two (Ibn Kutaibah, 99). On account of this dualism the orthodox then called *even* the advocates of free-will "Qadarites"; while these with more etymological correctness called the orthodox so. (Ibn Kutaibah, *Mukhtalif* 97; Ibn Hazm, 1, 54). In the 4th/10th century Mukaddasi mentions the Qadariya sect as having been absorbed into that of al-Mutazilah (Eng. tr. p. 54 text p. 37). Even Ashari places the Mutazilah and the *ahl-el-Qadr* side by side (Spitta, 131). But no one with discrimination can fail to see, says Mukkadasi, the difference between the two; adding at the same time the fact that the 'Qadriyya' have been absorded in the larger whole of the 'Mutazilah.' And yet about 400/1010 the most celebrated Mutazilite then, Abdul Jabbar, the Qadhi of Rai, will not give the appelation of the 'Qadariyya' to his school and sought to establish—naturally with the help of the sayings of the Prophet—that by the 'Qadarites' the orthodox fatalists were meant (Schreiner, ZDMG, 52, p. 509 f.).

(1) Horowitz, *uber den Einfluss der griechischen Philosophie auf Entwicklung des kalam,* Breslau, 1909.

(2) Becker, ZA, Vol. 26, 176 ff.

the essence and attributes of God, has, through Spinozism, affected, Western thought.

The Mutazilites says Ibn Hazm, have invented the term *Sifat* (attributes)—the older term being *nu'ut*, (descriptions)[1]. Mukaddasi considers subtlety, knowledge, lewdness and scoffing as the chief features of the Mutazilites[2]. That they were regarded as particularly prone to contention and disputes is palpable from their very system itself which is wholly based upon dialectic[3].

The Mutazilites say : "When the learned dispute, they are both in the right'[4]. But despite their contentious spirit they were so firmly knitted together that in the 4th/10th century "clinging one to another like Mutazilites" became a proverb[5].

These scholastics drew everything into the meshes of their speculations and "craved for all knowledge[6]." The so-called philosophers looked slightingly down upon them ; not unlike an empirical psycologist upon the metaphysician[7]. Besides being narrow-minded the philosophers suspected the scholastics of an irreligious trend of thought, nay of positive scepticism[8]. These scholastics rejected magic, astrology, even miracles of saints. "Of this band three stand out conspicuously in the world of Islam : Jahiz, Ali Ibn Ubaid-ullah al-Lutfi, and Abu Zaid al-

(1) Bukhari, *Kit. al-tauhid* ; according to Goldziher, *Zahiriten*, 145 note 1.

(2) p. 41; Eng. tr. p. 69.

(3) In their hey-day Ibn Raffal (d. 355 or 356) is said to have composed the first work on the art of controversy (Jadal); Abulmahasin, II, 321.

(4) Samarqandi, *Bustan al-arifin*, p. 15.

(5) Khwarezmi, *Rasa'il*, 63.

(6) Jahiz, *Kit al-haywan*, IV, 109.

(7) Goldziher, *Kit-Ma'anl en-nafs*, AGGW, N, F. 10. p. 13 ff.

(8) Goldziher, ZDMG, vol. 62 p. 2 ff; Ahmad b. Yahya, ed. Arnold, 51.

Balkhi[1]. Of these, Jahiz and Balkhi, the second is not known to me, were men of rare liberality and breadth of vision. In Jahiz there is more eloquence than substance; in Balkhi, a happy union of the two, Jahiz is the Voltaire; Balkhi (d. 322/933),[2] the more sober and the more solid, is the Alexander Humboldt of this school. Besides philosophy Balkhi studied astronomy, medicine, geography, natural sciences. He wrote a work on the Qur'an in which he considered—without speculation or digression— only the actual meaning of the words. His book of allegory caused the forfeiture of a pension which he drew from a Karmathian magnate.

Ibn Kutaibah tells us what the opponents of Jahiz thought of him. "Of all the scholastics he is strongest in this: he makes trifles great and great things trifles".

He can defend opposite propositions with equal dexterity. Now he will vindicate the pre-eminence of the black over white. Now he will fight with the Shiahs on behalf of the party of Uthman and now against the Othmanites and the Sunnites for the Shiites. Now he will exalt Ali and yet again lay him low. He composed a book adducing the reasons urged by Christians against Muslims but instead of meeting their charges he withheld proof suggesting thereby that he wanted to drive the Muslims to a corner and to cause doubt in those of weak faith. His writings are full of jokes and fun to attract youths and wine-bibbers. He ridicules the tradition[3]—as all learned men know—when he speaks of the liver of the whale which supports the earth; of the horn of the devil, and, equally so when he asserts that the black stone was originally white, only the heathens had made it black, and that the faithful would restore its original

(1) Yaqut, *Irshad*, 1, 148.

(2) *Irshad* 1, 142.

(3) Ibn Kutaibah *Mukhtalif el-hadith*, (Cairo 1326), pp. 71 ff.

colour when they become truly so. And in the same scoffing tone he speaks of the scroll, on which was inscribed 'the Revelation concerning Suckling'; which lay under the bed of Ayesha and was eaten up by a sheep and of other Christian and Jewish traditions such as the traditions of "the cock and the raven drinking together" "the hoopoe burying, its mother, in its head," the history of the hymn of the frog and 'the scarf-ring of the pigeon'. And yet others which gravely offended Muslims.

Once on Firday Thumamah, their leader, saw the people rushing in emulation to a mosque to be in time of prayer. See 'the cattle,' 'the donkeys,' he cried out and told a friend; 'what has this Arrab made of men'[1].

In the 3rd/9th century the ecclesiastical circles were riven with hatred and contempt for each other. In 300/912 the Mutazilites Ashari went over to the enemy and waged war with the Mutazilites with their own weapons. And thus in the 4th/10th century the official scientific dogmatics of Islam came into being. Like every official system it was a compromise and was called the *Madhab ausat* (the middle course)[2]. Ashari flattered himself on being able to reconcile the most orthodox teachings with reason and declared himself a Hambalite. In his articles of faith he wrote : "we teach what Ahmad ibn Hanbal has taught and refuse credence to those who differ from him. He is an excellent Imam and a perfect master and through him has God revealed the truth when error got the upper hand"[3].

This notwithstanding—the Hanbalites adopted an

(1) Ibn Kutaibah, *Tawil mukhtalif el-hadith,* 60.

(2) *Spitta, ashari,* 46. Their nearest predecessors, among the dialecticians, were the Kallabites who were now merged in the Asharites and who were reproached for their rigid doctrine of predestination. Muk. 37 (Eng. tr. p. 55).

(3) Spitta, 133.

attitude of hostility towards him[1]. With justice, Ibn al- Jauzi says, that he really always remained a Mutazilite[2]. His system had the common fate of all compromise—theology. Its prominent disciples strongly leaned towards the left—notably so Al-Baqilani (d. 403/1012) who introduced the ideas of atom, of empty space, etc., into dogmatics[3].

Another who began as his disciple but went over to the Mutazilites and became its prominent leader was Qadi Abdul Jabbar of Rai[4]. He owed his success in life to Sahib ibn Abbad but, dispite this, he refused ecclesiastical benediction to him, after death, because he had died without repentance[5]. Ibn al-Athir is quite indignant over it and regards him as a type of perfidy and faithlessness. From all this it is mainfest that the Mutazilites as a whole deserve but little the title of the 'Free-minded'.

During the 4th/10th century the representatives of the old Sunnah opposed the arrogant Shiahs at Baghdad. In the Provinces they made the position of the Mutazilites difficult. But though they stirred the people up against them—they met with little success in this direction. We hear, indeed, of a very few persecutions[6].

The Asharite system was not yet strong enough to stand as a rival to the Sunnah. Not until 380/1000 does it at all assume any importance in Mesopotamia[7] when it has to reap the consequences thereof. The Hanbalites forbade the Khatib al-Baghdadi admission into the chief mosque at Baghdad for his Asharite leanings[8]. Under Toghril Beg the

(1) Spitta, III.
(2) fol. 71 b.
(3) Schreiner, p. 82 according to Ibn Khaldun.
(4) Ahmad ibn Yahya, ed. Arnold.
(5) Ibn al-Athir IX, 72.
(6) Two specially characteristic ones in Goldziher ZDMG, 62 p. 8.
(7) Maqrizi, *Khitat*, I, 358.
(8) He was consistently unjust to the Hanbalites (Ibn al-Jauzi, fol. 118 b).

leading Asharite teachers were persecuted and banished and towards the end of the century an influential Asharite, Al-Qushairi (d. 514/1120), was compelled to leave the capital (Baghdad) on account of a riot fomented by the Hanbalites[1].

From this event Ibn Asakir dates the real split between the two parties[2]. This new theology which was destined to be the theology of Islam slowly spread over the empire. In the extreme East it entered into competition with the system of Al-Maturidi—though the two systems had much in common. But apart from this it had to fight the Hanbalites whose leader is said to have solemnly anathematised Ashari in 400/1010[3], and the Karmathians who, just at this period, denounced the Asharites to Government as those who maintained that the Prophet was dead[4].

In the west, indeed, Ashariism made its way from one cultural seat to another—Sicily, Qairwan, and Spain where thier cause, at the time of Ibn Hazm, 'Praise be·to God', was not in a very flourishing condition[5]. In North Africa[6] it was entirely unknown and as not introduced until about 500/1107 by Ibn Tumart[7].

At the beginning of the 5th/11th century theological differences were in a measure officially settled. In 408/1017 Caliph Al-Qadir issued an edict against the Mutazilites. He commanded them to desist from teaching their doctrines and stopped them discussing views at variance with the orthodox Islam on pain of punishment. Of the Amirs—the newly risen Star in the East, Muhmud of Ghazni, gave effect

(1) Goldziher, 9 f.
(2) Spitta, *Ashari*, III.
(3) Subki, III. 117.
(4) Subki, III, 54.
(5) Milat, IV, 204.
(6) Qairwan is in N. Africa.
(7) Goldziher ZDMG, 41, 30 ff.

to the command of the Caliph.

He persecuted the schismatics, killed them, banished them and had them cursed from the puplit. "*Such Cursing became this year the practice in Islam*[1]". At Baghdad a similar edict was once more issued and promulgated. In 433/1041 the very same Caliph (Al-Qadir) issued a *Confession of Faith* which was solemnly read out at Baghdad and subscribed to by the theologians in order that "one may know who is an unbeliever". This was the first official announcement of its kind. It meant the end of theology. The intelligent mind perceives in every word here the germs of age-long disputes." It is necessary for man to know that there is one God who has no Companion, who neither begets nor is begotten, who has no equal and has accepted none as His son or companion and who has no co-ruler of the universe with him. He is the first and, as such, He has always been. He is the last for He will never, cease to exist. All powerful—He needs nothing. When He wishes a thing—He has only to say—'be' and it is there. There is no God besides Him. Living—no sleep overtakes him, no, not even a casual slumber. He gives food but does not take it Himself. He is alone and yet never feels lonely. He is friendly with none. Years age him not! and how can they affect Him for He is, indeed, the Author of the year and time, day and night, light and darkness, heaven and earth, and all the creatures that are therein, of land and water and all that is within them and, verily, of all things, living and dead. He is the only one of his kind—there is nothing near or about Him. No space encloses Him. By His sheer power He has created every thing. He has created the throne though He does not need it. He is on the throne because He so wills it and, not like human beings, to rest on it.

He is the Director of heaven and of earth and of all things

(1) Ibn al-Jauzi, fol. 16, 56.

there and of all things on land and water. There is no director save him and no protector either. He controls mankind. He makes them ill and well again, makes them die or keeps them alive. But weak are created beings, Angels, Prophets, Apostles, all creatures. He is knowing through his own knowlege. Eternal and incomprehensible is He. He is the Hearer who hears and the Seer who sees. Of His attributes men only apprehend these two and none of his creatures attains them both.

He speaks but not with organs like those of human beings. Only those attributes should be ascribed to Him which He has Himself ascribed or those which His Prophets have ascribed to Him and every one of the attributes which He has himself ascribed is an attribute of His being which man should not overlook.

Man should also know : the word of God is not created. He has spoken through Gabriel and has revealed it to his Prophet. After Gabriel had heard it From Him—he repeated it to Muhammad, Muhammad to his companions his Companions to the community. And, therefore, mere repetition by man does not make 'the word' created for it is the very word of God and the word of God is not created. And 'uncreated' it remains whether repeated or retained in memory, written or heard. He who asserts that it is in any way 'created' is an unbeliever whose blood it is permissible to shed—should he refuse to repent of his error when called upon to do so.

One should also know that Faith is speech, action, and thought : Speech with the tongue, action with the *arkan* (members) and the limbs (*jawarih*). Faith may become greater or smaller—greater by obedience, smaller by refractoriness. It has different stages and divisons. The highest is the confession : 'There is no God but Allah !' Self-control is part of faith and patience is to faith what the head is to the body. Man knoweth not what is recorded about it with God and what is sealed there with Him. And for this reason precisely we say : 'He is believing if God will : and I hope, I am believing.' There is no other resource save hope. Let him not, therefore, despair because he is striving for something which lies hidden in the future. He should honestly carry out all laws and directions and do acts of supererogation for all these are part of faith. Faith never reaches an end, since supererogatory works never attain a limit.

One must love all the Companions of the Prophet. They are the best of human beings after the Prophet. The best and noblest of them after the Prophet is Abu Bakr as-Siddiq, next to him Omar ibn al-Khattab, next to Omar Othman ibn-Affan, and next to Othman Ali-Ibn Abi-Talib. May God bless them and associate with them in paradise and have compassion on the souls of the Companions of the Prophet. He who slander Ayesha has no part or lot in Islam. Of Moawiyah we should only say good things and refuse to enter into any controversy about him. We should invoke God's mercy for all. God has said : 'And they who have come after them *into the faith* say, O, our Lord, forgive us and our brethren who have preceeded us in the faith, put not into our hearts ill-will against them who believe. O, our Lord ! Thou verily art kind and merciful[1]'. And He said of them : We will remove what is in their breasts of rancour as brethren face to face on couches[2]. We should declare no one an unbeliever for omitting to fulfil any of the legal ordinances except the prescribed prayer; for he who neglects to pray without due cause is an unbeliever even though he does not deny the duty of praying, as the Prophet said : Neglect of Prayer is of unbelief, whoso neglects it is an unbeliever, and remains so until repents and prays. And

(1) Sura, 59, 10.
(2) Sura 15, 47.

were he to die before repentance he will awake on the day of judgment with Pharaoh, Haman, and Korah. The neglect of other injunctions does not make one an unbeliever even if one is so criminal as not to admit the duty. Such are the doctrines of the Sunnah and of the community ! He who stands by them stands in the clear light of truth, is under right guidance and on the true path. For such an one we may hope for immunity from hell-fire and admission into paradise, God willing! Some one asked the Prophet : towards whom one should be of good will ? He replied : all the faithful, high and low. And he said : Should a warning come from God to man through religion—it is but an act of God's mercy. Should he pay heed to the warning—it will be profitable to him—Should he not— it will be a witness against him. But by refusal (to pay heed) he multiplies his sins and draws down upon him the wrath of God. May God make us thankful for his favours and mindful of His mercies ! Let Him make us defenders of pious practices and let Him forgive us and all the faithful[1]".

The friendly intercourse with Christians and Jews—a toleration unparalleled in the Middle Ages—gave to Muslim theology an absolutely unmediaeval appendix. Thus the science of comparative religion took its rise from an altogether untheological quarter.

Naubakhti who wrote the first important book on the subject belonged to that group which translated Greek works into Arabic[2]. The very untheological Masudi wrote two books on 'Comparative religion'[3]. Then, again, the civil servant Musabbihi (d. 420/1029), who wrote, in his own long-winded way some 3,500 leaves[4] on 'Religions and cults', was a writer with distinct worldly interests. The

(1) Ibn al-Jauzi, 195 f.

(2) Masudi, 1,156 ; *Fihrist*, 177.

(3) Masudi, 1,200 ff.

(4) *Fihrist*, 92, 24.

explanation that we can offer for this work—the only work of his dealing with religion—is his Sabian interests ; for his family came from Harran, celebrated for Sabian associations[1].

Nor must we lose sight of the fact that theologians of inquisitive turn of mind also occupied themselves with this subject. And this is abundantly manifest from the *Kit. al-milal wan-nihal* (Book of sects and religions) of Abu Mansur al-Baghdadi (d. 422/1031)—a tittle which now comes into fashion[2]. Like a pious Muslim, the Spanish Ibn Hazm (d. 456/1064), in his similarly named works, has discussed a number of religious systems; while, in the beginning of the 5th/11th century Biruni (d. 400/1009) wrote him 'History of India' which is essentially an account of the Hindu religion from a purely scientific point of view not, as he says, in a spirit of opposition but with a view to bring facts to light"[3].

It is noteworthy that the 'historians of religion' were mostly men whose faith was not altogether above doubt or suspicion. Even Shahrastani is reproached for his heretical tendencies. In his preachings he is never once said to have quoted from the Qur'an[4].

---

(1) Tallquist, 102.
(2) Subki, III, 239.
(3) Sachau (Eng. Tr) 117.
(4) Yaqut, III, 343; Goldziher SWA 73,552.

XIV. THE SCHOOLS OF JURISPRUDENCE

In the history of Muslim Law the 4th/10th century constitutes an important landmark. Then the supreme source of legal development—the interpretation of the Qur'an and the tradition by the aid of individual light— is supposed to have ceased (*Ijtihad Mutlaq*)[1]. Then the creative period ended; the old masters were set down as infallible and only in matters of trivial concern were the Jurists allowed to form an independent judgment of their own. In other words the rabbis succeeded the scribes.

But such, indeed, is only the Islamic view of the position of affairs! In reality, here, as elsewhere, precisely the same thing happens—the outstanding feature is the introduction of the pre-Islamic legal conceptions—the revival of the old Greco Roman ideas. These ideas were represented by the Jurists (*Fuqaha*), in contradistinction to the upholders of the *Sunnah*, who sought to shape and regulate life in conformity with the word of God and His Prophet. The old school, however, would not yield straightway and was still predominant in two very important provinces—Fars and Syria—besides Sind.[2] Further, in Media it reckoned many supporters.

Of the schools of *Sunnah* the Hanbalites, the Auzaites and the Thaurites were the most important.[3] But as compared with later times it is necessary to note that the Hanbalites were not then regarded as Jurists at all. In 306/918 the schools of jurisprudence mentioned are : the

(1) Snouck Hurgronje, RHR 37, p. 176.

(2) Muk., 179, 395, 439, 481.

(3) *Fihrist*, 225. Muk., 37 (Se Lammens, *Islam*, Ch. V. Tr.).

Shafi'ites, the Malikites, the Thaurites, the Hanafites, and the Daudites[1]. And towards the end of the century : the Hanafites, the Malikites, the Shafi'ites and the Daudites[2]. On neither of these occasions are the Hanbalites referred to as a School of Law. There was a disturbance at Tabari's funeral (d. 310/922) because, in his work on the *Differences of opinion among Jurists*, he completely ignored Ibn Hanbal on the ground that he was no jurist but a mere traditionist.[3] Only later did the Hanbalites succeed in receiving recognition as Jurists[4]. The other schools of Jurisprudence could not hold out. Already in the 3rd/9th century the Auzaites had been overshadowed in Spain by the Malikites. The Qadi of Damascus, howover, who died in 347/958, was an Auzaite[5]. They even had a school in the great mosque of Damascus[6]. According to Muqaddasi Auzai failed only because the centre of his teaching was too far away: "Had it lain on the route of the pilgrims, the inhabitants of both East and West would have embraced it."[7] Muqaddasi even regards the teachings of Sufyan Thauri which, at one time, predominated in Isfahan, to have fallen into obscurity[8]. In 405/1014 died the last great jurist who delivered lectures in the Mansurah Mosque at Baghdad according to that school of Jurisprudence[9]. Although, according to tradition, some five hundred schools of Jurisprudence are said to have disappeared at or about the beginning of the 3rd/9th century—yet everything still was in a state of flux[10].

(1) Subki, II, 337.
(2) Muk., 37.
(3) Ibn Jauzi, *Muntazam*, Sub anno. 310 according to Thabit ibn Sinan: Ibn al-Athir, VIII, 98, according to Misk : Wustenfeld, AGGW 37, Nr. 80.
(4) According to Ghazzali about 500/1107, Kern, *Ikhtilaf* of Tabari, 14.
(5) Abu'l-Mahasin, II, 347.
(6) Muk., 179.
(7) Muk., 144. (Eng. tr. p. 234 Tr.)
(8) Muk., 37, 395 (on Sufyan Thauri, see Ibn Khall. I, 576 Eng. Tr.)
(9) Ibn Taghribardi, 126.
(10) '*Umdat al-arifin* in Kern's *Ikhtilaf* of Tabari, 14.

Daud of Isfahan (p. 270-883) founded the Zahirite school which in the 4th/10th century rose to great prominence in the East. In Iran it included within its circle some very distinguished names and in Fars even the Qadi and other Judicial officers subscribed to its tenets. The ruler 'Adad-ud-Daulah himself belonged to that school[1]. It rigorously proceeded against the compromise affected by Shafii' between the old traditional school of *Sunnah* and the new jurisprudence.[2] Like all extremists it aimed at purification. Its principle to stand faithfully by tradition was a scientific principle but it was soon apparent that jurisprudence was not an exact science. Its clear-cut method exercised by far the greatest influence in the historico-philological sphere. According to Muqaddasi the chief characteristic of the Zahirites are : Pride, acuteness, combativeness, prosperity[3].

The historian Tabari (d. 310/923) also founded a school of jurisprudence. For months after his death the pious came to his house to offer prayers at his grave[4]. Tabari's friend, Ibn Shajarah, who died at the age of ninety in 350/961, likewise, followed his own line of thought and acknowledged no master. Despite his independence (and it is characteristic of the tolerant conditions in the East) he became a Qadi (Yaqut, *Irshad*, II, 18). Even the Qadi of Old Cairo Ibn Harbawaihi (d. 319/931 over hundred years old)—belonging as he did to the Shafi'ite school—decided according to his own light, unfettered by any system or authority.

Had another done this, it would not have been tolerated

---

(1) Muk., 439.

(2) Khwarezmi, *Mafatih al-'ulum;* p. 8: Goldziher, *Za'iriten,* 110.

(3) p. 41.

(4) Wustenfeld, AGGXX 37, Nr. 80. Ibn Taghribardi mentions a jurist who died in 410/1019 belonging to the shcool of Tabari. The Egyptian Qadi al-Kha ibi (supplement to Kindi, p. 577), who died in 347/958, wrote a controversial work against Tabari.

for an instant but no one, in his case, took exception to it (Kindi, 528 ; Subki, *Tabaqat,* II, 303).

But, in point of fact, the four main schools held their ground—as is the case in the East to-day—except in the Shi'ite countries. In the 4th century the Hanbalites, for the first time, passed beyond the confines of Mesopotamia[1].

But the outstanding fact is the expansion of the Shafi'ites with their head-quarters at Mekka and Medina[2]. "Since the appearance of the Shafi'ites up to the present day, the offices of judge, of preacher, and of superintendent in the holy towns had been in their hands. For the last 563 years they have preached in the mosque of the Prophet according to the school of his cousin Muhammad ibn Idris el-Shafa'i. And the Prophet has been present and has heard what they have preached and therein lies the best proof that this school is the best school before God."[3] In Mesopotamia they received but little support. There the Jurists and the Qadis were mostly Hanafites;[4] although in 338/949 a Shaf'i was appointed the chief Qadi[5]. In the East they were more successful against the Hanafites[6]. In Syria and Egypt they managed to establish their stronghold. Abu Zurah (d. 302/914) was the first Shafi'te Qadi of Damascus and of the Egyptian capital. His successors in Syria remained loyal to his School[7]. In Egypt their opponents were the Malikites who had come to power there since the middle of the 2nd/8th century. In 326/938 the Shafi'ites and the Malkites had

(1) Suyuti, *Husnul-Muhadera,* 1, 228.
(2) Khwarezmi, *Ras'ail,* 63. Muk. is silent on this point.
(3) Subki, *Tabaqat,* 1, 14.
(4) Muk., 204 (Eng. tr.)
(5) Subki, II, 244.
(6) At Shash the extreme edge of the empire, the Shafi'ite teaching was introduced by a scholar who died in 335/948. Suyuti, *de interp. Corani,* 36].
(7) Kindi, 519 : Subki, II, 174 ; Suyuti, *Husnul Muhadera* 1, 186. An exception to this rule, p. 203.

each 15 circles of students in the chief mosque of Fustat ; the Hanafites only three[1]. At the time of Muqaddasi a Shafi'i, for the first time, acted as Imam of the mosque of Ibn Tulun. Till then this office was almost exclusively held by the Malikites. Even most of the Jurists there belonged to the Malikite school[2]. The circles of audience which formed round the Malikite Imam en-Na'ali (d. 380/990) covered seventeen pillars of the mosque[3]. For this reason precisely the Fatimid Government proceeded very severely against the Malikites. In 381/991, for instance, a man was scourged at Old Cairo and was taken round the town in disgrace for possessing a copy of the *Muatta* of Ibn Malik.

After the fall of the Fatimids—the Ayyubids, by their Shafi'ite leanings, helped this school on to victory. But, as is the cast to-day, the whole of Lower Egypt remained essentially Malikite. Further westward the Shafi'ite propaganda did not penetrate. Between them the Malikites and the Hanafites shared the Maghrib[4]—the latter being less rigid were more acceptable to the Fatimids than the former. But when in 440/1048 North Africa shook off the Fatimid yoke—not only the Shi'ites but also the Hanafites suffered; the province having passed into the hands of the Malikites who retain it even to-day[5]. In Spain the Malikites reigned supreme[6].

At Baghdad itself the Hanbalites, among the orthodox, kept the government fully occupied. With intense fierceness they fought the Shi'ahs. Whenever the latter built a mosque there was tumult and riot[7]. In 323/935 the Malikites assaulted

(1) Ibn Sa'id, Ed. Tallquist, 24.
(2) Muk., 202, 203.
(3) Suyuti, *Husnu'l Muhadera* 1, 212.
(4) Maqrizi, *Khitat*, 1, 341.
(5) Goldziher, *Le Livre de Ibn Toumert*, 23.
(6) Muk., 236
(7) Wuz, 335

Shafi'ite pedestrians in the streets[1] but they reserved their fury for the Shi'ahs and their theological foes. Even, according to Muqaddasi, the Shafi'ites were decidedly the most quarrelsome among the Jurists.

People in these matters have been misled, for most of the information regarding them comes from Shafi'ite sources. One thing is certain, wherever there was a juristic squabble, the Shafi'ite was never absent. Other disputants change and come to terms with each other.

On the whole, in the 4th/10th century, the schools behaved very well towards each other. The learned—such as Muqaddasi—recommended peace and concord (p. 366). The change from one school to another was still a matter of no great moment.

Ahmad ibn Faris (d. 369/980)—the most notable philologer of his day—went over from the Shafi'ite to the Malikite school out of indignation at the fact that at Rai where he resided there was not a single follower of this far-famed, school[2]. At Cairo a Shafi'ite was chosen as Imam of the Tulunid mosque—a position held hitherto by the Malikites—on the naive ground that no better candidate was available[3]. Even Muqaddasi assings purely personal reasons for his preference, in answer to the question, asked in amazement, why he, a Syrian, whose countrymen are Hanbalites and whose jurists Shafiites, attached himself to the Hanafite school[4].

---

(1) Ibn al-Athir, VIII, 230.
(2) Yaqut, *Irshad*, II, 7.
(3) Muk., 203.
(4) Muk., 127

XV. THE QADI

Of the principle of the separation of the judicial from the executive, Islam thought as little as Christian Europe till the most recent times. Not unlike the Prophet the Caliph was the supreme judge of the faithful. In the Provinces the Governors exercised this power for him. But their manifold duties necessitated help in 'this direction as is reported of Mukhtar : in the beginning, with great zeal and talent, he personally carried on the judicial work until it became too heavy for him and he was compelled to appoint Qadis (Judges).[1] And precisely, for this reason, the jurisdiction of the Qadi was never definitely defined or rigidly marked off from that of the Governor—the latter reseryering for himself all that "for which the Qadi was too weak." (Mawardi). Should the Governor refuse to accept the decision of the Qadi—the latter had no alternative but to resign, or at least to suspend work.[2] But such a contingency was of rare occurence. Kindi, in his *History of the Egyptian Qadis*, records only two such instances, from the whole of the first centuries, where the decision of the Qadi, on a question of personal law was set aside by the governor : one of these involved a principle of exceptional importance[3]. A woman had married one not of equal birth. Her relatives demanded dissolution of this marriage from the Qadi. But the Qadi, in defiance of the command of the governor, refused to entertain their request. The Governor, thereupon, parted the couple. Here, in this case, two principles stood face to face—the old Arab-world principle of aristocracy and the

(1) Wellhausen, *Die religios-politischen oppositions—parteien* 78.

(2) Kindi, *Qudat*, ed, Guest, 328, 358, 427.

(3) Kindi, 367. The other instance is to be found on page 427.

Islamic one of democracy—which rested no longer on blood but on faith and piety.

In accordance with the defeudalization of the Empire under the 'Abbasid the Qadi was removed from the authority of the Governor and was, now, either appointed direct by the Caliph or at least confirmed by him[1]. Mansur was the first to appoint judges at the capitals of the Provinces[2]. As illegally appointed inasmuch as he was not appointed by the Caliph[3]. In 394/1004 the otherwise all-powerful Baha-ud-Daulah wanted to make the registrar (Naqib) of the 'Alids chief judge, but as the Caliph had not nominated him it could not be done[4]. Among the few surviving prerogatives of the Caliph—the appoinment of the Chief Judge in Egypt is one acknowledged even today[5]. Ever since the days of the first 'Abbasid the position of the Qadi rose in importance. Though it had, hitherto, been the practice for the Qadi to attend the governor's levee— the Qadi appointed by Harun in 177/793 replied to the invitation of the Amir in so insulting a style that "the practice was done away with[6]." In the 3rd/9th century, things having changed, the governors are said to have waited upon the Qadis[7], until the year 321/933 when

---

(1) Yaqubi, II. 468.

(2) The Qadi of Egypt, appointed by Mansur in 155/772 was the first Qadi of Egypt to be appointed directly by the Caliph. Kindi, *Qudat*, 368. It was under Al-Mahdi that the first Qadi, sent by the Caliph, came to Medina. (Yaqubi, ii, 484). In early Islam Judges apparently were appointed by the Caliphs. The letter of 'Omar to the Qadis and officers admits of such a construction.

(3) Subki, *Tabaqat*. II, 113 ff.

(4) Jauzi, Berlin, fol. 141 b: Ibn al-Athir, IX, 129.

(5) Gottheil, *The Qadi*. SA of REES 1908. 7, note 3.—This is of course no longer the case (1929) Tr.

(6) Kindi, 388. The only two attempts to make the Qadi at the same time governor are : (*a*) the appointment of the Spanish Qadi Asad who died in 213 and (*b*) that of Sarh ibn 'Abdullah under Al-Mahdi (158-169) *Kit. al'uyun*, 372.

(7) Wustenfeld, AGGXX, 37 Nr. 91.

Qadi Harbawaihi, being too proud to rise to receive them, the Governors dropped the practice. (Suyuti, *Husnu'l Muhadera*, II, 101 ; supplement to Kindi, 528). A similar story is related of the Wazir Ibn Abbad. The Qadi of Baghdad refusing to rise to receive him, the Wazir offered his hand to help him in getting up. (Yaqut, *Irshad* II, 339. But this story is related of another also). This Qadi was a prince of justice. He refused the title of Amir to the Governor and always addressed him by name and in a case before him he called upon the powerful fieldmarshal Munis to produce testimoney from the Caliph to the fact that the Caliph had emancipated him and that he was no longer the Caliph's slave. He was a great stickler for dignity. No one ever saw him eat or drink or wash his hand or sneeze or spit, or even pass his hand across his face. All this he did in private. He decided cases wholly according to his inner light—without reference to any particular school of law—a thing which would have been greatly resented in others. His learning was indisputable. No suspicion of corruption ever rested on his name[1]. When someone once laughed, during the hearing of a case, the Qadi called him to order in a voice which filled the room : "What art thou laughing at in the court of God where the matter against thee is proceeding? Laughest thou when the Qadi trembles between heaven and hell?" The Qadi so terrified the offender that he lay ill for three months[2]. The Baghdadi Qadi al Isfraini (d. 406/1015) could say to the Caliph Qadir that he dare not dismiss him. On the contrary he—the Qadi—need only write to 'Khorasan to shake the Caliph's throne[3]. It is, indeed, indicative of respect for the judicial post that while, about that time, we often and often hear of princes and wazirs languishing in jail—we hear of but few such instances from the judicial circles. Only one Qadi is said to have died in

(1) Subki, *Tabaqat*, II, 302. ff : *supplement to Kindi*, 528.

(2) Subki, II, 306.

(3) Subki, III, 26 : AGGW, 37 Nr. 287.

jail and this one Abu Umayyah, was an exception. He was not a trained lawyer but a dealer in cambric. When a reverse of fortune had overtaken Ibn al-Furat he concealed himself at Abu Umayyah's house and, while in concealment, he promised him a Government post—should he again become wazir. Ibn al-Furat became wazir for the second time and Abu Umayyah had to be provided with an important post, but he lacked qualification for a governorship, for the collectorship of income-tax, for the head-ship of police. The jovial wazir, therefore, made him the Qadi of the great towns of Basra, Wasit, Ahwas to spite the jurists. The new Qadi was simple and honest, two qualities which atoned for his ignorance. He behaved very coldly towards the Governor and never paid his respects to him, with the result that as soon as the news of the fall of the Wazir reached Basra the Governor forthwith put him in jail[1].

Theoretically the jurists did not look approvingly upon the office of the judge. Even in the 4th/10th century Samarqandi (d. 375/985) tells us[2]: "On the question of the acceptance of a judicial post there is no unanimity of opinion. Some maintain that it should not be accepted ; while others that it may be, provided it has not been sought or striven for." They reported fearful denunciations of the Prophet even against a righteous judge[3].

A man whom the Caliph 'Omar I, desired to appoint Qadi in Egypt rejected the suggestion on the ground that 'God had not rescued us from heathenism and its evil ways to go back them[4].' When in A.H. 70/689 a Qadi was appointed for Egypt—his father, hearing of the appointment, said 'May God help us ! The man is lost[5].'

---

(1) Jauzi, Berlin, fol. 7 b. The news came through the pigeon-post.

(2) *Bustan al-'arifin,* 38.

(3) Ibn Khall. 1, 135 note 5 : *Mishkat,* (Eng. tr.) 221 Tr.

(4) Kindi, 302. This does not agree with a statement above that Mansur was the first Caliph to appoint provincial judges. Tr.

(5) Kindi, *Qudat,* 315.

I am not aware how the early Christians looked upon this question, but Islam manifestly clung to the principle of 'Judge not' of the Sermon on the mount. We are told how pious people hurried away from Mesopotamia across Syria to Arabia to escape their threatened appointment as judges: such, among others, where Sufyan Thauri, who died in concealment, and Abu Hanifa, who inspite of the lash, would not accept a judgeship[1]. According to Tabari, the traditions taught by Abu Yusuf were suspect, because he was a friend of a Qadi[2]. Under Al-Mahdi the Qadi of Medina was made to accept the post by public flogging[3].

And yet about this very time the Qadi Sharik, having received a draft on the court-banker for his services, insisted on being paid in coin of full weight; and when the banker told him that, after all the difference would not suffice to buy him a suit of clothes, he answered "And yet I have for it something better than a suit of clothes; I gave up for it my religious convictions[4]."

A savant is even said to have feigned madness to avoid appointment to the post of a Qadi[5].

In striking contrast to the Qadis (representative of the '*Ilm ed-dunya*) stand the sufis. On the day of Judgment the true savant wi'l rise from the dead with the Prophet—the Qadi, however, with the wielders of temporal power. Isma'il ibn Ishaq was a friend of the Sufi Abu'l-Hasan ibn Abi'l-Ward. When Isma'il became Qadi, the latter broke off his

---

(1) *Bustan al-'arifin* 30 : other instances in *Kushf al-Mahjub,* tr. by Nicholson, 93.

(2) Ibn Khall, Nr. 834.

(3) See the life of lyas al-Qadi in Ibn Khall (Eng. tr.), Vol, I, 232. Two men refuse to act as juges. Tr.

(4) Ibn Khall Tr. 290. (Eng. tr. Vol I. p. 23 Tr.).

(5) Further examples, Amedroz. *Office of the Kadi in the Ahkam Sultaniyya.* JRAS 1910. 775.

friendship with him. Summoned as witness before him Abu'l-Hasan put his hand on Isma'il's shoulder and said : Oh Isma'il ! the knowledge which has borne thee here is worse than ignorance[1]. Isma'il drew his mantle over his face and wept until the mantle became wet.

The Hanafites were the first to yield to the exigencies of the age. At least the Shafi'ite Ibn Khairan (d. 310/922) thus taunted a colleague on his appointment as Qadi : Only the Hanafites accept such offices ! The critic himself had refused the Qadiship of Baghdad. A guard, accordingly, was placed at his house by the Wazir where he was kept confined[2].

But even the chief of the Hanafite school—Al-Razi (d. 370/980)—twice, refused the office of chief judge[3]. Indeed, up to the end of the 4th/10th century convention demanded but a hesitating acceptance of the Qadi's post.

On the appointment of a new judge in 399/1009 a poet sings:

"I have been compelled, says the one—the other, (the dismissed one): Now, I can breathe. Both lie. Who can believe all this[4]?"

The question whether a Qadi should accept a salary was very keenly debated. 'Omar I is said to have forbidden it. The Hanafite jurist Al-Hassaf (d. 261-874) seeks to establish the contrary proposition by sayings of the Prophet and examples from the early times. The Qadi Ibn al-Hujairah,

(1) Makki, 1. 157.

(2) AGGW 37, Nr. 81. Similar had been the fate of Ibn Suraij [d. 305/919] who had formerly been the Qadi of Shiraz [Subki. II, 92]. According to Subki the confinement of Ibn Khairan was a mere sham. According to the Egyptian historian Ibn Zulaq [d. 387/998] people looked at the sealed door and pointed it out to their children. Subki, II, 214.

(3) Jauzi, fol. 118 a.

(4) Ibn Taghribardi. 103 : Jauzi, fol, *adab al-qadi.* Leiden 550, fol. 25 a.

appointed in Egypt in 70/689, got an annual salary of 200 dinars (about 2,000 marks). But in addition to this appointment, he held the posts of treasurer and state-preacher. Each of these offices brought him 200 dinars a year. Over and above these he received a gratuity of 200 dinars and a pension of equal amount— making up an annual income of 1,000 dinars (that is, 10,000 marks)[1]. Even in the year 131/748 the judge of the Egyptian Captain drew a salary of 20 dinars a month (about 200 marks)[2]. But this amount obviously was not sufficient for the up-keep of his office and staff.

Of his 10,000 marks the above-mentioned Ibn Hujairah hardly had anything left by the end of the year[3].

A man turned up at the meal-time of the Qadi of Fustat (appointed in 90/709). The meal consisted of old lentils, served on a rush mat, biscuit and water. Bread he could not afford, said the Qadi[4]. The Qadi of Fustat, appointed in 120/736, carried on an oil-trade, along with his judicial work. When a young friend in astonishment questioned him about it, he put his hand on his shoulder and said : "Wait until thou feelest hunger through other stomachs than your own." The young man only recognised its meaning when he had his own children to bring up[5].

The Egyptian Qadi (appointed in 144/761) was extremely scrupulous about his pay. "When he washed his clothes, attended a funeral, or did some other private work of his own, he reckoned the time so taken and made a deduction therefor from his pay." Along with his judicial work he worked as a bridle-maker and daily made two. He used the sale-proceeds of one for himself ; while that of the

(1) Kindi, 317.
(2) Kindi, 354.
(3) Kindi, 317.
(4) Kindi, 331.
(5) Kindi, 352.

other he remitted to his friends in Alexandria who were fighting the infidels there[1].

The 'Abbasids, who conferred a higher and independent status on the Qadi, placed him also financially in a better position. Thus the Qadi in Egypt, now received a monthly salary of 30 dinars[2]. Of this sum, at least under Mahdi, a third was paid in kind ; namely, in honey[3]. In the liberal days of Mam'un the Egyptian Qadi drew from the governor a monthly salary of 168 dinars (1680 marks)[4]. He was the first to draw as much. When Tahir—noted for his generosity—came to Egypt and appointed a Qadi—he allowed him seven dinars a day (70 marks)— "which is the judge's pay to-day."[5] "Before his appointment the Qadi of Aleppo had been a poor man who had struggled with poverty, accepting it with resignation from God and rating it higher than riches. When I met him in 309/921 as Qadi of Aleppo he was a changed man who exalted wealth over poverty. I learnt that he gave to his wife on one single occasion 40 pieces of cloth from Tustar (Persia) and other valuable stuff[6]."

To prevent unjust acqusition of wealth on the part of the judge—the Caliph Al-Hakim doubled his pay on condition that he did not accept a single dirham from the people[7]. In the 5th/11th century the Persian traveller Nasir

(1) Kindi, 363.
(2) Kindi, 378.
(3) Kindi, 378.
(4) Kindi, 421. According to page 435 it was 163 : according to page 507, his successor also received 168 dinars from Mutawakkil.
(5) Kindi, 435. The amount is differently given. Subki, II, 302, reports, according to Ibn Zulaq [d.386/998], that the Qadi Harbawaihi of Egypt, who retired from office 321/933, only had a salary of 20 dinars a month—an amount which corresponds with the oldest arrangement.
(6) Mas'udi, VIII, 189 f.
(7) Kindi 597.

Khusru states that Egyptian chief Qadi drew a monthly salary of 2,000 dinars—the supplement to Kindi also mentions his annual income to be over 20,000 dinars[1].

In the East also the Qadi was paid from the State treasury (*Kit. al-Kharaj*, 115). But it is also stated that, either because of the insufficiency of pay or for reasons of conscience, the Qadi refused to draw his salary. The latter probably was the case. Hasan ibn 'Abdullah, a famous calligrapher, who, for fifty years, had been the Qadi of the great commercial town of Siraf (d. 369/978) made a living as a copyist[2]. Under Mahdi the Qadi of Medina refused to accept salary for his post. "He did not wish to be enriched by the hateful post."[3]

The Malikite chief judge of Baghdad, appointed in 303/915, made the following conditions on taking office : That he would accept no salary ; that he would not be compelled to pass an illegal order ; that he would, in no way, be approached on behalf of any one.[4] 'Ali ibn al-Muhasin et-Tanukhi (d. 447/1055), Qadi of some of the districts of Mesopotamia, and superintendent of the mint at Baghdad, received only 60 dinars a month as pay.[5]

In 335/945 robbers broke into the house of a *quondam* Qadi of Baghdad. As he was poor they did not find much and so they wanted to extort money by violence. The poor man fled to the roof, threw himself down, and was killed.[6] In 352/963 the judge of Baghdad received no pay.[7] The Baghdad Qadi Abu Tayyib (d. 450/1058) had only a turban

(1) Guest, 613. The 50,000 mentioned on p. 499 must be understood to be inclusive of his illcit again. The Fatimid budget in Maqrizi's *Khitat*, I, 398, assigns only 100 dinars a month as the qadi's salary.

(2) Haurt, Calligr. 77.

(3) *Tarikh-Baghadad*, JRAS 1912, 54.

(4) Kindi, 573, Jauzi, fol. 105 b : cf. Subki, III, 84.

(5) Yaqut, *Irshad*, V. 302.

(6) Jauzi, 75 a.

(7) Misk, VI, 257.

and a coat between himself and his brother—when one went out, the other stayed at home.[1] Even the chief judge of Baghdad, who died in 488/1095, lived on the rent of a House. It brought in 1½ dinar (about 15 marks) a month. He used a linen turban, a coat of coarse cotton, lived on crumbs soaked in water[2]. And a Spanish Qadi similarly lived on the produce of land he cultivated[3].

In 1852 Peterman reports from Damascus : Every year a new Qadi is sent from Constantinople, chosen by the *shaikh ul-Islam*. In the event of a death he receives a fixed share (I am told ¼ which is, indeed, too much) from the inheritance and 5 per cent on the value of every suit he decides. This is the amount payable by every subject of the Porte for a law-suit (should he lose it). The European subjects pay only 2 per cent[4].

In modern Morocco the Qadi, as a religious officer, is paid out of pious endowments. But as such payment is rare, they fall back upon presents from the parties[5].

In 350/961 the office of the chief judge at Baghdad was auctioned for 200,000 dirhams a year for the benefit of the Amir's treasury[6]. The first purchaser combined "an ugly figure with an ugly conduct." They imputed the vices of pederasty, licentiousness and drink to him[7]. But thing did not pass off quite smoothly for him. The Caliph refused to receive him and two years later he was removed from office.

(1) Ibn Khal, Nr. 306.
(2) Subki III, 84
(3) Ibn Bashkuwal, *Bibl his arab* I, 60
(4) *Reise in orient,* 98.
(5) *Revue du monde Musulman*. XIII, 517. (See also Burton's East Africa, 1, 88, Tr.)
(6) Misk, VI, 249. Eng. tr. V. 205.
(7) *Tadhkirah* of Ibn Hamdun, in Amedroz, JRAZ, 1910. p. 783. Passion for boys was regarded as a special vice of the Qadis (*Yatimah*, II, 218, *Mahadarat al-Udaba*, I, 125 : *Mustatraf*, II, 199). The chief Qadi of Mam'un was notorious pederast. Bhuturi charges the chief Qadi Ibn Abil-Shawarib with the same vice (*Diwan*, II, 175).

His successor set aside all his judgments on the ground that he had bought his office. (Misk, VI, 249; Ibn al-Athir, VIII, 399, 407). For the Prefect of police, see, Misk, (Eng. tr.) Vol. V. p. 42; for his pay, Vol. V. 205.

Already the Qadi Taubah (d. 120/738) had laid his hands on pious endowments which earlier were administered either by the donor or his heirs. On his death the pious endowments had become an important branch of administration[1]. In addition to the pious endowments the Qadi was put in charge of the estates and effects of orphans which, since 133/751, had been placed under the control of the treasury, a receipt being granted therefor[2]. In 389/999, on the death of the Cairene Qadi, a deficit of 36,000 dinars was shown in the accounts of the orphans. There was a severe and searching enquiry. At the instance of the Caliph a Christian officer pursued and seized the properties of the Qadi and his assessors (the most influential believers of the town), but only half of the amount was recovered. Since then all orphans' money came in into the treasury in a chest sealed by four assessors to be opened in the presence of them all[3].

Only in the 4th/10th century was the jurisdiction of the Qadi in matters of inheritance definitely settled. Finally he supervised the prisons of civil debts within his jurisdiction, in contrast to the police prisons (Habs al-Ma'unah).

In 402/1011 on the first night of the Fast the Wazir inspected the prisons under the jurisdiction of the Qadi of Bhagdad. Whowever was imprisoned for one to ten dinars was released but whoever was indebted for more was released for the festival on the Wazir standing bail for his return after the festival[4].

(1) Kindi, 346.
(2) Kindi, 355,
(3) *Supplement to* Kindi, Guest, 595.
(4) Jauzi, Berlin fol. 157 b. In the police prison he set at liberty offenders imprisoned for slight offences.

Tickets (Riqs), bearing the names of plaintiffs and defendants, with those of their respective fathers, were used in calling out cases. The clerk of the court collected them before the court's work began and the judge disposed of some fifty cases, on an average, per day[1]. The court work was conducted with absolute publicity. When the Caliph lets a case be tried in his palace the Qadi has the doors opened and lets the public in. And, thus, in the presence of all, the court-carrier, according to the tickets, called out the parties[2].

And precisely for this reason the Qadi Originally sat in the chief mosque leaning against a pillar—the chief mosque being public place, open to the entire Muslim community[3]. The Qadi could also hear cases at home. And thus the Qadi of Egypt, appointed in 120/738, heard cases in room overlooking the street, over the porch of his house, while the parties down below discussed matters among themselves[4].

Indignant at his injustice the Egyptians flung the praying carpet of the Qadi, appointed in 204/918, out of the mosque into the street ; after that this Qadi decided cases at home and never came to the mosque again[5]. The Egyptian Qadi, appointed in 219-834, sat in winter in the porch of the chief mosque, leaning against the wall with his back towards Mekka. He would not let any official approach him.

Even his clerks and the parties were allowed only to sit at a certain distance from him. He was the first to introduce this rule. In summer he sat in the courtyard of the mosque by the western wall[6].

About the middle of the 3rd/9th century the orthodox

(1) Al Hassaf (d. 261/874), *Adab al-Qadi* Leidan, 554, fol. 9 a.
(2) Baihaqi, ed. Schwally, 533.
(3) *Aghani*, X, 123.
(4) Kindi, 351.
(5) Kindi, 428.
(6) Kindi, 443.

reaction regarded the use of the mosque as the court of the Qadi as a desecration of God's and forbade it[1]. But this prohibition was ineffectual. About 320/932 the chief judge heard cases at his house[2] and in Egypt now at the mosque and now at his house. A Qadi (d. 407/1016) at Nisapur, immediately on the announcement of his appointment, was taken to the place set apart in the mosque for the Judge[3]. And Ma'arri complains that there are robbers not only in the desert but also in the mosques and the bazars:[4] only these are named assessors and merchants[5]. On another occasion he calls the assessors "Beduins of the towns and mosques"[6].

During the Fatimid period the chief Qadi of Cairo sat on Tuesdays and Saturdays in the wing of the mosque of 'Amr ibn al-As on a dais with a silken cushion. To the right and the left of him sat the assessors according to seniority. In front of him set five court servants and four court clerks, facing each other in twos. A silver inkpot from the citadel treasury[7] was placed before him.

In the earlier days the parties conducted their business before the Qadi standing. When under the Omayyads, a prince of that dynasty refused to stand and do business before the Qadi, he was compelled to withdraw his suit[8]. Later was introduced the practice of sitting in a row before the Qadi. When the Caliph Mahdi had a law-suit with his mother, a Qadi from Egypt was brought to Baghdad. The queen-mother appointed a representative on her behalf and,

(1) Abu'l-Mahasin, II, 86.
(2) Subki, *Tabaqat*, II, 194.
(3) Subki, II, 113.
(4) Subki, III, 59.
(5) Von Kremer, ZDMG, XXX, 49.
(6) ZDMG, XXXI, 478.
(7) Maqrizi, Khitat, 1. 403.
(8) Kindi, 356.

at the trial, the Qadi required the Caliph to take his seat among the litigants. Whereupon Mahdi stepped down from his seat and sat in front of the Judge[1]. When the Caliph Ma'mun—so an old authority relates—appeared as a suitor before the Qadi and took his seat on a carpet, the Qadi intimated that the opposite party too should be supplied with one[2]. And when the representative of the powerful Zubaida—wife of Harun—sat impudently at the trial of a case before an Egyptian Qadi he had him laid on the ground and ordered ten stripes to be administered to him[3].

The theorists discussed all kinds of things calculated to affect the partiality of a judge. Should the parties greet the judge? If they did so, should not the Qadi respond to the 'Peace on thee' as is the practice, not "on thee be peace" but only "on thee"? To say "peace" would be an improper anticipation of events[4].

And the pious theory similarly declaimed against any influence that the judge might seek to bring to bear on the parties. He should not shout at them nor is he to force them to give any definite answer.

By reason of these theories and of the difficulty in getting money from an Egyptian—Egyptian witticism has invented the story of a Qadi who fastened two horns to his cap to give a dig therewith to the obstinate and refractory suitor (*an-nattah*). the Caliph Hakim, hearing this, reproached the Qadi for it. Thereupon the Qadi invited the Caliph to take his seat behind the curtain of the court-room to be convinced of the perversity of the people. The Caliph came. Two litigants presented themselves before the Qadi—one claiming 100 dinars from the other. The Qadi suggested a

(1) Kindi, 357.
(2) Baihaqi, 538.
(3) Kindi, 392.
(4) Al-Hassaf (d. 261/874): K. *Adab al Qadi* , *Leyden*, fol. 22 a.

monthly instalment of 10 dinars. The debtor objected. Then he suggested an instalment of 5 dinars a month ; then 2 ; then 1 ; then 1/2. The debtor, finally, proposed : "I will pay ¼ of a dinar every year but I wish the plaintiff to be put in jail for, if he is free and I fail to carry out my promise, he will simply kill me." Hakim enquired of the Qadi : 'How many blows had he given the man'? Only one, replied the Qadi. Give him two more, commanded the Caliph, or give him one and I will give the other[1].

The Qadi wore the black colour of the 'Abbasid officials. The Egyptian Qadi, appointed in 168/784, used a thin black band round his long cap[2]; the Qadi who acted from 237/851 a black mantle (*Kisa)* but, this, indeed, only when it was pointed out to him that he would, otherwise be mistaken for a partisan of the Omayyads[3]. In the course of the 3rd/9th century the high conical hat—*qalan suwah,* called *danniyah* "pot-hat" like the English top-hat became the official head gear of the judges[4]. It was used along with the *Tailasan.* When the 85 year old Qadi Ahmad at-Tanukhi resigned his post as judge he said : he would like an interval between service and the grave. He would not go straight from the *Qalansuwah* to the grave[5]. A Qadi without the *Qalansuwah* has been likened to a glorified clerk[6]. In 368/978 an accused women was frightened at the sight of a Qadi with a beard a yard long and a face and a top-hat of equal length. To quiet her the Qadi removed his hat and covered

---

(1) de Sacy. *Religion des Druzes,* CCCCXXVIII.

(2) Kindi, 378.

(3) Kindi, 469. The Qadi of Cordova at the time of the Caliph Al-Hakam sat in court, like a fop, in a yellow mantle and with parted hair. *Ajbar Mahkumah,* 127: *Bayan al-Maghrib* (tr. by Fagnan) 128.

(4) *Aghani,* X, 123 *Irshad,* 1, 373 : VI, 209 : Hamadani, Rasa'il, 168: *Supplement to Kindi, 586.* (See Khuda Bakhsh, *Islamic Civilization,* Vol, 1, pp. 96-97 Tr.)

(5) Yaqut *Irshad,* 1, 192.

(6) *Shabushti* Berlin , fol 81 a.

his beard with his sleeve and said: I have done away with two yards, now answer the charge preferred against you[1].

The Fatimid Qadis carried the sword (Kindi, 589 596, 597).

About 300/912 the staff of the Qadi's court consisted of :-

1. The clerk (katib), salary 300 dirhams a month.
2. The court usher (Hajib), salary 130 dirhams a month.
3. The Munsif deciding cases at the gateway of the court, salary 100 dirhams a month.
4. Superintendent of the court premises and the police ('Awan), monthly salary 600 dirhams collectively (Kindi, 574; Jauzi, fol. 105 b).

To these was added, since the time of the Caliph Al-Mansur, the most remarkable of legal institutions—a permanent body of "witnesses". Al Kindi's excellent authority tells us: "Formerly only witnesses known to be of good repute were accepted. Others were either openly rejected or, in case they were absolutely unknown, inquiries were made regarding them from their neighbours. But now, as there is such a lot of false swearing, secret inquiries are made regarding the witnesses; that is to say, a list of men, fit to be called as witnesses is prepared. The result is that not reliability but inclusion in the prepared list is now the passport to the witness-box; the word 'witness' (*Shahid*)

(1) Dhahabi *Tarikh al-Islam*, JRAS, 1911, 659 note 1. In the first half of the 4th/10th century the Egyptian Qadis had to use a blue *Tailasan* (Shabushti, Kit. ed. Diyarat, fol. 131 a). Even at Baghdad a Qadi, about 400/1009 used this kind of blue *Tailasan* (a cover for the neck). Yaqut *Irshad*, V, 261. Even the assessors used the long black hat. A poet of the 4th/10th century, thus, mockingly refers to them, "On their top-hats the wingless raven of Noah." *Muhaderat al-Udaba*, 1, 129.

signifying such a definite individual (Kindi, 361)."

An official list of these witnesses was drawn up at the instance of the Qadi appointed in 185/801; a practice which has continued up to the present day. People made fun of this judge for admitting 100 Egyptians (non- Arabs) into this list and for removing 30 old ones and replacing them by as many Persians (Kindi, 396). From among these witnesses were chosen the fixed number of assessors (bitanah) who assisted the judge in his work. Every six months—so ruled the Qadi about 200/815—fresh nominations were to be made and the undesirable ones to be removed (Kindi, 422). A later Qadi is reported to have taken this part of his duty so seriously that he roamed about the street at night with covered head enquiring about the character of the "witnesses" (Kindi, 437). Even in the letter of appointment of a Qadi in Qodamah (written some what later than 316/928) the selection of witnesses is set down as one of his main duties[1].

When 'Adud-ud-Daulah's (d. 327/982) general asked him to direct the Qadi to include a name in the list of witnesses he received the reply: "You must speak about the promotion of soldiers. The inclusion of names[2] in the list of witnesses is the Qadi's business. Neither you nor I have any voice in that matter."

It is said of Al-Hakim that in this matter too he restored the old practice. In 405/1014 he made more than 1200 people "witnesses" at their request. But when the chief Qadi reproached him, saying that many of them were not fit to be placed on the list, he allowed him, with his usual fickleness, to retain or strike off the names he pleased[3].

---

(1) Paris, Arabic, 5907 fol. 12 b.

(2) Ibn Al-Athir, IX, 15.

(3) Ibn Sa'id, fol. 124 a : *Supplement to kindi*, 612.

The assessors, being personally appointed by the Qadi vacated on the removal or dismissal from office[1]. The Egyptian Qadi, in the year 321/933, insisted upon his "witnesses accompanying him on his rides[2]." At that time four "*witnesses*" sat with the Qadi at the hearing of a suite—two to his right and two to his left[3].

In the 4th/10th century the transformation of the "witnesses" originally respectable, trustworthy men of the circuit, into a permanent body of officials takes place. The substitution of this new institution in place of the old is a creation of this century. In the 3rd/9th century a Qadi nominated no less than 36,000 witnesses[4] but of these only 16,000 availed themselves of the honour. About 300/912 Baghdad counted some 1800 such witnesses. In 322/934 the Egyptian Qadi had to intimate to the "witnesses" that they need only come when sent for. He did not assign any salary to them[5], the position being that they wanted to be officials in the proper sense of the term but the Qadi stood by the old view. In 383/993 the number of 'witnesses' at Baghdad was cut down to 303 but even this figure was felt to be too high[6]. The chief Qadi at Cairo too had very few

(1) Mawardi. 128.

(2) *Supplement to Kindi*, 545.

(3) *Ibid*, 552,569, 590.

(4) Amedroz, JRAS 190, 779 ff, according to the Paris Ms. of *Nishwar* of *Tanukhi* printed at p. 128). See also , Sabi, *'Rasa'il*, 122 Kindi calls the substitutes of the "witnesses" *(Shuhud)* for the year 327/939 "witnesses" who represent them. In 339/951 Mas'udi, written in Egypt, speaks of the *'Shuhud* of Baghdad (VIII,378. In the East and in the Maghrib, in the 2nd half of the 4th/10th century, court assessors were called *'udual Yatimah*, III 233 : Misk, V, frequently this word is used : Dozy, Sub, *udul* : Ibn Khaldun , *Proleg.* (Slane's tr.) p. 456. This term has been retained to this day in Morocco (*Revue du monde musulman, XIII*, 517 ff).Witnesses who are not officially so are now called *Mu'amin bil' adalah* (Kindi, 422 : Sabi. Ras. 122.

(5) Kindi, 549 : Amedroz, JRAS 1910, 783 : according to Ibn Hajar, fol. 128 a.

(6) Jauzi,*Muntazam, fol.* 63a : Berlin 134a : Amedroz, JRAS, 1910, p. 779 ff according to *Raf al-Isr* and Dhahabi.

witnesses[1].

These "witnesses" apparently are the resurrected notaries of the pre-Islamic empire. It is recommended to the wise business man to look round among the "witnesses" and to choose the best reputed one for notarial confirmation of his papers. A black sheep not infrequently creeps in among them with the result that all notarial work done by him becomes invalid in law[2].

Over each of the five petty courts of Cairo a 'witness' presided in the name of the Qadi[3]. In the Cairo of Lane the 'witnesses' (*Shuhud*) sat in the porch of the High Court. The plaintiff brought his case to one of them who happened to be free. The 'witness' (*Shahid*) noted his case down for a piastre or so. If it was an unimportant one and the defendant submitted to his jurisdiction, he forth with passed judgment. Otherwise he referred the parties to the Qadi.

In the appointment letter of the chief Qadi[4], drawn up by Ibrahim es-Sabi in 366/976, in the name of the Caliph, the Caliph recommends constant study of the Qura'n ; punctual fulfilment of prayers; just treatment of the parties; that is to say, he is to show no preference or partiality to a Muslim as against a Jew or a Christian. He is to walk with dignity; speak little and gently; not to look round too much,

(1) *Raf al-Isr in* Kindi, 596.

(2) *Mahasin at-ijarah,* 36.

(3) Maqrizi, *Khitat* , 1, 333.

(4) The first who bore this title was Qadi Abu Yusuf, the Qadi of Harun al-Rashid. This Caliph conferred this title upon all the Qadis of the more important provices. (Maqrizi, *Khitat,* 333). Ma'mun's chief Qadi had to examine all the judges (Ibn Taifur, ed. Keller, fol. 100 a). He questioned them regarding the Law of Inheritance and other intricate rules of Muslim Law. (Ibn Kutaibah, '*Uyun,* 86. To appoint four chief Qadis—one for each school of jurisprudence—became a necessity in the post-crusade period) Zahiri *Kashf el-Mamalik, ed. Ravaisse,* 92. Baibars appointed four chief Qadis at Damascus in 664/1266. Subki, *Tabaqat* 11, 174.

and be restrained in his movements.

He is to employ an experienced, legally-trained *Katib* (clerk), an incorruptible court-usher (*Hajib*), and a trustworthy deputy for work he cannot personally attend to. He is to pay them adequately. He is to select witnesses discreetly and to keep a watchful eye over them. He must protect orphans and supervise charitable institutions, and regarding such matters as he cannot decide according to the Qur'an and the *Sunnah* he is to consult the learned. Should they agree among themselves that the Qadi has erred in his decision—he (the Qadi) must set the decision aside.[1]

This body of learned men, absolutely independent of the State, thus constitute the highest tribunal. Through them democracy, the sovereignty of the community of the faithful, maintained its position in the important sphere of Law.

All offices had a tendency to become hereditary from sire to son. And, indeed, such is most strikingly the case with the judicial service. In the 3rd and 4th centuries one single family, that of Abu Shawarib, supply no less than eight chief Qadis at Baghdad, besides sixteen Qadis. From about 325/937 the descendants of Abu Burdah were, for several generations, chief Qadis of the Province of Fars and from about 400/1010, for centuries, Qadis of Ghaznah. (Ibn Al-Balkhi, JRAS, 1912, 141). For eighty long years similarly, in Fatimid Egypt, the highest judicial office was retained in the family of An-Nu'man.[2]

---

(1) Sabi, *Rasa'il*, 115 f. At the beginning of the 4th/10th century the Qadi dissolved the marriage of a young woman on the ground that her consent had not been asked by her father. But the woman's consent being only required when she has already been married, the savants attacked the decision of the Qadi. *Supplement to Kindi*, 566.

(2) Gottheil, a distinguished family of Fatimid Cadis in the Xth century, JAOS 1906. p. 217 ff.).

In the 3rd/9th century the power of these judicial dynasties rose to an immense height by the introduction of the practice of subletting the judicial jurisdiction—a practice already in vogue in the case of governorships.

From the beginning of the 4th/10th century the court records show that there was only one Qadi in Egypt and that in Khuzistan and Fars all the courts were placed under the jurisdiction of one judge[1]. The chief judge of the Iranian Buwayyid held the judgeship of the Capital Rai along with that of Hamadan and the hill-tracts[2].

The Qadi of Mekka in 336/947 was also the Qadi of Old Cairo and other districts[3]. At times, under the Fatimids, the Egyptian territories, Syria and the countries of the West were placed under one Qadi[4]. The appointment letter of the chief Qadi of Egypt, in the year 363/974 indeed, confers jurisdiction over almost the entire empire west of the Persian mountains. Under him were placed subjudges *(hukkam)*, over whom he exercised supervision[5].

By the side of the court of the Qadi stood the temporal court (*An-Nazar fil mazalim)*[6].

All matters, for which the Qadi was considered too week or for which a masterful hand was needed, came up before this Court.

In all Muslim countries these two courts existed side by side[7]. But their respective jurisdiction was nowhere clearly

(1) Wuz, 157.
(2) *Irshad*, II, 3 14.
(3) Mas'udi, IX, 77.
(4) Qalqashandi, 184.
(5) Jauzi, fol. 105 b.
(6) Maqrizi, *Khitat*, II, 207. (Khuda Bakhsh, *Orient under the Caliphs*, 283-292 Tr.) Amedroz, JRAS, 1911, 635.
(7) For Turkistan, see Schwarz., *Turkestan*, 210. For the Egypt of

defined. It merely came to this : Which was the stronger of the two, Islam as represented by the Qadi or the world and the wielder of the wordly power?[1] Most police matters came up before the *Mazalim* which was sometimes presided over by a Qadi—especially the court of the sovereign by the chief judge[2].

The Wazir appointed temporal judges in the provinces[3]. Twice, indeed, did the canonical law attempt the control of the police. In 306/918 the Caliph directed the police commissioner at Baghdad to appoint a jurist in every quarter of the town to receive and deal with complaints and petitions : these then were[4] legally trained police-commissioners. "By this, fear of the Government was very much lessened and the impudence of robbers and loafers very much increased." (*Zubdat al-fikrah*, Paris fol. 186 a.) Also al-Hakim associated two jurists with the police in every town, who had to investigate every offence reported to them within their jurisdiction[5]. The attempt miscarried. Indeed in entire opposition to the juristic theory appeal lay to the *mazalim* from the decision of the Qadi; especially to highest court, that of the sovereign[6].

"There are many people (so are the frequenters of this

Mohamed Ali, see Lane, *Manners and Customs,* Chapter IV. For Mekka, see Snouck Hurgronje, *Mekka,* 1, 182.

(1) Amedroz, JRAS, 1911, 664.

(2) For Egypt the Qadi appointed by Ikhshid in 324/936 Subki, *Tabaqat,* II, 113. There was even a special Qadi for the *Mazalim* in 331 (*Supplement to Kindi,* Guest 572). For Baghdad in the year 493/1004. Jauzi, fol. 149 b. About 317/929 the Qadi-at Tanukhi in Ahwaz. *Irshad,* V, 332, Even when such was not the case, the decisions were drafted by the Qadis. Wuz, 151.

(3) *Arib,* 50 : *Irshad,* V, 332.

(4) *Arib,* 71.

(5) Yahya ibn Sa'id, 205.

(6) Miskawaihi, Vol. IV, p. 75 (Eng. tr.). I am indebted to Prof. Margoliouth for this reference. Tr.

court described) who come from distant lands and make their complaints—some against an Amir, others against a collector of taxes, and yet others against a Qadi or a ruler.[1]"

About 420/1029 a Qadi at Cairo sought the hand of an heiress and was refused. With the help of four witnesses he, in retaliation, declared her to be of unsound mind and attached her property. She appealed to the wazir, who imprisoned the false witnesses and directed the Qadi to restore her property and other unjust misappropriations, confined him to his house and appointed his son (the Qadi's) to do the duties of his office[2].

The viceroy Ibn Tulun administered justice so scrupulously that 'people almost ceased to go to the Qadi's court'. For seven years, during his administration, there was no Qadi in Egypt. All matters were taken up and disposed of by the secular court[3]. Even under the negro viceroy Kafur, the Qadi in Egypt disappeared from the scene because Kafur frequently heard cases himself[4]. In 369/979 there was a conflict of jurisdiction between the two courts—spiritual and temporal—the Wazir deciding that they should not interfere with each other[5]. About 400/1000 the Qadi was constrained to object to the police interfering in matters relating to the canonical law. The Caliph ended the dispute by placing the temporal Court under the jurisdiction of the Qadi[6]. About 320/932 it seems that the tickets were thrown into the box in the presence of the presiding judge[7]. The judgment was a

(1) Wuz, 107.

(2) Amedroz, JRAS, 1910. p. 793. accordig to Paris, Arab. 2149, fol. 60 : Cf. JRAS. 1911, 663 : *Supplement to Kindi*, 499, 613.

(3) Kindi, 512.

(4) *Supplement to Kindi*, 584. Kindi, 591.

(5) Kindi, 604.

(6) Wuz, 52, 107. Every week an abstract of all complaints was to be laid before the President of the Mazalim. Qodamah., Paris , 907, fol. 236.

(7) *Supplement to Kindi*, 541.

written judgment. Some of these have become classics of literature—not unlike the marginal notes of Frederick[1].

At court a day was fixed for hearing cases. Such indeed, was already the practice under the Byzantine rule. In 494 A.D. the governor of Edessa sat every Friday in a church to hear cases (Josua Stylites, 29). Under Al-Ma'mun Sunday was the day set apart for hearing cases (Mawardi,143). For this purpose Ibn Tulun set twice a week (Maqrizi, Khitat, II, 207). Ikhshid, the viceroy of Egypt, held his court[2] every Wednesday in the presence of the Wazir, the Qadi, the jurists and other dignitaries; Kafur every Saturday[3].

But after Al-Muhtadi (255-256/868-869) the Caliph no longer held such courts[4]. This last Caliph heard and decided cases and, being a pious man, preached every Friday. He built a special domed hall with four doors where he administered justice. This 'Palace of Justice' was called (*"Qubbat al-Mazalim."*)[5]

On cold days he arranged for coal-pans to heat the place—"so that the suitors may not be turned into stone by cold together with his Majesty's presence.[6]"

Among other promises the Caliph Qahir, when trying for the throne, promised personally to attend the *Mazalim*[7]. Under Al-Mutadid (279-289/829-602) the chief-Marshal

---

(1) Such as those of Tahir in Ibn Taifur , *Kit. Baghdad, fol.* 50 b : of Ma'mun in Baihaqi, 534 f : of *Sahib ibn Abbad in Tha'alabi, Khas al-Khas,* Cairo 1909, p. 73.

(2) Ibn Sa'id, Tallqist, 39.

(3) Kindi, 577.

(4) Maqrizi, according to Mawardi. There Saturday is mentioned as the court-day of Ikhshid and his son. The brief historical survey of Maqrizi is drawn from Mawardi. (Ed. Enger, 131).

(5) Masudi, VIII 2.

(6) Baihaqi, 577 Amedroz, JRAS, 1911, 657.

(7) Amedroz, JRAS, 1911, 657.

presided over the sovereign's court in lieu of the sovereign—the wazir, every Friday, over other courts (Wuz, 22).

At the beginning of the 4th/10th century the Wazir heard *Mazalim* cases every Thursday—the *divisional chief* sitting with him[1]. In 306/918 actually a lady presided over *Mazalim*[2]. The *Mazalim*, being free from juristic hair-splitting, enjoyed greater freedom and Mawardi reckons ten points on which it differed from the Qadi's court. Most important of these are: that here the parties could be forced to come to terms, a thing which the Qadi was not competent to do; witnesses also could be put upon their oath here. Moreover, unlike, the Qadi, the judge could in this court, of his own motion, call and examine witnesses; whereas before the Qadi only the plaintiff adduced evidence and questioned witnesses (Mawardi, 141 ff.)

But all this was mere theory. Local law and local practice actually prevailed and the old tested method such as corporal punishment, though forbidden to the Qadi, continued in full force.

---

(1) Wuz, 22.

(2) *Arib*, 71 : Abu'l-Mahasin, II, 203. Openion was divided whether a woman should be appointed judge. At least the famous Tabari (d. 312) spoke in favour of such a proposal. Mawardi, 107. Later was imposed the condition that the Qadi should be a man. For the *Mazalim* no such restriction was imposed.

XVI. PHILOLOGY

In the two main branches of Arab philology—in grammar and in the preparation of dictionaries—the 4th/10th century struck a new path. Like theology, it was then emancipated from the shackles of juristic method—in external form entirely. Suyuti thus describes the old philology : "Their mode of dictating was absolutely similar to that which obtained in theology. The listener (*Mustamli*) wrote at the beginning of the page : Lecture delivered by our Shaikh So-and-So on such-and-such a day. The lecturer mentioned something, with a chain of traditions, which the old Arabs and the orators had said and which contained something striking and called for an explanation. The lecturer explained, made comments and, in addition, cited passages from the old poets. The quotations had to be well authenticated; comments and explanations were matters of more or less indifference. Such was the widely-diffused method of lecture in philology in the early times. But when the *Huffaz* died out, dictation in philology ceased. The last, of whom I heard that he dictated lectures in this fashion, was Abu'l-Qasim az-Zajjaj. The notes dictated by him were so copious that they made up a stout volume. He died in 339/950. No later students' note-books of lexicographical contents are known to me."

These old savants were discursive and their lectures were not well-knit together. Their interest centered in an individual fact, in an individual form, in one word or in one proposition; as is the case with* Mubarrad (d. 285/898) or even with Qali (d. 356/967). Their books are a variegated

* *Muzhir*; See Godziher, SWA, 69, 20f.

assemblage—philology, anecdotes, history.

Ghulam Tha'lab (d. 345/956) allowed himself to be led by questions from his pupils ; for instance : O Shaikh !

What is *al-qantarah* among the Beduins?[1] The leading philologers of the 4th/10th century on the other hand, felt the need of method, the systematization of their material. In the initiation of this new method the study of Greek grammar played the chief role. At the court of 'Adad-ud Daulah (d. 371/981) differences between the Arabic and Greek grammar were discussed and Abu Sulaiman ibn Tahir has pointedly[2] characterized the new tendency as profane and untheological: "The grammar of the Arabs is religion ; our grammar is reason."

And, thus, when, for the first time, an *'introduction to grammar'* appears (*Muqaddamah fin-nahw*) ; namely, that of Ibn Fairs (d. 395/1005) it is naught else but the Arab descendant of the *Isagogik* (introduction) of the Greek philology.

The outstanding achievement consists in fixing and elaborating the meaning of words. The model is apparent.

The philology of the old type was nothing more or less than a handbook for orators—an aid to rhetorical flourishes, a mine of synonyms. It ends with Hamzah al-Isfahani (d. between 350-60/961-70). In his *Kitab al-muwazanah* he has put together 400 expressions for "the unlucky" and, in his '*Book of Sayings*' he has collected so many parallels of rhetorical phrases 'whiter than snow,' 'more voracious than an elephant' that later centuries could add nothing to them.

His predecessor had amassed 300 of such comparative terms, but he 1800. Maidani (d. 578/1178) has merely copied

(1) Jauzi, 85 a.

(2) Kifti, ed Lippert, 283.

him and has added only one or two, or at the most four, idioms to every chapter. Even all his explanations he has borrowed from his predecessor[1].

Even in the sphere of proverbs proper, the chief work was done in the 4th/10th century by Al-Hasan al-'Askari (d. 395/1005).

A generation later, in the dictionary of Jauhari (d. 302/912), the new school shows its impress. A comparison with the great dictionary of Ibn Duraid (d. 321/933) shows what steps forward in method and elucidation had been effected. 'To make clear and to bring nearer home' —so says Ibn Faris (d. 395/1005) himself—'was from the beginning to the end, the aim of his own dictionary[2].'

So supreme was Jauhari, in his own realm of knowledge that an entire literature—pro and con—has grown up round him through the centuries[3]. Even Suyuti (d. 911/1505) wrote a book in Mekka in his defence against Jaujari and Abdul Barr in which he is said to be particularly hostile toward the former—his contemporary (d. 889/1484[4]).

All later lexicographies stand in relation to Jauharis as supplements and commentaries. Here, too, we note the end of one epoch and the beginning of another which lasts for centuries. Similarly, etymological inquiries too now enter upon a serious course and continue for long. Their chief was Ibn Jinni of Mosul (d. 392/1002), son of a Greek slave, who is said to have introduced into this science the so-called great etymological rule of the original bi-radical

---

(1) Mittwoch, MSOS, 1910, 184 f.

(2) Goldziher, *Beitrage zur gesch. der sprachgelehrsamkeit bei den Arabern*, SWA, *phil. hist.* KL. 73, p. 518.

(3) Goldziher, SWA, Vol. 72, 587. *Zur gauhari- Literatur.*

(4) Suyuti, *de interp. Corani' 24 f.*

roots—even important today[1].

The etymological work of the Arabs has not achieved anything greater. The language of ordinary parlance subsisted by the side of the written language, but with such enormous difference that in the Baghdad of the 3rd/9th century people were surprised to find a man effortlessly speaking correct grammatical Arabic with case terminations[2]. The interest, awakened in literature, brought philology home to the people at large; making them no longer insensible to linguistic errors and irregularities. Spanish Az-Zubdani (died about 330/941) wrote a book on "*the dialect of the People*[3]." Ibn Khalawaihi in Aleppo (d. 370/980) composed '*Kitab Laisa'* the book of '*not so*'. How much he left to the later philologers, notably Hariri, to do, yet remains to be investigated !

---

(1) Goldziher SWA 67, 250 according to Suyuti's *Muzhir* , 1, 164. *This* passage in the *Muzhir*, says Prof. Margoliouth, does not refer to this. In his *Khasais*, Chapter 30 of book II deals with *Ishtiqaq el-Akbar* (O. Rascher, *Stud'en ubr Ibn Jinni,* ZA, 1909, 20.)

(2) Masudi, VII, 131.

(3) Al-Dabbi, *Bughjat al-Mutlammis, 56, Bibl. His Arab.*

XVII. LITERATURE

The transformation of the race, the exhaustion of the ruling class, and the stepping-forward of the old population of mixed blood most strikingly show themselves in literature. About the year 200/800 literature was in a state of ferment. The tried form of *Qasidah* in which the old Arab poets had sung their lofty emotions, had become too tedious, too pathetic and had lost its hegemonic position. The townsfolk, assuming the lead, had relegated the heroic language and the epic material more and more into the background. The gloomy wildness yielded to clear sentences — the shorter metres won the day. The poet is deposed to produce excitement through fresh material, subtle thoughts, and fine words and images, rather than exaltation into a more vigorous world. Realism, fatal to all heroic poetry, is awakened and literature rediscovers real life. Once again literature takes note of the present and rejoices in the manifold aspects of the life around . The people, notably the unlettered townsfolk, now interest themselves in Arabic literature, not only to see Arab poetry with Arab eyes or to sing it in Arab rhythm, but to employ prose for the expression of the manifold, fresh object encountering and surrounding them.

Thus prose, hitherto confined to learned and ecclesiastical treatises, or at the most to a few popular books translated from the Persian, enters the domain of literature.

About the year 250/864 prose is said to have supplanted poetry.

1. Prose

Respect even for non-rhythmic language, which is the beginning of all good prose, was the great virtue of the old Arabs. Therein they excelled all other nations. Along with the poet stood the orator of the tribe, equal in rank with him. The gift of oratory was regarded as some thing superhuman, and hence the belief that the orator of a tribe must needs die before another can rise with the demoniac spirit within him[1]. And thus the talent for prose was looked upon as something so absolutely different from poetic talent that people were astonished when a poet shone in oratory or showed epistolary excellence[2].

So keen was the love of elegant diction that when in 208/823 a flood devastated Mekka and the Caliph sent money for relief and a letter of consolation, they said that the letter was of greater moment to the Mekkans than the money[3].

Interest in the contemporary world reveals itself first and foremost in the study of popular manners. About this time one Abu 'Aqqal wrote the first book on "the manners of the illiterate". The Qadi of Saimar "(d. 275/888)composed the "History of the Lower Orders" *(Akhbar es-Siflah)*[4]. While the description of town-life is a favourite theme of Jahiz[5]. This man of whose ugly exterior many interesting stories are told, his name meaning the goggle-eyed,[6] and his grandfather having been a negro, is the father of the new Arabic prose. Tha'labi calls him the first great prose-writer. The wazir Ibn al-'Amid, master of the diplomatic style, used to question every one whom he examined for state-service

(1) *Aghani* XVIII, 173.
(2) *Aghani* XX. 35: Ibn Kutaibah *Liber Poesis*, 'ed. de Goeje, 549.
(3) Baihaqi. ed. Schwally, 475.
(4) Mas'udi, V, 88 *Irshad*, VI, 402.
(5) e.g. *Tiraz el-majalis*, 67 ff.
(6) *Irshad*, VI, 56. His grandfather was an African.

regarding his views on Baghdad and Jahiz[1]. And for this he was nicknamed the second Jahiz[2]. The famous Thabit ibn Qurrah is said to have envied tree men: 'Omar I, the saintly Hasan of Basra, and Jahiz[3]. Abu Hayyan et-Tauhidi, perhaps the greatest master of Arabic prose, wrote a book in praise of Jahiz[4]. He took the subject so seriously that he dealt individually with the writers who highly esteemed Jahiz[4]. His respect for the master was so great that he actually adopted his scholastic lead[5]. On every subject Jahiz has written : from the schoolmaster[6]. to the Banu Hashim ; from robbers to lizards[7] ; from the attributes of God to libaldry regarding[8] the wiles and snares of womankind[9]. His style is entirely his own. It is chatty and, not infrequently, clumsy. But it is precisely this which appeals to his admirers. They appreciate its comparative freedom from literary pedantry which until his time was in the ascendant in learned circles. They treat the leisurely *causerie* as conscious art. Even Mas'udi in 323/943, applauds, in these terms, the perfect arrangement and the solid structure of his works : "When he fears that the reader is weary, he instantly passes from the serious to the humorous, from sublime wisdom to elegant oddities". Mas'udi places Jahiz' intricate work, *Kitab ul Bayan*, first on the list on account of its many-sidedness and versatility,[10] and often compares a good writer to one

(1) *Yatimah* III, 338 Tha'labi himself is spoken of by Bakharzi as the Jahiz of Nisabur, *Intro.* to Tha'labi's- Kit. *al-Ijaz.*

(2) Lata'if al-ma'arif, 105; *Irshad*, I, 686.

(3) *Yatimah* III, 3.

(4) *Irshad*, VI, 69.

(5) *Irshad.* V. 282.

(6) *Irshad* V, 380. Bakharzi mentions the voluminous Tha'labi.

(7) *Mustatraf* II, 199. How far the jokes there came from Greek witticism, in which the school-master is the central figure, yet remains to be investigated, see Reich *Mimus*, 1, 443.

(8) Husri, *Iqd*, 1, 561.

(9) *Faraj ba'd al-Shiddah* quotes from his *'Book of Robbers'*.

(10) VIII, 34. This alternation between seriousness and jesting is pointed out in all literary histories. Khwarezmi, 183.

who gathers wood at night and collects unexamined all that comes to his hand[1].

About 200/800 Mysticism, following the exhaustion of Arabism, powerfully helped the popularization of letters and largely contributed—as it did in other literatures too—to naturalism by despising pedantry and parade of learning, by even actually opposing it in and by casting in its lot with common people. It preached to them ; it regulated their lives for them ; it entered into their needs and aspirations; it allowed itself to be moulded by their very mode of expression itself. And, indeed, only by the decline of the old Arab tradition can the introduction of rhymed prose in Muslim literature be explained. The Muslims were still familiar with the heathen flavour of rhyme, but detested it, as the Christians of the Roman Empire detested the antique metres. Jahiz (d. 255/868) says: "As the reason for the prohibition of rhymed prose, *viz* the heathen soothsayers, who employed it, have disappeared, so has the prohibition too[2]."

The Christian converts to Islam, now exercising a decisive influence, were familiar with rhymed prose in their sermons, and thus in the 3rd/9th century rhymed prose appears in official sermons. We find it in a large measure in an address of the Caliph to his loyal supporters, although it is not consistently sustained through[3]. In epistolary style too rhymed prose made its way.

There always were writers who, putting aside religious scruples, wrote in rhymed prose, so admired in old Arab orators. The people of Baghdad knew by heart the letter which Ibrahim wrote to the Barmakid Khalid in the time of

---

(1) For instance Mas'udi, IV, 24.
(2) *Kit. ul-Bayan 1*, III.
(3) Goldziher, *Abhandlungen zur Arabischen Philologic*, 1, 65 f.

Harun[1].

The official Arabic was the standard language. About 200/800 the Chancellor of the Caliph Ma'mun wrote simply and without rhyme[2]. Ibn Thawabah(d.277/890), whose rhymed letter to the Wazir has been preserved was well-known for his ornate style. Even the famous curse on the Omayyads, which was meant to be solemnly read out from all the pulpits, was composed without the singsong of rhyme; and yet it shows faint indications of it[3]. About that time, however, a State-Secretary writes in quite unrhymed prose to the Wazir[4].

But about 300/900 rhymed prose becomes the fashion among the aristocracy of Baghdad. The Caliph Muqtadir writes in it to his subjects[5]. The Wazir 'Ali ibn 'Isa ornaments his letters with a great deal of rhyme (Wuz, 277). Abroad in the provinces they did not, however, yet soar so high. The rhymed letters of the Wazir Ibn Khaqan sounded Chinese to the authorities (for instance the letter of the Sahib el-Khabar (Secret service agent in Dinawar, *Arib*, 39 f). The officials in the provinces still wrote in the usual unrhymed style (*Irshad*, II, 418).

But now the passion for rhymed prose grows and spreads; while 'Amid and his contemporaries now use and now do without-rhyme, at the end of the century, in stylists like Sabi and Babagha,[6] it is never absent[7]. The Buwayyid

(1) Jahiz *Bayan*. II, 114. I have taken this quotation from Prof. Margoliouth's *Letters* of Abu'l Ala XLIII.

(2) E. G. al-Kindi, 446, and Ibn Taifur often. A rhymeless letter of Mu'tasim to Abd. b. Tahi in *Kit. fi's-Sadaqah* of Tauhidi Const. 1301. p 5 : *Irshad*, II.

(3) Tabari, III, 2166 ff.

(4) *Irshad* VI, 463.

(5) *Wuz.' 337 Irshad* VI, 280.

(6) On Sabi, see Browne, *Persian Lit.* Vol. I, 372 : Nicolson *Hist of the Arabs*, pp. 327-8 Tr.

(7) Ibn Khafagah, in the introduction to the *Khutbah of Ibn Nubatah*, 16.

Wazir, Sahib ibn 'Abbad,[1] is said to have had a mania for it! So possessed was he by it that he would not miss it were he even to ruin everything thereby or to risk the greatest danger. On one of his journeys he shifted from nice to miserable quarters merely to date his diary 'From Naubahar at noon' (*Nisf en-nahar*)[2]. At least such is the report of an evil-tongued dependent. On one occasion the Sahib showered so much rhyme upon an 'Alid who had come to see him that the 'Alid nearly fainted away, and had to be brought round by sprinkling rose-water on him[3]. And to this day has rhymed prose retained its position in the Muslim Orient[4].

The letters of the 4th/10th century are the finest products of Muslim art, working upon the noblest material—human speech. Were all the things which artists fashioned out of glass and metal to perish, these letters alone would proclaim and establish how light elegance and easy mastery of difficult figures were prized among them. It is no accident that many Wazirs of that age were masters of style, and as such their letters were deemed worthy of preservation in book-form—Khasibi, Ibn Muqlah, Muhallabi,[5] Ibn el-'Amid, the Sahib Ibn 'Abbad, the Samanid Wazir el-Iskafi. The last was distinguished in state-despatches but worthless in private correspondence—so fine then was the distinction between the two[6]. The more important documents—such as deeds of appointment—were drawn up at a special department of the Government, the *Diwan er-Rasa'il.* At Baghdad they went the length of placing at the head of this

---

(1) On Sahib, See Browne, *Persian Lit.* I, 374-5. Tr.

(2) *Irshad,* II, 298.

(3) *Irshad,* II, 304.

(4) With very few exceptions. Thus a famous Chancellor of the first Almoravid—true to the wisdom of the old Chancellors—avoided it. Marrakeshi, Transl. by Fagnan, 139.

(5) *Fihrist, 134.*

(6) *Yatimah,* III, 119 ; IV, 31: *Irshad,* V. 331.

department the most brilliant stylist of the second-half of the century, although he openly professed the sabaean religion and declined to accept Islam when offered the Wzarat[1]. And when he died, no less a person than the chief of the ‘Alids sang an elegy on this non-Muslim, showing how much higher then literary accomplishment stood than mere orthodoxy[2]. This Ibrahim Ibn Hilal es-Sabi (d. 384/994) knew his worth and was fully cognizant of the fact that he was “the eye of the Caliph through which he surveyed the contemporary world”, and that he possessed ideas of which Kings were in need[3].

His letters fall into two parts: the first recapitulates the contents of the letter in answer. Here the opportunity for courtly compliments is offered and made use of. Thus does a letter of the Wazir to the Chief Qadi begin: The letter of the chief Qadi come with words which make the sea sweet when mixed with it and ideas so clear that it illumines and chases the night away[4]. Then follows the reply prefaced by ‘I have understood’. Even to-day the letters of Sabi can be read with relish and admiration for the command of language which enlivens even purely business correspondence with delightful diction, adorns it with pleasing rhymes and embellishes it with wit and humour. And despite all this splendour the sense is never lost in the mere tangle of words or sweet-sounding cadences. Unlike the letters of the later ages, we instantly perceive and understand here what is said. Stripped of all adornments, even in a clumsy translation, they are eminently readable.

A congratulatory letter, drafted by Sabi, from Izz-ud-Daulah to his cousin ‘Adud-ud-Daulah, in answer to a

---

(1) *Irshad*, I, 343.
(2) Ibn Khalikan, Eng. tr, Vol. I. 31, T.
(3) *Rasa'il* Ba‘adba, 1898 p. 8.
(4) *Yatimah*, II, 277.

communication of the latter announcing the conquest of Beluchistan and the mountain range of Qufs in 357/968, may serve as an example of a state-despatch. "The letter of the Amir 'Adud-ud Dawlah has arrived—May God maintain his power and glory!—with the news of his success which the Almighty has granted him by reason of his faith and piety ; namely that he—May God maintain his greatness!—has conquered the mountain-range of al-Qufs and al-Belus and the inhabitants who were hostile; to our faith and had strayed away from the path of God ; that he chased them from one hiding place to another that he subdued them wherever they sought shelter or refuge; that he slew their guards ; destroyed their heroes, laid waste their fields and pastures; effaced all traces of them with the result that he left them no option but to submit to him, to sue for peace, to give hostages, to surrender their treasures , to take up a correct attitude towards our faith and to enter its fold. I have understood and praised God for the favours He has shown to the Amir 'Adud-ud-Dawlah for I knew what booty God has given him. I rejoice over his success. I share with him what he has and I stand by him, for even the sense of sharing his glory is an honour because of the greatness of the man that has achieved it. We are accustomed to see the Amir—May God strengthen him!—chastise the unbeliever until he mends his ways and the obstinate until he softens down. We are accustomed to see the Almighty help him and ensure good luck to him and lead him to a successful issue. When information of some great deed of the Amir reaches me, I wait to hear of the next which swiftly follows, and every thanksgiving that I offer for the past glory is a pledge of another to come. And it does speedily come. I pray to God that He may strengthen him with His kindness, overwhelm him with His gifts, so that he may attain his temporal and spiritual ends. I pray that He may grant everything lavishly to him in the two worlds—temporal and spiritual ; that He may crown his banner with victory—be it small or great ;

that He may exalt him over his enemies—whatever be their number ; that He may place their forelocks in his hands in war and peace, and that He may reduce them under his authority—be they willing or not[1].

The use of ornate, flowery, rhymed styled passes from official [*Sultaniyah*] into private correspondence. In the 3rd/9th century, the poet-prince Ibn al-Mu'tazz condoles with the prince 'Ubaidullah' 'Abdullah ibn Tahir in rhyme—less prose and receives a rhymeless reply. But a century later such a thing was unthinkable[2]. At the end of the 4th/10th century the art of studied letter-writing acquires such steem and popularity that a living could be made out of it, as it could from time immemorial out of poetry. After the days of the first 'Scribes' of the Arabs Abu Bakr el-Khwarezmi (d. 383/993) is the most famous of such private letter-writers. He visited almost all the Muslim courts of the East : Bukhara, Nisabur, Herat, Isfahan, Shiraz[3]. He wrote to princes, wazirs, generals, qadis, officials, theologians and philologers. The contents are of the usual kind : Felicitations on festive occasions, on promotion in rank, on success ; consolation on bereavements, dismissal, illness or perils of war ; thanks for gifts. Even a complaint to the Director of Taxes finds a place among them. The complaint is regarding too high an assessment of his land-tax. The director is to remedy this grievance *if he would not rob Khorasan of its tongue.* Upon this the tax is remitted for a year[4]. His fame apparently drew many pupils to him, notably jurists (*Fuqaha*). In his collected correspondence we find many a letter to his pupils, past and present; and even one in which he gives thanks for the appointment of a pupil[5].

---

(1) *Rasa'il of Sabi*, 571.
(2) Shabust. *Kit. ed-diyarat, Berlin.* fol. 46 a ff.
(3) *Yatimah*, IV, 123 ff.
(4) *Rasa'il, Const.* p. 81.
(5) Rasa'il, 119 ff.

Among others here is one : Thy letters, my son, are apples and incense, flowers and bouquets to me. I rejoice at the receipt of the first but I wistfully long for the second. I am thankful to thee for the one that has come, but I count days and nights for the one yet to come. Therefore write long and write many letters and know that I am firm and steadfast in my love.

> With such intensity do I love thee,
> That it would make an enemy friend.

Thy presence I enjoy—in thine absence I fret. Wert thou only aware of my longing for thee, a sense of pride would come over thee and men would cease to have any value in thine eyes and thou would'st only look at them scornfully and speak to them contemptuously.[1]

Compared with these, the letters of Sabi are simple and matter of fact. Rhythm and lightness of touch are the central features of Khwarezmi. The contents are merely so many pegs on which the artist hangs his chaplets. This method, again, has very much in common with the old Arab method—the sheer joy in sweet-sounding words, in metaphors and similes, in violent, tumultuous emotions. But there is this all-important difference : that the chivalrous strain of the Arab has now become grotesque, as it was bound to became in a prosaic age.

Grotesque is the rhetoric of Khwarezmi. Exaggeration and accumulation are restored to as deliberate forms of art.

"Someone has offered me—I know not if the wind has swept him away, or the earth has devoured him, or the serpent has bitten him, or the wild animals have torn him to pieces or the sorceress of the desert has seduced him, or the devil has enticed him away, or the lightning has burnt

(1) *Rasa'il*, 76.

him, or the camels have trodden him under foot, or the guide has misled him. Has he fallen from a camel or has he rolled down from a precipice, or has he been flung into a well, or has a mountain tumbled over him, or have his hands withered, or his feet been paralysed, or has elephantiasis seized him or diaphragmitis either? Or has he chastised a slave, and in retaliation been killed by him? Has he lost his way in the mountain, or has he been drowned in the sea, or has he died of heat, or has he been swept away by a torrent, or has a deadly dart pierced him, or has he done Lot's work and been stoned?[1]

To one who wishes to buy a copy of his letters he writes: If I only could, I would make the skin of my cheek, paper; a finger of mine, the pen; and the pupil of my eyes, the ink[2].

Sometimes his rhetoric furnishes us with a very useful list of contrarieties of the times; for instance, when he describes how perversely and unhappily things have fared with him:—

"I have ridden a strange animal. I have taken food out of a strange bowl (lit. bag). I have stayed in a hired house; I have taken raisin-wine. In summer wool have I worn, in winter with paper have I covered myself. In writing courtesy has been shown to me, but, face to face, I have been addressed as 'thou'. In the line of worshippers, mine has been the very last place. Things have even gone so far, that my female slave has treated me unkindly and my horse has became restive. My companions with whom I have journeyed have arrived before me, and even a good dirham in my hand has become counterfeit. Cloth purchased for dress has looked like stolen stuff on my person. When I

---

(1) *Rasa'il* 68.

(2) *Rasa'il* 106, also p. 68.

washed my clothes in July the sun vanished and clouds covered the sky. When I travelled in June, the wind below and the mist obscured my vision. Everything I had I lost, my honour included."[1]

By accumulation he achieves splendid flattery, and at the same time, supplies us with a list of books out of which a fine rhymed letter may be composed: 'The Sahib[2] has said that he has written the reply to my letter between the midday and the evening, but this length of time was unnecessary, for is not his mind as full and deep as the sea? To write this letter I, on the other hand, closed my door, let my curtains down, brought my books to my elbow, sat between the tax-gatherers and the Buwayyids, Khasibi and Ibn Muqlah, summoned the race of the Yezdads and the Sheddads from their graves, called the Basran Ibn Al-Muqaffa from the other world, the Persian Sahl ibn Harun, the Egyptian Ibn 'Abdan Hasan ibn Wahb, Ahmad ibn Yusuf. To my right I placed the Life of Ardeshir ibn Babekan, to my left the book *At-Tabyan Wul-Bayan,* in front of me the Savings of Buzurgmihr ibn-al-Bakhtikan and above them all the letters of our Lord and Master Sahib '*Ain ez-Zaman'*, etc., etc.

By his contemporaries Khwarezmi[3] was regarded as antiquated and far too simple, for he wrote 'like ordinary people with an ordinary pen'.

Abu'l Fadl of Hamadan is the protagonist of the new advanced school. At the age of 12 he came to the Sahib ibn 'Abbad at Rai;[4] 12 years latter to Nisabur, where both orally and in writing he measured his strength with

(1) *Ras'ail*, 30.

(2) *Ras'ail*, 35.

(3) Hamadani, *Ras'ail* Beyrut, 76 (for Khwarezmi See Ibn Khall. Eng. tr. I, 366: Vol. III, 108. Khwarezmi died A.H. 383. According to Ibn al-Athir, A.H. 393 Tr.)

(4) For the life of Hamadani, see , Prondergast's tr. of his *Maqamah* Introduction. Tr.

Khwarezmi[1]. On the death of his rival he left Nisabur, and began his grand tour in Khorasan, Sijistan, Afghanistan, where he visited and reaped a harvest in every town. Finally he took up his residence at Herat, where he formed a rich matrimonial alliance and acquired landed properties. In 398/1067 he died a little over forty[2]. He was famous for his memory. He could accurately repeat a poem of fifty verses on hearing it once[3].

Among the feats he could perform and Khwarezmi could not, he reckoned writing a letter which served as a reply even when read with the lines reversed ; writing a letter without certain letters or groups of certain letters, or without the article; writing a letter which was a poem read sideways; writing a letter which may be interpreted both as praise or censure[4]—a performance then regarded as the highest triumph of authorship.

Hamadani also finds fault with the style of Jahiz as too simple too much akin to the language of the common folk, too jerky and abrupt, without ornamentation or rare expressions (*Maqamah*, 72, Beyrut edition). Fortunately the letters of Hamadani which have come down to us are free from literary tricks or jugglery, but they are far more ornate than Khwarezmi's and are strewn with far-fetched allusions and grotesque puns upon words. But something new which has forced its way into the epistolary style now comes to

---

(1) We should read 392 as in *Irshad* (1, 97) instead of 82 as in *Yatimah* (Damascus edition).

(2) *Yatimah*, IV, 168 : Ibn Khall, Wustenfeld's edition, 1, 69.

(3) *Yatimah*, IV, 167.

(4) *Rasa'il*, 74 (There is one such *Ghazal* ascribed to the poet Khusru of Delhi. Here are some of the lines:—

تو خوش خفته بودی ومن کرده ام ـ دعا وثنابا بوقت سحر

ترا میکنم هم زنت را کنم ـ چنان خدمت مادران را پسر

light. It is the *pleasure in sheer narration.* Here and there we now come across in letters, anecdotes, more 'or' less elaborate, by way of illustration—a thing never met with in Khawarezmi. Thus the man from Basra, who had lost his donkey, personifies him who takes a long journey to find what is near home. "He set out to find him and looked for him at every inn. When he failed to find him he marched through Khorasan, came to Tabaristan and Mesopotamia, went round the *Bazars,* but the donkey was nowhere to be found. Then he gave up the quest, and after a long and tedious journey returned home. One day he sees the donkey in his stable, and lo and behold, he is there with his saddle and bridle, crupper and girth, nibbling away at his fodder."[1]

And to illustrate one's incessant longing for home, Hamadani says: The camel, despite his coarse texture, longs for his town; the birds fly across the sea to return home. He relates of Tahir ibn el-Husain: When he came to old Cairo he found domes set up in the streets, carpets laid out, houses artistically decorated, people on horseback, and on foot, gold scattered to right and to left. But Tahir bent his head, said nothing, interested himself in nothing and felt pleased with none. When questioned about it he replied : The old women of Buseng (his native town) were not among the spectators."[2]

A merchant supplies his son with money in a foreign country and, at the same time, gives him advice. He administers special caution against generosity. "Let people say, God is generous! But His generosity enriches us without impoverishing Him. But with us it is different. " Abroad, the son developed a passion for learning. He spent all his money in its acquisition and returned home to his father with the Qur'an and its commentaries, and said: Father, I

(1) *Rasa'il*, 174 ff.
(2) *Rasa'il*, 370.

have come to thee with power over this and the enternal life to come. I have come to thee with Traditions and their *Isnad*; I have come to thee with jurisprudence and its tricks; scholasticism and its ramifications, prose and its elegance, grammar and its conjugations, philosophy and its principles —so, pluck flower and fruit from the tree of knowledge and things noble and beautiful from the fine arts. The father thereupon took the son to the *Bazar*, to the money-changer, to the linen dealer, to the spice-seller, and finally to the vegetable-seller and asked for a bundle of vegetables and said: Take in payment the commentary on any Sura you please. The vegetable-seller jibbed and rejoined: "We sell only for current coin and not for a commentary on the Qur'an." Then the father took some dust in his hand and put it on the head of his son and spoke: You child of misfortune, with money you left home and to home you have returned with learning which will not buy you even a bundle of vegetables[1].

Hamadani's leaning and propensity for the dramatic fitted in well with the lively interest in travellers, in their language and adventures, which marked the circle that gathered round the Sahib. The Wazir himself was an adept in the language of the common folk (*Munakat bani Sasan*) and loved to converse with Abu Dulaf al-Khazraji. Abu Dulaf had travelled to India and China 'in quest of knowledge and refinement'. To him we are indebted for valuable information on those countries. He collected MSS. for the Sahib and played the part of a negotiable instrument for his business[2]. Not only had he eye and ear for foreigners but also for the lowest strata of his own people; mostly as strange as the former to cultured circles. Even here in this sphere of activity Jahiz had preceded him by some 150 years.

---

(1) *Rasa'il*, 393 ff.

(2) *Yatimah, III*, 174 (See Ibn Khall., Eng. tr. I. 215: on Abu'l Firas , see Ibn Khall., I, 366 : see Ibn Khall., I, 114 Tr.).

Jahiz was the first to draw up a list of the arts and crafts of the common folk with their distinctive characteristics, which Baihaqi at the end of the 4th/10th century somewhat amplified[1]. But now Abu Dulaf composes a long poem on common folk with such exhaustive notes and comments that he leaves his two predecessors far far behind him[2]. To Ahnaf al-Akbari, himself a traveller, touchingly singing of his homelessness, belongs the credit of having inspired Abu Dulaf with the idea of that work. As a veritable poet Ahnaf could not compile a dull dictionary of slang but to Abu Dulaf he passed on the material for such a work[3].

In this circle Hamadani now makes his appearance with a special gift for short, rhetorical, lively, dramatic stories. A series of *Maqamat* is the result, of which one, the *Rusafah maqamat,* is a monument of slang, not unlike the poem of Abu Dulaf[4]. He himself shows the influence of Abu Dulaf, for the poem quoted in the first *Maqamah* is a poem of Abu Dulaf[5]. Khwarezmi asserted that, besides the *Maqamat*, Hamadani had achieved nothing, a statement strongly resented by the latter[6]. We do not know what impressed the critic so much then. For us the great advance lies in the grouping of scenes round one single individual, Abu'l Fath of Alexandria. The many-hued stories are woven round him as a centre. Here a new vein is struck, a fresh beginning made. Only a step was required to attain to Rogue-romances of the lightest and subtlest kind—such as have not been

(1) *Kit al-Mahasin*, ed Schwally, 624 ff.

(2) *Yatimah,* III, 175 ff.

(3) *Yatimah,* III, 175.

(4) He boasts of having composed (Rasa'il 390, 516) 400 of such *Maqamat*, of which none resembled the other in thought or expression. The number 400 is not to be taken too literally (Ras 74). He asserts that he could write a letter in 400 different ways .

(5) *Yatimah*, III, 176. The *Maqamat* are not dated. According to al-Husri, (Iqd., 1, 280) the Hamadaniya is said to have been dictated in 385/ 995 (Beyrut, 150 ff).

(6) *Ras*, 390.

attained even today. That step has not been taken. They failed, not because they lacked the power of weaving a story, for that power abundantly manifests itself in the popular stories, but because the *Maqamat* became a playground of rhetoric where a logical sequence of events was a matter of no consequence. They only developed a taste for rhetorical rockets which shot forth in rapid succession from the subject under treatment. The poems of Hamadani have also been collected—typical poems of a genuine man of letters—completely unlyrical, brimming over with rhetoric, redolent of deliberate art and laboured wit[1]. He beats time with his tears to the song of the nightingale; plays artistic pranks with grammar, even composes a poem without the letter *w* (and) — a feat which Sahib could not perform, although he could do without any other single letter of the alphabet in a poem.[2] The anthology of Husri (d. 453/1061) shows how Hamadani outdistanced his predecessors. It contains long extracts from his letters, whereas Khwarezmi is not referred to at all. Among the contemporaries of Husri was Abu'l 'Ala el-Ma'arri (363-449/973-1057), the most famous of prose writers. Thus writes Nasir Khusru who passed through Ma'arra in 428/1037 : "All writers of Syria, of the West, of Mesopotamia, agree that there is none who stands on the same level as he. One of his writings particularly the traveller extols, in which he has displayed such eloquence and powers of expression that one can only partially understand it and must needs have recourse to him for explanation."

Such, indeed, was the ideal of good prose! The most amazing subtleties Abu'l 'Ala reserved for his poems, but even in his letters the rhymed sentences are much shorter than in Hamadani, the comparisons and similes are far-

(1) Printed at Cairo, 1321. The Paris MS. is more correct and complete: *Rasa'il*, 390.

(2) *Yatimah*, III, 223 : *Diwan* Paris fol. 54 a.

fetched; in fine, the rhetorical artifices so overlay the letters that often it is difficult to decipher the meaning.

Sometimes a comparison takes an epic turn : "And my grief at parting from you is like that of the turtle-dove, which brings pleasure to the hot listener, retired in a thickly-leaved tree from the heat of the summer, like a singer behind a curtain, or a great man hedged off from the frivolous conversation of the vulgar; with a collar on his neck almost burst by his sorrow; were he able, he would wrench it with his hand off his neck, out of grief for the companion whom he has abandoned to distress, the comrade whom Noah sent out and left to perish, over whom the doves still mourn. Varied music does he chant in the courts publishing on the branches the secrets of his hidden woe, etc.,etc."[1] Here wit and learned allusions flash out, and in every word almost we hear their overt or hidden tone.

The longing for the addressee is the usual preface to letters. Where Hamadani expresses himself in a comparatively simple fashion: "I need thee as the body needs life, the fish water, and the land rain" (Rasa'il, 8), now the turtle-dove appears or some other uncommon simile. "My longing for all I have seen in Baghdad is not unlike the wind which is never still or the Persian fire which is never out. I need you like the verse which cannot do without rhyme;"[2] or "My longing for my master is as permanent as time, which is not exhausted by months and years and as often as one period elapses, another comes to take its place";[3] "I await thee as the merchant awaits the caravan from Persia";[4] "And I with my companions send you with every traveller on the highway, every wind that blows, every flash of lightning, every phantom that crosses

(1) *Letters*, p. 47 Prof. Margoliouth's tr. p. 54.
(2) *Letters*, p. 45.
(3) *Letters*, 54, Eng. tr. p. 60.
(4) *Letters*, p. 36.

the path, a salutation[1]." The art of flattery was cultivated to perfection. An abstract of a famous grammar is presented and 'one wonders how the Euphrates is made to flow through a needle's eye'. And similarly a letter to one residing in Egypt thus begins: "If scholarship emits any fragrance, or wit any flame, even at this distance we have felt the perfume of your scholarship, and your wit has turned our darkness into day[2]. ....Your letter is too grand to be kissed; kisses are for its shadow; too precious to be bandied about, let that be done with copies! For us it is a short of sacred thing[3]......The abodes wherein you take up your residence are like those northern and southern constellations, twenty-eight in number, which only are famous because the moon takes up its quarters in them, and to which in consequence the Arabs ascribe every rain-bringing mist[4]." He describes his native town Ma'arra to one proposing a visit there:

He would come to this city like the vulture , who is a King and a Chieftain among birds, and from whose limbs there issues a musk-like odour, falling on a foul carcase[5]. This is such an epithet as may be applied to Ma'arra, which the opposite of the Paradise described by the Qur'an, 'the garden which is promised to those that fear (Qur'an, XLVII, 16) wherein are rivers of water that does not corrupt.' Her very name 'mischief' is ominous; God save us from it ! The water-courses are blocked up; and the surface of its mould in summer is dry. It has no flowing water, and trees can be planted there. When a slaughtered beast is offered to the inhabitants by which they might hope to profit, you would fancy that it had been dyed with indigo, yet still they gaze at it as longingly as at the new moon that marks the end of

---

(1) *Letters*, p. 88, Eng. tr. p. 100 Tr.
(2) Prof. Margoliouth's tr. p. 1.
(3) Prof. Margoliouth's tr. p. 3.
(4) Prof. Margoliouth's tr. p. 7.
(5) *Letters*, p. 61-62.

the fasting month. And there comes a time when a goat there is as precious as capricorn, and a ram of inferior breed as rare as a crow with two chicks; when a man standing by a milk-seller fancies himself standing in Paradise asking for the water of life."

The great art of these pyrotechnists has made the language uncommonly supple and vigorous while terse, and this art is at the back of all those who combined freedom and spontaneity of expression with utmost brevity and concentration. In this sphere Abu Hayyan et-Tauhidi (d. 400/1009) stands unexcelled. He is, one sees, conversant with the secrets of the elegant style, but there is little trace of mannerism in him. A simpler, a more balanced, a more forcible prose has never been written in the Arabic language. But fashion favoured and honour fell to the other style. Abu Hayyan stands alone, in advance of his age and his people. Says he: Exceptional is my position, exceptional my language, exceptional my beliefs and manners. I am wedded to loneliness; to solitude and silence I am resigned. Familiar with affliction, I patiently endure grief. I distrust mankind. Often have I prayed in the mosque without noticing my neighbour and, whenever I did notice, I found him a shopkeeper, a tripe-man, a dealer in cotton or a butcher who sickned me with his stench."[1] Towards the end of his life he burnt his books,[2] for " I have no child, no friend, no pupil, no master and would not leave my books to people who would trade with them and smirch my honour.

How am I to leave my books behind to those with whom I have lived for twenty years without receiving love or regard; by whom, often and often, I have been driven to privation and hunger and galling dependence or reduced

(1) *Fi's-Sadaqah,* Const. 130. p. 5.

(2) See Prof. Margoliouth's *Arab Historians* pp. 96, 97. There is a letter of Abu Hayyan of about 400 A. H. wherein he defends his conduct in doing this by citing the example of many eminent men, Tr.].

to the necessity of bartering away my faith and honour"[1]. He put so much venom and sarcasm in his '*Book of Two Wazirs*' that people, for long, believed that it would bring ill-luck to him who owns it.

The decline of pure Arab taste is finally evidenced by the fact that from the 3rd/9th century onward the delightful stories of other nations fill a large space in Arabic literature[2]. Jewish legends (Israiliyah) and sea-fables had hitherto supplied the need; but fresh translations from Persian and Indian are added to them— the most important being the '*Thousand and One Nights*' or , as they were then called by their Persian title,'*Thousand Fables'(Hazar Afsan).* They consisted of 200 stories spread over 1,000 nights[3]. Those accustomed to inflated and ornate prose found the new style 'dry and insipid' (*Fihrist,* 304). The great Abu'l 'Ala speaks slightingly of *Kalila Wa Damna (Rasa'il,* 120). The new un-Arab style was really meant for foreigners, and yet savants and authors of repute did not consider it unworthy of them to write simple historical works for entertainment.

The well-known writers Ibn Abdus el-Jahshijari imitated the '*Thousand and One Nights*' but died when he had got to 480 nights. The striking thing about him is that he disregarded the interweaving of the stories, precisely the

---

(1) *Irshad,* V, 387 f.

(2) Tradition says that Quraish were famous for their ready reply and the Arabs generally. The non-Arab could only answer them after deliberation and effort. (*Amali* of Murtada, 1, 177).

(3) Were the stories of Sindbad there ? They existed independently of these '*thousand fables*' in large or smaller versions and were known even then to have come from India (Mas'udi, IV, 90 *Fihrist* 305). Suli, at the beginning of the 4th/10th century (*Auraq, Paris* 4836, 9),and the poet Ibn al-Hajjaj (d. 391/1,000 Gotha, fol. 11 a) speak of them as particularly popular fictions. An Indian physician Sindbad is said to have been the author. Their contents were:- The *Seven Wazirs, The Teacher and the Boy,* and *The wife of the King* Mas'udi. I, 162 : Eng. Tr. I, 175, Tr.

thing so appealing and attractive to us[1]. He brought every story to an end each night. To this class belong the entertaining works of the Qadi et-Tanukhi (d. 384/994), and, finally, the most important work of the century—Miskawaihi's (d. 420/1029) *Uns el-Farid (Companion of the Lonely),* the finest book of stories and anecdotes. (Kifti, 331 ff).

There are other collections still older, such as those of Ibn Kutaiba and the '*Iqd.* In them, for the first time, we notice a style of story-telling not purely Arab. Along with these, there grew up a whole host of anonymous books: Romances of chivalry like those of 'Urwah ibn 'Abdullah and the limping Abu 'Omar; books of witticism and anecdotes such as those of Jiha, the Beduin wag, and of Ibn Ma'mili, the famous singer; comical books such as those of man who fell in love with a cow, the stories of the 'cat and the mouse' (Suli, *Auraq*, p. 9), of the bird lime, of the well scented one, and a heap of love-tales, first and foremost among them being the romances of poets and of cunning and passionate women.

Love-stories between men and demons also fill a large space[2]. The historian Hamzah of Isfahan speaks of some seventy widely-read books of amusement in his time, about 350/961[3]. There were love-stories too of the elegant world of maudlin sentimentality. They evinced great enthusiasm for Udhrah, who "dies when he loves," and for the pale, sunken hero whose very bones wither away for love's longing[4].

And there Arabic prose has remained up to this day!

---

(1) Mez means the process of inserting one story in another: Tr.

(2) *Fihrist*, 303-313.

(3) *Annales, ed. Gottwald*, 41,

(4) *Muwassa*, 42 ff.

2. Poetry

The great towns of Mesopotamia were the centres of the new school of poetry. Bashshar b. Burd of Basra (d. 168/784) was regarded as its founder[1]. He was the son of a digger. He was stone-blind but tall and well-built, and his listeners burst into laughter when, in a love poem, he referred to himself as one so worn out by love's woes, as to be blown away by a breath of wind[2]. Before reciting, he clapped his hands, cleared his throat, spat right and left, and then began[3].

Then, at Basra, every lad and every girl in love sang Bashshar's songs; every wailing women and every songstress made money thereby; every man of importance feared and dreaded his tongue(*Aghani*, III, 26). Even to Baghdad he went and declaimed *Qasidahs* before the Caliph Al-Mahdi. He is said to have composed 12,000 *Qasidahs*. Like the ancient poets he sang in purest Arabic. To the Bedouins of the tribe of Qais Ailan, then encamping at

(1) (Ibn Khall.Vol. 1, 254 ; Nicholson, *Lit. Hist. of the Arabs* (1st Ed.) p. 373 Tr). Marzubani (d. 378) wrote a lengthy history of the modern poets. He placed Bashshar first and Ibn al-Mu'tazz last on the list (see Prof. Margoliouth's Arab Historians, p. 79 Tr.) *Fihrit*, 132 Ibn Khallad sings: The modern whom Bashshar leads' (*Yatimah*, III, 235). He calls him 'father of the moderns' (Hamzah el-Isfahani in the *Diwan* of Abu Nuwas, p. 10: Al-Husri, Margin of '*Iqd*, p. 21).

(2) *Aghani*, III, 22, 65. Some one found him, resting in the passage of his house, like a buffalo.' *Ibid*, 56.

(3) *Aghani*, III, 22. The poet Bahturi also behaved very disgustingly at the recitation of his poems. He walked up and down the room, backwards and forwards, shook his head and shoulders, stretched out his arm and shouted: 'Beautiful, by God !' and attacked his audience, calling out to them: 'Why do you not applaud?' (Yaqut *Irshad* VI, 404). In the 4th/10th century there were poets even in the provinces who simulated the ecstatic emotions of the poets of former times. One such appeared at Mosul with his face smeared with red earth, dressed in a red felt mantle, with a red turban, a red staff in his hand, red shoes (Shabushti, *Kit.-ed-diyarat*, Berlin, fol.86 b). For the line of Buhturi see Ibn Khall., Vol. III, 657, 74).

Basrah, he recited his poems. He was so conversant with the intricacies of the language that philologists cited him as an authority (*Aghani*, III, 52). Bashshar was over sixty or seventy years of age and had the misfortune of losing all his friends before his death. "Only people remainde who knew not what language was." On account of a venomous verse he was beaten to death by order of the Caliph, and his body thrown into the Tigris. The body was eventually recovered, and his bier was accompanied to the grave only by his black slave-girl crying *Wa Sayyida! Wa Sayyida!* (O my master ! O my master!).

But all this was old style. They found no new forms scarcely even fresh materials. What they did do was to introduce into poetry flowers of trimmed gardens instead of heather blossoms[1]. Instead of the wild ass they sang of the goat, as did Qasim, brother of the famous Katib ibn Yusuff[2]. Or of the domestic cat, as did Ibn al-Allaf (d. 318/ 930)[3].

But if nothing else, one thing certainly was new—the ingenuity which now characterises Arab poetry. (The word 'Tayyib' now comes into fashion and is a favourite word of Jahiz. Van Vloten: *Livre des Avares,* p. 111). It was the manifest result of a decadent culture, inevitable consequence of the lead taken by the heterogeneous population of the great towns. And precisely the same happened in prose. The passion for things new and

(1) Ibn Rashiq, '*Umdah*, 150.

(2) *Aghani,* XX, 56.

(3) Damiri, II, 321. That famous poem is a long elegy on a cat. Some took it to be an elegy on his royal friend and poet, the slaiṇ Ibn al-Mu'tazz for whom, from sheer fear, the poet substituted a cat. Others would have it that a slave of the poet who fell in love with a slave girl of the wazir was meant by it. They were both killed. By the cat crawling into the dove-cot the slave was meant. (Abu'l Fida, *Annales*, year 318). Ibn al-Amid later wrote a poem on the cat in which he emulated the glory of Allaf (*Yatimah*, III, 23).

interesting destroyed once and for all the taste for bardic lay. Jahiz is praised as the creator of this new style in prose because he alternated between moods gay and serious. In Bashshar, father of the new poetry, what delighted the philologist Abu Zaid more than anything else was his mastery over things both serious and gay ; whereas in the old masters naught but one mood, gay or serious, manifested itself.[1]

Similarly Asma'i applauded the versality of Bashshar,[2] whereas Ishaq al-Mausili fanatical admirer of the old style, thought little of him. He found fault with Bashshar for great disparity in his writings : notes lofty and notes trivial subsisting side by side. The poet once compared the bones of Sulaima to Sugar-cane adding that if an onion were brought near them its odour would be overpowered by that of the musk.[3]

The older poets regarded witticism as a false note in poetry. Now, however, it gains ground. In poetry the shibboleth of the 3rd/9th century was 'originality' or 'innovation' (bida'), something unlike others.[4] One of the outstanding poets of the age, Ibn al-Mu'tazz, actually wrote a book on this subject.[5]

As in all "ingenious" poetry thought preponderates ; so what they wanted was expressiveness and all sorts of allusions in the verse. And thus the ideas (*ma'ani)* to which Bashshar and his followers now gave currency were ideas which had never found a place in the Pagan or even the

(1) *Aghani*, III, 25.
(2) *Aghani*, III, 24.
(3) *Aghani*, III, 28
(4) Etymologically allied to the words for 'to be alone' and 'to begin'.
(5) This book (*Kit. al-badi'*) was an anthology of bacchanalian piecese, the first important work on poetics. Nicholson, *Lit. Hist. of the Arabs*, p. 325 (1st Edn.) (Tr.)

Islamic poets of earlier times[1]. And in this sphere Bashshar was supreme for "he not only accepted what nature and talent offered him but searched for the very root of ideas, the mines of truths, and niceties of comparisons and used them with a powerful mind".

As a typical specimen of modernity were regarded the blind poet's verses addressed to the voice of one of the women who talked with him:—

"You people, my ear loves one of the tribe,
"And often in love the ear takes precedence of the eye.
"They say: Foolishly you rave of her whom you have not seen.
"To them I reply : To the heart the ear speaks as effectively as the eye".

And this very idea is simplified and intensified in another passage:—

"How foolish you talk? You have never seen her !
"To them I say: The heart sees what the eye sees not"[2].

Ordinarily they spoke of rosy cheeks, but now one is enraptured to hear the roses likened to "cheeks closely pressing each other"[3]. The witty poem of Ibn Rumi[4] (d. 280/893), addressed to one who had his hair cropped "his face grows at the expense of his head like the summer day at the expense of the night", secured the warmest applause ; the night and the day referring respectively to the black

(1) *Umdah* of Ibn Rashiq, Cairo, II, 185.
(2) '*Umdah* 188. A third variant in *Aghani* III, 67. The popular style: "I said—they said—" 'Omar ibn Abi Rahi'ah developed.
(3) Shabushti. MS. Berlin, fol. 5 b.
(4) (Ibn Khall., II, 29 Tr.).

hair and the shining skin of the head[1]. Extreme in his views, Ibn Rumi (*i.e.*, son of a Greek) declared Bashshar to be the greatest poet of all times[2]— a statement which staggered the philologists of his age. And yet 200 years later the critic Ibn Rashiq (d. 463/1071) proclaimed Bashshar the most brilliant of modern poets. 'He made beautiful what he wanted', said Ibn Rashiq referring to the poem quoted above[3]. Bashshar's example gave a lively impetus to gifted poets to develop their own powers of observation and expression, and to keep off the beaten track.

To this new vein we owe that effortless sweetness which marks Bashshar's elegy on his little girl:—

> "O daughter of him who had wished for no daughter,
> "Only five or six were you.
> " When eternal leave you took of me,
> "Shattering my heart to pieces for love or you.
> "Fain would I have had you a boy,
> "Drinking at dawn, flirting at eventide"[4]

And again in the poem on the girl bidding farewell:—

> "Lo! She suppressed a sob and white were her tears
> "On her cheeks and yellow were they on her neck[5]".

And to this vein again we owe such forcible images as the one in Abu Nuwas (d. circa 195/810), recalling our own popular songs to mind[6]:—

---

(1) *Umdah*, II, 187.
(2) Hamza al-Isfahani in the *Diwan* of Abu Nuwas.
(3) *Umdah;* 188, 194.
(4) *Aghani*, III, 63.
(5) *Helbet el-Kumait*, 191.
(6) He grew up at Basra and had taken Bashshar as his model Hamza

"Love plays with my heart not unlike a cat with a mouse[1]".

Or the imposing metaphor in Ibn al-Mu'tazz (d. 296/909):—

"A thunder-roll in the distance, like the Amir's speech from the hill-top to the people[2]"

And again:

" I have committed my soul to God's keeping and there it rests like a sword in the scabbard[3]".

And once again in a song of the spring which begins:—

"Behold ! the spring approaches not unlike the fair ones, decked out for their lovers!"

The verse:

"The cupping-glass of the yellow truffle shows itself, and all over is the carnival of life[4]".

Or:

"He visited me in absolute darkness when the Pleiads, like a bunch of grapes, hung in the west[5]".

Or:

Against my will I tarried helpless like one in

---

al-Isfahani in the *Diwan* of Abu Nuwas. Jahiz regarded him the most important poet after Bashshar and so did Ibn Rumi (Intr to the Cairene Ed. of the *Diwan* of Abu Nuwas, 91).

(1) *Diwan*, Vienna MS., fol. 176b.

(2) *Diwan*, Cairo, I, 15. Abu Tammam, *Diwan*. 370.

(3) Ibn al-Mu'tazz, 1, 16

(4) *Ibn al-Mu'tazz*, II, 34.

(5) *Ibid*, II, 110.

an old women's embrace[1]"

Not infrequently do these great poets become much too original. Thus Abu Nuwas on a jilted girl:—

"And a tear adorned her. And out of her tears
a cheek grew on her cheeks and a neck on
her neck[2]".

Or:

" The new moon is like a silver crescent
moving the Narcissus, the flowers of
darkness[3]"

Or oi the rainbow:

"The hands of the cloud have flung a grey
veil on the earth,
"And the rainbow has adorned it with
colours, yellow, red, green and white.

"It resembles the train of a fair one who comes in coloured mantles, one shorter than the other" (Ibn al-Rumi in Ibn Rashiq, '*Umdah*, II, 184).

Striving after uncommon metaphors and similes marks the entire poetry of the 4th/10th century. It powerfully stimulated the tendency to penetrate into the most hidden secrets of things and to see the oddest peculiarities in them. Above everything else we note the function of plastic art assigned to poetry. Much of it is pure word-painting Sheer visual pleasure now gains the upper hand, bringing in its train the desire to see things artistically and to express them clearly. This the genuine Arab had never known. But the fashion set by them place the red-pen instead of the brush in the hands of a people of very different temperament. And these now become the exponents of the new style. The

(1) *Ibid*, II, 122.
(2) *Diwan Cairo*, p. 8.
(3) Ibn *al-Mu'tazz*. Diwan, II, 122.

Sifat—descriptions, which Abu Tamman, in the VIIth Chapter of his Anthology of the Arab poets, disposes of in a few lines, have immensely developed. Very cursorily indeed did the Arab poet deal with land-scapes. They dealt, instead, as was their practice from time immemorial, with wine, with the description of the dull, rainy day when drink was particularly delightful.[1] Even later poets have given us the subtlest comparisons in this sphere. Ibn Rumi:

> "The overcast heaven was like the darkest silk,
> "And the earth like the greenest damask".[2]

And the Wazir Muhallabi fondly sings:—

> "The heaven looked like a dark stallion."

In the older days they preferred their carouses at night or the earliest dawn: "when the cock crows, hand the morning draught[3]".

In the few passages where the drinking-songs of Abu Nuwas give details we invariably find:

---

(1) Ibn al-Mu'tazz, *Diwan*, II, 122.

وتقصير يوم الدجن والدجن معجب   ببهكنة تحت الخباء المعبد

We find these as constant themes in Eastern poetry.

تندو پرشور وسیہ مست زکھسار آمد   می کشان مزدہ کہ ابر آمد وبسیار آمد

And our Indian Poets.

جم کہ پانی برس کے کھل جائے   باغ جانے کا تب مزہ آئے

Tr.)

یہ بہار آئی ہوئی ایسی گھٹا چھائی ہوئی   توبہ کر زاہد کروں میں توبہ ایسے وقت میں

(2) *Yatimah*, II, 21.
(3) Ibn al-Mu'tazz, II, 33.

"The morning has rent the veil of darkness", or some such thing.[1]

A hundred years later, Ibn al-Mu'tazz gives most variants on this subject:-

> "Arise, carousing boon companions, let us take the morning draught in darkness for the dawn is well-nigh on us!"

Or:

> "In the heaven I see the Pleiades like a bare foot emerging from a mourning dress"[2]

And again:

> "Above the crescent of the new moon the whole zodiac is visible like the head of a negro with a grey beard"[3].

But just about the time of Ibn al-Mu'tazz, this remarkable carousing hour was getting out of fashion. The poet ridicules it as unsuitable: "When the shivering wind blows, the saliva freezes in the mouth, the servant curses, and cares capture the heart".[4]

In Ibn al-Mu'tazz, love for natural scenery begins to assert its claim in drinking songs. The wine-bibber begins

---

(1) *Diwan*, 349. The first two verses of the poem are quite modest: "The time is happy, the trees are green, the winter is over, and March has come". The talk of green gardens and singing birds does not exactly fit in with what follows. They are obviously subseqent interpolations. And such also is the case with the Battle of Flower's which Mas'udi (VIII, 407) ascribes to Abu Nuwas. It is not to be found in his Diwan and comes from a later time.

(2) *Diwan*, II, 37.

(3) Ibn al-Mu'tazz, II 110.

(4) Diwan, II, 110 ff. (The wine bibbers in the East have never really give up the early morning-draught which they consider the best of all drinks.)

now to enjoy, with his drink, the green of the garden, the trees, the roses, the narcissus, the singing birds, and in the spring the feast of life'. (*Diwan,* II, 34, 51, 110).

And in the first half of the 4th/10th century two Syrian poets, both friends, developed the poety of the garden and its myriad charms and carried it to its highest point.

Mohammed Ibn Ahmed[1] Abu Bakr, born in Antioch, was the Librarian of Saif-ud-Daulah[2]. His surname As-Sanaubari suggests that either he or his father was a cutter of pipe-wood[3]. He was also called 'Skittle' on account of his figure (*Mafatih el-'Ulum, ed. Van Vloten, 207).* The second surname Al-Sini, the Chinese, does not necessarily imply that he was personally in China. In Kufa a merchant who traded with China was so called (Yaqut, III, 444). He died in 334/945, being at least fifty years of age (Abu'l Mahasin, II, 313; Yaqut. II, 664). Of his life we only know that he was friendly with the poet Kushajim to whom he was a stream of boundless beneficence (*Diwan*, of Kushajim (Beyrut, 1213 p. 116): that Kushajim married one of his daughters (*Diwan,* 74 f.) and comforted him at the death of another who died unmarried (*Diwan*,71). He sang chiefly of Aleppo and Raqqah, the two capitals of Saif-ud-Daulah. But he also resided at Edessa, where, at the house of a book-dealer, he used to meet a circle of Syrian, Egyptian and Mesopotamian literati. (Yaqut, *Irshad*, II, 23). At Aleppo he owned a garden with a summer-house full of plants and trees, flowers and oranges. (Diwan of Kushajim, 74). For this he was called

(1) This according to *Fihrist* 468. According to Alal Mahasin (II, 312) : Ahmed ibn Mohammed ibn al-Hasan al-Dalbi. According to Yaqut (II, 311): Moh. ibn al-Hasan b. Marrar. According to Kutubi (I, 61): Ahmed Ibn Mohammed.

(2) *Guruli Malali el-Budur*, II, 176

(3) At Hisn et-Tinat, by the sea near Alexandria, many pine-forests were cut down and pines shipped to Syria and Egypt (Ibn Haukal, 221). Also there was a pine forest. 12 square miles, south of Beyrut along Lebanon,—Idrisi, 23.

Al-Halabi. Too Young for the *Aghani* and too for the *Yatimah*, his Diwan, which was once alphabetically arranged in 200 folios by Suli has been split up into fragments and does not exist except in small selections. The fragments had therefore to be collected from all quarters.

On a bed of blood-red anemones fringed by pale red roses:-

"Roses encompass the anemones in your beautiful garden, not unlike human faces gazing at a conflagration[1].

"When the red anemones wave up and down, they resemble hyacinth banners tied to emerald shafts[2]"

And again Spring in the garden:—

"Rise and gaze, O Gazelles, the flower-beds
revel their miracles!

"The spring has rent the veil which had
wrapped their faces divine.

"Roses like cheeks, narcissus like eyes, which
greet the loved ones.

"Anemones, like silver mantles, with blank legends; cypresses like singing-girls tucked up to the knee; one looks like a gentle maiden playing with her companions at midnight. The gentle breeze has made the brook tremble and filled it with leaves. Had I the power to guard the garden—no mean soul would ever tread its soil[3]"

Sanaubari regards the narcissus as the "Queen of

---

(1) Shabushti, MS., Berlin fol. 96.
(2) Khafaji, *Rathanat el-alibb*, 256.
(3) Al-Kutubi, 1, 61 and Tha'alibi. *Kit. Man Gaba.* 25 (For his life See Ibn Khall., Vol. II. P. 129, Tr).

flowers",—"camphor eye-lids fringe the saffron eyes"[1]. And indeed, narcissus is the chief flower of Syria which not infrequently completely whitens its meadows[2]. Even of a 'Battle of Flowers' he has sung in which the rose, the self-satisfied lily, the anemone 'whose cheeks bear the scar of warfare' the violet in mourning attire and the carnation as war-crier march in the cover of the whirling dust against the narcissus, —until the poet, anxious for his favourite, unites them all peacefully in a salon where 'birds and harps sing'[3].

In the previous century Buhturi (Ibn Khall., Vol. III. 657) had sung of a lake in the Calip's palace:

"The envoys of water discharge therein
hastening from the starting line.

"Tis as if white silver flowing out of ingots were running in its channels. When the wind passes over it, it produces billows like cuirasses with polished edges.

"At night when the stars are reflected therein—we might take it for the starry heaven; only fishes, instead of birds, fly therein" (*Diwan,* I, 17, Mez has mistaken the sense of these lines. Prof. Margoliouth, Tr.)

But as a poet of gardens he adds:
"And the flowers shine like stars—now in clusters, now single and apart" (*Iqd.* 1,183).

---

(1) Kutubi, *Fawat el-Wafayat,* (Cairo, 1299) I, 61.

(2) Nasir Khusru, ed. Schefer. Tr. 39; Schefor reminds us of the Narcissus-island of the Syrian Tripoli.

(3) Kutubi in Mas'udi VIII, 407; a 'Battle of flowers' is ascribed to Abu Nuwas in which red flowers (Rose, Pomegranate and Apple-bloom) oppose the yellow ones (Narcissus, Camelia, Citron). For internal reasons this cannot be accepted as correct . The poem, morever, is not to be found in the Beyrut edition of the *Diwan.* Nor can the poem be ascribed to Sanaubari for the Mesopotamian vineyard of Baturunga plays a role therin and the rose is preferred to narcissus.

The first landscape poet of Arabic literature is equally a passionate lover of the sky, of light and air, with an eye for their sweet secrets.

A song of the spring:

> "When there is fruit in the summer, the earth is aglow and the air shimmers with light.
> "When in autumn the plam trees shed their leaves, naked is the earth, stark the air.
> "And when in winter rain comes in endless torrent, the earth seems besieged and the air a captive.
> "The only time is the time of the radiant spring, for it brings flowers and joy.
> "Then the earth is a hyacinth, the air a pearl, the plants turquoises, and water crystal."

He was the first to sing of snow:—

> "Gild the cup with wine, lad , for it is a silvery day.
> "Veiled in white is the air, bedecked in pearls, as though in bridal display.
> "Do you take it for snow? No, it is a rose trembling on the bough.
> "Coloured is the rose of spring, white the rose of December."[1].

Sanaubari has left his mark on Arabic literature. There is, to begin with, his countryman Kushajim,[2] who followed in the footsteps of his more renowned friend— namely, the path of visual delights. Kushajim was attached to Sanaubari like water and wine. Sworn friends in sunshine and gloom; comrades of joy , sober and rictous; to be seen in the heaven

---

(1) Tha'labi, *Nasr en-nazm* (Damascus, 1300 ; p.137)
(2) He was a Katib. And in addition astrologer and master of the kitchen of Saif-ud-Daulah, *Yatimah*, IV, 157.

of fine arts like sun ana moon in harmony like lute and flute[1]. Thus sings Kushajim:

> "In a blue garment she came, that blue which
> we call 'running water'
> "A full moon is she, and in the colour of
> heaven resplendently she shines[2]."

He call a girl in violet-mourning dress 'a rose in violet', and of a mourning youth he thus sings:— He rent his cheeks until its roses veiled themselves in violets[3].

He sings of the Quwaiq, the river of Aleppo, flowing in its emerald meadows, through red anemones and lilies like a loosened string of pearls, flashing like an Indian sword, now bare and now in the sheath. He likens the lotus of the meadows to a hanging lamp, now alight and now extinguished by the wind[4].

When the Nile rises in Egypt, shattering the dams, it encloses the villages, like the sky whose stars are the farm-houses[5].

Also songs of snow he has penned. One of them begins thus:

"Is it snow or is it silver that comes pouring down?"

In this poem he has the bad taste to say:

"White is the land as though everywhere white teeth were smiling."[6]

He had a large circle of admirers, one of whom sang:-

(1) *Diwan* of Kushajim (Beyrut, 1313) p. 74.
(2) *Diwan* p. 6.
(3) *Diwan* pp. 21, 22.
(4) *Diwan*, p.48.
(5) Shabushti, *Kit. ad-diyarat*, Berlin, fol. 115 a.
(6) *Diwan*, p 140.

> "Woe to the luckless who enjoys not a cup
> of wine, the letters of Sabi, and the poems of
> Kushajim[1]."

In the middle of the 4th/10th century Kushajim was the 'flower of the cultured' at Mosul. The Khalidi brothers and Sari poets of this town, however much they might wage war with each other; followed whole-heartedly in the footsteps of their Syrian master. They not only plagiarised each other's verses but Sari inserted the best poems of his opponents in Kushajim's 'Book of Poems' with a view, at once, to charge more for the transcript and to annoy Kalidi[2].

Once at Mosul the poets were sitting together when it began to hail, covering the ground with hail-stones. Khalidi threw an orange at them and invited the company to describe the picture. Sulami (d. 394/1004) began straightway: 'Khalidi has placed a cheek on the teeth' (*Yatimah,* II, 158).

One of the Khalidis sings thus of the dawn:

> "The stars in the firmament stand like lilies
> in violet meadows.
> "Orion staggers in the dark like a drunken
> man.
> "Veiled in a light, white cloud,
> "She now conceals herself behind it.
> "Like the breathing of a fair damsel on a
> mirror, when her charms are perfect and she
> is unweded"[3].

---

(1) *Yatimah,* II, 24.

(2) *Yatimah* I, 450. In the letters of Sabi (Leiden) there is one in which he defends himself against the suspicion of the Mosul poets, that he aided with Sari: on the contary he asserts that, when Sari begged him to be allowed to compose a panegyric on him, he was permitted to do so provided he said nothing offensive about Khalidi in it.

(3) The name of this constellation is feminine in Arabic. See Pliny's *Natural History,* VII.* 64 for the explanation of this . I am indebted to Prof. Margoliouth for this note,. Tr.

And again : "Hand me, from a white hand, yellow wine in a goblet blue—

"Beverage is the Sun, forth the moon, hand
the axis of the earth, vessel the sky[1]".

Himself more than a poet of moderate attainments and founder of a distinguished literary line, the Wazir Muhallabi popularised in Baghdad Sanaubari's gleeful poetry of nature and of wine. He used especially to recite, as the Sahib[2] states, in the diary of his Journey to Baghdad, a great many poems of Sanaubari and of his school[3]. He even imitated the poem of his master on snow, which is a miracle in Baghdad:—

"Like Confetti falls the snow. Come, let us
enjoy the pure, virgin daughter of the vine."

The inspiration is from the school of Sanaubari, too, when the Qadi et-Tanukhi, belonging to the circle of Muhallabi, sings of a girl in a fire-red garment:—

"She coyly covered her face with her sleeves,
like the setting sun in the evening glow[4]"

And again:

" I have not forgotten the Tigris. The darkness descended and the full moon went under. A carpet of blue was the river with golden embroidery[5]"

When Saif-ud-Daulah, the Prince of Aleppo, likens the crimson-blushes of a virgin, wrapped in a grey veil, to glowing embers, he sees her with the eyes of Sanaubari. And such also is the case when Wathiqi in Turkistan sings of the incipient charcoal fire:

(1) *Yatimah,* I, 519.
(2) Ibn Khall, Vol. I, 214 Tr.
(3) *Yatimah*, II, 12.
(4) *Yaqut Irshad*, V. 338.
(5) *Yatimah*, II, 109: *Irshad*, V. 335.

"Jet in red-gold in between blue lotus[1]".

When , at the end of the century, Ibn 'Abbad sang in Khorasan of the winter:—

> "Do you not see how December scatters its roses and the world seems like a piece of camphor"?—

Khwarezmi discerned at once that all this was traceable to Sanuabari[2].

About the year 400/1009 'Uqaili in Egypt represented the style of Sanaubari. "He had summer-houses in the Island of Old Cairo, took no service of princes, eulogised no one"[3].

The following is a specimen of his verse:—

> "On the brook the hand of the wind has flung fiery anemones, beneath whose red, the water looks like a swordblade, sprinkled with blood[4]".

Little attention is paid to the sensations of sound.

Sulami (d.394/1004) describes the mighty dam of Shiraz but there is not a word in his description about the rushing of water[5]. The only thing of the kind that I have found is in a verse of the Buwayyid Izz-ud-Daulah relating to a banquet on the bank of the Tigris:

> "And the water babbled between the branches like female singers round the flautist[6]".

---

(1) *Yatimah*, IV, 113.
(2) *Yatimah*, III, 95.
(3) Ibn Sa'id,ed. Tallquist, p. 52.
(4) Ibn Sa'íd 78.
(5) *Yatimah*, II, 179.
(6) *Yatimah*, II, 5. (It is double whether this rendering is correct. For "babbling" we should probably render "flowing". Prof. Margoliouth, Tr.)

Towards the end of the century most heterogeneous things were put together for the pleasure of the ingenious, for the eaves and one's own reflection in a mirror[1]. Maimuni in Bukhara describes the entire pantry: cheese, olives, roast fish, mustard sauce, scrambled eggs[2]. Another sings of a candle in the centre of a fish-pond, and compares a fountain with an apple floating in it to a blow-pipe of fine glass, whereby a ball of a gate is made to revolve[3].

The Egyptian 'Abdul Wahhab ibn al-Hajib (d. 387/997) thus speaks of the two great pyramids:—

"Tis as though the country, parched with thirst, had bared her two towering breasts, invoking God's help, like a woman bereft of her child.

"And then the Almighty made her a gift of the Nile which supplies a copious draught to her[4]"

Only in the 4th/10th century—and it is very significant —do tramps find a place in Arabic Poetry :

"Theirs is Khorasan and Qashan unto India.

> "Theirs (the country), up to the Roman frontier, up to the land of the negroes, up to the territory of the Bulgarians, and Sind.

"When the warriors and travellers find the road insecure for fear of the Bedouins and Kurds,

> "We spring across without sword; nay, even without a sheath[5]".

---

(1) The *Qassar*, known as *Ṣari ed-Dila* (d. 410). *Tatimmat al-yatimah, Vienna,* fol. 28 b.

(2) *Yatimah*, IV, 94, ff.

(3) *Yatimah*, IV, 316.

(4) Maqrizi, I, 121.

(5) *Yatimah*, II, 286. *Chevaliers d'industrie* called in Arabic *Banu sasan*. Prof. Margoliouth. Tr.

With these tramps there is ushered in light and lively songs—indeed lyrics, which make no pretence of ingenuity. Al-Ahnaf of Ukbara in Mesopotamia was their chief bard. His drinking-songs take no note of the joys afforded by nature:—

> "I caroused in a tavern to the accompaniment of tambourine and zither:
> "The drum sounded 'Kurdumta'—the flute "tiliri'.

"We sat hard pressed as in a baking-oven, so hot was the room, and from the blows which rained we were like the blind and one-eyed.

"I felt seedy in the morning[1]— Oh, how seedy !"

He sang of the miseries of the tramps too.

> "Despite feebleness the spider spins a wed to rest therein,
> "I have no home.
> "The dung-beetles find support among their kind, but neither love nor support have I"[2].

No artifice ! no epigrams here! It is the style which characterises French literature from Villon to Verlaine. To this circle belongs Mohammed ibn 'Abdul Aziz, of Sus, who in a poem of more than 400 verses described his changes in religion, sect, and employment. It begins :— "No luck have I, no clothes in my trunk[3]". Alongside of him stand the popular poets of the great Mesopotamian towns such as

---

(1) *Yatimah,*II, 287. The Caliph al-Mutamid had already sung :"The Amir is on the march and the drum is sounding :*Kurdum, Kurdum!"* Shabushti, Berlin, fol, 42 b.

(2) *Yatimah,* II, 286. Tha'libi, *Kit. al-'Ijaz,* 236: Tha'libi, *Book of Supports* DMG VIII, 501, I have not discovered the Arabic name of this work. Tr.

(3) *Yatimah* III, 237.

Ibn Lankak at Basra, 'whose poems rarely go beyond two and three verses and who is rarely felicitous in Qasidahs [1]'; Ibn Sukarrah[2] who is said to have composed over 50,000 verses, of which 10,000 are addressed to his black singing-girl Khamrah, and finally, one who surpasses them all, Ibn al-Hajjaj in Baghdad (d. 301/1001)[3].

He was slim and slender:—

"Fear not for me because of my narrow chest,
"Men are not measured by the bushel[4]".

And once, defending himself for running away from his creditors, he sang:—

"Many say : The wretch has fled,— were he a man he would have stayed behind.
"Revile him not! Revile him not for running away!
"Even the Prophet made his escape to the cave[5]".

To this unhappy time probably belong the proud verses:—

(1) Ibn Lankak has collected the short love-poems of the Basran rich-baker (d. 330/941) in front of whose shop people assembled to listen to him . (Ibn al-Jauzi , fol. 70 b). These poems were mostly pederastic. The youths of Basra felt proud of being referred to by him. They appreciated his language for its clarity and intelligibility (*Yatimah*, II, 132). After his death he became popular at Baghdad. Also Mas'udi writes in 333/944 (Mas'udi VIII, 374) that his songs were sung most frequently.

(2) *Yatimah*, II, 188.

(3) Abu Abdullah al-Hasan Ibn Ahmad died at Nil in Mesopotamia on Tuesday the 27th (according to *Wuz*. p. 430, on the 2nd) Jamada I of the year 391. As a zealous Shi'ite he was burried by the grave of Musa ibn Ja'far es-Sadiq. He chose the inscription for his grave : 'And at the threshold lies the dog with paws outstretched'. Surah 18.17 (Al- Hamadani, Paris, fol. 340 b. He resided in Suq-Yahya, of which he sang a great deal).

(4) Yaqut, II, 242 .

(5) *Yatimah*, II, 228.

"When I praised them in the morning, they thanked me not,
"And when I reviled them in the evening, they ignored it.
"I hew my rhymes out of their quarry,
"Whether the blockheads hear or heed them, is no concern of mine".
Rich and influential alike dreaded his evil tongue,

Filth procures me money and honour', he himself says[1]. He became tax farmer and later even Inspector of Industries (Muhtasib) in the capital, for which his less successful contemporary Ibn Sukkarah envied him most[2].

In his poems he loves to use the language of the tramps and charlatans[3]. In him and his companions the disgusting obscenity or Oriental towns reveals itself,—a thing kept in check in literature by the influence of sober and continent Bedouins[4].

Like one freed from some unwelcome restraint, Ibn al-Hajjaj rejoices in and boasts of his license. Indeed his licentious boast is but a reaction against the maudlin sentimentality of others. He says:—

"Necessary too is the levity of my songs, for are we not ingenuous and shameless?
"Can one live in a house without a privy?
"When silent I am laden with fragrance but when I sing the bad odour exhales.

---

(1) *Diwan*, 10. Baghdad, Marghanah, my copy, p. 258.
(2) *Diwan*, Baghdad, 240: *Wuz*,430, *Yatimah*, II, 219.
(3) *Yatimah*, II, 211.
(4) When one examines the descent of the more famous representatives of this literature of fifth one finds it in most cases like the descent of Rawandi (d. 298-911): Son of a Jewish magian or heathen convert (Abu'l Mahasin, II, 184).

> "Cleaner of a privy am I and my song is
> naught but a sewer[1]"

It was precisely for this reason that in a later police-manual the work of this poet is banned to boys[2], but its filth never worried the contemporaries. The highest dignitary of the 'Abbasid Caliphate—the Registrar of the 'Alids—al-Rida, was an ardent admirer of Ibn al-Hajjaj and edited a selection of his poems[3]. He even mourned his death in an elegy. The Fatimid Caliph in Cairo purchased for 1,000 dinars his works in which he was praised[4]. His *Diwan* not infrequently fetched 50 to 70 dinars[5]. Al-Haukari, court-poet of Saif-ud-Dawlah in Aleppo, begged the Mesopotamian poet for a song which he might recite before his master (*Yatimah*, II, 226).

Ibn Hajjaj says himself:—

> "If my song were to strike a serious vein, the
> stars of the night you would see resplendent
> therein.

"But generally it is jocular and redolent of the trivial round of things[6]".

And he achieves his purpose with effortless ease. He calls everything by its right name, defies the laws of metre and of rhyme. And thus his *Diwan* brings together a whole heap of expressions from the colloquial language of the Baghdad of the 4th/10th century[7]. For him the traditional poetic model exists only to be parodied, as for instance on the death of Subuktagin:

---

(1) *Yatimah*, II, 24.
(2) Mashriq, X, p. 1085.
(3) Ibn Khall, Vol. III, p. 418 Tr.
(4) *Diwan* X, 237 : Wuz., 430.
(5) *Yatimah*, II, 215.
(6) *Yatimah*, II, 213.
(7) Unfortunately these are explained only partially in the British Musuem copy . No other explanation exists elsewhere.

"May always the privy in which he is buried.
"Be watered by the rain of the stomach[1]".

And through the mist of filth shine here and there the stars of the night which manifestly made his contemporaries regard this utterer of obscenities as a poet of great distinction.

Of Mesopotamian origin but of Syrian training Mutanabbi[2], in contract to these poets, staunchly adheres to the Arab tradition[3]. While they, being realists, sang of their experiences, Mutanabbi is the academician, to whom the universal appeals. Invited once to join a hunting party which possessed a remarkably intelligent dog that brought to bag a gazelle, without a hawk—the poet sang praises of him. But he thought that that çould be done without reference to the hunting-party, and therefore, simply sang of the dog in the customary fashion (Mutanabbi, Diwan, Beyrut 1882 p.128). Ibn al-Mu'tazz was the only modern poet of whom he approved. Yatimah, I, p.98). The Mesopotamians were unfriendly to him. Both Ibn Sukkarah and Ibn Lankak (Yatimah, I, 86, II, 116) and Ibn al-Hajjaj (Diwan, Baghdad, 270) satirized him, and there is extant a malicious account of the meeting of the Syrian Court-poet

(1) *Diwan*, Baghdad, 80.

(2) Ibn Khall, Vol. I. p. 102 Tr.

(3) Abu Tammam (d. circa 230/845 and al-Buhturi (d. 284/897)—also Syrian poets—were conservatives and followed in the wake of their Damascene predecessors al-Akhtal, Jarir, and Farazdaq. But Buhturi had poetic sense to prefer the more modern style of Abu Nuwas to that of the conservative band. He met the objection of the philologists with the report: Yours is only the science , but not the making of poetry. Only those understand the making of it who have passed through the toil of poetic composition (Goldziher, *Abhandl zur Arabischen Philologic* p. 164, note (4). In Syria also there was a notable representative of Ibn al-Hajjaj's style : Ahmad ibn Mohd. al-Antaqi, known as Abu'l Raqamaq (d. 359) who, however, succeeded in composing only a few lively verses *Yatimah*, I, 238-261). For further particulars about him—*Ma'alim al-Talkhis*, Berlin, fol. 156b.

with the literati of Baghdad. He is made to appear supercilious, and despite intense heat, he wears seven coloured robes, one over another, to increase his proportions, but before a Baghdadian critic he has to trim his sails. (Yaqut, *Irshad*, VI, 506; *Tiraz el-Muwashsha*, Cairo, 1894, II, 65 ff; *Yatimah*, I, 85). In 400/1009 the Syrian poet Abu'l 'Ala left Baghdad on account of a quarrel with the influential supporters of Ibn al-Hajjaj. He sided with his countryman Mutanabbi as against them.

(Letters, ed. by Prof. Margoliouth, p. XXVIII. Abu'l 'Ala also wrote a copious commentary on the poems of Mutanabbi, (Von Kremer on the philosophical poems of Abul 'Ala, SWA, 117 , p. 89). There is a copy of this in the British Museum Tr.)

Even the Syrian Abu Firas (d. 357/968) distinctly pursues the old path. But the most remarkable thing about him is that he very sparingly alludes in his poems to the wild warfare on the western frontier of the empire. A cousin of the Hamdanid Prince Saif-ud-Daulah, he must have been mixed up a great deal with those events and yet the larger portion of his glorification is naught but poetical fiction. And one who is not conversant with the facts will find it impossible to make out from his poems that Syrians and Greeks, Muslims and Christians fought in such large numbers and with the most perfect military equipment of their age. They might equally well be dealing with the petty warfare of two Bedouin tribes. Even the poems relating to his Greek captivity appear to me mere rhymed prose[1]. And when writers like the Sahib[2] and Tha'libi[3] praise it extravagantly it offers but one more proof that faint then was the line between the writer and the poet.

(1) Few will agree with this. Tr.

(2) Ibn Khall, Vol. I, 214, Tr.

(3) Ibn Khall, Vol. II, p. 129 (d. 429/1037-8) Tr.

The Sherif Ar-Rida[1], born at Baghdad in 361/970, was only thirty when Ibn al-Hajjaj died. Himself a poet, he made a selection of Hajjaj's poems[2]. But he was too great a gentleman with too distinguished a pedigree to descend, like Hajjaj, against all convention, into the seamy side of life. His father had been Registrar of the descendants of 'Ali. On his death in 400/1009 he succeeded to all his honours and official preferments, although a younger son. He lived in great style; established a private academy where savants studied and were entertained at his cost; and boasted of having never accepted a present even from a Wazir. Proud was he of being a judge over his 'Alid kinsmen.

An 'Alid woman once complained to him against her husband of gambling away his fortune instead of providing for wife and child. When witnesses confirmed her statement the Sherif summoned him, ordered him to lie face downward, and had him flogged. The woman thought that they would stop beating, but when they exceeded 100 strikes she cried out : How would it fare with us if he died, and my children became orphans? Upon this the Sherif called out: 'Did you imagine that you were complaining to a school-master? He was the first 'Alid aristocrat who publicly abandoned resistance to authority, who exchanged the white dress, which his father had worn with as much pride as grief for the black uniform of the 'Abbasid courtier and official[3]. He traces his reserve and shrinking to his melancholy temperament:

"I might justify myself before men from whom I keep aloof. I am more hostile to myself than all men put together.

"They say : Comfort thyself, for life is but a sleep; when it ends, care, the nightly wanderer, vanishes too.Were it a

(1) Prof. Margoliouth, *Arab Historians*, p. 90 : Ibn Khall, Vol. III p. 418. Tr.

(2) *Diwan*, Cairo, 1307, p. 1.

(3) *Diwan* pp. 1 and 929.

peaceful sleep, I would welcome it but it is a disquieting, dreadful sleep[1]".

Never does one common, ugly expression escape from the mouth of this genuine aristocrat, such as we find in the state-secretary Ibrahim es-Sabi, the Wazir Muhallabi and Ibn 'Abbad. Even in satires where the poets have allowed themselves a free rein the following is the strongest that we have found in this poem:—

"When he makes his appearance the eyes blink and the ears vomit at his song.

"We would rather listen to the roar of contending lions than to thy song[2]".

That such an one should be at pains to make selections of the few decent verses in the works of Ibn al-Hajjaj and even compose a panegyric on him, is a fact creditable to both[3].

Moreover Rida is more on the side of Mutannabi, whose commentator, Ibn Jinni, was his teacher. Through the entire programme of the old school of poets Rida goes: congratulatory poems on the new year, Easter, Ramadan, the end of the month of Fast, *Mihrajan,* birth of a son or daughter, panegyrics on Caliphs, Sultans, Wazirs, elegies on death of men prominent or closely allied to him, and above all, poems on the anniversary of the death of Husain, the Ashura Day. Nor does he forget to glorify his house and its nobility and to complain of the world and of old age. And this he does, according to convention, from youth

(1) *Diwan,* 505, ff. Before the Sultan Baha-ud-Daulah he declined to recite : I do that only before the Caliph (p. 954). Regarding his melancholy it is to be observed that he was born when his father was already 65.

(2) *Diwan,* 504.

(3) *Diwan,* 864.

onward. Luckily, in his twentieth year, in consequence of a vow which necessitated the cropping the front part of his head, he discovered grey hair,— a discovery *which* gave him right to speak of old age[1]. In literary history Rida stands out as a master of elegy[2]. He is a stern stylist and is very sparing of personal details in individual cases. In 392/1002 he lost his friend and teacher Ibn Jinni. The elegy opens with a lament on the poet:—

"Little chips are we, borne by the torrent, rolling between the hillock and the sandfield".

Then a long Ubi sunt:—
"Where are the Kings of Yore?"

Then the reference to the special gifts of the dead:—

> "Who will now undertake to lead the refractory camel of speech to drink ? Who will now fling words like piercing darts? When he summoned words they came with necks as camels come to their driver. He led them to graze, with glossy backs, as though they were chargers of the blood of Wajeh or Lahik. The marks of his branding sank deeper into their pasterns than the brandmarks of camels. Who is there now to deal with poetical conceits which were flung in sacks before him? Who would unlock the secret of such conceits? He would ascend their highest peak, never stumbling; he would traverse their most slippery places and never slide."

And all personal references end here. The rest may be applied to any one. Though a resident of the capital and a

---

(1) This very story is to be found in the work of the Syrian prince and poet Abu Firas. The Arab collector there observes that the expression comes from Abu Nuwas (Dvorak, *Abu Firas*, p. 141.)

(2) *Yatimah*, II. 308.

peaceful man of letters, he ignores town-life and loves to dwell upon war, camels, noble horses and the desert. Many a poem is doubtless the fruit of personal experience, deeply left and characteristically expressed; betraying the pupil of Ibn al-Hajjaj behind the rolling verse. Splendid was the Qasidah which he declaimed at a solemn audience where the Caliph received the Khorasanian pilgrims. The opening lines express in powerful language the dangers of pilgrimage and the woeful fate of those that are left behind:—

> "Whose are the howdahs, tossed about by the camels, and the Caravan which now floats now sinks in the mirage?"
>
> They are crossing the sides of Al-Aqiq:
>
> "One goes to Syria, whose fancy drivers his mounts that way ; another to 'Iraq.
>
> "They have left behind a prisoner (i.e., the poet himself) not to be redeemed of his passion and a seeker who never attains his goal[1].

One of his most charming poems describes a beautiful woman in a nocturnal caravan:—

> "She looked out —when night was all embracing, trailing its long garments—from the chinks of the howdahs, while the driver's notes were sounding across a wide valley,
>
> "And the necks of the travellers were bending from the remains of the drunkenness of sleeplessness.
>
> "At sight of her they raised themselves erect in their saddles, their gaze following the light (of her countenance).

(1) *Diwan*, 541.

"We were in doubt; presently I said to them:
this is not the rising of the moon[1] ".

Thus in the 4th/10th century Sanaubari and Mutanabbi, Ibn al-Hajjaj and Ar-Ride stand side by side —each at the very height in his own sphere, gazing from one high, at the unfolding centuries of Arabic Literature.

---

(1) *Diwan* 394. "Mez seems to have mistaken", says Prof. Margoliouth, "the sense of these lines, which are an ordinary erotic prolouge in which the poet sees his lady-love in a howdah emigrating with her tribe". Tr.

XVIII. GEOGRAPHY

Marked are the progressive steps in Geography. But here, we shall only deal with its literary aspect. It is a child of the Renaissance of the 3rd/9th century. The works of al-Kindi (circa 200/800), one of the prominent interpreters of Greek learning, occupy[1] the place of honour and next to them "The Book of Roads' of Ibn Khuradadbih, composed, according to his own statement, about the year 232/846 on the basis of Ptolemy[2]. 'Masudi' in 323/935, refers to Ibn Khurdadbih's book as the best book on the subject[3]; but Mukaddasi, (even in 375/985) regards it as far too brief to be of much use[4] . Mukaddasi finds fault with Jaihani (end of the 3rd/9th century), the successor and plagiarist of Ibn Khurdadbih, for introducing learned, astronomical, and other matters, unintelligible to ordinary readers; for describing the idols of India and the wonders of Sind; for giving merely an itinerary and no more. Balkhi (he states) omits many large towns, he was not a traveller at all, and his introduction is faulty. Ibn al-Faqih (end of the 3rd/9th century) mentions, on the other hand, only large towns; collects all kinds of heterogeneous matters, making us alternately laugh and weep[5]. And, indeed, between the description of Yaman and Egypt he refreshes himself with two chapters "from seriousness to levity" and "laudation of friends". He makes the description of Rome and occasion

(1) Masudi, 1, 275.

(2) *Bibl. Geogr.* VI, 33. Khurdadbih means 'bumper' (Matali el- budur, 1, 189. Maqrizi. *Khitat*, 414 reads *Khurdadbih bellur* (English Tr. of Masudi p. 201 on Ptolemy. Tr.)

(3) Masudi, II, 71.

(4) p. 4.

(5) Muk, 3 ff.

for a criticism on architecture and, again a discussion on love for one's country. To his contemporary Ibn Rostah the strange and rare things of the world appealed most : the strange and rare things in South Arabia, Egypt, Constantinople, India, among the Magyars and the Slavs. Hamdani (d. 334/945) describes Arabia as a philologer and Qudamah (d. 310/922) deals with the Empire and the neighbouring countries in a manual for administrators.

Yaqubi (end of the 3rd/9th century) for the first time, deals with the countries in a true and proper spirit and treats them from the point of view of their own intrinsic interest.

" I set out young in years ever since been travelling in foreign countries". He visited the whole of the empire—was in Armenia, Khorasan, Egypt and the West, even India. He never tired of questioning people, on and off pilgrimage, regarding countries and towns, the distances between the stations, the inhabitants, agriculture and irrigation, dress, religion and their system of education. " I have worked long at this book; I have gathered information on the spot; and I have checked my information by interviewing reliable witnesses[1]". He gives a well-arranged and wonderful accurate account of the empire beginning with Baghdad. But be that as it may, his book is not a personal account of travels ; for in that age the personal aspect of travel was not in vogue. Masudi himself, writing about 333/944, is not more personal; though his curiosity took him much further afield, to Africa and even to China. And yet he does furnish, in his historical works a great deal of his personal experiences—a thing which Yaqubi sternly avoids. The work of al-Mukaddasi and Ibn Haukal in the 4th/10th century mark the summit of Arab Geography.

Both were borne on the current of the Muslim intincrant

---

(1) *Bibl Geogr.* VII, 232 f.

spirit—both were widely travelled. Mukaddasi experienced everything that a traveller could experience except actual begging and the commission of capital offences and spent 10,000 dirhams on his travels[1]. Ibn Haukal, too, visited every place except the western Sahara[2]. Both, however confined. themselves to the Empire of Islam (*Mamlakat al-Islam*)[3]. Mukaddasi himself confesses that he never went beyond the Empire of Islam and that his own personal observations were the basis of his work[4]. Both were intimate with the Literature on the subject. Mukaddasi makes this quite clear. Ibn Haukal read all the well-known and famous books but found none that could satisfy his thirst for the conditions and customs of the empire. Ibn Khurdadbih, Jaihani, and Qudamah never left his side[5]. The language of this period being more polished and refined, both these writers used it, in a masterly fashion, to serve their own ends; Ibn Haukal, indeed with lighter grace than Mukaddasi. The scholastics of his time applaud Mukaddasi for dividing and sub-dividing his material and for establishing from the Qur'an that there are only two seas[6]. He even added a map to his work which unfortunately is lost, where the familiar routes were painted red, the desert yellow, the seas green, the rivers blue, the mountains drab[7]. He had seen such a map in the work of Balkhi (d. 322/934). He had also seen one in the Library of the Samanid Prince at Bukhara, another at Nisabur, and yet another in that of 'Adad-ud-Daulah and the Saheb ibn Abbad; besides the sea-charts in the hands of Arab sailors[8]. By the chief of the merchants at Aden he had the Indian Ocean with its gulfs and bays sketched on the sand of the

(1) p. 44 f. He published his book when he was forty.
(2) p. 111.
(3) P. 9. (on the 'Empire of Islam', see M'S Eng. tr. P. 103. Also see p. 12 Tr.).
(4) *Bibl. Geogr.* II 5, 235.
(5) pp. 41, 270, 16. According to Sura 55, 19.
(6) p. 9. Eng. tr. p. 12.
(7) p. 8.
(8) p. 11 :Eng. tr. p. 15 Tr.

beach[1]. A physician in Jaricho, pointing out, said to him: Do you see this valley? It runs to Hijaz and on to Yamamah and on and on again to Oman and to Hajar, to Basra and to Baghdad where it rises, leaving Mosul to the right, up to Raqqah. It is the valley of Heats and of Palms[2]. And Ibn Haukal even maintains the continuity of the desert from Morocco to China[3]. He also holds that the Chinese chain of mountains merges into the Tibetan, Persian, Armenian, Syrian, the Mukattam and the North African ridges[4]. Of these two works later geographers took that of Ibn Haukal preferably for their model. Both indeed were far more critical, for instance than the later Idrisi who has used the 'Book of Wonders' of Hassan b. al-Mundhir despised alike by Mukaddasi and Ibn Haukal.

The scientific impulse, awake and active, shows itself in every direction in the 4th/10th century of the Hegira. The experiences and tales of the Seamen regarding China and the Indian Ocean were eagerly listened to (*Silsilet et-tawarikh, Ajaib al-Hind*). About the middle of the 3rd/9th century the Caliph sent an expedition by land to the Chinese Wall . (The report of the leader of the expedition Sallam is preserved in Idrisi and has been edited by de Goeje. *De murr Van Gog en Magog)*. In 309/921, Ibn Fudhlah wrote an account of his travels to the Volga Bulgarians[5] and about 333/944 Abu Dulaf wrote his to the Central and East Africa[6]. About this very time Istakhri reports on the authority of a

---

(1) p. 179.

(2) pp. 30, 104.

(3) 194, 110 f. see Bekri ed Slane 160. The first indication of this view appears in Ibn Khurdadbih, p. 172, Masudi, II, 71.

(4) Abul Fida, ed. Reinand, p. 2.

(5) Yaqut, Text and trans. by Frahn, 1823. (Viel Thompson in his *Origin of the Russ* has shown the great importance of this work for the history of Russia on the Volga Bulgarians see Vol. V (Helmholt's *World History* pp. 326, 328 Tr.

(6) cf. Marquart, *Schau-Fest-Schrift*, p. 272 note.

preacher from the Volga-Bulgarians that 'there the nights are so sort in summer that one can only do a *parasang* through them; in the winter on the contrary, that is the case with the days'[1]. The "traveller to the west" set out from Lisbon "to survey the ocean and its extent"[2]. In 377/987 the author of the Fihrist derives his information about China from a Nestorian monk who, along with five other *Katholicos* was sent to China and had resided there for seven years (Fihrist, 349). The merchants brought news of Germany and the Frankish Empire. In 375/985 one Muhallabi drew up an itinerary for the Fatimid Caliph al-Aziz which, for the first time, gave accurate information about the Sudan of which the other geographers of that century knew very little. (His book was named Azizi after the Caliph, to whom it was dedicated. It is the main source of Yaqut for the Sudan).

The spanish geographer Mohamad el-tarikhi (d. 363/973) described North Africa. (He is the main source of Bekri, Slane, 16) and the Muallam Khwasir Ibn Yusuf al-ariki, who in 400/1009 made a voyage along the Nubian and the South African coast, in the ship of the Indian Daban Korah, laid the foundation of the Sea-charts (Rahmani), elaborated in the 6th/12th century. (Ilm al-bahr, Paris, 2292, fol 3 a).

About this time in connection with the raids which started from Sayna, Beruni wrote the first and only work on India. He finds fault with the Indians for a lack of intelligent method in their works, for digressions and fairy-tales, for "mixing up precious crystals with pebbles"[3] a fault to be found even in Jahiz and Masudi. The criticism of Beruni shows the progress in restraint achieved by Arabic Literature.

Abu Zaid Ahmad ibn Sahl al-Balkhi. He was of

(1) *Bibl. Geogr.* 1, 225.

(2) Idrisi , 184. See the chapter on "Sea -Faring.

(3) India. Translated by Sachau, 1, 25.

Shamistiyan, a village in the neighbourhood of Balkh, and died 340 H. His work is entitled Suwar-ul-aqalim, on which al-Istakhri has chiefly based his treatise on it .

Abu Bakr Ahmad ibn Muhammad al-Hamdani commonly called Ibn-ul-Faqih. The author of the *Fihrist say* that he compiled his book from various works, and chiefly from that of al Jaihani, but from internal evidence it is conclusively shown that the work could not have been written later than 290 H. that is, some years before al-Jaihani wrote his. See de Geoge's Preface to *Kitab-ul- Buldan,* where the date of Ibn-ul Faqih's death, as given by Yaqut, *i.e.* about 340. H. is impugned.

I may refer here to two other important works on Muslim Geography: Beazley's *Dawn of Modern Geography* Vol.1 (1897) and Wright's *Geographical Lore of the Time of the Crusades* (New York, 1925,) Tr.

NOTES

Abu Abdullah Muhammad ibn Ahmad al-Jaihani, native of Jaihan, a town in Khorasan on the bank of the Oxus. In 301 H. (913 A.D.), al-Amir Abu Nasar Ahmad ibn Ismail as-Samani, Lord of Khorasan and Ma-wara an-nahr, was murdered by his slaves while on a hunting expedition; and his son Abul Hassan Nasr, then only eight years of age, was raised to the Amirship. Abu Abdullah al-Jaihani was charged with Government in the name of Nasr , and ruled with firmness and wisdom . Al-Jaihani's work was entitled *'Kitab-ul Mosalik fi Marfati-ul-Mama'ik*: but having died before he could complete it, the work was remodelled and abridged, according to Reinaud (Introduction, Ed. Abulf, p. 64), by Abu Bakr Ahmad ibn Muhammad al Hamdani commonly called Ibn-ul-Faqih; probably he adds, the abridgment caused the original work to fall into neglect. See however, de Coeje's preface to his edition of *Kitab-ul-Buldan*, part V of the *Biblio, (feo. Arab Series.)*

XIX. RELIGION

Even the inner religious consciousness of Islam felt fresh needs from the 3rd/9th century onwards. For the satisfaction of those needs the old religions, always simmering beneath the surface. Christianity, preeminently , offered their aid. By 'Christianity, we mean the Christian world tinged with Hellenism. The entire movement which in the course of the third and fourth centuries, transformed Islam, is nothing more or less than the penetration of Christian thought into the religion of the Prophet[1]. The new religious ideal is described as *Marifat Allah* (knowledge of God) which for the Prophet would have signified nothing but blasphemy. As its very name betrays, it is the old *Gnosis* which return to life once in the land of its birth and, in these two centuries, secures ascendancy over the entire domain of spiritual life. In the camp of the free-thinkers it shapes itself as Rationalism and scientific theology; elsewhere it assumes the grab of mysticism. And, despite the vicissitudes of world history, clear is the kinship between mysticism and rationalism.

All the distinguishing features of the *quondam* Gnosis now reappear: the esoterism, the mystery-organisation, the different grades of knowledge, the theory of emanation, the parallelism of the two worlds, the fluctuation between

---

(1) The neo-Plationism would not by itself have been able so universally to effect the mind. Bit it must not be forgotten that it was itself a child of the old oriental wisdom. In his *Lectures of Islam* Goldziher (Eng. Tr. 171) has dealt with the clear but secondary Indian and specially Buddhistic influences on Islam. It is to be noted that besides Hallaj, now and then, a sufi is mentioned who is familiar with Indian wisdom. (E.G. Kushairi, 102, and Hujwiri 272. On Kushairi, see Goldziher's Lectures (Eng. tr.) p. 188, Tr.

asceticism and libertinism, the conception as a 'path' to salvation.

The oldest sufistic writing that have come down to us—the writings of Muhasibi (d.234/848)—show unmistakable traces of strong Christian influence. One of these begins with the parable of the sower and the other may characterized as an extended sermon on the mount[1]. The old sufi Shaikh al-Hakim et-Termidi (d. 285/898) has placed Jesus higher than the Prophet[2]. Never before or after was the Islamic world so "full of Gods". The boundary between Allah had his servants was effaced . The Sufi professed the doctrine of merger with him. The Hululi actually saw Allah walking in shoes at John's Market at Baghdad[3]. The Mahdites played with the idea of the 'Divinity of the Ruler' as never before or after[4]. The poet ibn-Hani called out to the Umbrella-holder of the Fatimid Caliph Muiz (341/365 A.H.):—

O thou who turnest the parasoal wherever he promenades, terribly indeed under his stirrup

thou art rubbing shoulders with Gabriel.

And concerning the Caliph when he stopped at a place called Rakkada he said:-

The messias alighted at Rakkada, there alighted Adam and Noah.

There alighted God, the Lord of Glory, save
whom everything is empty wind[5].

(1) Margoliouth, *Transactions of the third Religious Congress*, Oxford, Vol. I, 292.
(2) Massignon, *Kit at-Tawasin*, 161, note 2.
(3) Abul Ala, *Risalat el-Cufran*, JRAS, 1902, 349, 350.
(4) (See Hopkins *Alexander Severus*, pp. 166 sq; Friedlander, *Roman Life and Manners*, III, 119 ff tr.)
(5) Much later Ibn Athir says (VIII, 457) that he did not find these verses in the *Diwan* of Ibn Hani. But they are to be found in the Beyrut edition, p.46.

And at the end of this period stands the Caliph Hakim, still worshipped as God by the Druses.

The first Sufi community makes its appearance about the year 200/815 and, indeed, in Egypt, the very cradle of Christian monasticism . "In the year 199/815 a party, called the Sufiyah, steps into light at Alexandria, which commanded, according to its view, commission of acts pleasing unto God, and, thereby, set itself in opposition to Government. Their chief was Abdul Rahman, the Sufi[1]. The very same name, Sufiyah, is applied by Ibn Qudaid (d. 312/925) to the band which "commanded the commission of acts pleasing to God and forbade those vexations unto Him". Enjoying the favour of the Egyptian Qadhi Ibn al-Munqadir (212-215/827-829) this band distracted him from his work and, eventually, ruined him by causing him to oppose the heir to the throne[2].

There were pious people too of active habits who very seriously took to the old duty of a good Muslim ; namely, to effectively interfere with the life of the community. These first gave the name of Sufi to those "whc kept their hearts free from frivolities"; a name already widely-speard before the year 200[3]. In its inception it had nothing to do with the later Sufi doctrines. But even Epiphanius in the fourth century A.D. deplores the existence of a very considerable number of disorderly gnostics in Egypt[4], whose views had passed into the Sufi community. Prof. Nicholson has pointed to the great influence which the Egyptian alchemist Dhun-Nun (d. 245/859) exercised on the Sufi doctrines[5]. As a

(1) Al-Kindi, ed. Guest, 162. Meqrizi, Khitat, I, 173. Also two Hadith quoted in Goldziher, ZA, 1909, 343 give the year 200 as the beginning of Sufiism.

(2) Kindi 440. (He wrote to Mamum objecting to the government of Mutasim).

(3) Kushairi, Risala, (written in 437/1045), Cairo, p. 9.

(4) Hilgenfeld, *Ketzergeschichte*, 283.

(5) JRAS, 1906, 309 ff.

matter of fact many of the old Sufi shaikhs of the East did come under the influence of Egypt[1]. It was only when Zaqqaq died that the reason for the derweshes to go to Egypt ceased to exist[2].

If the Sufi system developed completely in the East, notably at Baghdad, its progress was rapid[3]. The first Sufi of Baghdad was Sari es-Saqati (*i.e.* second-hand dealer). He gave up his trade, lived at home and died in 253/867 (*Zubdat el-Fikrah, Paris, 56;* Schreiner, ZDMG, 52, 515). He attained fame by being the first to speak at Baghdad of *Tauhid* (Monism) and of *Haqaiq* (inner religious truth). (*Tadhkirat-ul-Auliya*, 1, 274 apud Nicholson, JRAS 1906, 322; al-Watari, *Raudat en-Nazirin*, 8). He is said to have been first to tea·:h of *Maqamat* (Stations) and Ahwal (States). (*Kashf el-Mahjub, tr.* by Nicholson, p.110). The first who is said to have used the mystic terms : "Friendship, Purity of thought, Unity of Effort, Love, Suffering", was Abu Hamzah es-Sadafi (d. 269/882). He was the desciple of Ahmad Ibn Hauqal who addressed him : O Sufi, (Abulmahasin, II, 47; Zubdat el-Fikrah, fol. 73, a) He is said to have just spoken about it on the pulpit of the Rusafa-mosque when he had a stroke. His contemporary Taifur al-Bistami apparently was the author of the allegory of "intoxication", which, along with Love, has profoundly influenced Muslim mysticism[4]. The essentially un-Islamic prayer (?) of Ali Ibn Muwaffaq (d. 265/878) has come down to us: "God, if I serve thee for

(1) et-Tustari (d. 283), Kushairi, 17; Nakhshabi (d. 245) heard the Egyptian el-Attar (Kushairi, 20) and transmitted many of his views. Ibn .el-Jalli, the Sufi Shaikh in Syria, heard Dhun-Nun (Kush, 24) and similarly, Yusuf Ibn el-Husain, Shaikh of Rai and Media (d. 30 A. H:) and Abu Sa'id el-Kharraz (d. 277). Kushairi, 25 f.

(2) Kushairi, 25.

(3) The Baghdadian tradition says nothing of Egypt. The oldest historian of this religious order-al-Khuldi (d. 384/994) traces the Sufi doctrines, through the Baghdadian Maruf al-Karkhi (d. 207/922) to the celebrated old ascetic Hasan of Basra, *Fihrist*, 183.

(4) *Kashf el-Mahjub*, 184.

fear of Hell, punish me, then, with Hell; if I serve thee for the gain of Heaven, deprive me then of it, but if I serve thee out of pure love, do then with me what thou willest"[1]. The Baghdadian Abu Sa'id al-Kharraz (d. 277/890), pupil of the Egyptian Dhun-Nun, first propounded the doctrine of self-annihilation, of complete merger in God (Fana); a very ancient Gnostic doctrine which, to be sure, has nothing whatever to do with the Indian *Nirvan*[2]. At Nisabur Hamdun el-Qassab, the butcher, (d. 271/884) first persued the "path of blame", preferring the incurring of ill repute to honour which diverted him from God. This was the beginning of the extraordinary school of the *Malamatis,* 'the shabby saints' (*Kashf, pp. 66, 125*). Even this is no new idea. In his Republic Plato, in the beginning of the second book, describes truly just bearing the reputation of injustice (Jowett's tr. III pp. 40-41).

And, thus the Sufis deflected from their old path. In the earlier days they, in their pious zeal, interfered with the life of the community "bidding them do good and keeping them back from evil" and thus they did, at times, even in opposition to Government. But Ibn al-Nakhshad (d. 366/976), defines, Sufiism to be the very reverse of its former self"; Namely, as "patient endurance of command and

---

(1) *Zubdat al-Fikrah,* Paris, fol. 47 a. (I don't quite understand why Mez calls this prayer un-Islamic. One of our poets has expressed this very idea in language of superb beauty:
Ghalib,

طاعت میں تار ہے نہ مے وانگبین کی لاگ

دوزخ میں ڈال دو کوئی لیکر بہشت کو

(2) *Kashf el-Mahjub,* 143, 242 ff. Even in the 5/11th century the "unlettered Sufis" were attacked for teaching among other things the doctrine of complete annihilation (fanai Kulliyah). It is significant that Hujwiri criticises this idea p. 243.

prohibition"[1]: *i.e.* indifference towards the life of the community.

As in philology and scholasticism, so in this sphere too, Basra and Baghdad stood in striking contrast to each other.

Baghdad was the headquarters of the Sufis ; whereas Basra was the centre of *Zuhad i.e.* the pious of the old type. Even at the time of Mukaddasi Basra was the town of the *Zuhad.* Hasan, the chief of their school, was credited with a nasty fling at the woolen cowl of the Sufis[2].

But this fact has not stood in the way of the Sufis claiming the most famous of their opponents as their own and accepting the very same Hasan of Basra, the most popular saint of Mesopotamia, as the first teacher of their school. The genealogy was yet further extended. The attempt to trace the beginning of the Sufi principles to the Prophet himself shows itself in assigning to Hasan a teacher from among his companions; one Hudaifa, recipient from him of a secret doctrine of the gift of singling out "hypocrites". And indeed—so goes the report—whenever the Caliph Omar

---

(1) Kush, 34 "es-Sabr taht el-Amr wan nahy".

(2) Even the founder of the malikite school is said to have disapproved of the woolen cowl because of its ostentatious display. There was rough cotton wool at once cheap and undemonstrative. Ibn al-Hajj, *Madkhal* II, 18; Goldziher, WZKM 13, 40. Even here there was a contrast. (Our Literature is full of such attacks.

HAFIZ:—

دلم زصومعه بگرفت وخرقه سالوس کجاست دیر مغاں وشراب ناب کجا

زاہد ظاہر پرست از حال ما آگاہ نیست ہرچہ گوید در حق ماجاے ہیچ اکراہ نیست

WAHSHI:—

پش رندان حق شناسی درلباس دیگرست بربما منمائے زاہد خرقہ پشمینہ را

Tr.)

was called to a funeral prayer he always made sure of the presence of Hudaifa before leading the prayer[1]. About the end of the 3rd/9th century the disciples of Sari carried the Baghdadian Sufiism throughout the empire: Musael -Ansari (died circa 320/932) from Merv to Khorasan; al-Rudbari (died circa 322/934 in old Cairo) to Egypt; Abul Zaid al-Adami (d. 341/952 at Mecca) to Arabia[2]. With Thaqafi (d. 328/940) Sufiism entered Nisabur[3] and about the end of the 4th century of the Hegira Shiraz was particularly full of Sufis[4]. In the first half of the 5th/11th century the Afghan al-Hujwiri met in Khorasan alone 300 Sufi Shaikhs who had such mystical endowments that a single man of them would have been enough for the whole world[5]. About 300/912 there lived at Baghdad three Sufi Shaikhs side by side : es-Shibli,

---

(1) Makki, I, 149 (Goldziher, *Muh. Studien*, II, 14 "There are statements, says Goldziher, in the sunni tradition that the prophet favoured certain campanions' with teachings which he withheld from the others. Hudaif, one who also bears the title of *Sahib al-Sirr* or *S. Sirr al-nabi* (possessor of the secret of the prophet), was specially favoured in this respect. (Bukh, *Istidan*, No. 38. *Fada'il al-ashab*, No. 27). It is now interesting to see that this notice, which of course can mean nothing but that Hudaifa received esoteric instruction from the prophet, is interpreted by the theologians to mean that Mohamed gave this companion the names of persons of doubtful standing (*Munafikun)*, not therefore any esoteric religious teaching (Nawawi, *Tahdhib*, 200, 5). But we find Hudaifa actually the authority for a number of apocalyptic and eschatological *Hadiths*. In the canon of Muslim (V. 165) in the section 'Prerogatives of Abdullah Ibn Jafar' the following statement about this man is included: "One day the prophet made me mount behind him, he then secretly whispered to me a *Hadith* that I was not to communicate to any one". Bukhari has not included this utterance. It is to be noted that this Abdullah Ibn Jafar was only ten years old when the prophet died". Goldziher. *Lectures on Islam*, p. 206 Tr.) Though reading and visions of hell played a great role among the Sufis of the fourth century Kushairi, 125 ff.

(2) *Raudat en-Nazirin*, 13.

(3) *Kushairi*, 13.

(4) Muk, 439.

(5) *Kashf el-Mahjub*, 174.

his father had been a court-marshal and he himself had held several offices, famous for allegories (*Isharat*); Abu Ahmad el-Murta'is (d. 328/939), master of Sufiistic aphorisms; and, al-Khuldi (d. 348/959) at the age of 95), the first historian of that school who prided himself on crying three hundred Sufi *Diwans* in his head[1].

Even anterior to Sufism there had been Muslim hermits and cloisters. In one case Christian model is manifest: Fihr Ibn Jabir (d. 325/936) had widely travelled, had come much in contact with Christian monks and , at the age of fifty, had retired to the mountain chains of Damascus. He wrote a book on "Asceticism" containing a history of Christian monasticism and presented it to the mosque of Damascus[2]. In the Syrian mountain range of Jhaulan Mukaddasi met Abu Ishaq el-balluti with forty men. They wore wool and shared a common dormitory. Their chief was a jurist of the school of Sufyan Thauri. They lived on acorns , meal of which they mixed with wild barley. The largest cloistral organization stands to the credit of the Kirramites, followers of Mohammed Ibn Kirram[3]. They had cloisters (Khanqah) in Iran and Transoxiana[4] and one in Jerusalam[9]. A Kirramite settlement (mahalla) is reported in the capital of Egypt[5]. Mukaddasi read at Nisabur in the letter of a Kirramite that the order had 700 cloisters in the *Maghrib* but the traveller confesses that there was not even one[6]. At Jerusalam they performed *Zikr* at the Kirramite cloister at which something was read out from a book (*dufter*), not unlike what the

(1) *Fihrist,* 183; Abulmahasin, II, 292: *Raudat en-Nazirin,* 12, 13, 15.

(2) Masriq, 1908. pp.883 ff.

(3) The name is to be read thus according to the *Dict. Tech. Terms. p.* 1266,

(4) Muk. 323, 365.

(5) Muk, 179: Ibn Hazm, IV, 204, in Khorasan and Jerusalem. The founder a Sijistanian, died in 255/868 in Syria (Abul Fida, *Auntles,* year 255.

(6) Muk, 202; 235.

Hanafites did at the mosque of Amr[1]. They were an order of mendicants and preached renunciation of things worldly and put forward fear of God, humility, poverty as their faith and practice[2]. The Sufis had no cloisters then. They, then, at best, had huts intended for devotional purposes which they called by the military term 'Ribat' (fortress). The pious seem to have resided in these huts. When the Sufi al-Husri (d. 370/980) became old, he, only, with difficulty, could go to the chief mosque. The people, therefore, built for him a 'Ribat', opposite to the Mansur-mosque, named after his disciple ez-Zauzani. (See Maqrizi's observations. Khitat, I, 414. The cloister (Khanqah) came into existence about the year 400/1009 see Muk, 415; Kushairi, 17; Ibn al-Jauzi, Berlin, for 119 a).

They wore the special dress of their order; namely a woolen coat and a piece of cloth hanging down from the head. Later blue was adopted as their colour because it was the colour of mourning or possibly because it was best suited to a wandering people[3]. The first supposition seems to be right; for the *futah* (the head-cloth) too was used in mourning as covering for the head[4].

"I took a prayer rug. long as a day, and shaved off my moustache which I had allowed to grow" sings Ibn Abdel Aziz es-Susi in the 4th/10th century of his sufi days (*Yatimah,* III, 237). As with the German pietists, so with the Sufis, spiritual songs play a great part in their divine service. As

(1) Muk, 182.

(2) Muk, 41: Kalabadi, fol. 94 a: Goldziher, WZKM 13, p. 43 note 2 (see Hannah. Christian Monasticism pp. 78-79 Tr.)

(3) Kashf 53.

(4) Subki, II, 257. In the 5/11 century the Sufis rarely used wool, the usual garment being the patched coat (muraqqa). Kashf 45 ff. The patched coat and the woolen cowl early indeed became the costume of the ascetics. When the woolen coat became the distinguishing feature of the Sufis—the patched coat became the dress of the irregulars. Khushairi, 23, 198; *Irshad,* II, 292, 294.

already stated by Jahiz (d. 255/869) the truly spiritual poet must be a sufi (*Bayan*, 1, 41). "Now I wept with them and now I declaimed poems to them"- Mukaddasi says of the gatherings of the Sufis at Sus (p. 415). In the 5/11 century dance was superadded to songs. Hujwiri reports that he met a group of Sufis whose sufiism mainly consisted in dancing (Kashf, 416). Ma'arri (d. 449/1057) too, taunts them thus : Has God ordained your devotion to consist merely in dancing and gorging like animals? Women from the roofs or elsewhere used to watch them practice singing and Hujwiri, therefore, warns the novices against this (Kashf. 420). But soon the Sufi imagination provides paradise with stools (Kursi) which relieve the pious from the obligation of dancing for these stools, fitted with wings, beat time, gently or violently, as the case may be, with music, causing ecstasy thereby[1].

There was, indeed, no obligation to beg but Khwarezmi speaks of the Sufi "as one who exacts from us without us exacting anything from him"[2]. Such Sufis are also called "Faqir" (Poor)[3]. Mukaddasi tells us that as a Sufi he required but tittle money in Shiraz; for every day he had an invitation and "What an invitation[4]. Rudbari II (d. 369/979), chief of the Syrian Sufis, rich and influential, who traced his descent from the Sassanids, never announced an invitation to a meal to his fraternity but, when invited, he fed them first to prevent them from gorging outside and, thereby, disgracing the order[5]. His grandfather, Rudbari I, who lived at Old Cario (d. 322/933), "once purchased loads of white sugar, sent for a band of confectioners, and had a wall made out of the sugar with pillars and battlements with decorative inscriptions. He, then, invited the Sufis to attack and plunder

(1) Samarqandi, *Qurrat al-Uyun, on the margin of Raud,* 173.
(2) Rasail, 90.
(3) Muk, 415; Kushairi, 14, 32, 33.
(4) p. 415.
(5) Kushairi 36.

it[1]. His brotherhood soon won the reputation of eating well. "The appetite of the Sufi's" became proverbial[2].

Even then the gravest danger to the brotherhood was precisely the same as that which threatened the order of the mendicants in the Mediaeval Europe: the combination of contraries and the friendship of women. To this, as a peculiarly oriental danger was added "the intercourse with young boys"[3].

A Shaikh, who died in 277/890, is reported to have said: I saw the devil at a distance as he passed by. And I spoke to him: what do you want here? He rejoined: What shall I do with you ? You have rid yourself of that with which I used to tempt. And what was that? I questioned. "The world", he replied. When he proceeded a little, turned round to me and spoke: but one temptation I still possess for you—the intercourse with young boys"[4].

And al-Wasiti (died after 320/932) is reported to have said: "When the almighty wishes to make a servant of His contemptible, He drives him to this sink, meaning, "intercourse with young boys"[5]. Even Hujwiri in the 5/11th century concedes[6] that ignorant Sufis made pedarastic intercourse a religious rule, with the result that common people shunned the order.

The mystics have always shown a tendency to disregard the laws along with things earthly. "Among the Sufis there are always some who maintain that for him who "understands God laws do not exist, others even add that

(1) Subki, *Tabaqat*, II, 102.
(2) The alibi *Book of support*, ZDMG. V. 302
(3) *Kushairi*, 26.
(4) Kushairi, 27.
(5) Kushairi, 29.
(6) Kashf. 416, 420. (Khuda Bukhsh Islamic Civilization, Vol. I, pp. 108-109, 2nd Ed. Tr.).

such an one is united with God". We have heard it said that there is a man at Nisabur to-day, called Abu Zaid, belonging to the circle of the Sufis, who, at one time wears wool and at another silk which is forbidden to men, who makes 1000 prostrations one day and never prays at all the next, neither the compulsory nor the optional prayer (*Ferz* and *Sunnat*). But this indeed, is manifest infidelity[1]. Ibn Hazm further complains that a party of the Sufis contend that 'for him who has attained the summit of holiness, religious commands such as prayer, fasting, alms etc. are unnecessary. In fact things forbidden such as wine, incontinence etc. etc. are permissible to him. And for this reason, the members of this party permit association with other men's wives. They affirm that they see God and hold conversation with him and that whatever He puts in their heart is true[2].

Hujwiri states the doctrine "where the truth (Haqiqah is revealed, the Law (Shariah) is abrogated" to be the doctrine of the heretical Carmathians and the Shiites and their bewitched followers[3]. It was related of a Sufi to Rudabari (d. 322/933), the Shaikh of that order, that he listened, with rapt attention, to cheerful music, because he had reached the stage at which the differences of "conditions" (halat) did not matter. To this the Shaikh replied: He has indeed attained something, *viz.* Hell.

Most of the old Sufis were married. A brother was actually saved by a miracle from "the wiles of a wicked wife"[4]. A rennowned Sufi shared a female servant with two other Shaikhs. Her name *Zaitunah* (olive) suggests that she was a slave-girl[5]. He made a gift of a slave-girl who had

(1) Ibn Hazm, IV, 188
(2) Ibn Hazm, IV, 226 Schreiner, ZDMG 52, 476.
(3) Kashf, 383.
(4) Kushairi, 31.
(5) Kushairi, 198.

been presented to him for a wife to a companion[1]. Shibli was married[2]. Ibn abil Hawari (d. 230) 'the flower of Syria', had four wives and likewise his contemporary Hatim al-asamm, a great sufi of Khorsan, who left behind nine children[3]. It is, therefore all the more surprising that outside sufiism there were ascetic circles who practised the entirely non-muslim institution of celibacy. In the *Bustan-el-arifin* of the Hanafite Abul Laith es-Samarqandi (d. 383/995) it is recommended to him who came to remain single (*hasur*) and to serve God with an undivided devotion[4].

In the 4th/10th century this view triumphed and captured suffism; for in the 5th/11th century Hujwiri says: "It is the unanimous opinion of the Shaikhs of this sect that the best and most excellent sufis are the celibates, if their hearts are uncontaminated and if their natures are not inclined to sins and lusts. In short sufiism is founded on celibacy ; the introduction of marriage brought about a change"[5]. This is the very reverse of the truth.

Hujwiri is also the first to report of mock-marriages among the Sufis. He reports of a Shaikh of the 3rd/9th century who lived for five and sixty years without touching his wife[6] and of the famous Khafif in Shiraz (371/981), of royal descent, whom women wished to marry for the blessing which he brought. Thus he concluded 400 marriages only to part with his wives without touching them[7]. Hujwiri himself was unmarried. "After God had preserved me for eleven years from the dangers of matrimony, it was my destiny to fall in love with the

(1) Raud. en-Nazrin, 12.
(2) Ibid p. 12.
(3) Ibid, 198.
(4) Amedroz, Notes on some sufi lives, JRAS, 1912, 558.
(5) Kashf, 363, 364.
(6) Kashf, 362.
(7) Kashf, 247.

description of a woman whom I had never seen, and during a whole year my passion so absorbed me that my religion was near being ruined, until at last God in His bounty gave protection to my wretched heart and mercifully delivered me[1].

With the development of this doctrine of celibacy there was much dissatisfaction in the ranks of the Sufis. The first historian of the order (d. 341/952) has completely distorted his history and inverted the order of events. He has dealt with the Basran, the Syrian, the Khorasanian and the Baghdadian ascetics and has concluded with Junaid who, according to him, was the last sufi teacher; adding that "what came after him can only be mentioned with shame"[2]. The Sufi saint Sahl el-Tustari (according to Kushairi he died in 273/886 or 283/896 is credited with a prophecy that after the year 302/914 there will be no such thing as sufiism, for there will come a people to whom dress would be of greatest moment; language, a mere affectation, and God, their belly[3]. And in 439/1047 Kushairi addressed his circular letter to all the Sufis in the empire of Islam because contentment had ceased, covetousness had assumed gigantic proportions, prayer and fasting had lost all seriousness and they looked to common folk, women and Government for patronage and support and regarded the alleged union with God as an annulment of all laws, temporal and spiritual[4]. In these later times as a counterpoise to the spreading demoralization severe exercises of penance were ascribed to the old Sufi Shaikhs. Es-Sari never took meat and always reserved the last bit of his food for a little bird[5]. For sixty years he never lay down but when sleep overwhelmed him he dropped

---

(1) Kashf, 364.
(2) Makki, 126.
(3) Makki 126.
(4) Risalah, 3.
(5) Qazwini, *Cosmography*, ed. Wustenfeld 216.

off in a sitting posture in his parlour[1]. An anecdote, not unlike that of Diogenes, is related of him. His pupil Junaid states: One day I came to Sari es-Saqati and found him in tears. I asked the reason and he replied: Yesterday a girl came to me and said : Father, it is a hot night. Here is a cup of cold drink. I leave it here. Thereupon I dreamt of a beautiful girl descending from heaven. I questioned her: to whom do you belong? She rejoined : to him who drinks not a cold drink out of a cup. Then I took the cup, threw it on the ground smashing it into bits[2].

Ruwaini (d. 305/917), passing at midday through a street of Baghdad, felt thirsty and asked for a drink at a house. A girl came out with a cup of water and said: A sufi who drinks during the day! Since then he fasted perpetually (*i.e.* only ate or drank between dark and dawn)[3]. Junaid is reported to have prayed 300 Riqahs and counted *Tasbihat* every twenty-fours hours[4] and to have had food once a week[5]. It is also reported that being corpulent, people doubted the genuineness of his love for God[6]. Bishr passed by some people who said : This man keeps awake all night and eats but once in there days. Then Bishr began to weep saying : I do not at all remember keeping awake all night or fasting a day without breaking the fast at night : but God out of goodness and generosity, gives greater credit to his servant than he deserves.

The Sufi system is unthinkable apart from the scholastic system (mutazilah) for it has taken up its problems and has adopted its methods. Look for instance, to the saying of the Sufi Saint Ibn al-Katib who died about 340/951: the

(1) Watari *Raudat en-Nazirin*, 8.
(2) Kushairi, 12.
(3) Kushairi 24, Qazwinni, 218.
(4) *Zubdat al-Fikrah*, 164 a.
(5) Qazwini, 216.
(6) *Raudat in-nazirin* 12. Other instances of renunciation from later sources in Amedroz, JRAS 1912, 559.

scholastics (mutazilah) have purified the idea of God through reasoning and have missed the mark; the sufis have purified it through knowledge (Ilm) and have succeeded[1]. And thus in the mutazalite Persia sufiism spread most rapidly[2]. They made the favourite mutazalite theme, the freedom of the will, the centre of their doctrine and taught consistant determinism, thus : he, who is indifferent alike to praise and censure, is an ascetic (zahid); he, who faithfully fulfills his religious obligations, is pious (Abid); he who sees everything as happening from God, is a monist (ez-Zakariyyah in Kushairi 24)[3].

But the Sufi fatalism is not, indeed, the mechanical determinism of average philosophy. They have imparted to it religious content. The old Islam, indeed inculcated trust in God; but the Sufis now taught, with the greatest emphasis, that unconditional trust which suppresses all personal initiative for "the pious before God is like the dead before the corpse-washer"[4].

---

(1) Kushairi, 32 that is to say : the Mutazalite deny in God the deductive method of man; whereas the Sufi deny in Him the inductive. cf. massignon, Hallaj. 187.

(2) A poet, who was at once a mutazalite and an ascetic, for instance, *Yatimah*, IV, 324. Abu Hayyan et-Tauhidi, the best progs writer of the 4th/10th century, was also a mutazalite and an ascetic, Yaqut, *Irshad* V, 382.

(3) It is difficult to see how they can have made the freedom of the will and determinism their main themes.

(4) The expression 'Perinde ac Cadaver' appears here for the first time. In the 4th/10th century it could not have been common expression for whereas Kalabadi (d. 380/990) uses it Makki (386/996) does not. On the other hand Kushairi, 90. (Goldziher, WZKM 1899, 42. In this paper Goldziher discusses the importance of the doctrine of *Tawakkul* for the ascetic). It will be difficult to find a more luminous exposition of the doctrine of *Tawakkul* than in Hafiz:-

HAFIZ:-

تکیه بر تقوی و دانش در طریقت کافری ست

راهرو گر صد هنر دارد توکل بایدش

The outstanding feature of the Sufiism in the 4th/10th century is this unbounded trust in God which for ever opens the treasure of God to the pious *i.e.* the protestant doctrine of the grace of God. No fewer than four stages (stations) of their spiritual doctrine were connected with it; besides "trust", "patience", "contentment"; "hope". These views have profoundly influenced Islam ; in fact, they have impressed upon it that character which is designated to-day as Muslim Fatalism. Neither the Fatalism of the theologian nor yet of the astrologer has achieved results which the sufi doctrine has; for it drew the logical consequences of this doctrine and applied then to practical and daily life.

The terminology of the Muslim fatalism did not come into existence first at this time but was collected and emphasized as it is still. (The root *fatah* which is later used exclusively in this connection (Goldziher, WZKM, 1899,48 ff), only occasionally appears now). And indeed, everything has always turned upon it.

Through Sufi precepts and examples it was dinned into every Muslim ear that for every human being his success and failure has been irrevocably fixed long before his birth and to seek to evade it was as ideal as to evade death for what writ was writ; that to worry in the morning for the evening was tantamount to sin[1]; that neither force nor

---

AND SAYS SHAHI:-

تادر رهش طریق گدائی گرفته ام　　　　دانسته ام که سلطنت بے زوال چیست

AND SAYS TAWFIQ:—

کجا ما و سلوک راه عشق و اختیار ما　　　　در پر ره بسته آوردند مارا همچو محلها
آن روز که کردند نگار من و تو　　　　بردند زیست اختیار من و تو

(1)

فارغ بنشین که کارساز دو جهان　　　　پیش از من و تو ساخته کار من و تو
رضا به داده بده وز جبین گره بکشا　　　　که بر من و تو در اختیار نکشاید

cunning would lure fate to alter the portion assigned to us[1]; that it would be heathenism to provide for the morrow even if the heaven were to become copper and the earth lead; that individual subsistence was allotted 2000 years before the creation of the body[2]. And finally they fortified and sanctified the servile trust in God and this is most important from the religious point of view into submissive cheerfulness in the divine dispensation, into *amor fati* (Rida) with the result that "ill luck became as acceptable as good luck" and "hell no matter of discontent, if so willed by God"[3].

The indifference of the genuine sufi is illustrated by the well-known story of the Dervish who fell into the Tigris. A man from the bank saw that he could not swim. He called out to him if he should offer him help. No replied the unfortunate man. What, do you wish to be drowned? No. What, then do you want? That which is the will of God. What else should I want?[4].

Already at the beginning of the Sufi movement Muhasibi (d. 234/848) is said to have been the first to teach *amor fati* sheer joy in the divine dispensation, a doctrine which is distinct from the ordinary trust in God and is reckoned as a special gift of the divine illumination (hal)[5]. In fact Muhasibi who regarded this as a central doctrine may, indeed, be set down as the founder of the Islamic Fatalism.

---

(1)

غم ناموس خوردن بے تقدم رنجہ میدارد

همان بہتر کہ باخود واگزارم کار فردا را

(2) Makki, II, 7, 9; Makki, *Qulb al-Qulub*, III, 9.

(3) Kushairi, 106, 107.

(4) Kashf, 180. 379 ff.

(5) Kashf, 176.

The Sufi doctrine of Fatalism is by no means logical or consistent. They confined themselves, however, to matters of practical and religious importance and avoided the pedantry which might have hampered them in their doctrine of predestination[1].

The second most important doctrine of the Sufi is allied to Christian-Gnostic doctrine of saints. 'Wali', saint , really a 'friend of God', is a sufi[2]; a conception which the sufi school has imposed upon the entire Islam. And this, indeed, is to be reckoned its greatest visible triumph coming to the front in the 4th/10th century. Already in Muhasibi (d. 234/848), strongly influenced by Christianity, the hierarchy of saint appears as the stages of pious life[3]. And Tirmidhi (d. 285/898) is said to be the person who introduced the chapter of saints in sufi doctrines. He it was who placed Jesus before Mohamed[4]. The historians and biographers of the 4th/10th century know only the *Abdal* as a special kind of saints[5].

---

(1) Makki, 7.

(2) The earlier meaning of the word in Goldziher Muh. Studien, II, 286. (In the 4th century it was invariably used in a profane sense ; *e.g. Letters* of Subi (Leiden, fol. 2156 ; 219a : 220a ; 226b) ; *Letters* of Khwarezmi (Const. p 26) ; Kushairi p. 206 : "One was of the awliya of es-sultan, the other of the subjects" (Raayvah). The former is also called 'Jundi' (*i.e.* of the army).

(3) Prof. Margoliouth *Transaction of the 3rd Congress of Religious History*, Oxford, 1,292.

(4) Kashf, 210.

(5) This is the arabicised form of the Persian word for 'Father' which from the Gnostics to the Yezidis (Pir) has been used to signify the spiritual guide. Abu Taubah (d. 241), who was born at Damascus and who lived at Tarsus, is said to have been one of the *Abdals*, (Dhahabi. *Tabaqat al-huffas* ed. Wustenfeld, II, 18). In 242 died Tusi, one of the *Abdals* (Ibid, 33). Apparently his idea is that badil stands for *pidar*. In 265 died Ibrahim ibn al-Hani al-nisaburi who belonged to the circle of *Abdals*, (abul Fida, *Annales*, Sub 265). In 322 died al-Nassagh (Ibn al Athir VIII, 222) and in 327 Ibn Abi Hatim (Subki *Tabaqat*, II 237) of a spanish savant of the 4th century it is said 'if any one belonged, at his time, to the class of *Abdal*, it must be he. Ibn Bashkuwal, 1, 92.

Ibn Duraid (d. 321/933) notes *Abdal*, singular *badil*, a kind of saints (*Salihun*) the world is never without. There are seventy of them—40 in Syria and thirty elsewhere in the world[1]. Hujwiri, in the 5th/11th century, already mentions a larger number of the grades of holiness: 300 called *Akhyar*, 40 called *Abdal*, 7 called *Abrar*, four called *Awtad* , who every night make the circuit of the whole world, three called *Nuqaba*, and one called *Qutb* or *Ghawth*[2] who rules and superintends the world with his bands of holy men. It is manifest that the *Qutb* is the heir of the Gnostic Demiurgos. The "Desert of the *Israelites*" was then the place of audience of the *Qutb*[3]; Ubullah the home of the *Abdal*[4].

Only the orthodox of the old type, despised by the Sufis, as 'Hashawiyyah' authropomorphists kept away from saint-worship. They only recognized the Prophets as favoured of God. The mutazalites, on the contrary, denied that God favoured one believer over the other and maintained that all Muslims who obey God are his *Awliya* (friends)[5]. Society favoured sainthood so strenuously that in process of time there were none but sufi saints. The older ones like Maruf-el-Karkhi and Bisr al-Hafi were simply annexed to the circle of the Sufis.

Hasan al-Basri was placed at the head of this band the very same Hasan to whom sufi doctrines had been an abomination[6].

Against the Sufi uniform, with which he was afterwards credited, one of his bitterest sayings is reported: He was Malik Ibn Dinar with a woolen coat and asked: Are you pleased with it? Yes, said he. Well, before thee a sheep had

(1) Lane *Sahah*, see the word.
(2) Kashf, 214, 228, 229.
(3) Kashf, 229.
(4) Khwarezmi, Ras'ail, Const. p. 49.
(5) Kashf, 213, 215.
(6) *Raudat en-nezirin* 5.

worn it [1]. During the first two centuries of their existence the Sufis counted many who satisfied the two claims of holiness : the efficacy of prayer (*mujab-ud-Do'ah)* and the gift of *Karamat* (suspending the laws of nature).[2] And such were, indeed, the classical saints of Islam. Under the heading Baghdad Qazwini, for instance, mentions besides Bishr al-Hafi only such saints as had lived about the year 300/912 (*cosmography*, Ed. Wustenfeld 215 ff). The *Tabaqat es-Sufiyah* of Sulami (d. 412/1024) are the first lives of Saints. In reading Abul Muhasin who has used this work we receive the impression that the Saints only come into existence (W, II, 218, *Tarikh-eṣ-Sulami*) from the 3rd/9th and abound in the 4th/10th century (Yaqut, IV, 202).

Manifold indeed are the miracles of saints: generally efficacy of prayer, wonderful production of food and water, traversing of distances in an incredibly short time, rescue from enemies, strange happenings at the death of saints, hearing of voices, and other unusual things. (Kushairi, 188, cf. Nicholson, *mystics of Islam*, pp.120 sq). On the forehead of the dead Dhun-Nun was foud inscribed: This is beloved of God, who died in love of God, salin by God[3]. At his funeral the birds of the air gathered above his bier and wove their wings together so as to shadow it. When Barbeheri died in 324/936 his house was full of figures clad in white

(1) 'Karamat' is the doing of something in contravention of the *Laws of Nature* but without any claim to prophetship. I think Mez has misunderstood the sense of *Durub-el-Karamat* in the passage quoted from Sabi (Leiden, fol. 228). Says Professor Margoliouth : (The best rendering of *Karamat* is "spontaneous miracle", *i.e.* one which nature executes to do honour to a saint, without the saint's willing it). With regard to the efficacy of prayer—a poet says:

زو دعائے شیخ مثل ہر دعا ست   فانی است و گفته اش گفت خدا ست

چون خدا از خود سوال و کد کند   کے سوال خویشتن را رد کند

(2) *Kashf*, 100.

(3) Ibn al-Jazi, Berlin, fol. 356; Abul Mahasin, II, 233.

and green garments although the door was shut[1]. The Egyptian Bunan (d. 316/928) was thrown to the lions by Ibn Tulun but they did him no harm. A Syrian Shaikh, whom wild animals followed, was called Bunani cleared after him. A miracle- worker could walk on water at Qasibin and stop the current of Jaihun. Another brought forth jewels from the air. Round a black *Faqir* at Abadan the entire earth glittered with gold. His visitors ran away with fright. He performed on his ass the miracle of Balaam. To one in answer to his prayer the river Tigris throws back at his feet the signet which had fallen into the water; for the benefit of another who seeks to repair the roof of a mosque with too short a plank the walls draw close enough to help him in his purpose; of yet another the corpse laughs with the result that no-body ventures to wash it. Another Sufi, suffering a ship wreck, manages to save himself and his wife on a plank. The wife gives birth to a child and calls out to her husband: 'thirst is killing me'. The husband devoutly replies: He sees our plight. Raising his head he sees a man in the air holding a gold chain in his hand to which is attached a cup of red jacinth. He offered the cup to them and it was more fragrant than musk, cooler than ice, sweeter than honey. At the Ka'abah a charter of absolution was flung down from heaven to a Sufi absolving him from all sins, past and future. A Sufi lived in a loft to which were neither stairs nor a ladder when he wanted a wash he flew in the air like a bird. Like Abraham he also passed through a fiery furnace. Another after the wedding felt himself unable to cohabit with his wife; it transpired later that she was already a married woman.

At the command of the Egyptian Dhun-Nun his sofa moved round the room[2]. Another sufi changed the position of a mountain. For es-Sari (Egyptian founder of an order) the world, in the form of an old women, swept the floor

(1) Abulmahasin, II, 235, see also II, 37.

(2) Nicolson, mystics of Islam, 145. Tr.

and cooked the food. When a sufi died on a boat the water parted and the boat went aground to enable the burial of the saint. The burial being over—they got into the boat—water heaved up and the waves rolled over the grave.

Already now and then the eternally youthful Khidr makes his appearance the very Khidr who is even to-day the patron of the Dervishes. According to Ibn Hazm[1] widespread was the belief among credulous sufis that Elias and Khidr were alive—the former having jurisdiction over the desert, the latter over gardens and meadows. The credulous sufis believed that Khidr appeared to those who invoked his aid.

Indeed the more remarkable the miracle the further off is its date from the reporter's time. Kushairi professes to have known only one, namely, that Daqqaq, though suffering from irretention of urine, could always go through his lecture undisturbed. But only after the death of the master did this strike him as something extraordinary[2].

The miracle of calling the dead to life[3], practised by contemporary Christian miracle-workers, is not found in the Islam of that age. The only thing of the sort that we do find is the calling of dead animals to life[4]. The interest in miracles was mainly confined to the sufi community, but even the cultured among them set no store on them as compared with the wonderful powers of the spiritual life. When it was reported to Murta'is (d. 328/940) that so and so walked on the water, he said : I consider it much grander if God granted one strength to resist one's passion than the power to walk over the water[5]. A sufi related ' I was thinking of a miracle

(1) IV, 180.
(2) Kushairi, 203.
(3) E.G. Michael Syrus, 260 ff.
(4) Kush, 205.
(5) Kushairi, 30.

when I took a fishing rod from a boy, stood between two boats and said: By thy omnipotence if a fish, three pound in weight, does not come out now, I shall drown myself; and verily, a three pound fish did come out. When Junaid, the Chief of the school, heard this, he said : an other should have come out of the water and bitten him[1]. The sufi saint Bistami who died in 261/874 said on hearing that a miracle-worker did the journey to Mekka in one night: The Devil goes from sunrise to sunset (i.e. from East to West) in an hour under the curse of God[2]. When he heard that some one walked on the water and flew in the air he said: the birds fly in the air and the fish swim in water. Tustarì (d. 273/886) disbelieved in miracles but, as fate would have it, he is himself credited with them. He declared that the greatest miracle is to alter an ugly trait in one's character[3]. One day a man said to him : you walk on the water. He replied: ask the *Muezzin* of the quarter. He is God—fearing and will not lie. The questioner turned to the *Muezzin* who stated : That I do not know, but only that today he went to the pond to wash himself and fell in the water and had it not been for me, he would have been drowned[4].

Indeed a large section of the sufi thinkers contend that saints should not be credited with supernatural powers and that therein lies the fundamental difference between them and the prophets who are endowed with such a gift, the gift of Mujezah i.e. of working miracles[5]. Even on the question whether a saint should consider himself as such there was a divergence of opinion[6]. Sari, the father of sufiism,

(1) Kushairi, 193.
(2) Kushairi, 193.
(3) Kush, 193.
(4) Kush 203.
(5) A further difference between the prophet and the saint is that whereas the latter is regarded as incapable of sinning, the former is not Kashf, 25. (See Burton, Pilgrimage (memorial Ed. Vol. 1, 340 note 2 Tr.)
(6) Kush. 187.

is said to have felt great doubt on this score. If one were to come to a garden where were many trees and on every one of them many birds and were these birds to call out to him, in clear language : 'Peace be on thee, O ! Saint of God' and he feared no deception even in such a case verify there was a possibility of deception[1]. We have clear proof from Literature that saint-worship, after all, is merely the affair of Sufis and lower order.

No geographer of the 4th/10th century speaks of a single saint, no great poet either.

Finally sufiism developed a doctrine of incalculable religious force and vitality; a doctrine which satisfied the need for reverence, a need which existed long-before Islam. It raised Mohammed into a supernatural Being, almost into a divinity. The earliest tradition was extremely modest and circumspect. By the dead-body of his friend and teacher Abu Bakr is reported to have said in his prayer: God will not inflict upon you two deaths. You have gone through the one death which was appointed for you[2].

Already Hallaj, for whom Jesus was still the ideal figure, inserts in the first chapter of the *Kitab at-Tawasin* a rhapsodic hymn on the prophet: All lights of the Prophets—this too is a gnostic figure come from his light. He was before all—his name anticipated the pen of destiny he—was known before all history and all being and will endure after everything has ceased. Above and below him lighten clouds, flaming , pouring, fructifying (the world). All learning is but a drop from his ocean, all wisdom a handful from his rivulet; all times are but an hour from his life[3].

With these three central doctrines: the so-called fatalism,

(1) Kushairi, 189.
(2) Bukhari (Bab ul-Juna'iz).
(3) Massignon, 10 ff. The doctrine of Pre-existence is likewise of gnostic origin.

the worship of saints and of the Prophet, Sufiism has set its abiding impress on Islam.

But sufiism did not offer certainty of salvation nor yet did it allay the uncertainty of our lot after death.

When Makki , a very pious man and author of a textbook on sufiism, lay dying in 386/996 he spoke to one of his disciples : should you find out that I am saved, strew sugar and almonds on my corpse when borne to the grave saying: this is for the wise. I asked him, says the pupil, how should I ascertain that? Give your hand to me when I die . If I clasp it—know that God has saved me. But if I let it go know that my end has not been happy. And so I sat by him and he seized my hand firmly as he died. I strewed sugar and almonds on the bier as it was borne along saying : This is for the wise[1]. The very same story is related of Mawardi (d. 450/1058). He had not published any of his writings but when he was nearing death he said : my writings are all before me here and there. I had not published them because I felt no real satisfaction with them. When death is upon me and I lie unconscious, put your hand in mine, if I seize and press it, take the books and throw them into the Tigris but should I stretch my hand out and do not clasp yours, know that the books have found favour with the Almighty. And the letter happened[2].

It is touching to note how at the end of many strange biographies—the dead saint appears to a friend or a disciple in a dream, clad in the livery of the blessed and how he is anxiously questioned as to the way in which he found grace. The only sacrament in Islam—the only sure road to paradise is death in a holy war against the infidels. The Emperor Nicephorus, the greatest opponent of Islam in the 4th/10th century, realized the military import of this doctrine. He,

(1) Ibn Jauzi, Berlin fol. 139 b.
(2) Subki, III, 304.

likewise, wanted to declare as martyrs all who fell in war against the infidels. But the church, offended with him for financial reasons, declined to be a party to it[1]. In other forms the sufi movement transgressed the legitimate bounds of Islamic teachings. These forms constitute the un-European and specifically Oriental side- track. Their authors were not satisfied with defying the emotions, they wished to do the like for the will, and consistently claim the divine omnipotence for this divine will[2]. This gravely menaced the peace of the empire and explains the rise of the numerous heresies about 300/912. In 309/921 Hallaj, the wool-carder, was cruelly executed at Baghdad[3]. He had heard the discourses of many sufis, Junaid among them. Beruni calls him a sufi[4]. According to the *Fihrist* he gave himself out to the authorities as a shiite and to the common folk as a sufi[5]. He is reported to have prayed 400 *Riqas* a day[6]. Sixty-six years after his death the *Fihrist* registers 47 books by him[7]. One of these has been edited and commented upon by Massignon.

With an amazing skill which bears the stamp of the old gnostic tradition he lays bare the subtlest processes of his mind and the powerful results of his pantheistic

(1) Krumba cher, *Gesch. der byz. Lit.* 2, 985.

(2) (The sense is far from clear, but I fancy this must be what is meant) (Prof. Margoliouth Tr.).

(3) On Hallaj, see schreiner, ZDMG 54,468 ff and de Goeje; *Arib*, 86 ff. and above all Kit. al-Tawasin by Hallaj (Paris 1913) and *Ana al-Haqq* in Islam, III, 248 (for further information see Nicholson, *Mystics of Islam*, Ch VI and Lamens, Islam Ch VI Tr.

(4) *Chronology*, 194.

(5) p. 190

(6) *Kashf*, 303.

(7) 192 Beruni, India, tr. 125 mentions a "Book of the concentration of the greatest and a "Book of the concentration of the smallest". This is interesting on account of the terminology. The *Kit. es-Saiher fiaqs eddubur* has evidently drawn upon the work of Sulami (d. 412/1021). "It was a small square volume containing th : poems of Hallaj. Subki III, 61.

inspirations. It often reminds us of the most beautiful passages in the gnostic hymns. Even the method of Hallaj is positively that of the Mutazilah. He has taken over from them the idea of God, stripped of all human and fortuitous elements. He has borrowed from them too the term 'Haq', 'Being', to indicate this critically purified conception. But when two different aspects are distinguised in God—human and divine, *nasut* and *Lahut*, two foreign words drawn from the Syrian treatises regarding the nature of Christ—when God in human form is made to judge on the day of Judgment—when God is conceived of as projecting himself as man before all creation—the origional man, the Greek: *Proon anthropos* of the Gnostics[1]—when he distinctly appears as eating and drinking until His existence becomes a palpable reality[2] we find ourselves in the curious old world of the Christian gnosis which, in its turn, was simply a pale reflection of the ancient myth. The analogy extends to the minutest detail. According to Basilides of Irenaeus "from the father proceeds the Logos, then Wisdom (Phronesis), then power (Dynamis), then knowledge (Sophia)[3]. In the Tawasin[4] Hallaj draws four circles round God which no one can investigate : 1. His will (mashiah); 2. His Wisdom (Hikmah); 3. His power (kudrat).4. His knowledge (Malumah) *i.e.* his revelations. This pictorial method of instruction by circles which Celsus found among the gnostics is also to be found in the only extant book of Hallaj. As is well-known, we find the same thing in the Books of the Druses. The understanding (Synesis) is represented there as a "Rhomoboid"[5] and in the Kit. al-tawasin as a rectangle.

At a house-search Hallaj's books were found: Some were written on chinese paper and others with the tincture of

(1) Hilgenfeld, *Ketzergeschichte*, 294.
(2) Massignon.
(3) Hilgenfeld, 199.
(4) ed Massignon, 56.
(5) Hilgenfeld, 278.

gold, and were lined with silk and brocade and bound in costly leather[1]. The sacred Books of the Manichaeous were also beautifully got up[2]. This too, was a gnostic practice. Even the gnostic stages of common purification are there with special reference to Jesus as the highest ideal. "He gave himself up to a life of piety and rose from stage to stage. He believed that he, who purified his body through obedience, occupied himself with good works refrained from all lust, would ascend higher and higher in the scale of purity until his nature is rid of all things carnal. And when nothing carnal is left the spirit of God, from whom Jesus came, would settle in him making all his acts and behests the acts and behests of God. "Thus does a latter contemporary describe the teachings of Hallaj who, according to him had attained that rank[3].

Hallaj himself sings:

> Thy spirit is mingled in my spirit even as wine
> is mingled with pure water[4].

And again :

> "I am He whom I love, and He whom I love
> is I:
> We are two spirits dwelling in one body—
> If thou seest me, thou seest him,
> And if thou seest him, thou seest me"

In rare and beautiful figures he describes the idea of deification:

> The butterfly flies into the Light and, by its

---

(1) *Arib*, 90, according to misk.
(2) Ibn al-Jauzi, 59 a (Khuda Buksh, *Islamic Civilization, Vol.* 1, 104 Tr.)
(3) Istakhri, de Goeje, 184 ff.
(4) Massignon 134. In the *Tawasin* curiously this idea is not to be found. The idea in *Tawasin* developed on different lines. (See Nicholson, *Mystics of Islam*, p. 151, Tr.)

extinction becomes the very flame itself[1].
Thou art with me between my heart and the
flesh of my heart;
Thou flowest like tears from my eye-lids[2].

Suli, who constantly speaks of Hallaj, refers to him as an unlettered man, who simulated wisdom. But, indeed, he secured disciples in the highest circles[3]; even the household of a Prince and specially the powerful court-marshal. Nasir were suspected of leanings towards him. Indeed a Qadi appointed by the Caliph refused to condemn him. For eight years he lived in mild custody at the Caliph's Palace and the general impression is that his death was due solely to palace intrigues. Most of the reports regarding him come from hostile sources. But this much is clear that in the higher circles of Baghdad Hallaj exercised a potent spell. A further proof of this is to be found in the fact that both Jauzi and Dhahabi wrote his biography. Though neither of these works have come down to us; yet the honour of a special biography has not fallen to the lot of many men in Islam.

Powerful, indeed was the influence of Hallaj on Sufi theology. Despite martyrdom, many of his disciples carried on his teachings; notably the sect of salimayyah. In the 5th/11th century Hujwiri saw 4,000 men in Mesopotamia who called themselves the flowers of Hallaj[4]. And the very same Hujwiri testifies that Hallaj was dear to him and that there were but few Sufi shaikhs who could deny the purity of his soul or the severity of his asceticism[5]. And, indeed, at the time of Abul Ala (d. 449/1057) there were people at Baghdad who expected him to rise again and stand upon the shore

(1) Massignon, 17.
(2) Massignon, 133
(3) According to Istakri (p. 149) specially in Babylon, Mesopotamia, media. According tc Ibn Haukal he began as a Fatimid emissary.
(4) *Kashf*, 260.
(5) Ibid, 155 f.

of the Tigris where he was crucified[1].

Christian speculation stands at the background even of the other heresies of the time. The so-called Kisf (Mansur at Ijli who was regarded by some as a Prophet) taught in Kufa that God created Jesus first and after him Ali[2]. And Shalmaghani, belonging to a Mesopotamian village in Wasit, professing himself to be the bearer of the divine spirit taught likewise[3]. At the instance of the Wazir Ibn Muqlah, he, along with two disciples, was put upon his trial. To prove their innocence they were bidden to strike their God : one actually dealt a blow but the hand of the other shook while trying to strike him. The latter then kissed the head and beard of Shalmaghani with the words: My master. Thereupon the master and the pupil were placed on the pillory, scourged and burnt. Shalmaghani taught that God resided in everything according to its capacity and that He has created for everything its opposite for instance with Adam He created *Iblis* and he dwelt in them both. The opposite of Abraham was Nimrod; of Aaron, Pharaoh; of David, Goliath. That the opposite of everything stands nearest to it; as for instance, the opposite of truth exists to point the way to the truth itself[4]. Masudi regards him as Shiah[5] but though he accepts Ali as his precursor in the incarnation of divinity he refuses to believe in Hasan and Husain as his sons, for God can neither have a father nor a son. The last precursor of Ali—so he taught—who united in himself the

---

(1) JRAS 1902, 347.

(2) Ibn Hazm IV, 185 (Goldziher, *Muh, and Islam*, p. 171 Tr.)

(3) The Literature on the subject is in schreiner, 472. It is wanting in Ibn Haukal and is only to be found in Yaqut's *Irshad*, 296 (which was edited later), where Yaqut gives an extract from a letter of the Caliph Radhi to the Samanid Nasr Ibn Ahmad regarding the legal proceedings against Shalmaghani. Yaqut had come across the letter at Merv.

(4) Yaqut, *Irshad*, I, 302.

(5) *Tanbih* 397.

human and divine nature in Adam was Jesus; whereas Moses and Mohamed were referred to by him as deceivers who had overreached their senders and Ali.

The obvious meaning of the Qur'anic Laws symbolically interpreted: Paradise because the recognition of the truth and the acceptance of their sect; Hell, ignorance of their teaching and aloofness from their community. His followers gave up prayer, fast, ablution. They were charged with immorality and credited with community of wives. They even considered the love of boys as indispensable for through it they pretended to illuminate the love—one by their own light[1] .This sect was, by no means, a sect of common-folk. Its founder was a clerk, who at Baghdad stood high in the esteem of Ibn al-Furat and had held all kinds of offices. The disciple, who died with him, was Ibrahim Ibn Abaun, poet, author, high placed official, and the Wazir of the Wazir-family of Banu Wahb is said to have believed in the divinity of this man[2].

Of a wholly different kind were the movements inspired by the idea of the Mahdi. The persons with whom we have been dealing were individual seekers after God who followed the lead of the old theology. The most amazing thing about them was that they found response for their strange preachings. But mahadism from the commencement had been political in its essence. It appealed to the masses and thus had very different success. Already about the middle of the 3rd/9th century Hamdan Qarmat[3] had collected together the turbulent elements of Mesopotamia but all their risings were suppressed by the Caliph al-Mutadid[4].

(1) This is affirmed by *Kashf,* 416. The *Haluliyan* i. e. the adherents of incarnation have made the love of boys ; a stigma on the saints of God and the aspirants to sufiism.

(2) Kit al-Uyun, IV, 184 b.

(3) *Kit al-Uyun*, IV. 184 b.

(4) Of the numerous etymologies of this name I consider the conjecture

But it was only when the propaganda turned to Arabia that it rose to real political importance. There was the centre of the rebels of all shades of opinion, eager to follow a leader, plundering and murdering, into rich agricultural estates. On account of the Qarmatians the competent Caliph al-Mutadid died in 219/901 of a broken heart[1]. They possessed two brilliant generals who knew how to organize the wild forces of Arabia and to guide them to greatest expedition which the Peninsula had witnessed since Islam. About the beginning of the 3rd/9th century Syria was ruthlessly devastated. And again about the beginning of the 4th/10th century Mesopotamia suffered from their attacks; Basra and Kufa were conquered and plundered; Baghdad reeled with paralysing fear and the connection between Mekka and the East was interrupted.

From the Syrian deserts in 316/928 flowed the Qarmatians' predatory raids right up to the mountain chains of Sinjar[2]. In 317/929 they let in unmolested the pilgrim caravan to the Holy city but, then, with an incredibly small band of 600 cavalry and 900 infantry, stormed the city, entered the Ka'aba slaughtered all, rifled the treasures of the temple and made away even with the Black Stone. Only the nomadic Beduins resisted the invaders, the town-folk of Mekka riotously revelled in the plunder of their own sanctuary. Contrary to our expectation this event made little impression on that age. Only the latter ages viewed it with intense horror; the religious indifference being then much too pronounced to assume pious, gathering round the aspiring Sufiisim, set before them something higher as an ideal than Black Stone. And even the strictly orthodox did

of Vollers, coupling it with Greek Grammata (letters) to be the most probable because it finds support in the Mesopotamian Jargon of the 4th/10th century. In the poem of Abu Dulaf (Yat. IV. 184 a Qarḿat appears as a "writter of amulet.

(1) Maqrizi, *Ittiaz, ed. Bunz.* III.

(2) Ibn al-Athir, VIII, 133; Arib, 134.

not feel quite at ease in their respect for that stone. The plunder of Mekka marks the highest point of the Qarmatian rebellion. Further predatory incursions to the East, as far as the interior of Persia, followed. The desert had become almost impassable and more than once, for fear of them, the Bazars of Baghdad were closed down. The diplomacy of the Court, however, tried to counteract the danger. Qarmatian troops were admitted into the army of the Caliph and in 327/938 the rebels concluded a treaty with the Government to let the Pilgrim-caravan through as against the payment of a fixed sum for every litter and every camel-load. In 339/950 the Black Stone was restored to Mekka. A lean camel could now carry it and even become fat in doing so—whereas 12 years ago three strong camels broke down under its weight. The ill-luck of the Black Stone does not end here. In 413/1022 an Egyptian—suspected of being a partisan of Hakim—smashed it with a club. The culprit was killed and the stone patched up with musk and gum[1]. By the invasion of Egypt and Syria the Qarmatians helped on the onward march of the Fatimids but in 358/968 they finally, concluded peace with the Caliph of Baghdad for whom prayer was now offered from all their pulpits; the Caliph supplying them with money and arms[2].

As at the outset of their career, Syria once again becomes the goal of their invasion but the enemy now is their old ally, the Fatimid. Wherever they succeeded, they unfurled the black flag of the Abbasids[3]. Their advance was, however, checked and they returned to Arabia on payment of an annuity. Some years later they were finally expelled from Mesopotamia by the Buwahids. At the end of the century they formed only a small state on the East Coast of Arabia which gave no serious trouble to the Mekkan pilgrims but

---

(1) Jauzi, 170 b.
(2) Sabi, in Qalanisi, ed. Amedroz, p. 11.
(3) Maqrizi, Ittiaz, 133.

merely kept its customs house at the gate of Al-Basra where imposts were levied[1]. As late as 443 when the Persian Nasir Khusr visited their capital, Lahsa, be found in front of the grave of the founder of this Qarmatian State, a saddled-horse in readiness, day and night, to enable the founder to mount it immediately on his return to life[2].Travellers reported to Abul Ala that there were quite a number of people in Yaman—each of whom regarded himself as the expected mahdi and, as such, found people to pay tribute to them. It is impossible to assess how much faith or how much love of booty entered into their minds. Nor are we in a position to judge the precise proportion of sincere religious spirit in this movement. It is, however, to be noted that Yaman has always been famous for its highly-strung spiritualism. "It has always been a refuge for the most daring views and a mine for those who traded with religion or sought sordid gain by hypocrisy[3]".

The Mahdism of the Qarmatians was by no means good Islam; the Christian-gnostic doctrine of the incarnation being always there in the background. "One sect teaches the divinity of Muhammad ibn Ismail ibn Jafar and these are the Qarmatians. Among them are those who teach the divinity of Abu Said el-Jubbai and his sons; others teach the divinity of Ubaidullah and his successors up to the present day; others teach the divinity of Abul Khattab ibn Abi Zainab in Kufa whose supporters exceed one thousand there. Another section teaches the divinity of the wheat-dealer Ma,mar in Kufa, a follower of Abul Khattab, and actually worships him. May God curse them all"[4]. At least according to Beruni[5] even the Qarmatian mahdi the

(1) Muk, p. 133 (Eng. tr. p. 217).

(2) Muk Trans. p. 228. This was related to Abul Ala also JRAS, 1902, 829.

(3) Abul Ala el-ma arri.

(4) Ibn Hazm, IV, 187. cf. de Geoge in *Arib*, p.111 note 3.

(5) p. 196

Zakariyya claimed to be God. Like the black Alps behind the green Jura those tower behind the Qarmatian their age-long masters the Fatimid who exploited the idea of the mahdi with a force and success which never fell to its lot again. This back-swell of Arabism to the west, the entry of the Caliph into Cairo with the coffins of his ancestors, is the most romantic phenomenon of this stirring age. It is indeed as the Caliph puts it: "the sun rose where it generally sets"[1]. Its progress is the most striking incident in the politics of the 4th/10th century. Some 100 years after the appearance of their first Mahdi, their rule, about the year 360/970, extended over the whole of North Africa and Syria up to the Euphrates and "their mission filled every valley"[2]. In 362/972 the Caliph Muiz thus wrote to the Qarmatian leader: "There should be no Island or climate on the earth without our teachers and missionaries to promulgate our doctrines in every tongue"[3]. The Qarmatians obeyed his orders. Baluchistan, atleast by payment of gold, acknowledged the suzerainty of the ruler at Cairo[4]. And when the poet Hamadhani went in the 80's of the 4/10th century, to Jurjan, up high in the north, always understanding where the greatest power and wealth were to be found, he attached himself to the Ismailites (Yaqut, Irshad, 1, 96). Spiritually they had nothing new to give but it is spirit and not the number of the soldiery that makes for lasting power. Only 20 years after its meridian splendour the propaganda ceases: "There are but few missionaries and I see no book written for their guidance. Such at least is the case in Mesopotamia, possibly in Persia and Khorasan things remain unaltered. In Egypt, however, things are very doubtful, the present ruler proves nothing that is related of him and his father gives no evidence by his own conduct[5].

(1) Maqrizi, Ittiaz, 141.
(2) *Fihrist*, 189.
(3) Maqrizi, *I'tiaz*, Rai was the residence of the Government of Mahdi in the East. Even the Mesopotamian recruiting agents were under him such as the Banu Hammad at Mosul, *Fihrist*, 189.
(4) Ibn Haukal, 221.
(5) *Fihrist*, 189.

We know but little of the Ismailite doctrines in the 4th/10th century. Our chief source of information, dating from this period, is the report of Akhu Muhsin, preserved by Nuwairi and Maqrizi and translated by the Sacy (*Expose de la religion des Druzes,* LXXIV ff). But it is tainted at its source for it is drawn from the polemics of Ibn Rezzam against this sect which both the Fihrist (p. 186) and Maqrizi designate as "a compound of truth and fiction". The fragments edited by Guyard give no idea as to their date. Old names prove nothing for in all these circles literary forgeries were the order of the day. Even in the 4th/10th century most of the writings ascribed to the oldest Ismailite Shaikhs were pure forgeries[1]. But the main thing, indeed, which we learn from Shahrastani is that there is a great difference between the Ismailities of the 4th/10th century and those of the later 5th/11th century and that we should keep severely apart the catechism of the Caliph Muiz from that of the old man of the mountain.

Unfortunately Ibn Hazm is absolutely reticent on the Ismailites. He only tells us that they and the Qarmatians have notoriously fallen away from Islam and teach pure Zoroastranism[2]. Abul Ala says also very little about them. In his *Resalat el-Gufran* we seek in vain for information on the Ismailites. Possibly their proximity enjoined silence. Thus for authentic information we have to fall back on the *Fihrist.* They had seven grades of development as against nine of Akhu Muhsin— the instruction regarding each grade contained in a book. The first two grades could be completed in a year; annual then, was the progress up to the sixth. It is not stated when the last grade could be reached. Ibn Nadim claims to have read the Book of the

(1) *Fihrist,* 187, II.

(2) Ibn Hazm, II, 116. We should not take the expression literally. It stood then for a heresy. Kushairi, 38, even attacks something quite unzoroastran. It is pure magianism.

seventh grade and found in it things, terribly immoral and in violation of the orthodox teaching[1]. This sect, even then, had recourse to allegorical interpretation (ta'wil). A rich Qarmatian took away the pension from Balkhi (d. 322/933) for writing his "Examination of the allegorical method"[2]. Thus the conception of Religion as the Rational knowledge of God; the gradation according to the state of knowledge; in later authorities the elaborately worked-out Dualism and parallelism of the world all, once again, point to the old gnosis.

Even the *Fihrist*[3] has reproached the Fathers of the Ismailites doctrines as Bardesamians. Their doctrines could be got together from the Mutazils and the Shiah', but this fact only enabled them to adopt anything that was not-Abbasid or Sunni.

New , indeed, was the stern discipline for which the oriental has a special aptitude when sanctified by religion. The conversion of Hamdan, the Qarmat, by the Fatimid missionary al Husain al-Ahwazi offers a typical illustration of the way wherein this discipline served as a mode of approach "when Ahwazi was proceeding as a missionary to Mesopotamia he met Hamdan ibn al-As'ath, the Qarmat, in the neighbourhood of Kufa. He had an ox which carried something for him. When they had walked for an hour Hamdan spoke to Husain: I see you are coming from a great distance and you look tired, sit on the ox. Husain rejoined: I have no such order. Then, said Hamdan it appears you do what you are bidden to do. He replied, yes. Then rejoined Hamdan, who commands and forbids thee? My king and thine to whom this and the other world belong was the reply. Hamdan was surprised. He paused and said : God

(1) *Fihrist,* 189

(2) *Fihrist* 138; Yaqut, *Irshad I, 142.*

(3) *Fihrist* p. 187.

alone is the king over this and that world. Thereupon the other rejoined. You are right but God gives his kingdom to him whom He will; and he began to canvass him. He (Husain) went to him (Hamdan), to his house, took from the people the oath of allegiance for the Mahdi and stayed in Hamdan's house, the latter being pleased with his cause and its importance[1].

Husain was very keen in devotion. He fasted during the day, kept awake at night, and people envied anyone who was allowed to take Husain into his house for a night.

As a tailor he earned a living. His person and his tailoring brought blessing to his customers[2].

This sect, incorporating within its bosom many old Mesopotamian doctrines, followed the Mesopotamian method too, in setting its records down on clay tablets. Their Missionaries made over to their followers a seal of white clay bearing the inscription: Mohammed Ibn Isma'il, the Imam the friend of God (Wali allah), the Mahdi[3].

Now also in the Fatimid Empire was the introduction of officially recognised and remunerated clergy : a thing nowhere to be found in Islam till then. These were the quondam missionaries of the sect (Du'at) who, now became its pastors with a general superintendent over them[4], who counted as one of the highest officers of State.

Where so many mahdis and Gods flourished—the claim to be a prophet would be out of date. Even a century

---

(1) The great success of the sect in the year 260/875 coincides with the death of Hasan ibn Ali whom the majority of the Shiites venerated as Imam and who, to their greatest embarrassment died childless that year, Ibn Hazm, IV, 93.

(2) Maqrizi, *Ittiaz* 101 ff.

(3) Jauzi, *Muntazam*, fol 296.

(4) Nasir Khusru tr. 160.

before poor jests were made on this subject. The biography of the Caliph Mamun is enlivened by several conversations with false prophets.. But even now, here and there, occasionally, such a claimant came forward in a province. In 322/934 far away in the pious Transoxiana some one managed by alleged miracles to secure a large following. He dipped his hand in the water and fetched it out full of gold. When he became troublesome the Samanid Governor ordered his execution[1].

On the other hand a year later in Ispahan a colleague *i.e.* another pretender to the prophetic office is said to have been asked by the head of the state if he could establish his claim by a miracle, to which he replied: If one has a beautiful wife or a daughter, let him bring her to me and she will, in a single hour, be presented with a son. This is my miracle. To this the presiding *Katib* replied: I believe in you and can dispense with your proof. (But this anecdote is already reported of the Court of al-Mamum)[2]. Another however , proposed, as they had no beautiful woman, to furnish a she-goat instead : whereupon the prophet made preparations to go. When questioned, whither ? he answered: I am going to Gabriel to report to him that these people want a he-goat and need no Prophet. Thereupon they laughed and let him go[3].

The term (prophetaster) (mutanabbi) had already become a nick-name among boys and hence the poet Mutanabbi was so called (d. 354/965)[4].

There was no lack in this century also of men who put forward no such high pretentions but sought simply and humbly to serve God in the ways of the faithful of yore. A

(1) Ibn al-Athir, VIII, 216.
(2) Baihaqi, ed. Schwally, 31.
(3) Yaqut, *Irshad*, I, 130 f.
(4) Jauzi, fol 96.*
In the "Table talk of a Mesopotamian Judge (Islamic culture) the

very popular form of higher piety, then, was never to leave the house save for the Friday prayer[1]. The uneclesiastical poet Abul Ala (d. 449/1057) vowed never to leave his house. Many lived in a mosque[2]. The Caliph al-Qadir daily distributed to those living in mosques one-third of the food provided for him. In 384/994 died a pious man who for seventy years had never leaned against a wall or had used a pillow[3]. Hujwiri met a pious man in the interior of Khorasan who never sat down for 20 years except when required to do at prayer. "It does not seem proper to sit down while contemplating God"— said he[4]. Another for forty years never lay on a bed[5]. Another, in his life-time, had made his grave by the side of the resting-place of the pious Bishr and there very often read the Qur'an through[6]. For forty years Saffar al-Ispahani (d. 339/950) never looked up to the sky[7]. In 336/947 died at Mekka, a holy man who had lived a whole year through on 30 dirhams, given by his father[8]. A savant, who died in 348/959, fasted during the day, ate a flat cake of bread (garif) at night from which he always saved a bit. On Fridays he gave his bread as alms and ate the saved-up bits[9]. In 404/1013 died a pious man who at night surrounded himself with dangerous utensils so that he might hurt himself should he drop off to sleep. He always had traces of injuries on his head and forehead. He never took a bath, never cropped his hair. When the hair, indeed, grew too long he cut it with clipping shears. He never washed his clothes with soap[10]. Another (d. 342/

poet admits that he actually claimed to be a Prophet.

(1) Jauzi, fol 158 b; 169 a.

(2) Jauzi, fol 158 b.

(3) Ibn al-Athir IX, 74.

(4) Kashf, 335.

(5) Abu Nu'aim, Tarikh *Ispahan, Leiden,* fol. 98 a.

(6) Yaqut, *Irshad*, 1, 247.

(7) Jauzi, fol. 82 a: Subki *Tabaqat, II*, 166.

(8) Jauzi, fol 80 a.

(9) Jauzi, fol 88 a.

(10) Jauzi fol 160 b.

953), while at prayer, use to knock his head, weeping against the wall until it bled[1]. Al-Baihaqi (d. 438/1046) fasted for the last thirty years of his life *i.e.* he never took anything during the day[2].

Strict compliance with Law was reckoned as part of asceticism. In 400/1009 lived a savant who would not hammer a nail in the wall of the house which he shared with another for fear of interfering with his proprietary rights. He even paid the taxes twice a year apprehending that he might have been too lightly assessed[3]. A man, who died in 494/1101, refrained from taking rice on the ground that it needed so much water for cultivation that the cultivator could not do without *unlawfully* during water from his neighbour's field[4]. A third one gave emetic to his little child because he had taken milk from a neighbour women, thus unjustly depriving the women's child of his portion[5]. In al-Hakim an ascetic sat, at last, on the throne, who strove to revive the stern primitive practices of Islam, and wished to banish the world out of religion.

About the year 400/1009 he closed the royal kitchen, ate only what his mother sent him, forbade prostration, kissing of hand and the use of the term 'maulana' (our Lord) in addressing him. He let his hair grow; did away with the "umbrella", the royal ensign; abolished titles; removed all illegal exactions; restored the properties confiscated by him or his grandfather, manumitted in the *mohurrum of* 400/1009 all his male and female slaves and provided them with a dower; threw into the Nile his female favourites after nailing them down in boxes, weighted with heavy stones. And this to renounce all lust: His crown-prince rode in full

(1) Subki, *Tabaqat*, II, 80.
(2) Subki, Tabaqat, III, 5.
(3) Subki, III, 208.
(4) Subki, III, 222.
(5) Subki, III, 251.

royal splendour but the Caliph, on a donkey with an iron harness by his side, clad, at first in white and later in black wool, carrying a blue *futah* (napkin) on the head with a black band[1].

We have frequent reports of "conversions" and the consequent withdrawal from the world. A savant and poet, pupil of the lexicographer Jauhari, repented, undertook a pilgrimage to Mekka and Medina, withdrew from the world, begged Tha'alibi to publish nothing of his earlier love and laudatory poems[2]. A Khorasanian Qadi thus express himself in a poem: Like a dream youth has flown and now that death draws nigh, others will soon be wrangling for his inheritance. He concludes his poem with a six-fold farewell.

> "Farewell, O Books, which I have composed and adorned with clear thoughts,
> Farewell, O Praise, which I have ingeniously wrought and woven together during long nights.
> To you bides adieu a man who never found what he sought nor attained what he wished.
> To his Lord, penitent he turns, seeking forgiveness for his sins in lowliness of heart[3].

Sudden conversions were mostly caused by Qur'anic passages which do not make a very effective appeal to us. In the first half of the 4th/10th century a high official of the Sultan while passing through the town like a Wazir in stately pomp hears a man recite the 57 "verse of Sura 15". Is it not time for those who believe to humble themselves and think of God? And lo : the official cries out: It is, O God, it is: He dismounts, takes off his clothes, rushes into the Tigris,

(1) Ibn Said, fol. 123 a ff. Even the Emperor Nicephorus Phocas (963-969) wore a hair shirt and a girdle of penance at night.

(2) *Yatimah*, IV, 310.

(3) *Yatimah*, IV, 320.

covers his body with water, gives all his possessions away. A passerby gives him his shirt and coat to enable him to come out of the water[1]. Others, on the other hand, only sought at the hour of death to ensure themselves against the Day of Judgment. When the Samanid Nasr Ibn Ahmad felt, in 331/942, the approach of death, he cuased a tent to be pitched in front of the gate of the palace and named it the "House of Divine Service" where, clad in a penitent's grab he performed religious duties[2]. Even Muiz-ud-Dawlah repented before his death, sent for Jurists and theologians and questioned them regarding the true atonement and whether he could duly perform it. They replied in the affirmative and told him what to say and to do. He gave away the major portion of his wealth in charity and emancipated his slaves[3].

By reason of the insecurity of the Arab roads pilgrimage, in those times, became not only dangerous but impossible. Since the time of the Qarmatians the Beduins were paid to let the official pilgrim pass in peace (qafilat es-Sultan): The Usaifir, for instance, got at least 9000 dinars[4]. Apart from the Baghdad Government, other princes too contributed towards the amount paid for safe passage; the prince of Media, in 386/996, contributed 5000 dinars[5]. In 384/994, the Beduins refused safe passage on the ground that the dinars of the previous year were merely gilded silver pieces. They, therefore, claimed the amount for both the years. The negotiations broke down and the pilgrims returned home[6].

---

(1) Jauzi fol. 89 a.

(2) Mirkhond, *Hists. sam,* 50.

(3) Misk VI 295; Jauzi, 100 a.

(4) Jauzi, 136 b; Masudi. *Tanbih,* 75. I cannot verify this reference : Moze does not quote Mas'udi's *Tanbih*, which is about a different matter).

(5) Jauzi, 139 a.

(6) Jauzi, 135 b; Ibn al-Athir, IX, 74 where, according to Jauzi instead of dirhams, "dinars" should be read.

In 421/1030 only such made pilgrimage from Mesopotamia who used desert-camels and were given escorts from tribe to tribe. Every one of these escorts got four dinars as remuneration[1]. Even in peaceful times pilgrims passed through severe hardships for want of water in the desert; those who lived near Arabia themselves were not immune from such hardships. Ibn al-Mutazz compares a disagreeable man, whose company was unavoidable, to the water of the pilgrimage over which people used abusive language at every halt but which one could not do without[2]. "He died on the pilgrimage" is the uncanny refrain in many biographies. In 395/1004 the pilgrim caravan, on the return journey, suffered so terribly from scarcity of water that people urinated on their hands and drank it[3]. In 402/1011 a bag of water cost 100 dirhams[4]. In 403/1012 the Beduins let the water run out of the cisterns provided on the pilgrim-route and threw bitter-weed*[5] in the wells: 15000 pilgrims thus perished or were taken captives. The Governor of Kufa[6], who was responsible for the pilgrim roads undertook a punitive expedition, killed many Beduins, and sent fifteen of their ring-leaders as prisoners to Basra[7]. There they only got salt to eat and were tied up by the Tigris were they perished of thirst. Years after the Banu Khafagah, the worst offenders then, were attacked and the captive pilgrims released. Till their release they had to tend the flock of sheep of their Lords and Masters. They returned home only to find "their properties distributed and their wives re-married"[8] In 405/1014, 20,000 pilgrims are said to have perished and 6000

(1) Jauzi fol 181 a.
(2) p. 5.
(3) Arib, 24.
(4) Jauzi, fol. 158 a.
(5) p. 301 line 13 from the top.
*(I cannot verify this passage. Prof. Margoliouth Tr.)
(6) Jauzi, fol. 158 a.
(7) Misk, V 247.
(8) Jauzi. fol. 159a.

to have themselves saved by drinking camels' urine and eating camels' flesh[1]. The well-known swelling-up of torrents during the rains also claimed its victims. In 344/960 the Egyptian pilgrims camped in a valley near Mekka. The torrent suddenly rose, no arrangement could be made, and the Egyptians were drowned. A great number of them perished, the rush of water sweeping them and their possessions into sea[2].

The ultra-pious pilgrims travelled on foot; some, indeed praying two *Rakahs* at every mile-stone[3]. For a Sufi it was meet and proper to set out on this perilous journey without outfit or money[4]. The very reverse of the Sufis were those who made this pious journey for money on *behalf of others for their heart is perverse* and becomes more so still on return. They drive but little benefit from their journeys. Some have done two or three pilgrimages and yet I have known this class of people to thrive[5] or to possess and goodness." The return of the pilgrims was always the occasion of a festive celebration. To enter Baghdad fresh the next day for the festivity they even passed the previous night in the suburb of al Yasiriyyah[6]. Those proceeding further east were received by the Caliph. In 391/1000 al-Qadir availed himself of this great celebration for declaring his son as successor to the throne[7]. The numerous local sanctuaries endeavoured to divert people from the great pilgrimage[8]. The statement that ten visits to the mosque of Jonas at Nineveh were tantamount to a pilgrimage at Mekka is significant[9]. More

(1) Jauzi, fol. 162 b.
(2) Misk VI, 240.
(3) Ibn Nu'aim *Tarikh, Isfahan* Leiden, fol. 71 b.
(4) Yaqut, Irshad, II, 357.
(5) Muk 127. (Eng. tr. p. 205).
(6) Masari, al-ushaq, 109.
(7) Wuz, 420; Jauzi, 146 a.
(8) Muk, enumerates the places of pious visitation (Eng. tr) pp 154 sq Tr.
(9) Muk, p. 146 (Eng. tr. p. 236).

important sanctuaries, doubtless, offered still better terms[1]. Above them all Jerusalem moulded its old attractive powers to new conditions. From the 5th/11th century comes the report that, at the times of the pilgrimage, those who could not proceed to Mekka, came to Jerusalem and there performed their sacrificial feast. More than 20,000 assembled there. They even brought their boys there for circumcision[2]. Even reproductions of holy places are mentioned. The Caliph Mutawakkil built a Ka'aba at Samarra, surrounded it with a walk for circumambulation and also places in the fashion of Mina and Arafat[3] to enable him to dispense with granting leave to his generals to go on pilgrimage for fear of desertion and disloyalty.

In mysticism a powerful current had set in *then* against pilgrimages[4]. Even earlier still a Sufi is said to have induced a pilgrim to return home and look after his mother[5]. The following words are put into the mouth of one who died in 319/931:— I wonder at those who cross the deserts and wildernesses to reach His House and sanctuary, because the traces of His Prophets are to be found there : why do not they traverse their own passions and lusts to reach their hearts, where they will find the traces of their Lord[6]? Abu Hayyan et-tauhidi, mutazalite and sufi, wrote, about 380/990, a Book on "Spiritual Pilgrimage" (Hajjaqli), recommending it when the legal one becomes too troublesome[7]. When in the 5th/11th century the wazir

(1) Ibid.
(2) Nasir Khusru, tr. 66.
(3) Muk. mentions Mutasim Eng. tr. p. 169 Tr.
(4)

حاجی به ره کعبه و من طالب دیدار

او خانه همی جوید و من صاحب خانه

(5) Kashf, 91.
(6) Kashf, 140.
(7) Yaqut, *Irshad*, V. 382.

Nizam-ul-mulk was making arrangements for a pilgrimage a sufi wrote to him in the name of God: Why do you go to Mekka? Your pilgrimage is here. Remain with these Turks (the Seljukian Turks) and help the needy ones of your community[1].

In the 5th/11th century Hujwiri (the typical sufi of compromise) declares: Any one who is absent from God at Mekka is in the same position as if he were absent from God in his own house, and any one who is present with God in his own house is in the same position as if he were present with God at Mekka[2].

We get the impression, indeed, that the cultured circles, in response to the growing reverence for the Prophet, attached greater importance to the visit to *Medina*. The famous Bukhari wrote his "chronicles" (*Tarikh*) by the grave of the Prophet[3]. Says the disciple of the philologist Jauhari: I have come on foot but fain would I come on my eyes to the grave where the Prophet of God lies[4]. Even the Wazir Kafur of Egypt, patron of the far-famed traditionist Daraqutni, purchased a house in Medina along-side of the grave of the Prophet for his burial[5].

A *quondam* Wazir (d. 488/1095) served in the "Garden of the Elect" swept the mosque of the Prophet, laid the mats, cleaned the lamps[6].

The obligation of the Holy war now, as ever, was very seriously taken. "Through the path of God" many God-fearing people sought paradise. To Tarsus, the base of

(1) Subki, III, 140.
(2) Kashf, 329.
(3) Abulfida, Annales, year 256.
(4) Yaqut, *Irshad*, II, 357.
(5) *Irshad*, II, 408.
(6) Subki, III, 58.

operation against the Byzantines, the hereditary enemies of Islam, trooped in the faithful from all sides for war-service. To Tarsus also streamed in pious gifts and donations from those who could not personally take part in the war. "From Sijistam to the Maghrib there was no town of importance which had not its station (dar) there for its warriors to rest before the actual campaign. To them poured in considerable money and rich presents from home as well as from the Government. Every distinguished man endowed property or made other provisions for them[1]. The inhabitants of the frontier fortresses were always accorded a warm welcome at Baghdad and it was for that reason that the philologist al-Qadi (d. 356/967) is said to have given himself out to be the child of the Armenian Qaliqala[2].

At once lucrative and effective was the fraud practised in the Islamic Empire in the shape of collecting funds for the Holy war or for ransoms of captives. To make a better or stronger impression many of these swindlers went about collecting subscription on horse-back[3]. In Egypt the frontiers (Mawahiz) were garrisoned by soldiers (ahled-Diwan) and volunteers (muttawwiah). The pious donations for the war (sabil) were collected every year and administered by the Qadhi who forwarded the amount to the frontiers in the month of Abib. Transoxiana, whose inhabitants, among Muslims, were noted for their unrivalled self-sacrificing zeal, was the second most important military centre. "In the Islamic countries" says Istakhari, "the prosperous spend, by far the greatest part of their wealth, in pleasures and in objectionable practices but, with rare exceptions, in Transoxiana the rich utilize their money in keeping the roads

(1) Ibn Haukal, 122.

(2) Yaqut, *Irshad,* II, 353. (It rests on a mistake : these people were respected because of their relationship to Armenian King (*thagavor)*: they supposed the word to be a misprint for *thughun* "frontier"). Prof. Margoliouth Tr.

(3) The *Beggar-Muqamah* of Abu Dulaf. Yatimah, III. Kindi, 419.

in repair, on Holy war and in other commendable objects"[1]. The town of Bikend —between Bokhara and the Oxus—is said to have had about 1000 hostels for soldiers fighting in the cause of the Faith; the town of Asbighab even 1700 where food for the needy was found and fodder for their animals. The zeal for the Holy war drove the Easterners, at the time of the great Byzantine successes, even to the western front. In 355 some 20,000 religious warriors appeared with elephants on the Eastern frontier of the Northern Buwayyid Empire. But their attitude was wholly unlike that of the warriors fighting for the Faith. The Commanding Officer of the frontier reported that they had no common leader but the warriors of each town had their own Chief. The Wazir hoped to satisfy them with little, as they were wont to do with people warring for their faith, but they claimed the entire land-tax of the country: you have hoarded the land-tax in the Treasury of the faithful to meet cases of need and emergency but what need or emergency can be greater or graver than to see the Greeks and Armenians Masters of our frontiers and the Faithful too weak to withstand them. They also demanded that the troops of the Prince should effect a junction with them. When their demands were rejected these tribes revolted charged the Government with infidelity, harried the town all night, marched about with swords, lences, bows and arrows and robbed the people of their head-gears as it was the month of Ramadhan and the people were out in the streets. They beat drums all night in their camp and threatened battle. In the morning they attacked the house of the Wazir who, in course of the attack, received a lance-wound and was constrained to seek safety at the castle of the Prince. His house, stables, store-rooms were rifled and when the Wazir returned home at night the found nothing to sit upon—no, not even a cup to drink from. Eventually he managed to suppress the rebels and avert the danger. Had they marched

(1) Istakhri, 290.

on with the resources at their command they would have defeated the Greeks. But God had willed otherwise[1].

SERMONS

When a man remarked to the Caliph Abdul Malik "You have become prematurely old". The Caliph replied: "No wonder, every Fridays I have to set my wits against that of the people"[2]. He is further reported to have said : "It would be splendid to rule without the clatter of the post-horses and the hard wood of the pulpit"[3]. Even for other leaders the weekly appearance before the community was an irksome duty—leaders more familiar with swords than with books. They, for instance, put forward before the community verses of the heathen poets as words of God[4].

Harun al-Rashid is said to have been the first who committed to memory sarmons prepared by others. His son Amin got his teacher, the grammarian al-Asmai, to prepare ten sermons for the mosques[5]. In the 3rd/9th century even in this small matter the good old simple ways of Islam had ceased.

High dignitaries gave up the weekly sermons and committed them to the charge of professional preachers[6]. It is related as something extraordinary of the devourt Muhtadi (255-256/866-867) that every Friday he ascended the pulpit

(1) Misk, VI, 283 ff; Amedroz, *Islam* III, 331 ff. Istakhri, 314; Muk, 273; Istakhri, 220.

(2) *i.e.* he had to speak in public, and might make a mistake in his Arabi.

(3) *Muhadarat al-Udaba* p. 821.

(4) Yaqut, *Irshad*, VI, 94.

(5) Tanukhi, K. *al-Faragh ba'd essiddah* 1, 19.

(6) With many governors their defective knowledge of Arabic stood in the way of discharging their ecclesiastical duties. The last Arab Amir of Egypt (238-242) was also the last who led the prayer. Kindi, 202 (Ed. Guest).

of the chief mosque[1]. Towards the end of the 3rd/9th century Mutadid led the prayer on the battle field, but never actually delivered a sermon[2]. Only on festive occasions did the ruler ascend the pilpit: but when the Caliph Muti (334-363/945-974) desired to preach at Bairam which concluded the month of Ramadhan, precedent was wanting as to how he was to act on the occasion[3]. A sermon of al-Tael, which he delivered in the year 363 on the occasion of the sacrificial feast, has come down to us. It is very brief and refers merely in a sentence to the legend relating to the feast. His sermon[4] slightly abridged runs thus: "God is great, God is great. There is no God but Allah. He has placed me as the administrator of my community etc. etc. God is great. He has entrusted me with the protection of my people, their goods and chattels and their wives and children. He has destroyed my enemies in the desert and in the country and has placed me as a good deputy over the earth and all that is within the earth. God is great. He commanded his prophet and friend to slay our father Ismael and without shrinking he was ready to do so. Come, therefore, to God on this great day with animals for sacrifice and you should come full of faith within you. God is great. My God bless Mohamed, the elect, his house, his followers and my fathers, the noble Caliphs. Help me in my Government and strengthen me in the caliphate which he has given unto me. I warn you, O Faithful, against the love of the world. Do not surrender your heart to that which passes away. I fear for you the Day of Judgment—when you will stand before God. Your page in the Book will be read out to you. May God help you and us in doing things pious: I pray God for forgiveness for myself, for you, and for all the faithful.

The Fatimid rulers, on the other hand, stressed the

(1) Masudi, VIII, 2.
(2) Abulmahsin , II, 87.
(3) Yaqat, *Irshad*, II, 349.
(4) Jauzi, fol. 106 b. The conclusion is the usual one as in Ibn Nubatah.

ecclesiastical aspect of the Caliphate and mounted the pulpit every Friday. They read out the sermon from a manuscript prepared by the *Diwn el-Insha* (drafting department)[1]. Until the construction of the mosque named after him Al-Hakim, for instance, preached one Friday at the Amr Mosque, another at that of Ibn Tulun, on the third at Azhar and rested on the fourth[2].

The *Khutbah* is not a sermon in the western sense of the term. It is merely a piece of liturgy which offered greater liberties to the officiating persons than the rest of the service (*i.e.* it was not stereo-typed,) like the prayers: For this reason precisely they did not expect anything new every Friday. It is specially noted of a preacher at Nisapur (d.494/1101) that he delivered a fresh sermon each time[3]. Ibn Nubatah, (d. 374/984), the court preacher of Saif-ud-Dawlah at Aleppo was the most famous preacher of the 4th/10th century. The collection of his sermons shows the art of preaching at its best in that age. The fact that the prophet Mohamed himself was no great orator, as the Muslim tradition affirms, has, at least, saved Islam, if not from all other dangers, at least from idle chatter. He has cammanded[4] to pray long but to preach little and, hence, it is that in Ibn Nubatah the actual sermon never lasts more than five minutes. A short praise of God and prayer for the Prophet preceded the sermon. The preacher, then, sat down soon to rise again to read the *Khutbah Thaniyah*, (second Discourse). 'Brief as the sitting of the preacher' was the complaint made by the contemporary poet Ibn Hamdis against a hasty meeting with the loved-one. The sermon proper always opened with a passage from the Qur'an, followed up with a stereo-typed

(1) Maqrizi, *Khitat* II, 55. Even of earlier times we hear that sermons were read but in Egypt, *Khitat*, II, 390.

(2) Suyuti, *Husnul Muhadhera*, II, 155.

(3) Subki, III, 285.

(4) Jahiz, *Bayan*, 1,117. p. 42—In the old Islam sermons were always short ; eloquence consisted in hitting off the point.

conclusion: "May God bless us and you through the verse quoted and through our pious meditation. I pray God for forgiveness for myself, for you and for all the faithful.[1] Even the ordinary service was much shorter than it is to-day[2]. Specially solemn was the passage where the preacher turned first to the right, then to the left, then straight in front invoking the blessing of God on the Prophet[3]. This part of the service was of great importance to the preacher as he had a number of texts to select from[4]. In the time of war the preacher prayed for victory for the ruler. For instance:—

God, grant to the Amir so and so victory over thy enemies, the refractory infidels, who have strayed away from thy path; who have denied thy revelations and have contradicted thy messenger. Let them have no army that is not destroyed. Let them have no desert to flee to; no blood left to be shed; no fugitive to escape; no fortress to capture or destroy; nothing holy which may not be profaned and nothing noble which may not be humbled and venquished.

O God grant him victory over thine enemies and place their forelock in his hands so that he may humble and eject them from their fortifications and they, in subjection, render tribute to him from near and afar[5].

The time allotted to the sermon was much too short to permit of a commentary on the text. From old times the

---

(1) Sermons. Ed. Beyrut, 6. Sahban (d. 54 H/673) was the most celebrated preacher and orator of the early days of Islam. One of the earliest extant specimens of an arab *Khutbah* in rhymed prose is by him. Chanery's *Hariri*, 1,309 Tr.)

(2) Two sermons (translated into English) from India and Egypt, Hugnes, *Dict. of Islam*, under *Khutbah* Lane, *Manners*, 73 (Ch III p. 84ff). One at the Court of the Almohades in Fagnan's tr. of the *Hist. of the Almohades* by Merrakechi p. 295ff.

(3) In Khorasan he did not do this, Muk. 327.

(4) Ibn Nubatah, 287ff.

(5) p. 321ff.

usual Friday sermon has but one theme: the end is near. For man, death and the grave; for the world , the Day of Judgment. And thus does the sermon run in a concise, nervous way. The little joys and sorrows of life are of no moment. Those that see the fire of Hell behind worry not about the flowers on the road-side. Already Ali is reported to have fervently preached: "Flee! Flee! Save yourselves, save yourselves. Behind you is the arch-enemy, intent on his work, hurriedly advancing towards you".

To describe the blessedness of heaven or even the tortures of Hell would have been too agreeable. Now all the rhetorical powers are concentrated on the moment when this life and this world would, with a fearful crash, come to an end. The important matter was to cry out *respice* finem (think of the end) to people who lived for the day more sensually and naively than we do.

Thus Ibn Nubatah (p. 69 ff):—

Rid the heart of thoughtlessness and the soul of lustful desires. Subdue licentiousness by the thought of the onrushing death. Fear the day when your sins will be recognized by their scars. Think of him who up on high calls from heaven; who makes the bones alive; who gathers mankind at a spot where illusions cease but where sorrow and repentance endure. A caller, indeed, who makes decayed bones listen; who gathers together vanished bodies from the eyrie of birds of prey and the flesh of wild animals; from the bottom of the sea and the ridges of the mountains until every limb finds its proper place and every part of the body is restored.

Then, a fearful trial will be your lot, O men, your faces will be covered with dust from the reeling of the earth and you will be livid with fright. You will be naked and bare-footed as you were on the day you were born. Then the

Caller will demand your attention. His look will pierce you through and through. Full of perspiration you will be covered with dust. The earth will tremble with all its burden—mountains will totter and fall and will be swept away by the rising wind.

> Wide open were the eyes,
> Not an eye could close:
> The station was crowded with heavenly and
> earthly folk:
> And whilst the creatures standing were
> awaiting the realization of what had been
> told them.
> With the angles[1] in their ranks all around:
> So, there surrounds them hell's darkness,
> There covers then smokeless flame,
> They hear it roar and gurgle,
> Showing forth wrath and anger,
> Here upon those that were standing sink on
> their knees.

The guilty then will receive their certain doom and even the pure will be in fear and trembling. And the Prophets will bow for fear of the Lord.

Then they will hear: where is the servant of God; where the son of his hand maid? Where is he who persisted in his delusion? Where is he who was torn away by death when unprepared? They will all be detected and called to account for the use they made of their lives. They will plead and prevaricate; they will stand in terror before Him who knows their most secret thoughts. Like lightning, then, God will thunder and with an iron rod He will rule. All their excuses will melt away before a Book regularly kept, the precise register of their sins.Then, indeed will the soul realize its plight, will have no companion or helper save the just but severe judge.

(1) Following Mary's emendation.

"And the wicked shall see the fire and shall have a fereboding that all shall fall into it, and they shall find no escape from it"[1]. May God lead you and us to the path of salvation and take away from you and us the burden of gloom and make the pure doctrine of the unity of God or light in the darkness of the Last Day! The word of the Creator is the richest source of wisdom and the brightest light in darkness.

"When one blast shall be below on the trumpet, and the earth and the mountains shall be lifted up and shall both be dashed in pieces at a single stroke. On that day the woe that must come suddenly shall suddenly come.

> And the heaven shall cleave asunder, for on that day it shall be reft;
> And the angels shall be on its sides, and over them on that day eight shall bear up the throne of thy Lord.
> On that day ye shall be brought before Him:
> No hidden deed shall remain hidden from you[2].

Of heaven there is very little talk and none at all of a theme very popular with us—meeting again after death. Much too engrossing was the fear of the last day and of Judgment! The words of a distinguished Arab lady: "I long for the Last Day to see my husband's face again" are often quoted as an amazing proof of a love which conquered the greatest of all terrors—the terror of the Day of Judgment[3]. All the sermons of Ibn Nubatah are in rhymed prose. The words all end on the same note. Even the introduction of rhymed prose in sermons is an innovation which dates from about the middle of the 3rd/9th century and, now, attains

(1) Qur'an, Sura, 18, 51, Rodwell's tr.
(2) Sura 69, 13-18.
(3) For instance. *Thufat el-Arus*, 162.

its highest point. Ibn Khallikan mentions a later preacher who, though aware of the new style, preferred the simpler one of the earlier days[1]. But noteworthy it is that even in this sphere the 4/10th century fixed the rules and settled the standard for later Islam[2]. If the rhetorical sermons of the Christians, delivered on important feast days, were nothing more or less than hymns in prose—the Muslim Sermons of the 4th/10th century were no different. The similarity between the two is too striking to permit any one to deny the influence of the Christian over the Muslim style. Possibly the Qur'anic style too was influenced by it.

The collected sermons of Ibn Nubatah contain sermons which he delivered on New Year's Day, on the anniversary of the death of the Prophet, on the Holy months of Rajab and Ramadhan, on the Feast of Bairam. His sermons on the Holy War, fruits of the warlike days of Saif-ud-Dawlah, are in no way inferior to the most famous models of the earlier days[3].

> You people, how long will you hear the warning without heeding it?
> How long will you allow yourself to be scourged without bestirring yourself?

Your ears seem to dissipate the words of the preacher or else your hearts are too proud to listen to them. Your enemies are up and doing and this because you are more lazy and languid than they.

---

(1) Intro. to Ibn Nubatah, 19.

(2) The sermon-Book of Abul Ala has preserved a fragment of the old style. It contains sermons for the Fridays, for the two festivals, for the eclipse of the Sun, for praying for rain, for mourning. They are alphabetically arranged. But they only represent rhymes in b,d,r,l,m,n, because other letters were too artifical and the style of the sermon demanded easy flow. Yaqut, *Irshad*, I, 182.

(3) Norden, *die antike Kunstprosa*, II, 844. The *Khutab al-Jihadiyyah* are said to have been composed in 348 when the Byzantines occupied Mayfariqin. Abulmahasin II, 349.

And the devil has roused them to maintain
his lies, and they have followed him.
Whereas the Almighty has called you to his
Truth and you have ignored the Call.
Beasts fight for wife and child and birds die
in defence of their nests.
And they have neither prophets nor
revelations.

Like camels, you, who have insight and intelligence. Law and wisdom, scatter away before your enemies or meet them in the mask of weakness and cowardice.

You should rather have attacked their country for you have the assurance of God's words and you believe in His reward and punishment.

God has distinguished you with power and strength and has made you the best of mankind.

Where is the undying ardour of Faith?
Where the Faith that shields and shelters you?
Where the dread of Hell-Fire?
Where the trust in the Almighty?
In His Holy Book verily has God said:—
"If ye be steadfast and fear God, and the foe
come upon you in hot haste, your Lord will
help you with five thousand angels in their
cognizances.

And this, as pure good tidings for you, did God appoint, that your hearts might thereby be assured—for only from God, the mighty, the wise, comes victory[1].

God claims faith and perseverance of you and He, in return assures help and victory.

---

(1) Sura, 3, 121 ff.

Do you not really trust him?
Do you doubt his justice and goodness?

Thus vie with each other in the Holy War with a pure heart and steadfast soul, with joy and promptitude.

Resolve firmly and tear the ribbon of sloth and shame from off your forehead.

Give your soul up to Him whom it belongs!
Rely not upon prudence, for it will not stave
of death.

"Be not like the infidels, who said of their brethren when they had travelled by land or had become combatants "had they kept with us, they had not died, and had not been slain!". God purposed that this affair should cause them heart-sorrow! And God maketh alive and killeth; and God beholdeth your actions"[1].

War, War, you men of courage!
Victory, Victory, you men of unflinching
resolve!
Paradise, Paradise, for you that go forward!
Hell, Hell, for you who fly!

The surest foundation of faith, the widest gate to Heaven and the steps that lead to the fairest garden there, is the Holy war.

He who stands by God, stands between two
rewards, universally coveted and worth
striving for:
the crown of victory in this and the martyr's
crown is the next world.
And of these the latter is by far the sweetest.
Thus stand by God for the War on behalf of

(1) Sura, 3, 150.

God is the surest citadel against perdition.
"And him who helpeth God will God surely
help; verily, God is strong, mighty[1].

The word of God is the most illuminating thing for chasing the darkness of the heart away.

Read: "O Believers: What possessed you, that when it was said to you, march forth on the way of God" ye sank heavily earthwards? Are you contented with the life of this world instead of the next? Yet the fruition of this mundane life, in respect of that which is to come, is but little. Unless you march forth, with a grievous chastisement Will He chastise you, and place another people in your stead, and ye shall in no way harm Him: for over everything is God potent"[2].

Only the colour of preacher's attire did the Government prescribe. When prayer was offered for the Abbasid Caliphs the Official black colour was used; in Fatimid countries the white colour. Since, however, there was no clergy or special ecclesiastical dress the preacher generally confirmed to the provincial tradition. In Mesopotamia and Khuzistan the preacher wore full military uniform : tunic and girdle[3]; whereas in Khorasan he used neither a mantle nor a tunic but only a coat (Durr'ah)[4]. In 401/1010 a Fatimid preacher preached at Mosul in a tunic of white Egyptian linen, a yellow head band, trousers of red brocade and shoes. The white tunic was regarded as sufficient official colour[5]. Only at Basra, the center of piety and Pharisaism in Mesopotamia, the official preacher preached every morning a practice which Ibn Abbas had followed. Elsewhere the official

(1) Sura 22, 41.
(2) Sura 9, 38 ff.
(3) Muk, 129 (Eng. tr. p. 207).
(4) Muk, 327.
(5) Ibn, Tagribirdi ed Popper, 107.

preacher preached only on Faridays leaving the rest of the week to private preachers who always were much too eager to volunteer their services. These were called *Qussas* "narrators" Goldziher has written their history[1]. Maqrizi, too, in one of his beautiful sketches, has collected a good many story about them. He makes an old tradition distinguish between the 'story-teller' (Qass) who was not *Makruh* (undesirable) and the official one such as was already appointed by Mu-awiya whose duty it was to pronounce the *dhikr Allah* after the morning prayer, to praise God, to say prayers for the prophet, the Caliph, and his supporters and to curse the enemies and the infidels[2]. In addition to these duties, after the Friday sermon he had to read and explain the Qur'an. This office was first held by the Qadhi. But, this fact is only attested regarding Egypt ; the office probably being an institution of the Egyptian church[3]. Even the Egyptian Qadhi, appointed in 204, was a *Qass* (Popular Preacher[4]. Then the union of the two offices ceases; while the Qadhi rises in importance, the other sinks into insignificance.

The Qass, appointed in 301/913, wanted to read the Qur'an daily but his superior officer would only permit this three days a week[5]. At the time of Mamun, in the East, the activity of a *Qass* and giving alms for his subsistence are

(1) Muh, Studien, II, 160 ff. There is a characteristic joke in *Aghani* regarding their method of preaching. Bashshar ibn Burd passing by a *Qass* heard him say: " For one who fasts in Rajab, Shaban and Ramadhan God will build a castle, the court yard of which will measure 1000 *parasangs* (1200 Kilometers) and doors 10 *parasangs* broad and high. Bashshar, turning to his guide said: The place must be very uncomfortable in January.

(2) *Khitat*, II, 253.

(3) *Khitat*, 253. The Qadhi of Misr appointed in the year 70 was also the official reader. He drew the same salary for this work as for his judgeship, namely 200 dianrs a year for each office. Kindi, 317.

(4) Kindi, 427.

(5) Maqrizi, *Khitat*, II, 254.

mentioned along with the building of a mosque, maintenance of orphans and donations for the Holy war as pious works[1]. In the West the *Qass* was a rare phenomenon (Muk 236). Malik ibn Anas, leader of thought there, was not favourably inclined towards him. (*Madkhal* of Ibn al-Hajj, 11, 21 ff.). In the 4th/10th century the *Qussas* had come down in the world to the level of the populace, to whom for money they related pious stories, legends and made jokes in mosques and on the streets. They prayed with the people and were much liked by them, (for example Makki 149. In 335/946 one such *Qass* at Tarsus described the Majesty of God so powerfully that out of sheer fright he fainted away and died. Subki *Tabaqat*, II,103).

For protesting against the heresies preached by a *Qass* at Baghdad the gate of the house of the theologian Tabari was pelted and barricaded with stones with the result that access in and out became impossible[2]. At the end of the 4th/10th century they were the Chief fomenters of the eternal riots between the Sunnis and the Shiahs[3]. The Sasanid-Maqamah of Hamadani simply classes them under buffoons. By this time they had completely forfeited the esteem and good-will of the pious circles who, now turned to their successors, the *Madakkirin*. Their devotional meetings were called *majlis ed dikr*[4]. It grew out of the voluntary litanies recited by the pious after the conclusion of the divine service[5]. The Sufis gave this name to their preachers. The following statement of Abu Talib al-Makki (d. 386/996) belongs to the period of rivalry between the

(1) Ibn Taifur, ed. Keller, 100. The Qass should be blind, grey-haired and have a powerful voice Jahiz, *Bayan* 141.

(2) Goldziher, M. S. II, 168 (see notes at the end of this chapter Tr.).

(3) Jauzi, fol, 152 f.

(4) Muk. 182, 13, I find the oldest reference in point of time to the *Mudakkir* in the poem on the siege of Baghdad under Amin, 198/813 in Masudi VI, 448.

(5) Muk 182.

Mudakkir and the *Qass*: the *dikr-meetings* are more valuable than the ritual prayer and the ritual prayer more valuable than *Qass*[1]. Already a distinction was made between the two: "There are three classes of religious teachers: those who sit on the stairs are the *Qassas* those who sit by the columns are the *Muftis*; those who sit in the corner of the mosques are the enlightened ones (die Leute der Erkenntnis). The *dikr-meetings* are the meetings of those learned in the lore of God, emphasising the unity of God and of the people of enlightenment[2]. The *Mudakkir* assumed a more dignified attitude than his predecessor the *Qass*. And this consisted above all in this that he never extemporised but always read out from a copy book. (Muk, 182, 327). Even to-day at Baghdad the bards invariably read out the heroic legends from a little book; whereas the Jewish Ikhbari, despised by them, always relates his stories freely.

The demands made of a Mudakkir by Abu Zaid es-Samarqandi (d. 375) show to some extent the procedure at their discourses, "he should be pious, contemptuous of the world, neither proud nor coarse. He should be conversant with the commentaries on the Qur'an with history, with the decisions of the jurists. He should report no tradition which he does not believe to be true. He should not be covetous but should only accept what is voluntarily given to him. In his lectures he should not excite only hope or fear but both. He should not be so lengthy as to exhaust the patience of his audience, for in that case, the benefit of knowledge vanishes. When required to be lengthy he should introduce matter which relieves the strain or which provokes laughter. The audience on the other hand, should punctuate his discourse with: 'good', 'true', to encourage the *mudakkir*. They should, further, repeat the formula of blessing each

(1) Kashf, 235, Ibn al-Hajj, Madkhal. II, 23. I could not find this in the *Kut al-qulub*.
(2) Kut al-qulub of Makki, p. 152.

time the name of the prophet is mentioned and should not drop off to sleep during the lecture hour[1]. The meeting for Edification dissolved when the members thereof rose to pray[2].

The legal digest, drawn up in the 3rd/9th century, do evidently know of litany-like repetition of certain words of prayer but attach not the slightest importance to it. After every prayer the prophet is said to have enjoined the repetition of *Subhan Allah* thirty-three times and of "thank God" and of "God is great" for the same number of times[3]. As early as the 2nd/8th century a man is contemptuously reproached for having learnt nothing at Mekka save old women's traditions, *viz.*, to invoke God from a copy book and to pray with pebbles[4].

In the collection of Darimi (d. 255/869) people are described sitting in a mosque, grouped in circles, with small pebbles in their hands, awaiting the morning prayer. Every such circle had a leader who directed. Repeat 100 times, God is Great! Then 100 times, *Subhan Allah*. The pebbles served as counters. A shaikh passing by them, angrily addressed them saying: They should rather count their sins[5]. Throughout the 3rd/9th century *dikr* (devotion) was regarded as of very little value. In fact theological works scarcely mention it. Only the fourth century distinguished *Du'a* (voluntary prayer for a fixed purpose) and understood thereby short pious ejaculations to God, the salutation, prayer before meals, morning and evening (Called *tasmiyah* "naming Allah"), and the hundred fold invocations to Allah which accompanied the faithful through the day's work[6].

(1) *Bustan el-arifin*, pp. 25 ff.
(2) Jauzi, fol. 896.
(3) Bukhari, 1,100.
(4) Yaqut, *Irshad*, VI, 109.
(5) *Sunan*, ed. Cawnpore, p. 38 cited by Goldziher, RHR, 1890, p. 299.
(6) The Iqd. which reflects the views of 3rd/9th century deals with these slight rites under the heading of prayer, I, 322; whereas Samarqandi

To this religious practice they attached an enormous value and ascribed to the Prophet the saying : "He who enters the Bazar and says: There is no God but God. He has no companion. To him belongs all power and all kingdom. He vivifies and kills. He lives for every and dies not. In his hands is goodness and He is supreme over everything". Whoever repeats this prayer God credits to his account 1000 times 1000 good deeds; wipes away 1000 times 1000 evil deeds and raise him 1000 steps higher[1]. The Egyptian Qadhi Abu Zur'ah (d. 302/914) presented[2] to the Prince Khumarwaihi a loaf of bread which he had blessed by repeating ten chapters of the Qur'an and 10,000 times the formula 'there is no God but God'. The lips of Bushengi (d. 467/1074) never ceased "mentioning God". Once a barber begged of him to keep his mouth shut to enable him to crop his beard but he replied: "you may as well ask the time to stand still"[3]. A savant appeared in dream to another after his demise with a diadem set with precious stones. He had secured forgiveness by uttering repeated blessings on the Prophet[4]. And a sufi authority even gives the assurance of the Prophet to the effect that no one would fare badly at the last hour of the Day of Judgment who would say Allah! Allah![5] In the place of little pebbles (or olive-berries) the rosary (Subhah) is now imported from the East for counting prayers[6]. Historically its practice is first referred to in a poem of Abu Nuwas who under the Caliph Amin (193-198/

---

devotes a special chapter to meditation (Andacht).

(1) Samarqandi *Tanbih*, 255.

(2) Abu Zulaq (d. 386/997), supplement to Kindi, 519.

(3) Subki, III, 229.

(4) Ibn Bashkuwal 1,134.

(5) Kushairi, 119.

(6) Mubarrad, (Cairo 1308). d. 367. (The story here rather refers to olive *plants*—a yet earlier reference is in Mubarrad, Kamil II, 80 in a line of Basshar Ibn Burd (d. 167 A.H.) and one yet earlier in a story about Uthman b. Hayyan (Governor of Medina 93 A.H.) Kamil, 1, 380 Prof Margoliouth, Tr).

808-813) begged for release from incarceration of the Wazir Ibn Rabi:—

You, Ibn Rabi, you have taught me piety......the rosary hangs from my arm and the Qur'an, like a chain from my neck[1].

In the 3rd/9th century theologians and savants derided the rosary, then only used by women and hypocrites. They found fault with better men, like Junaid (d. 297/909) for using it. Even in the 5th/11th century the rosary is mentioned as a special equipment of Sufi women[2]. From the very earliest times *Mau'izah*, the preaching of penance, has been the most favourite practice of men, lettered or unlettered, endowed with rhetorical gifts. Most common, indeed were these preachings during the Ramadhan, and on Fridays after the Prayer. And such indeed, is still the case in Egypt[3].

Great magnates sent for well-known preachers and asked them to preach so as to inspire fear in them and often enough they got more than they had bargained for[4]. For a public keenly alive to the charms of eloquence, a public preacher possessed amazing powers of attraction. With military or religious processions, with festivities, with jugglers and poets he shared the glory of feeding the popular imagination. Not infrequently they fell into the snares of their profession and made good business out of it, although the remark of Jaubari regarding these preachers that "they constituted the highest class of charlatans" (*Banu Sasan*) is not yet applicable to the period under consideration[5]. In the 4th/10th century, however, there were pious people who did not at all approvingly look upon these preachers[6] and

(1) *Diwan*, 108.
(2) Subki, III, 91.
(3) Mohammad Omar Hadir el-Misriyyin. Cairo 103.
(4) A number of such anecdotes, which show at least the current view, will be found in *Iqd*, I,290.
(5) *Revealed secrets* (Vienna, fol. 17 b).
(6) Samarqandi, *Bustan*, 22.

with just cause. The great preachers were artists by nature and, as brilliant orators, loved the brilliant fashions of the day. The most renowned popular preacher (Wa'iz) of Baghdad in the 4th/10th century was Abul Hasan ibn Sam'un (300-317/912-997)[1]. He used to dress and eat well for he declared that if you are at peace with God you may wear the softest garments and take the finest food without any harm to yourself. According to the Diary of the Sahib who heard him at Baghdad he was sufi. While preaching he sat on a stool of costly teakwood (Yaqut, *Irshad*, II, 319). When Adud ud-Dawlah forbade all preaching at Baghdad to prevent tension between the sunnis and the shiahs Ibn Sam'un defied the order. He was taken to the prince and he moved the stern soldier to tears by the verses of the Qur'an—the only time that he shed tears in his life[2]. He could also perform miracles. He cured a lame little girl by stepping on her. On one occasion member of the audience, sitting close to the preacher's stool, dropped off to sleep at a sermon. Thereupon Ibn Sam'un stopped for quite an hour (The Arabic probably means "for a time") until the man woke up. The preacher addressing him said : You were seeing the prophet in your dream and hence I stopped so as not to disturb you or interrupt your good fortune[3]. The Caliph Tai who frequently suffered from fits of passion sent for the preacher while in one of such fits. He related the history and repeated the sayings of Ali to him until Tai wetted his handkerchief with tears. The preacher, then, stopped and the Caliph presented him a packet containing perfume and other things[4]. Ali ibn Mohammad (d. 338/949), called Misri, on account of long residence in Egypt, used a veil to cover his face lest the women, hearing him preach, might be led

(1) He himself reports that his grand father Ismail called him Sim'un with 'i', *Tarikh Baghdad,* Paris, fol. 85 (See his life in Chanery's *Hariri,* Vol. I, p. 456-458) (Tr.).

(2) Jauzi, fol. 112 b.

(3) Jauzi, Berlin, fol. 141 a.

(4) *Tarikh Baghdad*, Paris 1, fol. 85.

astray by his handsome appearance[1]. Another popular preachers Abdullah es-shirazi (d. 439/1047) lived at first in a deserted mosque, collecting a number of poor people around him. Then he flung the ascetic's grab aside and donned fashionable garments. Finally he preached holy war, put himself forward as the leader and headed a considerable army to Adherbaijan[2]. Even a lady preacher of penance appeared at Baghdad in the 4th century—Maimunah bint Sakulah (d. 393/1002) "with a tongue sweet in preaching". She was an ascetic and once said : today is the 47th year that I have been wearing this shirt without tearing it. My mother had spun it for me. A dress in which no offence against God is committed, is never torn"[3]. These preachers had no official status at all. We do not hear even of an acknowledged savant of the century as a popular preacher then, whereas 200 years later a crowd of hundred thousand assembled to hear the preachings of Ibn al-Jauzi[4]. So unecclesiastical was Islam, indeed, that it let these unofficial preachers peacefully occupy the pulpit, the only difference—as they point out—between the official Friday preacher and these unofficial ones—was that while the former preached standing, the latter did so sitting on a stool. The great preacher of penance—Yahya b. Ma'd er-Razi (d. 258/872) for instance, ascended the pulpit at Shiraz, quoted some verses to the effect "the unrighteous preacher is he who does not act up to his preaching", and, then, stepped down from the stool (*Kursi*) and, for a whole day, said nothing[5]. At least in Egypt their old colleagues—Qassas—first read the Qur'an standing and then delivered their discourse sitting[6]. Even this practice must have had its

(1) Jauzi, fol. 89 a. It is reported that he said that the Kassas were a thing of the past.
(2) *Tarikh Baghdad,* f. 112 a.
(3) Tagribirdi (ed. Popper) II, 93.
(4) Zerkawi, 1, 63.
(5) *Zubdat al-fikrah*, Paris, folio, 20 a. Goldziher, ZDMG, 55, p. 607 note (1).
(6) Maqrizi, Khitat, II, 254.

origin in the Christian practice; for even today the Roman Catholic Lent-preachers do not address from the pulpit but from a dais in the centre and mostly seated on a stool.

A set of questions was handed over to those preachers which they were expected to answer. Of this practice I find proof only from the sixth century[1]. The Fatimid Court, strongly ecclesiastical in its tone and colour, actually had a preacher of penance as Court Official. He came next in rank to the Cabinet Secretary of the Caliph. His duties were to preach to the Caliph regarding the word of God and the histories of the Caliphs and prophets. Each time that he preached he received a paper (Kagid), put in an inkpot, with ten dinars and a parchment (Qirtas) with costly perfume to perfume himself for the next lecture[2].

MOSQUE

The mosques, with rare exceptions, were open day and night[3]. According to law they could be used as shelters for homeless, for travellers, for penitents and this employment of the mosque considerably lightened the hardships of life. There is a story told how, among others, a snake-charmer once spent a night at a mosque and how his basket got loose and the uncanny reptile crept about in the dark with the result that the narrator of the story spent an anxious night standing on the base of a pillar[4]. Even during the day the "Houses of God" were rarely empty (Baihaqi, ed.

(1) Ibn Jubbair, 221; Jauzi, Kit. a-Adkiya, 95; Qazwini, Cosmography, 214.

(2) Maqrizi, *Khitat*, II, 403.

(3) Thus in the Tulunid Old-Cairo the Chief mosque was closed after the evening prayer because the State money-chest stood before the pulpit (Ibn Rosteh *Geography* 116) (He should have said Fustal: Cairo is a Fatimid foundation). But when in 295 H the Governor again wanted to close it and only open it for prayers the people rose in revolt, Kindi, 266.

(4) Maqrizi, Khitat, 319.

Schwally, 483). They served as clubs or popular meeting-places, notably the Chief mosque where the Qadhi held his court and the savants lectured[1]. The places of the latter were marked by their prayer - mats. In case the authorities disapproved of any savants or his followers they simply threw the mats out of the mosque. Liveliest were the evening, for it is then that the tide of life is at its highest in the East.

It was about this time that Mukaddasi found the lectures of Jurists of Qur'an-readers, of literati and of philosophers thronged in the chief mosque at Fustat. I used to go, says he, with a number of people from Jerusalem and sometimes when we were sitting and chatting we would hear cries from behind and from front. "Turn towards the assembly", we would, then turn round and see that we were between two circles'. I counted 120 such circles[2]. In the mosques in Egypt people enjoyed great licence. The Easterner Ibn Haukal was surprised that at Fustat people had their meals in the mosques and that bread and water-sellers freely carried on their trade within their precints[3]. The Syrian Mukaddasi reports that the Egyptians spat and blew their noses in the mosques and deposited the stuff under their mats[4]. The small neighboring mosque was like a second house to the faithful, living under its shadow. Thither the merchant carried the shutters when he opened his shop[5]. In Persia in case of bereavement they sat three days in a mosque for comfort and consolation[6]. The mosque remained what it originally

(1) The orthodox reaction of the 3rd/9th century regarded this as a desecration. The Government forbade the Qadhi to hold his court in the Chief mosque and also forbade book sellers to sell books on philology and dialects. Abulmahsin, II, 86.

(2) p. 205.

(3) p. 341.

(4) p. 206

(5) Tunukhi, *Kit. al-faraj* II, 10.

(6) Muk. 400.

was the Bait *en-Nida* (Men's house), known to anthropology. There they found constant company for gossip and entertainment[1]. There the events of the night were related in the morning[2]. There poems were declaimed and even the web of love-intrigues woven[3]. There too the swindlers found a happy hunting ground for their activity as the two well-known collections of Maqamahs testify[4].

The following story comes a later time: "In the year 613/ 1216 I saw a pedlar at Harran who had trained a monkey to salute, to count the beads, to pick the teeth, to weep. On a Friday he sent a handsome, richly - dressed Indian slave to spread a fine prayer mat close to the prayer-niche. At the fourth hour the monkey rode to the mosque on a mule with a gilded saddle accompanied by three well-clad Indian slaves and greeted the assembly. To every one who enquired it was reported : that he was the son of king so and so, a mighty Indian ruler, but was be-witched. The monkey prayed in the mosque. He took his handkerchief out of his girdle. He picked his teeth. While doing these things the eldest slave rose, greeted the people and said: By God, friends, once there was none more handsome or more God-fearing than this monkey who is, now, before you. But the faithful is under God's decree. His wife has bewitched him and out of sheer shame his father has turned him out. For 100,000 dinars his wife will recall the curse but hitherto he has only collected 10,000. Pity, then, this youth, homeless and kinless. Only with that amount can he be transformed again. No sooner was this said than the monkey took his hand-kerchief to his face and wept. There, the hearts of the people softened and every one generously contributed to

(1) Hamad. Maqamah, 157.
(2) *Aghani*, XVII, 14.
(3) *Ya'imah*, II, 160; Jauzi Berlin, fol 48 a.
(4) A quick-change-artist who delivers his beggar-discourse on the most diverse good objects in all the mosques of Basra, in constantly changing figures, suggests to Hariri his work. Yaqut, *Irshad*, VI, 168.

the fund. The pedlar left the mosque with plenty of money. And thus he roamed about the countries[1].

Not till the 3rd/9th century did piety become sufficiently mundane to demand that the mosque should be worthily furnished and service asthetically conducted. Mamun is said to have ordered more costly illumination of mosques[2]. Syria specially, in imitation of the Christian example, distinguished itself by permanent illumination of its mosques. Lamps were hung by chains as in Mekka[3]. In the 4th/10th century huge oven-shaped lamps had come into fashion in the mosques. They were, indeed, called *Tanur* (baking ovens) and they offered ample scope to artists for skill and ingenuity. The guardian of Hakim presented to the Amr-mosque one such lamp and in 403/1012 Hakim himself put up there a huge silver baking-oven, 100,000 drachms in weight. To let it in the entrance door of the mosque was temporarily removed[4]. A part of the inventory of a great 'House of God' the Azhar-mosque, in the 4th/10th century is set down in its deed of endowment, dated 400/1009:—

Abbadan mats

Plaited mats

Indian aloe, camphor and musk for perfuming in Ramadhan and on other festive occasions.

Candles

Two for lamps

Charcoal for incense—burners

4 ropes, six leather water bags, 200 brooms for sweeping the mosque.

Oil for lamps

(1) Jaubaris, *Revealed secrets,* Vienna, fol. 25 a.
(2) Baihaqi, 473.
(3) Muk. 182.
(4) Suyuti, *Husnul Muhadhera,* II, 151.

2 huge silver lanterns
27 silver candle-sticks.[1]

The Azhar, indeed, was founded by al-Hakim[2]. The mosques stood under the supervision of the Qadhis. In the Fatimid Cairo they used to inspect them on the 4th of Ramadhan every year to see if they were in good repair and the mats and lighting arrangements were satisfactory[3]. Their upkeep was not very costly. They reckoned 12 dirhams in Egypt as their monthly expenditure. And yet an account of the year 403/1012 shows that there were 830 mosques in Egypt without any resources at all. In 405/1014 the Caliph, therefore, assigned as endowment a number of landed properties to meet, at least, the expenses of cathedral mosques where preaching was done; such expenses as their up-keep and the wages of the Qur'an readers, theologians and the muezzins. As regards the internal arrangements in the "Houses of God" I have unfortunately very little to say. In Aramaic countries the old tenacious cult of Baal with its true-worship has left its traces behind. The Palestinian-Tiberias had a jessamine mosque named after the trees which filled its court-yard[4]. In the mosque at Raqqah there were two vines and a mulbery tree[5]. In Egypt it was usual to use canvas-awning in mosques at the time of preaching,

(1) Maqrizi, *Khitat*, II, 274, of Suyuti, H.M, II, 151.

(2) 'Under the Fatimid Caliph, Moizz (359 AD, 969/970 AH) says Von Kremer, the great mosque of Cairo, Al-Azhar, was built and endowed. The endowment was considerably enlarged by Hakim. Khuda Bukhsh, *Politics in Islam*, p. 229. There is an article on *Al-Azhar* in the Oct, 1925 of the '*Nineteenth century* and after'. Tr.

(3) *Maqrizi, Khitat*, II, 295.

(4) Nasir Khusru, 56.

(5) This is typically German. They start a theory, and then, collect facts to support it. The existence of trees in the court-yard of the mosque does not at all establish any traces of the cult of Baal or any other cult. The planting of trees may have been pure accident and the naming of the mosque equally so. In India almost every mosque has trees within its compound Tr.

such as was done in circus in Hellenic days. And the same is reported of Basra and Shiraz (Muk, 205, 430). The Palace mosque at Baghdad had two pulpits (Jauzi, *Muntazim* fol. 67 b). In a mosque in Khurasan there were two huge brass pitchers for drinking water which was cooled with ice on Friday (Muk. 327) Already the mosque of Ibn Tulun had the typical court-yard fountain: ten marble columns supported a dome, underneath which was marble basin 4 yards in diameter. In the centre of the basin was a playing fountain, fringed by trellis work[1]. This domed- fountain took the place of the little domed-house which in other mosques served the purpose of the state-treasury. 100 years later the first fountain was built in the Amr-mosque on the spot where the little domed-treasury had stood[2]. Such a fountain with copper pipes was seen by Nasir Khusru 100 years later at Amida and the Syrian Tripoli[3]. Collections for the constructions of mosques were also made. In 226/841 some one collected subscription in Ispahan for the extension of a mosque. He appealed to each individual present in the mosque and collected a large amount, not disdaining to take even a ring or its value, a ball of yarn or its worth[4].

CHURCH MUSIC

In different countries the form of divine service developed somewhat differently. But at no important centre was the puritan tone of old Islam preserved; for the pre-Islamic cults made their way every where. In this respect the most striking development, now, is that of the liturgical music—the church choir. Even in the South Arabian San'a there were 22 *muezzins* (*i.e.* those who call to prayer). Out

(1) Suyuti, HM II, 153. That this was an innovation is evidenced by the fact that it was criticised. Ibn Tulun did not build the usual place for ablution in the mosque.
(2) Suyuti, HM, II, 151.
(3) Tran. 28, 41.
(4) Abu Nu'aim, Leiden, fol. IIb.

of this institution grew the official choir[1]. It was already the practice for the choir in Khorasan to sit on the bench, opposite to the pulpit and there to play the music with 'skill and melody'[2]. The sing-song recitation of the Qur'an, and imitation of the ecclesiastical practice, is forbidden by Malik but is sanctioned by Shafi'i and is today in vogue in the Muslim orient.[3] In 237/851 in some of the mosques of the Egyptian Capital but not in the great mosque, the Qur'an was sung with melody, a practice; which the Qadhi who had been sent thither by the orthodox reaction, forbade[4]. The Qadhi al-Adami at Baghdad (d. 348/959), called *Sahib al-alhan* (master of melodies), heard, once on a pilgrimage, a *Qass* (Preacher), in Medina in the mosque of the prophet, relate false stories. He, then along with another "Reader" began to recite the Qur'an and did so, so beautifully, that all left the *Qass* and gathered round him[5]. In 394/1003 two Qur'an readers secured a brilliant triumph. They found their pilgrim-caravan encompassed by the Muntefiq Beduins. "They recited the Qur'an before the Beduin Shaikh in a manner never recited before and lo! the Saikh let the caravan pass. Turning round to the two "Readers, the Shaikh said: For your sake I have lost a million dinars[6]. In the face of this, the miracle of Arion is naught but a mere trifle. From among these "Readers " the voluntary preachers of later days formed a choir who sat on stools opposite to the preacher[7]. To display his cleverness the preacher used to announce to the choir the rhyme of his sermon to enable them to employ the same cadence in their opening song. In the sermons

(1) Ibn Rosteh, III.
(2) Muk, 327.
(3) Muh, Omar Hadir al-masriyyin, Cairo, 1320, p. 106.
(4) Kindi, 469.
(5) Jauzi, fol. 88 b.
(6) Ibn al-Athir, IX, 129.
(7) Ibn Jubair, 221. The "Readers" of the Christian Church, serving at the altar were also called (Qurra). They sang the psalms of David in a tremulous voice. (Abu Nuwas supplement, Cairo, 1316 p. 80).

the clauses often rhyme throughout with the same letter[1].

Ibn Taifur (d. 278/981) makes Mamun say:- " A man comes to me with a piece of wood or board, perhaps worth a dirham. He reports : on it has the Prophet laid his hand or out of it has he taken a drink or he touched it and without any guarantee or proof I take it out of sheer love and veneration for him for 1000 dinars, more or less. I, then, place it on my face or on my eye to obtain the cure of an illness and yet nought else is it but a piece of wood which really can do no good nor yet has any virtue save the alleged touch of the Prophet"[2].

In the 4th/10th century the relic-worship of the *Sunnah* was distinctly confined to what was left by Mohamed or the earlier prophets, an indication that saint-worship then was still in its infancy[3]. The Sufi Shaikh al-Sayyari of Merv (d. 349 ff) gave a large fortune for two of the Prophet's hairs and directed that those hairs should be placed in his mouth when on the point of death (*Kashf*, 158). And indeed imposture throve in full swing. Thus as the beginning of the 4th/10th century a Jew offered for sale the treaty of the Prophet in which he remitted the capitation-tax of the Jews of Khaibar. The Wazir instantly declared it a forgery as it was dated 60 days before the capture of the town[4]. In a religion, exclusively based on a Book, the only

---

(1) Jaubari, Vienna, fol. 17 b.

(2) Ed. Keller, 76.

(3) To the relics mentioned by Goldziher, in his *Muh. Studien*. II, 356. ff. I may add some more : the bed of the Prophet which was purchased by a client of Muawiya after the death of Ayesha, for 4000 dirhams (*Kit. Alif Ba*, 1, 131, according to Ibn Kutaiba); the mantle and a treaty, inscribed on leather, entered into by the prophet, preserved in the Syrian *Edroh* اذرح Muk, 178.

(4) Wuz, 67 f. A similar story is related of the Khatib al-Baghdadi who declared the treaty of Khaibar as forgery. Yaqut, *Irshad*, 1, 248 (See Prof. Margoliouth, *Arab Historians*, p. 149). (Tr.)

unchallenged relics, in mosques, would be the old copies of the Qur'an which had passed through the hands of Othman and which, as such, would be regarded as genuine words of God. Of such there were five copies, the famous Qur'an of Asma in the Amr-mosque at Misr from which they read out three times a week and which the Fatimid Caliphs venerated[1]. Next in the great mosque of Damascus—the information only dates from the 6th/12th century—was shown the only Qur'an which the Caliph sent to the Capital of Syria. After prayer the public was permitted to touch and to kiss it to obtain a blessing[2]. The Qadhi sent to Misr, in 237/851, appointed, for the first time, an officer to inspect the Qur'ans in the mosques which had amazingly multiplied in the 4th/10th century —a fact, indicative of the credulity of people in these matters[3]. A Mesopotamian came with a Qur'an which he passed off as that of Othman. The blood stains on the book were shown as proof of its genuineness It was preserved in the mosque and was, henceforward, read alternately with the other. In 378/988 the intruder was removed[4]. In 369/979 a Qur'an of Othman was also found in the possession of the caliphs of Baghdad[5]. And, finally, in the State treasury, at the mosque in Cordova, there lay a Qur'an which was so heavy that two men were required to carry it. It contained four folios of the Qur'an of Othman Ibn Affan with his blood stains. Early on Fridays, this Qur'an was fetched out by two servants of the mosque; while a third preceded it with a candle. It was covered with a finely-embroidered cover and used to be placed on a stool in the *Mussalla*. The Imam would read half a section (Hizb) and, then it would be taken back to the treasury[6].

---

(1) Abulmahasin, II, 472.
(2) Ibn Jubair, 267.
(3) Kindi, 469.
(4) Maqrizi, *Khitat*, II, 254.
(5) Jauzi, fol. 116a.
(6) Idrisi. *Description de Afrique* at de Espagne, 210.

Other relics were sparingly preserved in the Provincial mosques; for their theology had no room for these Christianisms. In the mosque of Hebron lay a shoe of the Prophet[1]; in the *Mehrab* of the mosque of the commercial town of Qurh there was reported to have been a bone which administered a warning to the Prophet; 'Eat me not for I am poisoned'[2].

SPIRIT OF MOCKERY

Alongside of a heightened religious tendency there subsisted a contempt of all things religious and ecclesiastical. And this spirit of derision and raillery reveals itself now in a manner, never revealed before. Form the standpoint of 'Rationalism' the Syrian poet Abul Ala attacks everything Islamic (born 368/974; d. 449/1057). He descended from a clever stock, a family of Qadhis[3]. At the age of four he was blinded by small pox[4]. He studied philology and composed a number of philological works. At the age of 37 he returned from Baghdad to his native town "without God or gold" intent on accepting no service and on keeping himself aloof from the world "like the little chicks who separate themselves from their shell" and determined to leave his town no more even when the inhabitants were flying away therefrom for fear of the Greeks[5]. He resolved to fast continually; omitting to do so only on two "festivals"[6]. He lived on an annual stipend of a little over 20 dinars, half of which he gave away to his servant. Despite this he declined a pension which the highest ecclesiastic at Cairo offered to him and, indeed, with

(1) Goldziher, 362.
(2) Muk, 84.
(3) Yaqut *Irshad*, I. 163.
(4) JRAS, 1902, 296.
(5) Letters ed. Prof. Margoliouth, 34.
(6) JRAS 1902, 298.

perfect sincerity[1]. In old age he was so crippled that he had to pray sitting.

A philosopher in the technical sense he was not. He lacked the mentality of the Greek school. He did not feel the need of profound investigation. He was essentially a man of Letters, a reformer, a kind of Tolstoi. He preached Rationalism and the gospel of simple life . He was a strict vegetarian abstaining not only from flesh but also from milk, eggs, honey[2]. He was an opponent of superstition, astrology, indeed of everything that smacked of theology. "Awake, awake, you fools, your religions are but an imposture of your forbears[3]. "Men expect an *Imam* to rise — a vain delusion. There is no *Imam* save "Reason" "Religious doctrines are naught but means to enslave man to the mighty"[4]. "All religions are equally in error. They are fairy tales invented by the cunning of the ancients". "The most undesirable denizen of the earth is the theologian"[5].

> "Worst villians dwell in the Valley of Mekka,
> While drunk they lead the pilgrims by twos
> into the Holy House."

(1) JRAS 1902, 304. Just at the time when this happened and when Abul Ala's fortune was so very slender the Persian traveller Nasir Khusru passed through Ma'ura. He stopped there only a day, did not see the poet, but he relates: " He was regarded as the Chief of the town, had great wealth and numerous slaves and servants. All the citizens are his subjects. He himself has renounced the world, uses garments of hair and never goes out of his house . His nourishment consists only half of a mann (weight) of barley-bread. His door is always open to visitors. His officers and adherents administer the town. Only in matters of importance they consult him. He never refuses monetary aid. He always fasts, keeps awake all night, and has nothing to do with wordly affairs". The poet, however, himself complains: 'People think I have money and hence, they expect money of me. Kremer, 101, Bombay Edition p. 40.

(2) JRAS 1902. 304.

(3) Kremer, ZDMG 30, p, 40.

(4) Kremer, p. 43.

(5) Kremer, pp. 5, 53.

For cash they let in Jews and Christians there[1]. In vain did his Egyptians Correspondent expect "Some light on religion" from him[2]. The poet had nothing to offer as moral lesson save simple life and cheerful resignation. The same idea is expressed in his answer to a famous letter of Ibn al-Qarih[3] in his highly ingenious but badly composed *Risalat el-Gufran* in which he speaks of many things, even of heaven and hell, of heresy and rationalism. And precisely, for this reason his teaching seemed to many of his disciples vague and shadowy.

While the theologians disputed whether the Qur'an was created or not; while Ibn Furak (d. 406/1015) could not sleep in a house where a copy of the Qur'an was, out of respect for the word of God[4]; Rawendi (d. 293/906), one of the most accursed names among Muslim heretics, maintained that the orator Aktam ibn Safi wrote finer prose than was to be found in the Qur'an. "How can we prove the prophetship of Mohamed by the Qur'an? Had Euclid asserted that a book like his could not be produced by man—would he, thereby, establish himself as a Prophet"[5]. Abulhusain ibn Abi Bagl, a high official, was reproached for ridiculing the Qur'an and writing a book on its imperfections (Uyub)[6]. But, now, Abul Ala composes a rhymed parallel to the Qur'an, divided into suras and verses[7]. The literary historian al-Bakharzi has preserved a fragment which shows its veiled sarcasm. To the objection that it lacked the grandeur of the Qur'an the author replied: You will judge its worth when its language has been polished for 400 years in the prayer-niches[1]. There

(1) ZDMG 30 p. 45.
(2) JRAS, 1902, 308.
(3) Yaqut, *Irshad*, V, 424.
(4) Subki, III, 53.
(5) Abulfida, *Annales*, Year 293.
(6) Wuz, 270.
(7) Several fragments are collected by D.S.M in the *Centenario dit M. Amari*. A portion of the work is said to be still in existence Tr.

was also the tolerant irreligion of the man of the world and the incessant raillery of the frivolous. Abu Hurairah, an Egyptian poet of the first half of this century sings:—

"Let me be impious, O God, let me be unlucky
Only let one of my hands all my life rest on the loved one's thigh and the other hold the cup of wine"[2].

His contemporary and countryman the court-poet of the Prince ventured the prayer:—

"We pray to the call of the Zither and listen to the note of the string.
The leader of our prayer prostrates himself before the cup and bends over the *flute*[3].

In his wine songs Ibn al-Hajjaj blasphemes more than ever:—

Outwardly a Muslim am I but really a Christian when flows the wine.
We like to pray with the Zither—the first prayer a *Suraigiyyak* and the last a *Makhuri melody*.
Reach sweet wine unto me—the wine which Qur'an forbids, the wine which enlists me into Satan's band.
Give me wine to drink on the day of the Mihrjan and even on the last day of Ramadhan[4].
Hand me a drink—with my very eyes I have

(1) Goldziher, ZDMG, 29, 640.
(2) Tallquist, 103.
(3) Sulami (d. 394); *Yatimah*, II, 171.
(4) He probably means Ramadhan 27th. (ليلة القدر)

seen my place in the deepest depth of hell[1].
Give me wine to drink which the Revelation
forbids, Give it unto me—the Christian
priest and I will then discharge it in hell[2].

On the piety of the common-folk we possess but slight information. It had many firm beliefs and marked tendencies which led to religious riots. A Karmathian leader was executed in 289/901 at Baghdad and his body was suspended at the pillory. "The people spread the rumour that before his execution he told one of them: take off my head-band, keep it, for I will return after forty days! Heaps of people used to gather near the pillory where he was suspended, counting the days and quarrelling over the matter. When the forty days were over—there was a great consternation. Some said: 'There is his body'. Others said : It has disappeared. The Government has killed and impaled another in his place to avert trouble. And there actually was trouble[3]. Even Mohamed al-Fergani (d. 362/972), who was closely related to the Prince, thought it worth his while to thus record the event in his history. Abu Sahl ibn Yunus es-Sadafi (d. 331/942) whom Ikhshid, the Prince of Egypt, very much revered and whose blessings he sought in writing, for he never met him in person, relates in 330/941: at Maifariquin a Christian hermit saw a bird dropping pieces of flesh and then flying away. Of themselves the pieces jointed together, forming a human body. And lo! the bird came and started picking at it. The unfortunate one begged the monk's aid and represented himself to be Ibn Muljam, murderer of Ali. The monk thereupon, left his tent, accepted Islam and related the incident to Abu Sahl[4].

A Bukhara poet, at the end of the 4th/10th century,

(1) *Yatimah*, II, 242. According to Muslim belief the dead sees the place which he will occupy in heaven or hell after the Day of Judgment.
(2) *Yatimah*, II. 263.
(3) Masudi, VIII, 204 f.
(4) *Kit al-Uyun*, IV, fol. 207b.

reflects that aristocratic spirit in religion which dominates the Muslim Orient to-day, a spirit which leaves the strict fulfilment of prayer and such like duties to the rich and prosperous. The poor do not even regularly pray[1]. Says the poet:—

> My wife taunts me that I do not pray to God.
> I reply : get thee gone, thou art divorced,
> Prayer is not for the poor but for the rich and the powerful.
> It is for Tash, Bektash, Kanbash, Nasr ibn Malik and the patricians.
> It is for the war-lord of the Orient whose store-houses are full to overflowing.
> Naturally Nuh, the ruler of Bukhara, prays—
> Verily the Orient bows to this authority.
> Why should I pray? Where is my power, where my house,
> My horse, my harness, my house, my girdle?
> Where my moon-faced slaves, where my pretty charming slave- girls?
> Where I to pray, when not an inch of the earth is lawfully mine, I would be naught else but a hypocrite.
> I have left the prayer for those that are

---

(1) This is anything but true of India where the rich ignore and the poor sedulously fulfil the religious obligations of Islam. The piety of the poor stands, here in striking contrast to the scepticism and irreligion of the rich. One of our Indian poets has his fling at the Almighty in the following lines incomparable beauty:

کہیں کہیں نہ عدو مجھکو دیکھ کر محتاج
یہ ان کے بندے ہیں جنکو کریم کہتے ہیں

(This is quite false in reference to Egypt writes Prof. Margoliouth to me Tr.)

prosperous.
Fool is he who censures me for not praying.
Yes! if the Almighty should bless me with prosperity I would never cease praying so long as lightning shimmered in the sky.
But the prayer of the poor is naught but a fraud.

The wavering fortune of War in the west made, indeed, severe demands on the faith of the faithful. When in 322/934 the Byzantines captured Malatia their general is said to have put up two tents, one bore the cross. In this tent took shelter those inhabitants who, by accepting Christianity, sought to save their wives, children and money. The other was meant for those who persevered in their Faith. To such as took shelter there, only their lives were spared. Most of them, indeed, became Christians[1]. After the reconquest of Laodicaea by the Greeks, many Muslims emigrated but many remained behind and paid, in their turn, the capitation-tax, 'I think, says ibn Haukal, they will accept Christianity because of the horror of this humiliating exaction and of the desire, enforced by duress, for honour and pleasure"[2]. The echo of the victory of the unbelievers should but faint in the heart of the Empire. They had indeed too great a trust in Allah. The explanation of the misfortune was, indeed, the usual one. It serves indeed, if anything, as a proof of the truth of Islam. And the explanation was that Islam must atone for the sins of its professors[3].

(1) Ibn-al-Athir, VIII, 221.
(2) p. 127.
(3) Subki, *Tabakat II*, 184.

NOTES

I

Qass, Qassas, Pl. Qussas.

Goldziher : Muh, Student, Vol. II PP. 161-170

Qass or Qassas (Pl. Qussas) were those who collected people round them in the streets or in the mosques without any official sanction to amuse or edify them with traditions. They were only distinguished by the subject-matter of their discourse from those profane story-tellers who collected the public around them in street corners to amuse them with funny stories and anecdotes[1]. These latter apparently performed the same function as the comic papers do in our days. They were even attached to the Caliph's Court. In the earliest days of Islam the term 'Qass' was not associated with that uncomplementary significance which, in the course of its historical development, was later associated with it. Indeed the name was inherited from worthy forbears; the Prophet having himself used the word 'Qass' in reference to his own pronouncements[2]. And, in traditions, the Prophet refers to pious preachers, called 'Qass' in terms of highest appreciation[3]. The Muslim tradition traces this institution to the earliest times of Islam. Omar is said to have expressly permitted the pious Temim al-Dari, according to others, Ubayd b. Umeyr, the first 'Qass; in the real sense of the term, "to narrate to men"[4]. And up to the Omayyad period—specially the well-known Ka'b under Muawiyah—pious men are mentioned who, with the consent of the orthodox authorities, carried on the calling of independent preachers and who, by pious stories and exhortations, sought to

(1) We meet such story-tellers in the circle of Wits. *Aghani* XXI. p. 90 line 7; al-Mubarrad, 356.

(2) Sura 7 : 175; 12 : 3.

(3) Jauzi, fol 9: Masudi, VIII, 161 ff.

(4) Jauzi, fol, 16-17.

strengthen faith, to encourage virtue, to brighten the hopes held out by Islam. We meet them on the battle-fields. Like poets, in the[1] Heathen times, then, by pious admonitions, animated and inflamed the courage of the religious warriors. One of the oldest notices that we possess on this branch of Muslim society, is the account of the three 'Qassas' in the camps of the warriors who in the seventies of the Higra marched out, in the caliphate of Merwan I, under the leadership of Sulaiman b. Shurad, to avenge Husain. They fanned the fanaticism of the warriors by thus arranging the plan of their work. While two of them worked at definite units of the army, the third wandered to and fro, now here and now there, constantly inciting the troops with fiery words[2]. In the third century, too, we hear of this activity of the 'Qassas'. A man, called Abu Ahmad al-Tabari, received the surname of 'al-Qass' because in the wars against the Dailamites and the Greeks he accompanied Muslim troops and fired them with pious stories[3]. Even as expounders of Qur'an they were well thought of.

In this connection to men of the third century—Musa al-Uswari and Amr b. Kaid al-Uswari—stand out conspicuous in Iraq. The former delivered lectures on the Qur'an simultaneously in Arabic and Persian; the Arabs sitting to his right, the Persians to his lift. He spoke in the two languages with equal ease and fluency. "This constitutes a world wonder, observes Jahiz, for when two languages are spoken by one person he generally mixes up the two to the detriment of both. This Musa, however, was a rare exception to the rule". The other Uswari delivered such through lectures on *Tafsir* that he required forty-six years

---

(1) Cf. Goldziher, Vol. I, p. 44. According to Dinaweri (p. 128, line 15) Sa'd employed the old poets Amr b. Madikarib, Kays, b. Hubayra and Shuahbil b. al-Samt before the Battle of Qadasiyya to encourage and inflame the Arab warriors.

(2) Tabari II, 559.

(3) Ibn Mulakkin (Leiden Ms) fol. II a. *Tandib*, p. 741.

to go through the whole of the Qur'an. He devoted, indeed, several weeks to the elucidiation of a single verse[1]. Till now the "Qussas" had served their religious purpose either as homiletic preachers or narrators of pious stories. In their activities they were left free and unhampered. The official theologian, indeed cheerfully tolerated these voluntary preachers and popular theologians. The 'Qassas' whether they preached in the mosques or in the streets, adapted themselves to the mentality of the people and spread, among them, those ascetic tendencies which the official theologians, nursed first and foremost on law, shelved and ignored. Among the 'Qussas', indeed, these tendencies found their champions and exponents. Jahiz gives us extracts from the preachings of these men[2]. We are not informed that in the exercise of their calling, which supplied a lacuna in the religious life of Islam, they were any where or in any way opposed or interfered with.

II

The opposition was only against the use and misuse of the Qussas-system. The measures, of which we hear, are measures directed against those unscrupulous charlatans, who, in defiance of religion, amused people by the invention and circulation of false traditions or sought to give a false colouring to religious stories. The wrath of the conservative theologians was directed only against this unwatranted use of legends.

We are in possession of information regarding the earlier times. The oldest notice is the information of Sa'id b. Jubayr[3], preserved in Bukhari, which says that a 'Qass' called Nauf.

(1) Kit *al-bayan*, fol. III b.

(2) *Bayan*, fol 127 b. (for instance from the prechings of Abd al-Aziz al Qass).

(3) *Tafsir*, No. 163 to Sura 18 : 60.

b. Fadala, worked in Kufa—Ibn Abbas calls him an enemy of God—who denied the identity of the Prophet of Israel with the Moses referred to in the Qur'an in connection with Khidr (The reference is to Surah XVIII, 59 and 99). This report projects later conditions into those earlier times[1]. As soon as the danger was perceived, which threatened the correct preservation of traditions from the side of the 'Qussas'—they tried to discredit them by linking up their early history with Kharijites[2].

The persecuting zeal began against them only when these street preachers multiplied to such an extent in Iraq that Ibn Aun (d. 151 H) reported that in the mosques of Basra while only one single group gathered round the Lecturer in Jurisprudence, countless groups formed round the 'Qussas'. Indeed the mosques were full of them[3]. The following story illustrates the credulity of the populace : The poet Kulthum b.Amir. Al-Attabi, who lived in the days of Harun and Mamun, once collected a crowd around him in a mosque and *seriously* quoted the following tradition to them: "He who can touch the tip of his nose with his tongue will not go to hell". Immediately as though on a signal, all present there stretched out their tongues to see if they possessed that mark of predestination[4]. It is not difficult to see that the light, entertaining stories of the 'Qussas' possessed far greater attraction for the people than the heavy stuff of the pedantic theologian, specially so as the 'Qussas' never shrank from any means or method to draw the folks to them. Jahiz gives us an illustration of the unbounded

(1) To this class also belongs the information in Al-Yaqubi (II 270) according to which Al-Hasan took a man to task who worked as a 'Qass' in Medina before the mosque of the Prophet for only the Prophet could assume such a title.

(2) Jauzi, fol. 18.

(3) Jauzi, fol II.

(4) *Aghani*, XII, 5.

frivolity in the stories of a 'Qass' called Abu Kab[1]. We, hear, now of measures initiated by the Government against the 'Qussas'. In 279 H it was proclaimed in the streets of Baghdad that neither in the streets nor in the mosques a 'Qass', an astrologer, or a sooth-sayer, would be allowed. In 284 H the proclamation was repeated[2]. The juxtaposition of the 'street-preachers' with astrologers and sooth-sayers indicates the view which the official circles took of the profession of the Qass'. Shortly after this Government measure, Masudi unfolds a lively picture of the common-folk of his time. "They only collect round men with bears and monkeys. They pursue false-saints and miracle workers. They lend ear to the lying 'Qass' or flock to see one sentenced to flogging or condemned to the gallows"[3]. As to the reasons that led to the Government measures referred to—more illuminating than even Masudi's account is a document, dating from the fourth century, which comes from the pen of the poet and humourist Abu Dulaf al-Khazragi. He composed a *Qasida*, immensely instructive from the point of view of cultural history[4]. He described in it the acts and deeds of the so-called *Mukaddin* or as they were still otherwise called '*Banu Sasan*'. Its commentory constitutes a mine of rich and diverse information on the social conditions of those times[5]. We have made the—

---

(1) *Kit al-Haiwan*, fol 121 b.

(2) Tabari, III p. 2131, line 3 p. 2164. Abulmahasin, II 87 line 2. In this very proclaimation the bookseller is also forbidden to sell philosophical and dialectical works.

(3) Masudi, V, 86.

(4) Also in lexical sense. By this *Qasida* the dictionaries have been extraordinarily enriched. Even before him Ahnaf al-Okbari, called 'Shair al-Mukaadin' had composed a similar but shorter Qasida. In both of these *Qasida* these charlatans are brought in speaking.

(5) On the origin of the appellation 'Banu Sasan' see Commentary to de Sacy's Hariri p. 23. These interesting excerpts, belonging to this literature, serve as a commentary. Houtsma has published them. We see from p. 250 how these charlatans were connected with 'Qussas'.

acquaintance of these *Banu Sasan* from the XLIX maqamah (Al-Sasaniya) or Hariri. Abu Zaid, in his testament, dedicates his son to the adepts in the Sasanian art[1]. In the treatise of Abu Dulaf a picture is drawn of swindlers, buffoons and impostors of the worst types. Everywhere the 'Qass' is found side by side with miracle-workers and amulet-writers:—

Among us are such who tell us of Israel (commentary: the stories of the Prophets) or span on span (*i.e.* short stories, about a span square) such stories, on that account, they call, al-Shibriyyat[2]. Then there are among us those who had down *Isnad* to fill almost a library[3].

Among others they practice the following trick. They collect a large crowd around them. One 'Qass' takes his stand at one end of the street and quotes traditions regarding the excellence of Ali[4]. At the other end, at the same time, stands his colleague who glorifies Abu Bakr with exceeding glorification : capturing thus at once the dirham of the Nasibi[5] and that of the Shiite[6]. They then share the proceeds among themselves. This state of affairs continued on. In the VIth century the rhetorician Ibn al-Athir speaks of the 'Qussas' and the buffoons in one and the same breath[7]. This grouping of the two under one classification is not strange, when we read the characteristics of these 'Qussas' drawn by Jauzi, in his treaties, composed about this time. "There

(1) De Sacy's Hariri, 659 ff.

(2) *Yatimah*, III, 179. One might understand by the expression '*Spanne auf spanne*" (short stories about a span square) that these "Qussas" pretended to know the minutest details of their stories cf. *Ja'rif bishibr*, ZDPV p. 166, I fancy the word SHIBR here is a HEBRAEISM and means "fragment". But see LEVY , NEU HEBRAISCHES WORTER BUCH, IV 502 for the full explanation.

(3) *Yatimah*, III, p. 184, line 4.

(4) They also mourn over Al-Ḥusain. We learn from *Yatimah III*.

(5) ZDMG, XXXVI, 281 note 1.

(6) *Yatimah*, III, 182.

(7) *Al-mathal al Sa'ir*, 35.

were among them those who smeared their faces with all kinds of spices to make their complexion yellow, the ascetics distinguishing sign. Others used stuff to cause the flow of tears at any desired moment. Others went even so far in playing to the gallery that they would throw themselves down from the pulpit which, contrary to the usual practice, they decorated with variegated rags; or, in contravention of the Eastern Orators' Convention, would display false pathos by gestures and postures, striking the pulpit with their feet etc etc. Others attracted women by fine dresses and effeminate ways—opening up, thereby, opportunities for unchaste practices[1]. Their immodest exterior corresponded with the contents of their lectures. "While the Qussas" of the earlier times won the esteem and regard of the pious theologians by the moral and religious tone of their preachings—the street preachers of the later days rioted and revelled in the profanation of religious materials for public entertainment. By charlatanism and far-fetched etymology[2] they imposed upon the unlettered and created the impression of profound learning.

Biblical legends, adorned and amplified by fables and fictions, formed the staple of their preachings. They loved to relate their fabrications regarding Biblical persons; that particular branch of study, 'Israiliyyat',—traditions concerning the heroes of the Israelite times which made their way even into serious exegetical works—found in them its most assiduous promoters[3]. They sought to make it attractive by weaving all kinds of frivolous stories into it. And, thus, they gave appearance of being intimate with the minutest details of the sacred History. They left no question unanswered; for a confession of ignorance would have shaken their authority with the people. A 'Qass', for instance,

(1) Jauzi, fol. 101-106.
(2) Yaqut, I, 293, II, 138.
(3) *Itqan*, II, 221 *Tawarikh Israiliyya*.

knew the name of the golden calf and, when questioned as to authority, he mentioned the 'Book of Amr b. al-Asi' as the source of his information[1]. Another knew the very name of the wolf which had devoured Joseph and when it was pointed out to him that Joseph was never devoured by a wolf he got out of his embarrassment by saying; never mind, that was the name of the wolf that did not devour him[2]. With equal levity they encountered profound theologians who unmasked their imposture. It is easy to understand that in the pedantic theologians they saw their worst opponents. As at Basra, so every where, the common folk flocked to the 'Qussas'. Their lectures were far more crowded than those of the trained theologians who found in them their dangerous rivals. By the cunning and imposition referred to above they managed to pass for savants and indeed, they were rated much higher than learned men by training and profession. The mother of Abu Hanifa, wanting an explanation of some religious question, first applied to her learned son for the explanation but, not satisfied with it, she went with him to the Qass Zara and only when he confirmed, in Abu Hanifa's presence, his opinion, was the mother satisfied[3].

But not all were so meek and mild as Zara towards acknowledged savants. Generally they opposed them with a marvellous imperturbability and, indeed, had the people always on their side. We have quoted such examples in the foregoing pages and they may be indefinitely multiplied. Their mutual relation is, indeed, illustrated by a number of anecdotes The traditionist Al-Sha'bi (d. 103H)—so it is related—saw on a Friday, Palmyra, an immense crowd round an old man with flowing beard, taking notes of his lecture. Among other things he spoke, with Isnad, going

(1) *Mubarrad*, 356; *Iqd*. II, 151 Cf. Masudi, IV, 23, 26.
(2) Jauzi, fol. 129.
(3) Jauzi fol. 129.

up to the prophet, of the two trumpets on the Day a Judgment from which two sounds will issue: One laying down all in a state of lifeless prostration and the other recalling them all to a new life. The traditionist could not endure this falsification of the Qur'anic eschatology and reprimanded the preacher by telling him that he had made two trumpets out of one. The preacher reported: Thou, evil doer, how dearest thou challenge what I have narrated with correct chain of traditions right up to the Prophet. And he took up his shoe and called upon the crowd to strike Sha'bi. And the people agreed to beat him until he swore that God created thirty trumpets[1]. Even if this story is not strictly historical, it is characteristic atleast, of the attitude of the learned theologians towards the 'Qussas' and the part taken by the populace in the frequent encounters between them. In a somewhat similar position Tabari found himself by his energetic opposition to a lying 'Qass'. A 'Qass' was preaching all kinds of things to the people. Among others he explained verse 81 of sura 17 as meaning that God assigned a place to Mohamed on His throne by His side. When Tabari heard of this un-Islamic doctrine he thought it his duty to enter a protest against it. He wrote on the door of his house : God be praised! who needs no compa-nion and has none to sit with Him on His throne. When the people of Baghdad saw this inscription, aimed as it was, against their popular street-preacher they besieged the house of the much-esteemed *Imam* and pelted his door with stones blocking the entry[2].

From all that has been said the reader may draw his own conclusions regarding the danger which the activity of such a class of preachers spelled to the correctness and integrity of the *Hadith* and the share, which their levity, contributed in the invention and circulation of false

(1) Jauzi fol. 107.
(2) Suyuti, *Tahdir al-Khawass* (Leiden Ms) fol. 46-49 Ch. VII.

traditions. This class, in the earlier times, seems to have been widely-spread in Iraq and, later in middle Asia. Rarely was its representative found in Hejaz. Malik Ibn Anas, as it is reported, is said to have forbidden them to enter the mosque of Medina. Also in the Maghrib where a tendency to be scrupulously true and loyal to traditions (Hadith) always prevailed this class was but rarely met with[1]. Their falsification of traditions is to be distinguished from the kind of falsification hitherto dealt with. The 'Qussas' wore no political, religious or pray colours. What they did, they did solely for the amusement of their audience. We may, indeed, add that all this they did for pure, personal gain. And because they had primarily an eye to personal gain—professional jealousy arose among them, "One 'Qass' does not love another" became a by-word[2]. The collection of money seems to have been of old, the end in view of such street-preachers. At least the following report, ascribed in later times to the Companion Imran b. Hasim, suggests it. He passed by a "Qass" who, after the conclusion of the reading of the Qur'an, was begging from his audience. At the sight of this scene Imran cited the following saying of the Prophet: "He who reads the Qur'an should invoke God with it but a time will come when people will make the Qur'an a means of begging"[3]. *Kawwaza* was the term used for such collection and he who was charged with such collection was called *Mukawwiz*. The artful way, in which this collection was made, may be seen from an account which comes from the IVth Century[4]. The common folk reposed such faith in the 'Qussas' that they even applied to them to pray for them. A father has prayer said by a 'Qass' on the successful return-home of his son. All this, to be

---

(1) Muk 236 line 18.

(2) *Yatimah, III,* 3, line 17.

(3) Trimidhi, II, 151; Jauzi gives very interesting examples of this practice. Folio, 147-149.

(4) *Yatimah*, III, 123.

sure, meant money[1]. In the 5th century these 'Qussas' apparently traded in a kind of indulgence for sins[2].

We meet these irresponsible preachers even now in Muslim towns[3]. Schack notes in his diary of 1870 (Damascus): "The most interesting to me was a characteristic scene which I witnessed at the Omayyad mosque. By a pillar stood, surrounded by a large audience, a Shaikh, delivering a lecture with lively gestures. My guide told me he was no ecclesiastic but a man from among the people who was preaching for money". This scene reminded Schack of Abu Zayd, the hero of Hariri. And indeed, the XLIst maqamah describes a corresponding scene.

---

(1) *Yaqut* II, 123.
(2) Jauzi. fol. 115.
(3) For instance on Bukhara, Petermann's *Geog Mittheilungen* 1889, p. 269 a (India is specially full of them. They constitute greatest menace to progress. And so great is their power and influence with the people that their word is law to them. Their stock-in trade consists of a few texts of the Qur'an and *Hadith* which they have committed to memory and which they quote in season and out. They invent false traditions, pervert facts, distort truth. Their audience listen to all kinds of lies and distortions with rapt attention. I have heard these sob and sigh; I have even seen them weep at these gatherings; so impressive apparently is their own preaching, so historic their method, or so accommodating their faith. Frequently, indeed, I have been amazed at the ignorance or the audacity of these preachers. But my co-religionists listen without questioning and obey without hesitation the direction which they give and the interpretation which they put upon legal or religious questions.

No reform is possible or conceivable where the people are so entirely under the influence of such irresponsible men. The only hope is in the spread of education which may, perchance, restore Reason to its proper sphere of activity. The Muslim preachers, who are so conspicuous to-day in every town and in every village in India, are apparently the direct discendant of the 'Qussas' of later days' Caliphate Tr.)

XX. MANNERS AND MORALS

In the ancient Orient and the Byzantine world custom required the employment of eunuchs in distinguished households[1]. Castration of men and animals was, however, severely forbidden alike by the Qur'an and the *Hadith* (Tradition). The *Muhtasib* (trade-Inspector) was enjoined to see that this prohibition was not broken in upon[2]. But here too, in the Muslim Orient, about the year 200/800 this old oriental custom engrafted itself upon the waning Arabism, despite the clear prohibition of the Prophet. The Caliph Amin, son of Harun, was mad after eunuchs. "He purchased them from wherever he could. He collected them round him by day and night, at meals and drinking bouts, even at business hours and would have nothing to do with women, free or unfree. He called the white ones, grasshoppers; the black ones, ravens"[3]. Hence the satire of a contemporary poet:—

> He has introduced the eunuchs; he has ushered in the cult of impotence.
> And the world follows the practice of the Prince of the faithful[4].

The faithful evaded the prohibition against castration by purchasing eunuchs and leaving the actual operation to Jews and Christians[5]. A report, dating from the 6th/12th

---

(1) Their origin is pious. For the sake of the gods this third sex came into existence. Both the Council of Nicea and the Prophet felt constrained to oppose its religious significance Sachau, MSOS, 2,83 f.

(2) Mawardi, *Const. Political*, ed. Enger, 431.

(3) Tabari, III, 950 f.

(4) Abu Nuwas in Tabari, III, 956.

(5) In this connection it is strange that their laws forbade the Jews to

century, speaks of the Christians Abysinnian Hadjah as the only place where castration was carried on as a trade[1]. Even at the beginning of the XIX century there were two Christian (Coptic) cloisters in upper Egypt, the main income of which was drawn from castration and this was so extensively done that it supplied the whole of Egypt and a part of Turkey with eunuchs[2]. Some Copts of Siut made a trade of purchasing young negroes and of castrating them. Many died at the operation but the survivors were sold at a profit of twenty-times their original value[3]. They divided the eunuchs, then, into four classes : Blacks, Slavs, Greeks and Chinese[4]. The white eunuchs, according to Mukaddasi (p. 242), were of two kinds :

> (a) The Slavs whose home-land was behind Khwarizm. They were imported to Spain, where they were castrated and exported thence to Egypt[5].
>
> (b) The Greeks who came to Syria and Armenia. But this source was exhausted owing to the devastation of the frontier.

" I questioned a number of them regarding castration and learnt that Greeks remove the testicles of boys, intended for dedication to the church[6]. This they do so that they may

---

castrate stallions and bulls with the result that they had to purchase their oxen from the Christians, Krausz, Tal. Archaologic, II, 116.

(1) Ibn Fadlallah in Marquart, *Dse Beniusami* lung, CCC VI.

(2) Furst Puckler, *Ans* Mehemed *Alis Reich*, Vol. III, 159.

(3) Maltzan, *Meine Wallfahrt nach* Mekka 1865, 1, 48.

(4) Masudi, VIII, 148.

(5) Even according to Ibn Haukal (p. 75) all slaves brought to Khorasan were uncastrated. Such also were the Slav-eunuchs exported from Spanish Gallicia. The voices of the Slavs are said to alter more than those of others after *castration* (Jahiz, Hayawan, 1, 51) (see Dozy, *Spanish Islam, 430 Tr.)*

(6) In contrast to the Latin Church, eunuchs served in the orthodox churches not only as a choir but also as priests. At the beginning of the 4th/10th two eunuchs even held the position of the Patriach of

not run after women or be assailed by lustful passions. When the faithful made their incursions they attacked the churches and carried away the boys. The slaves were brought to a town behind Bagganath (Pechina, the old capital of the Province of Almeria), where Jewish inhabitants castrated them[1]. Accounts differ regarding the actual process of castration : some assert that at one and the same time they remove the penis and the testicles, others that they make an incision in the scrotum and remove the testicles and place a little piece of wood under the penis and cut it off at the root. " I said to the eunuch Arib, a truth-loving savant : Master, tell me about the eunuchs for the learned are at variance with each other on that subject. Even Abu Hanifa speaks of their marital capacity and credits them with children, born to their wives[2]. On this question you are, therefore, the one to consult. He replied: Abu Hanifa is right. In the process of castration the scrota are opened up and the testicles removed. Often, indeed, the patient takes a fright and one of his testicles disappears in the body, is looked for but is not instantly found. Eventually it reverts to its proper place after the incision has been cicatrized. Should it happen to be the left testicle—the eunuch recovers his passion and semen-should it be the right, he grows a beard like a normal man. Abu Hanifa has stood by the word of God : The child belongs to the husband, and *that* is possible with those eunuchs who retain one of their testicles. (I related this to Abu Sa'id at Nisabur. It is, indeed, possible. One of my testicles is small and the hair on it is light and

---

Constantinople in succession (Ibn Sa'id, 83, 86) . And the same was the case about the year 370/980 (Barhebracus, *Chron.* ecclesiast, 1, 414) and 410/1019 (Ibn Sa'id, 227).

(1) Even the Jews of the Frankish empire practised castration these of Verdun were specially famous for it (Dozy, *Mcors in Spain,* II, 38).

(2) A eunuch's wife is mentioned in Ibn al-Athir, VIII,191. Love intrigues between the slave-girls and eunuchs of Khumarwaihi are said to have been the cause of the murder of the Prince. One of Adad-ud-Dawlah's eunuchs was married to an Abysinnian slave girl, but "another actually owned her heart'. Ibn al-Athir, IX, 39.

scanty). When castration is over, they insert a leaden peg in the urinal passage so that the passage may not be closed up in the process of healing.

This serious operation considerably limited the number of eunuchs. In the Byzantine Empire eunuchs worth four times the price of an average slave[1]. About the year 300/912 the tender appellation of 'servant'. (*Khadim*) or "Master" (*Muallim, Ustad, Shaikh*) came into vogue for these wretches, whereas, in earlier times, they were called by the offensive term '*Khasi*' the castrated ones[2]. They had to suffer much mockery from the populace. People called out after them : ungrateful son, pour out water and fling in meal : or, ungrateful child with your long legs[3].

On a Friday evening, in the year 284/987, a eunuch was hurrying across the Bridge of Baghdad with a message from the Caliph. By reason of such contemptuous terms being used against him by the people, a quarrel arose and the eunuch was beaten. In the tumult the letter containing the message was lost. Thereupon the Caliph directed that behind the eunuch some cavalry and infantry should proceed through the streets of Baghdad and arrest and punish those who insulted him[4]. Stories regarding eunuchs were the enduring themes of public actors, mimicry of their voices and caricature of their gestures were the surest road to popularity[5]. Their endurance on horse-back, however, is praised and here they excelled the Turks[6]. They are even

(1) Vogt. *Basil*, I, 383.
(2) Jauhari, noting the older expression, does not bring out the specific sense of 'eunuch', but says that all male and female, were called 'servants' Elias V. Nisibis, on the other hand, always translates it as 'Sarisha', Muk, 31.
(3) Masudi, VIII, 180 (The exact import of the jest is obscure. Tr.).
(4) Tabari, III, 2164.
(5) Masudi, VIII, 262, 164.
(6) Baihaqi, 610.

mentioned as good shots[1]. By the side of the Byzantine Narses and Solomon the Muslim orient of the 4th/10th century might place the Field-marshal Munis and the Samanid general Fa'iq, a eunuch likewise[2]. To their circle too belonged the victorious Muslim admiral Thamil of Tarsus[3]. The Byzantine admiral Niketas, defeated off Sicily, was a eunuch too. In the naval engagement of the year 307/919 between the Fatimids and the Byzantines, both the admirals were eunuchs[4]. The Officer, who was daring enough to taunt the Caliph Hakim over the singing and burning of his black slaves and who hinted that even the Greek Emperor would not have embarked upon such a course of action, was a slay eunuch. He paid for his independence with his death[5].

Only a black eunuch, named Shakkar (sugar), succeeded in securing the confidence of the suspicious and tyrannical Adud-ud-Dawlah, an honour coveted by all. When on his death-bed, none else but he dared to approach him. His eldest son was instantly banished by the angry father to another province for forcing his way into the room.[6] A white eunuch even became regent during the minority of the Fatimid Caliph Hakim. Only from religious offices they were shut out, until the time of the later Crusades when one was appointed Qadhi of Damiettu[7]. Oriental experience found in them persons who never became bald or indulged in pederasty[8]. One notable feature of theirs was an extreme passion for singing-birds and hence they were constantly seen at the bird-markets[9]. The training of pigions as letter-

(1) Jahiz, *Haywan*, 1, 62.
(2) Hamadhani, *Ras'ali*, 19.
(3) *Kit. al-Uyun*, IV, 99 a.
(4) Kindi, 276.
(5) Yahya, fol. 130, a, b.
(6) Yahya, fol. 107 a; Ibn al-Athir IX, 39.
(7) Suyuti Awalil.
(8) Jahiz, *Haywan*, I,48, 62; Baihaqi, 609.
(9) Baihaqi, 611; Maqrizi, *Khitat*, II, 96.

carriers was the one work in which they excelled[1]. Long is the list of their defects; offensive perspiration (the reverse of castrated animals)[2]; heavy clumsy bones (castrated animals have fine ones); long feet; crooked fingers; liability to rapid decay, although they are longer-lived than ordinary men (in this respect they are not unlike the mules among the animals); shrivelled skin; rapid changes in their tempers, being like women and children easily moved to tears; quick to anger; eager for chat and gossip; liable to wet the bed; voracious in appetite.[3] It is specially noted that their one craving is to serve distinguished people and to look down with contempt on all without wealth or power[4]. In Barjawan the Egyptian guardian of Hakim, haughtiness rose to its height. Off hand he was even with his ward when grown-up. One day the Caliph sent for him. He put his foot on the neck of the Caliph's horse, almost touching the Caliph's nose with his shoe[5]. For this and similar acts he was stabbed to death in the Caliph's garden.

With the eunuchs came into vogue another kind of sexual perversion. To cure her son of his passion for eunuchs the mother of the Caliph Amin smuggled among them several slender, handsome maids with short hair, dressed up as boys in tight jackets and girldles. Court circles and common-folk all alike followed this fashion and similarly dressed-up their slave-girls and called them *Ghulamiyyah*[6]. At the age of seventeen the sweet, seductive female-singer Atrib, "the most beautiful of God's creation," stood before the very same Caliph dressed up as a boy and reached him the cup[7]. Even a century later girls dressed up

(1) Jahiz, *Haywan*, I, 53.
(2) Masudi, however, praises their want of smell in the arm. pit. VIII, 149.
(3) *Haywan*, 1, 48, 61, 72; Baihaqi, 611.
(4) *Haywan* 1, 72.
(5) Maqrizi, *Khitat*, II, 3.
(6) Masudi, VIII, 299.
(7) Sabushti, K *ed-diyarat*, Berlin, fol. 70b.

as boys were found in the Caliph's Court[1]. This practice was extended even to the waiteresses on duty[2].

In times when the Arabs set the fashion intrigue with boys played no part in social life. The old laws and regulations scarcely concerned themselves with this subject. Conflicting thus are the views of the Jurists in this matter in the 4th/10th century. Some regarded it as tantamount to adultery; others made a distinction between pederasty with one's own slaves and strangers. Most of them held that[3] there was no legal punishment (*hadd*) for it—the Judge must act therefore according to his Judgment.

The real pederasty, according to Muslim tradition, came from Khorasan[4] with the Abbasid army. Even in the third century Afghanistan is noted for it. (Tha'alibi's *Book of Support*, ZDMG, VIII, 56). In the 4th/10th century it becomes general. Of love-songs there are as many addressed to boys as to girls. Few, indeed, are like Mus'ab and Sulami (d. 394/1003)—avowed pederasts—who sing only of boys[5]. Not many, indeed are of the class either who dedicate their muse exclusively to girls. Even a sober and distinguished poet like Abu Firas has poems addressed to boys[6]. In the third decade of this century the most popular song was the song of the poet Khubzarruzi (singing behind the baking-oven), a short, passionate lyric, addressed to a boy:—

Were I but a reed-pen in his hand or ink

(1) Masudi, VIII, 300.

(2) Abu Nuwas. Diwan 234,240. When this very poet (p. 370) used "he" of a girl the reference is to this custom.

(3) Qodamah, Paris, Arabe 5907, fol. 29 b; Subki, III, 18.

(4) Jahiz (d. 255/868) explains this, in his "Book on the School-master" by the fact that Abu Muslim forbade his army for the first time, to have anything to do with women. Hamza al-Isfahani in the *Diwan* of Abu Nuwas (Berlin, 7532 fol 193b) printed by *Mittwoch, Die literararische Tatigkeit al-Isfahanis*,MSOS, 1910.

(5) Saboushti, Berlin, fol 83 a; Yatimah, II, 163 f.

(6) Dvorak 165 ff.

threin, he would at least take me up once
and kiss me with his mouth if a hair got into
the pen[1].

Pervasive was this passion in circles high and low, and yet we do not know of a single instance of a Caliph's passion for a boy. The otherwise ill-reputed Buwayyed Amir Bakhtiyar was more hit by the captivity of his Turkish favourite than by the loss of his empire,—a fact which "brought him into contempt with all"[2]. Even the renowned soldier, Saif-ud-Dawlah, had a boy in Aleppo, called by a female name 'Thamil', whom he dearly loved[3]. Fashion claimed from these boys a lisping tongue and delicate speech.

In the inventory of an inn on the Tigris we find, apart from wine, a boy or a girl—all told costing two dirham a night[4]. At Cairo the Caliph Hakim was greatly pleased with a lusty pederastic street-figure[5]. Even pretty romances sprang up in his sphere. The famous jurist Naftawaihi (d. 323/935) loved the son of the famous Daud, founder of the sect named after him. But the youth cared for another Naftawaihi being sloventlly and offensive in smell. This notwithstanding, Naftawaihi persisted in love and died for it. While dying he lisped the words of the Prophet; He who loves and remains chaste in love, who keeps his love a secret and dies for it, dies a martyr. A whole year, for grief, Naftawaihi suspended his lectures[6].

---

(1) Masudi, VIII, 374; *Yatimah,* II , 133.

(2) Misk, VI, 469; Ibn al-Athir. VIII, 495.

(3) Misk, VI, 81.

(4) Yaqut, *Irshad,* II, 340.

(5) Yahya, Paris, fol. 127 b. (Practice of unnatural lusts was one of the two abominations of Carthage (in the 5th century A. D.). In the foot-note 42 I find following passage:— The streets of Carthage were polluted by effiminate wretches who publicly assumed the countenance, the dress, and the character of women" Gibbon, Vol. III (Bury's Ed) p. 435 Tr.

(6) Yaqut, *Irshad,* 1, 309.

The Spanish Grammarian Ahmad ibn Kulaib (d. 426/ 1035) studied together with one Aslam, the handsome son of a Qadhi. Ibn Kulaib won his love, composed poems on him which flew from mouth to mouth and were sung at weddings. Aslam, thereupon kept away from his lectures. Ibn Kulaib then paced up and down by the door of his house to have his fill of joy when he came out for a stroll in the evening. Finally Ibn Kulaib came disguised as a Beduin with eggs and fowls. When Aslam stepped out of the house Ibn Kulaib kissed his hand, pretending to be a peasant from one of his estates who had come with some presents for him. In course of the conversation Aslam recognised him and complained that for his sake he was kept so confined. Ibn Kulaib then went away but fell very seriously ill. He begged a friend to get Aslam to visit him "He took his mantle and started with me. Ibn Kulaib resided at the end of a long street. When half way Aslam halted blushed and said : By God, no further will I proceed and pray, expect me not to do so. I pressed him : you have not far to go; you are already at the house. But said he: I must return. Then he hurriedly turned back; I seized him by the mantle; he pulled: the mantle tore and a piece reminded in my hand. And thus alone I proceeded to Ibn Kulaib. Our arrival had already been announced to him by a servant who had seen us in the street. When I reached him alone, Ibn Kulaib changed colour. He enquired where Abul Hasan was? I related the entire story. On hearing me he became delirious, incoherent in speech. I left. Hardly had I got to the middle of the street when I heard the lamentation announcing his death. Later when the street was empty. Aslam was seen by his grave, mourning his death. In these terms did Ibn Kulaib dedicate his *Kit. al-Fasih* to him:

> " This is a Book of good Arabic and all its
> idioms, Like myself, I humbly dedicate it to
> you."[1].

(1) Jauzi, fol. 190 a; Irshad, II, 19 ff.

The Syrian poet Sanaubari (d. 334/945) relates another story: There was a book dealer called Sa'd in Edessa in whose shop the literati met. He was clever and well-read, and wrote sentimental verses. I, the Syrian poet Abu Mi'waj and other Syrian and Egyptian poets never left his shop. A Christian merchant there had a son, named Isa. He was the handsomest of God's creation; of the finest build and endowed with the richest gifts of mind and conversation. He was wont to sit with us and take down our poems. He was then a mere school boy and we liked him very much. The book-dealer Sa'd conceived a vehement passion and wrote verses on him, with the result that his passion for him became widely known. When the boy grew up he showed a marked tendency for monasticism. He spoke to his parents on the subject, and pressed them until they yielded and purchased a cell for him, paying its price to the superintendent of the Monastery. The boy then took up his residence. For the book-dealer the world then lost its sunshine. He closed his shop, abandoned his friends, betook himself to the cloister where the boy was and wrote verses on him. The monks disapproved of this sort of intimacy and forbade the boy to bring him there any more on pain of expulsion. When Sa'd saw that his friends was avoiding him—it broke his heart. He personally begged permission from the monks but in vain. They said: "It would be a sin and shame to grant permission. Moreover they feared the Government". And when he came to the cloister they shut door against him and would not allow the boy to speak to him. His longing grew; his passion became uncontrollable. He tore his clothes, went to his house, set fire to all that was there, lived in the desert close to the cloister, naked, mad, tearful, composing verses. Once Mi'waj and I, returning home from a garden where we had passed the night, saw him sitting with long hair and altered appearance in the shade of the cloister. We greeted and taunted him but he said: "Leave me alone with these devilish promptings! Do you see this bird? Since the morning I have been beseeching him to fly down to Isa with a message from me". Then he left us, went to the door of the cloister but found it closed. After some time he was found dead by the cloister. Abbas ibn Kaigalag was then the Amir of the town. When he and the people of Edessa heard of this, they came to the cloister and said : The monks have killed him, —Ibn Kaigalag adding: "The youth's head must be chopped off, the cloister burnt down and the monks whipped". He proved unrelenting and the Christians had to redeem themselves and the cloister on payment of 10000 dirhams. When after this incident the youth returned to Edessa to visit his family the boys shouted after him: The murderer of Sa'd, the book-dealer, and threw stones at him: in consequence thereof the youth left the town and settled down at the Sam'an cloister[1].

For fear of such love intrigues some professors would not let beardless youths into their lectures; the diligent students had therefore to use false beards to obtain admission[2].

Prostitution is not, as our thinkers on social problems imagine, a makeshift for the unmarried but, in its inception, is not unlike the institution of eunuchs, a curious religious institution. It even flourished in Islam, although polygamy and custom had so contrived as to make unmarried men and women exceptions to the general rule and the law *in theory*, penalised it with death by stoning. But indeed, so strict was the proof required for adultery that no conviction could ever be had[3]. A Muslim traveller (about the year 300/912) describes the regularly-organised prostitution in China with a staff of officers and a system of taxation and concludes: "We thank God that He has saved us from such

(1) Yaqut *Irshad* II, 25.

(2) Wustenfeld, AGGW, 37, Nr. 88.

(3) Jokes regarding it in *Muhadarat al-Uda* 1, 129.

seductions"[1]. But only fifty years later Adud-ud-Dawlah (d. 372/982) was un-Islamic enough to tax prostitutes and dancing girls in Fars and to lease out the Tax[2]. The Fatimids of Egypt followed his example[3]. According to a legend, dating about 400/1002, Adud-ud-Dawlah compelled the princess Jamila to go into prostitutes' quarters for rejecting his offer of marriage; whereupon she drowned herself in the Tigirs[4]. A curious practice at Laodicea was for the market-superintendent to publicly auction the prostitutes every day to foreigners, who received rings as tokens of their purchase called the Bishop's rings. If any foreigner was found with a woman at night without such a ring he was punished. This practice, however is reported of the time when the town had once again passed into the hands of the Byzantines[5]. Mukaddasi found even in Sus, Capital of Khuzistan, brothels near the mosque-gate[6]; whereas Ibn Haukal reports that there were no brc .hels in the maghrib[7]. In the year 323/934 the Muslim *ultras*, the Hambalites, vigorously proceeded in the capital against immorality. They attacked the houses of influential men; let the wine run out of the casks; assaulted female singers; destroyed musical instruments and *forbade men to walk in the streets with* women and boys[8]. If she is thy wife—so was one reproached who was found talking to a woman in the street it is unseemly; if she is not thy wife, it is worse still[9]. The orthodox morality was extremely unwilling to let women out of their homes; the Caliph

---

(1) *Silsalet et-tawarikh* ed. Reinaud, 70; supplement to Abu Zaid es Sirafi; compare Masudi, 1, 295.

(2) Beruni, India tr. by Sachau , II, 157; Muk, 441.

(3) Maqrizi, Khitat, 1, 89.

(4) Guzuli, Matali,el-buder, II, 48.

(5) Qifti, 298.

(6) p. 407.

(7) p. 70 (Prostitutes taxed in the Roman Empire, Gibbon, Bury's ed, Vol. II, 210, Tr.

(8) Ibn al-Athir, VIII, 230.

(9) Mawardi, 418.

Hakim, intent on restoring the original Islam, forbade them to go out and cobblers to make shoes for them. Women-nurses and cropse-washers were enjoined to take out a written license[1]. From the pious circles this system passed on to the people of rank and distinction even in Spain and, through Spanish influence, it came about that about the middle of the XVIIth century no woman was ever seen in the streets of Itlay[2] . In the 4th/10th century three stripes, it is said, was the punishment for a guest who told his host : "Call your wife to eat with us"[3]. As among the old Greek so here, the wife's place, in social circles, was taken up by the *hetairas,* who were trained women, endowed with wit and beauty, equipped with culture and accustomed to the free-talk of men. We feel that both the home and society benefited by this division. Most of these *hetairas* were slave-girls, but there were among them emancipated ones as well who offered their services for payment[4]. A famous female flute-player worked for two dinars *per day* and one *per night.* To the fool who worried the Baghdadian lady with love-letters and told her that, for her sake, he was robbed of food, drink and sleep, and implored her to come at least in dream, she sent a message to the effect that he should send her two dinars and she would bodily present herself to him[5]. In this sphere too the popular custom held its ground alongside of the canonical doctrines. The Arabs noticed the great freedom which the Copts allowed to their women. It was explained thus : After the disaster of the Pharoah and his army in the Red Sea only women and slaves survived, and these intermarried. But the women imposed a condition, namely, that henceforward they would remain

(1) Yahya, Supplement to Kindi, (Guest, 606). According to Wustenfeld *Statthalter Agyptens,*II, 58 this prohibition was in force, for the first time, in 253/867. Kindi, (d. 350), however, states otherwise.

(2) Stendhal, Promenades, II, 358.

(3) Iqd 1, 218.

(4) Aghani XIX, 36.

(5) Abulqasim, 73.

their own mistresses[1]. Some of these privileges the Muslim ladies of Egypt have still retained. A women has two husbands, says Mukaddasi[2]. Even the women of Shiraz get a bad certificate[3], and so do those of Hirat, who "in spring become as lewd as cats"[4]. About 300/912 the claims of women to higher callings was apparently put forward and pressed, for says Ibn Bessam : 'What have the professions of clerk, tax-gatherer, preacher to do women? They belong to us"[5]. There were women theologians whose lectures were eagerly listened to, and so also there were women preachers[6]. There were also jurists who declared women eligible for judgeship. All reports and stories suggest that the middle class was monogamous. In the *Maqamah* of Hamadhani a merchant invites a guest to whom he thus praises his wife: Sir, if you were to see her working in the house with a tied apron, running backward and forward from the baking-oven for utensils; pounding spices with her hand; smoke covering her comely countenance and leaving traces behind on her tender cheeks, you would witness something worth witnessing. I love her and she reciprocates my love[7]. The Fatimad Caliph al-Muizz is said to have counselled his nobility to have one wife only : "One wife is enough for a man"[8]. Even the poet Abul Ala considers it better "to associate" none other with a wife, "for if there were any gocd in companions, God would not be without companions" (Kremer, ZDMG, Vol. 38, p. 509). Polygamy among the rich was only due to the slave-girls who played the part of concubines. All the Caliphs of the 4th/10th

(1) Maqrizi *Khitat*, 1, 39.
(2) p. 200.
(3) p. 427.
(4) p. 436.
(5) Qalqashandi, *Subh al-Asa*, Cairo, 1, 40.
(6) Ibn al-Jauzi, 126 a. 146 a. Renowned like Kariman in Mekka, who taught the whole of Bukhari in five days. Yaqut, *Irshad*, 1, 247.
(7) *Maqamah*, Ed. Beyrut, 103.
(8) Maqrizi, *Khitat*, 1, 352.

century were born of slave-girls. They, in their turn, rarely married free women, who were called by the special term 'al-Hurrah'—the free[1]. An old writer asserts that slave-girls were more popular than free-women, for men personally selected the former while the latter were selected by women who know nothing of female charms[2].

Though sanctioned by law, remarriage of widows was highly disapproved by custom. A story of the 3rd/9th century mentions the writing of a letter to a friend whose mother remarries, when a widow, as the most difficult of tasks. He solves the difficulty thus : Fate follows a course different from man's desire. May God, who determines his servant's destiny, grant you her death for the grave is the noblest of husbands[3]. In a similar strain wrote Khwarizmi (d.393/1003) to the historian Miskawaihi when his widowed mother remarried : before I could have prayed God to keep her alive long for thy sake; but now , I pray that He may take her away as speedily as possible; for the grave is a better husband and death a more coveted honour. Thank God, the want of dutifulness and affection is on her side, not yours[4].

The birth of a daughter was indeed generally an occasion for congratulation. Thus writes the poet al-Rida to his brother:

> The charger of good-luck has come prancing
> on a bright, happy day.

A little child—all who see her beauty, kiss her, and thou, the envied one, holdest her in thy arm! But a letter wherein khwarezmi condoles on the death of a little girl, concludes

---

(1) Jauzi, fol. 121 b.
(2) Fusul al-Jahiz, Brit, Mus. Nr. 3138 fol. 61a.
(3) Baihaqi, 449; Jamhara, of Saizari, Leiden, fol. 200b
(4) Rasa'il ed. Const 173.

with a wish : And may God compensate her loss by the birth of a brother[1].

It is not only the seclusion of women from men which is the cause of the unpleasant license in language which is noticeable among the Southern people. When we compare the stories and witticisms, the conversation and poetry of the 3rd/9th and the 4th/10th centuries with those of the old Arabian times, the sheer joy of the later times in filth and vulgarity fills us with amazement. *Here, in this sphere, the fashion of the Pre-Islamite, an Arab orient asserts itself.* The Beduin even today, is chaster and far more continent than the others[2]. The defamatory poetry becomes particularly lewd now. The collection in the *Hamasa,* compared with the poems of Buhturi[3]—who was then regarded as old-fashioned—is severely modest and restrained. The Abbasid prince and poet Ibn al-Mutazz (d. 296/909) wrote his reply on the back of his love-letter "so that my writing may carry on unnatural offence with his"[4]. In 319/931 a *wazir* might have forfeited his office "for frivolous talk or vulgar expression inconsistent with his exalted dignity"[5], but by the end of the century the *Wazir* of Rai, Sahib-ibn-Abbad, indulged in the coarsest allusions and clothed literary criticisms in the grossest obscenity[6]. On a State-visit to Baghdad when the *Wazir* did not immediately receive him, he addressed the following lines to the State-Secretary Sabi:

Like a eunuch impotent am I at the door—while others go in and out *Sicut membra virilia*[7]. And even this very Sabi—

(1) Rasa'il, 61.

(2) Landberg *Proverbes arabes, XVI.*

(3) Ibn al-Rumi altogether outdoes Buhturi in his lampoons on the latter Tr.

(4) *Diwan,* 87.

(5) *Arab,* 161.

(6) *Yatimah,* III, 102 ff; III, 130.

(7) Yaqut, *Irshad,* II, 338.

the pride of Arabic prose—rioted and revelled in smuttiest expressions in attacking an enemy[1]. Well may we imagine the filth of a real *Magin* (loose-liver) such as Ibn al-Hajjaj!

A poet tells us how he seduced a number of boys at the great mosque of Basra, and concludes with the advice that if any one be difficult to get at :

> Go with a current dirham and you will get him ; for the dirham brings down what floats in the air and captures what lives in the desert[2].

Hamadhani too has his fling:

> You are a day-labourer by nature who falls on his knees when he sees a penny[3].

And this applies to many of his contemporaries. Once again the old ways are reverted to and money supplants everything else, and venality becomes the key-note of life. Sordid passion for gold taints the highest circles in the empire.

In 321/933 the Caliph Qahir forbade wine and song and enjoined the sale of musically-trained slave-girls. On the issue of this order prices fell. And while the market was thus depressed he purchased slave-girls for himself through some men of straw, for he was fondly devoted to music[4]. Somewhat amusing, indeed, are the stories of the then Amir of Egypt. He took away the things of his people without the slightest qualms of conscience. Muzahim ibn Raiq relates: I had a fur made for 600 dirhams. I very much liked it for its beauty. I put it on at Damascus when I went to Ikhsid. As soon as he saw me he began to examine and

---

(1) *Yatimah*, II, 63 ff.

(2) *Yatimah*, II, 130, Yaqut, *Irshad*, VI, 317.

(3) Cairo, Ed. p. 65; Paris, fol. 59a .

(4) Ibn al-Athir, VIII, 204.

admire it and said: I have never seen the like of it. Hardly had Ikhsid retired to his room, when Fatik came to me and said: 'Be seated, Ikhsid will confer a robe of honour on you". Then they brought a parcel, took the fur off me, folded it, carried it away and left me. After a while they returned and said: Ikhsid is resting now, come again tomorrow evening. When I rose and asked for my fur they said: What fur? We have no fur of yours. I came back to Ikhsid in the evening and saw him wearing the fur. When he saw me, he laughed and said: You look so impudent but you are, indeed, the son of your father. What sums have I not offered you, but you were shameless in your demand! I have, therefore, taken the fur without thanking you[1]. At a garden-party which the Madera'i gave to Ikhsid carpets were spread on a table; gold and silver ornaments and figures of camphor and amber were placed before the Amir and singers, male and female regaled him with music. Finally two silver-bowls were set before him, one full of gold, the other full of silver-coins. Putting the gold coins behind him he gave away the silver-pieces. When he left, everything on which the food was served or which was placed before him, everything indeed out of which he had eaten or taken his drink, was sent to him on two horses with gold saddles and bridles[2].

The absence of a sense of personal honour corresponds with a feeling of indifference for the honour of others. In 268/884 Ibn Tulun punished the insurrection of his son Abbas. A high scaffold was erected where, on a raised seat, sat Ibn Tulun, his son in striped *Kaftan, in turban* and shoes, with a bare sword in hand standing before him. Opposite to him were arrayed his friends and helpers in the insurrection, now in custody. The son was made to cut off their hands and feet, their bodies were, then, thrown down

(1) Maghrib of Sa'id, ed. Tallquist, 34.
(2) Tallquist, 29.

from the scaffold[1].

The son of the Wazir Ibn al-Furat, getting his father's predecessor in office into his power "acted in an inhuman way towards him which was condemned alike by all". He dressed him up in a monkey-skin and made him dance at his driking-bouts[2]. While arranging the line of battle before the Battle of Badr the Prophet rudely touched an Arab getting out of the line; the Arab claimed compensation whereupon the Prophet bared his breast and called upon the warrior to avenge him self[3]. This story reflects the Arab sense of honour. But now, corporal punishment was scarcely regarded as dishonourable. In the second half of the 4th/10th century a Wazir is whipped for the first time at Baghdad, and then quietly resumes office[4]. In the 5th/11th century even one whose hands had been cut off for embezzlement becomes a Wazir. Indeed the standard of the negro is reached according to which only those that have been whipped can become leaders of the caravan[5].

The treatment of prisoners taken in possession of weapons depended upon the measure of their guilt and the wrath they excited; at least the treatment of foreign war-prisoners differed from that of the rebels within the empire. The Beduin chiefs who filled up the wells with earth on the caravan-route, and thereby consigned thousands of pilgrims to the torture of the thirst, were tied up along the banks of the Tigris, where they languished and died. In 289/901 the teeth of a captive Qarmatian chief were extracted, then one of his hands was tied to a high post and the other was weighed down by a stone. In this position he was left from sunrise to sunset: then his hands and feet were chopped

(1) Kindi, 224; Irshad, II, 416.
(2) *Arib*, 112.
(3) Ibn Hisham, 444.
(4) Mez, *Ren. des Islams*, 85.
(5) Zintgraff in *Vierkandt*, Naturvolker, 264.

off, then his head; his trunk was eventually impaled[1].

In 291/903 the dreaded Qarmatian general, 'the man with the wart, who had slaughtered the faithful like cattle, was brought with some of his lieutenants to Baghdad. The Caliph could not exhibit him high enough to the people. At first he thought of taking him round the town on an elephant, tied to a long pole. The Caliph, accordingly, issued orders to pull the archways down through which the procession was to pass. But this he found to be too dull and uninteresting. He, therefore, had a stool 2½ yards high tied to the elephant and seated 'the man with the wart' there. Ahead of him passed in procession the rest of the prisoners on camels in chains, clad in silk coat and burnoose. Second in rank among the prisoners was a beardless youth. In his mouth they placed a piece of wood and with a ribbon, like a bridle, they tied it to the hind part of his head. On his entry at Rakkah the people cursed him, insulted him, spat on him. The rebels were then taken to prison where a ten yards high scaffold was erected. While in prison 'the man with the wart' broke a cup, and with the broken pieces cut his veins. They dressed his wounds and deferred the execution until the recovery of his strength. As for the lieutenants their hands and feet were cut off and heads, limbs and trunk flung down from the scaffold. After the hands and feet of "the man with the wart" were cut off, a big fire was lighted before him; a wooden bar was made red hot and with it the body was branded. He opened his eyes wriggled, fainted away, expired. On his death the head was severed from the body and was fastened to a pole, all shouting : God is great. The rest of the prisoners were simply beheaded. The head and trunk of "the man with the wart" were exhibited at the Bridge[2]. In 397/1007 the Egyptian

(1) Tabari, III, 2206.

(2) *Arib*, 3 ff for other (instances of cruel punishments, see Chapter VIII, of this Book. Also Gibbon (Bury's ed), II, 490; Valentinian's

Caliph al-Hakim subdued the rebel Abu Raqwah who had violently shaken his empire. He put him on a two hundred camel, in a pointed cap of rags, with a monkey behind him, who was trained to clout him. And thus was he taken to the place of execution. But when they tried to bring him down they found him dead[1]. Instead of this interesting report from later sources, the contemporary Yahya says: He was shown in the town and then slain at the mosque of et-Tibr, where his body was impaled and burnt[2].

Such fierce punishments were dealt out to cruel and dangerous rebels stained by countless deeds of bloodshed. But when we consider that the cutting off of hand and foot was an old canonical law, which even to-day is used against rebels in Morocco, and take into account the horrible punishments meted out in Europe in the Middle Ages the Baghdad and Cairene Governments show a refreshing restraint and moderation. Rebels taken prisoner were usually carried round the town on mules[3], elephants[4], particularly on a two-humped camel[5]. They dressed the offenders up differently, now in a penitent's garb in a felt burnoose and a red hair coat[6] : now in a jester's costume of silk and brocade[7], with a fox's tail or ribbons or little bells tied to the burnoose now in a long burnoose such as is worn by women.

---

cruelty Vol. III, 21, 22, 50, 52. For further examples Lca, *Inquisition*. 1, 233 ff. Tr.)

(1) Ibn al-Athir, IX, 144; Ibn Taghribirdi, 93.

(2) p. 191.

(3) Yahya, 121.

(4) Ibn al-Athir, VIII, 49; Masudi, VIII, 169, *Arib*, 77.

(5) *Arib*, 64, Masudi, VIII, 169, 138.

(6) Zubdat al-fikrah, Paris, 179 b; such as Munis did to the captured Hamadanids.

(7) The Qarmatians the Kharijite (Masudi, VIII, 169) and the eunuch Wasif (Masudi, VIII, 198), the Hamdanid Husain (*Arib* 57), Yusuf ibn-Abisagh (*Arib* 77).

Besides being carried round the town the offenders in the 4th/10th century were pilloried. They put a wooden frame on the camel and tied the offender to it (Masudi, VI, 17). A man, concealed under the silk coat of the offender, turned the wooden frame of the Hamadanid Husain, now to the right and now to the left, while being taken round Baghdad in 303/915. When the power of the Caliph declined and the Amirs entered the House of Islam no longer as rebles but as belligerents this mode of punishment fell into disuse. In 307/919 Yusuf ibn Abissagh, who rose against the Caliph and established a kingdom of his own in the north-west, was taken prisoner. When he was taken round Baghdad on a two-humped camel in a brocade coat and a long burnoose bedecked with ribbons and little bells, the people of Baghdad took it amiss on the ground that he had never insulted his prisoners[1]. Already then people had ceased to realize that it was the case not of dealing with an enemy but of chastising a rebel.

The general who marched against Imad-ud-Dawlah in Faris carried with him a fur burnoose, with fox's tail, and hand-cuffs for his adversary to bring him thus apparelled back to Baghdad in triumph. But he was beaten and taken captive. They advised the Buwayhid ruler to dress him with the infamous things he had brought with him. But Imad ud-Dawlah thought it petty and wicked to do so[2].

The cruelty of the enquiring Magistrate was effectively restrained by the canonical law of Islam, which regarded confession extorted by torture or intimidation as illegal. The temporal court could, however, resort to corporal chastisement when interrogating an accused. Lash, cane stripes on the back, belly, posterior, feet, joints, muscles, could be administered[3]—the cane being regarded as milder

(1) *Arib*, 77.
(2) Ibn al-Athir, VIII, 205 f.
(3) Masudi, VIII, 154.

than the lash[1]. Other forms of torture only show themselves for purposes of administration or of collection of taxes. The most approved method was to stretch aloft an arm or foot of the offender and kept it so suspended until it became sore and tender[2]. The severest punishments in the Islamic Law are stoning in case of adultery, but the exacting evidence required made conviction an impossibility; cutting off of hand and foot for highway robbery;[3] cutting off of head for theft. But as the soul, after death, was thought to be connected with the body—an insult to the corpse was regarded as aggravation of the punishment. Often was a corpse placed in a pillory with out-stretched arms. At night it was watched and fire was lighted in front of it[4]. *At this time no one alive was crucified or impaled to death.* Of the schismatic Hallaj, who was executed in 309/921, some authorities aver that he was impaled to death[5]. The more correct report is that he suffered pillory at the beginning of his career and was then imprisoned. It was indeed eight years before his death, that he endured the lash. Among the inhuman atrocities which the rebellious negroes practised at Baghdad Ibn al-Mutazz mentions "impaling before death"[6]. The heaviest punishment was the burning of the corpse for it signified destruction of the soul. This final stage of distruction is evidenced by the fact no blood-money might any longer be paid for one so burnt[7]. In 312/924 a Persian traitor, caught in the very act of treason in the

(1) Wuz, 102.
(2) Wuz, 381; *Arib*, 184.
(3) *Kit. al-Kharaj*, 108.
(4) From the poem of Anbari this appears to have been done to one who was impaled in 367. According to *Uyun es-Siyar* of Hamadhani in Nadim al-Arib of Ahmad Sa'id Baghdadi, 143.
(5) Istakhri, *Bibi.* Geog 1, 149. Ibn Haukal copies him p. 210.
(6) *Diwan*, 1, 129.
(7) This is so today as it was in the old days. Compare the conditions imposed by Abu Bakr on the insurgent Arabs. We keep what we have taken from you but you return what you have taken from us. *You shall pay blood-money for our dead, but yours are to be in*

place, was executed, then crucified, and finally, wrapped up in a mantle of hemp and oakum, smeared with naphtha, was set fire to (Misk, V, 208). In 392/1001 the body of an unpopular officer was fetched out of the grave and burnt (Wuz, 471). *No one to my knowledge was burnt alive at this period.* (Only one single anecdote is found which casts suspicion on the Caliph al-Mutadid of such an act. (Yaqut; *Irshad*, VI, 494 f). Of flaying we hear only among the African Fatimids. A rebel who had laid waste the entire West and had cut down in Biskrah alone 300,000 palm trees, was taken prisoner in 341/952 and flayed alive. His skin stuffed with straw was exhibited (*Kitab al-Uyun*, IV, 252 b).

A rebel who had given much trouble to Jauhar, the Fatimid conquerer of the country, committed suicide in prison. After his death he was there flayed and then exhibited between Cairo and old Cairo[1]. The Fatimid Muiz is said to have ordered a pious man to be whipped and flayed alive for seditious speeches. But the flayer, a Jew, for sheer mercy, instead of flaying, plunged a dagger into his heart—a story entirly unlike all that we know of Muiz. Maqrizi relates something equally incredible. At the time of Malek en-Nasir the most favourite form of torture was to place dung beetles-on the head of the offender and then to tie a flame-coloured cloth over it. After an hour the skull was pierced through and through and the offender was dead[2]. Only in egypt could a mad Caliph, wishing to have no more wives, nail a number of them down in a chest and consign them to the Nile[3]. The Christians specially invented

---

hell fire. Beladhuri in Futuh, 95 (Eng. tr. Vol. I. p. 144 Tr.). The Muslim leader then actually burns the corpses of his opponents (Beladhuri, 96). The disappearance of 'blood-money' among the Greeks is also connected with the growing practice of burning the corpses. Yahya, fol. 100a; Maqrizi, *Khitat*, 413.

(1) Jauzi, fol. 111a.

(2) *Khitat*, 1, 426.

(3) Yahya, fol. 123 b.

all kinds of cruel stories about him. Thus it is said that Orestes, the Patriarch of Jerusalem, was terribly tortured and killed. In May the church celebrates the martyrdom of St. Orestes, but his Christian contemporary Yahya 'three times assures' us that Orestes died at Constantinople[1]. The dynastic troubles at Baghdad did not pass off without atrocities. This was mainly due to the religious fear of shedding the Caliph's blood[2]. But actual cases of such tortures were really isolated. In the oldest reports popular imagination actively co-operated. In 255/869 the Caliph al-Mutazz was deposed. Masudi, born soon after the event, writes that opinion was divided regarding his death. According to some he died a natural death in prison; according to others he was starved to death. According to yet others boiling water was poured on him causing his death, and according to others still they choked him in a hot bath,—others add that while there he was given ice water to drink which burst his liver and entrails[3]. The later Abulfida even says that he was immured alive[4]. Still wilder reports were circulate about the death of his successor. He is said to have been throttled or stifled in carpets and cushions. Again we are told that his testicles were pressed until he died. And again, he was placed between too wooden frames which were pulled by strings until he expired[5]. The later Ibn Al-Athir, likewise, mentions in the account of the Caliph, Ibn Mutazz's death in the year 226/902 that his testicles were squeezed until he died, but the older authorities know nothing about this[6].

(1) Schlumberger, Epopee Byz. II, 208.

(2) Many atrocities, seemingly unnecessary to us, were due to this fear. Marco Polo (II, 5) relates that the great Khan wrapped up *Nayan* in a carpet and rolled him up and down until he was dead 'because he was his own blood which he would not shed on the earth and in the light of the sun'.

(3) Masudi, VIII, 4.

(4) *Annales, 255.*

(5) Masudi, VIII, 11.

(6) Ibn al-Athir, VIII, 13.

In conformity with the Byzantine practice in the 4th/10th century they began to blind the claimants to the throne, making thereby their accession impossible. The first of the line to suffer this fate was the deposed Caliph Qahir, when he refused to release the people from their oath of allegiance and to abdicate before the Qadhi and the notaries (322/934)[1].

Ahmad ibn Abulhasan, the Sabian, blinded him with a red-hot nail[2]. Al-Muttaki, the second, was blinded by the Chief of the Turkish guards who, to drown his shrieks and those of his wives, caused the drum to be beaten during the operation of blinding (333/944)[3]. About 400/1000 this was a very favourite practice among the Buwayhids and yet a Caliph in 357/967 was satisfied with merely cutting off the nose of a dangerous Abbasid prince, and in 366/976 a Buwayid Sultan dealt similarly with a deposed *Wazir*[4]. This too, was an importation from Byzantium.

Death by hanging was not common; only one such case I know of in 450/1058[5]. Even poisoning does not play the role which one might expect it to play by reason of its usage extending for centuries. He who is familiar with the imaginative powers of the modern orient will be inclined to reduce by quite one-half the number of reported cases of poisoning. Here is an instance in point. Poisoning by baked eggs is hinted at in the oldest contemporary authority as a *possible* cause of the death of a victim over eight years of age[6]. In a later authority it is asserted as an actual fact[7]; whereas in the Kitab al-Uyun, drawing from best sources, it

(1) Yahya, 86 a; Misk V, 456; Ibn al-Athir, VIII, 211.

(2) *Uyun al-hadaiq*, IV, fol. 142 a.

(3) *Masudi*, VIII, 351; Elias Nisib, 212 according to Thabit ibn Sinan.

(4) *Ibn al-Athir*, VIII, 431; 499; Yaqut, *Irshad, V, 349.*

(5) Subki, *Tabaqat*, II, 293.

(6) Amedroz in Wuz, 19.

(7) For instance *Zubdal al-fikrah*, Paris, 193.

is stated that he died of diarrhoea[1]. Even as regards one of the earliest cases of poisoning under the Caliph al-Hadi (169-170/785-786) it is stated; "There are other version as well"[2]. The contemporary Masudi thus relates the gossip regarding the death of the Caliph al-Mutadid. Some ascribed his death to poisoning by Ibn Bulbul; others to the exhaustion upon the strenuous campaign against Wasif; yet others to a slave-girl poisoned him with a handkerchief with which she wiped his perspiration. Besides these there were other reports as well[3].

According to the later Mirkhond poisoning palys the greatest role relatively in the royal house of Bukhara. A careful comparision with the older reports will considerably modify the quantities employed. Among the rulers of their times al-Mutadid and al-Qahir are said to have been of a cruel disposition. It is reported of the first that he was wont to stuff the mouth, the nose, the ears of his victim and then have air pumped into the intestines until he swelled like a bag. The next thing done was to make an incision in the veins out of which air, along with blood, escaped whistling[4]. The misdeeds of al-Qahir were of a piece with his wicked character. In his presence he had two men thrown into a well and when one of them hung on to edge he ordered his men to cut off his hand, which they did[5]. On the fall of the field-Marshal Munis he caused, at first, the head of the son Yalbaq to be cut off and brought to his father. Then Yalbaq's throat was cut, and his head with that of his son was sent to Munis. Munis was then dragged by the foot to the gutter and there slaughtered like a sheep, while Qahir looked on[6]. The three heads were brought out in three basins to the

(1) fol. 107 a.
(2) Masudi, VI, 266.
(3) Masudi, VIII, 211.
(4) Masu'di, VIII, 116, 16.
(5) Misk, V, 446.
(6) Misk, IV, 604; Misk, III, 304 Eng. tr. Tr.

parade-ground, to be seen by the people, that of Yalbaq's son Ali was carried round the city on both sides, then brought back to the palace, and in accordance with custom placed in the magazine of skulls. The later Ibn al-Athir reports that the soldiers reluctantly helped him in this act of cruelty[1]. Qahir was also the only one who caused a man—an Abbasid prince and pretender—to be immured alive[2]. The Amir Adud-ud-Dawlah (d. 372/982) had a *Wazir* and his associates, who had played the traitor, trampled to death by elephants—the only instance of the kind in that period[3].

Throughout the century two instances of suicide, apart from those under sentence of death, are recorded[4]. Poor and shunned by all for his venomous satires a clerk, son of a Samanid Wazir, committed suicide[5]. The other the physician Ibn Gassan, drowned himself in Kalwada being disconsolate for the love of a foreign slave. He, however, was a Christian[6].

Already about the year 100/700 the Caliph is said to have forbidden the use of iron neck-chains for prisoners[7]. The Canonists at the time of Harun were agreed that the prisoners should be fed and clothed at the cost of the exchequer and that a monthly allowance of 10 dirhams *per head* should be sanctioned. Even their dress was determined according to the season, and according to their sex. It was forbidden to prisoners to go out in chains and beg[8]. In a

(1) Misk, V, 423; Ibn al-Athir, VIII, 194.
(2) Misk, V, 421; Jauzi, 45 a; *Zubdat al-fikrah*, Paris, fol. 225 b; Ibn al-Athir, VIII, 193.
(3) Misk, VI, 481, 517 Adud-ud-Dawlah was also the first to revive the use of war-elephants in war (Misk, VI, 464).
(4) But see index to the *Eclipse of the Abbassid Caliphate* S.V. suicide. Tr.
(5) *Yatimah*, IV, 7.
(6) Abulqasim, 83.
(7) *Fraq hist arab.*
(8) *Kit. al-Kharaj*, 83.

Budget of the Caliph al-Mutadid (279-289/892-902) a monthly allowance of 1500 dinars is shown for the prisoners of Baghdad[1], namely for their provisions, water and other necessities.

The embroidered girdles (tikak) are said to be the special work of the prisoners[2]. It is, even today, the finest work that is done in Baghdad. "I learnt in the prison[3] how to embroider trouser-bands".

In the beginning of the 4th/10th century the *Wazir* appointed doctors for prisoners, who were to visit them daily and render them medical aid[4]. In Egypt on the other hand, prisons were leased out. It was the most coveted of Government leases for it yielded large income. The lessees exacted six dirhams a month from every prisoner. This amount was paid in on admission and was not refunded even if the prisoner was detained for a shorter period[5].

The minimum charity, canonically fixed for a Muslim, is 2½ per cent on his property, not on its income[6]. Examples of benefactions are given, both of the pious and the wordly, showing a sense of great refinement in charity. A rich savant at Heart (d. 378/988) had gold struck, worth one-and-a-half times as much as the current coin. "The poor rejoices when I make over a small packet to him for he thinks that it contains a silver-piece. On opening it he is pleased to see the yellow of the gold, and more pleased still when he finds

(1) Wuz, 21.
(2) *Tikak*, Lane: "the band (that is inserted in the double upper border) of the drawers or trousers. Generally a strip of cotton, which is often embroidered at each end; sometimes of net-work and sometimes of silk Tr.
(3) Ibn al-Muttaz. Baihaqi, *Mahasin*' ed. Schwally 571. It is not to be found in the *Diwan*.
(4) Ibn al Qifti, 193.
(5) Maqrizi, Khitat, 1, 89.
(6) Eg. Kashf, 315.

it heavier in weight than the ordinary current-coin[1].

A rich merchant, who happened to be at the same time a man of learning (d. 361/962) sent to another a book with a gold-piece between every two folios[2]. A goldsmith at Baghdad sent the following day to a popular preacher, who had preached on "sweets", 500 biscuits with a gold-piece in each[3]. Living in cheerless house afflicted by poverty the poet Jahizah (d. 324/936) was visited by an official who brought with him all that was necessary; carpets, utensils, provisions, slaves. After chatting through the night the made over 2000 dirhams to the poet, took him round the house and on leaving said: "Take care of your house. All that is in it is yours"[4]. The pious mother of a clerk accustomed her son from his childhood to place at night a pound-weight of bread under his head and to give it in charity the next morning. And indeed he did so all his life[5]. In Kirman rich in date-trees the custom is never to pick up fallen dates, but to let the poor have them, with the result that when a violent wind blows the poor get more than the owners[6].

In making small presents, among lovers there was delicacy and discrimination. To send a lemon was considered improper, for it was nice to look at but was sour within. Often the loved-one sent an apple where "her bite seemed like the claws of a scorpion"[7]. This practice obtained in the Roman world[8]. Or again a poet had a valuable piece of cloth embroidered with his verses for his favourite female musician[9]. Though they established no orphanage yet, since

(1) Jauzi, 128 a; Subki, 11, 165.
(2) Subki, 11, 222.
(3) Jauzi, fol. 142 b.
(4) Jauzi, fol. 56a.
(5) Wuz, 64.
(6) Ibn Haukal, 224.
(7) Ibn al-Mutazz, 1, 68, 73.
(8) Gleichen-Russwurm, *Elegantiac* 277.
(9) Shabushti, 117a.

the Prophet had been an orphan, they took a very kindly interest in them. In Isphahan, for instance, a pious man was wont to take them home every Friday, to get their heads oiled[1]. On the other hand the establishment of hospitals was a purely wordly affair—the pious having nothing to do with medical treatment. Its very name 'Bimaristan' is Persian and comes not from the Qur'an. Walid, son of Abdul Malik, is said to have been the first to found a hospital in Islam[2]. Then the Barmecides, anything but orthodox, founded one, with an Indian physician as its Superintendent[3]. In his famous letter Tahir enjoins on his son: Build houses for the faithful that are ill, appoint a Supervisor to look after them and physicians to treat them[4]. In 259/873 Ahmad ibn Tulun built the first great hospital in Egypt. It had a bath for men and one for women, and was exclusively meant for poor folks—no soldier or courtier being admitted there. On admission the clothes and money of the patient were deposited with the Superintendent. Before discharge the patient received bread and chicken as his parting meal. The Prince spent 60,000 dinars for the hospital and visited it every Friday[5]. Ahmad even established a dispensary in his Court-mosque where a physician treated every Friday free of charge[6].

There was also a section for the lunatics in the hospital. Baghdad however, possessed a particularly large lunatic asylum—the Ezechiel monastery of Yore—a few days journey southward on the way to Wasit[7]. Chains and whips

(1) Abu Nuaim, 161 a.
(2) Maqrizi, *Khitat* II, 409.
(3) *Fihrist*, 245.
(4) Ibn Taifur, ed. Keller, fol. 20 b.
(5) Maqrizi, *Khitat*, II, 409. An opponent, however, ridicules it: "Fasten the hospital to his back-side with all the clumsy ruffians within (Kindi, 217).
(6) Maqrizi *Khitat*, II, 267.
(7) Yaqubi, *Bibl Geogr.* VII, 321; *Iqd, III, 240.*

as was the case with us a few decades ago; were the chief requisites of such an institution[1]. At Baghdad under al-Mutadid (279-289/982-902) 450 *dinars* a month were allotted for the remuneration of physicians, attendants and eye-doctors—the only specialists of that age,—for warders, gate-keepers of the asylum, for food, bakery and medicine[2]: The hospitals of the capital received powerful support from a non-Muslim. In 304 Sinan ibn Thabit assumed charge of "the five hospitals of Baghdad"[3]. Under the influence of this famous physician two other large hospitals were opened in 306/918, one by the Caliph himself at "the Syrian gate", and the other at the cost of his mother on the valuable building site on the eastern side of the town by the St. John's market and the Tigris. Both were placed under the direction of Sinan. For the up-keep of the Caliph's hospital 2000, and for that of his mother 600 dinars a month were assigned by endowment[4]. In 311/923 the Wazir Ibn al-Furat too established a hospital at Baghdad, for which he paid 200 dinars a month[5]. At Sinan's suggestion his patron Bejkem started in 329/941 the construction of a third hospital on the delightful little hill on the western bank of the Tigris where once stood the castle of Harun but it was never completed. In 368/987 Adud ud-Dawlah completed the building, and in 371/987 the hospital was opened with a staff of physicians and attendants, servants, porters, supervisors, administrators[6]. Muiz-ud-Dawlah founded in 355/965 yet another hospital by the Bridge of the Tigris and

(1) *Aghani*, XVIII, 30.
(2) Wuz, 21.
(3) Jauzi, fol. 14 a. Here he is particularly good as an authority for he has used the chronicle of Thabit. The oldest was the Sa'idi at Muhawwal-gate (fol. 66 a).
(4) Qifti, 194: Usaibiah, 1, 222; Jauzi, fol 16 a—according to him the figure is 2000; Abul Mahasin, II, 203.
(5) Jauzi, fol. 23.
(6) Qifti, 193; Jauzi, fol 69 a, Ibn al-Athir, IX, 12; Ibn Khall II, 485.

endowed it with landed properties yielding an income of 1000 dinars[1]. Even provincial towns such as Shiraz, Isphahan and Wasit had their hospitals[2].

In 319/931 the Caliph Muqtadir was informed that a physician had treated some one on wrong lines, with the result that the patient had died. He ordered Ibn Batimah, his Inspector of Professions, to prevent any one from practising as physician who was not examined by Sinan, his physician in ordinary and who had not obtained a certificate of competence from him. Apart from those who commanded confidence by their great reputation or were actually in Government service, there were more than 800 qualified medical practitioners. Their examination was conducted in the politest form: "I desire to hear something from the gentleman which I would always like to remember"[3].

In this century on single instance is on record of a physician-in-ordinary paying with his life for the wrong treatment of a prince. In 324/935 the Christian physician Bukht Jesu fell under the suspicion of having purposely treated the deceased brother of the Caliph wrongly. He atoned for it merely by banishment from Court.

---

(1) Jauzi, fol. 98b.

(2) Muk, 430; Jauzi, 69a. The one at Wasit was called an *Inn dar al-Diyafah)* and was a feeding-house for the people as well. It was founded by the Bejkem at the time of a famine (Jauzi, 69 a; Qifti, 193). Wasit got a hospital proper only in 413 (Jauzi, fol. 193 b.)

(3) Qifti, 191.

XXI. THE STANDARD OF LIVING

300 dirhams (300 franks) were reckoned at Mosul at this time as the annual requirement of a married couple in a humble station of life[1], 5-7000 dinars (50-70,000 marks) as a decent competence[2]. A young man, belonging to an official circle, who had run through his patrimony in women and songs, inherited from his maternal side 40,000 dinars but, now, having grown wiser, utilized his money thus : for 1000 dinars he repaired and restored his ancestral home; for 7000 he purchased the household needs : carpets, dresses, three slave girls *et cetera*; 2000 he invested in a business; 10,000 he buried under-ground for a rainy day and with the balance 20,000 he acquired a landed estate on the income of which he lived[3].

The excavations at Samarra have familiarized us with the Mesopotamian houses of the 3rd/9th century. "The houses at Samarra were built according to a definite plan: a covered passage led from the street or the lane to a spacious rectangular courtyard the proportion being 2 : 3. On the shorter side lay a ⊢ shaped hall with smaller rooms in the corners. The Courtyard, moreover, was surrounded by rows of rectangular residential and other rooms intended for household purposes[4]. In most of the houses there were a number of subsidiary court-yards with our houses (Wirthschaftsraumen). The houses invariably had baths and

---

(1) Masari-al-Ushaq, 159.

(2) Ibid, 5.

(3) Kit. 'al-.Faraj, II, 17.

(4) Sarre and Herzfeld, *Erster Vorlaufiger Bericht uber die Ausgrabungen Von Samarra* Berlin, 1912, p, 14.

sewerage and not infrequently wells. Occasionally they had open halls with colonades and under-ground living rooms with ventilation-chimneys. The houses were one-storied. Where the ground was uneven—it was skilfully turned into terraces. There were as many as fifty rooms in a house. Windows were set with bull's eye-shaped coloured glass of 20 to 50 CM in diameter".

In the Mesopotamian Literature of the 4th/10th century we find no reference to summer underground dwellings. Not a single one of the numerous stories of the time suggests it[1]. The practice of sheltering oneself in this way from the intense heat comes from Central Asia where in 981 A. D. WANG YEN TE remarks that the Uighurs reside in summer in uderground dwellings[2]. Of the Muslim countries—Zereng, capital of Afghanistan and the Persian town of Arragan were the first to build *Sirdabs* with running water for summer dwellings[3]. Even in the 5th/11th century it appears as a peculiarity of Arragan to Nasir Khusru to have as many rooms below[4] as above the earth. Through these underground dwellings (*Sirdab)* flowed water—ensuring thereby coolness and comfort in summer. Some centuries later Maqrizi can boast of Egypt that "in summer there people need not as at Baghdad go into underground dwellings"[5]. Instead of the Sirdab the summer-luxury of the day was the *"Bair or Qubbat al-Khaish* (House or dome of felt)[6].

---

(1) *Sirdab* at this time, is an underground excavation: *e.g.* Muqtadir dug a pit in the palace in front of the Plant-House (Baum-house?) for Munis. It was then to be said that he was thrown into a *Sirdab Kit ul-Uyun*, fol. 113 b. In Arib (p. 10) "in a house enclosed by iron gates". Already at the time of Mansur some one has been imprisoned in a *Sirdab.* He could not distinguish the light of the day from the darkness of the night". Masudi, VI, 200.

(2) JRAS 1898, p. 819.

(3) Ibn Haukal, 299.

(4) Ed. Schefer, Text, 91; tr. 250.

(5) *Khitat* 1, 28.

(6) (The usage of the authors suggests that this was something like a punkha. Tr.)

In summer the Persian kings are said to have taken their siesta in a room with double walls, the intervening space being filled with ice. And such too, it is said, was the case with the Omayyads, but under Mansur a different cooling process was introduced. They spread the coarsest felt and kept watering it; the evaporation produced a cool breeze[1]. At first they spread the felt over a tent, later over the Venetians[2]. In the palace of Adud-ud-Dawlah at Shiraz the felt was kept constantly wet by water-discharging pipes[3]. At Baghdad apparently this was the approved cooling-process. At the beginning of the 4th/10th century a general considered a levy coming from Baghdad as unfit for a strenuous campaign on the ground that "they were accustomed to houses on the Tigris, to wine, to ice, to wet felt and female musicians[4]". To these summer houses *Mirwahat el-Khais*, (fans made of felt), brought further coolness. Deeply scented pieces of cloth were fastened to these fans not "unlike a sail to a ship"[5]. Ice and wet felt were even taken to the pleasure-boats on the Tigris, curtains of coloured gauze draping it[6]. During the summer nights people of Baghdad slept on the roofs of their houses[7].

In the north, at Amul, by reason of the incessant rain the roofs were generally sloping[8]. In Yaman even in summer

(1) Tabari, III, 418, Yaqut, *Irshad*, VI, 99, in verses from the time of Tahir.

(2) Tha'alibi, Lat al-Ma'amit, 14.

(3) Muk, 449,

(4) De Geoje, *Carmathes*, 218, according to Misk.

(5) Guzuli, *Matali el-budur*, 1, 60, for the 4th/10th century we have a proof of this in a passage in Sari.

(6) *Jamhara*, of Saizari, Leiden fol. 199 a; Baihaqi, ed. Schwally; 447.

(7) This is manifest from the story of this animal Zabzab which finds a place in all the chronicles under the year 304. Further Ibn Jauzi (18, b) says : "chronicles under the year 308 it became so cold that people came down from the roofs and covered themselves as in winter".

(8) Istakhri, 211.

it was so cool in the houses that they had to cover themselves at Siesta. They returned to bed and drew the curtain. This was explained by the fact that the interior of the houses was white-washed with lime. The roof and the wall being of marble, houses were always full of light. Indeed where pure marble was used for the roofing—the shadow of the flying birds was visible within[1]. In the middle of the 3rd/9th century for larger buildings the Hirah style of architecture was adopted; in other words Hellenistic style; three sided frontage with a door in the centre and in each of the two wings. The Caliph Mutawakkil built his palace with three hugs gates "through which a rider could pass lance in hand"[2]. This style found favour and the people generally built houses in the Hirah style[3].

According to the preliminary report on the excavations at Samrra the central (archway) was larger and broader than the others. This, indeed, was an imitation of the Hellenistic triumphal arches[4]. The Palace, the Taj, built forty years later, is likely to have been an extension of this style. Its front consisted of five vaults or arches resting on ten marble columns, each five ells (or about 8 feet) in height[5]. The frontage of the Palace of Ibn Tulun in Egypt had three doors side by side : only on great festive occasions were all these opened[6]. From the East, indeed, did Ibn Tulun borrow this as well as the style of the Minarets.

The palace, with its enclosure, on the east side of

(1) Hamadhani, 196.
(2) Yaqubi, *Bibl, Geog* VII, 266, 16.
(3) Masudi, VII, 192 f.
(4) p. 34. The Suburb, on the east side of Baghdad, where the military Road to Persia leaves the capital, was called the 'Three Gates" by reason of this style of architecture (See Guy Le Strange, Baghdad, p. 203, Tr.)
(5) Yaqut 1,809. Thus is this somewhat obscure passage is to be understood (Guy Le Strange *Baghdad*, 254 Tr.).
(6) Maqrizi, 1, 315.

Baghdad, constituted quite a little town. Encircled by a wall, it stretched 12 kilometers inland from the Tigris[1]. The places of the aristocracy also consisted of several buildings. The Wazir Ibn al-Furat who (about 300/912) spent about 300,000 dinars on his Palace, had a garden house built close by (Dar-ul-Bustan) at a further cost of 500,000 dinars, where his women-folk, nieces and his small children resided[2]. Behind the gates towered[3] the tallest portion—the *Bahw*—adorned with battlements:

Its battlements rose like Veiled women squatting in a row at prayer[4].

The Caliph's palaces possessed gardens, houses bowers, cupolas, courtyards, ponds and rivulets enlivening the scene. In the 'Lead-House' the Caliph held his official audiences. There flowed a brook in front, discharging itself into the Tigris[5]. Courtyards, for accommodating guards, were called after the later forty, sixty, ninety[6] Among the rotunda the 'Citron-House' (dar-el Utrujjah)[7], and the dome of the Ass' are mentioned[8].

---

(1) Istakhri 83. This might have been like Shiraz, (according to a traveller) which about the end of the 4th/10th century was for the most part, intersected by waste lands. *TARIKH BAGHDAD* Text, 49.
(2) Wuz, 179.
(3) Jauhari, under Bahw, Abulqasim, 36.
(4) Ibn al-Mutazz speaking of the "Seven-Star Palace".
(5) Wuz, 420.
(6) So were the division called because their month for salary counted 40 or 90 days. (Thses seem German rather than English formations) Tr.
(7) Misk, V, 324: Hamza Isphahani, 1, 204; Ibn al-Mutazz, Diwan, I, 136 lines 6 is to be read so.
(8) Jauzi, 160 a. In Ibn al-Mutazz it is referred to as "a high rotunda 1, 139. line 6. The name is said to be due to the fact that the Caliph could on his round, mount up to the top on a donkey. But this is stated only in a latter source (Yaqut, 1, 806) and is likely to be an invention after the fashion of the Alexandrian light-house which was similarly called, Ibn Khurdadbih, 115.

The Amirs used to ride in the labryinth of palaces as far as the Dar es-Salam, where they dismounted (Jauzi, 160 a). Later authorities speak of underground passages connecting the Palaces one with the other. Nasir Khusru also tells us that the Fatimid palaces consisted of large and small buildings interconnected with underground passages. In the many detailed stories, referring to the palaces, however, we never hear of such secret inlets and outlets. In any case there is exaggeration. Mukaddasi visited the palace of Adud-ud-Dawla at Shiraz after his death. He reports that he heard from the Chief Chamberlain that it contained 360 rooms—the prince using one every day of the year[1]. The Light-house at Alexandria is said to have had 366 rooms[2]. The Palace of Eldenburg at Brandenburg had as many rooms as the days of the year[3].

As a forerunner to artificiality in Literature we notice, towards the end of the 3rd/9th century, fanciful innovations spreading from Court to Court.

In the Tulunid Palace in Egypt there was a quick-silver pond, 50 cubits square. At its corners were massive silver pillars to which were attached silver cords with silver rings, holding a leather mattress filled with air. On this slept the ruler, one of the sublimest of regal devices ! It was marvellous to see it on a moon-lit night when the moon-beams mingled with the sparking quick-silver[4].

In 305/907 the Caliph showed to the Greek Ambassador at Baghdad a lake of tin, more resplendent than polished silver. It was 30 x 20 yards with four beautiful pleasure boats, covered over with gold-embroidered Egyptian linen[5]. "At

(1) p. 449.
(2) Khurdadbih, 114.
(3) Fontane, *Funf schlosser, 96.*
(4) Maqrizi *Khitat,* 1, 365.
(5) *Tarikh Baghdad,* 53.

the time of Augustus the so-called Egyptian garden came into fashion in Rome[1]. It approximately represented what was later understood by an English Park. It was a reaction against the severe architectural style which built gardens on the same lines as houses".

And when the ruler of Spain built his Pleasure-Palace of Zahra at Cordova—it could not, of course, be without a quicksilver pond[2].

In the Tulunid Khumarwaihi this Egyptian tradition was united to the Turkish delight in flowers; making him the greatest garden-builder among Muslim princes. On his father's drill-ground he had all kinds of flowers and trees planted: rare grafts such as almonds on apricot stem, various kinds of roses, red, and blue and yellow lotus. In laying out the garden patterns of pictures and letters were followed. The gardener had to see that no leaf overlapped the other. Ponds, fountains, artificial wells—similar to those of the Egyptian style of gardening—and pavilions enlivened the garden. The idea of an 'English Park' , which was little known even in ancient history, was so far remote that the garden-loving Egyptian Caliph of the subsequent century ordered the paths of his gardens to be covered with Babylonian mats[3]. The palm-stems were covered with guilded metal plates—an old oriental taste! Already the Persian kings, held audiences under plane—trees, entirely wrapped up in silver[4]. Indeed even in the "modern Pavilion" at Baghdad there stood some 400 palms—all five yards high and all covered from top to bottom with carved—teakwood,

(1) Gleichen—Russwurm, *Elegantiae,* 387.
(2) Abulmahasin, II, 281.
(3) On the continent 'English, Parks or English Gardens signify wild growing bushes and trees which seem more like a forest than an artificial well-cared for park. The latter is styled : franzosichen Garten. Tr. Maqrizi, *Khitat,* 1, 487.
(4) *Khitat*, 1, 316; Abulmahasin, II, 56.

supported by gold girders[1].

The supremest pleasure of the Caliph Qahir was in his orange-garden for which he imported trees from Basra and Oman, only recently brought there from India[2]. And about this very time flourished in Syria two poets—Sanaubari and Kushajim—interpreters of the charms of gardens, flowers and trees. But the field was a limited one roses, narcissusses, deep-red anemones, white poppies, violets, jasmin, granates, mint, carnations, lilies, ruyrtles, the yellow camomiles and lotus on the ponds. The tulip had not yet come down from Central Asia. The rose-cultivation was already well-developed. The author of the Nishwar al-Muhadarah (d. 384/994) professess to have seen a deep-black rose with delicious scent and, likewise, at Basra a rose half deep-red and half pure-white, the dividing line appearing on each petel as if marked by a red-pen[3]. The cypress was then the only garden tree along with the palm. The passion for gardening, originating in Egypt, remained ascendant throughout this period. In the 5th/11th century Nasir Khusru found in Cairo market—gardeners who had fruit-bearing plants in tubs in stock for ready transplantation. He had not seen anything like it elsewhere. A rich Jew had on his roof 300 plants in silver pots[4].

In the midst of a round pond of clear water in the Palace at Baghdad there was a tree of eighteen branches with boughs of silver and some few of gold. It had multi coloured leaves which, like real ones, trembled in the breeze. All kinds of birds made of silver sat and twittered on the branches. In 305/917 this is said to have amazed the Byzantine ambassador more than anything else[5]. At the

(1) *Tarikh Baghdad*, p. 63 f.
(2) Masudi, VIII, 336.
(3) Suyuti, *Hush al Muhadarah, II, 237*.
(4) Schefer's tr. 160, 172.
(5) Tarikh Baghdad, ed. Saloon.

Imperial Palace at Byzantium there were several pieces of furniture round the Caesar's throne on which, Bishop Liutprand, ambassador of the German King Otto, saw and heard birds sitting and singing. The Greek Emperor even had large gilded lions stretched before him watching his throne. During the audience they occasionally opened their mouths, roared and struck the ground with their tails. Further, the Imperial throne could be lifted, by a machine, to the roof of the saloon : a piece of bad taste, foreign to the orientals[1].

Ibn al-Mutazz, Prince and contemporary, praises the tree at Baghdad[2].

The houses at Baghdad mostly had projections and bay-windows on the ground floor which[3] an indifferent donkey-rider could not always avoid and which as dangerous corners had an evil reputation[4]. In the narrow streets of Shiraz where two animals could not pass side by side people were always colliding with these projections[5].

The house door was of a tastefully carved wood—a ring served as a knocker[6]. Wood, indeed, was very widely used in rich houses—the Indian teak being the greatest favourite. Like the rooms of our peasants the interior was, as the Germans say, "Cozy". The room which stands in the Cairo Museum has that effect[7]. The rooms however, were somewhat empty-looking but the figure, the dress, the movement of the inmates showed to great advantage. Colour and design had a free play on carpeted walls and floor. The

---

(1) Ebersolt, *La Grand Palais de constantinople*. Paris. 1910, 68.
(2) *Diwan*, 1, 138.
(3) Kawasik, Abulqasim, 33.
(4) Yatimah, II, 253, Jamh, al Islam Leiden, fol 77 a.
(5) Muk, 429.
(6) Hamadhani, *Maq*, Beyrut, 105.
(7) I think Mez refers to an antique *room* preserved in the Museum Tr.

only piece of furniture was the trunk which also was a depository of clothes[1]. Cupboards and bedsteads were unknown. The table was brought in for meals only. In the rich houses of the 3rd/9th century an onyx plate was used for meals[2]. Later tables with legs came into fashion[3]. In Abulqasim tables made of red-white Khorasanian Khalang-wood resembling "a bunch of Carnations" are praised. By and by the tables became more and more massive. In 305/917 the Caliph sent to a Wazir three tables—the largest of which had a circumference of fifty spans with the result that the door had to be enlarged to let it in[4].

At the Fatimid Court quivers of Khalang-wood were likewise used[5]. They were specially prepared at Jurjan on the Caspian Sea[6]. Already in the 3rd/9th century Jahiz praises for the east utensils made of Kaimakish (Turkish) Khalang-wood alongside of the Chinese utensils, then popular all over[7]. The cooking utensils are simply called *Sufr* (Copper)[8]. In the Cairo of the 5th/11th century a women owned 5000 heavy copper water-tubs which she let out on hire for a dirham per month[9].

In the numerous arrangements for warm baths Islam carried forward a beautiful inheritance of the Greco-Roman world. In the old Orient this side of life was not developed. The Persian king Balas (484-488 A.D.) incurred the wrath of his priesthood by building public baths in the towns of his empire[10] "for in the bath lay a desecration of the holy

(1) Wuz, 172: *Yatimah*, III, 237, *Kit. al-faragn,* 1, 20.
(2) Jahiz, *Bukhala*, ed. Vloten, 56; Masudi VIII, 269.
(3) Hamadhani, maq, 113; Abulqasim, 38, *Maqrizi* Khitat, I, 419.
(4) Wuz 65.
(5) Yaqubi, *Bib-Geog*. VIII 277.
(6) *Maqrizi*, Khitat, I, 420.
(7) *Bukhala*, 57, Khalangwood utensil, in the poem in *Iqd*, III, 296.
(8) *Irshad*, I, 392.
(9) Nasir Khusru, 152.
(10) Joshna Stylites, ed. Wright, 19.

elements"[1]. When Kobad visited a public bath, after the capture of Amida, he was so greatly pleased with it that he ordered the construction of baths, similar to it, in all the Persian towns[2]. An old Arab writer even reports that the Persians had no baths before Islam[3]. But even stern Muslims always looked askance at the public bath system. Abu Bakr es-Sulami (d. 311/923) was not quite sure whether the prophet ever went to *Hammam*[4]. The husband is not to provide his wife with money for visiting a public-bath since, he, thereby, helps her in something culpable[5].

The Caliph even in 322/934 called them the "Grecian Baths" (*Hammamat Rumiyyah*)[6]. Their decoration was entirely un-Islamic . In the baths of Sammarra, instead of the stucco-work which is Syrio-Hellenic tradition, the pedestals were painted (Sarre and Herzfeld, 24). Masudi observes that often in the baths the fabulous bird Anqa was painted[7]. It is an old oriental cherub : a bird with human face and on eagle-beak, with four wings on each side and two hands with claws. It is put into the mouth of Ali that he never saw a Qura'nic inscription in a bath[8]. In the 3rd/6th century on the Eastern side of Baghdad alone there were 5000 baths[9]. In the first half of the 4th/10th century Baghdad still counted 10,000 baths[10], in the second half of the century

---

(1) Noldeke, *Tabari*, 134, note 5.
(2) Land *Anecdote III, 210*; Joshna Stylites, 75.
(3) Yaqub, History, 1, 199.
(4) Subki, Tabaqat, II, 131.
(5) Guzuli, *matali el-budur*, II, 17 according to Zan akhshari.
(6) Misk, V, 449. For the dressing room at the baths the Arabs used a Syrian loan-word, *maslah (Mughrib, ed Tallaquist,* 43). The Syrians in their turn, called the bricks of the baths by the special Greek term Keramedi Mu'arrab, ed. Sachau, 116.
(7) Masudi, III, 29.
(8) Guzuli, II, 17.
(9) Yaqubi, *Geogr*, 254.
(10) *Tarikh Baghdad,* 76 ff.

the number is said to have dwindled to 5000[1]. The number, indeed, steadily declined. In the 6th/12th century 2000 is the figure stated[2]. They were covered with asphalt which came from a place between Kufa and Basra and looked like black marble[3]. Baths were not as popular in Egypt as in Syria. Old Cairo is reported to have had 1170 warm baths—new Cairo only eighty[4]. The bath-staff consisted of at least five officers: the bath-master (hammami); the attendant (Qayyim); the dung-man (Zabbal)—the baths were mainly heated by dry dung—the stoker (Waqqas) and the drinking-water carrier (Saqqa)[5].

Mansur (2nd/8th century) introduced at his Court the girdle and high cap which the heathen Arabs had regarded as Persian fashion[6]. A courtier has his fling at this;—

> "We expected an increment for the Prince for
> he has enjoined the high cap;
> which sits on the skull like the cup of the
> Jews, enriched by a veil"[7].

(Through the crusades this high cap with veil became the head-gear of women in the West[8]. Under Mustain (284

(1) *Tarikh Baghdad*, 76, ff. The figure 60,000 for baths then is fantastics. Mosques might number 27000.

(2) Maqrizi, Knitat, II, 80; Ibn Jubair, 230.

(3) Ibn Jubair, 230.

(4) Maqrizi, *Khitat*, II.

(5) *Tarikh Baghdad*, ed. Salmon, 74.

(6) Jacob, *Altarab*, Beduinleben. 237; (Khuda Bakhsh, *Islamic Civilization*, 1. 96 ff. Tr.)

(7) They were propped up from inside with staves. *Aghani* IX, 121 ; *Lubb al-adab,* said to have been the first to adopt this costume. Beladhuri, 434.

(8) Rashid was against this innovation. He is reported to have sent away a poet who wanted to recite poetry in a high cap. He had to come back in the Arab costume with the head-band. Jahiz, Bayan, 1, 42. Mustain is said to have restored the high cap to fashion again. Masudi, VIII, 302. About 230/845 the Qadhi of Egypt alone claimed for himself the right of using a high cap and ordered its disuse by

252/862-866) hats again became shorter ; the Qadhis only retaining the long hood (Aqba) (Masudi, VII, 402). This very Mustain is said to have introduced sleeves three spans wide, a thing unknown before. These sleeves served as pockets for all kinds of necessary things : money, books[1].

The mathematician wishing to note something, fetched his pencil out of sleeves; the banker slipped his cheque-book therein ; the tailor his scissors ; the Qadhi his MS from which he read out at the pulpit and the clerk his petition[2]. The shoe served as a depository with others. Out of his shoe the Wazir of Mustain pulled out the inventory of the Treasury[3]. The Court Officials took to the palace in the shoes of their slaves flasks full of broth for their meal[4]. From the beginning and from the end of the 4th/10th century we hear that it is not good taste to use coloured dresses which are intended for women and slaves. At most it was permissible only in the privacy of the house when they were *cupped* or when they were at drinking-bouts but it was considered vulgar in the street. The nobleman's dress should be white. Even the theologians recommend this. In Paradise white will be worn[5]. In coloured clothes, however, roamed about the musician ibn Suraij (during the Ommayyad period) in the streets of Medina, holding a grasshopper tied to a thread

---

others. Kindi, 460. Even the strange fashion of the girdles, which prevailed in the Frankish empire of the XIIth century, came from the East, Jac. Falcke, *Gesch-des Geschmackes im mittelatter*, 66.

(1) Yaqut *Irshad* 1, 254 : Bibl-hisp. Arab. III, 49. Tauhidi (d.400):— Some one questioned : Can one of you put his hand in the sleeves of his friend and fetch out as much gold and silver as he wants ? They answered in the negative. Thereupon he said : Then you are no brothers. (Fis-sadaqah was-sadiq. Constant. 1301, p. 11).

(2) Yaqut *Irshad*, II, 49; Yaqut, *Irshad* 1, 399; Masudi, VI, 345 : Maqrizi, *Khitat*, 390; Kit, *al-faragh*; 1, 69 ; *al-arifin* 90.

(3) Fakhri, Ahlwardt's ed. 298 (During the Mutiny in India letters were placed between the sole of the shoes to ensure safety Tr.)

(4) *Adab en-nadim*, 15 a.

(5) Samarqandi, Bustan *al-arifin*, 90.

which he now let fly and now, again, quickly pulled back[1]. It was reckoned inelegant to wear washed with unwashed, new with used clothes, linen or wool with silk[2] : "The best dress is the one that matches". Besides men white was the colour worn by divorced women ; the rest of the women avoided it except for loose white trousers. They, however, used natural and not artificial colours—the later were only used by peasant and singing slave girls. In the East blue was the colour for mourning and for widows[3] ; in Spain, on the other hand, white[4]. Trousers, an entirely unarab piece of dress, formed part of a better outfit for men[5]. Even the three great official circles were distinguished from one other by their dresses : the "scribe" wore the *durra'ah*[6], a coat spilt at the breast ; the theologian the wrapper (tailasan)[7]; and the military man the short Persian jacket. This jacket came into fashion as court-dress about 300/912. At divine service the Courtiers used black jackets. One of these tells us how he sought admission into the official circle of the mosque in a *durra'ah* and how the dusky porters sent him back saying that admission there was only in a black jacket. And such, indeed, was the case in all official circles in the mosques. But the Khatib adds that about 400/1009 the practice had altered—*Now* only the preacher and the *Muazzin* (one who calls to prayer) appear in black[8]. The

(1) *Tadkirah Hamaduniyyah*, Paris, fol. 148 a.

(2) Kit *al-muwassa,* ed.Burnnow, 124; Tha'alibi, *Kit. al-mirwah al-muruwwah*, Berlin, Petermann, 59, fol. 129 b.

(3) *Kit. al-Muwassa*, 126; Kushajim, *Diwan,* ed. Beyrut, 169; *Kit. al-Uyun wal hadaiq* Berlin, fol. 209.

(4) *al-Tiraz, al-muwassa* 202.

(5) E. G. misk. V. 528; Wuz 176. From *Sarawil* a further plural *Sarawilat* is formed Muwassa, 126, 15.

(6) Misk, VI, 308.

(7) Only in Shiraz *tailassan* was so commonly used, that even the drunkard stumbled over it? (p. 368 line 2 from the bottom of the notes). Mnkaddasi was not allowed admission before the Wazir in *tailasan.*

(8) *Tarikh Baghdad,* Paris, fol. 15 a.

rich merchant and the private gentleman worę two shirts (Qamis) and a mantle over the trousers. And thus was the Prince Qahir attired when in 320/932 the news of his election as Caliph was announced to him[1]. And the Sufi at Ferghani (d. 331/943) who pretended to be rich, although actually poor, likewise used two shirts, a mantle, trousers, fine shoes a band (Binde) and carried a key in his hand though he had no house of his own[2]. Already the *Khafṭan* takes the place of the Arab mantle. At the beginning of the 4th/10th century an Egyptian poet rides, on a wintry day, to the Court in a *Khaftan*[3]. It formed part of the dréṣṣ of the Syrian literati[4]. In a *Khaftan* the Caliph Muqtadir mounts his horse on the occasion of his solemn death-ride (320/932).

Waterproofs of oil-cloth—protection against a heavy shower came from China[5]. Already the poet Buhturi (d. 284/897) begs his patron for one such water-proof[6]. In describing the rainless Yamam Mukaddasi tells us that no one ever talks of a water-proof there[7]. Stockings were used both by men and women[8]. Red-shoes were not in good taste though the Greek emperor and the ordinary Muslim folk used them. But like the Byzantine crown prince the fops might uses yellow and black shoes[9].

For a long time the fashion continued for boys and girls to make up[10] the hair on the temple "like a nun" (ن) or like a scorpion coiled up because of the proximity of the fire of

(1) *Arib*, 182.
(2) Abulmahasin II, 303.
(3) Ibn Sa'id, *Mughrib*, ed. Tallquist, 33.
(4) Sanaubari in *Jamharat ul-Islam of Saizari*, Leiden fol. 113 a.
(5) *Lataif el-ma'arif*, 12.
(6) *Diwan*, 1, 185.
(7) 96.
(8) *Aghani, IX, 85; Yatimah*, III 54 of flowered silk.
(9) Muwassa, 125: Ibn Khurdadbih. 109.
(10) Ibn al-Mutazz; 1, 66.

the cheeks[1]. Already a century before this had been sung by Abu Nuwas[2].

The ostrogoths had once terrorised the people of southern Europe by their green-dyed hair. The Thracians dyed their blond hair blue[3]. In the orient, too, in Arabia and Persia, the practice of dyeing hair had spread and the theologians disputed its canonical sanction. Abu Nu'aim (d. 430/1039) for instance, in his *History of Isphahan*, meticulously reports in every individual biography whether the hero dyed his hair or not. Even an ascetic who, for forty mortal years, had never used a bed, dyed this hair and beard[4]. In the higher society, however, the use of dye seems to have been exceptional (Mez, Text, p. 370 line 3 from the top). The Fihrist, in the short biography of the Courtier and literature al-Munajjim, expressly tells us that he used the dye till his death[5]. The artificial taste of the later Roman Empire introduced into the arena purple-dyed sheep, white-washed oxen, lions with gilded manes, ostriches dyed with vermillion[6]. No such practice in the 4th/10th century is recorded in any Arab report. But in the modern Baghdad I have seen donkeys painted half red and delicate rose-tinted pigeons. This, indeed has an affinity with the practice of the antique world[7].

In the 4th/10th century an absolutely un-Islamic practice, for the first time, grew up in burials. The great built mausoleums for themselves (turbah). The mother of al-Muqtadir, a Greek, was the first to build one at Rusafa[8]; the

(1) Ibn al-Mutazz, 1, 70.
(2) *Diwan*, 82.
(3) Gebhart, Italie mystique; Tomaschek, *Die Thraker*
(4) MS Leiden, I fol. 98 a; other instances 108 a; 122 a; II, 25 b.
(5) p. 144.
(6) Gleichen-Russwirm. *Eleguntice*, 461.
(7) (And such, too, is the case in India) They dye horses, pet, birds, cats. Tr.)
(8) Abulmahasin II, 203.

Caliph Al-Radi (d. 329/940) likewise built one there[1]; Muiz-ud-Dawlah (d. 356/966) built one over the graves of the Quraish[2]; the Caliph Tai, again, built one at Rusafa[3]. Apart from this in this sphere a series of practices entirely foreign to Islam tenaciously held their ground. Despite the prohibition the practice of loudly lamenting the dead continued. Thus in Egypt about the year 250/804 the tearing of clothes, the blackening of faces and the clipping of hair were forbidden and women, employed for lamenting the dead, were imprisoned. Similar steps were taken in 994/907. Indeed al-Hakim forbade unveiled women to follow a funeral. He forbade weeping and howling and procession of mourning women with drums and pipes[4].

With blackened faces and loosened hair women mourned the death at Baghdad[5]. When in 305/916 the brother of the Caliph's mother died she caused[6] a green pavilion which he had built, his boat, his "Flyer" on the Tigris to be destroyed. In the year 329/941 the Caliph al-Radi took the death of his eunuch Ziruk so greatly to heart that, for a few days, he removed from his own to another's house—a well-known custom among many nations—and, as a sign of mourning, caused 400 casks of old wine to be poured into the Tigris[7]. In a draft will Hamadhani directs that no one should loudly mourn him; that no one should strike his cheeks, scratch his face; that no door is to be blackened; no furniture smashed; no plant uprooted and no building destroyed; that he is to be buried in three white Egyptian pieces of cloth which should neither be silk nor

(1) Jauzi 69 a.
(2) Jauzi, fol. 102 a.
(3) *Dewan* of Rida 606.
(4) Kindi, 203; 206. Yahya, b. Sa'id, fol. 115 b.
(5) Wuz 49.
(6) *Kit. al-Uyun*, Berlin, fol. 137 b.
(7) *Kit. al-Uyun*. fol. 180 b.

embroidered nor yet worked with gold[1]. With the dead bodies of the rich strange un-Islamic luxuries came into fashion ; notably in matters of shroud and embalming. In 356/967 died the Hamadanid (his ancester was حمدان) Saif-ud-Dawlah—he was washed nine times, first with *aqua pura*, then with the essence of lotus, then with *sandal*, then *Derirah*, then with amber, then with camphor, then with rose-water and twice finally with distilled water. He was wiped with a *Dibiqan* piece of cloth, worth fifty dinars, which was made over along with his remuneration, to the Qadhi of Kufa, who had washed the body. He was embalmed with myrrah and camphor. His cheeks and throat were done with 100 *mithqal of Galiah*; his ears, nose and neck with 30 *mithqal* of camphor. His shroud cost 1000 dinars. He was laid in a coffin , strewn with camphor[2]. The son of the Caliph al-Muiz, who died in 371/984, was wrapped up in 60 shrouds[3]. The embalming of the Egyptian Wazir Ibn Killis (d. 380/990) is said to have cost 100,000 dinars.[4]

Lamentation for the dead was given a legal form when criers proclaimed at the funeral of scholars; it is he who defended the messenger of God, who shrank from falsehood who knew the traditions of the messenger of God[5], or when they said "those only will be pardoned who love the Law and the community"[6]. Frequently theologians were buried in their own houses first but a few years later were transferred to a cemetery[7]. In the second half of the 4th/

(1) Ras'ail, 536 ff.

(2) Ibn Saddad, Beyrut, fol, 51 a. I am indebted to Dr. Sarasin for this passage.

(3) Ibn Khall, ed, Wustenfeld. II 23.

(4) Ibn Taghribirdi; 46, according to Dahabi.

(5) Subki. *Thabaqat,* III, 15.

(6) *Bibl hisp-arab,* Ibn Bask, 1, 134. In Spain this was wide spread custom.

(7) For instance Imam al-Haramain (Subki, II, 257); the eighty years

10th century grew up the practice of the Shiahs—prevalent even to-day of taking their dead for burial to Najaf and Kufa. Even this was an adoption of an older practice. The Shiite theologian al-Qummi (d. 381/991) tells us that his contemporary Jews and Christians still inter their dead in Palestine (Kit:al-Ilal, Berlin 8327, fol. 115 b. Ikhshid, with his two sons, was buried in Jerusalem. Kindi, 296).

The invitations to parties had necessarily to correspond to the rhetorical tendencies of the day. Many strange literary freaks show themselves here[1]. Thus writes the Sahib (*i.e.* Ismail b. Abbad) to a friend : We are, in a company which is blessed by everything save thee. Besides thee we have all that we need for our contentment. The eyes of the narcissuses are open; the cheeks of the violets are ablush; the censers of lemon and orange trees are spreading their perfume—eloquent are the lutes, fragrant the cups. The fine market-hall is open—the herald is there to announce you. The stars of the carousing companions have arisen and well outstretched is the amber-sky. By my life, when thou comest—we would be in a heavenly paradise and thou wilt, verily be the very centre of the pearl string[2]. At the beginning of the 4th/10th century the Wazir Ibn al-Furat had nine councellors daily to meal among them were four Christians. "They sat in front and by his side. First a plate was placed in front of each containing all kinds of seasonable fruits in delicate, artistic pieces. A huge plate with similar contents stood in the centre. But this was merely ornamental. On each of the small plates lay a knife for cutting and pealing quince, pears and peaches. Each guest was served with a glass dish for the pealings. When they had done with fruits—

old Chief Judge Abdullah ibn Maruf (d. 380), (Jauzi, fol. 336); Isfaraini (d. 436 at Baghdad) removed to a cemetery in 410 (Ibn Khall I, 35); the Mutazalite chief Qadhi Abdul Jabbar of Rai (d. 410). Subki (1, 220). Qudurl, Ibn Khall, 1, 38.

(1) For example, see *Yatimah*, III, 80 f.

(2) *Yatimah*, III, 81.

plates were removed and bowls and jugs of water were brought in for washing the hands. This was followed on a leather tray, covered with a lid of bamboo pieces over which was spread Egyptian linen. Round the dish were the serviettes.

With the removal of the lid—the meal began.

Ibn al-Furat conversed with them, kept them feeding on. Continually for two full hours one dish after another was served. Then the guests proceeded to a side-room to wash their hands. The servants poured water and the eunuchs stood, with Egyptian linen, for them to dry their hands and flasks of rose-water to sprinkle their faces with[1]. The fact of bringing the courses one after another is reported for the obvious reason that it was an innovation. The old Muslim practice was to serve up the entire food leaving to each individual to take what he pleased[2]. And such, indeed, was the French practice too in the eighteenth century, namely, simultaneous serving of all the dishes; now, however, exchanged throughout Europe for the general Russian practice. Generally they washed the hand *together* at the table before the meal. And usually this was done with one and the same bowl, the master of the house leading so that "no one need feel ashamed" *i.e.* of undue haste in starting the meal. Ablution after meal was a real-washing. It began from the left of the host and proceeded on with the result that the host's turn came last[3]. But if one was not among his equals his superiors, as is the case here, with the Wazir—the practice was for the guests to wash in a side room. Even the Adab en-nedim rules ; do not wash before

(1) Wuz, 240.

(2) Mustatraf, 149 and all the older stories.

(3) Qummi (d. 381) *Kit. al-ilal*, Berlin, fol. 112 b; Kushajim, *Adab en-nedim*, Paris, fol. 48 b. Qummi a Khorasanian, testifies to another custom : after food thay began right from the door whether a slave or a freeman.

kings and superiors, but spare them the sight of that which is unpleasant for one to see in *himself*, much more in others. The host, sometimes, requests his guests not to trouble but to wash at the table; but only a fool listens to him.[1] This custom was universal. In Mesopotamia they expected an inferior to rise after meal and wash his hands aside.[2] And, indeed, because Afshin would not comply with this practice he is said to have fallen into disfavour with the Caliph[3]. Even in Egypt a distinguished Barbarian had his guests shown into a room for washing their hands[4]. This practice as the following story shows sprang up in the 2nd/8th century. Ibn Da'b did not take his meal with the Caliph al-Hadi : " I do not eat where I cannot wash my hands"; for at Al-Hadi's they were wont to withdraw for washing hands. Ibn Da'b, however, obtained permission to wash hands in the presence of the Caliph[5]. And similarly one was to pick his teeth only when alone[6].

Ibn al-Mutazz, thus describes an undesirable table-companion: " he continually picks his teeth with a tooth-pick"[7]. He, likewise, describes the custom of his age when he says that the Wazir conversed with his guests at the meal. It was a moot-point, however, whether one should talk at meals[8]. If at all, it was the duty of the host to carry on the conversation, to enable the guest to enjoy their meal undisturbed[9]. Even to say "God be praised" after food was disapproved; for by saying so one might perhaps, compel others to get up before they had finished[10]. Jahiz (d. 255/

(1) Kushajim, *Adab en-nedim*. fol. 48 b.
(2) Baihaqi, ed. Schwally, 497; Masudi, VIII, 104.
(3) Guzuli *Matali el-budur*, II, 67.
(4) Ibn al-Athir, IX. 85.
(5) Yaqut, *Irshad*, TI, 105.
(6) *Adad en-nedim* fol. 48 b.
(7) *Diwan*, II, 6.
(8) The different views, *Adad en-nedim*, 44 b et spq.
(9) Ibid, fol. 45.
(10) Tha'alibi, *Kit. ahsan ma Sumi'a* 103.

896) recommends as a table-companion one who does not pick marrow from the bone; who does not grab at the egg lying upon vegetables; who does not appropriate to himself liver and breast of the fowl, brains or kidneys, even the choicest piece of mutton in the Balkan—and young spring chicken[1]. It is stated a hundred years later : the better class despiste entrails, tendon, veins, kidneys, stomach, cartilage, diaphragm, or broken bits and green herb in soup. They do not sip their soups; they do not look for the marrow, they do not their hands with fat, nor do they take much salt which they regard vulgar. They do not dabble about in vinegar. They do not make the bread lying before them greasy: they do not reach out from their places; they do not lick their fingers; they do not stuff their mouth full; they do not take huge pieces which make their lips greasy; they do not take two morsels of different kind into the mouth nor do they eat salted Hors-d' oeeuvre. This is considered vulgar. At the most singing-girls and fashionable ladies sometimes coquetishly took salted things at the house of their[2] lovers professing to despise food in by a dish of food in general. Single plates were never served—only the philologer Abu Piyash (2nd half of the fourth century in Besra) who used to put back on the plate meat into which he had bitten—received a special plate for himself. But even so he scandalized the guests of the Wazir by spitting and blowing his nose in the table-cloth[3].

Culinary art received great literary notice. A Courtier like Munnajjim, a royal musician like Ibrahim ibn al-Mahdi; a genuine poet like Jahizah wrote cookery-books in the 3rd/

(1) Tha'alibi, ZDMG, VIII, 518. Animals was mostly slaughtered and eaten on Friday. What was left was enten on Saturday specially the head. For this reason, long after the Muslim time, sheeps' head was eaten in Spain on Saturday. Mendoza, *Lazarillo de Tormes, Reclam*, 31.

(2) *Kit. al-Muwassa*, 129, f.

(3) *Yatimah*, II, 120.

9th century[1].

Even the historian of the 4th/10th century, the librarian Miskawaihi (died after 400/1009) wrote a book on dietary "dealing with the principles of the culinary art and its rare ramifications"[2]. Hamadhani (d. 334/945) gives us to understand that there was a vast culinary literature: "The food and drink of Yaman are to be preferred to the recipes of the cookery-books (Kutub al Matabikh)"[3]. Unfortunately all this literature seems lost. The Arab cookery books, that have come down to us, are all of later dates. They recommend a hideous mixture of meat, musk, camphor, rose-water[4] such as was popular at the time of the Italian Renaissance. The recipes of the earlier times, that have come down to us, show better taste[5]. They reserve musk, camphor, and rose-water for confectionary,. which of all foods on festive occasions always claimed and received the highest culinary skill. Towers, made of sugar, served as centrepieces. Mutanabbi, for instance, thanks for a fish made of sugar and almond[6].

The actual conversation was strictly separated from the meal. Sternly it began only *inter pocula*. Even, in the most dissolute period, wine was never taken with meals. Like the Greek *nogalmata* and the Latin *nuclei, nuql* (highly-pungent thing) served as an introduction. It was not in good taste to take much of it. On account of their smell radish, celery, garlic, onions were avoided and, likewise, everything, having a stone such as olive, dates, apricots, grapes and peaches. These later were considered unsightly to, eat. Pomegranates, figs, water-melons, being much too cheap

(1) *Fihrist*, 14. b.
(2) Qifti, 331.
(3) p. 198.
(4) Abulqasim, XXXIX f.
(5) Masudi, VIII, 392.
(6) *Diwan*, 18.

were left to the common folk. And similarly sour wheat, black raisins like "Goat's dirt", acorns, chestnut, roasted sesam-seeds. Only costly delicacies such as Indian olives, edible earth[1] from Khorasan, pistachio-nut, sugarcane washed with rose-water, quince from Balkh and apple from Syria[2] were acceptable to the higher circles.

Inspite of the Quranic prohibition drinking became widely-diffused. In this respect the provinces, however, differed. In 169/785 an Alid was punished for drinking wine in the Arabian Hijaz, whereas in Mesopotamia they found no foult with wine-drinking[3]. Wine-shops continued precisely as they had been before Islam. The innkeeper, the waiter and witresses were mostly Christians (they were often Jews):—

> "Like carnation shone the cross on their breasts"[4].

And things were no different in Egypt. At old Cairo Mukaddasi complains that even the most estimable ones (*Masha'ikh)* shrank not from wine[5]. All police prohibition was ineffective. Under the Fatimids they were content to close the wine-shops before sunset in the Holy month of *Rajab*[6]. In Morocco, rich in vines, women are said to be very particularly fond of drink[7]. Says a modern traveller : at harvest a large part of the population gets drunk[8]. When the famous philologer Azhari came to the yet more famous Ibn Duraid (d. 321/938 at the age of ninety) he found him drunk and, hence never visited him again. When Ibn Duraid

(1) Also called "Clay of Nisabur", described at length by Ibn Baitar, Tr.
(2) *Kit. al-Muwassa*, 131 ff. Abulqasim, 48 f.
(3) Tabari, III 552.
(4) Ibn al-Mutazz, II, 64.
(5) p. 200.
(6) Maqrizi, *Khitat*, 1, 490.
(7) *Zinad al-Wari*, Leiden. 1053 fol. 63a.
(8) Rohlfs, *Mein erster aufenthalt in'Narokko*, 75.

was lying on his death-bed visitors were shocked to find lutes hanging and vessels of wine standing in his house[1]. In the same year the Caliph al-Qahir forbade muşic and wine—though he himself was never sober[2]. His successor al-Radhi had vowed never to drink. To this vow he remained true for two years, only taking syrup in company but, then his resolution gave way. He copied out the words of his oath and placed them before Jurists who found the usual solution. "He sent writes Suli, 1000 dinars. I was to spend the money in alms and the Caliph, freed from his oath, took to drink again"[3]. In 333/944 the Caliph al-Mustakfi ascended the throne. He had given up wine but, after accession, he resumed his old way[4]. In rich houses along with the cook there was a master of the Cellars (Sharabi) who was in charge of the wines and the cups, fruit and perfune[5]. Even high dignitaries indulged in wine. "At the residence of the Wazir Muhallabi Qadhis—among them Ibn Ma'ruf the Chief Qadhi and the Qadhi el-Tanukhi—met twice a week, all with long grey beards like that of the Wazir. At the summit of their merry-making each, holding a golden cup in hand, filled with Qatrabul and Ukbara wine[6], would dip his beard into it and they would sprinkle each other with it and dance, dressed in veriegated dresses and adorned with garlands"[7]. In a company at the house of a clerk of the Caliph a Qadhi of Baghdad (d. 423/1031) took only fruit juice, while the rest of the company indulged in wine. The host, then sent for a flask which was sealed and bore the inscription: "Fruit-juice from the shop of Ishaq al-Wasiti" but which really contained wine. The Qadhi saw the inscription and the seal,

---

(1) Jauzi, 49b; Abulmahasin, II, 256.
(2) Misk, V, 424; Abulmahasin, II, 254.
(3) *Auraq*, Paris Ar. 4837, 63.
(4) Masudi, VIII, 390.
(5) *Kit. al-faragh*, 1, 11.
(6) Places near Baghdad, famous for their wine : in an anecdote in the Table-talk, ph ii the former is shown to be of surpassing merit.
(7) Yatimah, II, 106.

drank a little, found it excellent and enquired what it was. Answer : Fruit juice. He drank a second and a third cup, always enquiring, what it waş. He got angry and some one said : wine. Finally he fell flat on the ground, was wrapped up in his *tailasan* and was carried home[1]. The Registrar of the Egyptian Alids (d. Circa, 350/961), a religious Officer of the highest rank, composed wine-songs such as this[2]:—

> Shall I give up drinking? The rain continues
> and the drops are spread over the leaves,
> the branches: for sheer joy, shake themselves
> like drinkers
> the rose now shrink and now unfold
> themselves.
> Never; by her who left me on the day of our
> parting as though sand had been flung into
> my eyes[3].

On the other hand the poet Mutanabbi (d. 354/965) abstained from wine and declared that he would rather drink what the vine drinks: namely, water[4] but this was not due to piety on his part as he had no connection with Islam[5]. The Caliph, al-Hakim, who sought to restore the original Islam, enacted stringent measures against wine-drinking. The reports show how very just Mukaddasi was with his complaint against the Egyptians; that they all drank. When al-Hakim's Christian physician Ibn Anastas prescribed wine and music for his melancholy, people reverted with joy to the old vice. But the physician soon died and the Caliph became a yet greater opponent of alcohol. He even forbade the sale[6] of raisins and honey and destroyed the casks

(1) Yaqut, *Irshad*, V, 260 ff.
(2) Ibn Sa'id, p. 49.
(3) The text of Ibn Sa'id is full of misprints, which have been corrected.
(4) *Diwan*, 50.
(5) He feared it might injure the health Diwan, p. 242.
(6) Ibn Sa'id, fol. 118 a.

wherein wine was kept.

Drinking in twos is not commended. It is termed "Saw" (Minshar) as two persons are seated to use that implement[1]. Just as antiquity had recommended a number between those of the muses and the graces, so Abu Nuwas would have liked a drinking bout consisting of three or four:—

> Besides the host and the musician—three
> make a delightful company ;
> if the number reaches six—it becomes a
> disorderly mob[2],

And this number with the approval of later times too:—

Below five is solitude—beyond it a market[3]. And a guest, who drank not, is thus ridiculed : Six, with him, make only five, and five v ith him only four[4].

As with ancient and Byzantine banquets—the floor of the banquet-room was strewn with flowers. Wreaths crowned the heads of the revellers[5].

> On one a wreath of roses, on one a wreath
> of eglantine[6].

They threw flowers at each other as a symbol of greeting. It was bad taste to present one with a single rose. No refined women would ever say to another : "This is thy rose". This would have been a gross breach of etiquette[7] being the language of the vulgar. At the drinking bouts they also presented fruits:—

---

(1) Kushajim, *Adab en-nedim,* fol. 32 a.
(2) *Diwan,* 356, 358.
(3) *Muhad al-Udada,* 1, 428.
(4) Ibid, 429.
(5) *Yatimah,* II, 170.
(6) Sanaubari, *Jamaharat al-Islam,* fol. 113 a.
(7) *Kit. al-Muwassa,* 131, *Yat* II, 40.

> The cup was handed over to me and in the hand of the loved one was a rose and a lemon;
> I was quaffing the wine and, while so, she presented me with my own colour and with hers[1].

To wine belong music and dancing. Four instruments were mainly used then as now[2]. Slave-girls sang behind the curtain. But as a mark of special honour to the guest they even sang in the hall. About the year 300/912 at a feast the Wazir's some singing-girls sang in front and some behind the curtain[3]. Music made a powerful appeal to them—"the soul of many flew". When the musician Mushariq sang in the middle of the Tigris, all wept[4]. He sighed so beautifully that he gladdened every heart (p. 379 lines, 6 and 7). When the princely musician Ibrahim ibn al-Mahdi, convicted of high treason, sang before the Caliph Mamum, an officer kissed the lapel of his coat and excused himself by saying "that he could not help kissing it even if he had to atone for it by his death"[5]. In the middle of the 3rd/9th century Al-Mutazz entertained Ubaidullah Ibn Abdullah ibn Tahir with many wonderful things: the songs of the female musician Shanah; the music of a renowned flute-player; the copper water-organ[6] of Ahmad ibn Musa; a fight between lions and elephants. Ubaidullah, himself a poet, declared the songs of Shanah the most wonderful of all[7]. For the Fatimid prince Tamim (d. 368/978) a female singer was purchased at

(1) *Yatimah* III, 129.

(2) Ibn al-Mutazz, II, 118; Lyre, lute, Zither (Qanun), flute, Altanukhi, *Mustatraf*, II, 144; Lute, Guitar, (tanbur) flute, lyre. On the melody for dance and the musical scale see Masudi, VIII, 100 ff.

(3) Wuz, 193.

(4) On Mushariq, see Ribera's *music in Ancient Arabia and Spain* pp. 56. et sqq. Tr.

(5) Ibn Taifur, 74 a.

(6) See H. G. Farmer "The organ of the Ancients" 1931 p. 87.

(7) Shabushti, fol. 44 b.

Baghdad. Being exceedingly beautiful the prince fell completely under her spell and promised all she asked for. She felt home-sick and sought permission to sing at Baghdad once again. The prince kept his word and allowed her to travel there across Mekka where she disappeared[1]. A number of similar stories were in circulation. Specially impressionable people flung themselves on the ground, sobbed and foamed, bit their fingers, struck their faces, tore their faces, tore their garments, knocked their heads against the wall[2]. At wine parties short droll stories were told. Already Tahir (about 200/800) when merry after meals, used to relate current, popular stories. (Ibn Taifur, fol . 43 a). "Long stories were more suited for the story-teller than for the company of the cultured" (Kushajim, Adab en-nedim, fol, 43; Mesudi, VI, 139).

> "Between the cups naught but short chant
> stories. When the cup bearers, like the

(1) Jauzi, fol. 115 b.

(2) Abulqasim, 78 ff. The word 'tarab' is likely to be a further development 'Taba' to be *in good health.* Few philologists will agree with this. Stendhal, *Vie de* Rossin, 18; Real melo-mania is rare in France. There usually it is a mere pretence. But in Italy it is met with everywhere. When I was in the barracks of Breseia they showed me an Italian who was most powerfully affected by music. He was of a quiet temperament and was generally well-behaved but, at a concert, if the music aroused his sensibilities he would unconsciously take off his shoes. At specially fine passages he invariably flung there at the audience behind him. At Bologna I have seen the most miserly of men scatter his money on the ground and look like one possessed when music stirred his soul. (In India we see *particularly* at the shrines of saints wonderful samples of actual or feigned ecstasy. The music that produces this ecstatic condition is generally sacred music. The person affected by it flings his turban, dances, yells, gives himself up to extraordinary acrobatic performances and not infrequently faints away. In most cases it is feigned for it brings at once esteem and money to the reeling, fainting *Shaikh.* But genuine cases are not unknown. This nervous condition is mainly produced by lonely habits, continuous fasts and prolonged night vigils Tr.).

towering Alif on the lines, stand amidst the
tipplers"

sings Ibn al-Mutazz (Diwan, II, 63). This form of enjoyment was also passionately pursued. If one is to elect between conversation with men, music and privacy with women — let him elect conversation with men *(Adab en nedim, fol 40 b)*. Even for Masudi the entire life lies in having a conversational friend (Masudi, VI, 132). The Prince of Egypt, like a child, craves for "a story, a tiny, tiny story, no bigger" than a finger (Ibn Said Mughrib, 33). Men, endowed and unendowed with poetical talents improvised rhymed toasts to flowers, to beautiful cups to male and female musicians, to heaven. Mutanabbi's carousing companions made an automatic doll which lifted one leg and held a bouquet of flowers in one hand. Any one, towards whom her face turn while stopping to revolve, had to drink her health and given her a push causing her to revolve again. Each time that his turn came Mutanabbi composed verses on her (Diwan, 160).

Wine drinking checked the spread of other narcotics. The enjoyment of hemp (Hashish) first emerges in Juristics literature in the 3rd/9th century. The Shafiites forbid, the Hanafites allow its use[1]. Even in the 4th/10th Assassins it finds no place in any story. The history of the century shows that it was something quite new as a means of popular enjoyment. Chinese tea had no yet come into vogue although an arab account of China, written in 237/831, speaks of it, among other taxable articles[2]. We have nowhere of smoking as a form of enjoyment. "Edible earth" (see. below Chapter XXIV) was chewed. At the beginning of the 4th/10th century the practice of betel chewing-passed from

(1) *Mikhlat*, 186.

(2) *Silsilat et-tawarikh*, Reinad, II, 41. It had not been even long in use in China and was, for the first time, taxed in 793 A. D. Pfizmaier, SWA 67, 422.

India into Mekka and Yaman[1]. In Summer iced-water constituted the chief luxury. In 304/915 the newly-appointed Wazir Ibn al-Furat used for the entertainment of those that had come to congratulate him 40,000 *Ratl* of ice. It was a hot day[2]. The rich even took a supply of ice to the boats[3]. For cooling the drinks ice was supplied from Syria to the Egyptian Court[4]. The richest private gentleman of Egypt—the *quondam* administrator of the realm—Ibn Ammar (d. 390/999)—daily used, at the end of the 4th/10th century, half a camel-load of ice[5]. This luxury was, however, not to be at Mekka and Basra[6]:

At the Squalid Basra we drink the foulest drink, Lemon water, yellow, nasty, heavy, thing like the Cholera stool[7].

A story of the 4th/10th century describes the reception which some officers, travelling to Egypt, received, while looking for accommodation at Damascus, at the house of an *unknown* gentleman who conducted business—on a great scale. They were taken to the bath of the house where they were attended by two beardless slaves and two very handsome boys. A meal was then served and two beardless slaves massaged their feet. Then the host conducted them to a hall in a beautiful garden where they took wine. He, then, touched a curtain with his hand behind which were slave-girls and called out to them: Sing and they began to sing beautifully exquisitely. While drinking he called out : Why this shyness before our guests come out: He divided

---

(1) Masudi, II, 84.
(2) *Arib,* 61.
(3) Baihaqi, 447.
(4) Guzuli,, II, 71.
(5) Maqrizi, Khitat, II, 36.
(6) *Kit. al-Faragh*, 1, 15.
(7) *Yatimah*, II, 47. Adab-ud-Dawlah, had a monopoly of ice and silk fabrics. Ibn al-Athir, IX, 16 according to the *Taji* of his contemporary al-Sabi.

the curtain and young women, comely, delicate, ravishing, such as we had never seen, stepped out. One had a lute, another a flute, a third a lyre, yet another Castanets. Nor was a dancer wanting. All were splendidly bedecked and bejewelled. They sang to us. When they were almost inebriated the master said: he had sent slaves to them at midday but he had heard that they had not entertained them. Would they behave similarly now: It was his wish, said he, that each one should provide himself with a partner for the night. The next morning they were again conducted to the bath and were served and perfumed by beardless slaves. The host, then enquired whether they preferred to ride to one of the gardens and amuse themselves there till the meal or play chess or backgammon or read books. They chose chess and backgammon and books and with these whiled away the time till the midday meal[1].

With the game of chess—once treated with hostility—the theologians came to terms. Sahl-ibn Abi Sahl (d. 404/1013) declared : "When property is secure from loss and prayer from neglect—then the game of chess is an act of friendliness between friends". To Suli, who about 300/912, ruled as the indisputed sovereign in this game, his talents secured admission to the Court[2]. At the end of the 3rd/9th century special variety of this game was played at the Court of the Caliph al-Mutadid, called the *Jawarihiyya* (Literally "Organic" Mas'udi describes it) in which all the six senses of man were ranged against each other (Fihrist 131; Masudi, VIII, 314). Sitting patiently and silently side by side at a game was *unarab* and was resented as such by genuine Arabs. According to the Medinites "Chess is only meant for the barbarians who in company merely stare at each other like

(1) *Nishwar al-Muhadharah* of Tanukhi (d. 384/99) in the *thamrat* al-awraq (margin) of *Mustatraf*, II, 143 ff. (Edited by D.S. Margoliouth R.A.S. pp. 193—199 of Arbic Text).

(2) Subki, II, 172, a Variant of *Muh. al-Udaba*, 1, 447.

cattle. For this reason, precisely, they invented this game" (*Muh al-Udaba,* I, 448). The Arab's special trait always remained: rhythmically expressed proverbs, witticism, anecdotes, pitty expressions. When, after his accession, the Caliph Mamun had the best chess-players of Mesopotamia brought to the Court, they acted so stiffly and formally in his presence that the Caliph, impatiently broke out : "Chess and politeness do not go well together. Talk naturally as if you were among yourselves"[1]. The chess scenes in Abulqasim are taken from such *nawadir es-shatranj*[2]. The winner had even an eye on some gain; for instance a meal was used as the stake.[3] On the other hand *nerd* was backgammon played on 12 or 14 squares with thirty stones and two dice, a pure game of chance, often likened by the poets to the inscrutable ways of fate. Hence the curse of the pious on it. Along with donkey-races, dog-baiting, ram and cock-fighting Abul Laith es-Samarqandi calls it a work of Satan[4]. It was openly played for money. 20 dinars, at a time, were won at *Nerd*[5].

"Three games the angels witness : the game of the man with women the race and the shooting competitions"—so runs through literature in many varaints a saying of the Prophet. The Prophet is also reported to have had race horses[6]. The theologians, however, imposed a condition on their favourite sport, horse-raching, namely, that there was to be no betting. In Egypt we hear most of races. About 190/806 the winner, for instance, got the horse of his

(1) Masudi, VIII 311. Red leather served as chess-board (Masudi, VIII, 316. Ibn Taifur, fol. 112 b. Besides the square board, now in use, Masudi mentions a rectangular one, a round one which he calls 'Roman' yet another round one in which the seven planets and the twelve signs of the Zodiac move . VIII, 313 ff.

(2) *Muh. al-Udaba*, 1, 449.

(3) Shabushti, 3b.

(4) *Qurat al-nyun*, on the margin of *Raud* 192 f.

(5) Shabusti, 3b.

(6) See Damiri, under the word 'Khall'.

competitor as prize[1]. The fanatical Governor, appointed in 242/856, forbade horse-races for money and sold the race-horses which, according to the Pre-Islamite custom, were maintained at Government cost. But in 249/863 races were once again renewed. Under the Tulunid Khumarwaihi "races were regarded as a festival by the people"[2]. Ikhshid, however, again restrained such practices.[3] There was even a 'Book of Stallion and race-courses' which described every race-course and the horses that had run there before and after Islam[4]. Despite theological disapproval pigeon-racing was keenly practised[5] and pre-eminently so in Egypt. In the 5th/11th century it was very largely indulged in. The Caliph Muiz grew jealous of his Wazir because his pigeon flew better[6]. And likewise cock, dog, ram-fighting[7]. Sabuktigin, the Turkish general of Muiz-ud-Dawlah had a champion-ram, which the poet Ibn-al-Hajjaj suggest should be pitted against the husband of a songstress whom she and he jointly, deceived[8]. Quails were pitted against one other[9]. In Tarkistan even today the fight between these birds is so enjoyed by the people that the owner of a famous fighting quail is a made-man earning a rich living from the bets made upon his quail[10]. The game of chance was mostly played with dice[11], and was everywhere indulged in despite the Quar'anic prohibition. Already at the time of the Prophet

(1) Kindi, 402.
(2) Kindi, 203; Maqrizi, *Khitat*, I, 316.
(3) Ibn Sa'id, 18.
(4) Masudi, IV. 25.
(5) Goldziher, AFR, VIII, 422.
(6) Guzuli, II, 220 (In the *Musaddus* of Hali the reader will find a catalogue of these vices in India Tr.)
(7) Ibn Taifur, 38a; *Tadhkirah* of Ibn Hamdan, Paris, fo.l 25a; Masudi, VIII, 230, 379.
(8) Ibn al-Hajjaj, MS. Baghdad, 141.
(9) Masudi, VIII, 397.
(10) Schwarz, *Turkistan*, 290.
(11) Ibn Taifur, 38 a.

an Arab Sheikh ended by gambling away his freedom[1]. At the time of Harun the Singer Ibn Jami said: were it not for gambling and love of gods which take up my time—I would not have let any singer earn his bread[2]. At the end of the 5th/10th century an Alid is punished for gambling away all that he possessed and for leaving his children destitute[3]. The gambling dens are constantly recommended to the supervision of the Trade-Inspectors[4]. In Egypt old men were paid to encourage gambling. Ikhshid once ordered taverns and gambling-dens to be closed down and the gamblers to be arrested. A number of people were, accordingly, placed before him, among them a decentlooking old man. When he enquired if the old man was a gambler too—the answer was: he is called "the merry maker" and is the cause of the immense activity in the gaming house. Whoever has gambled away his gold, he tells him, play for your mantle, possibly you may win. When the mantle is gone he tells him, play for the coat, with it you may, perchance, recover all that has been lost and so on and on until comes the turn of the shoes and these even go. The old man receives a daily wage from the lessor of the gambling-den. Ikhshid laughed and said : Turn to God and repent of your sin. He repented and Ikhshid gave him a coat, a mantle and 1000 dirhams and ordered him a monthly salary of 10 dinars. The old man went away thanking and blessing. Then he said: bring him back to me, take from him what we have given him, lay him flat on the ground and give him 100 stripes. After all this was done he said : let him go![5] How does this compare with your encouragement of the gamblers?[6].

Polo, borrowed from the Persians, was the most

(1) *Aghani*, III, 100.
(2) *Aghani*, VI, 70.
(3) *Diwan* of Rida 3.
(4) Mawardi, Enger's Ed. 404.
(5) Ibn Sa'id, 30.
(6) I have varified the passage, and corrected Mez's rendering BSN Tr.

aristocratic sport then, as it is today[1]. The Caliphs played it in their race-course (Wuz, 138). A Wazir of the 3rd/9th century played it on Friday, when free from work, in the race course of his palace[2]. After the game the Wazir had a bath with message[3]. One had suddenly to stop the horse while at full gallop and at the top had to be careful not to injure the other players or smash the ball, even though half a dozen balls were worth only one dirham.

Nor were the spectators, sitting on the wall, to be sacred away. Indeed to prevent any interference with them they made the courses 60 yards broad[4]. As mountain-folk the Dailamites loved simple games. Thus Muiz-ud-Dawlah introduced wrestling matches at Baghdad. He set up a tree in the race-course with valuable things hanging there on . At its feet he placed purses with dirhams. Musicians with drums and flutes sat on the well. "All were invited to compete and thus wrestling took place in every part of the town. When Muiz-ud-Dawlah saw the winner he gave him a reward. "In the struggle many eyes were lost, many a leg broken." His people also took to swimming. The Baghdaddians enthusiastically practised and vied with each other in it; and so ultimately could perform the most difficult feats in swimming. Youths used to swim standing, carrying, in their hand, a utensil with fire in which food was cooked. In water they ate the food so cooked and then landed at the palace[5]. Alongside of all these games and sports hunting

(1) A good account of the game by a Greek author in Quateremere. *Hist, de mom*, 1, 11 ff. Polo is the name of the ball (Pers-Arab 'Kurah, *Saulajau* that of the stick.

(2) Abulmahasin II, 38. In 315/927 a Governor of Jurjan fell off his horse while playing polo and was killed *Zubdat al-Fikrah*, Paris fol. 203 a.

(3) Tabari, III, 1327.

(4) Ibn Kutaibah, *Uyun al-Akhbar*, ed. Brockelmann p, 66 according to the Kit al-Uyun.

(5) Jauzi, 34 b.

retains its position unimpaired. Now it is even celebrated in special poems[1] but most of this poetry is description and laudation of dogs used for hunting purposes (Jagdhundes), The Lion, the noblest of wild animals, was not rare either in Syria or on the Euphrates and the Tigris. Indeed he was met quite close to the capital. In 331/943 the Caliph proceeded to the suburb of al-Shammasiyah for lion-hunting (Jauzi, fol. 71 a; for Syria see the poems of Mutanabbi on hunting). Even in Egypt the Viceroy Khumarwaihi could not hear of a lion without searching for it (Maqrizi, *Khitat*, 316). Stories of lion-hunting constituted a great part of entertainment (Kit. al-farag, II, 70 ff).

It is naturally conjectured of one who had disappeared that he was devoured by a lion[2].

Already the places of Samarra had zoological gardens[3]. About the middle of the 3rd/9th century al-Mutazz showed to his guests, as a great marvel, a fight between lions and elephants[4]. Later curiosity became a really keen interest. About the Tulunid Khamarwaihi built a fine zoological garden with a water-basin for every cage[5]. There was even a menagerie at Palace of Baghdad[6], where about the year 300/912 oddities were sent from all over the world. The Egyptian Wazir Jafar ibn al-Furat took a very keen interest in snakes and all kinds of vermin. In a huge marble courtyard stood their baskets attended by servants and tamers. All the snake-charmers were in his pay. Once he wrote to a

(1) Poems on hunting are called 'tardiyyah'. The root *trd* is only later used for hunting. Lane vouches for his meaning only after *Zamakh snari*. It is Syrianism. The west-Syrians use instead of *sad, tad* for hunting. Barhebraeus, Book of Rays, tr by Moberg, p. 30.

(2) Abul Ala, Letter V. For lion stories see especially the Autobiography of Usamah, and table-talk of a Mesopot Judge, Part II.

(3) *Aghani*, X, 130.

(4) Shabushti, fol, 44b.

(5) Abulmahasin, II, 60.

(6) *Tarikh Baghdad* ed. Salmon, 56.

neighbour that rare and poisonous vipers had crept over to the latter's house and begged him to keep them there to enable his men to catch them. The neighbour replied : "may his wife be divorced three times should he remain with his family even for a night in the "house"[1]. The shadow play *i.e.* wherein the acting is behind a curtain, which shows the shadows of the actors. The wit Abdullah, son of the Chief of the Caliph Mamun, threatened the poet Di'bil when he thought of satirizing him : "I shall produce thy mother in the shadow play"[2]. In Egypt, too, shadow plays enlivened festive occasions[3]. The real actor, the mimic, was not wanting either. Indeed mimicry was always regarded as an art worth cultivating Ibn al-Majazili collected a crowd round him and related to them stories of the Beduins, Nabatians, Gypsies, Negroes, Sindhis, Mekkans, eunuchs and always with their peculiar gestures and intonation. He was even admitted to the presence of the Caliph al-Mutadid[4]. In the 4th/10th century the poet Abulward, a companion of the Wazir Muhallabi, enjoyed the greatest reputation as "mimic". He held his audience spell-bound. In the 5th/11th century Mohammad al-Azdi raised mimicry into literature and embodied and manners and foul-language of the citizens of Baghdad in the person of Abulqasim (Abulqasim, ed. by Mez). At Hadramaut V. Wrede saw a Jester who parodied the Turks, the sea-faring people and even the Beduins[5]. Sachau speaks of such an artist even in recent times[6].

(1) *Yaqut* Irshad, II 412 Maqrizi, *Khitat*, 319.

(2) Shabushti, fol. 81 a.

(3) al-Mussabbihi (d. 420/10) 29 in Maqrizi, *Khitat*, 1, 207.

(4) Mauardi, VIII, 161 ff. in *Mustatraf.* II, 203 this anecdote is already laid to the credit of Herun a more attractive personality. Of other mimics Jahiz speaks in his *Bayan*, 1, 31 and Tha'alibi in his "*Book of support*" ZDMG, V.

(5) V. Maltzan, II, 119.

(6) *Am Euphrat und Tigris*, 65 ff. (They are very common in India. They mimic of perfection and are often found at wedding-parties and social-gatherings. They not only mimic men and women but also

Finally we hear of actors too (samagat); in Egypt on festive occasions[1]; at Baghdad on the new year's feast at the Caliph's court when they appeared in masks.

---

animals and always with a skill which not only delights but challenges unbounded admiration. Not to speak of grown-up artists, I have seen little boys and girls who were perfect adepts in this art. One instance specially struck me as amazing. This was a little girl—hardly seven—who took off an English lady with astounding skill and dexterity. She reproduced her talk, her jesture, her movements, her typical little ways and all with perfect skill and mastery. Tr. (al-Musabbihi d. 420/1029) in Maqrızi, Khitat, 1, 207.

(1) Sabushti, 15 a.

XXII. MUNICIPAL ORGANIZATION

The only division of towns, coming from the fourth century, is one without a political basis and may be thus stated:—

(a) 16 metropolises (Amsar)[1].

(b) 77 fortified Provincial Capitals (Qasabat)

(c) Provincial towns (madain or mudun)

(d) Tracts of Country (nawahi)-such as Nehawend and Jazirat ibn Omar.

(e) Villages (Qura)[2].

The distinguishing feature of a town was the pulpit (minbar). Specially the Hanafites insisted that only in really important towns the Friday service should be held and that in a Friday-mosque. For this very reason there were many villages in Transoxiana, where this school predominated, where only a Friday-mosque was needed to confer upon them the status of a town. "How the citizens of Baikand tried and tried until they were allowed to put up a pulpit (mimbar)[3]. Despite its small size there were more than twenty pulpits in Palestine[4]. The importance of the pulpit for the town is evidenced by the fact that even in large towns

---

(1) Muk (Eng. tr. pp 84, 85) Tr.

(2) Muk, 35, 47. Also we have Psychological classifications then. In *Tarikh Baghdad* (ms. Paris fol. 15a). We have the largest list of our period : artistic skill in Rasra, eloquence in Kufa good living at Baghdad, trick and counting in Rai, envy in Herat, sin in Nisapur, avarice in Merv, pride in Samarqand, chivalry in Balkh, trade in Misr.

(3) Muk, 282.

(4) Istakhri, 48.

the populace would go to no other than the Friday-mosque that happened to be[1]. About the year 300 there were at Baghdad some 27,000 places of worship[2]. Yet the chief service was held only in one Friday-mosque, on each side of the river and from the year 280 in the Palace Chapel as well[3]. These could not hold the pious band and thus Fridays, week after week, offered the spectacle of the rows of worshippers swelling beyond the mosque-gate, lining the streets right up to the Tigris, the late-comers even joining the faithful on the canoes and the signallers, posted at intervals, echoing the words and imitating the gestures of the *Imam* (*Tarikh Baghdad* Paris ms. fol. 15 a). Even Fustal had only two Friday-mosques—that of Amr and of Tulung (Istakhri, 49). Basra, likewise, had two Friday-mosques in the 3rd century—though it counted 7000 places of worship—and in the 4th century had but three. (Yaqubi, *Geography*, 361 ; Muk, 117). This indeed, is strange for in this century the old Islamic conception of a town vanishes. The importance of this period lies in this that *then* in every sphere the thin Islamic veneer fades—the old onent reasserts itself assuming the shape which it has ever since retained. In the 4th Century the number of Friday-mosques begins to

(1) In this the Shafietes were insistent, Suyute, Husn-el-muhadarah II, 155. (The conditions of primitive Islam are reflected in the teaching of the Hanafis, who only permit the Friday Service in large towns. As to the towns, the Shafais, on the other hand, have retained the original condition, since they permit the Friday service in only one mosque in each town. Istakhri mentions as innovation in Islam that Hajjaj built a *djami* in Wasit on the west bank, although there was already one on the East bank. Tr.)

(2) *Tarikh Baghdad.* ed. Salmon p. 70 where the number of baths and mosques have been mixed up. According to Yaqubi (p. 25) the Eastern half of the Capital in the 3rd century had 30,000 place of worship.

(3) (Of the three Friday-mosques one stood in Mansurs "Round City", another in Rusafa and the third in the Royal Precincts. There was still another Friday mosque at Kalwadha, in a bend of the river on the east bank, below the city Levy, A *Baghdad Chronicle p. 158* Compare Guy Le Strange, *Baghdad during the Caliphate* p. 320 Tr.)

adjust itself to the need of the people. At old Cairo Mukaddasi saw close to the Amr mosque six other Friday-mosques and yet on Fridays—so he tells us—the rows of worshippers from the Amr mosque extended more than 1000 yards into the street; even ware-houses small mosques, booths on entire side being full of them[1].

In 440 Nasir Khusru found close to these seven old mosques for others in New Cairo[2]. Slow, however, was the march of events at Baghdad. In 329 a fourth Friday mosque came into existence at Baratha, once a shrine of the Shiites[3]. At the beginning of the century this shrine was destroyed. It was at its site that a Friday-mosque was established when in 379 they wanted to build a fifth Friday-mosque[4] it was represented to the Caliph that, with its parish lying behind einen graben(?), it could constitute a sort of town by itself (Text p. 389 lines 3 and 4 from the top). A sixth Friday-mosque was added at the Hazbiyah Gate at Baghdad in 383 to meet the extension of the town[5]. In the sixth century Ibn Jubair found eleven Friday-mosques and yet "almost nothing

(1) p. 198.

(2) Schefer's Ed. 145.

(3) Guy Le Strange, Baghdad, p. 320 Tr.

(4) *Tarikh Baghdad*, Ed, Salmon.

(5) The high road from the upper Bridge of Boats to the Syrian gate of the Round City crossed daigonally the eastern part of the great northern suburb, the whole of which in early times had been known as the Hazbiyah. In later times, however, the name Hazbiyah came to be used in a more restricted sense, and was applied solely to that part of the northern suburb lying immediately below the Hazb Bridge, which was traversed by the road of the Hazb Gate. This quarter by the 4th/10th century came to possess its own Friday-mosque which had originally been built for an oratory by one of the Abbasid princes during the Caliphate of Muti, who had some scruple in allowing congregational prayers to be said here. It was , therefore only in the reign of Kadir namely in the month Rabi II of the year 383/993, that a decree was obtained erecting this minor mosque into a *Jami* (as a great mosque for the Friday prayers is termed); and Khatib, writing in the following century, adds that he

was left of Baghdad except its famous name" (Ed. Wright, 230).

Official registers were kept of those who were liable to the Capitation-tax. In the year 306 a Census, however appears to have been taken of the male and female singers[1] of Baghdad and also of the poor[2] (p. 389 text 2nd parra). The geographers of the 3rd and 4th century gave us all kinds of figures; number of gates and doors, mosques and baths but they seem indifferent to human population, regarding it seemingly as unnecessary. Eventually a naive method of calculation reveals itself. Ibn Haukal once mentions that in Palermo there were 150 butchers' shop and from this fact he would have us fix the number of its inhabitants[3]. And the authority of the Khatib-al-Baghdadi calculates the number of the inhabitants of Baghdad in the third century from the fantastic statement that there were then 60,000 baths arguing thus: if five Muslims used every bath and five, at the very least, every mosque—the total-male population then, would be at lowest calculation 1500000[4]. In the 5th century all this changes. The traveller

---

himself had frequently attended the Friday prayers here. When Yaqut wrote in 623/1226 though many of the surrounding quarters had in greater part then fallen to ruin, the later Hazbiyah, namely the suburb of the Hazb Gate remained a populous Quarter, shut in by its own wall, with the Friday-mosque and many well-supplied markets. It stood, he adds like a township in the midst of the waste and a distance of almost two miles covered by ruins, seperated it from the quarter of the Basra Gate to which belonged the great mosque of Mansur. In the previous century, when Ibn Jubair visited the Hazbiyab, it is described as the highest up of the then inhabited quarters of west Baghdad, and beyond it there were only to be seen some villages that were considered as outside the City limits. Guy Le Stange, *Bhagdad* pp. 125-126 Tr.).

(1) *Abulqasim* Ed. Mez 87.

(2) *Et-tuhfah el-bahiyyah*, Const. 1306, p. 37.

(3) p. 83.

(4) *Tarikh Baghdad*, 74.

Nasir Khusru[1] estimates the population of Arrajan just over 20,000 males; of Jeddah at about 5,000; whereas he fixes the male population of Mekka only at 2,000—all having fled on account of famine. He estimates the male population of Jerusalem and of the Syrian Tripoli at 20,000, apparently his favourite figure. Most illuminating, indeed, is the estimate of Cordova about 350: 113000 houses of the subject population. 3000 places of worship[2].

In the empire four different types of towns existed side by side: the Hellenistic Mediterranean town; the South-Arabian town, such as Sana, to this type also belonged Mekka and Fustal; the Mesopotamian and the Eastern town. The Arabian towns were essentially of narrow but high houses. At Fustal there were houses five, six, seven even eight-story high. The ground floor was never occupied. Often two hundred people lived in one house[3]. And Nasir Khusru loves to say : he, who sees the town from a distance, takes it for a mountain for some houses are fourteen storys high, others seven. There are Bazars and streets which are constantly lighted up by candles for the sunlight never enters there[4]. The Iranian towns consisted of a citadel, the official quarter, which generally had four gates and the Commercial quarter where the Bazars were. Each of these three divisions was well-fortified by its own special wall. Between the official and the other quarters there was constant friction. Since the middle of the 3rd century a fifth type came into existence close to the Capital the rulers built their own residences: Samarza and Jafariyah on the Tigris, the Aghlabide town of Raqqadah, Mansuriyah, Mohamadiyyah and Qahira, the most successful creation of the century, nay of Islam. In Spain Abdur Rahman built Zahra at Cordova

(1) 65, 67.

(2) Adhari II, 247.

(3) Istakhri. 49; Ibn Haukal, 96; Muk, 198.

(4) p, 50.

and issued a proclamation that any one building in the neighbourhood would receive a reward of 4000 dirhams. This proved an effective bait[1]. And three kilometres from Shiraz Adad-ud-Dawlah found (d. 372) the suburb of Fana Khusru. He constructed a water-channel extending (Mez, p. 390 line 14 from the bottom?) over a whole day's journey and on its bank built a park one parasung long. His generals built there residences for themselves. There the Amir established a fair where rows of booths were erected and people met for "pleasure and sin". After his death this suburab rapidly declined[2]. Spaciousness was the striking of feature of these new towns and it is this fact which Yaqubi is never weary of pointing out regarding Samarra. The main street of Jafariyah was 200 yards broad with a canal flowing on either side[3]. Cairo, in its inception, was a veritable garden-town. The houses stood single and apart the trees of one never ove· lapping the walls of another, says Nasir Khusru[4].

However much the Islamic world emphasised the importance of drinking-water (p. 391 line 1) its acqueducts never equalled those of antiquity. Like the Middle Ages in the west it honestly did not feel justified in lavish extravagance for the care of the body. The old achievements, thus, amazed them all the more. In the Kitab al-Mawali of Kinḍi (d. 350)—the question as to what is the most wonderful thing in the world is thus answered; the light-house of Alexandria and Aqueducts of Carthage[5]. Yaqut (IV, 58) praises their arches and minaret-like pillars. Old Cairo used the Nilewater, the water carriers supplying it at the

(1) Ibn Haukal, 77.

(2) Muk, 431 and Yaqut, Compare Schwarz, *Iran*,50.

(3) Yaqubi *Geography*, 266.

(4) p. 45. Later the fate of large town overtook Cairo. Ibn Sai'd complains in the 7th century, of narrow, dark ditry streets or the high houses where light and air cannot come in. Maqrizi, Khitat, 1 365.

(5) Maqrizi, *Khitat*, 1,066.

uniform rate of half a Daniq per skin of water[1]. About the year 400/5200 camels are reported to have brought skins of water into Cairo and Misr[2]. In 382 an order was issued to the effect that those who brought water on camels and mules were to so wrap up the skins that the clothes of the peoples were not wetted[3]. Baghdad, for the most part, drink water from the Tigris. It was either directly fetched from the river or was taken to the houses of the well-to-do by water carriers. The canals, too supplied water to the cisterns which served as reservoirs (p. 391 2nd para line 3). Even two covered aqueducts.

They were much more modest than the stone aqueducts of the Romans. These were built of bricks jointed with lime[4]. As the cistern-water in Mekka was bitter, and such was unfit for consumption—it soon became an object of pious benevolence to provide the Holy City with good water. The underground aqueduct, built by Zubaida, often gave trouble; as for instance, about the middle of the 3rd century when a skin of water in the town cost 80 dirhams. It continued to do so until the mother of the Caliph Mut-awakkil had it restored[5]. The Wazir Ali ibn Isa, an exile at Mekka purchased a great number of animals and endowed a sum of money for their up-keep. At the same time he had a large well dug which supplied sweet water and bought a spring for 1000 dinars and widened it so that there may be plenty of water at Mekka[6].

---

(1) Muk, 307.
(2) Nasir Khusru. 44.
(3) Maqrizi, *Khitat*, II, 108 according to Musabbibi.
(4) Yaqubi, *Geography, 250.*
(5) Tabari, III, 1440.
(6) Wuz, p. 286 (Ali ibn Isa found the water-supply in particalar very defective in Mekka. It was usual to bring water from Jiddah (the Red Sea port) by Carvan, and the necessary animals were obtained by a periodical impression. Ali now bought out-right a troop of camels and donkey and set aside a fund for their up-keep. At the

At Samarqand Muslim piety made even better provision for the thirsty. "Rarely did I see an inn, a street corner, a square or a number of men at a well (p. 392 line 5 from the top) without some arrangement for iced water in God's name. Water was regularly supplied at 2000 places either at brick-built shelters or from brass buckets (Istakhri, 290; Ibn Haukal, 339).

In the town water circulated in an old moat of the fortress. It was carried to the middle of the market by a stone dam whence it was distributed further by means of lead pipes. The arrangement was pre-Islamic the water supply was kept up from the income of the nighbouring lands. The supervisors were Zoroastrians who, for their work as such, were relieved of the Capitation-tax[1]. Specially North-Iranian towns such as Qumm[2] and Nisapur, then the greatest town of the East, had under-ground water-courses. Various conduits ran under-ground (p. 392 line 16 from the top); some supplied water to the suburban gardens and some to the houses of the town. They were of various depths. Special passages led to them : sometimes one had to go down 100 steps. And thus a wit has his fling: "Nisapur would be a lovely town if its water-courses ran above and its inhabitants under the ground"[3]. Even these water-courses had their own supervisors and administrators[4]. The mountainous town of Dinawar, rich in springs : signalised its refinement by supplying water in cool pitchers with mouth-pieces.

In the commercial town of Basra the definite operation

---

same time he had a well dug, called after him at *Jarrahiyah*, in the millers' market. He also caused another abundant spring to be opened and its channel widened. Bowen, Life and Times of Ali ibn Isa, p. 128 Tr.)

(1) Istakhri 216; Ibn Haukal, 366.

(2) Yaqubi, *Geography* 274.

(3) Nasir Khusru, 278 (French tr)

(4) Muk, 394.

of night-soil seems to have been disposed of in a most off-hand fashion. It was left in the hands of contractors (p. 392 line 7 from the bottom). Here and there we come across witty sallies on this system[1].

Already in the 3rd century donkeys were let out to the middle class of the town on hire for transit. At Baghdad their chief stand was at Bab-al-Karkh, at the entrance of the business quarter[2].

At Fustal there was a stand at Dar-el-hurm. The ride cost two dirhams[3]. At Baghdad and Basra—towns by the river—boats were used for communication between places. At the time of Al-Muwaffaq (256-279) a census was taken of the Baghdadian ferry men. They numbered, 30,000 and their daily income was assessed at 90,000 dirhams[4].

The town administration, for the most part, was in the hands of Government officers. Of these, for example, in every district town of Khorasan, there were four; the Qadhi, the post master, the Inspector of taxes and the head of the police[5]. At Baghdad the Eastern portion was under the direct administration of the Court—while the Western was under the prefect of the district of Baduraya—whose post was reckoned as the most one rous and influential of the kind[6]. In the second decade of the fourth century one and the same *Katib* acted in Isphahan as the chief of the inland revenue office and the town administrator (Tadbir el-beled)[7]. Alongside of the municipal hierarchy there existed

---

(1) Yaqut, 1, 248; *Uyun cl-Akhbar, ed.* Brockelmann, 265.
(2) Jahiz Bayon, 1, 31.
(3) Ibn Sa'id, 39. In 440 Nasir Khusru speaks of 50,000 donkeys for hire in Misr, p. 53.
(4) *Tarikh Baghdad* 73.
(5) Ibn Haukal, 309
(6) Wuz 75.
(7) Yaqut, Irshad, 1, 130.

a peculiar organization (p. 393 line 15 from the top?). From the very foundation of Baghdad every quarter of the town was specially placed under a courtier for administration. Apart from this arrangement every community, the Persian pre-minently had its own foreman (Rais) and chief (Qadi)[1]. The Commander of the Body-guard (Sahib-us-Shurtah) was responsible for public safety at the residences of the Prince and of the Governors—in other towns the chief of the Police had the same responsibility (Sahib-el-Maunah), (Daneban Stand (p. 393 line 12 from the bottom?). About the year 300 he is a well-established officer who, as his title shows, is one of the highest in rank at Baghdad[2]. Mawardi[3] and Ibn-el-Tuwais[4] for the first time, tell us what his manifold duties were. Often enough analogous duties such as the supervisor of the slave-market, of the mint and of weaving were imposed upon him.

Von der ersteren? (p. 393, line 5 from the bottom). A Baghdadian edict of the year 366 enjoins instant removal from the salve-market of all disreputable purchasers and the prevention of all shady practices and calls upon the Inspector of Industries to see that weaving was good, sound and durable and that the name of the Caliph was duly inscribed on clothes, carpets, banners and borders[5]. Mutasibs were mostly recruited from the jurists. When in 318 the Caliph appointed a courtier, who was also chief of the Body-guards, to that position—Munis insisted on his dismissal on the ground that only Qadis and men connected with law could be appointed to that post[6].

The distinguishing mark of the police was a long knife

(1) Yaqut, *Geography*, 248, Karkh was split up into twelve villages (Qaryah), Wuz, 258.
(2) Wuz. 158.
(3) Engeris ed. pp. 404.
(4) Maqrizi, *Khitat.*
(5) Rasail of Sabi Baabds 1898, 113.
(6) Arib, 147; Ibn al Athir, VIII, 165.

which they carried in their girdle[1]. Their patrol at night continued till the early morning-prayer[2].

In the second century there was no statistics in the East of the foreigners passing through the town-gate[3]. A report of the third century speaks of the gate-pass, customary in China, as something quite new[4]. For the first time in the fourth century Adud-ud-Dawla introduced a gate-pass in his Capital, Shiraz. Mukaddasi points out that the arrival of strangers were carefully noted(?) and none was allowed to leave the town without a permit[5].

---

(1) Hamadhani *Maqamah*, Beyrut, 162.

(2) *Khitat-al-Faragh tad es-siddah,* I, 19.

(3) Aghani, XIX, 147.

(4) *Silsilet et-towarikh*, ed Rainaud, 42. Egypt had, even in the earliest Muslim period, a strick pass system for inland intercourse (Becker, Papyri Scott-Reinh. 140). Even no one permitted to leave Tulnid Egypt without a permit (Jawas). Ibn Said Mugrib, ed. Vollers, 52.

(5) p. 429.

XXIII. THE FESTIVALS

The festivals show how thin was the Islamic varnish over the popular life. The Muslims celebrated all the Christian festivals—most of which were nothing more or less than rivals of much older practices. Indeed many Christian places of pilgrimage in Mesopotamia and Egypt were old heathen places of worship. The festivals of patron saints of the Christian cloisters, which grew up, were merely new labels on old pagan celebrations. The local Muslims insisted on celebrating the days which had brightened the lives of their heathen and Christian ancestors. But in contrast to the church they generally disdained to forge new legends and left the Christians to settle their religious affairs as best they could. They simply shared in the social side of the festivals. The festivals, as, for example, of the Baghdadians, were almost all positively Christian festivals. Of them the feasts of the patron saints of the various monasteries were the most popular. Even on ordinary days these pious centres were not free from worldly visitors.[1] With their fine gardens and cool drinking-places they were popular rendezvous of the Baghdadians, intent on pleasure. Cloisters and taverns are often and often mentioned in one and the same breath: "On a rainy day it is delightful to sip wine with a priest."[2] And particularly commended is the sacramental wine (*Sharab al Qurban*).[3] Things were not very different in Cairo.

(1) Sabushti, 8 a.

(2) Ibn al-Mu'tazz, II, 46 (The old Arab preferred sipping wine with a girl "in a tent" on a rainy day Tr.)

(3) Ibn al-Mu'tazz, II, 50 Schiltberger found the Greek priests in the Muslim empire as inkeepers. (Bibl des literar, vereins, 50). In the Syrian villages also Christian priests brought wine for us concealed in their mantle.

At the end of the 4th/10th century the favourite pleasure-resorts of the Cairenes are mentioned: The gazelle-hunt near the Pyramid monastery; the Bridge and Taverns of Gizeh; the garden at Maqs with a view of the canal and the palace; the play-ground at the Mar Hanna monastery and, above all, the monastery of al-Qusair, high up on the Muqattam with its delightful prospect: "how often was I day and night at the monastery of al-Qusair without recovering from the effects of wine."[1] The Tulunid Khumrawaihi had a watch-tower built there with four bow-windows, one for each point of the compass.[2]

Palm-Sunday (Sha'nin-Hosannah) was a day of universal festivity or the people. It must have been an old feast of the trees notably of olive-trees.[3] In Egypt it was simply called the "Olive festival"[4]. At the court of Baghdad slave-girls appeared on Palm-Sunday in gay dresses with palm and olive branches.[5]

In Jerusalem of the 4th/10th century on olive-tree was

(1) *Irshad*, 1, 291.
(2) Abu Salih, *Churches and Monasteries* ed. Evetts, fol. 49 a.
(3) Already in the 4th century A.D. children used, on this day, to go round and round the mount of Olives at Jerusalem with branches of palm and olive-tree in their hand *Silviae Peregrinatio* 91). And even today among the Maronites a finely decked out tree is brought on Palm-Sunday into the church and is auctioned. The purchaser places his son or some other youth on it and carries him round the church amidst the acclamation of the people. After this the people rush at it to get some of its twigs which bring a blessing. The Copts (p. 395, line 6 from the bottom) weave twigs of palm and olive into a large olive tree which the Patriarch places on the alter on Palm-Sunday—he then takes it to the four corners of the church where each time the Palm-Sunday service is read before it. Similarly the olive is taken in procession round the monastery mill and baking oven. *Mashriq*, viii, 342. In the Western churches the holy oil is consecrated on Palm-Sunday.
(4) *Maqrizi*, I, 264.
(5) *Aghani* XIX, 138.

carried in solemn procession from the Church of Eleasor to the Church of the Resurrection—the *wali* of the town with his entire staff heading the procession.[1] All the churches of Syria and Egypt were adorned with olive leaves and palm branches which the people took home for a blessing. Hakim forbade this. He would not see any olive-branches or palm-leaves 'in the hand of a Believer or Christian either.'[2] In Egypt the Monday-Thursday was called Lentil-Thursday because all ate lentils on that day. Lentils were a mourning food and, hence the Egyptian Christian ate lentils every Friday.[3] On this day (Monday-Thursday) the mint turned out gold carobs[4] and distributed them at Court.[5] The Alexandrians celebrated this festival at their light-house where they held a banquet.[6] In Syria this day was called blue or egg Thursday. Coloured eggs were sold in the streets; slaves, boys and fools gambled with them.[7] At Baghdad on Easter-day Muslims and Christian marched in procession to the Samalu monastery at the Shammasiyah gate, at the north-end of the Eastern town, where a lively carouse took place: "until I took the earth for a ship and the walls danced round us."[8] On the last Saturday of September was held the feast

(1) Yahya ibn Sa'id 194.
(2) Yahya, 194. It was a special Christian practice to wear white garments on this day (Radi, Diwan, 917).
(3) Razi translated by Steinschneider in Virchows Archiv 36, p. 574.
(4) Name of a coin, one fortich of a dinar.
(5) Maqrizi, *Khitat*, I, 450.
(6) Maqrizi, I, 157.
(7) Maqrizi, I, 266 : *Mudkhil*, 305.
(8) Sabushti, 4 b. (In the early days of the Abbasid Caliphate the Samalu monastery occupied a considerable tract of ground beside the river...The Dayr is described as a magnificent edifice, inhabited by many monks, and it took its name from Samalu, a town of the Armenian frontier, which Harun had captured in the expedition of the year 163/A.D. 780. The Caliph caused the whole population of this place to be transported to Baghdad, for by the terms of the capitulation it had been stipulated that none of the families were to

of the Monastery of Foxes (Dayr-ath-Tha'alib) at the Iron Gate on the West side of Baghdad. It was fondly frequented by Muslims and Christians alike, for in the midst of the town it possessed its own park, trees and flowers.[1] On the 3rd of October, at the monastery of Ashmuna, was celebrated one of the great festivals of Baghdad. This monastery was in the Katrabbul District to the north-west of the Round City (Guy Le Strange, *Baghdad*, p. 209). People came there—according to their position—in 'flyers', barks or ordinary boats (Sumariyyat) with wine-skins and singing-women. The well-to-do pitched their tents and caroused for three days and nights on the banks of the Tigris "amidst candles and pretty faces" (Sâbushti, 18 a, b; Beruni, 310). A stranger, who enquired of this sights worth seeing at Baghdad, was consoled with the promise of this feast which was to take place within a month. (*Kit. alsin ect.* Florence Laurent, fol. 99 a). St. Barbara ushered in the winter. Her day, the 4th of December, was celebrated alike by Christians and Muslims, and Mukaddasi thus states the maxim of the peasants: "when the Barbara Day arrives the masons should take to the flute."[2] He also boasts of having taken part in this feast.[3] Christmas, the 25th of December, the Nativity of Christ (al-milad) and

---

be seperated and they were settled on the lands to the north of East Baghdad where was built the monastery which afterwards went by the name of their native place. With lapse of time and monastery fell to ruin, and the author of the *Marasid*, who wrote about the year 1300 A.D., states that all trace of its buildings had then long since disappeared. Guy Le Strange, *Baghdad* pp. 202-314, Tr.)

(1) Subushti; 8 a; Beruni, 310 (There was much dispute concerning the position of this monastery. Some authorities state that it stood nearly two miles distant from Baghdad on the Kufah highroad towards Sarsar and near the village of Harithiya: while according to shrine of Ma'ruf Kakhi and hence was either to be indentified with the Dayr al-jathilek (the monastery of the Catholicos or Patriarch), being merely its other name, or else was a second monastery which had stood alongside of it. Guy Le Strange, *Baghdad*, p. 210, Tr.)

(2) p. 182.

(3) p. 45 (Eng. tr. p. 77, Tr.)

the feast of the Sun was celebrated with bonfires. Why do the Christians light up fire on Christmas night and play with nuts? asks the Shi'ite Babagwaihi al-Qummi (d. 381/991) and thus answers: To warm Mary when in travail, Joseph lighted a fire and cracked nine nuts for her which he found in his saddle-bag and he fed her with them.[1] The Muslims also celebrated the yule-feast (*Sadaq,* Arabic *Lailat el-wuqud,* Night of the fire)[2] which according to the Canon of Mas'ud[3] was celebrated on the 5th or the 10th of Bahman[4] but which, according to Ibn al-Athir and Abulfida coincided with Christmas.[5] Ibn al-Jauzi, speaking of the year 429/1038 says: "People lighted fires on Christmas Day as usual."[6] In the 4th/10th century they used "to fumigate their house to keep off mishap,"[7] so that finally it has become one of the customs of the kings to light fires on this night and to make them blaze, to drive wild beasts into them and to send the birds flying through the flames, and to drink and amuse themselves round the fires. May God take vengeance on all who enjoy causing pain to another being, gifted with sensation and doing no harm!" The most famous Christmas feast of its time was that of the year 323/935. The Condottiere Merdawig—Prince of the west Iranian mountain tracts—caused fagots to be collected in the *Wadi* of Zerinruz at Isfahan, set up huge candles and gathered together a large number of naphta throwers and marksmen. At every elevation about the town a huge castle of trunks of trees was built and was filled up with oakum and fagots. He had birds captured and caused nuts, filled with oakum and naptha, to be tied to their beaks and fect. In the hall of his

---

(1) *Kit. al-ilal*, Berlin, fol. 32 a.
(2) Misk, V. 479.
(3) Name of a work of Al-Beruni.
(4) Beruni tr. 213.
(5) Ibn al-Athir, VIII, 222 ff; Abulfida, *Annales'* 323.
(6) Fol. 192 b.
(7) Beruni, 226.

castle he set up powerful wax-pillars and figures made of wax for illumination. He arranged that the fire might be lighted up simultaneously on the hills, in the desert and in the castle. The birds, too, were to be released in the darkness of the night. He arranged for a great feast for which 100 horses and 200 cattle apart from sheep—were slaughtered. But when he inspected the arrangement he found it all petty and trifling, for to the eye—set on the wide, wide expanse—everything seems small and petty. He became angry; wrapped himself up in a mantle and uttered not a word[1]. On Christmas Day the Fatimid Caliph presented their officers with sweets, rose-water and codfish. They illuminated shops and streets with lantern[2] (fanus) and gave them to beggars at a cost of one dirham for a lantern.

In Egypt Epiphany was specially celebrated with great splendour. It was called the "Feast of Diving" (*Id-al-Ghitas*) because the Christians bathed in the Nile. Even today on the very same day the Greek church blesses holy water. It was an old custom for the Commissioner of Police of the Lower Town to go about the streets in the evening in a gorgeous dress with candles and fire-baskets proclaiming: "On this night Muslims should not mix with Christians." At dawn the Christians proceeded in a splendid procession to the Nile singing Psalms and carrying crosses and burning candles. Many actually dived into the Nile. "Officials and savants had greater Pleasure and fun at this feast than on any other day of the year."[3] Mas'udi states: "The night of the diving"[4] is a great night for the people of Misr. They do not sleep all that night. In 330/941 I took part in this festival at Misr.[5] Ikhshid Mohammad Ibn Tughj was in his residence

(1) Misk V, 479 ff: Ibn al-Athir, VIII, 222 : Abulfida, anno. 323. gives the figure of animals slain as 100 horses and 2,000 cattle.
(2) Maqrizi. 1, 265.
(3) Maqrizi, 1, 266.
(4) Ibn Sa'id, 196.
(5) Mas'udi, II, 364 ff.

called 'the chosen one' on the island of the Nile. He had the banks of the island and of the town lighted up by 1,000 fire-baskets. The people themselves adding their own candles and fire-baskets to this illumination. There were 100,000 Muslims and Christians on the Nile that night—some on boats, some in the neighbouring houses, some again on the banks. They vied with each other in eating, in drinking, in gaudiness of dress and apparel, in gold and silver ornaments in precious stones, in music, in piping and in dancing. It is the most beautiful and the most enjoyable night at Misr. The streets are not closed. Most people bathe in the Nile and think that they, thereby, secure immunity from illness." Specially the candle-market was lighted up on a grand scale. It was, as a rule, open till midnight,[1] was, much frequented at night and was a resort of prostitutes distinguished by special attire, pantaloons of red leather.

In 415/1025 the chief police officer of Cairo pitched a tent on the Nile bridge on the Epiphany for the Caliph and his women-folk to see the festival. The Caliph himself gave the signal for the lighting up of the fire and lanterns and "it was a beautiful, and prolonged illumination."[2]

The night of the first Sunday in Lent was also a great day of festivity for Muslims at Baghdad. It was celebrated with great *eclat* at the *Dair-al-Khawwet* (monastery of the sisters) at Ukbara, a village noted for wine. The pleasure-making reached its culminating point on the *Lailat-ul-mahsus* (night of the touch)" when women mixed freely with men, no one shrinking from anything. There was plenty of drinking, dancing and fun."[3] The later Ibn Khaldun even knew of men, dressed up in women's clothes, riding wooden horses, with faces turned towards the tail, and

(1) Maqrizi, *Khitat*, II, 96.
(2) Musabbihi (d, 420/1029) in Becker, *Beitrage*, I, 62.
(3) *Ibid.*

having mock fights.[1] On the fourth Sunday of Lent people of the two faiths went to the monastery of Durmalis and gave themselves up to festivities for several days.[2] A great Christian festival of the Egyptians was unhesitatingly adopted by the Muslims: The deliverance of Joseph from prison at Gizeh. Previously people, with trumpets and drums, went round the bazars and the streets collecting subscriptions for the festival. But in consequence of a rise in prices the merchants in 415/1024 refused to pay subscription. The Government, thereupon, consented to double its usual grant. Everywhere amusement, acting and shadow-plays were arranged. For two days the Caliph himself came to inspect the show.[3] He also was present, three months before at the dedication of a church when Christians and Muslims pitched tents on the banks of the canal and enjoyed themselves with food, drink and other pleasures. Women, on this occasion, drank so heavily that they had to be carried home in baskets.[4] On the 8th of May was the martyr's feast in Shubrah near Cairo. A box containing the finger of a martyr, which was kept in the Christian church at Shubra, was annually thrown into the Nile.

All Cairo and the whole band of Egyptian musicians joined this celebration—often, indeed, wine, worth over 100,000 dirhems, was sold that day. Only in the 8th/14th century was this festival done away with.[5]

There were three New Year feasts:

(a) The Persian and the Syrian which fell in spring;

(b) The Coptic in Egypt which fell at the end of

(1) Sabushti, fol. 37 b.

(2) Mashriq, IX, 200.

(3) Sabushti Ia: Musabbihi in Maqrizi, *Khitat*, 1, 207.

(4) Musabbihi, apud, *Khitat*, II, 1355.

(5) Maqrizi, I, 60.

August;

(c) The beginning of the Muslim year which varied from year to year.

(d) Besides these,—there are traces of the ancient Persian New Year which occurred at the summer solstice.

Generally the pre-Islamic New Year's day, at the beginning of the solar year, was celebrated by mutual gifts. Among other things the Caliph at Baghdad distributed objects made of amber; as for instance, red roses.[1] The Samanids in Bukhara presented summer clothes to their soldiers;[2] the Fatimids robes and eatables to their folk.[3] Even before the Caliph they acted with masks at Baghdad. The Caliph flung money at the actors and it so happened once that one of the actors actually looked for a stray coin under the flaps of the royal coat. This provoked the displeasure of an old courtier ; for this close intercourse with masked people offered too many opportunities for assassination. Henceforth the Caliph witnessed the performance from a height.[4] It was customary both at the Persian and the Coptic New Year for people to sprinkle water over each other. In 282/895 this was forbidden in the East.[5] But Beruni, about 400/1008, testifies to the renewal of this practice.[6] The Chinese traveller Wang Jente who travelled westward between 981-83 A.D., observed this practice even in Turfan (Kan-tschang) : The inhabitants of Kan-tschang make silver and copper pipes, fill them with water and sprinkle each other with it. Sometimes for fun they do so with their hands. They assert that they, thereby, cool the humours and thus keep illnesses away.[7] In Egypt people nominated a prince

(1) Sabushti, 22b.
(2) Beruni, 217.
(3) Maqrizi, *Khitat* , 268 f.
(4) Sabushti, 15 a, b.
(5) Tabari, III, 2144.
(6) pp. 215, 218.
(7) JA. 1847, I, 58.

for the new year (amir un-nauroz) who besmeared his face with flour or lime, went through the streets on a donkey, in a red or yellow coat with a copy-book in hand like a *Muhtasib* (market-inspector) collecting money from the well-to-do. He who did not pay had water and dirt thrown at him. They hit each other with straps (julud) and twisted leather-ropes (anta), the poor in the streets, the rich in their houses. The police, therefore, entertained no complaint on that score. In the school the teacher was attacked by his students and sometimes thrown into a fountain where he remaind until he redeemed himself by payment. In 335/945 the Governor forbade the "throwing of water." In 363/974, the Caliph prohibited the feast, but, despite the prohibitions, it was celebrated with greater zest than ever, for three days—the punishment proving ineffectual.[1] Only in the eighties of the 8/14th century was this festival suppressed by the Sultan Barquq.[2] The Egyptian custom can easily be recognised as the carnival: celebrated on the intercalated day which everywhere came at the end of the old year, were under the dominia of a King of fools, and faithfully followed the migration of the new year[3]—through the calendar.[4]

Of the old Persian New Year, at the beginning of the summer solstice, the sprinkling of water still survived about the year 400/1009.[5] Today it is associated with the Christian Feast of Ascension which falls about this day and the day is named the "sprinkling Thursday."[6] Khamis er-rishash). I

---

(1) Kindi, 294 : Maqrizi, *Khitat*, I, 266. The new year in Egypt falls in August. People light fire and throw water at each other. Calendar of Cordova for the year 961 A.D. ed. Dzy. p. 85.

(2) Maqrizi, *Khitat*, I, 269, 403.

(3) This seems to be the sense.

(4) Even in Europe; Saturnalia, time between X'mas and Epiphany etc., etc. In some parts of Germany on the 4th day after X'mas children give a beating to their parents and kinsmen. In Bulgaria on New Year's day, servants do likewise to their master.

(5) Beruni, 266.

(6) Mashriq, III, 668.

have witnessed this custom myself at Baghdad. A "Prince Carnival" is also at Al-Kausaj (the thin bearded man). His day, once at the end of February, now falling at the beginning of November by reason of the shifting of the Persian calendar, coincided with the five intercalary days of the Persians. He rode about the streets of Mesopotamian and Persian towns on a mule and he who would not give him something had his clothes smeared with red glue. "On this day God was said to fix the good and evil fortune of man"[1]—as was the old belief, concerning the New Year's day. These were days of jubilation and rejoicing for the Persians. About three months later followed the old winter solstice of the Persians (Mihrjan)—now falling at the end of September—which, along with the *Nauroz*, has always remained their most important feast. It was, like the *Nauroz*, celebrated by mutual gifts—the Court and the army donning the winter uniform.[2] The people, on this day, too, "changed carpets, utensils and clothing."[3] It is specially noticed as a peculiarity that on this feast-day even subjects made presents to their Prince. The *quondam* State-Secretary As-Sabi sends to his prince presents from jail on the Mihrjan day—a Khusrowan dirham and a book "as big as my prison and as firmly bound as myself."[4] On the other hand the constantly shifting Muslim New Year never became a popular festival but remained merely a court-holiday on which mutual gifts were made.[5]

The custom of the Abbasid Court to strew roses is also traceable to nature-worship. The splendour-loving Mutawakkil is said to have had five million dirhems struck

---

(1) Beruni, tr. 211. Mas'udi III, 413: Tha'libi, *Book of the Props* ZDMG VI, 389 : Qazwini, on the margin of Damiri, 1, 127.

(2) Beruni' 223 : Yat. IV. 65, *Diwan Kushajim*.

(3) Mas'udi. III, 404 : *Sukkardan* on the margin of *Mikhlat*, 163.

(4) Yat, III, 58.

(5) For North Persia, Ibn al-Athir, IX, 41 : for Egypt, Maqrizi *Khitat*, 1, 490.

and painted in various colours: red, yellow black, etc., etc., for showering upon court officers.[1] They built for the Cairene ruler at Qalyub—where was special rose cultivation—a castle of roses where a great banquet was held.[2].

The two canonical festivals are the sacrificial festivals at the conclusion of the month of Fast. They, along with the *Nauroz*, constituted the three principal festivals of the people of Baghdad.[3] At Basra sheep were fattened for a year for the sacrificial feast and were sold at 10 dinars each.[4] At Cairo, amidst a huge crowd, the state table of the Caliph was carried through the main streets under the guidance of the Trade-Inspector and Chief of the Police. The table was adorned with many mounted pieces as for instance in the year 415/1024 with seven huge towers; in 439/1047 with an orange-tree—all made of sugar. Chains of cracknels and other dainties were heaped up in the tower which the people were allowed to plunder.[5] These two *Ids* were the only great festivals which could be celebrated as Islamic festivals with official Muslim splendour. They were most solemn where Muslim sentiment was at its highest such as in Tarsus,[6] where Muslim warriors from the entire empire streamed in. After the loss of Tarsus—Sicily later became renowned for its most beautiful *Id* celebrations.[7] The sacrificial feast, by its wholesale slaughter of defenceless animals, must always have been repulsive.

Ramadan was the time of the greatest hospitality. The Wazir Ibn 'Abbad entertained some thousands on these nights in his house and gave more away in one month than

(1) Sabushti, 68 b.
(2) Maqrizi, 1, 488.
(3) Tabari, III, 1170.
(4) *Aghani*, III, 62.
(5) Musabbihi in Becker, *Beitrage*, 1, 70 : cf. Nasir Khusru, tr. 158 : Maqrizi, *Khitat*, 1, 387 : Abul Mahasin, II, 473.
(6) *Tarikh Baghdad*, Paris 14 b : Abul Mahasin, II, 67.
(7) Muk. 183.

he did during the rest of the year put together.[1] The growing veneration for the Prophet, in the pietistic circles, introduced about the year 300/912 his birthday celebration—a vexatious innovation to the faithful of the older type.[2] The pious Karaji (d. 343/954) broke his fast only on the two *Ids* and the birthday of the Prophet. In the 6th/12th century the Fatimid Caliphs even forbade four birthday celebrations as unlawful; those of the Prophet, of Ali, of Fatima and of the reigning Caliph.[3]

But the first to celebrate the birthday of the Prophet on a grand scale is said to have been the Prince Abu Sa'id Muzaffur-ud-din of Arbela (d. 560/1233).[4] At this feast, legends relating to the Prophet, notably the history of his night-journey to heaven (mi'raj) were fondly recited, leading inevitably to the luxuriant development of his biography.

Of the family feasts the circumcision was by far the most important. It had not yet become a 'private' feast; for it still retained many features of the old feast of puberty. They felt shy of circumcising one child alone. The Caliph al-Muqtadir had five of his sons circumcised at the same time, besides a band of orphans whom he loaded with rich presents. The entire cost is said to have been 600,000 dinars (Jauzi, fol. 10b.) Isma'il Ibn Qa'im (the Fatimid) ordered

---

(1) *Yat*, III, 36.

(2) Goldziher *Moh* and *Islam* p. 198 Tr.

(3) Maqrizi, 1, 432.

(4) To the celebration, arranged by him, streamed in from Baghdad, Mosul, Jazirah, Sinjar, Nisibis, even Persia, Sufis, preachers, Qur'an-readers and poets and remained at Arbela from Mohurram to the beginning of Rabi' I. The Prince had 20 finely adorned booth shows, 4 or 5 storeys high, erected in the principal streets and manned them throughout with singers, musicians and shadow-players. The people, at this time, did nothing but roam about and enjoy the pleasures offered to them. On the night of the *Milad* the Prince himself rode through the streets. Many burning candles—each tied to a mule—waved to and fro in front of him. The festival concluded with a parade and a banquet. Ibn Khail, ed. Wustenfeld, 2, 16.

that the sons of the Commanders and Superintendents—nay, even those of the slaves, soldiers and poor-folks of Qairwan and other towns should be registered for circumcision and gifts. The figure showed more than 10,000. Every day 500 to 1,300 were circumcised, fed and rewarded. He gave to everyone according to his position—from 100 dinars to 100 dirhems and even less. The feast lasted for 17 days. "I have heard a courtier say that the total cost was 200,000 dinars. Such expenditure and extravagance had never been experienced before.[1]" And so also was the greatest court-feast of the 3rd/9th century—the circumcision of the Caliph al-Mu'tazz. It cost his father the fabulous sum of 86 million dirhems.[2] But fates had willed that the son, so blessed with his father's joy, should be murdered after a brief reign and that his son should end his days in poverty and indigence.

Along with these circumcisions, weddings were the most renowned court-feasts of the olden times. The wedding of Harun cost 50 million and that of Mamun 70 million dirhems.[3] In 3109 22 the Chief Stewardess fell into disfavour for celebrating the wedding of her niece with an unheard of splendour.[4] On these occasions people liked to show themselves richer than they actually were. They hired[5] ornaments, carpets and utensils.

Finally an important feast was the feat of cupping, when presents were received and a special meal was served. (Irshad II. 141). The operation was done by a barber who, about the year 300/912, received half a dirhem as his remuneration.*

(1) *Kit al-Uyun wal-hadaiq*, IV, Berl. 252 a.

(2) Sabushti, 66 ff.

(3) Sabushti, 66 b.

(4) *Zubdat al-Fi Krah*, 192 a.

(5) *Aghani*, V, 119. At Baghdad the first wedding dish, according to the custom there, always was the *Harisah* a kind of mince. Ibn al-Hajjaj, X, 70. The throwing of canfetti was also a custom at weddings there. *Yat*, II, 20.

(*) *Irshad*, 1, 370. Distinguished people had a barber of their own. Misk, VI. 247.

XXIV. LAND PRODUCTS

The citizens of the Muslim Empire were almost all bread consumers in contrast to the Hindus and Eastern Asiatics who lived on rice. From the latter they were specially distinguished by the fact that they all drank milk. These two articles of food formed as in Europe, their staple food. Only in the East the bread retained the shape of thin, round cakes, not any different from what was given to it by the European lake-dwellers.

In domestic economy of medieval Europe the most important event was the supplantation of millet and barley by wheat. In the East, however, wheat had established its position long before. Everywhere, where there was sufficiency of water-supply it was cultivated. Millet (durrah), on the other hand, was confined to the dry regions of the South (South Arabia, Nubia, Kirman) because "like sesame or oats it needed little water."[1] "Millet resembles wheat but is eaten like rice."[2] Mesopotamia was essentially a wheat cultivating province; the high price of wheat there is invariably adduced as a proof of famine. After barley, rice stood third on the list there. This fact attracted the attention of the Chinese; Ling Wai tai ta (1178 A.D.) thus[3] reports of

---

(1) Mashriq. 1908, 614.

(2) Yahya b. Adam, 86.

(3) Chau ju kua tr. Hirth, 137, 144. Already Strabo (XV,I) mentions the cultivation of rice in Mesopotamia but it must have been very slight for in the Talmud it never plays any part at all. At least in Krauss's *Tal. Arch* it is not even mentioned. The corn that was cultivated in Syria, before the Mesopotamian wheat, was called Qamh and finds its place in the Old Testament by the side of chittah, the Mesopotamian wheat, which, under this very name, was imported into Egypt. (Kremer, S.W.A. 1889). In the Arabian period wheat in

Baghdad: The people here eat bread, meat and Su-lo but seldom fish, vegetables and rice. Another Chinese thus writes of Egypt about 1300 A.D. The people live on bread and meat and eat no rice. In Khuzistan, likewise, wheat occupied the first place but they also made bread of rice-flour and rice was an article of popular food.[1] Only the marshy neighbourhood of Mazenderan[2] depended entirely upon rice.

In Palestine and Egypt a vegetable, corresponding to our potato, the Quloqas, was cultivated.[3] In the old Greek time its existence is attested in the Greek Isles, Asia Minor and Egypt. It is the thick, pulpy root-stock of Colocasia esculenta which in Polynesia was the staple food before the advent of the Europeans. "It has the shape of a round radish and has a rind. It is pungent in taste and is fried in oil."[4] "The Quloqas is peeled and cooked. The cooking-water is then poured off and it is fried in oil."[5] There are two varieties of these, one called the "fingers" and the other the "heads". The former is dearer[6] and more tasty. It is specially appreciated in winter with mutton.[7]

Grapes were the most cultivated of fruits. Mawardi[8] mentions even in Mesopotamia the cultivation of the vine as holding the first place (Karm in Ancient Mesopotamia was the general word for the cultivated field.) There were grapes of widely different varieties. "Even if one were to

---

Syria is called Qamh; in Mesopotamia Hintah: in Arabia Dhurr (Jahiz, *Bayan*, 7, 9).

(1) Ibn Hauqal, 173.

(2) Ibn Hauqal, 272.

(3) Muk, 203; Abdul Latif saw it at Damascus where it was not plentiful. *Relation* tr. by de Sacy, 23.

(4) Muk, 203.

(5) Abdul Latif, 23.

(6) Ibn al-Hajj, *Madkhal*, III, 143.

(7) *Hazz al-Quhuf*, 160.

(8) Ed. Enger, 304.

set out from his early youth to old age travelling through the countries—valley by valley and town by town—going from vineyard to vineyard—to learn their varieties and to master their peculiarities, he would not be able to do so even in a single climate, or a single region. It would be too much for him."[1] South Arabia possessed giant grapes. A Governor of Harun is said once to have brought from there two bunches of grapes on a camel, in a howdah apiece. Table-tops, twenty spans in circumference, were made of vine wood from the Armenian and Indo-Persian mountains.[2]

The name of the different varieties of grapes were popular names such as cow-eyes, sugar, nun's fingers tip, tiny flasks, but mostly they were named after their place of origin such as Mulakhite, Gurakhite' Slav.

The vine which, according to Strabo,[3] the Macedonians first brought to Mesopotamia and Persia, spread throughout the empire; the Arab conquest in its turn carried fresh sorts to the East. Thus the Raziqite grapes from Taif were cultivated in Mesopotamia[4] and near Herat in Afghanistan.[5] A report from the Dead Sea calls attention to the fact that the peasants artificially fecundate the vine(?) there just as they do with the palm and the Maghribines with figs.[6] To the fruits grown in the empire in the 3rd/9th century two were added, the orange and the lemon. At a court-feast at Samarra about the middle of the 3rd/9th century these, along with other costly fruits, were served for the guests. The reporter, writing about it in the 4th/10th century, particularly speaks of the orange, as exceedingly rare at that time.[7] The

(1) Ibn al-Faqih 125.
(2) *Ibid.*
(3) XV, 3.
(4) Ras'ail by Khwarezmi, 49.
(5) Istakhri 266.
(6) Ibn Hauqal, 124.
(7) Shabushti. *Kit. al-diyarat*, Berlin, fol. 66a b.

Prince Ibn al-Mu'tazz sings of them both at the end of the 3rd/9th century[1] but they seem to be confined to a small circle. In 323/935 Mas'udi writes: The orange and the round citron tree (utrug mudawwar) were imported from India after the year 300/912 and planted in Yaman. They were then taken to Basra, Mesopotamia and Syria until they became plentiful in the houses of Tarsus, of Antioch, of the Syrian Coast, of Palestine and Egypt, where they were unknown before. But the fine fragrance and the beautiful colour which they had in India has passed away from them.[2] The Caliph Al-Qahir (320-322/932-934)—to whom orange-trees were dearer than any other—had them planted in his small palace-garden. They were imported across Basra and Oman from India. In Muqaddasi's time they were cultivated even in Palestine.[3] In the 4th/10th century Ibn Hauqal had to describe the lemon for the benefit of his readers. "In Sind, the extreme south of the empire, there are neither grapes, nor apples, nor nuts nor pears; but there is sugar-çane. There they have a fruit, like an apple, which they call lemon. It is very sour."[4] Similarly Muqaddasi states; "among the specialities of Sind is lemon ; a fruit like apricot, but very sour."[5] Throughout the 4th/10th century it remained an imported fruit[6] and only later found a home from India across Oman in Mesopotamia.[7] Later in Egypt they cultivated "apple-lemon" (limun tuffahi)" so little sour that it could be eaten without sugar;[8]" "winter-lemon" and "weeping-lemon" (Sa'il)[9]. Not yet was this fruit utilized for preparing

(1) *Diwan*, II, 106, 119.
(2) Mas'udi, II. 438 f.; Maqrizi, *Khitat*, 1, 28.
(3) p. 181.
(4) p. 228.
(5) p. 482.
(6) *Yatimah*, III, 82.
(7) Qazwini on the margin of Da miri, II 30 f. In the Calendar of Cordova, under the year 961 A.D. where fruit culture of Spain is mentioned; both orange and lemon are wanting.
(8) Maqrizi, *Khitat*, II, 237.
(9) Thamarat el-Awraq, II, 224.

lemonade. The fashion in the higher circles in the 4th/10th century was rather to take iced drinks as in Baghdad. But in Basra "we drink the foulest drink; citron-water (?), sallow, distasteful, thick, horrid like cholera-stool."[1] Water-melons were the most commonly sold fruit and hence the fruit-market of the town was simply known as the "melon-house."[2] The water-melons of North Persia were most famous. They were brought to Mesopotamia from Merv, cut into pieces, a thing not done with melons of other places.[3] Marco Polo confirms that the melons from Shubarqan (between Merv and Balkh) were cut spirally into thin slices, as we do with pumpkin. And when they dried in the sun, they were sent out in large quantities for sale to the neighbouring countries.[4] Others were brought to Baghdad in leaden ice-chest. On safe arrival they fetched 700 dirhams apiece.[5] The part which the American tomato plays in the kitchens of Southern Europe was played then by the pomegranate. Consignments of oil and wood, along with big quantities of this fruit, were imported into Baghdad in vessels which came from the Euphrates.

The Syrian apples were regarded as the best.[6] They were

---

(1) Ibn al-Sabi, *Yatimah*, II, 47.

(2) Tha'alibi, *Umad al-mansub*, Z.D.L.G. VIII; 524. The foul-mouthed Baghdadians named a poem of Ibn el-Rumi, where many names of places occur, "Water-melon House," Fakhri, ed, Ahlwardt, 299. And Ibn Lankak reviles one thus: He is the son of all the world; The names of his father is merely an abbreviation like "Water-melon House" where all sorts of fruits are stored, *Yatimah*, II, 122.

(3) Istakhri, 262.

(4) 1, 24

(5) Tha'alibi, *Lat el-Ma'arif*, 129. Merv, to-day, for the most part, is a desert; but the melons of Bukhara, similarly placed, are famous. They tell us that the Department of Agriculture in Washington has imported Bukharan species of melons to the United States and crossed them with happiest results. They are the best melons in the Union, Busse, *Bewasserungs wirthschaft in Turan*, 241.

(6) Mas'udi, VII, 270.

imported into Egypt—the yearly supply, which was sent in skins, to the Caliph's Court being 30,000.[1] In the East they failed "since they could not stand the hot, dry desert wind."[2]

The date trade involved immense transport. Mesopotamia, Kirman, North Africa were the chief date-producing centres.[3] Finest was the Mesopotamia date; the lists mentions several varieties. In the date-producing districts of North Africa one could buy, in good years, a camel-load for 2 dirhams.[4] In Kirman the price of 100 mann (a measure) of dates sometimes fell to one dirham. It provided the whole of Persia with dates. Year by year some 100,000 camels, in huge caravans, marched south-ward to fetch the favourite fruit. The camel-drivers were wild fellows. "Fornication was freely indulged in these caravans" and all this was so unpleasant to the Kirmanians that they gave one dinar to every one of these Khorasanian drivers on condition of his departing.[5] Likewise the caravans which proceeded through the Sahara to the country of the negroes mainly carried dates. In return they brought slaves and gold. The chief centre of this date trade was Sijilmasah in Southern Morocco.[6]

The oilve tree is a Mediterranean plant, Syria and Mesopotamia provided the whole empire with olive oil. The best came from Syria;[7] Nablus[8] especially possessed many

(1) Suyuti *Husn ul-Muh*, II, 229.

(2) Busse, *Bewasserungs wirthschaft in Turan*, 316.

(3) While Anah on the Euphrates and Tekrit on the Tigris mark to-day the border of date-growing regions—Sinjar, then, was centre of date-palms. Ibn Hauqal, 149; Muq, 142.

(4) Muq, 228 "In the Wadi Dra'a dates are so cheap that in good years they get a camel-load for half a dinar," Rohalfs, *Mein erster Aufenthalt in marrokka*, 442.

(5) Muq, 469.

(6) Idrisi, 4, 6, 21.

(7) Zamakhshari, *Kashshaf*, Comm, to Sura 24, 35.

(8) Muq, 174.

olive trees. It was kept in Aleppo in huge cisterns. At the capture of this town in the year 351/962 the Greeks poured water into these cisterns causing the oil to over flow.[1] Already Tunis had provided Rome with olive oil. At Sfaz so much olive oil was to be had in the 4th/10th century that one could get 90 and 70 Qafiz for a dinar.[2] Even to-day the olive tree is more carefully looked after there than anywhere else in the Mediterranean region.[3] People of other provinces imported radish and rape-seed oil from Egypt;[4] sesame oil from Mesopotamia and Afghanistan.[5] In Fars olive trees were planted anew. By reason of the high price sugar fetched, sugar cane was cultivated at every conceivable place—even in Galilee and Tyre.[6] Although its cultivation in Egypt is attested by papyri for the 2nd century, no geographer of the 4th-10th century speaks of it at all. In the 5th-11th the sugar industry seems, however, to have assumed some importance there. This, probably, was due to the political separation of Egypt from the East. Nasir Khusru, in 400/1048, tells us that "Egypt produces plenty of honey and sugar" (p. 51). The chief centre of the sugar industry was Khuzistan—in the district of Jundaishapur grew the best sugar-cane (Muq, 408). In Mesopotamia the neighbourhood of Basra was the most famous centre of the sugar industry. Even in Spain the faithful had made sugar a household

(1) Misk, V. 255.

(2) Ibn Hauqal, 47.

(3) Fischer *Mittelmeerbilder*, 1, 432.

(4) Nasir Khusru, 153. At Alexandria, in the Mediterranean region, olive oil was prepared (Muq, 197). According to Qalqashandi (Wustenfeld, 34) the few olives of Egypt were eaten specially with salt.

(5) Krausz, *Tal Arch.* II, 226; Marco Polo 1, 27. According to the Talmud "Mesopotamia also showed some olive-trees." Krausz, 215.

(6) Muq, 162, 180. At the time of the Crusades the Venetians possessed a cane-sugar plantation at Tyre, Tafel and Thomas. *Urkun den zur alteren Handels und Staatsgeschichteder Republik Venedig*, Wien. 1856, II, 368.

commodity.[1] The Yamanite table-sugar was packed in a special way. It was dried in the sun, stuffed in osier-rods and was kept a few days in cold storage until it hardened. The openings of the rods were sealed with gypsum. On arrival at the destination the rods were broken and the sugar was cut with a knife on a dish or on a loaf of bread. This sugar was exported to Mesopotamia and Mekka.[2]

Sturgeon took the place of our dried cod. They were caught in Lake Van and were taken pickled to Aleppo, nay even the Afghanistan.[3] In the west the tunny (Arab tunn, Greek thynnos) took its place. It was caught near Spain and the opposite coast of Africa (particularly Ceuta). It was chased with harpoons[4]. The people believed that it travelled every year from Africa to the Mediterranean, making pilgrimage to a certain rock.[5] "Edible earth" was a favourite food. They took it as desert. The best variety was green like the rape but more shiny[6]—even the ordinary white sort was praised[7]. The green was chiefly found in Quhistan[8]. In Egypt and the Maghrib it sometimes cost one dinar a pound.[9] From Toledo "edible earth" was exported to Turkistan.[10] Its use, however, was forbidden by various savants (*Kunjel-ummal*, on the margin of Ibn Hanbal's *Musnad* VI 191 ; Qummi, *Kit. al-llal*, Berlin, fol. 207a).

(1) For the 4th/10th century *The Calender of Cordova*, ed. Dozy, 25, 41, 91 and the Cron. Moro Rasis in mem. Acad. Madrid, VIII, 37, 38, 56.

(2) Hamdani, ed. D.H. Muller, 198.

(3) Ibn Hauqal, 248 ; Yaqut, 11, 467; Abulfida, *Geography*, ed Reinaud, 54. Lake Van has salt water (Le Strange, Mustawfi, 51).

(4) Idrisi p. 168.

(5) Abulfida, II, 215.

(6) Ibn Hauqal, 213. Not "that tasted like beetroot" (Le Strange, *Lands of the Eastern Caliphate* 258....??

(7) *Yatimah* IV, 107, "like pieces of camphor"...

(8) Istakhri, 274.

(9) Tha'alibi, lat. el-Ma'arif, p. 214.

(10) Idris, 188.

"The people of Sijistan used *asafoetid* in all their food. It grows in the desert between Sijistan and Mekran[1]. Even today this offensive smelling spice is a chief article of export from the Punjab across Quette to Afghanistan[2] whence it was taken to China in the Middle Ages.[3] The Muslim sailors brought from Borneo and Sumatra camphor, one of the most costly and favourite spices, both to the west and to China.[4] On the other hand, incense, the chief export of Yaman in earlier times went out of fashion in the Islamic world. It is still mentioned[5] but its place is taken up by ambergris—the best of which came from South Arabia.[6] The picturesque variety of oriental costume was due to the fact that every place adopted the colours most easily obtained locally. Thus the Beduin dress combined black goat's hair with the white sheep's wool. In the 4th/10th century the people of North African Barqah—where the entire ground is red[7]—were distinguished from the rest of the Westerners by their red dress.[8] But commerce exercised an equalizing effect. The two chief colouring materials, for fine blue and red—indigo and *Kermes* (whence our word crimson)—soon became popular throughout the Empire. Kabul, alone, annually imported two million dinars worth of Indian indigo.[9] By reason of its popularity this precious substance—like sugar—cultivated at every place at all favourable seasons.

It was cultivated in Upper Egypt. It constituted the main

(1) Istakhri, 244.
(2) *Revue du monde Musulman*, V, 5, p. 137.
(3) Chu Ju-Kua tr. by Hirth, 224.
(4) Reinaud, *Relations*, 36; Chau Ju-Kua, 193.
(5) Ishakhri, 25; Hamadani, 200.
(6) Ya'qubi, 366.
(7) Mutahhar, ed Huart, IV, 72; Bekri, ed Slane p. 5.
(8) Ibu Hauqal, 13.
(9) Ibn Hauqal, 328. Even in the sixth or quite late in the seventh century indigo was known to the Chinese as the product of the Persian province of "Tsan (Kabul), Hirth, Chau Yu Kau, 217.

industry of the oases.[1] It was cultivated at Zoa in Palestine, at Basanitis,[2] at Kirman, on the Dead Sea, where a lively trade in indigo supplanted the imported indigo from Kabul.[3] The Egyptian indigo could be cut every hundred days, but it had to be watered once in ten days the first year; thrice in ten days the second year and four times in ten days the third year.[4] Apparently its cultivation originated in the land of the decimal system. For *kermes* Armenia, notably the province of Airarat,[5] was the main source of supply. It was exported as far away as India.[6]

They used genuine saffron (za'fran), safflower ('usfur) and the Arabian saffron (wars) for yellow colouring. The Arabian saffron was a sesame-like plant which grew only in Yaman.[7] Yamanite camels, "marked completely yellow" by their valuable load, carried it to the north. Alongside of the other two—*wars* (the Arabian saffron) was scarcely of any account, still the Italians designated the Brazil wood after it as verzino. Saffron was so highly prized that in 246/860 the Caliph's ambassador to the Byzantine Court took it with him as a present for the Emperor.[8] By reason of its dearness it was cultivated at numerous places: in Syria, in South Arabia: but the ancient Media was its chief centre.[9] From Toledo it was exported to the west in large quantities.[10] Of inorganic stuff—Borax was found only in Lake Van in

(1) Idrisi, 14. Still the Egyptian indigo considered inferior to the Indian, Abdul Latif, 36.

(2) Muq, 185.

(3) Ibn Hauqal, 124; Muq, 174: Idrisi, 5.

(4) Maqrizi, *Khitat*, I, 272. On further preparation of indigo in Indian Marco Polo reports, III, 25.

(5) Istakhri, 188.

(6) Istakhri, 190.

(7) Jauhari, under *Wars* : Tha'alibi, *Fiqh el-lughah*, Cairo, 113 Hamdani, p.100 ; Qazwini, *Aja'ib*, II, 76.

(8) Tabari, III, 1449.

(9) Karabacek, *Die Persische Nadelmalerei*, 52 ff.

(10) Moro Rasis. 50; Maqqari I, 48.

North Persia and was exported for the use of bakers in Mesopotamia. It was called Bread Borax (Boraq el-Khubz) and was used for glazing pastry.[1] White jeweller's Borax was obtained from the Lake of Armia and was imported as far as Egypt with great profit.[2] Alum was the chief product of the country round Lake Chad. It was exported to Morroco and Egypt.[3] The salt of the Sahara-mines set thousands of camels and carriers in motion and the sea-salt of the Atlantic made its way deep into the interior of the Sudan. The only important places where sal-ammoniac (naushadir), a substance much used in contemporary chemistry, could be found were in the opposite ends of the Muslim Empire in Transoxina and Sicily.[4] But Transoxiana was by far the more important of the two, and after it, since the earliest times, the drug has been named in Europe "tartar salt." In the Buttam mountain there is a cave over which a house with closed doors and windows has been built. Out of this cave rises a vapour lik : smoke at day and like fire at night: when the vapour is precipitated, sal-ammoniac is got out of it. The people, entering the house, must cover themselves in wet felt or without it they may be hurt.[5] This vapour shifts from place to place. In the open it evaporates and is harmless but when it is encompassed whithin walls its heat burns.[6] Masudi in the year 322/944 gives us a remarkable account of the sal-ammoniac valley. In China, at the source of the great rivers, is the mountain which yields sal-ammoniac. Here in summer fires can be seen at night from a distance of 100 parasangs; at day-time owing to the greater power

(1) *Traite d'alchimie arabe* in Berthelot, *La chimie au moyen age*, II, 63, 145 note 4.
(2) Ibn Hauqal, 248.
(3) Idrisi, 39.
(4) Even on the summit of Demawend, northern Tehran, sal-ammoniac was found. They filled it in ox-hide and rolled it down. Nasir Khusru, Tr. p. 10: Richthofen, *China*, 1, 560.
(5) Istakhri, 327; Ibn Hauqal 38 d.
(6) Ibn Hauqal, 363.

of the sunlight they appear as vapour. The sal-ammoniac is obtained thence. Travellers in summer take their road from Khorasan to China by this mountain ; for there is a valley through it, which is forty or fifty miles long. At the entrance of the valley wait some men who offer themselves to carry the baggage, if they are well paid. They use sticks to drive the passengers on their journey; for any stoppage or rest would be fatal to the traveller, in consequence of the irritation which ammoniacal vapours of this valley produce on the brain, and on account of the heat. At the end of the valley are marshes and water, into which they throw themselves, to obtain relief from the depressing influence of the vapours of sal-ammoniac, and of the heat of the air. No animal can pass through the valley. In summer the sal-ammoniac throws out flames, and in that season no one can venture into this valley. In winter much snow and rain fall, which extinguish the heat and flames: at that time men can enter it, but not animals on account of the heat. Those who are coming from China are as hard hit as those who are making their way thither."[1]

In the year, 982 the Chinese traveller Wang-jen-ti visited the ammonia mine and reports as follows:

[Here ends my brother's translation. What follows is the work of Professor D.S. Margoliouth].

"Ammonia is obtained from a mountain north of the Pe-thing, whence columns of fire constantly ascend. At night flames are seen such as proceed from torches; one can see birds and field-mice coloured red all over. Those who collect the substance have to wear shoes with wooden soles, since soles of leather would be burned. According to Chinese authorities the place where ammonia is obtained lies in eastern Thenschan, 200 Li north of Kucha." In a Chinese

(1) Mas'udi, 1347 (Eng. tr. pp. 359-60 Tr.)

work of the year 1772 the following statement occurs: "The sal-ammoniac comes from a mountain called after it to the north of the town Kucha, which is full of caves and crevices. In spring, summer, and autumn these cavities are filled with fire so that at night the mountain looks as if it were illuminated with thousands of lamps. No one can then approach it. Only in winter when great masses of snow have subdued the fire, can the natives occupy themselves with collecting the sal-ammoniac."[1] The Afghan Hujwiri who wrote in the 11th century narrates in a mystical work that on the frontier of Islam in a Turkish town he had seen a burning mountain out of which vapours of sal-ammoniac issued, and that in the midst of the fire was a mouse which died if it got away from the glowing heat.[2] This sal-ammoniac was so highly prized in China that the natives paid their tribute to the emperor with it.[3] Thirty years ago this sal-ammoniac mountain was explored. The official Turkestan Gazette reports about it as follows: "The mount Peishan or Paishan is not a volcano, as was ascertained by a Russian expedition despatched for this purpose. The smoke comes from layers of burning coal. The slopes of Paishan are covered with crevices out of which smoke and sulphuric gas escape with terrible noise." I find this in the essay of Friedrichsen just cited; he adds: with this there agrees the information given by Regal[4] on the authority of a gardener named Fetiow who had been sent to make botanical investigations: Paishan, he says, is a conical mountain, with no crater at the top, but only lateral aperturies. Hence Friedrichsen would regard the mountains as a seam of burning coal.[5]

(1) V. Richthofen, China I, 560.
(2) *Kashf al-Mahjub*, tr. Nicholson, p. 407.
(3) Friedrichsen, Zeitsch. Gesell Erdkunde, Berlin, 1899. p. 246. From Kalproth, *Tableaux histor.* p. 110.
(4) *Gartenflora*, 28th year, 1879, p. 40.
(5) L. c.p. 247.

In the two precious metals the different parts of the empire supplemented each other admirably. The east provided silver, the western half gold. The Klondyke of the time was the arid desert east of the Upper Nile, between Assouan and Aidab. The metropolis of the gold-miners was al-Ullaqi, fifteen days' journey from Assouan.[1] They would start out on nights when there was little moonlight, and mark the places where they saw anything glitter.[2] The next day they would wash these portions of sand, mix the gold with quicksilver, and melt it down.[3] Adventurers crowded thither after the middle of the 3rd/9th century, after the rebellious Bujjah had been brought to reason in the year 241/855 by an energetic expedition consisting in a small but picked force of imperial troops. From that time dates the absorption of this indigenous population by Arab tribes.[4] In the year 332/944 the chieftain of the Arab tribe Rabi'ah is ruler of the gold country.[5] Abu'l-Ala el-Ma'arri (ob. 449/1057) says to the Egyptian Caliph who offered him money; I am as wealthy as a man can be, the mine of Assouan is nothing to me.[6] The second great source of gold was the Sudan: "Gold is the chief product of the blacks, rich and poor live on it.[7] All the caravans which marched from the south through the Sahara carried gold and slaves; the bearers brought salt and took back gold, all on their heads, so that

---

(1) Fullest account in Ya'qubi, *Bibi Geogr*, VII, 334. seq.

(2) With ashes or chalk. Petakhya J.A. VIII. p. 384. This method of getting at the gold sand seems to have been practised over the whole of the near East Chang-af, who travelled to the west in the year 1259 A.D. reports: In Egypt (Mi-sirh) there is gold in the ground. At night sparkling is observed in certain places. The people mark these with a feather and coal. If they dig in these places in the daytime, they find large nuggets. (Bretschneider, *Mediaeval researches* I. p. 142.)

(3) Edrisi, ed. Dozy, p. 26.

(4) Istakhri p. 288.

(5) Maqrizi, *Khitat*, I, 196/7.

(6) Yaqut, *Irshad* I, p. 178.

(7) Edrisi, ed. Dozy.p. 8.

they got quite bald."[1] In the year 390/1000 a gold mine was discovered in the east, in Afghanistan,[2] but nothing more is heard of it. The richest silver mine of Islam lay in the eastern extremity of the empire, in the Hindu-Kush, the "five hills" of Benjehir. It counted at the time 10,000 miners, "all of them scoundrels."[3] "Silver coins are there so plentiful that anything almost costs a whole silver dirham, even a bit of vegetable. The silver is to be found at the peak of a mountain which towers over the city and looks like a sieve owing to the number of shafts. The miners follow only those veins which show signs of leading to ore. When they find a vein of this sort they continue to dig till they come upon the silver. A miner can make as much as 300,000 dirhams; many a man finds enough to enrich himself and his posterity, many another obtains enough to pay his expenses, but many too are impoverished and even reduced to beggary, if water and other obstacles get the upper hand. At times it happens that one miner follows a vein and another the same vein in a different fissure, both commencing to dig at the same time; it is the rule that whichever of the two first reaches the ore has a right to the mine and its output. The rival miners in such cases work harder than any demon, for if one of the two arrives first, the other loses all that he has expended. If they arrive simultaneously, they go shares equally. They mine only as long as their lamps or lanterns keep burning ; if they go so far that these are extinguished they proceed no further. Any one who ventures to do so dies in a very short time. A man may be poor in the morning, and rich in the evening, or rich in the morning and poor by evening."[4]

---

(1) J. Marquardt, *Die Beninsammlung*, p. CII from a Protuguese report. In Marquardt's Index of Contents everything is to be found that is worth knowing about the production of and the trade in gold in the south.

(2) Mutahhar, ed. Huart IV. p. 73; Ibn al-Jauzi, Berlin, fol. 144 a; Ibn al-Athir IX, p. 116.

(3) Ibn Hauqal p. 327.

(4) Yaqut *Geogr*, I. p. 773 foll.

The silver mines near Isfahan had been long abandoned in the 3rd/9th century,[1] and the yet more distant silver mine in Baghagis (Afghanistan) had to be given up, because fuel failed.[2] On the other hand, the copper mines near Isfahan paid in the 3/9 century a tax of 10,000 dirhams.[3] The copper used for the bright caps of the minarets came from Bokhara.[4] The country where most iron was produced and wrought was Persia,[5] but Beirut,[6] Kerman[7] and Kabul[8] also had iron mines. The iron tools of Ferganah had so high a reputation that they were exported as far as Babylonia ; "the iron of Ferganah is easily worked".[9] In the west there was a great iron mine in Sicily"[10] and iron continued to come from Africa, the original home of the iron industry, out of which the most costly articles were wrought in India.[11] In Western Asia iron was always a rarity. In the year 355/964 the Qarmatians of the Arabian desert sent an expedition to Saifeddaulah at Tiberias asking him for iron. This prince ordered the iron gates of Raqqah to be unhinged, took all the iron that he could find, even the weights of the shopkeepers and gave it all to them. They conveyed it down the Euphrates as far as Hit whence they carried it through the desert.[12] By far the most important quicksilver mines of the Muhammedan

---

(1) Ibn Rusteh, p. 156.
(2) Ist, p. 268.
(3) Ibn Rusteh, p. 156.
(4) Muq. p. 324.
(5) Ibn Hauqal, p. 214: Ibn al-Faqih, p. 254.
(6) Muq. p. 184; Edrisi ed. Brandel, p. 22. Seetzen furnishes some details for the year 1805 about the production of iron in the Lebanon. (U.J. Seetzens *Reisen*, I, 189).
(7) Muq. p. 470.
(8) Ibn Hauqal, p. 328.
(9) *Gartenflora* 28th year 1879 p. 40.
(10) L. c. p. 247.
(11) Ya'qubi, *Bibl, Geog.* VII. 334 foll. gives the fullest account.
(12) With ashes or chalk, Petachya J.A. VIII. p. 384. This method of obtaining gold-dust seems to have been practised all through the nearer East. Chang-te, who travelled to the West 1259 A.D. reports

territory lay in Spain, near Toledo. "More than a thousand men work in the mine. Some go inside and hew the rock, others fetch wood in order to burn the mineral, others construct vessels for melting and distilling, while yet others attend to the ovens. I have myself seen this mine, and ascertained that the floor is at a depth equal to the stature of 250 men."[1] Coals, "black stones which burn like charcoal" were found in Bokhara and Ferganah,[2] but treated mainly as natural curiosities. Asbestos, which was found near Farwan in Khorasan, was called "wick-stone," because it was chiefly employed (as at present) for the wicks of lamps. Besides this, table-cloths were woven of it which had merely to be put in the oven to be cleaned. The values attached to precious stones were different in those days from now. A writer of 4th/10th century places the most precious in the following order: turquoise from Nisabur, *yaqut* from Ceylon, pearls from Oman, emerald from Egypt, ruby from Yemen, and *bizadi* from Balkh. Biruni about 400/1009 groups them similarly : *yaqut*, emerald, pearls. The diamond had not the surpassing value which it has in our time the coloured gems which gently glow were esteemed more highly. In Khorasan and Babylonia the diamond was only used for cutting and poisoning.[3] The higher classes employed the diamond in

---

as follows ; In Egypt (Mi-si-rh) there is gold in the soil...In the night sparkling is seen in certain places. The people mark such places with a feather and coal. The following day when they dig there, they find large nuggets. (Brestchneidor, *Mediaeval Researches*, I. p. 142.)

(1) Edrisi, ed. Dozy, p. 26.

(2) J. Marquardt, *Die Beninsammlung* after a Portuguese report. Under "gold" in his Index of contents everything worth knowing about the gold industry and trade in the South is to be found.

(3) Al-Dimashqi, *Mahasin et-tijarah*, Cairo, 1318. p. 16. Benvenuto Cellini II. 13 : They bethought themselves of mixing pulverized diamonds with the food. This is not in itself poisonous but owing to its incalculable hardness retains very sharp edges, and is unlike other stones which when broke up are to a certain extent rounded. If it enters the body with other food, owing to its sharp points it

suicide ; if they fell into the hands of enemies and might expect torture and abuse, they swallowed the gem and died therefrom. The blue turquoise (Firuzaj) was found only in the neighbourhood of Nisabur;[1] in 1821 Fraser visited the hill which lies about 60 kilometres NW of the city. The gem was extracted in the most primitive fashion with hammers and in small trenches. Yet it is clear that at an earlier period work was carried on there on a larger scale.[2] 200 years later taste changed, and the gem was so much in use for signet rings that the higher classes no longer employed it.[3] Much the same was the case with the ruby which was so highly prized in the 4th/10th century. In the 6th/12th century it was so commonly worn that the higher classes use only large pieces and these for perfume-pots, goblets, etc.[4] The finest sort was mined in South Arabia near San'a, where "at times they get a piece as big as a rock, at times nothing at all."[5] The Alps of Afghanistan furnished valuable rubies,[6] which were mined for like gold and silver.[7] The only emerald mine in the empire was in the desert of E. Egypt, seven days' journey from the Nile, where the stone was broken by excavating deep into the mountain[8],[9]. Starbo already

---

adheres during the process of digestion to the skin of the stomach and the entrails, and gradually, as other food presses on it, perforates these parts, in time causing death. No other stone, nor even glass, can thus adhere, but passes out with the food.

(1) Tha'alibi, *Lat. 'el-ma'arif* p. 15. Marco Polo, Lemke, p. 93 also mentions turquoises of Kirman.

(2) Fraser, *Journey into Khorasan*, London 1825, p. 407 foll. Grothe, Persian , p. 19, states that Bricteux, *Au pays du lion et du Soleil*, pp 251-255 gives a description of the present mining operations for turquoises near Nisabur.

(3) *Mahasin et-tijarah*, p. 16, probably from the 6th/12th century.

(4) *Mahasin et-tijarah*, p. 17.

(5) Muq., p. 101.

(6) Ibn Hauqal (near Badhakhshan).

(7) Marco Polo I., cp. 27.

(8) Maqrizi *Khitat* I, 196 after Jahiz.

(9) Mas. iii 43 foll. India produced smaller emeralds. *ibid.* p. 47.

mentions it ; in the year 332/943 it belonged to the chieftain of Rabi'ah, Ishaq, who also was in possession of the gold-bearing lands.[1]

In manufacture the many coloured lined onyx exported from Yaman was favoured. It was made into plates,[2] pommels, knife-handles, and saucers and with its sheen of many colours adorned almost all the tables of the upper class.

Precious coral was fished for in N.W. Africa (Marsa el-kharaz) as it is still (Ceuta, etc.)[3]. From 20 to 50 men were ordinarily employed with the yield.[4] They threw out wooden harpoons wound round with loose flaxen threads and in the form of corsses. These would stick in the coral reefs, and when the ship moved backwards would tear out great masses, worth from 10 to 1,000 dirhams.[5] Coral formed the chief article of commerce in the Sudan[6] and was in particular favour with Indian women :[7] in Marco Polo's time it was exported to Europe from Kashmir[8], and in our time the Italian coral which is intended for Russia, in order to avoid the duty levied at the western frontier, has to make the vast circuit over India and Turkestan.[9]

The pearls of the Arabian (? Persian) Gulf counted in China too as the best.[10] Fishermen worked, as they do still,

---

(1) Mas. iii 33.
(2) Hammadani. p. 203.
(3) Mas. iv. 97 ; Muq., p. 228; Biruni, *Kit. al Jawahir* in "Islam" ii. p. 317. The Chinese author Chau-Ju-Kua (about 1300 A.D.) also states that the coral industry is to be found in the western Mediterranean (Transl. Hirth, pp. 154, 226).
(4) Ibn Hauqal, p. 51.
(5) Muq., b. 236; Edrisi, ed. Dozy, p. 116.
(6) Edrisi ed. Dozy, p. 168.
(7) Biruni, l.c.
(8) Bk. I, cap. 29.
(9) M. Hartman, *Chinesisch Turkestan*, p. 63.
(10) Chau-ju-jua p. 229.

from April to October, and especially in August and September.[1] The fisher was worked on the capitalistic system, a contractor hired divers for two months of 30 days, and paid them regularly. The profit, which at times was enormous, remained with him undiminished.[2] At the time of Benjamin of Tudela (about 1170 A.D.) the industry was in the hands of a Jew ;[3] in our time the produce belongs to the boats of a tribe or group of tribes, and is shared by them in common. The profit goes to the Indian dealers, who purchase the shells at extremely low prices.[4] The labour was exceedingly severe. The pre-Islamic poet el-A'sha portrays the pearl-diver as "leader of four differing in colour and physique embarking in a flimsy boat, then closing his teeth and discharging oil from his lips, and so letting himself down into the sea, which had slain his father. Men crowd round him, urging him to sell ; but he clasps the precious treasure to his neck with both hands."[5]

Mas'udi reports as follows at the beginning of the 4th/10th century : The fishermen maintain themselves with fish, dates, and the like ; nothing else. The inside of their ears is bored in order that the breath may issue thence instead of through the nostrils. Over these latter something like a broad arrow-head made of tortoise-shell of horn, not wood, is placed, to press them together. Their ears are plugged with cotton wool, steeped in a certain oil. A little of this is squeezed out in the water, and serves to give them light. They paint their feet and legs black, in order not to be bitten

---

(1) Mas. I. 328 ; Edrisi-Jaubert I. 373 foll; Palgrave in Zehme, *Arabien*, p. 208. Benjamin of Tudela is mistaken in asserting that fishing begins in October.

(2) *Merv. de l' Inde*, p. 135 Edrisi I. 373.

(3) ed. Asher, p. 90.

(4) Zehme, *Arabien*, p. 208 ; Grothe, Persian, p. 19, mentions a small monograph of Perez ("Six semaines de dragages sur les bancs perliers du golfe Persique." (Orleans, 1908).

(5) *Khizanat al-adab* I. 544 ; transl. Lyall, J.R.A.S. 1902. p. 461.

by the sea monsters, which flee away from that colour. Down in the sea the divers yell like dogs so as to be heard by each other.[1] In the 4th/10th century the pearl-fishery of Ceylon had lost its importance; few shells were found there, so that it was supposed the oysters had migrated from Ceylon to Africa.[2] This is the reason why the geographers and travellers of this time say nothing about pearl-fishing. At a later period the oysters came back, whence we have exhaustive reports from the 6th/12th century. More than 200 ships leave the town together, each ship housing 5 to 6 traders in separate cabins, each of whom had his diver and assistants with him. A leader sails in front of the fleet, stops somewhere and dives; if the result seems satisfactory, he drops anchor. The others do the like all round; the divers proceed to plug their nostrils with wax melted in oil of sesame, take with them a knife and small bag, and then mount on a stone which an assistant holds by a rope, and on which they descend into the deep. Working time is two hours in the day. On a special market day the pearls are measured under government supervision and then sold. Measurement is done with three sieves of different mesh, one above the other[3]. Benjamin of Tudela (p. 89) adds the details that the divers can hold out in the water from one to one and a half minutes.

There is a Chinese report from the same period. "Thirty or forty boats are employed, each with a crew of a dozen or so. Pearl-divers, with ropes would round their bodies, and with ears and noses plugged with yellow wax, are let down into the water 200 or 300 feet or even deeper. The ropes are fastened to the vessel. When a diver signals by shaking the rope, he is drawn up. A soft blanket is previously heated as much as possible in boiling water, to be thrown over the

(1) Mas. I, 329 foll.

(2) Biruni *India*, transl. Sachau I. 211.

(3) Edrisi, Jaubert I, 373 foll.

diver the moment he comes up, lest he should die of a paroxysm. They are apt to be attacked by huge fishes, dragons, and other sea monsters, which rip open their bodies or break limbs."— "It often happens that the diver gives a signal with the rope but the man on board who is holding it cannot draw him up. The whole crew then pull with all their might, and find when they have brought him up that his feet have been bitten off by a monster."— "In general a pearl is regarded as of value when it is perfectly spherical. This is proved by its rolling about a plate continuously for a whole day. Foreign dealers who come to China usually conceal pearls in the lining of their clothes or the handles of their umbrellas in order to escape the duty."[1] The Chinese author Chang-te, who is on the whole well informed and who visited the West in the year 1259 A.D., obtained the following account. "The divers get inside a leathern bag, so that only their hands are free. A rope is wound round their loins, and thus equipped they descent to the bottom of the sea. They take up the oysters together with sand and mould, and put them into the bag. They are often attacked by sea monsters in the deep, but frighten them off by discharging vinegar upon them. When the bag is full of oysters, they signal to the people above by the pulling the rope, and are then drawn up. It often happens that they perish in the sea."[2] Ivory was purchased by the Arabian traders in East Africa and taken by them as far as China;[3] it fetched higher prices than the ivory of Annam and Tongking, which was of smaller and reddish tusks.[4] Mas'udi asserts that the supply from Islamic countries would be ample, if the Eastern demand were not so excessive.[5]

---

(1) Chau-Ju-Kua, transl. Hirth, p. 229 foll. after the Ling-waiteira (written 1174 A.D.).

(2) Brestchneider, *Mediaeval researches*, I, 145.

(3) Mas. III' 8.

(4) Chau-Ju-Kua, p. 232.

(5) III. 8.

Tortoise-shell came from East Africa, and of this the better sort of combs was manufactured, whereas common combs were made of horn; the same country furnished great panther skins for saddle coverings.[1] Indeed the negroes provided leather for all the Near East. Probably Egypt and Syria learned from them the skilful treatment of leather in which they distinguished themselves.[2] Muqaddasi, who understood how to bind books in the Syrian style, boasts that he had often got two dinars for a volume in South Arabia;[3] the taste for this sort of work was so highly developed there. It would be interesting to think that the present form of the book, which has superseded the ancient roll, had originated in the black continent. In the 3rd/9th century Islam retained traditions of the kind : "To the negroes three things are to be ascribed ; the daintiest perfume, known as *ghalliyah*; the form of bier called *na'sh*, which conceals females most completely, and the form of book called *mushaf*, which preserves its contents most faithfully.[4]

Even in antiquity the Western portion of the empire had been denuded of wood ; in the East however the less accessible parts still had forests. The crippling of the mining industry in the East through lack of wood was mentioned above. "The country of Bukhara was so copiously irrigated that no tall trees were to be found there."[5] "On the other hand the grass there grew so high that a horse would disappear in it entirely."[6] Compensation was found in a vast trade in timber. Afghan wood, in particular cypress, was

---

(1) Mrs. III. 2.
(2) Muq., pp. 180, 203 ; Benjamin of Tudela, ed. Asher, p. 30; Istakhri, pp. 24, 35.
(3) Muq.,p. 100.
(4) Jahiz, *Opusc.*, p. 71.
(5) Istakhri, p. 312.
(6) Muq., p. 283.

sold throughout Khorasan.[1] Timber for ship-building came from Venice and Upper Egypt.[2] For house-building in Baghdad and the whole of the East the timber made from the Indian teak tree (saj) counted as the most valuable, and of this the ornamental wood-work of all the best houses was made. In the Mediterranean regions the same part was assigned to pine wood (sanaubar) ; Fort el-Tinat near Alexandretta was the centre for the trade in Syrian pine wood, whence it was exported to the other ports of Syria, to Egypt and to Cilicia.[3] In Spain the pine Forest of Tortosa was the most celebrated. Its timber "is red with bright bark, solid, does not easily rot, and does not house beetles like other wood. The ceiling of the Mosque at Cordova was made of this timber."[4] The forests of Mazanderan, some of which still exist, furnished the pinkish wood of the chalang tree, favoured for furniture by the fashion of the 4th/10th century.[5] The mountaineers of Tabaristan carved vessels and plates out of this hard wood[6]; from Qumm came the famous chairs which were imitated in the metropolis of Kirman to the South[7], and from Rai came painted salvers.[8]

The parts of the empire in which irrigation offered grave problems for solution where Egypt, South Arabia, Babylonia, North-east Persia, Transoxiana, and Afghanistan. The legislation on this subject often formed a complicated mass of the most subtle regulations; all however had in common the principle of the canon law, that water might neither be bought nor sold. Hence neither the individual nor the State

---

(1) Istakhri, p. 268.
(2) See the chapter on Navigation.
(3) Istakhri, p. 63.
(4) Edrisi ed Dozy, pp. 190, 280.
(5) Ibn Hauqal, p. 272.
(6) Istakhri, p. 212.
(7) Muq., p. 470.
(8) Ibn al-Fakih, p. 254.

might make a profit by irrigating only[1]. The largest part of European regulations concerning water is traceable to the East. In different places they have developed different technique. Unfortunately we have little exact knowledge, and so are unable to answer the questions how they are connected and whether they radiated from a single point. In Babylonia the government had to see to the maintenance of weirs, dams, and sluices,[2] and for this there was a whole class of official engineers (muhendis). It was a troublesome business, as the dams were made of reeds and mould, so that "the hole of a mouse was often the cause of a breach, since the water inundated; and an hour could destroy the work of a year."[3] The able ruler Mu'izz-ed-daulah took this matter so seriously that once when a dam had been breached he carried earth with his own hand in the lappet of his cloak, to set an example to his troops.[4] The regulations concerning water in East Persia were very elaborate. In Merv there was a Water-bureau (diwan el-ma)[5]; the head of this bureau had a staff of 10,000 men under him, and was a higher official than the chief of police in the region.[6] The unit of measurement was the quantity which issued from an aperture one *sha'irah* square.[7] Further the amount to be distributed in a day was divided into 60 parts. The water-meter was placed at a distance of one parasang from Merv; this was a board with a longitudinal slit, in which a barley-corn moved up and down. If the gauge stood at 60 barley-corns, there would be a fruitful year; there was general rejoicing, and the rations of water were increased. If it stood

---

(1) For Turkestan Basse p. 55.
(2) *Kit. al-Kharaj* p. 63.
(3) Misk. VI, 376.
(4) Misk. VI, 219.
(5) *Mafatih ul-ulum* ed van Vloten, p. 68.
(6) Istakhri p. 261 foll Muq., p. 330.
(7) *Mafatih ul-ulum* p. 68 (The author substituted *yards* for the original, which is here restored Sha'irah (barley-corn) was a measure, very much smaller than a yard).

no higher than two barley-corns, there would be a famine. The state of the gauge was at each time reported to the water-bureau, which then fixed the ration, and sent it to all the sluice-keepers. "At the weir below the city 400 keepers were employed, who watched it day and night. They had often to plunge into the water when it was bitter cold, and then they would smear themselves with wax. Each of them had to hew a definite amount of wood per day, and to gather brushwood for the time when it might be required."[1] The regions of East Persia which lay at a distance from the main rivers were cared for by ingenious systems of irrigation. Here, where there were only insignificant rivers or brooks, it was necessary to collect such water as trickled down the precipices as the result of rains, as well as the groundwater, to the last drop. Here what is now called the Karis system was employed. Long tunnels with easy gradients which even now reach as far as 50 kilometers were driven through the ground; at definite intervals airshafts lead to the surface. There were famous works of this sort at Qumm, and especially at the East Persian metropolis Nisabur, where people had to descend flights of as many as 70 steps to reach the tunnel which thus furnished the city also with pure water for drinking which was always cool.[2] The execution of such works requires great skill; "the water-bearing strata must be tapped by the management at a point where they strike an underlying impervious stratum, and this latter must have a sufficient fall to admit of a rapid flow."[3] Irrigating machines that were in use were the Dulab, the Daliyah, the Sarrafah, the Zurnuq, the Na'urah and the Manjanun[4]. Of these the Zurnuq (German *Star*) was a draw-

---

(1) Muq., p. 231.

(2) Ya'qubi, *Geogr.* 274; Muq., 329 ; Schefer in Nasir Khosrau; p. 278; see also above. 22.

(3) For the Karis of the present time see W. Busse, *Bewasserung in Turan*, p. 321 foll : Sven Hedin, *Zu Land nach Indien* I. 184 Grothe, *Wanderungen in Persien*, 1010. p. 105.

(4) *Mafatih al-ulum*, p. 71.

well of the simplest sort, worked, *e.g.* in Medinah, by camels;[1] the Daliyah was a drawing machine moved by beasts, the Na'urah a water-wheel driven by a river,[2] and Dulab was the Persian name for the Greek *manganon*. The Na'urah appears not to have been in use west of Babylonia.[3]

The weirs were all wanting in solidity, being made of wood, even the famous weirs of Bukhara; on the other hand the civilized area of South Persia, Khuzistan, and Fars had the advantage of stone water-works. Below Tustar there was the dam which according to the legend King Sapor I., had made the captive Roman Emperor Valerian execute,[4] according to the Arabs 1,000 yards long, according to Europeans 600 paces, which served to divert the Mashruqan Canal from the river Dujail. In the 4th/10th century one of the most famous irrigation works was that organised by Adad-ud-daulah on the river Kur in Fars. By a mighty dam, of which the foundations were filled up with lead, the water was raised into a lake. On both sides of the river he set up draw-wheels driven by the water; there were ten of these and under each was a mill. He thus irrigated 800 villages by the aid of pipes.[5] These weirs had sluices; "at high water the sluice-gates were opened, and the roar of the rushing water for a great part of the year prevented people from sleeping. High water was in winter time, because it came from rains, not from glaciers."[6] On the other hand in S. Arabia, where the object was to collect running water for use, they had pools (masani')[7] bordered with pebbles; but further up the mountains (as in San'a) they had dams (sadd), with openings below; the water was distributed by means

(1) Ya'qubi, Geogr. p. 313.
(2) Jauhari, s. V. *dlw*.
(3) Muq., pp 411, 444.
(4) Tabari, I, 827 ; Noldeke, Tabari, p. 33 Note 2.
(5) Muq., p. 444.
(6) Muq., p. 411: Abu Dulaf in Yaqut I, 411, 412.
(7) Hamdani, p. 138.

of canals. This method was such a speciality of S. Arabia that Ibn Rustah finds it necessary to explain the word.[1] In Transoxiana for the construction of canals they possessed the ideal material, loess, which when moistened is as plastic as clay, whereas when dried in the sun it becomes as hard as stone; it is the yellow earth of the skilful Chinese peasants. Nevertheless the reports express astonishment at the wonderful conduits which the peasant can fashion with his mattock (ketmen) and without the aid of any sort of level; "their specialists (ustad = master) have a wonderful knack of detecting the slightest differences in gradient, which would completely escape the ordinary spectator."[2] What is remarkable about these constructions is that they have not here to deal with a plain as in Egypt and Babylonia, but with a hilly country, where it is harder to conduct the water. The different canal systems often lie in several storeys one above the other, and frequently cross each other. In such cases the upper canal is conducted over the lower on a wooden platform in open wooden channels. Locks (?) are unknown. Here there prevailed water-rights dating from extreme antiquity, with which the Muslims did not interfere, and with which the Russians have only tampered to their cost. The classical point of this form of agriculture is the valley of Ferghanah, in the latitude of South Italy, but continental, and hence of almost tropical heat. The greatest breadth of the valley is scarcely 100 kilometers, between mountains which rise to a height of from 4,000 to 7,000 metres, whose glaciers with their streams do the irrigation in summer. The meadows there are manured, and fields watered, covered with mud, and at times even sprinkled with minerals. The water officials are elected by the peasants, and have a share in the harvest. The principle of irrigation is to divert the tributaries on both sides of the valley by dams, so that they do not reach the main river

(1) p. 112.

(2) W. Busse, *Bewasserungs wirtschaft in Turan*, p. 111.

which flows in the middle. Here too as in Afghanistan the dams are intentionally made unsubstantial so that high water at once carries them away, and so automatically prevents inundation. The small canals are all constructed with easy gradients, and only as they approach the level of the valley do they become rapid, so that the torrent can be used by mills.[1] In the 4th/10th century there were in Transoxiana vine-yards and ploughed lands which paid no land-tax, only the owners had to keep the weirs and the streams which flowed by their properties in order.[2]

The part of Afghanistan which is capable of cultivation coincides with the delta of the river Hilmand, which like the Jordan, and (with one exception) all the streams of Persia, has no outlet to the sea, but loses itself in vast marshes. Like other streams which meander in sands this river had often changed its bed, and in consequence confronted the irrigators with special problems. Major Sykes found it in the beginning of April as broad as the Thames in London.[3] A series of canals was diverted from the river, and at the end their was a weir to prevent the water flowing into the lake. When in consequence of a thaw high water came, the flood water tore into the weir, and passed through it, doing no other damage.[4] Hence it might not be solid, and was probably constructed like the chief existing dam, the Bend-i-Seistan ; some 1,000 workmen were employed, thin stakes of acacia were put close together, interwoven with brushwood, and covered over with rough fascines, while interstices were done over with clay.[5]

In the fourth century the Lower Nile had two dams, made of earth and reeds (Halfa) ; one near Heliopolis, the other,

(1) Von Schwarz, *Turkestan*, pp. 341 fol. : Busses, p. 32.
(2) Von Middendorf, *Mem. Acad. St. Petersburg*, VII. Vol. 29.
(3) *A travers la Perse orientale*, Hachette, 1907, p. 193.
(4) Istakhri, p. 244.
(5) Sykes, I c; Sven Hedin, *Zu Land nach Indien* II 331.

and the larger of the two, lower down near Sardos. The first was closed before the rising of the Nile, and turned the water on the fields. "At the Feast of the Cross, when the grapes had sweetened" the ruler of Egypt came out and ordered the weir to be dug through : the inhabitants closed up their ditches, so that the water should not flow back to their fields, and the whole bounty of the Nile was discharged northwards.[1] The hydrometers had from the earliest times been of the following construction ; the water was made to flow into a pond, and its elevation was read on a scale of yards and inches engraved on a stone. The most important was the hydrometer on the island Rodah near Cairo, where the officer in charge had to report daily to the government on the elevation of the water. If the water rose to 12 yards, a crier called out daily through the city: "God had caused the sacred Nile to rise to such and such a height ; last year the rise was so much ; God will complete it."[2] Since the restoration of 247/861 there was a grating on the building, and on this the black curtain of the Caliph was let down when the water reached 16 yards.[3] During the inundation Egypt was under water ; communication in the villages was by boat.[4] People laid in provisions for these four months as for a siege, even baking bread in advance drying it in the sun.[5]

Water-clocks, called in Persia *tarjeharah*, were everywhere in use ; there was a copper one in Biyar (in N. Iran) as in Arrajan (Persis),[6] others in N. Africa. In an oasis of the Sahara the three natural water-courses were first divided each into six brooks, and from these the separate irrigation canals branched off, all being of the same

(1) Muq., b 206.
(2) Muq., l c.
(3) Maqrizi, *Khitat*, II 185.
(4) Muq, I c.
(5) Nasiri Khosrau, Transl p. 118.
(6) Muq, p. 357 ; B G IV, p. 288.

dimensions, two spans broad and one inch deep, constructed of stone. "Each person whose turn comes to irrigate takes a vessel (*qadas,* Latin cadus, jug) at the bottom of which there is an opening no wider than the string of the bow used in carding flax ; the vessel is filled with water, and hung up, and the man irrigates until the water has all run out of the vessel. A whole day's irrigation was the equivalent of 192 jugs, so that 8 jugs went to the hour. Payment was made once a year at the rate of the *mithaqal* for 4 jugs.[1]

Only in Afghanistan had people to struggle with the shifts, and a special science arose to deal with them. The whole country there was sand, and the winds blew with tremendous force and persistence. Thus in the year 359/970 the chief mosque of the metropolis Zaranj was filled with sand, and the whole city was seriously endangered, till someone for a fee of 20,000 dirhams turned the wind in another direction. This was told to Ibn Hauqal by a traveller who came from the country. He added the following details: when the people there wish to drive the sand away without forcing it into the neighbouring estates, they build a wall of wood and twigs, high enough to outtop the sand; in the lower part of the wall they leave a door open. Through this the wind penetrates; and the sand flies high like the waves in a storm, and disappears beyond the range of vision to a place where it does them no harm.[2]

Agriculture, of which almost every village and valley had devised its special variety, was in the empire of the Caliphs of a very varied character at that time. In the district of Ardebil *e.g.*, (between Tabriz and the Caspian) eight oxen

(1) Bekri, ed. Slane, p. 48. At the present time in Sus the time during which each family may irrigate is measured by the time it takes a perforated platter to get to the bottom of a large vessel containing water (M. Zeys, Une Francaise au Marco, p. 78).

(2) Ibn Hauqal, p. 299.

were used in ploughing, and each pair had a driver, not because the ground was particularly hard, but because it was frozen.[1] "On the other hand in the Persian locality Aberquh no oxen were used for ploughing although they had great numbers in the region."[2] Manuring was everywhere carried out energetically, both with cow's and sheep's dung, but also with human excrement. The former was sold by the hamper in Babylonia[3] reference has been made above (§22) to the eagerness with which human manure was employed. In the neighbourhood of the Persian Siraf, in Kuran and Irahistan the palms had to be planted in so deep a hole that only the top projected above the ground. The water of the winter was retained in the depth and nourished the tree. Hence people used to ask the question: Where do palms grow in well? The answer was : In Irahistan.[4]

The scarecrow was never known anywhere in the whole Muhammadan world any more than it is now. In Babylonia the Qarmatian children handed over to the communistic society the pay which they received for scaring the birds from the fields.[5] In Turkestan at the present day "the natives try to protect their fields and gardens from birds by erecting in the middle of each field a pyramid of earth some two meters high, on which lads are posted, generally half naked or entirely so, whose duty it is to pass the whole day under the burning sun and scare the birds by shouting, beating tomtoms and old slavers, or throwing earthen balls. Since these living scarecrows in summer time are posted in every field and garden, often in pairs or trios, each lad trying to outdo the other, from morning to evening there is such an

---

(1) Yaqut, *Dict* I 86.
(2) Abdellatif *Relation* p. 3.
(3) Yaqut, *Irshad* V 303.
(4) Ibn al-Balkhi (about 5006/1107) : J R A S 1902, p. 329.
(5) De Geoje, *Mem. sur less Carmathes*, p. 29.

infernal din that it might drive one mad."[1] For Morocco see the description of the painter Franz Buchser in his *Marokkanische Bilder*[2].

In the 4th/10th century Babylonia was still a cattle-rearing country. The "Nabataeans" who lived there were ridiculed as "Cow-knights"; only with the increase of the marshes has the buffalo superseded the ox. This animal was brought by the Arabs from its Indian home; and under the Omayyads was made to migrate from Sind into the Babylonian marshes. The government went to the length of establishing 4,000 buffaloes at the North Syrian frontier, because the inhabitants complained of the damage done by lions, and the buffalo was supposed to be the mortal foe of the lion. In the 4th/10th century Mas'udi asserts that the mode of harnessing the buffalo in use at Antioch was the same as in India.[3] The Syrian Arabs brought this "domestic animal," which enjoys marshes, to Italy and Spain. In Babylonia in the 2nd/8th century people still ate beef, but afterwards this was discontinued,[4] and the animal was kept only for its milk.[5] The meat was thought bad[6] and was even regarded by physicians as poisonous : Razi recommends only cow's milk and mutton.[7] Ibn Rusteh recounts with

(1) Von Schwarz, *Turkestan*, p. 365.
(2) Berlin, 1861, p. 66.
(3) De Goeje, *Memoires* 3, p. 22 foll. In 270-883 Ahmed b. Tulun, ruler of Egypt and Syria, died of drinking too much buffalo's milk. (Abulfida, *Annals*, year 270). This milk was also to be had in Palestine in the 4th/10th century (Muq, p 181).
(4) Muq, p. 116. The change was ascribed to Hajjaj who is said to have forbidden the slaughter of cattle (Ibn Khordadbeh, Bibl Geogr VI, p. 15).
(5) Ibn Hauqal, p. 208.
(6) Abul Qasim ed Mez. The Kirgis also are under the influence of the Arabian medicine : "Beef is not eaten at all by the wealthy Kirgis, and the poor dislike eating it. They assert that beef is indigestible, and in consequence very bad for the health ; occasions stomach-ache and headache." Radloff, *Sibirien* (II p. 439).
(7) *Tibb al-fuqara* (Munich MS) fol 68.

surprise (about 300/912) that the inhabitants of Yaman prefer beef to fat mutton.[1] Even now it is considered an insult in that country to offer beef even to a servant.[2]

Importation of beasts for slaughtering from a distance is mentioned only in the case of Egypt, where such beasts are said to have mainly come from Barqah.[3]

For the camel with one hump Arabia was always the best nursery. The dictionary of terms connected with the camel, as compiled by the philologists, shows with what disagreeable craftiness the smallest movement or instinct of this animal was utilized, altered, or suppressed for the benefit of man. Arabian subtlety has very largely been developed on the camel. For camels with two humps Balkh maintained the reputation of the ancient Baktra.[4] Still, for breeding, stallions were imported from Sind, called Falij, which were bigger than the ordinary Baktrian camel. "Only the wealthiest possessed such animals.[5]" By crossing these two-humped stallions with Arab one-humped females they obtained the two-humped racing-camels called *bukhti*, and pacers (*jammazat*). These hybrids were incapable of interbreeding.[6] Horses were bred in numerous places ; Arabs and Persians had their own equine traditions and pedigrees. Blood horses came to Baghdad from Arabia, the other mainly from Mosul.[7] The trade in horses between India and Arabia which is now so important is mentioned, so far as I know, first by Marco Polo, and indeed as the most considerable traffic between the two countries. In south India according to him each horse could be sold for 100

(1) Bibl Geogr VII 112.
(2) Glaser ap Jacob, Altarabo *Beduinenlelen*, p. 94.
(3) Bekri, ed Slane, p. 5.
(4) Istakhri, p. 280.
(5) Muq., p. 482; Jauhari, s.v. flj.
(6) Mas. III. 41 For the performances of the jammazat see Trade.
(7) Muq., p. 145.

silver marks; every year 5,000 were imported, of which at the end of a year not as many as 300 survived. The Venetian writer supposes the reasons to be "that the climate of the country is unsuitable for the breed of horses, whence they are not reared in the country, and it is difficult to preserve them. They are given meat cooked with rice for food. A tall mare covered by a handsome stallion produces only an undersized foal of ugly shape, with crooked legs, and unfit for riding."[1]

In certain regions of N. Africa, such as Sijilmasa (Tafilelt) in accordance with pre-historic practice dogs were kept and fattened for slaughtering.[2]

Egypt had from ancient times been noted for its artificial poultry-farming, especially the ingenious incubators. The technique seems never to have been introduced into the other provinces ; as late as the year 1200 the Baghdad physician Abdellatif describes it as one of the many specialities of Egypt.[3]

Doves were kept in dove-cotes to preserve them against snakes and other harmful things,[4] owing to their valuable manure ; they were not eaten. With regard to pisciculture the only notice that I have is that carp were caught in the lake of Tiberias which had been put into it from the Tigris at Wasit.*

(1) Marco Polo, pp. 91. 454.

(2) Bekri, p. 148. See Marquardt, *Die Beninsammlung*, p. CLXVII, who derives thence the name of the Canary Islands.

(3) *Relation*, transl. De Sacy, p. 135 foll. In note 3 De Sacy has collected the earlier passages.

(4) *Geoponica* 13, 6.

(*) Muqadd., p. 162.

XXV. INDUSTRY

Of the three basic necessities of the human body, food, clothing and housing, clothing was the most important to the dwellers in the Near East. The clothier's art was more elaborated than any other, and interior decoration consisted almost entirely in coloured hangings for the rooms. Luxury meant to them in the main to be well dressed; comfort meant to have handsome carpets on the walls and on the floor. It was especially noticed in the case of the ascetic et-Tusi (ob. 344/955) that "he possessed no carpets."[1] So the manufacture of carpets was widespread and constituted far away the most important industry. Particular styles of carpet actually formed a constituent element of the national costume ; one who travelled through the empire could tell from the carpeting of the rooms in what province he was. Three main sorts were at that time distinguished: 1. Curtains for the walls (*sitr*) : 2. Carpets for the floor (*busat*) and long strips (*nakhkh*) : 3. Such as were not intended to be trodden (*namat*).[2] To these were to be added the smaller sorts: prayer-mats, quilts, pillows and various sorts of cushion.[3]

Although cotton had long been cultivated in Upper Egypt,[4] it is not mentioned in the 4th/10th century as an Egyptian product, and appears to have played no part in the land which now produces the best cotton.[5]

---

(1) Wustenfeld, *Schafiten*, AGGW 37 Nr. 129.

(2) *Ta'rikh Baghdad* éd. Salmon p. 52.

(3) Abu'l-Qasim, p. 36.

(4) Pliny N.H. xix 14.

(5) As late as the end of the 18th century Egypt exported flax to Syria and imported cotton thence (Browne, *Travels in Africa*, London, 1799, p. 354.

Egypt's speciality in textiles was flax, which was chiefly grown in the Fayyum,[1] and was exported as far as Persia.[2] The wrappings of mummies are invariably of linen: The 365/976 till 385/995.[3] There was besides a loose sort of linen fabric "comparable to a sieve,"[4] called *qasab*. This could be *coloured*; all the coloured *qasab* came from Tinnis, the white from Damietta.[5] It was made into turbans, but chiefly into cloaks and veils for women.[6] Further, in the 5/11th century a new speciality came in, *Abu Qalamun*, an iridescent material, exclusively manufactured in Tinnis.[7]

In the Delta industry was carried on in the home; women spun the linen, the men move it. They received a daily wage from the dealers, and might only sell to the official brokers. At the commencement of the 3/9th century a weaver's daily wage was half a dirhem, "which was insufficient for the bread of his mouth"—at least this was the complaint they made to the patriarch Dionysus of Tellmahre when he travelled through the region.[8] The article was raised to an

(1) Muq., p. 203. At the time of a severe famine the Egyptians had to eat linseed (Eutychius, p. 71).

(2) Muq., p. 442.

(3) Maqrizi, *Khitat* i. 229. At a later period there was a place in Babylonia called Dabiqiyyah (Yaqut s.v.), which is nowhere mentioned in the 4/10th century. This does not prove that the Egyptian industry was taken over, for the place is likely to have been called after the famous cloth, like the place Susanjurd near Baghdad (Karabacck, *Die persische Nadelmalerei*, p. 117).

(4) Yaqut i 190.

(5) Nasir Khosrau, ed, Schefer, p. 36.

(6) E.g. Abu'l-Qasim, pp. 53, 54 ; Nasir Khosrau, p. 36.

(7) Nasir Khosrau, p. 36; Abu'l-Qasim, p. 3. The authors of the 4/10th century do not speak of this in connection with Egypt. Muqaddasi (p. 240, thinks of *Abu qalamun* as "wool of the sea." *i.e.*, hairs of an animal which had been rubbed off on stones, and collected, and were so costly that a garment made of them fetched 10,000 dinars. In the 5/11th century the storehouse of the Fatimid Caliphs actually contained carpets made of Qalamun (Maqrizi, *Khitat* i. 416).

(8) Michael Syrus, ed. Chabot, p. 516.

absurd price by all sorts of duties.[1]

The East too had its seat of a linen industry in Persia ; the chief place being Kazrun, called "the Damietta of Persis."[2] Here too the Egyptian styles were distinguished, *Dabiqi, sharb* and *qasab*, which indicates that the two industries were not independent of each other. And since Muqaddasi (p. 442) asserts that in earlier times flax was imported from Egypt to the Persian maritime town Siniz, which was celebrated for its linen *qasab*, whereas in his own time the local product was chiefly employed for this manufacture,[3] this is evident that the linen industry had been transplanted thither from Egypt. And indeed it came by sea; at first it was localized on the coast, at Siniz, Jennabah, and Tawwaj: only at a later time, after it had become independent of the Egyptian material, did it penetrate into the interior. Hence the best sort of Persian linen was still called that of Tawwaj, when most of it was manufactured at Kazrun.[4]

Ibn Balkhi, who composed his description of Persis about 500/1106 portrays the manufacture of the Tawwaj linen in Kazrun as follows. The flax is soaked in ponds, then pulled apart and spun into threads. The linen thread is washed in the water of the Rahban Canal; though the water of this canal is scanty, it has the property of bleaching the linen thread, which becomes white in no other water. This Rahban Canal belongs to the royal treasury, and its earnings now belong to the house of the Emir, since the exchequer grants the use of it only to those weavers who are commissioned by it to weave. A fiscal inspects as overseer, and brokers fix the proper price of the fabrics, sealing the bales before they are put into the hands of foreign traders.

(1) See above 8.
(2) Muq., p. 433.
(3) Muq., p. 442.
(4) Muq., p. 435.

These relied on the brokers, and purchased the corded bales, just as they were lying, and in each town whither they were brought people merely asked for the certificate of the broker of Kazrun, and sold the bales without undoing them. Hence it often came to pass that a load of bales from Kazrun changed hands more than ten times without being opened. In these last days, however, fraud has begun to be practised. People have become dishonest, and all confidence has disappeared. For goods with the stamp of the exchequer have often been found to be of poor quality, whence foreign dealers avoid the products of Kazrun.[1]

With this single exception cotton was to the East what linen was to the west.[2] Even the *qasab* of Kazrun was frequently made of cotton. Cotton had travelled by a direct route from India to the north long before it came westward or eastward. In the 13th century A.D. it was still little known in China. The narrative of the travels of Chan Chung (1221 A.D.) mentions it in the valley of the Ili; "there is there a sort of cloth *lu-lu-ma*, which people say is woven from the wool of a plant. This hair resembles the catkin of our meadows, is very clean, fine and soft; people make of it thread, cord, cloth and quilts."[3] As late as the 4/10th century celebrated cotton stuffs (*sabaniyyat)* were exported from Kabul to China and Khorasan. In Babylonia cotton was not cultivated, but was brought thither from northern Persia and Mesopotamia;[4] even in our time Transoxiana produces cotton annually to the value of 400,000,000 Marks ; in Mesopotamia it was encouraged by the policy of the Hamadanids, which was hostile to the peasants.[5] In the

(1) JRAS 1902, p. 337 (This reference appears to be wrong. Transl.).
(2) "It is well known that cotton belongs to Khorasan and flax to Egypt" (Thaalibi, *Lata'if al Ma'arif*, p. 97).
Bretschneider *Medieaval Researches* i 70 ; also p. 31.
(3) Ibn Hauqal, p. 328.
(4) W. Husse, *Hemdsserungswirtschaft in Turan*, p. 72.
(5) See above 8.

4/10th century it had migrated to North Africa[1] and Spain.[2] All the chief seats of the cotton industry were in the Persian East: Merv, Nisabur, and Bemm (eastern Kirman). The speciality of the last consisted in veils, interwoven with wreaths, which travelled as far as Egypt,[3] costing about 30 dinars a piece. The product of Merv on the other hand was soft flannel,[4] too thick for clothing; hence it is called by Mutanabbi[5] "apes' raiment" and Abu'l-Qasim makes merry about "coarsely woven stuff of Merv, of domestic manufacture, each strand accompanied by a *crepitus ventris*[6]". On the other hand it was prized for turbans.[7] Even the cotton-growing area of Turkestan exported fabrics to Babylonia,[8] whereas in Transoxiana linen was one of the rarest articles; the Samanid Isma'il presented each officer with a linen garment as a valuable gift.[9]

Following the opposite course to the cotton industry that of silk had spread from Byzantium in the West Eastward. The tradition of this lasted to our time[10] Greek satin also continued to be imported, indeed it was the most important article which came through Trebizond.[11] In the 4th century it counted as the finest.[12] The greatest number of silk looms were still to be found in the province of Khuzistan, whither the Sasanids had transplanted the art from the Byzantine

(1) Bekri, ed. Slane, 59, 69.
(2) Moro Rasis, p. 56.
(3) Ibn Hauqal, p. 223.
(4) Muq., 323 ; *Lat. al Ma'arif*, p. 119 ; Ibn Hauqal, p. 316 : Ibn al-Faqih, p. 320.
(5) *Diwan*, Beyrut ed., p. 17.
(6) p. 37.
(7) Yatima ii, 62.
(8) Ibn Hauqal, p. 362.
(9) Vambery, *History of Bokhara*, p. 63.
(10) Mas'udi, II, 185 f.
(11) Ibn Hauqal, p. 2.
(12) *Lat. al-Ma'arif*, p. 131 ; satin was brought to the Muslims even from the land of the Franks (Ya'quti. p. 270).

empire.[1] Damask, satin, plush, and floss-silk were produced. On the other hand silk-throwing was localized in the North, on the former land route to China. There, in Merv, and especially in Tabaristan, the mountainous country south of the Caspian, the strong *abrishem* thread was thrown, which was exported every where,[2] and out of which in the neighbouring Armenia the famous knee-bands were made which fetched from 1 to 10 dinars.[3] The fabrics of heavy silk (*thiyab harir*) which Tabaristan exported show direct relationship with China; the Persian industry preferred the lighter textures.

Among woollen carpets the Persian, the Armenian, and those of Bokhara were especially distinguished. In Persia the "art Carpets" (*el-busut-es-sani'ah*) were woven, the choicest specimens of which were those worked with the technique of Susangird.[4] But that age set the highest value on Armenian carpets (*i.e.* of Asia Minor) the prototypes of our Smyrna carpets.[5] In the residence of the Umayyad Caliph Al-Walid II floor and walls were covered with Armenian carpets.[6] The consort of al-Rashid sat on an Armenian carpet, her women on Armenian cushions.[7] Armenian carpets and carpets of Tabaristan are mentioned with admiration among the possessions of the jeweller who about 300/912 was the richest man in Baghdad, as well as in the treasury of Muqtadir's mother.[8] A vassal presented this Caliph with

(1) Istakhri 212 ; Ibn Hauqal 272.

(2) Ibn Hauqal 246. This industry is the most valuable of modern Baghdad. It was known that floss-silk was imported from Merv into Jurjan and Tabaristan (Ibn Hauqal 316), and as late as the 4th/10th century cocoons came annually from Jurjan into western Tabaristan (Ibn Hauqal 272).

(3) Karabacek, *Die persische Nadelmalerei Susangird*, Leipzig, 881.

(4) Tha'alibi, *Lata'if al-marif*, pp. 111, 222, Abu'l-Qasim, p. 36.

(5) Ag. v. 173.

(6) Mas'udi, vi. 334.

(7) Arib, p. 48.

(8) Misk. v. 389.

seven Armenian carpets among other gifts.[1] The highest value was set on those Persian carpets which most nearly resembled Armenian workmanship[2], and in praise of the best Persian carpets, those from Isfahan, it was said that they matched particularly well with the splendid Armenian carpets, but looked sufficiently well by themselves.[3] Marco Polo (I.3) observes that the best and finest carpets are wrought in Armenia.[4] Probably the reason for the value set on them lay in the Armenian wool to which Tha'alibi assigns the first place after the Egyptian, and particularly in the Armenian red. "Red is the colour of children, women, and joy. Red suits the eye best, because it enlarges the pupil, whereas black narrows it[5]" —such is the doctrine of Mas'udi in the year 332/943. In the carpet store in Cairo red carpets were the most admired[6] and it is said of the crimson carpets of the Egyptian Siyut that they resemble the Armenian.[7] The rugs called *Tanafis* betray their Greek origin in their name (*lapetes*). In Babylonia they must at an earlier period have been manufactured especially in the Christian frontier town Hirah, since at a later time the manufacture of en-Nu'maniyyah bore the name "Carpets of Hirah".[8] The patterns remained the same: chalices, elephants, horses, camels, lions, and birds.[9] Throughout the empire mats were made of rush (*halfa*). Those most in repute were from Abbadan, a small island at the mouth of the Shatt el-'Arab.[10]

---

(1) Elias Nisib, p. 202.

(2) Istakhri, p. 153.

(3) Ibn Rusteh, p. 153.

(4) *Lata' el-ma'arif*, p. 128. Next comes that of Tekrit, and only than the Persian. According to ZDMG viii 529 this passage comes from the treatise of Jahiz on trade.

(5) Mas'udi ii 102.

(6) Maqrizi, *Khitat* i 416 f.

(7) Ya'qubi, *Geogr.*, p. 331.

(8) Ibn Rusteh. p. 186.

(9) Cp. *Ta'rikh Baghdad,* ed., Salmon, p. 52, with Kremer, *Kulturbesch.* ii 289 ; Marqizi i. 417.

(10) Muqaddasi, p. 118.

They were copied in Persia[1] as in Egypt.[2] Famous places had the words "product (*'amal*) of —"woven in the fabric as evidence of origin, a practice which naturally did not prevent fraud. Thus, *e.g.*, some unknown localities inscribed the well recommended name Basinna on their curtains, and similarly materials for garments which came from Khuzistan bore the stamp of Baghdad.[3]

A special branch of industry flourished in the Persian province Sabur, şimilar to one in the French Riviera: the preparation of perfumes. Ten essences were there made out of violets, lotus, narcissus, fragrant screw-pine, lilies, white jasmine, myrtle, marjoram, and orange-peel.[4] This lucrative industry was attempted in Babylonia also; Kufah added the essence of pinks, and surpassed the Persians in that of violets.[5] A similar industry, though quite separate from it, had its headquar'ers in the southern town of Jur. There fragrant waters were prepared, but from quite different flowers: roses, palm flower, southernwood, safflower, and willow. Thence rose-water was exported to the whole world, "the Maghrib, Spain, Yemen, India and China."[6] These important industries, of which the ancient reporters say nothing, must have arisen in the Islamic period.

We hear no more of the drudgery of the awkward handmill among either country or townsfolk; there were floating mills on the rivers,[7] and water-mills on the brooks.[8] The Devil's River of Jiruft in Kirman alone drove fifty mills,[9] and in Basrah one of the most modern problems of

(1) Muq., p. 442.
(2) Muq., p. 203.
(3) Istakhri, p. 93.
(4) Muq., p. 443.
(5) Istakhri, p. 153 ; Ibn Hauqal, p. 213.
(6) Ibn Hauqal, p. 213.
(7) E.G. Muq., p. 408 *Mafatih al-'Ulum*, p. 71.
(8) Muq., pp. 401, 406.
(9) Ibn Hauqal, p. 222.

hydraulics was tackled: mills were erected at the mouths of the canals which were almost entirely fed by the tide, and these were driven at the ebb by the falling water.[1] Animals were used for grinding only where there was no water.[2] The citizens of the Moroccan town Ijli felt pious qualms about enslaving the water: "They have no mill on the brook, and if they are asked what stands in the way they reply: How could we compel the sweet water to turn a mill ?"[3] The great floating mills of Babylonia were on the Tigris, not on the Euphrates; they were in Tekri, Hadithan, Ukbara, Baradan, and Baghdad. Some famous ones were also in Mosul and Beled. The last of these had its season ; it worked only during the days in which the harvest was being shipped for Babylonia. We have a more precise description of the mills of Mosul. They were made entirely of wood and iron, and were suspended on iron chains in midstream. Each mill had two stones, (*'arbah*) each of which ground fifty camel's load per day.[4] The largest mill of Baghdad, the Patricius Mill, had 100 stones, and is said to have earned 100,000,000 dirhems annually.[5] We hear nothing of sawmills for wood. It is stated that the murderer of 'Umar I, a Persian of Nehawand, offered to make a mill to be driven by the wind[6]. As late as the 4th/10th century the strong and abnormally steady wind (Called *bad-i-sad u bist ruz* because it blows for 120 days) was utilized in Afghanistan for windmills.[7]

---

(1) Muq., p. 125.

(2) Istakhri, p. 273, dealing with Khorasan. In well-watered Persia this clearly was not practised. The inhabitants of the village Khullar, which supplied the millstones for the whole province, had to have their grinding done in a neighbouring village, as they had no millstream (Ibn al-Balkhi, who wrote about 500/1107. JRAS 1902, p. 335).

(3) Bekri, p. 162.

(4) Ibn Hauqal, p. 147 f.

(5) Ya'qubi, p. 243.

(6) Mas'udi *Prairies* iv. 227.

(7) Ibn Hauqal, p. 299 ; Muq., p. 333.

Such still exist: "The North wind sets in about the middle of June, and blows continuously for two months. The windmills are erected for it exclusively. They have eight arms and stand between two posts, between which the wind penetrates like a wedge. The arms are vertical and stand on a similarly perpendicular rod, the lower end of which sets in motion a millstone which revolves over another stone."[1] This then is a genuine wind turbine. A statement of Guzuli (ob. 815/1412) shows that such a mill could be regulated like our waterwheels by opening and shutting the apertures. "In Afghanistan all the mills and waterwheels are driven by the North wind, and made to face it. This wind blows there constantly in both summer and winter, but is stronger and more constant in summer. Oftentimes it ceases blowing once or twice during the day or night, and then every mill and waterwheel in the region stops work. Then the wind starts again, and they start also. The mills have hatches (*manafis*) which can be opened or closed, so that more or less wind can pass in. For if it blows too fiercely, the meal gets burned and comes out black, and often the millstone becomes red-hot and crumbles.[2]"

In the manufacture of paper also the third and fourth centuries brought a great revolution, which liberated the process of writing from the monopoly of a single country, and materially cheapened it. So long as people wrote on papyrus, they were dependent on Egypt,[3] whereas now "the

---

(1) Seven Hedin *Zu Land nach Indien,* ii. 147.

(2) Guzuli, *Malali 'al-Budur*, Cairo, 1299, i. 50. The "Persian mills" of North Africa (Bekri, ed. Slane, p. 36 ; Abu Salih, ed. Evetts, fol. 63a: not in the dictionaries) served for chopping up the sugar-cane (Lippman, *Geschichte des Zuckerrohrs*, p. 110).

(3) It was ordinarily manufactured there in rolls of about 30 yards in length, and one span in breadth (Suyuti, *Husn al-Muhadarah*, Cairo, ii. 194). I cannot say what is meant by *qirtas quhiyyah* in Umar b. Abi Rabiah (*Diwan*, ed. Schwarz, No. 32, 3;) perhaps we should adopt the variant *qahwiyyah* "wince-coloured.

Chinese papers, manufactured only in China and Samarcand, displaced the papyrus of Egypt, and parchment on which our ancestors wrote."[1] Ya'qubi, towards the end of the third (9th) century, speaks of small towns in Lower Egypt in which papyrus was still fabricated.[2] Even the Sycilian papyrus was only wrought into writing material to a very small extent for the Government; most of it was wound into cables[3] as in Homeric times.[4] "The Egyptian manufacture of papyrus for writing material may with great probability be assumed in the main to have become extinct about the middle of the tenth century A.D. Dated papyri cease entirely with the year 323/935, whereas dated paper documents start in the year 300/912."[5] At that time the best paper in the empire was the *kagid* paper which had been transplanted from China, but experienced a change of world-wide historical importance in the hands of the Muhammadans.

They freed it from the mulberry-tree, and the bamboo, and invented rag-paper.[6] In the third (9th) century it was manufactured only in Transoxiana,[7] but in the 4th/10th century there were paper-mills in Damascus, in the Palastinian Tiberias,[8] and in the Syrian Tripoli.[9] Still Samarcand remained the headquarters. Khwarizmi jestingly

(1) Tha'alibi, *Latai'f al-ma'arif* p. 126.
(2) *Geogr.* p. 338.
(3) Ibn Haqal, p. 86.
(4) Hehn, *Kulturpflanzen*, 8th ed. p. 312.
(5) Karabacek, *Mitteilungen aus den Papyrus Rainer*, II, III, p. 98.
(6) Karabacek, loc. cit., 4. 11 foll.
(7) Istakhri, p. 288.
(8) Muq, p. 180.
(9) Nasir Khosrau, p. 12, Edrisi (ed Dozy, 192) in the 6th/12th century mentions the papermill of Xativa as the best in Spain. According to Karabacek, loc. cit. p. 121, a factory for the paper of Samarcand was erected in Baghdad as early as the end of the 2nd (8th) century. Against this there are the positive assertions of Istakrhi and Tha'alibi, who is here copying an earlier authority, probably the treatise of Jahiz on trade, and the complete silence of all ancient authors,

excuses a friend for not writing on the ground that he lives a long distance from Samarcand and so finds paper (*kagid*) too dear.[1] About the same time the librarian of the princely library in Shiraz is collecting the best paper "of Samarcand and China."[2]

The manufacture of accurate astronomical and mathematical instruments in Harran, the last refuge of the old Star-warship, was connected with the peculiar religious position of the city.[3] The accuracy of the Harranian weighing-machines was proverbial.[4] And the trade in rosaries which still flourishes in the city of pilgrimage, Jerusalem, was already then in full swing.[5]

---

among them those of accurate descriptions of the city of Baghdad. Karabacek's sole source is Ibn Khaldun, who is too late; the two other sources, both western and late, the *Diwan al-Insha* and Maqrizi, speak only of the introduction of paper into the bureaux of Harun ar-Rashid. Yaqut is the first writer who mentions (II 522) that paper in his time was manufactured in what was formerly the Silk Court in Baghdad. On the ground that the author of the *Fihrist* (p 10) finds paper documents made of *waraq tihami*, Karabacek, following Kremer, would find the third oldest paper-factory on the south-west coast of Arabia, which is a *priori* improbable, against the evidence of Istakhri and countered also by the silence of Hamdani and all later authors. This single notice then cannot be maintained; most probably we should read *sh ami* for *tihami*, which would give Syrian paper. Finally, if Tha'alibi (ZDMG viii 526) praises the paper of Egypt as the best, finest, and smoothest it is not clear from von Hommer's translation whether paper or papyrus is meant. Probably too Tha'alibi is speaking of earlier times. This is rendered almost certain by a good old report in Yaqut's *Irshad* (ii 412) according to which the Egyptian vizir Abu'l Fadl b. al-Furat (ob. 391/1001) used to import paper every year from Samarcand for his copyists, and an Egyptian savant, who came into the possession of part of his library, carefully cut out all the blank leaves from these books and put them together for a new book. This gives no indication of a local industry for the manufacture of paper.

(1) *Rasa'il*, p 25.
(2) Yaqut, *Irshad*, v. 447.
(3) Hamdani, p. 132.
(4) Muq., p. 141.
(5) Muq., p. 180.

XXVI. TRADE

The Near East, during the period wherein we are acquainted with it, is far removed from the division of labour which the natural forces suggest, and according to which the male should produce the goods and the female retail them. Only in Egypt did it attract the attention of Herodotus that retail business was carried on by women. It is reported of the north Iranian town Biyar that "the bazaar is in the houses, and women do the selling,"[1] and Marco Polo found that among the Tartars the women do all the trading.[2] Warlike nations successively and regularly looked down on trade with contempt. Tradition has ascribed to Omar I, the most thorough-going representative of the old Islamic community, the saying: No Muslim should be a salesman, as chattering in the bazaars draws men away form Islam.[3] The Umayyad world had no sympathy with the salesman, not because of religious zeal, but as knights and feudal lords. The commercial class plays no part in their annals. In this matter also the 3rd/9th century produced a revolution, and in the 4th/10th the wealthy tradesman has become the carrier of Muhammadan civilization, which by then had, from the material point of view, become very pretentious. Towards the end of the century a petty chieftain of Western Iran had not disdained to purchase a store in the city of Hamadhan, which belonged to a colleague, to conduct the business in his own name, which consisted in the sale of the choice products of his territory, and to obtain thence a profit of 1,200,000 dirhems. The local chieftain, fearing that the

---

(1) Muqaddasi, p. 356.

(2) I.4.

(3) Bukhari II, 4.

taxable wealth of the city would go "abroad", raided the agent of the merchant-prince, evicted him, and appropriated his money.[1] The enterprise and energy of the time had to some extent retreated into the bazaars and counting-houses; in these too there lived a good share of poetry with romantic possibilities and flutters. Since almost every trade was also a traveller, the prices of goods and the exchange of an immense variety of coinage got intricately mixed up with adventures in all countries, and with the most extensive experience of the world and knowledge of mankind. Muhammadan commerce in the 4th/10th century was a proud spectacle. It had become master in its own house; its ships and caravans moved in all directions; it had taken over the lead in world trade; Baghdad and Alexandria fixed the prices at any rate for the luxuries of the contemporary world. As late as the 3rd/9th century Jews of Province were designated simply "traders on the sea,"[2] who embarked in France with eunuchs, male and female slaves, brocade, skins of beavers and martens, other furs, and swords. They rode camels across the isthmus of Suez, embarked again at Suez, called at the ports of Medinah and Meccah, and then sailed to the Persian Gulf, India and China. For the homeward journey they took as freight musk, aloes, cinnamon, and other Oriental groceries, to bring to the Mediterranean; these they sold partly to the Greeks in Constantinople, partly in the capital of the king of the Franks. Often, too, they preferred the overland route from Antioch to the Euphrates, proceeding thence *via* Baghdad to the Persian Gulf. They spoke Persian, Roman, Frankish, Spanish, and Slavonic.[3]

---

(1) *Wuzara*, ed. Amedroz, p. 478.

(2) *Ibn al-Faqih*, p. 270.

(3) Simonsen in *Revue des etudes juives* 1907, p. 141 foll, suggested the rendering of *Radhaniyyah* by "people of the Rhone," which seems plausible, but was not approved by de Goeje (*Verslagen en Mededeelingen*, Amsterdam, 1909, p. 253). I too regard it as improbable Jewish ships in the Mediterranean are mentioned at this time (end of 9th century A.D.), by Notker balbulus in his tales of

There is no mention in the 4th/10th century of these successors of the Syrian traders, who up to the Middle Ages had been established on the Rhone. This can be no accident.[1] The rise of Muhammadan marine commerce drove the foreign middlemen out.

The second great triumph of the fourth century A.H. was the opening of the Rusian North to trade. We have a description of the route followed by "Russian," *i.e.*, Norman traders belonging to the 3rd/9th century. "They are a Slav race, and bring beaver skins and hides of black foxes from the most remote regions of the Slavs to the Greek Sea, where the ruler of the Greek takes from them his tithe. They frequently sail down the Don, which is the river of the Slavs, and proceed through Khamlij, the metropolis of the Khazars, whose ruler takes a tithe from them, to the Caspian Sea, where they disembark at any point they choose. They frequently bring their goods on camel-back from Jurjan to Baghdad, where the Slav eunuches serve them as interpreters. They profess to be Christians, and as such pay poll-tax."[2] In the year 309/921 the Caliph entered into diplomatic relations with the king of the Volga region;[3] in the following year the inhabitants of this region adopted Islam,[4] and it was of the greatest importance that now the Muhammadan North-east was united under a competent dynasty, which secured the frontiers, brought about prosperity and promised the foreign trader undisturbed profit. Most of the Arabic coins found in Northern Europe belong to the 4th/10th century, and more than two-thirds

---

Charlemagne: "Ships are to be seen in one of the coast town of Gallia Narbonensis, said by some to be Jewish, by others to be African or British merchantmen" (Book II, ch 14).

(1) Ibn Khordadbeh, p. 153; Ibn al-Faqih, p. 270.

(2) Ibn Khordadbeh, p. 154; Ibn al-Faqiih, p. 271.

(3) By the mission of Ibn Fudlan, whose report is in part preserved.

(4) Mas'udi II, 15.

of these are Samanid.[1] From this time and throughout the period of the Crusades Russia was the road between Scandinavia and the Orient.[2] As in the North so too in the East Islam won vast territories (See above, §1). In the year 331/943 the king of the Uigurs in Kan-chan enters into friendly relations with the Samanids in Bukhara, and this secures the route to China for the Muhammadan trader.[3] And about 400/1000 vast portions of India, of the utmost commercial importance, were added to the "Empire of Islam." On the other hand in the 4th/10th century there was much disturbance in the Slav North owing to the advance of the Normans, who sailed down the Volga into the Caspian in the years 270/883, 297/910, 300/912 (on this last occasion, it is said, with 500 vessels each containing 300 men), pillaged everything, and in the year 358/969 destroyed the metropolis of the Khazars.[4] This is probably the reason why their friendly visits to Muhammadan territory cease at this time; only the Persian trader continued to come as before[5] to the Khazars, who now became the agents for the northern goods. The only article of exportation which was the actual product of the land of the Khazars was isinglass ; everything else, honey, wax, felt, beaver skins, was conveyed by them from the North.[6] Jewish trade had a monopoly of the chief European commodity, slaves; still in the year 356/965 Prague, the chief slave-market of Europe, was frequented by Muslims, Jews and Turks from the country of the Turks with goods and Byzantine gold coins, who exported thence slaves, tin, and beaver skins."[7] With this development there corresponded the rise of Muhammadan colonies chiefly

(1) Heyd *Levantenhandel*, I, 69.
(2) Schlumberger, *Epopee Byzantine*, p. 9.
(3) Abu Dulaf in Yaqut, s v *Sin*.
(4) Ibn Hauqal, p 281 Cf Dorn, *Caspia*, Mem Acad St. Petersbourg 1875.
(5) Ibn Rusteh, p. 281.
(6) Ibn Hauqal, p. 281.
(7) Westberg, *Ibrahim ibn Ya'qub's Reiseberichte*, pp. 53 and 155.

under governments of their own, as Khazars, Sarir, Alani in Gana and Kuga (Africa),[1] as also in Saimur (India).[2] The case was similar in China;[3] even in Corea there was a colony of Muslim traders.[4] On the other hand Eastern traders were not allowed to remain more than three months in Byzantium;[5] the most important colony in the Byzantine empire was Trebizond.[6]

About the middle of the sixth century A.D. Cosmas Indicopleustes narrates how a Greek and a Persian trader disputed before the king of Ceylon which of their rulers was the more powerful. The Greek won ultimately by producing a fine Byzantine gold coin, which was current in the whole world, whereas the Persian could only produce a silver coin. There is this amount of truth in the story that there was a pact about coinage between Byzantium and the Sasanid realm whereby the latter might coin silver, but had to use the Roman solidus as its gold coin.[7] In consequence of this a gold currency prevailed in the provinces of the Caliphate which had formerly been Greek, whereas the Persian countries reckoned by silver dirhems. According to Yahya ibn Adam (ob. 203/818) in Babylonia the dirhem counted as currency, but in Syria and Egypt the dinar.[8] In our period, however, and this is the surest sign of the unification of Muhammadan trade, the gold currency makes its way eastward. At the commencement of the 3rd/9th century all the gifts of the Caliphs are reckoned in dirhems ; at the commencement of the 4th/10th century the

(1) (The original here is somewhat obscure. Transl.)
(2) Ibn Hauqal, p. 227; *Merveilles del' Inde*, pp. 142, 144, 161.
(3) See next §.
(4) Ibn Khordadbeh, p. 70.
(5) Vogt. *Basile*, I, 393.
(6) Muq., p. 123.
(7) Gelzer, *Byzantinsche Kulturgeschichte*, 1909. p 79. Byzantium had a similar pact with the Frankish king Chlodwig.
(8) *Kitab al-kharaj*, ed. Juynboll p. 52.

gold currency has been introduced into Baghdad, and the central government reckons by dinars. The decisive step was taken between 260/874 and 303/915; in the budget of the former year the tribute of Babylonia is still given in dirhems,[1] in the latter in gold.[2] Together with the silver currency—and this is an interesting point—payments in kind ceased; in 260/874 such payments still figure in the budget of Babylonia, but no longer in 303/915. A rule issued by the heads of the Babylonian Jews in the year 787 A.D. further indicates that more property was in the form of purely liquid assets. This was to the effect that personal and not only estate might be siezed for a testator's debts.[3] Still in private life the two sorts of coin were not yet reckoned together ; thus the savant Tha'lab who died in Baghdad in the year 291/904 "left 21,000 dirhems, 2,000 dinars, and shops at the Damascus Gate worth 3,000 dinars."[4] Only presents, such as those to poets, are still given in the old fashion in dirhems.[5] Doubtless this looked less like a matter of business. We are besides acquainted with the different sentiments attached to the old and new currencies. The Eastern provinces of the empire adhered to the silver dirhem even during the 4th/10th century ; "In Transoxiana the dirhem is familiar, the dinar not in use,"[6] or current only in the chief towns,[7] and "in Persis (Fars) all trade is carried on with the dirhem.[8]

The petty chieftains who sprang up at this time and struck coins either independently of or under the Caliphs saw to it that the greatest possible variety of both sorts was

(1) Qudamah, p. 239.
(2) Kremer, *Einnamebudget*.
(3) Gratz *Geschichte der Juden*, ed, 4, V. 196.
(4) Yaqut, *Irshad*, II, 153.
(5) *Wuzara*, ed. Amedroz, p. 202.
(6) Istakhri, p. 314.
(7) Istakhri, p. 323.
(8) Istakhri, p. 156.

in circulation, and the tables of exchange-rates kept by the great bankers looked interesting enough, as is suggested by the lists of coins in Muqaddasi.[1] At the beginning of the 4th/10th century the dinar was worth about 14 dirhems.[2] Owing to the separation of the West (which alone held gold) from the Eastern empire the value of gold in the latter region rose enormously towards the end of the century; Maqrizi however exagerates when the reports that in Egypt it was only after the impoverishment which took place under Saladdin that people for the first time talked of dirhems having previously always reckoned in gold.[3] In the middle of the 4th/10th century the Buyid Rukn al-daulah coined dinars which were half copper, and often entirely of the metal. In the year 420/1029 they were accepted for one-third the value of an ordinary dirhem.[4] In the year 427/1036 an attempt was made to assist the local currency by formally abolishing the Egyptian (maghribi) dinar; no contract in which it was mentioned could serve as the basis of an action.[5] On the other hand the silver coinage was reduced in weight, so that 25, 40 at one time as many as 150 went to the dinar.[6] In the year 390/1000 the guards mutinied before the vizier's palace on account of the debased gold coinage.[7] Just as in our own time bad money had a definite though modest value in exchange. Spurious dirhems were called quicksilver[8] *e.g.*, in Meccah where 24 went to a genuine

(1) See also Hamadhani in *Rasa'il*, Const. 1298, p, II.

(2) Amedroz, *Wuzara*, p. 36 Note 1. In the year 330/942 the Hamdanid Nasir al-daulah coined dinars of full value of 13 dirhems, whereas the old were worth only 10. J.A Ser, VII, Vol. xv 259. The dinar was worth 15 dirhems according to *Merv. de l'Inde*, p. 52.

(3) J.A. Ser. VII, Vol. xiv, p. 524.

(4) Amedroz, J.R.A.S. 1906, p. 475.

(5) Ibn al-Jauzi, p. 191 a.

(6) Amedroz, *Wuzara*, p. 36, note 1.

(7) *Wuzara*, p. 402.

(8) Jauhari s.v. *zabaqa*. All silver which was to be coined was smelted with quicksilver. Amedroz J.R.A.S 1906, p. 479.

dirhem, but were out of circulation in the *haute saison*, from 6 Dhu'l-Hijjah to the end of the pilgrimage festival.[1] Fraud could be practised with genuine coins also, as was done by the clippers among us. Only, as the coins were weighed, they could not be filed, but had to have their weight increased; this was done with antimony or quicksilver.[2]

The smaller coinage was graded on the sexagesimal system: 1 dirhem = 6 daniq = 12 qirat = 24 tassuj = 48 habbah (barley corns). Silver coins cut up had also to serve for petty commerce, though this was constantly denounced.[3]

Wholesale business demanded if only for safety's sake mediums of payment which were less cumbrous, and inaccessible to robbers ;[4] these mostly had Persian names. A savant who journeys to Spain takes with him a letter of credit (*suftajah*), and 5,000 dirhems in cash.[5] Nasir Khosrau received from an acquaintance in Asuan a blank letter of credit addressed to this agent (*wakil*) in Aidhab of the following content ; "Give Nasir all that he may demand, obtain a receipt from him, and debit the sum to me."[6] The Viceroy of Egypt sent his representative in Baghdad letters of credit for the cashiered vizier. The representative accepted them,[7] and put the money at the vizier's disposal.[8] A sort of bill of exchange was the *sakk*, originally a note of band;[9] a rich man would draw cheques on his steward (*sakka ala*).[10] In Audagusht in the western Sudan Ibn Hauqual saw a

(1) Muq., p. 99.
(2) Abu Yusuf, J.A. Ser, VII. Vol. xix. 26.
(3) Ibid. Vol. xix. 25 foll.
(4) This subject is treated by R. Grasshoff, *Die suftajah und hawalah, der Araber, Jur,* Diss. Lnoigsberg, 1891.
(5) *Fasari' al'ushshaq*, p. 10.
(6) Ed. Schefer, p. 64.
(7) This is the sense of *sayhaha*; see e.g., *Wuzara*, d. 296.
(8) Ibn Sa'id, ed. Tallquist, p. 32.
(9) Bukhari (1309) I, 14; Agh. V 15; (Ibn al Mu'tazz, *Diwan* I, 137.
(10) *Wuzara*, p. 77.

cheque 42,000 dinars drawn by a man of Sijlimasah on one Muhammad ibn ʻAli Saʻdun in Sijilmasah ; it was officially certified.[1] The paper had travelled through a great part of the Sahara.[2] In Babylonia the *sakk* was a regular cheque in connection wherewith the banker plays an important part. In the 3/9th century (whereto the anecdotes connected with Harun belong) a magnate drew cheques on his banker. About 300/900 a great man paid a poet in this way, only the banker refused the cheque, so that the disappointed man composed a verse to the effect that he would gladly pay a million on the same plan.[3] A patron of the same poet and singer (Jahizah, ob. 320/936) during a concert wrote a cheque (*ruqʻah* "note") in his favour on a banker (*sairafi*) for 500 dinars. When paying, the banker gave the poet to understand that it was customary to charge one dirhem discount on each dinar; *i.e.*, about 10 per cent. Only if the poet would spend the afternoon and evening with him, he would make no deduction.[4] Another banker (*jahbadh*), who was even a greater patron of the fine arts, not only made no deduction; but presented the poet with an extra 10 per cent.[5] There was therefore plenty of employment for bankers, and it is not surprising that in Isfahan there were 200 banks in the bankers' bazaar— for these too sat together.[6] About 400/1000 the banker had made himself indispensable in Basrah: every trader had his banking account, and paid only in cheques on his bank (*khatt-saraf*) in the bazaar.[7] This would appear to have been most important refinement of monetary

(1) Ibn Hauqal, pp 42, 70. From Sijilmasah to Audagusht was 51 days' journey (Bekri 156 foll)

(2) Baihaqi ed Schawally.

(3) Yaqut, *Irshad*, I, 305.

(4) *Ibid*, I, 399.

(5) Shabushti, *Kitab al-diyarat*, Berlin, fol 88a.

(6) N. Khosrau, who came thither in the year 444/1051 : ed Schefer, transl, p. 253.

(7) Ibid, p. 86.

oderation in the empire,[1] and it is significant that it arose in the port-town Basrah, on the frontier between Persis and Babylonia. For the people of Basrah, the Persians of Persis, and the South Arabians were the best traders among the Believers, and had their colonies wherever anything could be procured. In this matter they were like the Swabians and Swiss of our time. About the year 290/902 al-Faqih al-Hamadhani observes: "The people of Basrah and the Himyarites are the greatest money-grubbers. One who travels to the remotest region of Ferghanah or the Western edge of Morocco is sure to find a man from Basrah or a Himyarite there.[2]" The citizens of this world-port were famous for their immunity from home-sickness. Below is an inscription which contained the words.

> Strangers, however hardhearted they become,
> In time of sickness recollect their home

someone is said to have written "except the people of Basrah."[3]

In Jeddah, the port of Meccah' Persians had long been settled,[4] and in Sijilmasah (S. Morocco) a large colony of Babylonians (people of Basrah, Kufah, and Baghdad) carried on business.[5] Likewise the inhabitants of the active Syrian port-towns, Tripoli, Saida, Beirut, were Persians, transplanted thither by the first Umayyad.[6] Egypt was indeed a great commercial country.,[7] but even in our time the

(1) There were no *giros* (deposit-banks) such as had attained full development in Greek Egypt (Preisigke, *Girowesen in griechischen Aegypten*, Strassburg 1910).
(2) Bibl Geogr V 11.
(3) *Rasa'il* of Ma'arri, ed Margoliouth, p. 75.
(4) Istakhri, p. 19.
(5) Ibn Hauqual, p. 41.
(6) Ya'qubi, Geogr B.G. VII. 327.
(7) Muq., p 35. "He who looks for trade must go to Aden, Oman, or Egypt."

genuine Egyptian whether Muhammadan or Copt does not distinguish himself by any special talent for business. In the 4th/10th century he had the reputation like the Frenchman of our time) of rarely leaving his country.[1] In our time the cream of the trade in Egypt is absorbed by Greeks, Levantines, Persians, and even Hindus. As early as the end of the 2nd/8th century there was a numerous and influential Persian colony in the Egyptian capital, were the qadi received 30 Persians at once into the exclusive and greatly coveted list of Witnesses.[2] The greatest financier, though not the greatest merchant, in the country was at that time Abu Bekr al-Madhara'i (income 400,000 dinars = £20,000) whose family was originally of Babylon.[3]

The chief rivals of the Babylonians and Persians were the Jews. The Jewry of Isfahan was the business quarter of this Persian capital;[4] of Tustar headquarters of the Persian carpet-industry, it is expressly attested that the greatest dealers there were Jews:[5] A Jew controlled the whole or the pearl-fishery in the Persian Gulf.[6] Kashmir was closed against all foreigners; only a few such traders had access, expecially Jews.[7] In the Orient too their speciality was the money trade. Towards the end of the 3rd/9th century when the Patriarch of Alexandria was laid under heavy contribution by the government, he procured the money by selling to the Jews the church estates, and a part of the Mu'allaqah church.[8] There were so many Jews among the

(1) Tha'alibi, *Lata'if al-ma'arif*, p. 101.
(2) Kindi, ed. Guest, p. 402.
(3) *Mughrib* of Ibn Sa'id, ed. Tallquist, transl., p. 118 foll.
(4) Muq., p. 388. There are still 5,000 of them there (Jackson *Persia*, p. 205).
(5) Misk. 4 408.
(6) See above, § 24.
(7) Biruni, *India*, transl. I, 206.
(8) Petrus ibn Rahib (Corpus scr. or Christ.) p. 132; Abu Salih, *Churches and Monasteries of Egypt*, ed Evetts, fol. 48 n.

money-changers of the Egyptian capital that in the year 362/973, in consequence of acts of insubordination on the part of the guild, the governor makes a special order that no Jew thenceforth should show himself without his Jewish badge (*ghiyar*)[1]. In the 5th/11th century Nasir Khosrau was told about a rich Cairene Jew Abu Sa'id, on the roof of whose house 300 trees stood in silver tubs.[2] In Babylonia we hear of two Jewish bankers, Yusuf ibn Finkhas and Harun ibn 'Imran of whom the vizier borrows 10,000 dinars (£5,000).[3] These two persons must have constituted a firm, since the vizier Ibn al-Furat, who was cashiered in 306/918, asserted that he had deposited with these two Jews 700,000 dinars (roughly £350,000).[4] Yusuf was banker (*jahbadk*) for Ahwaz, *i.e.* he advanced money to the government on the taxes due from Ahwas ; he lamented in the usual style that he had nothing and had to disburse so much![5] Together with a third, probably a Christian from his name Zakariyya ibn Yuhanna, these two Jews bore the title Court-banker (*jahbadh al-hadrah*), and had a right to the complimentary formula "God preserve thee," the lowest in use; it was allowed, *e.g.*, to the spies in the small post-offices.[6] Moreover the Jews who played the leading part in the carpet industry at Tustar, were not, as might be supposed, manufacturers, but bankers (*sayarif*).[7] In the second half of the 4th/10th century a governor of Baghdad, before decamping into the marshes, obtains the necessary cash from the Jews of the metropolis.[8] Hence it is not surprising

(1) Maqrizi, *Itti'az*, p. 87.
(2) Translation, p. 159 foll.
(3) V. Kremer, *Einnahmebudget der Abbasiden*, Dkschr, der Wiene Akademie, XXVI, 343.
(4) Arib, p. 74.
(5) *Wuzara*, p. 178.
(6) Ibid., p. 159. The Jewish sources mention Joseph ben Pinkhas and his son-in-law Metira among the most eminent Jews of Baghdad (Gratz *Geschichte der Juden*, ed. 4. V. 277).
(7) Misk. V. 408.
(8) Ibn al-Jauzi. Berlin. fol 150a

to find the Yiddish of the Bourse in Arabic : *Muballit* (German *pleite*) for the Arabic *muflis* (bankrupt).[1]

Beside Babylonians, Persians, and Jews, Greeks and Indians were the most active traders in the empire. The Greeks had infiltrated into its remotest regions; in the interior of Kirman there was a Greek colony settled in the market-town Jiruft[2]. On the other hand Armenian traders play no part anywhere; in Byzantine we find representatives of this nationality chiefly in high military officies[3] and it furnished the Fatimids with soldiers and generals,[4] among others the Emir al-Juyush, who ruled their state in the 5th/11th century.[5] A change seems only to have taken place in the Turkish period.

Trade, like industry, was grouped in the bazaars, where members of the same branch sat together. They stayed there till past midday, took their meal at the cookshop, or had something brought into the office: they did not go home till evening.[6] In Babylonia the innkeepers of the bazaars had a lavatory with mats, tables, mirrors, servants, tankards, dishes, and sofa on the first floor. On coming down a man had to pay one *daniq*, about three halfpence.[7] "Then we came to the cookship, where the gravy was dripping from the roast meat, and the bread was almost swimming in sauce.[8] I said: Cut a slice off this joint for Abu Zaid, hand

(1) *Taj al-Arus* s.v. *blt*.
(2) This is attested only for the 6th/12th century. Houtsma. *Seldschuken* I, 48, foll.
(3) Gelzer, *Byzantinische Kulturgeschichte*, p. 80.
(4) Maqrizi, *Khitat* I, 94 line 2af.
(5) Ibid, p. 381.
(6) The Baghdad banker in the above anecdote had finished business at noon (*Irshad* I, 399). In Hormuz, the chief port of Kirman, which like the Bender Abbas of our time is troubled with the most frightful climate in the world, the trader lived scattered over the country as far as 6 miles (Istakhri, p. 166).
(7) Muq., p. 129.
(8) The roast meat was laid out and served on toasted slices of bread,

him a portion of the sweet, choose one of those plates for him, spread thin slices of the finest wheaten bread over it, and pour over it some *summaq* water.—We sat down;—when we had done, I said to the confectioner:[1] Weigh out to Abu Zaid two pounds of almond-cake.—When we had finished that, I said: Abu Zaid, now we want iced water to reduce this burning; do you sit quiet, while I fetch a water-carrier, who will bring you a drink." The meal cost 20 (probably daniq) which would equal about 2/5.[2] Even in those times the innkeepers' cooking was deceptive: "The fraternity of the present time resembles the broth of the cook in the bazaars, fragrant, but tasteless."[3]

In Asia Minor and Egypt the shops everywhere lined the streets; the old Arabic word for this was *saff* (row). Even when Baghdad was founded no special market-places were laid out for this purpose; the "Quadrangle of Haitham" was a wonder.[4] Particular markets, at any rate at the time when they received their names, were held only on certain week days; thus the Tuesday Market in East Baghdad, the Thursday and Monday Markets in Qairawan.[5] In al-Askar (Khuzistan) the market was on Friday; between this place and Khan Tauq there were six towns, named after successive week days, on which they respectively held their markets.[6] Many a place of this sort is likely to have consisted in the main of permanent booths, which were only filled on market-day, like the Wednesday Market in Algeria, first

---

which to the Oriental palate are almost more important than the meat.

(1) Who then must have been present in the cookshop.

(2) Hamadhani Maq., ed Beirut p. 57 foll.

(3) At-Tauhidi, *fis-sadaqah*, Const. 1301, p. 48.

(4) *Ta'rikh Baghdad*, ed Salmon, p. 28.

(5) Muq., p. 225/6.

(6) Muq., p. 405/6. Likewise in the Moroccan Wadi Dra'. (Bekre ed. Slane, p. 152).

described by Prince Puckler,[1] or the great Market of Bau'an (Yaman); "imagine three or four rows of veritable kennels, with Arabs in them on market days, squatting and haggling."[2] In the East on the other hand the shops were by custom collected in great galleries, as in the centre of the Persian linen-trade, Kazerun, where the Buyid 'Adudeddaulah built one which brought the government 10,000 dirhems daily.[3] A bazaar of this sort, if intended to be handsome, had to painted, whitewashed, paved, and roofed.[4] The West on the other hand had halls only for foreign traders, who offered their goods for sale below, and lived in apartments above. They could fasten their rooms with "Greek-locks." These houses were called *funduq* (Greek *pandokeion*). There were also storehouses such as the water-melon-house in Basrah, whither all the fruit was brought.[5]

In Islam as elsewhere capital and luxury were closely connected; the richest traders and industrialists were those who were occupied with the provision of luxuries. Muqaddasi advises as follows: "If you want to know the quality of the water in a town, go to the dealers in cambric and spices, and examine their countenances. The more lively these are, the better is the drinking water. If you see cadaverous faces and hanging heads, leave the place as quickly as you can."[6] In the 4th/10th century these were the two most respected guilds. In the Persian town Ram Hormuz they sat with the dealers on mats in the handsomest

(1) Semilasso in *Africa*, II, 107.

(2) Glaser, Patermanns *Mitteilungen* 1886, p. 41.

(3) Muq., p. 433.

(4) Muq., pp 413, 425.

(5) Muq., p 425. Such buildings were called *khan* in Persia *tim* in Tansoxiana (Muq, p. 31); a single shop *makhzin* (magazine) a storehouse *khananabar*, plural *khananabarat* (Ibn al-Jauzi, fol. 180b, 182 a).

(6) p. 101.

bazaar of the place.[1] There was a proverb current in the 3rd (9th) century : The best trade is in cambric and the best industry that in coral.[2] Ibn Mushahid (ob. 324/935) was in the habit of saying ; The man who reads the Qur'an according to Abu 'Amr, follows Shafi'i in jurisprudence, deals in cambric, and knows the poems of Ibn al-Mu'tazz by heart, is the perfect gentleman."[3] Farabi (ob. 339/950) contrasted as the extremes of the high class and low class industries the cambric trade and weaving (which had been despised from ancient times), and trade in spices and street sweeping.[4] The richest trader in Egypt about 300/912 was the cambric merchant Sulaiman, out of whose estate the exchequer alone appropriated 100,000 dinars.[5] In Baghdad the bazaars of the dealers in spices, colourmen, silkmercers, and jewellers were situated side by side.[6]

The hire-system was enormously developed ; in the town people not only hired their dwelling houses, but their outfit also. A woman possessed 500 of the great copper cisterns which were in use in Cairo, and hired them out at a dirham a month.[7] At weddings the *coiffeuse* (*mashitah*) brought ornaments with her,[8] and carpets were hired for such occasions too.[9]

According to canon law a sale was conducted "hand in hand;"[10] modern jurists still hold that a sale is not valid

---

(1) Muq., p. 413.
(2) As usual this was supposed to be a saying of the Prophet. Ibn Qutaibah (*Mukhtalif al-hadith*, p. 90).
(3) Subki, *Tabaqat* II, 103.
(4) *Musterstaat*, ed. Dieterici, p. 65.
(5) Tallquist, p. 17.
(6) al-Suli, *Auraq*, p. 91.
(7) Nasir Khosrau, transl., p. 152.
(8) Quatremere, *Histoire des Mameloucs*, 247.
(9) *Agh.* v. 119.
(10) *Jami'saghir*, margin of Abu Yusuf, *Kitab al-kharaj*, p. 79.

without express declaration.[1] This is what I saw in the Syrian desert: During the bargaining one of the parties had his right hand in that of the other party, and only when the vendor said *bai'tu* (I have sold) and the purchaser *ishtaretu* (I have bought) did they leave go, and the business was done. In the story of the tradesman who sells his property to usurers Ibn al-Mu'tazz (ob. 296/909) does not forget to mention this oath of sale (*yamin al-bai'ah*).[2] Otherwise however in this vast empire, which embraced the most various stages of civilization, almost all forms of trading are likely to have existed simultaneously. Unfortunately the geographers of this particular time have no interest in the matter, and the jurists are occupied with their dry principles, so that we have few trustworthy notices. Barter unaccompanied by speech, in which each party in the absence of the other deposits and removes his goods, was practised at the extreme ends of the empire on the Niger, and in furthest Khorasan.[3] In Babylonia Rabbi Petakhyah was struck by what he saw: "The Muhammadans are very trustworthy. When a trader comes thither, takes his goods into a man's house and goes away, they take them to all the bazaars and offer them for sale. If people are willing to pay the price agreed on, well and good; if not, they show the goods to all the brokers. If they find that the valuation is low, they sell them off.[4] And this is all done most conscientiously."[5] Muhammadan law from the beginning most emphatically forbade usury, and likewise speculation in food-stuffs. It required much juristic effort to obstruct the smallest and narrowest loopholes whereby these rules could be evaded. Then Jews and Christians stepped into the breach. A vizier had to pay 30 per cent interest on a loan of 10,000 dinars to

(1) Sachau, *Muhammedanisches Recht.*, p. 278.
(2) Diwan i, 135.
(3) Mas. IV, 93; J. Marquart, *Beninsammlung*, p. CLXXXII.
(4) (The translator is not quite certain of the meaning here).
(5) J.A. 1831, p. 373.

Joseph ben Pinkhas and Aaron ben Amran.[1] A Christian lawbook of about 800 A.D. allows a Christian to pay as much as 22 per cent interest to another Christian.[2] A specially remunerative form of usury consisted in advancing money to victims of governmental confiscations and extortions who were in straitened circumstances; as much as 1,000 per cent could be earned in such cases.[3] But Muhammadan society also in the 4/10th century was far removed from the grandeur of the law. As early as the year 200/800 two financiers speculated on so vast a scale in the Babylonian harvest that they might have gained nearly 12,000,000 dirhems: at the last moment however there came a "slump", and they lost 66,000,000.[4] Besides this the peculiar conditions of agriculture necessitated more or less speculative contracts on the harvest, the threshing, and the date-harvest, which the learned senselessly only permit against a pledge given by the vendor.[5] According to Wansleb, in Egypt 1664 the laws against usury were as openly defied as amongst us; the borrower was forced to take goods of poor quality at enormous prices[6].

(1) See above in this §.
(2) Sachau, *Syrische Rechtsbacher*, II, 157.
(3) Ibn al-Mu'tazz, 136, Yaqut.
(4) *Irshad*, V, 458.
(5) Muhammad ibn al-Hasan, margin of Abu Yusuf, *Kitab al-kharaj*, p. 78.
(6) *Beschreibung Aegyptens*, p. 63.

XXVII. INLAND NAVIGATION

In the technique of communications the chief difference between the empire of the caliphs and medieval Europe is to be found in the paucity of waterways in the former. Muqaddasi (p. 19) can enumerate only twelve navigable rivers in the whole of the vast empire; the Tigris, the Euphrates, the Nile, the Oxus, the Jaxartes, Saihan, Jaihan, Baradan, the Indus, the Araxes, Nahr al-Malik, and the river of Ahwal.[1] Of these neither the three in Asia Minor (Saihan, Jaihan, Baradan), nor the two Caucasian (Nahr al-Malik and Araxes), nor the Indian frontier-river[2] can strictly be included in the territory of Islam, so that with the exception of the Nile only Mesopotamia with its appendage Khuzistan and the extreme North-east offer systems of inland navigation.

(1) This is probably in accordance with actual practice, although Istakhri (p. 99) enumerates in his native province Persis only "eleven great rivers, which carry vessels, if they are launched on them." The river of Afghanistan the Helmand, which has its sources in the Hindukush and the other Indo-Afghan mountains, was navigable only when the water was high (Ibn Hauqal, p. 301). Strabo (XV,1) talks of the Jordan having been navigated upstream by the Phoenicians. In the Middle Ages this no more happened than it does now, and only small vessles sailed on the Dead Sea between Zoar, Jericho, and other district of the Jordan depression (Edrisi, ed, Brandel, p. 4).

(2) "It takes 70 days' journey for the Kashmirians to get to Mansurah. They sail down the Indus, where the water is highest at the same time as in the Tigris and the Euphrates. They pack cuscess roots in sacks, each of which contains from 700 to 800 pounds, insert these sacks in skins, which they smear with pitch so as to render them watertight and tie them together in pairs, so that they can stand or sit upon them. In 47 days they reach the port of Mansurah, no damp having reached the roots " (*Merv. de l' Inde*, p. 104). Apparently the 47 days refers to the distance from the mouth of the Indus (Transl.)

And of these northern Mesopotamia offer serious difficulties to such navigation, at any rate on the chief streams. One of the best explorers of the country observes that "in Ferghanah the Syr (Jaxartes cannot carry even a fishing boat."[1] Both the level of the water and the beds of the Oxus and the Jaxartes change so constantly and so seriously that the Russian steam navigation on the former has been stopped, and has the greatest difficulty in maintaining itself on the latter. "No vessel, however light, can negotiate the current at Kilif (middle course of the Oxus) when the water is high."[2] On account of the irregularity of the currents and the numerous sandbanks not one of the towns on the Oxus was built like Baghdad or Wasit on both sides of the river, with the exception of this Kilif.[3] Still, navigation was practised everywhere on the tributaries and main canals.[4] There are no lakes worthy of consideration for extended voyages, although the greatest, the Lake of Urmia, is some ten times the size of the Lake of Constance, and the Dead Sea twice the size. Thus Syria, Arabia, and Persia come between the systems mentioned above, being vast tracts wherein inland navigation is impossible. This was the case no less in the Middle Ages than now. On the other hand the conditions of Babylonia are exceptionally favourable for inland navigation, owing to the fact that the level of the Euphrates is somewhat higher than that of the Trigris, so that vessels are easily carried eastward on the canals which are derived from the former, and can without serious difficulty be propelled westward. In the 4th/10th century full advantage was taken of this convenience. A number of the most diverse forms of river-craft (of which a short list is given by Abul-Qasim, ed. Mez., p. 107, to which must be

(1) V. Middendorf, *Memoires de l' Academie de St. Petersbourg* VII vol. 29, p. 189.

(2) Von Schwarz *Turkestan*, p. 425.

(3) Muq., p. 291.

(4) Istakhri, p. 301, foll.

added in the 4th/10th century the "flier" *tayyar*, and the *hadidi*, pl. *hadidiyyat*, which *e.g.*, waits before the door of the Babylonian governor)[1] sailed about Irak; the noise made by the boatmen constitutes together with the creaking of the water-elevators the sound that is most characteristic of the national civilization. In the "twenties" of this century the general Ibn Ra'iq said: "To sail in a flier on the Tigris, and hear the cries of the boatmen is dearer to me than dominion over all Syria"[2]—a sentiment of home-sickness for which he paid with his life. The Euphrates, which is navigable from Samosata, served for the conveyance of goods between Syria and Baghdad, but passenger traffic despised the canals. A magnate travels from Damascus to Jisr Manbij, where he embarks on the Euphrates for the metropolis; visitors come out to meet him at er-Rahbah, then at Hit and finally at Anbar; here he takes to horse-back.[3] According to this, for speedy travel Anber corresponds with the modern Felujah, near which it lay; there as now, there was a bridges of boats over the Euphrates.[4] The distance from Baghdad is 12 parasangs.[5] There too the canal leading from the Euphrates to Baghdad started.[6] It should be added that in those days the course of the upper Euphrates was also different from the present; not only Hadithah but Anah and Alosah were on island.[7]

Goods carried in bulk on the Euphrates were timber from the Armenian mountains, and olive oil from Syria, which were floated down on rafts, further pomegranates, which rolled through the country on the mighty *qerqurs*,

---

(1) Misk, VI, 44, 57, 111,
(2) Tallquist, p. 29.
(3) *Wuzara*, P. 310.
(4) *e.g.* for the 4th century, Ibn al-Athir, VIII, 125.
(5) Ibn Khordadbeh, p. 72.
(6) Abulfeda, *Geography* p. 52; "At Anbar, on an estate called al-Felujah, the Nahr Isa starts."
(7) Mas III, 40, where the test has incorrectly *Tausah*.

mentioned as early as by Herodotus and Livy as Mediterranean craft.[1] They had a breadth of from 60 to 20 yards. Canal traffic flourished most luxuriantly in the neighbourhood of Basrah, where the old chronicles talk of 120,000 navigable brooks. Ibn Hauqal thought this an exaggeration, but afterwards admitted its possibility, when he had seen there within the distance of an arroshot a great number of brooks whereon vessels lay. For a length of two days' journey a continuous series of canals extended from the city to the sea, with palm groves, villas, and places of entertainment. Most of these channels held sea water, and at ebb the greater number of the Basran canals were empty.[2] Traffic was also in full swing on the Tigris; Armenian goods came through Mosul, which besides supplied Baghdad with the vegetables and fruit of its mild climate.[3] Even the pilgrims from the north came by water; in the year 348/959 "a thousand" of them, who were sailing down the Tigris in ten large boats, (*zauraq*) were drowned.[4] Baghdad itself was a sort of Venice; "the people in Baghdad come, go, and cross by water; two-thirds of the property of Baghdad lie in the river."[5] Barges could put in at several of the bazaars, and at every moment the narrow streets had to cross the water on tall arches of masonry. At the beginning of the 4th/10th century there were counted 30,000 boats employed in passenger and goods transport; the ferrymen's guild had to pay duty daily on earnings amounting to 90,000 dirhems. These public conveyances were neither in form nor in name identical with the round *guffahs* in use now; they were called *sumairiyyat*[6] "vessels of the people of Sumaira."[7] The

(1) *Wuzara*, p. 257.
(2) Ibn Hauqal, p. 158.
(3) Muq., p. 138.
(4) Misk VI. 234.
(5) Muq., p. 124.
(6) Shabushti, *Kitab ed-diyarat*, fol. 17 a, 26 b; *Kitab Baghdad*, ed. Salmon fol. 36 b; *Sumairiyyat ma' baraniyyat*.
(7) According to Dozy the word is a corruption of the Greek *sellarion* (Transl).

sum given is likely to be correct; even in these days a ferryman (*juffaji*) often earns a Mejidi (between four and five dirhams).[1] The court alone disbursed 500 dinars every month in payment for its boatmen.[2] Besides these a vast number of private craft were afloat; the wealthy citizen of Baghdad was obliged to have an ass in his stable and his flier (*tayyar*) on the river. The river played a dominant part in the social intercourse of the great world. About 200/800 the Caliph Amin had six pleasure boats (*harraqat* "burners") built in the shape of a lion, elephant, eagle, horse, dolphin, and snake.[3] In the year 333/944 the state "flier" of the Caliph was called the Gazelle.[4] The remains of the Caliph al-Radi were carried to their resting place in a gondola in the year 329/941.[5] After the defeat of the great Dailemite rebellion in the year 345/956 Mu'izz-ed-daulah sailed through the city in his boat with the captured ringleaders following behind; the populace stood on the bank, showering blessings on him and curses on the others.[6] In the year 364/974 a meeting took place on the water between the prince 'Adud-ed-daulah and the Caliph: "all the world was there in skiffs and gondolas; once could go from one bank to the other on the craft."[7] When in the year 377/987 the prince Sharaf-ed-daulah sailed for his coronation by the Caliph, tents were pitched on the banks of the Tigris, and the houses on both sides of the river splendidly decorated.[8]

In order to render passage possible, the bridges on boats in Baghdad had on their eastern side two movable pontoons

(1) *Mashriq*, IV, 992.
(2) *Wusara*, p. 19.
(3) Tabari, III, 952 foll. attested by a poem of the contemporary Abu Nuwas.
(4) Mas. VIII, 377.
(5) *Kitab al-uyun wal hadda'iq*, III, Berlin, foll, 183 b.
(6) Misk VI, 218.
(7) Ibn al-Athir, VIII, 477.
(8) Ibn al-Jauzi, Berlin, fol. 125 a.

(*zanbariyyat*), which could be drawn out.[1] The bridges of boats at Wasit had such passages on both sides.[2] A peculiar method was employed on the Tigris for towing vessels upstream. A long hawser was secured at some point upstream, the men engaged in towing stood on the vessels itself, having over their shoulders a noose[3] attached to the hawser, just as on Assyrian representations heavy loads were dragged on land. The men in front steadily pulled at the hawser till the whole of it was piled in neat circles on deck. The operation was naturally accompanied by incessant singing. Between Samarra and Baghdad, near the little town 'Alth, there was a difficult place, called al-Abwab "the Gates," where the river dashed down a rift between rocks. Vessels had to anchor there and hire a pilot (*hadi*). The pilot kept his hand on the tiller till the vessel had got through.[4] It was in South Babylonia that shipping was faced with the most serious obstacle which interfered with the navigation of the Tigris during the whole of the Arabian period. Between Wasit and Basrah cargo had to be transhipped to small boats, as the Tigris divided here, and entered the region of the marshes (*Bata'ik*). Here there were only isolated channels in which the boats seemed to be gliding through lanes of reeds, with only an occasional glimpse of clear water. Along these lanes huts were erected on reed mats each holding five men, whose buisness it was to see to the safety of traffic on these fantastic waters. Their guard-houses were circular beehives, without windows, since only thus could they protect themselves from the terrible plague of midges.[5]

In spite of vigilance Babylonia below Baghdad was by no means safe during the whole of the century. The robbers were mainly Kurds; in the year 328/940 as important a

(1) Ibn Abi Usaibiah I, 179; Gildemeister, NGGW 1882 p. 439.
(2) Muq., p. 118.
(3) *Qamaya*, Abulqasim, p. 108; not in the Dictionaries.
(4) Shabushti, *Kitab ad-diyarat*, fol. 38 b.
(5) Ibn Rusteh, p. 135.

personage as the Prince Bajkam was killed by Kurdish robbers near Wasit where he was hunting.[1] Khwarizmi uses "the Kurd attacking the pilgrim "quite as a proverbial phrase.[2] In the later 4th/10th century there is special mention of a Kurdish chieftain Ibn Mardan, who embushed the vessels, and secured ample plunder, although the vessels usually went in fleets — whole caravans of vessels (*kar*).[3]

Another famous robber chief of the 4th/10th century was Ibn Ḥamdun, who carried on his operations between Baghdad and Wasit. He was a romantic Rinaldo Rinaldini, chivalrous and generous towards the poor, and only fleecing the rich;[4] his splendid career became proverbial.[5] A robber king of the Marshed, 'Imran b. Shahun, rose to political importance. He demanded payment by the government officials for the convoy which he provided, and defeated Muhallabi, the vizier of the mighty prince Mu'izz-ed-daulah. There was nothing that the vizier could do but nominate him viceroy of the Marshes in the year 339/950.[6]

On one occasion the pirates attacked a very exalted company who were going downstream to meet a maganate. The company contained the vizier, and the two heads of the house of 'Ali er-Radi and el-Murtada. Attacking them from their *harraqat* ("burners", a sort of rivercraft) the pirates shouted: "Out with the cuckolds!" which gave the Caliph's secretary, who was one of the company, the opportunity for the witticism: "They must have spied upon us, else how could they know that our wives were unfaithful?"[7]

---

(1) Yahya b. Sa'id, fol. 85. a.
(2) *Rasa'il* p. 79.
(3) Ibn al-Hajjaj, *Diwan*, London, fol. 170 a; X, p. 218; *Kitab al-Faraj*, II, 107.
(4) et-Tanukhi, *al-Faraj ba'd esh-shiddah*, II, p. 108.
(5) Tha'albi, *Umad al-mansub*, ZDMG. VIII, p. 306.
(6) Misk. VI, 171, fol : Ibn al-Athir, V.II, 362, 368 foll.
(7) Yaqut, *Irshad* I, 235.

Still more serious damage was done to the inland commercial navigation by the official highwaymen, especially the Hamdanids in Aleppo, who were distinguished not only for their chivalry, but still more by their inordinately stupid system of taxation. The most famous prince of this house, Saif-ẹd-daulah, utterly ruined the chief inland port of Syria, Balis at the bend of the Euphrates, by the heavy transit duties which he imposed. In the space of a few months he is said to have extorted about a million dinars from traders who had their barges there laden with wheat and their rafts with oil.[1] In Babylonia also inland duties were imposed. About the year 300/912 duties were levied at two points between Baghdad and Basrah;[2] at night the river was closed by the tax-collectors. "On both banks of the Trigris two ships were tied together and made fast to the bank, and ropes stretched across the water, with their ends fastened to the ships so that nothing could pass.[3]

Navigation on the Nile was in such volume in the 4th/10th century that Muqaddasi was astounded by the numbers of the vessels which were at anchor or sailing at the wharf of Old Cairo. "An Egyptian asked me: Whence art thou?__ From Jerusalem, I replied.—A great city that, he said, but my friend, God prosper you? if all the vessels which sail hence to distant countries and to the Egyptian villages were to come to Jerusalem, they could remove its inhabitants, with their goods and chattels, and the stone and timber of the houses, so that people would say: Once there was a city here!"[4] The point at which the continuous navigation of the Nile ceased was also the point at which Egypt ended.[5]

(1) Ibn Hauqal, p. 119.
(2) Ibn Rusteh, p. 184.
(3) Ibn Rusteh, p. 185.
(4) Muq., p. 198.
(5) Mas, III, 40; Abdallah b. Sulaim (end of the 4th/10th century, cited by Maqrizi ; see Marquart *Dic Beninsammlung*, p. CCLXIX).

Asuan was the great mart for the Sudan trade was carried on not, as might be supposed, by Egyptians making their way to Nubia—trading was never a special characteristic of the inhabitants of the valley of the Nile,—but by Nibian traders from the Sudan, who disembarked their goods above the cataracts, and conveyed them on camels for twelve days by the side of the river.[1] The region south of the second cataract was strictly closed to all strangers, a measure which goes back to the history of ancient Egypt.

(1) Edrisi, p. 20/21.

XXVIII. COMMUNICATION BY ROAD

The Arab domination was not favourable to the development of road-making. The Arabs are a race of riders with no taste for military roads or vehicular traffic. They were so unaccustomed to vehicles that when chess was taken over from India the figure of the "chariot" *ratha* was not understood, and became a "rook"[1] The Tartars were the first to drive vehicles in the North.[2] Roads had indeed been constructed in a small part of Arabia by the Roman infantry but all that remained of them was the word "Street" *sirat* in devotional language, the very rare word *iter* "route,"[3] and a few milestones. The style of the "royal road" was like its name taken over from the Persian "king's highway."[4] It was probably what it is now, a more or less broad congeries of trodden paths and tracks. We hear little of any sort of upkeep of the roads; Egypt furnished 10,000 dinars annually for the highroad which followed the course of the Nile;[5] the pass between Ailah and the desert et-Tih, which was so steep as to be almost impassable for a rider, was levelled by the Tulunid Khumarwaihi, who in other ways showed some understanding for traffic, in the 3/9th century:[6] At the end

(1) This statement is infelicitous on more than one ground. In the first place *rukhkh* is not an Arabic, but a Persian word; in the second there is evidence that it bore the sense "chariot" in both Persian and Arabic. See H.J.R. Murray, *A History of Chess*, Oxford, 1913 pp. 159, 160 (Translator's note).

(2) Marco Polo, I. 48.

(3) Hamdani 183; *aitar* are the "ropes" *hibal* of a road (The "rope" in this context means "a long and elevated tract of sand". The indentification with *iter* seems hazardous. Translator's note).

(4) Information given by Hamdani ibid; "the Arabs called it *mulaiki*,' to which he gives a false etymology.

(5) Nasir Khosrau, p. 118.

(6) Maqrizi, I. 213.

of the 4th/10th century Subuktegin constructed in Southern Afghanistan the roads whereby his eminent son Mahmud afterwards penetrated into India.[1] Chenghiz Khan had military roads on a great scale constructed through the Alps of Central Asia, in this as in other ways resembling Napoleon; one of these pierced the gorges of the Tien-Shan south of the Lake Sairam; it had forty wooden bridges on which two vehicles could be driven side by side.[2] In most cases attention was confined to policing, to the provision of inns, or at the least to the provision of water. Thus there was a dome with a tank of water for every 12 of 18 kilometers (2 or 3 parasangs) on the shortest road through the desert of Eastern Persia.[3] By the Lake of Van in Armenia Nasir Khosrau found the path indicated by posts driven into the soil, serving as guides in snowy or foggy weather.[4] In the salt marshes of North Africa also the road was indicated by post:[5] The hostelries on desert roads were pious foundations; they were to be found most frequently in the religious Turkestan, which counted more than 10,000 of such hostels; in many of these the needy traveller was given fodder for his beast and nourishment for himself.[6] In general the East was more hospitable than the West. A Persian landowner on a large scale maintained hostels of his estates, endowed with a hundred or more cows, whose milk was freely offered to wanderers; even the Persian villages elected a *jazir*, whose duty it was to regulate hospitality within the

(1) Biruni, *India*, transl. Sachau I. 22.

(2) Journey of Chang Chun in the year 1221 ; Bretschneider, *Mediaeval Researches* I. 89.

(3) Istakhri. p. 197 ; Nasir Khosrau 256.

(4) p. 22.

(5) Bekri ed. Slane p. 48. In these days the "road" (as it is called) from Yezd to Tebes through the Persia salt desert is marked out with five stone pyramids, erected by Parsees of Yezd. Seven Hedin *Zu Land nack Indien* II, 6. In these regions stone pillars stand at the crossings of main roads, ibid. II 36.

(6) Istakhri. p. 290.

community, and assign strangers to the inhabitants.[1] In Khuzistan buckets of water, which often had to be fetched from a distance, were placed along the road at intervals of one parasang.[2] The monasteries practised lavish hospitality in the countries which had formerly been Christian; travellers' of importance regularly alighted at these.[3] The monastery of St. John near Takrit on the Tigris as also Ba'arba further north had special buildings for the entertainment of travellers.[4] It is only in what was formerly Persian territory that we hear of hospices in the town; thus there was a *Shebistan* "Night-house" in Nisabur, and another in Shiraz, whereas there were in Egypt no hostels nor inns before the time of the Ayyubids (period of the later Crusades).[5] Still in the wild and unsafe regions of the West there were foundations providing lodging and protection, whither "charity flowed from all countries."[6]

In the time of Sasanids there had been permanent bridges over the Tigris ; in the 4th/10th century Ibn Hauqal professes to have seen the remains of a bridge of brickwork near Takrit,[7] and the handsome arch of such a structure is still standing near Jazirah.[8] In the 4th/10th century all these fell to pieces, and were replaced by bridges of boats (*jisr*), some of them movable, as in Baghdad and Wasit. Such were not however very numerous; indeed in the North they are said to have been unknown ; at the commencement of the 5th/11th century Mahmud crossed the Oxus with an army

(1) *Fihrist*, p. 343.
(2) Muq., p. 418.
(3) Shabushti, fol. 95 b. 113 a.
(4) Shabushti quoted by Streck, *Landschaft Babylonien*, p. 179; Yaqut II, 645.
(5) Qalqashandi, transl. Wustenfeld, p. 82.
(6) Ibn Hauqal, p. 49.
(7) p. 168.
(8) Photograph ap Hugo Grothe *Geographische Charakterbilder aus der asiatischen Turkei*.

against the Turks "on a bridge of boats, fastened together with chains. This was the first time that a bridge of this sort had been seen in these regions."[1] The Chinese traveller Chan-Chung found a similar bridge over the Jaxartes at a later period, in the year 1221.[2] A permanent bridge with five "doors" one large and four small, led across the 'Isa canal at the point where it branched off from the Euphrates.[3] At the end of the 3rd/9th century the width of the large "door" was fixed at 22 yards, that of the small "doors" each at 8 yards, after it had been ascertained that so even the largest vessels could pass through. In Kuzistan the bridge of Dizful, east of the ancient Susa, was 320 paces long and 15 broad, and was built on 72 arches. Ibn Serapion calls it the Bridge of the Romans.[4] In Ahwaz there was the "Indian Bridge," built of brick, with a mosque erected on it ;[5] and over the upper Qarun was the bridge of Idhaj, spanning the stream at a height of 150 yards in a single arch of stone, held together with iron clamps. At the end of the 4th/10th century it was repaired at a cost of 150,000 dinars.[6] The specimen of European bridge building which won most admiration in the whole Muhammadan empire was the bridge erected by the Emperor Vespasian over the Geuk Su, a tributary of the Euphrates, near Samosata. It was regarded as one of the wonder of the World, because it "soared high above a ravine in a single arch of masonry, each stone being ten yards long and five high."[7] The most

---

(1) Ibn al-Athju IX, 210.

(2) *Bretschneider, Med. Res.* I. 75.

(3) *Wuzara*, p. 257.

(4) Le Strange, p. 239.

(5) Muq., p. 411.

(6) Yaqut, s. v.

(7) Tha'alibi, *Umad el-mansub* ZDMG, VIII. 524 foll. ; Istakhri 62; Mas'udi, *Tanbih* 64, 144 ; Muq., p. 147 ; see Le Strange *Lands of the Eastern Caliphate*, p. 124 note. It was noticed as important as early as in the Roman Itineraries, Tab Peut : *ad pontem Singe*. Miller *Itin. Romana*, p. 756.

important wooden bridge appears to have been that over the Tab, the stream which formed the boundary between Khuzistan and Fars; it rose some ten yards above the water. Finally, a single author of the 4th/10th century admires a bridge which soars from one mountain to another near Chotan in Turkestan; it was not, he says, built by the Chinese.[1]

I cannot say how old is the type of ferry which I saw on the Khabur in Mesopotamia in which the ferryman pulls with his hand at a rope stretched across the river. This method is also in use in the Tarim basin.[2]

The post (*berid*) is a very ancient invention; in any case it owes its development to the intensified consolidation of the great empire of the Nearer East by Darius I.[3] Almost the whole of the nomenclature connected with the post under the Caliphs is still Persian : *furani*[4] or *faij*[5] or *shakiri*[6] "postillion," *askudar* "docket," containing a register of the number of post-bags and letters, as well as times of arrival and departure at the different stations. It would seem that the post was invented at some definite point, as the Byzantine, the Muhammadan, and the Chinese posts all docked the tails of their beasts as a special badge. Only the Byzantines used horses for the post,[7] as was also the practice of the pagan kings of Arabia;[8] the Chinese and

(1) al-Mutahhar, ed. Huart, IV, 87.
(2) Sven Hedin, *Durch Asiens Wusten*, II, 152.
(3) The Arabic tradition agrees (Maqrizi, *Khitat* I, 229).
(4) This word occurs as early as in Imrulqais (Ahlwardt, *Six Divans*, p. 130, line 27).
(5) Properly "pedestrian" ; the root *ped* is the source of the word. An Indian form *batdk* occurs *Merv. de l' Inde*, p. 106.
(6) Properly "hunter." Attested by Khwarizmi, *Rasa'il*, p. 53 for the fourth century.
(7) Ibn Khordadbeh, p. 112.
(8) Mubarrad, *Kamil*, Cairo, 1308, I, 286.

Muhammadan[1] posts employed mules.[2] West of the Euphrates the Caliphs post reckoned by miles, but in the East by parasangs (*farsakh*).[3] For the milestone there is only the Roman name *mil*, used even in places where Rome never ruled.[4] The Persian post does not appear to have used the term.[5] On the other hand in both havles of the empire there were stations (*sikak*) with relays of mules or riders at uniform distances of 6 miles or 2 parasangs.[6] The postillions themselves rode the whole way; in the year 326/937 there is a notice of one who accompanied the post-bag the vast distance between Baghdad and Meccah.[7] In the East and the West there was international exchange ; the Turkish post (*berid et-Turk*) went as far as the Chinese frontier;[8] that of Asia Minor, which had a station every three miles, as far as Constantinople.[9]

---

(1) This appears not to be quite correct. In the papyri orders for the use of such beasts call them *dabbah*, which normally means "horse", and in the account of the *barid* in the *Fakhri* horses are specially mentioned. (Translator's note).

(2) *Silsilat et-tawarikh*, p. 113. The docking as a badge is pre-Islamic (Ahlwardt, *Six Divans*. p. 138, line 28). Hamza al-Isfahani (ob. between 350/961 and 360/970) derives the world *berid* "post" from the Persian *berideh dhanab* "docktailed" (*Annales*, ed. Gottwaldt p. 39) which is copied by Tha'alibi, *Rois des Perses*, ed Zotenbers, p. 398).

(3) The parasang was regarded as equivalent, to three miles, Ibn Khordadbeh, p. 83; Muq., p. 65; Mutahhar ed. Huart, IV 85.

(4) e.g., in South Arabia Qudamah p. 190; in East Persia, Ibn Rusteh, p. 168.

(5) In India from remote antiquity there had been pillars at every 10 stages, indicating by roads and distances (Strabo XV. 1).

(6) *Mafatih al'Ulum* p. 63. Muq., p. 66. According to the latter passage the stations were at distances of 12 miles 4 parasangs in desert and in Babylonia. This does not agree with Rudamah for Babylonia. The extension of the distance between the stations must have taken place in any case in the latest-period, when Babylonia became a desert. A post-book of the 3rd/9th century gives the number of all stations together as 930 (Ibn Khordabeh, p. 153.)

(7) Al-Suli, *Auraq* Paris, p. 136.

(8) Ibn Khordadbeh, p. 29.

(9) Ibn Hauqal, p. 130.

The following were the chief post-roads:

1. Up the Tigris from Baghdad to Mosul, Beled,[1] then through Mesopotamia passing Sinjar, Nisibis, Ras'Ain, Haqqah, Menbij, Aleppo, Hamat, Hims, Baalbek, Damascus, Tiberias, Ramleh, Gifar, Cairo, Alexandria, and then on to the Cyrenaica.[2]

2. From Baghdad to Syria on the western[3] bank of the Euphrates, which was reached at Anbar. At Hit it crossed to the western bank of the Euphrates. The traffic was enormous: in the year 306/918 the ferry at Hit brought the government an income of 80, 250 dinars.[4]

There is no mention in the books of routes of the road Damascus to Der via Palmyra, which was of importance in antiquity, and occasionally traversed in our time, being protected by guard-houses—not even in Muqaddasi, who gives a detailed list of roads of the Syrian desert. Neither was there at that time in existence the camel post between Baghdad and Damascus which in these days functions with such regularity. Still the road from Hit to Damacus which it follows, as being the shortest route from Baghdad to Syria, was traversed by occasional riders. In such cases convoy (*Khufara*) of Bedouins was provided by the official at Hit.[5]

3. The chief road to the East went behind Baghdad crossing the Nahrawan Bridge, mounted behind Hulwan

(1) The direct and magnificent desert road Ktesiphon-Hatra-Harran, as given in the Tabula Peutingerana, had long been deserted.

(2) Qudamah, p. 227 foll.

(3) In ancient times the road mounted on the Eastern bank of the Euphrates (Tab. Peut)

(4) V. Kremer *Ueber das Einnahmebudget des Abbasidenreiches, Denkschriften der Wiener Akademic*, vol. XXXVI, p. 307.

(5) Tanukhi, *Kitab al-Faraj*, II. 76. Others brached off higher up on the Euphrates, and made the circuit round Rusafah in order to reach Damascus; in the year 440/1048. Ibn Botlan did this to get to Aleppo (Ibn al-Qifti, p. 295). In this road too there was danger of plunder by Bedouins (*Kitab al-Faraj* II, 109).

the ancient Media by a famous staircase, and still mounting behind Asadabad reached the height of Hamdan. In the middle of the pass dates and cheese were for sale.[1] The road is marked on ancient maps, and was certainly that followed by the Persian kings between their winter residence in Babylonia and their summer residence which was high up in Ecbatana. Thence the road proceeded to Rai (not far from the modern Teheran), Nisabur, Merv, Bukhara, Samarcand, which already possessed a "Chinese Gate."[2]

Continuation through the frontier region between Turkestan and China depended on the security of the road, which was very unstable. During the whole of the earlier period of Islam, and even in the 4th/10th century, the nearest road, which went through Fergana and the Tarim basin, had been favoured by the Chinese in the 8th century A.D.[3] and was afterwards followed by Marco Polo, was disliked: at any rate there is no mention of it anywhere. Even from Uzkend in Upper Fergana no use was made of the Alai passes, as might have been expected; instead, people proceeded through the pass of Atbas or Tabas, "up a steep ascent, unpassable in snowy weather," to Barshan, which lies to the south-west of the Issyk Lake.[4] Here it made a

(1) Ibn Rusteh, p. 167.

(2) Muq., p. 278.

(3) Richthofen, *China*, I, 456.

(4) The pronunciation and situation of this place are now at last settled by Gurdezi (ed. Barthold, p. 89 foll.) The statement of Qudamah (p 208) that the pass of Atbash lies between Tibet, Fergana, and Nushajan, is probably the chief source of de Goeje's view that Nushajan was the country round Chotan (*De Muur von Gog en Nagog, Versl. der Amsterd. Akad*, 1888, p. 114). But even so the statement does not agree, since the road to the pass of Ush through Uzkend clearly diverges to the north. The solution of the difficulties is to be found in the fact that at that time the Tarim basin was still reckoned as belonging to Tibet, *e.g.*, by the traveller Abu Dulaf (Yaqut III. 447) ; in the work of Mutahhar (ed. Huart, IV) Chotan is actually called the capital of Tibet. This agrees also with Chinese

junction with the road Samarcand, China, which led to Barshan by a wide arc, through Shash (Tashkent), Taraz (Aulie-ata), and Birki (Merka).[1] The continuation is thus defined by the *Zein-el-Akhbar* of Gurdezi (written about 1050 A.D.) : People proceeded through Penchul to Kucha in the Tarim basin, and then eastward as far as Chinancheket at the frontier of China.[2] As early as about the year 630 A.D. this route was taken by the Chinese Hsuen-Tsang, who travelled from Kucha through Paluqia (doubtless indentical with Gurdezi's Pechul, and probably the modern Aqsu) to the Issyq lake.[3] Even in these days the main traffic of the middle of the Tarim basin with Tashkent goes over Asqu, the Bedel pass, Qaraqol, Pishjek, Aulie-ata.[4] We cannot unfortunately make out how Sellam travelled in the 3rd/9th century, or Abu Dulaf in the 4th/10th.[5] From the passage in Mas'udi where he states that "he had made the acquaintance of many travellers to China and learned that the road to China from Khorasan through Sogdiana traverses the mountains which yield sal-ammoniac" it is to be inferred that in the 4th/10th century the China road was the same as that mentioned by Hsuen-Tsang and Gurdezi; for according

sources; as early as the 8th century A.D. towns between the Altyn and Tien Shan paid tribute to Tibet (JA, 1900, vol, xv.p.24). which retained possession of them for the greater part of the 9th century and only then lost them to the Uigours and Kharluk Turks (JRAS 1898, p. 814). Eastern Turkestan is also assigned to Tibet in the statement of Ibn Khordadbeh (p. 30): "Atbash lies on lofty plateau between Tibet and Fergana, " Edrisi (ed. Jaubert I, 490) calls Chotan (about the year 550/1150) "the capital of Tibet." and a final argument against de Goeje's identification of Chotan with Nushajan is to be found in the fact that Biruni as well as Gurdezi and Sam'ani (ob. 562/1167) cited by Abulfeda (*Geogr*, ed. Reinaud, p. 505) call Chotan by its present name.

(1) Ibn Khordadbeh 28 foll. ; Qudamah 204 foll. ; Muq., p. 341.

(2) Ed. Barthold, p. 91.

(3) Richthofen, *China*, I. 540.

(4) Sven Hedin *Durch Asiens Wusten* I, 466.

(5) de Goeje, *de Muur van Gog en Magog*; Marquart, *Osteuropaische Streifzuge* p. 74 foll.

to Chinese statements these mountains are in Tien-tsan north of Kucha.[1] Not till a hundred years later, about 550/1155, does Edrisi, the first Arabic writer to do so, describe the road from Fergana over the Pamirs to the Tarim basin;[2] this is probably to be connected with the fact that at the end of the 4/10th century the Bogra princes conquered western Turkestan, and transferred their residence to Kashgar in eastern Turkestan, so that traffic had again to turn in the direction of the Pamir passes.

In Merv the post-road branches off through central Khorasan. It does not go directly to Balkh, but makes the tremendous circuit of 300 kilometers along the Merv river to Merv er-rud precisely as at the time of the Tabula Peutingerana. A parasang further there begins the mountain range, in which the road made use of a ravine as far as Talaqan. Beyond Balkh it crosses the Oxus near Tirmid, and enters Fergana at Rasht.[3]

The road which crosses Iran diagonally, from Shiraz through Yezd to Nisabur, is still noticed by Ibn Khordadbeh, p. 50, but is not found in Ibn Rusteh or Qudamah. In any case this is connected with the disturbances in the Persian East, which enabled robbers and highwaymen to become powerful in the great desert between Yezd and Tabas. 'Adudeddaulah (ob.372/982) first restored order in this region; after his time every governor of Fars regularly held hostages of these robbers, who were from time to time replaced by others, so that caravans travelling under government escort could pass through without danger. About the middle of the 4/10th century he had a guardhouse built there with an aqueduct of sweet water; Muqaddasi saw

---

(1) Richthofen *China* 7. 560. Wang-yen-te, who travelled in 981-983 (*Journal asiatique* 1847, I. 63) similarly.

(2) Richthofen, *China* I. 562.

(3) Ya'qubi, *Kitab al-Buldan* p. 287; Qudamah 209 foll.

no finer building of the kind in all the regions of Persia; it was constructed of masonry and plaster like the fortresses of Syria.[1] However the road was not improved, for Muqaddasi; who meant to travel from Tabas to Yezd, required 70 days for a distance which had been calculated by Ibn Khordadbeh at 68 parasangs; his caravan had missed the way. According to him the predatory Qufs, who infest the region are wild of face and hard of heart; they are not satisfied with money, but slaughter any one on whom they lay hands in the style wherein people put snakes to death. They hold the man's head down on a slab of stone, and hurl stones at it till it is smashed."[2]

The pilgrim-road from Baghdad crossed the Euphrates at Kufah, and entered the desert at al-'Udhaib.[3] In spite of its terrible remoteness Meccah at the season of the pilgrimage attracted the greatest concourse of the whole Muhammadan world. It was not only the pious act of pilgrimage which allured them; another attraction was the relative safety of the vast caravans of pilgrims, who converged thither from all directions. In the year 331/943 many traders of Baghdad emigrated with the pilgrim caravan to Syria and Egypt, owing to severe oppression by the government of Babylonia.[4] Conversely in the year 335/946 many Syrians wishing to flee from the Byzantines attached themselves to the pilgrim caravan and made the tremendous circuit through Meccah; among these was the Qadi of Tarsus, who had 20,000 dinars on him.[5]

---

(1) In the year 1881 and in 1892 some private individuals of Yezd built a magnificent edifice for wanderers at the point where the roads Teheran-Tebes and Yezd-Tebes cross and to the north of it (Sven Hedin, *Zu Land Nach Indien* II, 37 Foll.)

(2) Muq., p. 488 foll.

(3) Qudamah, p. 186,

(4) Ibn al-Jauzi, fol. 71 a.

(5) Abu 'lmahasin, I, 174.

In North Africa in the 3rd/9th century most of the roads led in the direction of Qairawan. At that time the competent Aglabite dynasty had introduced order, and bestowed special attention to the roads. Along the whole coast there were guard-houses, and communication was safe.[1] Two great roads left Lower Egypt for the west; one along the seacoast (as in antiquity), the other further to the south. At first the post followed the latter (*tariqessikkah*), then turned towards Tripoli, thence made directly for Qairawan, and then proceeded along the coast. The miles were marked; from Qairawan to Sus al-Adna on the Atlantic Ocean a distance of 2,150 miles.[2] This was the great highroad communicating between Spain and the East.[3] A south road led through the oases Dakhil and Kufrah[4] to the western Sudan, going to Ganah and Audagusht. In the 4th/10th century it was deserted owing to sandstroms and raids.[5]

The post was for the government; it "ran for the 'Abbasids,"[6] and being so cumbrous had to serve for the conveyance of passengers only in the most urgent cases.[7] Besides letters it accepted other more or less official objects for speedy delivery. Thus when the prince Ma'-mum was still governor in Khorasan, the post brought him fresh groceries from Kabul;[8] it brought the Caliph presents which could not stand lengthy transport[9]. When Jauhar had conquered Morocco for his Caliph, and had reached the Atlantic Ocean, he sent him a fish in a glass bottle as a sign of dominion of the sea by post.[10] A military post was

(1) This is why the coast road is not mentioned by Qudamah, p. 222.
(2) Ibn Khordadbeh, p. 89.
(3) Ibid p. 55.
(4) J. Marquart, *Beninsammlung*, p. CV.
(5) Ibn Hauqal, 42, 66.
(6) Mas'udi, VI., 263.
(7) Baihaqi, ed. Schwally, p. 429.
(8) Beladhuri, p. 402.
(9) Ibn Taifur, fol. 131 b.
(10) de Goeje, ZDMG LII, 76.

instituted for the benefit of the government during campaigns. Thus, *e.g.*, when in the year 302/914 the Baghdad general marched to Egypt in order to expel the Fatimid invaders, the vizier ordered the establishment of a fast camel-post to keep Egypt and Baghdad in daily communication.[1] Mu'izzeddaulah hurried up the post in order to accelerate communication with his brother who ruled in other provinces; he introduced the employment of express messengers (*su'at*) as postillions (*fuyuj*).[2] The youths of Baghdad took a great fancy to this new profession, and poor people surrendered their sons to the prince for training therein. Two of these express messengers especially distinguished themselves, both of whom did more than 30 parasangs (about 180 kilometres) between sunrise and sunset. They were popular favourites; the historian goes to the length of recording their names, and mentioning that one was a Sunnite, the other a Shi'ite. At each parasang of the road there was a fort (*hisn*)[3]. Probably they no longer employed posthorses, but fast camels (*Jammazat*). Such were the animals employed e.g., in the year 394/975 by the Buwaihid vizier when he hurried from Baghdad to his master in Persia.[4]

Besides this there was at any rate in certain districts and for shorter distances a private post, or organized body of messengers. As early as the fifth century A.D. the letter-carriers of Lower Egypt, called Symmachoi, were famous

(1). 'Arib, p. 53.

(2) Ibn al-Jauzi fol. 34. Quatremere. *Hist. Maml* II, 289, after the *Kitab al-insa*. The name *sa'i* for postillion still remains.

(3) Ibn al-Jauzi, fol.34: Ibn al-Athir, VIII, 425 (more than 40 parasangs).

(4) Ibn al-Athir, VIII, 480. According to the account given in Tha'alibi's *Lata'if al Ma'arif*, p. 15 they are "amblers", the verb *jamaza* meaning "to amble". The fastest camel in the Persian East is still the Beluchi racer called *jambas*, an ambler which without the slightest difficulty can do a hundred kilometres in one day (Sven Hedin *Zu Land nach Indien* II 346 foll). So *jambas* is likely to be a popular etymology from the Persian.

for their speed. They were still in existence in the 8th century A.D., as is shown by a Rainer papyrus. A traveller of more recent date, M. Wanslab says: "One who would become a messenger in Alexandria has to carry fire in a basket constructed like a warming pan and attached to a pole of a man's height, fitted with a number of iron rings, for a run of 27 miles on the road to Rosetta, and return to the city on the same day before sunset."[1]

The fire telegraph (signalling) which was in use in the Byzantine empire was retained by the Muslims in the countries which had formerly been Greek, but was not introduced into the other provinces. It is said to have worked particularly well on the North African coast. This statement holds good for the 3rd/9th century. A message reached Alexandria from Ceuta in one night,[2] and in three to four hours from Tripoli. The latter tine came to an end only in 440/1048 when the West revolted against the Fatimids, who could no longer protect the forts from the Bedouins.[3]

On the other hand the Muhammadans strenuously developed the carrier-pigeon post which had been known in Roman times.[4] The founder of the Qarmatian sect (3rd/9th century) seems to have been the first to organize it systematically and on a considerable scale. From the commencement of his career he had messages brought to him by birds from all quarters to his Babylonian station, in order to be able to prophesy with ease and certainty.[5] Towards the commencement of the 4th/10th century notices

---

(1) *Fuhrer durch die Ausstellung Rainer*, p. 53.

(2) Abulmahasin, I, 174.

(3) Marrakeshi, transl. Fagnan, p. 299.

(4) Diels, *Antike Technik*, p. 68.

(5) de Goeje, *Mem. sur l'es Carmathes*, p. 207. Carrier-pigeons are first mentioned in China about 700 A.D., and appear to have been introduced there by Indian or Arab traders (Chau-Ju-Kua, transl. Hirth and Rookhill, p. 28, note 2).

of its employment in Babylonia became more frequent. In the year 304/916 the newly nominated vizier announces his arrival by carrier-pigeons.[1] When in the year 311/923 the Qarmatians seized Basrah, they were able to inform the citizens of the change that had taken place in the vizierate four days previously, having received the news by their carrier-pigeons.[2] In the year 313/927 during the Qarmatian war Ibn Muqlah (afterwards vizier) sent a man with 50 carrier-pigeons to Anbar, and had intelligence sent by them to Baghdad at regular intervals.[3] In the same year the vizier eatablishes posts against the Qarmatians at Aqarquf of 100 men with 100 pigeons, and demands a message every hour.[4] In the year 321/933 a private individual is able to reassure the vizier concerning the fate of Kufah, because the carrier-pigeons of his neighbour, a citizen of Kufah, have brought more favourable report than the official birds.[5] In the year 328/940 the ruler of Baghdad is said to have caught a carrier-pigeon with which his secretary had intended to betray him to the enemy.[6] Raqqah and Mosul could communicate at this time with Baghdad, Wasit, Basrah, and Kufah through carrier-pigeons within 24 hours.[7] In the second half of the century the Alid Muhammad Ibn Omar kept carrier-pigeons in Baghdad and Kufah, in order to transmit intelligence between the two cities with rapidity.[8] When a Qarmatian envoy was announced, ʿAdudeddaulah ordered this magnate to have the man lodged with his representative in Kufah. The Alid sends a "Kufan" bird; the representative replies by one of Baghdad, and the business is settled in

---

(1) *Wuzara*, p. 33.
(2) Arib, ed. de Goeje, p. 110 foll.
(3) Misk V, 306; Ibn al-Athir VIII, 135; further ibid. VIII, 240.
(4) Misk. V, 298.
(5) Misk. V, 416.
(6) Misk. VI, 22. The word often occurs in later chronicles.
(7) Thaʿalibi, *Umad al-mansub*, ZDMG VIII, 512.
(8) *ʿUmdat et-talib*, Paris *Mscr, arab.* 636, fol. 171.a.

few hours.[1]

The government in general left the private traveller undisturbed ; it is certain that in the East, at least in the 2nd/8th century, there were no gate-clerks nor registers of persons who entered the city gates.[2] A notice of the first half of the 3rd/9th century also speaks of the passports customary in China as something strange.[3] In Egypt on the other hand, even in the earliest Muhammadan times, strict insistence on passports prevailed. No one was allowed to leave his district without permission of the authorities. About the year 100/720 the governor is said to have issued orders that "any one found without a passport (*sijill*) either on the march or removing from one place to another, or embarking or disembarking, is to be arrested, and the vessel with its contents seized and burned." Passports of the sort are preserved in the collections of papyri.[4] Under the Tulunids a passport (*jawaz*) was required for permission to leave Egypt, and in this even slaves who accompanied their masters had to be mentioned.[5] In the East on the other hand at the end of the 4th/10th century it is pointed out as a remarkable practice that in Shiraz, the capital of the Buwaihid 'Adudeddaulah, a traveller was detained, and could only leave the place with permission.[6]

---

(1) Ibn al-Jauzi, Berlin, fol. 145 a. Other "pigeon-telegrams Misk VI 13, 19, 412.
(2) *Aghani* XIX, 147.
(3) *Silsilet et-tawarikh*, ed. Reinaud, p. 42.
(4) C.H. Becker, *Islam*, II, 369.
(5) Mughrib of Ibn Sa'id ed., Vollers, p. 53.
(6) Muq., p. 429.

XXIX. MARINE NAVIGATION

Muhammadan navigation had to be divided into two quite separate areas: the Mediterranean and the Indian Ocean. The Isthmus of Suez stopped all connection between the two. One who wished to reach India or Eastern Asia from the Mediterranean had to load his goods on camels at Farama and then journey through the desert for seven days to Qulzum (Greek Klysma), where he could re-embark them.[1] Moreover the types of vessel were distinct. In the Mediterranean the planks were nailed together, whereas in the Red Sea and the Indian Ocean they were stitched[2]—doubtless the older and at one time universal mode of ship-building. Ibn Jubair reports for the 6th/12th century: "No nails are used in the vessels of the Red Sea; they are merely stitched together with cords made of cocoa-husk. The planks are perforated with stakes of palm-wood, and then saturated with mutton-fat, castor-oil or shark-oil: the last is best."[3] Marco Polo writes as follows of the vessels in use at Hormuz in the 7th/13th century: "The vessels built in Hormuz are of the worst sort, and very dangerous. This is due to the fact that no nails can be used in their construction. The planks are perforated as cautiously as possible with an iron auger near their ends, and wooden nails or stakes driven in; this is how they are put together. After this they are bound, or rather stitched, together with a sort of rope-yarn, which is obtained from the husk of the Indian nut. Pitch is not used; the planks are smeared with an oil that is prepared from

(1) Ibn Khordadbeh, p. 153; Edrisi ed. Brandel, Upsala, p. 2; Maqrizi I. 213.

(2) Mas'udi, I. 365.

(3) p. 29; Edrisi l. c.

the fat of fish."[1] This difference was the result of traditional usage, but as ordinarily happens utilitarian grounds were suggested for it. According to Marco Polo "the wood is of too hard a quality, and liable to split or crack like earthenware. When an attempt is made to drive in a nail, it rebounds and is frequently broken." According to Ibn Jubair "their object in oiling the vessel is to make the wood soft and pliable on account of the numerous eddies in this sea, which are also the reason why they allow no vessels constructed with nails to sail." A third reason was the fear that the water of the ocean might attack the nails[2] while others talked of the mountains of magnet which were to be found in the Red Sea, which attract the nails and so disintegrate the vessels[3].

The ships of the Mediterranean were larger than those on the Ocean. The Chinese inspector of customs Chau-Ju-Kua at the beginning of the 13th century A.D. reports with admiration how "a single vessel carries several thousand men, and there are wine shops and foodshops to be found on board as well as looms."[4] Only on the Mediterranean were there vessels with two rudders;[5] those on the Ocean had never more than one deck, and in most cases only one mast.[6] The vessels which sailed the Red Sea were broad and of small draught on account of the numerous reefs;[7] those of Basrah were white, being calked with fat and

(1) I.18.

(2) Mas'udi, I, 365.

(3) First found in Edrisi, Jaubert, I, 46, after the *Aja'ib* of Hassan ibn al-Mundhir, a full-blooded representative of the "Mirabilia" literature. Next comes Qazwini, ed Wustenfeld I, 172. Mutahhar who lived in the heart of Persia has transposed the story, asserting that no ship can sail in the *western* sea, because the mountains of magnet attract the nails (ed. Huart, I, 89).

(4) Fr. Hirth, *die Lander Des Islam nach chinesischen Quelen.*

(5) Ibn Jubair , ed. Wright, p. 235.

(6) Marco Polo, I, 18; III, 1.

(7) Edrisi, on Brandel, p. 2.

lime.[1] Of the eastern ship the "Chinese" were the largest. In the Persian Gulf they could not negotiate a strait which other vessels could pass;[2] in the Malabar ports they paid dues from 5 to 50 times the amount paid by others,[3] and as early as the 8th century A.D. they occasioned surprise in Canton as being particularly large, "towering so high above the water that people require ladders some ten feet long in order to get on board." They were however commanded by captains who were not Chinese (*fan*).[4] The most valuable timber for ship-building came from the Lebek tree, which grew only in Antina (Antinoe); a single plank cost 50 dinars. Two were regularly tied together and left in water for a year till they had so swollen as to become one.[5] In the 4th/10th century Venice also supplied the Saracens with timber for ship-building, so that the Greek emperor made complaints on the subject to the Doge. The Doge accordingly forbade it, and only permitted trade in harmless wood-boards of ash or poplar not more than five feet long and half a foot broad, and wooden utensils.[6] This caused such a scarcity of timber in Egypt that the girders of the mint and of the hospital in the dove-market had to be removed to make masts for a new fleet of warships.[7]

The rudder of the seagoing craft was turned with two cords like that of our pleasure boat.[8] The authors of our

(1) Mas'udi VIII, 128.

(2) *Silsilet et-tawarikh* ed. Reinaud, p. 16.

(3) Ibid, p. 17.

(4) Hirth and Rockhill, Chau Ju-kua, p. 9.

(5) Maqrizi, *Khitat*, I, 204, after Dinawari's Book of Plants' (the edition has incorrectly "benjtree".

(6) Scheube, *Handelsgesvhichte der romanischen Volker*, p. 23 fol. As late as the beginning of the 19th century Egypt imported all its timber for building from Venice, and some of its firewood from Asia Minor (U.J. Seetzens *Reisen* III, 207); even at present the masts of the Nile boats are said to come mainly from the Black Forest.

(7) Yahya b. Sa'id, fol. 113 a.

(8) Muq, p. 12.

times say nothing about the compass, which is described first by Kapchaki in the year 1282 A.D.,[1] and then by Maqrizi (pp. 845/1442).[2] There were several anchors (called by their Greek name *anjur*) on board;[3] a plummet (*sibak*) was used for sounding[4]. The boat (*qarib*) was used when necessary to tow the ship with oars.[5] Ibn Hauqal, who had travelled far and wide, was struck by the skilful seamanship that he witnessed at Tinnis in the Egyptian Delta, where "two ship met and touched each other, the one going upstreem, the other downstream, with one and the same wind, each of them with bellying sails and sailing with equal rapidity."[6] The crew had a diver for one of its members.[7] On the Chinese vessels of the 11th century A.D. there were black slaves who could dive with their eyes open.[8] An Arab of the 8th/14th century reports that the ships of the Indian Ocean ordinarily carry four divers (*ghattas*) who, if the water rises in the vessel, rub oil of sesame into their skin, stop their nostrils with wax, and proceed to swim round the ship as it sails, and stop the leaks with wax; they can deal with twenty to thirty in a day."[9] A Chinese authority of the 9th century relates as follows: "A number of doves are kept on the seagoing craft of the Persians. These can fly several thousand *li*, and when set free fly homeward in a single flight, bringing good tidings."[10] On vesels that sailed the ocean a bowl of rice with grease was put out daily for the

(1) Klaproth, *Letter sur l'invention de la boussole*, Paris, 1834.

(2) *Khitat*, I, 210.

(3) *Merveilles de l' Inde*, p. 87.

(4) Ibid., p. 30.

(5) Ibid., p. 46.

(6) p. 103. In the East when the wind was unfavourable the sails of the ship's boats were used for cruising (Marco Polo III, 2). (Marco Polo's words in the Marsden Wright edition are "provided the wind be on the quarter, but not when right aft." Translator's note).

(7) *Merveilles de l' Inde*, p. 7.

(8) Chau Ju-kua, p. 32.

(9) Gildemeister, GGN, 1882 , p. 444.

(10) Chau Ju-kua. p. 28.

guardian angles.[1]

In the 10th century Europe had no power over the Mediterranean; it was an Arabian sea. Any one who wished to achieve anything had to ally himself with the Saracens, as did Naples, Gaeta, and Amalfi. European navigation seems as wretched affair. In the year 935 A.D. the ships of the Fatimid Mahdi could raid and plunder the South of France, and Genoa, and in the years 1004 and 1011 Pisa: nevertheless the Fatimid fleet must at that time have been decidedly inferior to the Syrian, for in the year 301/913 eighty of their ships were completely defeated by twenty-five of the Syrian. The Arabs counted 36 days' journey for the Mediterranean 'from the Atlantic Ocean to the port of Antioch"[2] This "port' of Antioch was Seleucia, which in the 3rd/9th century was the most important trading of Syria;[3] the Caliph al-Mu'tasim had had it fortified.[4] It suffered indeed from the great disadvantage that there lay between it and Cyprus the famous shoal (*sofalah*) on which most ships were wrecked.[5] We are also told towards the end of the 3rd/9th century that the harbour of the Syrian Tripoli holds a thousand vessels; the military harbour against Byzantium was at that time Tyre, which was protected by massive fortifications[6]. However the advance of the Byzantines in the 4th/10th century altered all these conditions in Syria. The eastern half of the north African coast is as ill-suited for navigation as possible. The only natural roadstead between Alexandria and the Gulf of Tunis is that of Tripoli. And this was of insufficient depth even for the shallow draught of the vessels of time; the inhabitants

(1) *Merveilles de l' Inde*, p. 46.
(2) Edrisi, ed. Dozy, p. 214.
(3) Antioch is *e.g.*, with procopius still the first of all the Roman cities of the Urient (Heyd *Levantenhandel* I 24).
(4) Ibn Khordadbeh, p. 153, Michael Syrus, ed. Chabot, p. 521, 537.
(5) Mas'udi, I. 332.
(6) Ya'qubi. *geogr.*, p. 327.

used their boats free of charge to help strangers in their difficult landing.[1] Next in order came Tunis, the port of Qairwan, near the site of the ancient mistress of the sea, Carthage. The story of the "voyagers to the West" in Lisbon probably belongs to the 4th/10 century. "They started out to explore the ocean, and discover what it contained and how far it reached." They were cinht cousins; they built a passenger ship, victualled it and took water to last for months, and launched it as soon as the East wind began to blow. After a voyage ,of some eleven days they entered a sea with heavy waves, murky air numerous reefs and little light.[2] Fearing disaster they shifted sail, and ran southward for twelve days till they came to Sheep Island. Thence for twelve days more they sailed to an island which was under cultivation. Here they were arrested, taken to the capital, thrown into prison, and after three days examined with the help of an Arab dragoman. When next the West wind blew they were taken blindfolded to the coast and allowed to sail away. After some three days they reached a country inhabited by Berbers. They required two months to get back to Spain.[3]

The Red Sea was dreaded owing to its reefs and adverse winds; sailing thereon was only possible in the daytime, and, owing to the peculiar laws which regulated its winds, at a particular season from north to south, and at another in the opposite direction. On this account the Nile water-way which runs parallel to the Red Sea maintained its great

(1) Ibn Hauqal, p. 46.

(2) In accordance with ancient opinion the Arabs supposed the extreme ocean to be dark. Thus in the East the furthest sea is called *al-bahr al-zefti* "The Pitchi Sea," because its water is murky, the wind are violent, and darkness is almost continuous. (Roinaud, Abulled, II, 26).

(3) Hdrisi, ed. Dozy, p. 184.
Istakhri. p. 30; Mas'udi, III 56: Edrisi ed. Brandel p. 1.

importance for marine navigation too. The port of exchange was 'Aidhab, deep and safe, with entrance through a gorge.[1] Here the wared of Abyssinia, Yemen and Zanzibar were disembarked, carried across the desert for twenty days of Asuan or Qus, whence they proceeded on the Nile to Cairo.[2] Towards the end of the 5th/11th century Aidhab attained a high degree of prosperity, and became one of the world-ports; "for unknown reasons the trade of North Africa passed through it on its eastward way; indeed from 450/1058 to 660/1258 the Egyptian pilgrims actually took the route through 'Aidhab; not before 823/1420 did it lose its importance to Aden."[3] At that time a tax of eight dinars was levied there on each pilgrim.[4] The traveller Ibn Jubair too in the early 579/1183 found 'Aidhab "one of the most frequented harbours of the world, since the ships from India and Yemen put in there, not to mention the pilgrim traffic." He mentions Indian pepper as the staple commodity.[5]

Mas'udi writes as follows in the year 332/943: "I have sailed a good number of seas, the Chinese, the Roman, that of the Khazars, the Red Sea and the Arabian Sea, and have experienced innumerable terrors, but nowhere have experienced anything more terrible than the African Sea." In the year 304/916 he sailed from Zanzibar (Qanbalu) to Oman: all the sailors with whom he made the journey out and back afterwards fell victims to the Sea.[6] The rulers of Zanzibar were already at that time Muhammadan ;[7] the furthest goal of Muhammadan travel in Africa was Sofalah (Mozambique), where they were attracted by the gold

(1) Wustenfeld, Qalqashandi, p. 169.
(2) Nasir Khosrau, p. 64, who visited the city in 442, 1050.
(3) Maqrizi, *Khitat*, I, 194-197; 202-203.
(4) Edrisi Jaubert, I, 133.
(5) p. 66.
(6) *Prairies*, I. 233 foll.
(7) Ibid III, 31.
(8) Ibid. III, 6.

treasures of Mashonaland,[8] and whence iron was mainly exported for fabrication to India, where products of high value were made of it.[1] Modern historians give some exact dates: about 908 Mahdishu "Mogadoxo in Italian Somaliland) was founded, as also Brawa; Kilwa in German East Aftica about 975.[2] This is based on Rizby's "Report on the Zanzibar Dominions," (p. 47) who follows the histories current there in these days. We have no ancient sources dealing with this subject; possibly the historians of South Arabia will furnish some information.

The "Persian Sea" to the Muhammadan mariner commenced at Aden, went round Arabia into the Persian Gulf, and ended somewhere about where Baluchistan commences. Everything else was Indian Ocean. The two seas were navigable at opposite seasons; when the one was clam, the other was stormy, and vice versa. The bad time of the Persian sea begins with the autumnal, that of the Indian with the vernal, equinox. The Persian sea is navigated at all season, the Indian only in winter.[3] Hence the former is the chief hunting-ground of the pirates, because of whom the Arabian coast was of the worst repute. As early as about the year 200/815 the people of Basrah had undertaken an unsuccessful expedition against the pirates in Bahrain;[4] in the 4th/10th century people could not venture to sail the Red Sea except with soldiers and especially artillery-men (*naffatin*) on board.[5] The island Socotra in particular was regarded as a dangerous nest of pirates, at which people trembled as they passed it. It was the *point d'appui* of the Indian pirates who ambushed the Believers there.[6] Piracy was never regarded as a disgraceful practice for a civilian,

(1) Edrisi Jaubert I. 65.

(2) *e.g.* Schurtz in Helmolts *Weltgeschichs*, vol. 3, p. 428.

(3) Ibn Rusteh, p. 86 foll.

(4) Michael Syrus ed. Chabot, p. 514.

(5) Muq., p. 12.

(6) Mas'udi III 37; Muq. p. 14.

nor even as a curious or remarkable one. Arabic has formed no special term for it; Istakhri (p. 33) does not even call them "sea-robbers," but designates them by the far milder expression "the predatory." Otherwise the Indian term *the barques* is used for them.[1]

The most important harbours of the empire on the Ocean were Aden, Siraf, and Oman. Of the second rank were Basrah, Daibul (at the mouth of the Indus), and Hormuz, the port of Kirman.

Aden was the great centre of the trade between Africa and Arabia, and the *point d'appui* of that between China, India and Egypt. Muqaddasi calls it the "vestibule of China."[2] There people could hear of a man starting out with 1,000 dirhems and coming home with 1,000 dinars and another starting with 100 and coming home with 500. A third started out with incense, and came back with the same quantity of camphor in exchange.[3]

Siraf was the world-port of the Persian Gulf, through which the imports and exports of all Persia passed.[4] It was especially the port for China; even the goods of Yemen intended for China were transhipped in Siraf.[5] About 300/912 the dues annually levied on the shipping there amounted to 253,000 dinnars.[6] The people of Siraf were the wealthiest traders in all Persia; they gave proof of this especially in their tall houses of many storeys, built of the costly teak wood; an acqaintance of Istakhri had expended 30,000 dinars on his dwelling-house. The merchant princes were, however, curiously simple in their attire; Istakhri

(1) Gloss Geogr, 195; *Merveilles de l' Inde*, p. 193.
(2) p. 34.
(3) Muq, p. 97.
(4) Istakhri. p. 34.
(5) *Silsilet et-tawarikh*, ed. Langles (composed about 300 A.H.) p. 51.
(6) Ibn al-Balkhi. JRAS 1912, p. 188.

(p.139) asserts that a man could be seen there who possessed four million dinars or more, yet whose dress was not different from that of his employees. Men of Siraf conducted business from Basrah also; Ibn Haqual met one of these traders, who had property of about three million dinars, an amount which the traveller had not seen elsewhere.[1] Many a man of Siraf spent his whole life on the sea, which led to the story that one of them for forty years had been embarking from one vessel into another, never treading on land.[2] To Siraf belonged the most celebrated shipowner of the time, Muhammad ibn Babishad, of whom and Indian king had a portrait executed, as the most eminent member of his profession. For "they have the custom of making protraits of the most distinguished men of all sorts."[3] This position of Siraf had for an effect that the chief language of the Muhammadan traders with India and Eastern Asia was Persian; at any rate even the Arabic works of our period offer a number of Persian nautical terms, such as *nachoda* "shipowner," *didban* "lookout-man", *rubban* (probably for *rah-ban*) "captain."[4] On the other hand the "caller" (the man who communicates the pilot's orders to the man at the helm) is designated by the term *munadi*, which is otherwise familiar in the life of the Arabs.[5] The captains had to swear that they would not wantonly surrender any ship to destruction so long as it was in existence and not overtaken

(1) p. 206.

(2) Istakhri, p. 138.

(3) *Merv. de l' Inde*, p. 98.

(4) Not "captain" as it is ordinarily rendered; his name is *ra's* or *rubban* (Muq., p. 31). The *nakhoda* Babishad, who voyages on his own vessel, has *e.g.* "the *rubban* of his vessel" with him, to see to the navigation. Tales of nautical skill are never credited to the *nakhoda* always to the *rubban*. At the present time on the Red Sea the *nakhoda el-bahr*, the person really in command of the vessel, who gives orders to the crew, and curiously enough is at once helmsman and pilot, is distinguished from the *nakhoda el-barr*, the shipowner (v. Maltxan, *Meine Wallfahrt nach Mekka*, 1865, I 71).

(5) *Merveilles de l' Inde*, p. 22.

by destiny.[1]

Basrah lay at a distance of two day's journey from the sea upstream.[2] In front of the river's mouth there was a sort of Heligoland, an island with the small fort 'Abbadan' whose inhabitants maintained themselves by the manufacture of *halfa* mats,[3] and whither people went to perform penance.[4] Dues were exacted from vessels at this place,[5] and it held a garrison against pirates. Six miles further seaward there was a building on piles: stakes (*khashabat*) were driven into the ground, and thereon stood a lighthouse, which was illuminated at night, so that vessels might keep away from the place.[6] A poet of Basrah satirized a lean and bony individual in the following line:

> "A face like 'Abbadan, after which nothing
> but wood comes for his lover."[7]

Mas'udi in the 4th/10th century speaks of three wooden towers of the sort;[8] Nasir Khosrau in the 5th/11th of two.[9] The latter writer describes them more accurately; "Four great stakes of teak wood are driven in, so as to form a square, only obliquely, so that the base is broad and the apex narrow. They rise fifty meters above the surface of the sea, and there built on the top a square cabin for the keeper." This indicates the weakness of the harbour on the Shatt el-Arab: its shallow and narrow entrance. "Of forty ships which

---

(1) Ibid, p. 22.
(2) Istakhri, p. 79.
(3) Muq. p. 118.
(4) *Wuzara*, p. 73.
(5) Yaqut, *Irshad,* I, 77.
(6) Istakhri 32; Muq, p. 12, who speaks of several "houses" which were illuminated.
(7) Yatimah, II, 134.
(8) Mas'udi, I, 230.
(9) p. 99.

enter one comes back" is what Muqaddasi heard stated.[1]

The history of the Muhammadan factories in the extreme East was somewhat troubled.[2] As early as the eighth century it is recorded that foreign captains had their names registered at the bureau of marine commerce in Canton, and that this bureau claimed the right of inspecting the ship's papers and exacting export duty[3] and freight dues before it gave permission for the disembarking of goods. The exports of rare and valuable articles are forbidden. Attempts at smuggling were punished with imprisonment.[4] Muhammadan factories may perhaps have already been in existence at other Chinese places as well; the western colony in Canton was already so populous that in the year 758 it could plunder the city, burn the warehouses, and make off with the spoil.[5] At the beginning of the 9th century A.D. we find again at the head of the Muhammadan colony in Canton a chief of the same religion appointed by the Chinese emperor who administered justice, preached, and offered prayers for the emperor of China at the service in the mosque.[6] "At that time if a vessel arrived, the Chinese would seize the cargo, bring it into the sheds, guarantee if for six months till the last of the sailors arrived[7] when three-tenths were taken always, and the rest given to the traders. Goods needed by the government were taken at top prices, and paid for in cash with no unfairness of any sort. Among such articles was camphor, for which the government paid at the rate of 50,000 pieces of copper the *mana*. When not taken by the government, camphor fetches only the half.'[8] Other

(1) p. 12

(2) The Chinese sources have been most recently collected by Fr. Hirth and W W. Rockhill Chau Jn-kua, St. Petersburg, 1912, p. 9 foll.

(3) Perhaps a slip for "import duty" (Transl).

(4) Chau Ju-kua, p. 9.

(5) Ibid. p. 14 foll.

(6) Reinaud, *Relation*, p. 14.

(7) It is not clear what this means, but the German cannot be rendered otherwise (Translators note).

(8) Reinaud, *Relation*, p. 46.

imports were ivory, copper bars, tortoise-shell, and rhinoceros-horn, 'of which the Chinese made girdles(?)".[1] At that time not only did Muslims voyage to China but 'Chinese vessels" did the like to Oman, Siraf Ubullah, and Basrah.[2]

Chinese annals confirm the Arab sailors' narrative of the destruction of the Muhammadan trading stations in China,[3] especially in Khanfu (the modern Canton).[4] With the fall of the Tang dynasty all was destroyed in South China[5] and the scene of marine commerce was shifted. The *Merveilles de l'Inde*, which essentially reflect the state of affairs in the 4th/10th century show that in their time Kalah or Kedah in Malacca, the predecessor of the modern Singapore, constituted the limit of Muhammadan navigation. Abu Dulaf says so expressly: "Kalah is the commencement of India, and the limit of navigation: the ship can go no further, else they come to grief.[6] Similarly Mas'udi, writing about 332/944 says: In Kalah at the present time the Muhammadans of Siraf and Oman meet the ships that come from China. There too the trader of Samarqand who is on his way to China embarks on a Chines vessel."[7] At the end of the 10th century, however, the Chinese government made great efforts to

(1) Ibid, p. 35. The query is the author's.

(2) Mas'udi, I 308; Hirth and Rochill in Chau Ju-kua, p. 15, n. 3. declare it to be most improbable that these "Chinese vessels" belonged to Chinese owners or were slected by such, since even the names, Aden and Siraf were unknown to the Chinese till the end of the 12th century. It agrees with this that the Arabs have no tales to tell of Chinese sailors and that with the destruction of the Muhammadan factories in China the "Chinese vessels" no longer came into Arabian waters. Hence Muhammadan vessels trading with China must be understood by the phrase.

(3) Reinaud, *Relation*, p. 62 foll, and Mas'udi, I. 302; Alulfeda, *Annals*, *anno* 264.

(4) For the identification see Hirth and Rockhill, Chau Ju-kua p. 15.

(5) Richthofen, *China*, I, 572.

(6) Yaqut, III, 453.

(7) I. 308.

attract oversea commerce once mere directly to the country. An embassy was sent "to invite the foreign traders of the South Sea and such as crossed the sea into foreign lands" to come to China, promising them favourable conditions for importation. In the year 971 the marine bureau in Canton was reorganized; about 980 foreign trade became a State monopoly, and private transactions with foreigners were to be punished with branding of the face and banishment. At that time and in the succeeding years a series of Muhammadan traders are mentioned, who visited the Chinese court, and were there received with remarkable friendliness. In the year 976 A.D. an Arab brought the first black slave to the Chinese court; in the 11th century wealthy people in Canton already possessed a number of such slaves.[1] Foreign traders had been established for some time not only in Canton, but also in Tsuan Chou; in the year 999 bureaux of marine commerce were further opened in the seaport towns Hangchou and Mingchou "at the request and for the convenience of foreign officials."[2] A Chinese writer of the year 1178 asserts that "of all the rich foreign countries which have a great store of varied and valuable goods none surpasses that of the Arabs. Next to them comes Java, the third is Palembang (Sumatra); aftér these come many others."[3] The same writer records a further renewal of navigation to China: "Travellers from the country of the Arabs (Ta-shi) sail first southwards to Quilon (Malabar) on small vessels; there they trans-ship into large vessels, and proceed eastwards to Palemabng (Sumatra.)"[4] The route to China was dictated by the direction of the monsoons, which alone rendered the navigation of the high sea without compass possible; it is described in the *Silsilet et-tawarikh* ed. Langles (cited by Reinaud. *Relation des Voyages*, Paris,

(1) Chau Ju-kua, p. 31. foll.
(2) Ibid., p. 17 foll., 119.
(3) Ibid., p. 23.
(4) Ibid., p. 24.

1845), p. 16 foll., and the Ibn Khordadbeh, p. 61 foll. and can be reconstructed from the *Merveilles de l' Inde.* They sailed along the Indian coast, or directly from Mascat in about one month to the Malabar port Kulam (modern Quilon), then left Ceylon on the right (?)[1] and went to the Nicobar Islands (10 to 15 days from Ceylon), then to Keda in Malacca—about a month's journey from Quilon—then to Java and the Sunda island Ma'it; thence in 15 days to Combodia then Cochin China and China. The Chinese coast alone demanded two months' voyage; further, since in those regions only one wind blows for half the year, they had to wait for the favourable one. On the return journey they sailed 40 days from Tsuanchou to Atyeh (north-west point of Sumatra), where they traded, and took to the sea again in the following year, in order to reach home in some 30 days with the help of the regular winds.[2] In the absence of all instruments for navigation such a voyager was an adventure; a captain, who had made it seven times, is mentioned with the greatest admiration.[3] "It was a miracle if any one remained safe and sound on the journey out; a sheer impossibility to come home safely."[4] Hence we are not surprised that at the first sight of home the look-out man shouts down from the mast: "God have mercy on all who cry: God is great!," and the crew all reply "God is great!", congratulate each other, and weep for joy and happiness.[5]

---

(1) The writer must mean the left (translator's note).
The Chinese Chau Ju-kua in the 13th century also reckons a month from Sumatra to Malabar with the monsoon (p. 87).
Marco Polo, III,. 4. As early as the fifth century A.D., the pilgrim Fa Hien had gone home from India by this route.

(2) This at least is what is stated in a Chinese report of the 12th century A.D. Chau Ju-kua p. 114.

(3) *Merv, de l' Inde*, p. 80.

(4) Ibid.

(5) Ibid., p. 91.